IDENTITIES AND INEQUALITIES

EXPLORING THE INTERSECTIONS OF RACE,
CLASS, GENDER, AND SEXUALITY

THIRD EDITION

DAVID M. NEWMAN

DePauw University

IDENTITIES & INEQUALITIES: EXPLORING THE INTERSECTIONS OF
RACE, CLASS, GENDER, AND SEXUALITY, THIRD EDITION

Published by McGraw-Hill Education, 2 Penn Plaza, New York, NY 10121. Copyright © 2017 by McGraw-Hill Education. All rights reserved. Printed in the United States of America. Previous editions © 2012, and 2007. No part of this publication may be reproduced or distributed in any form or by any means, or stored in a database or retrieval system, without the prior written consent of McGraw-Hill Education, including, but not limited to, in any network or other electronic storage or transmission, or broadcast for distance learning.

Some ancillaries, including electronic and print components, may not be available to customers outside the United States.

This book is printed on acid-free paper.

1 2 3 4 5 6 7 8 9 DOC 21 20 19 18 17 16

ISBN 978-0-07-802703-1
MHID 0-07-802703-9

Chief Product Officer, SVP Products & Markets: *G. Scott Virkler*
Vice President, General Manager, Products & Markets: *Michael Ryan*
Managing Director: *Gina Boedecker*
Brand Manager: *Penina Braffman*
Director, Product Development: *Meghan Campbell*
Product Developer: *Anthony McHugh*
Director, Content Design & Delivery: *Terri Schiesl*
Program Manager: *Marianne Musni*
Content Project Manager: *Jeni McAtee; George Theofanopoulos; Sandy Schnee*
Buyer: *Jennifer Pickel*
Design: *Egzon Shaqri*
Content Licensing Specialists: *Ann Marie Jannette, Jacob Sullivan*
Cover Image: *Samantha Craddock/123RF*
Compositor: *Aptara®, Inc.*
Printer: *R.R. Donnelley*

All credits appearing on page or at the end of the book are considered to be an extension of the copyright page.

Library of Congress Cataloging-in-Publication Data

Names: Newman, David M., 1958- author.
Title: Identities and inequalities: exploring the intersections of race,
    class, gender, and sexuality/David M. Newman, DePauw University.
Description: Third edition. | Dubuque: McGraw-Hill Education, [2016]
Identifiers: LCCN 2016017562 | ISBN 9780078027031 (0-07-802703-9: alk.
paper)
Subjects: LCSH: Equality—United States. | Group identity—United States. |
    Prejudices—United States. | Discrimination—United States. |
    Differentiation (Sociology) | Social classes—United States. | Race
    awareness—United States. | United States—Social conditions—21st century.
Classification: LCC HN90.S6 N45 2016 | DDC 305.50973—dc23 LC record available at
https://lccn.loc.gov/2016017562

The Internet addresses listed in the text were accurate at the time of publication. The inclusion of a website does not indicate an endorsement by the authors or McGraw-Hill Education, and McGraw-Hill Education does not guarantee the accuracy of the information presented at these sites.

www.mhhe.com

FOR MY MOM

ABOUT THE AUTHOR

David M. Newman is currently Professor of Sociology at DePauw University in Greencastle, Indiana. He received his PhD in sociology from the University of Washington in 1988. He teaches courses in deviance, mental illness, family, social psychology, and research methods and has won teaching awards at both the University of Washington and DePauw University. He has published numerous articles on teaching and has presented several research papers on the intersection of gender and power in intimate relationships. He has authored two textbooks, *Sociology: Exploring the Architecture of Everyday Life* (and co-edited an accompanying anthology) and *Families: A Sociological Perspective*. He is currently writing a book-length manuscript on the cultural ideology, institutional context, historical underpinnings, and personal experiences of "second chances" in everyday life. When not hunkered down in his third-floor office writing books, he enjoys running, swimming, crossword puzzles, and playing with his goofy Chocolate Labrador Retriever, Moki.

CONTENTS

PART TWO: INEQUALITIES — 157

I'm a regular visitor to the fitness center to my university's physical education building, which is open to people in the local community as well as
people affiliated with the school. You can always find an interesting mixture
of individuals there: professors, students, deans, administrative assistants,
local artists, sheriffs, UPS truck drivers, insurance salespeople, restaurateurs,
farmers, contractors, ministers, retirees, and so on. The locker-room conversation typically includes laments about the dismal play of local sports teams,
complaints about the weather or the economy, and of course advice on every
imaginable topic from the best way to strip old wallpaper to how to hit a
nine-iron out of the rough. Some professors can always be counted on to
grumble about lazy students, too many exams to grade, the puny size of our
pay raises, and so on.

To be honest, these topics bore me to tears. So I usually do more eaves-
dropping than talking. Every once in a while, though, someone will try to
engage me in casual chitchat. Since I began writing the third edition of this
book, I've had some version of this conversation a couple of times:

> *Other person:* So, David, how are your classes going?
> *Me:* Actually I'm not teaching right now. I'm on sabbatical.
> *Other person:* Sabbatical, huh? Must be nice, having a vacation, not
> having to work for months, and still getting paid!
> *Me:* [sounding annoyed] It's not a vacation! I work harder on
> sabbaticals than I do when I'm teaching.
> *Other person:* Sorry. Sorry. So what are you working on that's keeping
> you so busy?
> *Me:* I'm revising a book.
> *Other person:* Oh yeah? Impressive. What's it about?
> *Me:* Inequalities.

I realize that such a one-word description is totally insufficient, but
it's an effective way to squelch a conversation that I didn't want to have
in the first place. And since I'm usually dressed in a towel or less when
these exchanges take place, I want them to end as quickly as possible.

Most people respond with unpersuasive expressions of interest ("Hmm, that sounds . . . um . . . nice."), sarcasm ("Fascinating! But if you don't mind, I'll wait for the movie version."), or vacant, deer-in-the-headlights stares. A couple of brave souls have plunged past this conversational dead end, though. A soybean farmer once said he didn't realize that I was a math teacher. The owner of a local pizza joint suggested that if I wanted to sell more copies I should use some obscure science-fiction space alien's name in the title. A guy I'd never seen before complained that his own poor financial state—due to chronic unemployment—was recently made worse by the fact that his wife left him. The ex-mayor asked if I'd help him find a publisher for a book he wanted to write. Even colleagues from other departments have managed to convey their disinterest or downright disapproval:

> *Other professor:* What kinds of inequalities are you referring to?
> *Me:* Social inequalities. You know, race, class, gender, sexuality . . . stuff like that.
> *Other professor:* What do you know about social inequality? You're a white, male college professor with a PhD, for crying out loud!

Secretly, I have wished that I was writing about something a little more concrete and a little less threatening, like the history of staplers or an illustrated coffee-table book about lawn furniture.

Writing any book—whether it's a children's book, a romance novel, or a sociology textbook—is a daunting task. Writing a book about a hot-button topic on which everyone has an opinion—and usually a pretty strong opinion—is absolutely terrifying. Social inequality is not just an academic subject, described and explained dispassionately during a semester-long college course. It is a way of life with real and sometimes perilous consequences. It touches people directly, whether we're talking about their health, the availability of economic and educational opportunities, their access to political decision makers, their interactions with the law, the way other people communicate with them, or the prestige and power their group has in society. Some people want to deny the existence of inequality, hoping that if we simply say it doesn't exist, it will disappear; others wear it as a moral badge, making it a part of everything they do and say.

People's reactions to the topic of inequality are influenced by, among other things, whether they are harmed by it or benefit from it. Those who are members of groups that have historically been disadvantaged by social inequality—chiefly ethnoracial, religious, and sexual minorities, women, and poor people—are understandably sensitive (sometimes angrily so) about their position. Although they may be appreciative that their problems are being written about at all, many believe that they have a vested interest in how inequality is portrayed in books like this one. Some may even feel that the topic is private property that cannot be fully understood by outsiders. At the same time, some people from disadvantaged groups are sick and tired of talking about inequality. They see no value in perpetuating a dialogue of despair and hopelessness, preferring to see themselves as masters and not victims of their own fate.

On the other hand, those who have been historically privileged by social inequality in this society—namely, Whites, men, Christians, heterosexuals, members of the middle and upper classes—sometimes become defensive when the subject of inequality is raised, assuming that just talking about it will lead to their advantages being confiscated.

So you can see that the task of writing a book about race, class, gender, and sexuality is a formidable one. Ironically, however, my locker-room experiences have reinforced the importance of writing about this topic. A lot of people never get past sound bites and superficial rhetoric to develop a deeper and more useful sociological understanding of social inequality. It's my hope that this book will help you look at the issue with greater clarity.

IDENTITIES AND INEQUALITIES

Though we call attention to them to greater or lesser degrees, all of us have a race, a sexual orientation, an ethnic heritage, a gender, and a class status. All of these characteristics—not to mention religion, family membership, age, intellect, physical ability, sense of humor, attractiveness, and so on—combine to determine our identities, or who we are. But we live in a society that places dramatically different values on the various component categories of these identifiers. So at the same time that race, ethnicity, gender, sexuality, and social class combine to construct our identities, they also determine our place in society, or the inequalities that affect us. Our identities dictate our chances for living a comfortable life; our access to valued economic, educational, or political resources; the likelihood of being seen positively or negatively by others; and our susceptibility to victimization, either by crime or by illness.

For over a century, sociology has outpaced other disciplines in describing and explaining the ways in which race, class, gender—and more recently sexuality—determine people's experiences and their access to important life chances. These concepts are the bread and butter of our discipline. You'd be hard-pressed to find a sociologist who would deny the everyday influence or intellectual importance of these features of social life. No sociology course (or textbook) worth its salt would totally ignore the impact of race, class, gender, or sexuality. Our scholarly books and journals are filled to the brim with theoretical and empirical work that to some degree incorporates these concepts.

But that doesn't mean that all sociologists agree about the everyday influence of these factors or even how they're best defined. Are they personal traits or social groupings? Are they micro-level phenomena best examined as private lived experiences, or are they macro-level elements of culture best examined from the institutional perspective of the social structure? Are they primarily characteristics of difference or characteristics of inequality? As someone who has taught sociology courses for over 25 years, my answer to these questions is an unequivocal, shoulder-shrugging "I dunno." I think they are all of these things, simultaneously. They exert their influence on our lives at both the very personal and the very structural levels. They are the fundamental elements of our self-concepts and public identities, but they also shape the contours of our society and determine the history and quality of our lives.

Given the ubiquity of race, class, gender, and sexuality in our teaching and their popularity in our scholarship, it might seem . . . well . . . rather stupid to write yet another book about them. But as I combed through scores of books on the topic, I noticed that something was consistently missing. It seemed to me that the vast majority of books in this area treat race, class, gender, and sexuality as independent concepts, often occupying entirely separate sections of the book. That approach would be relatively useful if people were just male or just Asian or just heterosexual and nothing else or if people embraced the same identity in every situation throughout their entire lives. But that's not the way most people define themselves or experience everyday life. In fact, the determination of our identities is always a little like ordering from a menu in a Chinese restaurant: We select one item—or sometimes more than one item—from column A, column B, column C, and so on and then we mix everything together on our plate. The meal is not simply three or four or five separate and mutually exclusive dishes, but a mélange of our various selections. And the next time we order Chinese food, we may come up with a different combination of flavors.

So this book emphasizes the confluence of those four key social identifiers—race (and ethnicity), class, gender, and sexuality—from the perspective of individuals embedded in particular cultural, institutional, and historical contexts. I attempt to move away from the common "if it's week three, it must be gender" way of teaching this topic to a more integrated examination of how these four elements work together (or for that matter, in opposition) to form people's social identities and experiences with inequality.

Another complexity that cropped up as I was writing this book is that it's nearly impossible to account for—let alone explain—the experiences of everyone. It became clear early on that it would be impossible to address every possible combination of every race, class, gender, and sexual category. Instead, I've tried to consistently examine the experiences of people at all levels of the continuum of inequality. Too often sociologists focus on those who veer most obviously from the dominant groups: poor people, women, people who are members of non-white ethnoracial groups, homosexuals. I feel it is important to try to examine race, class, gender, and sexuality as variables with many constituent categories and not as single attributes. This book explores the experiences of white people as well as people of color; men as well as women; the wealthy and the middle class as well as the poor and working class; heterosexuals and bisexuals as well as homosexuals. It is about privilege as well as disadvantage, "otherness" as well as similarity, invisibility as well as visibility.

Trying to accomplish this balancing act hasn't been easy. And at the risk of giving away the punch line too soon, the overall message about inequality is not particularly uplifting. Although, as a society, we've made tremendous strides in acknowledging the problems some groups face and in improving their lives, we still face imbalances, injustices, and disadvantages. But perhaps by grappling with the sociological theories, research, and insight that inform this book, you will come to think of yourself and others as complex beings whose multifaceted identities offer both challenges and opportunities.

THE BOOK'S WRITING STYLE

Because so much of what you will read in this book is derived from research conducted by professional social scientists, it has the potential to seem rather cold and distant. So I have chosen to write this book in a style that I hope is simultaneously informative, accessible, and entertaining. I have tried to avoid baffling jargon wherever possible. At the same time, I have tried not to oversimplify the material. In short, I have tried to write the way I speak (hopefully with all my grammatical gaffes edited out). I truly believe that sociology has a great deal of useful information to offer, which people need to know simply in order to understand how their lives intersect with the social structure, and that a comfortable writing style helps to get that information across.

Each chapter begins with a small snippet of everyday life—often taken from my own experiences—to show you how the information contained in that chapter applies to understanding our personal lives. Indeed, the book is peppered with such examples, sometimes taken from contemporary headlines and sometimes taken from the lives of people just like you and me.

Moreover, you'll notice that the book is written primarily in the first person. I have purposely chosen to write the book this way to remind you that it comes from a real individual (me) who often struggles just like you to understand how and why things happen. I know it's heresy for an author to admit deficiencies in knowledge, but I am not so arrogant as to believe that I know everything. Most of the questions that crop up in a book about social identities and inequalities do not have easy, clear, straightforward answers. Indeed, the answers are usually frustratingly complex or even unanswerable. But that shouldn't stop us from asking them.

The first-person format of the book also serves as a reminder that as a real human being, I have beliefs, assumptions, biases, and values that I bring with me to every situation I encounter—including book writing. This book is about social inequalities because I believe that although we can debate their causes, educational, legal, political, cultural, and economic imbalances exist and create serious problems for some people while creating enormous advantages for others. That's not meant to be a blanket condemnation of those at the top or a blanket absolution of responsibility of the "downtrodden." Instead, it is my belief, based on the evidence that I have seen (and present in this book), that the way people are defined and treated in society—both by others and by the larger social institutions that govern everyday life—is not fixed and inevitable. In some ways, conditions are better than they once were; in other ways, they're worse. Sometimes people deserve the problems they bring on themselves; other times they truly are the innocent victims of circumstances that are largely beyond their control. Sometimes people who are advantaged are generous and helpful; other times they're callous and exploitative.

My purpose in this book is not to persuade you to believe exactly what I believe or adopt the same perspective on things that I have. On the contrary, my hope simply is that by reading this book you will begin to take a critical look at your life in relation to others and to the society in which you live. Some of what you will read will make you nod in agreement; some of it will make you angry and frustrated. But all of it will make you acknowledge and, I hope, examine your own beliefs, your own values, and the assumptions you make about others who are different from you.

THE BOOK'S ORGANIZATION

This book is organized as simply as possible. It's divided into two parts that, from the title, should be quite obvious. Part 1, *Identities*, examines the origin and utility of the concepts of race, class, gender, and sexuality. It focuses primarily on the nature of difference, the historical construction of these identifying concepts, the ways they are culturally presented and reflected in language and media, and the ways they are learned and incorporated into our personal identities. Where do our ideas about race, class, gender, and sexuality come from? How are they defined? How do we balance the features that make us different from others with those that we have in common? How do we learn to be a member of a particular gender, race, class, or sexual group and come to see ourselves accordingly?

Part 2, *Inequalities*, draws on the information in Part 1 and examines the everyday and institutional consequences of race, class, gender, and sexuality, paying particular attention to their relationship to social inequality. This part explores issues of prejudice and discrimination at the individual level and in the context of important social institutions: the economy, the criminal justice system, and the health care system. The final chapter examines the future of inequalities, paying particular attention to movements for social change.

To highlight the importance of examining the connections between race, class, gender, and sexuality, a feature called "Intersections" appears throughout the book. These features focus on specific areas of research or interesting social phenomena that illustrate the important combinations of two or more social identifiers. The goal is to enhance your appreciation of the importance of looking at race, class, gender, and sexuality collectively rather than separately. These sections cover such topics as mothering, single parenthood, bullying in high school, the response to natural disasters, the history of childbirth, body image, the death penalty, and workplace discrimination.

At the end of each chapter is an exercise titled "Investigating Identities and Inequalities," which will allow you to go outside the classroom and systematically observe some aspect of social identity and inequality. Some of the exercises require that you survey other people in order to gain some insight into their firsthand experiences. Others ask you to venture into your own past or into common social settings—businesses, local neighborhoods, hospitals—to examine the features that perpetuate social inequalities. I believe that learning is most effective and meaningful when it is active, not passive. These exercises are designed to bring you face-to-face with the everyday experiences of identities and inequalities from the perspective of both individuals and the social institutions they inhabit.

THE BOOK'S REVISED EDITION

The previous (second) edition of this book has a copyright date of 2012. In truth, I finished writing it in the summer of 2010 but a lengthy production process meant it actually first appeared in print in 2011. I think it might be one of the greatest understatements of all time to say that a lot has happened since 2010: Barack Obama's reelection; the killing of Osama bin Laden; the passage of comprehensive health care coverage reform; mass shootings in Aurora, Colorado, Newtown, Connecticut, and many other places; super-storm Sandy, the disappearance of a Malaysian Airlines plane; the ending of the wars in Iraq and Afghanistan; the Syrian refugee crisis; massive uprisings in the Middle East and the Ukraine; racial protests in Ferguson, Missouri, Staten Island, New York, and various college campus across the country; photobombing, selfies, the Red Wedding in *Game of Thrones,* and Miley Cyrus's twerking. So revising this book 5 years after I last revised it required a lot of updating!

I have revised all the relevant statistics in the book and have replaced outdated examples with new ones. I have added some new "Intersections" features and removed others. I have adjusted a great deal of content to account for the most recent events on the political, economic, and cultural landscape. In short, I have tried to make this book as up-to-date as possible.

MY CREDENTIALS

As I alluded to earlier, I am male. I am white. I am heterosexual. I suppose I am middle-class, though significant portions of my life would be better characterized as working class. Although I am a member of a religious minority, most people would say that I'm comfortably situated at the advantaged end of all the important dimensions that determine social privilege. What, then, can I possibly say about the intersections of race, class, gender, and sexuality and their contribution to the construction of social inequalities? What do I know about being the victim of subtle and wanton discrimination?

Some of you might think that my traits immediately disqualify me from writing this book. But although I can't truly know what it feels like to be a woman, an immigrant, a member of an ethnoracial minority, a homosexual, or a desperately poor person in this society, I do know what it feels like to *have* a gender, race, sexual orientation, and class standing. These characteristics are not invisible to me.

I went to college in San Diego, California, not far from the Mexican border. At the time, my parents lived in the Los Angeles area, about a 2-hour drive north up Interstate 5. I made this drive a couple of times a month throughout college, mostly to eat a decent meal and do my laundry. Fifty miles or so north of San Diego along the freeway was an Immigration and Naturalization Service checkpoint. Northbound traffic was required to slow down so INS officers could visually inspect the vehicles to see if any of the riders might be in the country illegally. Suspicious cars were instructed to pull over for a more thorough inspection. In the 4 years I made that drive, I never experienced any problems at this checkpoint. I was always quickly waved through by a smiling INS officer and allowed to go on my merry way. That is, except for the one time a dark-skinned friend of mine (whose parents had emigrated to this country from Pakistan) made the drive with me. Instead of being waved through as I expected, we were pulled over and the car searched. I was asked nothing. He was asked a series of intrusive questions about why he was traveling to L.A., why he was in the country, and how long he planned to be here. Eventually we were allowed to leave, but not before he got a serious dose of humiliation and I got a lesson about the unequal treatment people receive because of the color of their skin.

This experience made me realize that being a member of privileged social categories means that I have a special obligation to understand the systems of advantage and inequality that exist in this society. I have spent my entire academic life in the pursuit of this understanding, and I have spent my entire life as an adult citizen seeking ways to redress the disadvantages that others suffer. Now it is my privilege to be in a position to share some of what I've learned about inequalities in this book. I hope it helps you to understand how your own identities—whatever they may be—shape your experiences and how you can use your knowledge to shape a more just society.

ACKNOWLEDGMENTS

Just as I started writing the first edition of this book, I was invited to participate in a panel discussion with a few colleagues from other departments on the process of writing. In addition to me, there was a fiction writer, a psychologist, and a historian. We talked about how we write, why we write, when and where we write, and so on. Although our specific tastes and styles were quite different, we all had some things in common. When the topic came to the role of other people in the writing process, everyone around the table agreed that input from others is vital. I, however, broke ranks and stated rather bluntly that writing is as solitary an act as there is. When push comes to shove, I pointed out, it's just the author, alone with her or his keyboard, who's responsible for organizing a dense body of knowledge and creatively presenting it in a way that makes grammatical and substantive sense to the reader.

But that's not to say that others don't play a role. Indeed they do. Anyone who's written a book knows full well that books are always collective ventures. We get editorial help from some people and content help from others. Some people pitch in with the mundane responsibilities of everyday life to free us up to write. And the indebtedness we feel toward them is genuine and deserved. As weird and paradoxical as it sounds, the solitary act of writing cannot be accomplished without the help of other people. That said, let me acknowledge the people who managed to effectively avoid annoying me as I wrote this book.

First, I'd like to thank Gina Boedeker, Jamie Laferrera, Penina Braffman, Anthony McHugh, Kelly Hart, Jenilynn McAtee, and the rest of the McGraw-Hill team members for providing their time, energy, and useful suggestions during the planning and editing phases of the project. I'd also like to express my appreciation to Arpana Kumari for her production work and Tricia Lawrence for her work on copyediting the manuscript.

Special thanks to my research assistant, Kristin Otto. Any allusions and references I make to cutting-edge events that make me look hip are likely attributable to Kristin's keen eye and meticulous attention to detail.

In addition, thanks to the following instructors who provided valuable feedback in their reviews of all three editions of the book:

Julie Armstrong-Binnix, Bellarmine University
Todd E. Bernhardt, Broward Community College
Nelson E. Bingham, Earlham College
Michelle J. Budig, University of Massachusetts
Jan Buhrmann, Illinois College
Gloria Carpenter, Northern Kentucky University
Philip N. Cohen, University of California–Irvine
Patricia Drew, California State University, East Bay
Dr. Thomas P. Egan, University of Kentucky
Rachel L. Einwohner, Purdue University
Elizabeth B. Erbaugh, University of New Mexico
Dona C. Fletcher, Sinclair Community College
Sarah N. Gatson, Texas A&M University
Tom Gerschick, Illinois State University
Suzanne Hopf, University of Louisville
Judith A. Howard, University of Washington
Shayne Lee, University of Houston
Larry Lovell-Troy, Millikin University
Dr. R. Kirk Mauldin, Lake Superior State University
Peter Meiksins, Cleveland State University
Breny Mendoza, California State University, Northridge
Morgan Metzger Silk, Centenary College
Seth Ovadia, Towson University
Michael P. Perez, California State University–Fullerton
Craig T. Robertson, University of North Alabama
Sergio Romero, University of Montana
Deborah J. Safron, Michigan State University
Matthew Smith-Lahrman, Dixie State College of Utah
Jenny Stuber, University of North Florida
Theodore C. Wagenaar, Miami University
Janelle Wilson, University of Minnesota–Duluth
Idee Winfield, College of Charleston
Mark E. Woods, University of Akron-Wayne College

Several friends and colleagues provided suggestions and "raw data" along the way. In particular, my wife, Rebecca Upton, has been a rock of emotional support and especially helpful in providing numerous anthropological examples. Finally, I'd like to thank Mokolodi Underfoot for reminding me that no problem was too large to be fixed by a good belly scratch.

IDENTITIES
AND
INEQUALITIES

Identities

What would you say if someone asked, "Who are you?" Would you answer differently if this person asked, "*What* are you?" Both questions request that you reveal some component of your identity, but the second is particularly likely to probe your *social* identities, the group memberships by which you define and place yourself in relation to others.

These social identities consist of a variety of different components. Some mark us as unique, distinct from anyone else on the planet. Others highlight commonalities and connect us to larger communities of people, giving us a sense of belongingness and perhaps even collective pride. In Part 1, I will explore the nature, development, and intersections of our social identities, especially race, class, gender, and sexuality. ■

CHAPTER 1

Differences and Similarities

The National September 11 Memorial & Museum opened as I was starting to revise this chapter, serving to remind the nation—a decade and a half after the event—that 9/11/2001 remains the most significant day in American history. Close to 3,000 people lost their lives in the attacks that occurred that morning, and hundreds of thousands more died in the ensuing military actions in Afghanistan and Iraq and the sectarian violence that continues to plague the Middle East to this day. The events of 9/11 changed the political, social, economic, and ideological course of history like perhaps no other moment in our lives. Whether you were a full-grown adult at the time or a small child—like most of today's college students—that September day a decade and a half ago is one of those punctuating flashes that clearly demarcates the "before" and "after" of an entire country.

To varying degrees, all of us have seen the common rhythm of our daily lives change since 9/11. For instance, you've no doubt experienced that day's effects in your air travel behaviors—from the clothes you wear on flights, the liquids you bring with you in your carry-on, and the way you pack your luggage to the preflight time you allot yourself to get through TSA security checkpoints. Even if you don't fly, news reports of bombings or kidnappings or mysterious plane crashes or suspicious untended vehicles on crowded urban thoroughfares can easily trigger a wave of "not again" panic among those who remember 9/11. If, like me, you're middle-aged you might still get a little queasy when watching pre-2001 films set in Manhattan, hoping that casual shots of the World Trade Center towers won't appear in the background, conjuring up those recognizable feelings of sadness and lingering disbelief. At the linguistic level, terms like "homeland security," "ground zero," "terrorism," "Taliban," and "weapons of mass destruction" are now common components of our everyday vocabulary.

For our current purposes—that is, a book about identities and inequalities—what's especially important about 9/11 and its aftermath is that it serves as a powerful symbol of the common ways that Americans have always thought about themselves and others. I still remember a discussion in one of my courses the day after the attacks in which a student remarked that this national catastrophe, like others before it, would inevitably bring out the absolute best and absolute worst in us as a society and as a people. She was right, of course. In the days and weeks following the attacks, strangers came together like never before to weep, to grieve, and to share in the collective pain of this tragedy. Communities rallied to take care of their own. People began to feel a sense of solidarity, motivated not only by a swelling anger directed outward against the perpetrators but by a shared inward anguish. We were one. No matter what our ethnic, racial, religious, or class background was or where we fell on the political spectrum, we were in this nightmare together. Getting annoyed at the slow driver in front of you on the highway or fuming over the fact that your local grocery store was out of your favorite brand of ice cream didn't seem worth it anymore. All those trivial irritations that once drove us to distraction no longer seemed so significant compared to the powerful need to salve our psychic wounds and take care of one another.

And yet there was an unmistakable and predictable darker side that also emerged as a result of these attacks: a hideous unmasking of our deep-seated hatreds and prejudices. In the weeks and months following 9/11, individuals who looked "Middle Eastern" were beaten up on the street or taunted in their schools. Some people found themselves stopped and interrogated by law enforcement officials because they fit a stereotypical terrorist profile. Old friendships disintegrated; lives were destroyed by innuendo and mistrust. As one political scientist put it a decade later, "9/11 was this moment that we came together, and it lasted about three-and-a-half minutes" (quoted in Goodstein, 2011, p. A1). Nationwide, 762 Muslims were rounded up in the aftermath of the attacks and kept in jail, sometimes for months at a time. More often than not, they were arrested as a result of a neighbor or acquaintance calling law enforcement. One landlord reported several of her tenants, who were "Middle Eastern," to the FBI simply because she "would feel awful if [they] were involved in terrorism and she didn't call" (quoted in Neumeister, 2015, p. A5).

The anger and anti-Muslim rhetoric hasn't completely abated:

- In 2012, a Wisconsin man murdered six congregants and wounded a police officer at a Sikh temple because he thought the Sikhs were Muslim. A day later, a mosque in Joplin, Missouri, was burned to the ground (Beinart, 2012).
- A few years ago, the New York Police Department used a film, titled *The Third Jihad*, as part of its training program of new police recruits. The film depicted Muslim terrorists shooting Christians in the head and exploding car bombs; images of "executed" American children covered by sheets; and a doctored photograph showing an Islamic flag flying over the White House (Powell, 2012). Not until 2014, did the New York Police Department abandon a program—called the Demographics Unit—that sent plainclothes detectives into Muslim neighborhoods to compile files on where residents ate, prayed, and shopped (Apuzzo & Goldstein, 2014).
- One presidential candidate in the run-up to the 2016 election, proposed a ban on *all* Muslim immigrants.

It is still the case today that anyone whose apparent ethnicity even remotely resembles that of the people responsible for the attacks is subjected to subtle signs of suspicion: angry stares, apprehensive whispers, interpersonal withdrawal, or outright expressions of hatred. Twitter lit up with angry tweets in 2013 when Nina Davulri (who is actually of Indian descent and is not Muslim) was crowned Miss America (Broderick, 2013):

"[The anniversary of] 9/11 was four days ago and *she* gets Miss America?"

"Miss America or Miss al Qaeda?"

"More like Miss Terrorist."

Several years ago, a white colleague in another department was telling me about the intense scrutiny he was subjected to when he stopped at a border checkpoint while driving from Canada back into the United States. When he finished, he quipped, "Yeah, but if I was an Arab, I'd have been there for hours and they probably would have strip-searched me!" Though he meant his remark as a joke, there was certainly some truth to his contention that people from particular ethnic groups do not enjoy the same interactional privileges as members of other groups. The fact of the matter is that his coloring would always serve as a protective shield against others' fears.

In terrifying times when all people want is to feel safe and secure, the things that mark us as different take on added weight, overwhelming all the things that we might have in common. Easily visible distinctions become the chief criteria for deciding who is trustworthy and who is suspect, who is harmless, and who is dangerous. Out of a mistaken belief that those who look different pose the greatest risk to personal well-being, some people secretly and not-so-secretly long to surround themselves with others who are "like me." "You're either with us or against us" becomes a rallying cry used to quell any sort of difference or dissent.

September 11 wasn't the first time that we let our differences divide us, and sadly it probably won't be the last. A quick glance back in time reveals that virtually every minority group in this country—be it racial, ethnic, religious, sexual, gender-based, or class-based—has had or continues to have its own historical moment of suspicion and persecution:

- From 1619, when the first black slaves arrived, to 1865, when the 13th Amendment was ratified, outlawing slavery, millions of African Americans endured the hardships of forced servitude. After emancipation, they continued to be brutalized through the practice of lynching and other forms of violent intimidation.

- After centuries of mistreatment and forced relocation of Native Americans, the Homestead Act of 1862 gave any U.S. citizen the right to lay claim to 160 acres on land that had been recently cleared of Native Americans. The Dawes Allotment Act of 1887 granted parcels of reservation land to individuals rather than to particular tribes. It was believed that if individuals owned their own land, adopted white clothing and ways, and were responsible for their own farms, they would gradually lose their Indianness and be assimilated into the white population.

- In the mid-19th century, war with Mexico and westward expansion redrew national boundaries, enabling white settlers to freely move into lands previously inhabited by Mexicans.

- In the late 19th and early 20th centuries, several laws, such as the Chinese Exclusion Act, the Scott Act, and the Geary Act, barred Chinese immigrants from entering the country and stripped those already here of many of their legal rights.
- Early 20th-century immigrants from Ireland, Italy, Greece, Poland, Russia, and other Eastern European countries were subjected to varying degrees of hostility and discrimination. Business owners routinely prevented individuals from these groups from applying for jobs that were open to other Whites. The National Origins Act of 1924 established quotas on immigrants from southern and Eastern Europe.
- During the Great Depression of the 1930s, poor refugees from Oklahoma who moved westward in search of work were exploited, beaten, and forced to live in shantytowns known as "Hoovervilles."
- Japanese Americans (and some non-Japanese Asian people) were forcibly relocated from their homes to high-security internment camps after the bombing of Pearl Harbor and our entry into World War II.

In short, the tension between similarity and difference—what brings us together and pushes us apart—has been the hallmark of the American experience for centuries. While we take great pride in the fact that we are a nation of immigrants, the responses to people who are different are often tinged with tension, distrust, and hostility. In this chapter, we'll look at this phenomenon from a **sociological perspective**—a way of examining everyday social life that emphasizes the interplay between societal forces and personal characteristics—in influencing people's thoughts, actions, feelings, judgments, and interactions. Why do people distinguish between "us" and "them"? Are some aspects of difference more desirable than others?

SIMILARITIES AND DIFFERENCES IN EVERYDAY LIFE: DRAWING LINES

As a rule, I hate clichés. Several years ago, I (jokingly) told my university's student body president, who was preparing her speech for the commencement ceremony, that if she used any clichés (like "Today we embark on a life's journey filled with exciting new challenges" or "In my four years here, I learned to think outside the box"), I'd change the "A" she just got in my sociology class to an "F." But clichés always have some kernel of truth to them. Take *no two people are exactly alike*, for example. Obviously, no two people could ever be exactly alike. Walk down a bustling city street someday, and you'll no doubt see an eye-popping assortment of human sizes, shapes, skin colors, and ages. Spend a little time getting to know the people you meet and you'll unearth a vast range of different mannerisms, life experiences, attitudes, values, ideas, tastes, likes, dislikes, and so on. Even if you encounter identical twins you'll soon be able to distinguish one from the other. Your faith in clichés would soon be restored!

But let's imagine, in a science-fiction sort of way, what the world would look like if we take that trite statement to a ridiculously extreme conclusion. What if no two people were alike in *any* way? That is, what if we shared absolutely nothing with anyone else—no physical characteristic, no personality trait, no life experience? Imagine that every single human being was a unique sex, age, or race. Imagine if no two people had the same educational experiences, the same relationships with their parents, the same number of siblings, or the same socioeconomic status. What if no two people prayed to the same god, spoke the same language, told time the same way, obeyed the same laws, enjoyed the same music, or found the same food tasty? In this imaginary world, meeting someone for the first time would be like meeting a new life form from another planet. You wouldn't be able to place that person into any sort of existing social category. You wouldn't be able to draw on your past experiences with people who possess similar characteristics. You could assume nothing about anyone you meet . . . ever. In such a world, life would be utterly chaotic and unmanageable.

So, there are some limits to the applicability of this little cliché. Obviously, there's something more to this society than 330 million or so completely "unalike" individuals living in the same geographic region of the world. It turns out that each of us—even the most strikingly distinctive person you know—actually has quite a bit in common with other Americans. We're not clones, of course, but we do share membership in particular categories. With some people, we have a gender in common; with others, a sexual orientation, a race, an ethnicity, a religion, or a social class.

Although at times it's to our advantage to recognize and celebrate our individual uniqueness, at other times it's these similarities that provide us with the comfort of knowing that there are "people like us." Perhaps you've attended a festival devoted to the collective expression of pride in your ethnic group. If you're Irish, you're lucky enough to have one day a year devoted to your heritage: St. Patrick's Day. Or maybe you've found yourself in a different city and attended a religious service at your religion's local church, synagogue, or mosque, and felt reassured by the fact that these strangers shared your spiritual beliefs, prayed the same way you do, and knew the words to your favorite hymns. Or maybe you've had the experience of traveling somewhere far away and meeting someone who happens to hail from your hometown. You may not even know this person, but right away you're likely to feel a connection, a bond that can be reinforced by talk about neighborhoods, restaurants, and landmarks that only someone from your town could appreciate.

If you think about it, the fact that we're able to live together in a reasonably stable way most of the time is possible only because we have many things in common that we can easily count on. You can assume, for instance, that upon initiating a handshake with someone you've just met, this person won't slap or spit on your extended hand but instead will hold it for a second and release it. Indeed, our everyday lives rely on hundreds of these taken-for-granted bits of information that we assume others understand as we do. These things are so common, so immediately understood, that we rarely have to think about them.

We come to further appreciate these commonalities when we're faced with situations in which we *can't* assume that everybody knows what we know. If you've ever traveled to a foreign country, for instance, you probably felt some disorientation when you first arrived. Some of the confusion could no doubt be attributed to not knowing the language well enough to read street signs or ask people for directions or order from a restaurant menu. But you probably quickly realized that you lacked more than just an understanding of the vocabulary. You lacked knowledge of the common, taken-for-granted assumptions of everyday life. You didn't share the rules, the unspoken code of behavior that people with common cultural understandings unquestioningly live by. What's the acceptable way to greet people on the street? How do you tip in a restaurant? How close do you stand next to a stranger on a crowded bus? To some degree, we experience these differences when we come into contact with other groups in our own society.

So the trick to living in a society like ours where people differ on some social dimensions but share others is finding a way to balance the things that make us dissimilar with the things that make us alike. At what point, for instance, does strong pride in our heritage or ethnicity become exclusionary, intolerant, and maybe even intimidating to those who don't belong? Wearing a large crucifix around your neck or displaying a Confederate battle flag on your car may be expressions of pride that hold people of a particular community together, but they can also evoke extreme emotions in others who don't share those beliefs or sentiments and who may even feel threatened by them.

Deciding when, where, and with whom to highlight certain differences is a constant struggle of social life. Some distinguishing features are, of course, more important than others. We don't attribute much significance to differences in eye color or foot size or whether people have earlobes or not.

But differences in race, gender, social class, and sexual orientation carry enormous cultural, historical, and institutional weight in this society.

Some of the things that mark us as different may even be considered positive or even fashionable. For instance, when it comes to food, music, or art, many of us enjoy the diverse palette of ethnic influences. Neighborhoods become "trendy" or hip if they have an abundance of ethnic restaurants from which to choose or some chic shops offering collections of ethnic-themed goods different from what one finds at a generic shopping mall. These kinds of differences aren't threatening. Instead, they're safe because they give people an opportunity to taste another way of life without actually having to live it.

Other social differences don't carry the same cachet, however. Distinctive lifestyles associated with a lack of wealth, for example, don't have quite the aura of exotic desirability that ethnic differences can sometimes have. Poor or working-class people may wear clothes, eat food, or engage in leisure activities that distinguish them from, say, middle-class people. But these differences are not choices that express their pride in being poor; they're ways of life that reflect limited or nonexistent opportunities to live differently. Poor people have a different diet from wealthier people because they can't afford anything else. Have you ever heard someone say, "Hey, let's go get some poor people's take-out"? Unlikely. The former chief executive at the health food chain, Trader Joe's, generated controversy a few years ago when he opened a store called "Daily Table" that sells expired or cosmetically blemished food to low-income customers. Critics claim he is simply selling "poor people rich people's garbage" (Reeves, 2013, p. 16).

Indeed, any sort of celebration of a "poverty lifestyle" strikes many people as cruel and insensitive. For instance, when you think of vacation tours, what comes to mind? Visits to temples? Trips to monuments? Natural wonders? Over the past decade or so, however, chartered tours of some of the world's worst slums in places like Brazil, India, and South Africa have grown in popularity. On such trips—referred to as *slum tourism* or *poorism*—groups of Western tourists are guided through crowded, dirty scenes of human misery, ostensibly to learn about and empathize with those who live in abject poverty. But one study of tourists visiting a slum in Mumbai, India found that visitors were motivated primarily by curiosity rather than the desire to understand poverty (Ma, 2010).

When closer to home, the lifestyles of poor or working-class people are rarely seen for the photo opportunities they provide. More seriously, poor and working-class people are sometimes seen as a direct threat to the sensibilities and values of wealthier people. When a trailer park or a low-income apartment complex is feared to bring down the property values of an adjacent middle-class neighborhood, residents may mobilize all their energies to prevent the "intrusion."

"CLASSIFIED" INFORMATION: FORMING IMPRESSIONS

Humans have a powerful tendency to define, classify, and categorize. Among the ways they apply this tendency is to sort themselves and their fellow humans into groups. Every human society—from the simplest to the most complex; from the most uniform to the most diverse—has a means by which members differentiate themselves from one another.

People begin defining, differentiating, and ranking things early on. When children are first learning to talk, they begin to understand that tangible objects fall into broad distinct categories: Apples and oranges are "fruits," Chihuahuas and Great Danes are "dogs," Fords and Toyotas are "cars," and so on. They also learn that these categories can be distinguished from other categories: Fruits are different from vegetables, dogs are different from cats, and cars are different from trucks. Eventually, they learn that people can also be categorized and differentiated. As they get older, children spend a huge chunk of their lives ruthlessly making us/them distinctions and then ranking people in terms of those distinctions. Pre-schoolers often use racial and ethnic concepts to define others (Van Ausdale & Feagin, 2001). Indeed, judging and ranking others is probably the defining feature of social life in American elementary, middle/junior high, and high schools. As early as the third grade, children develop sophisticated ways of including some and excluding others that result in a clearly identifiable power hierarchy among 9-year-olds (Adler & Adler, 1998). Young people typically go beyond the most obvious types of distinctions (gender, race, religion, age, grade level) to more specific lifestyle traits and labels, such as jocks, preps, burnouts, emo, geeks, hip hop, metal-heads, punks, goths, health goths, gangstas, and so on.

When obvious distinguishing characteristics aren't available, young people will often invent them. When I was a pre-teen growing up in southern California, two broad groups dominated social life at my junior high school: *surfers* (who tended to be white) and *low-riders* (who tended to be Latino/a). The labels originally derived from specific recreational activities: surfing and driving cars that sat low to the ground. But one didn't have to surf or even have a drivers' license to be a member of either group. The labels were simply shorthand for creating broad divisions that sometimes—but not always—paralleled ethnic and social class differences. The two groups rarely interacted and fights between them were common. The creation and maintenance of such boundaries provided the interpersonal landscape on which everything else in school seemed to be built: friendship, romance, popularity, physical safety, and so on.

Eventually (and luckily!), most of us come to realize that the categorical cliques that are so vital to us as teenagers are based on rather superficial information—what a person wears, what kind of music a person listens to, what jargon the person uses, how a person carries her or his book bag, and so on. But other criteria maintain their importance throughout our lives. We never stop defining group boundaries in terms of countries, regions, religions, generations, races, sexes, classes, political groups, families, and so on (Epstein, 1997). We all know the powerful role that these differentiating characteristics play in everyday life.

Indeed, we highlight the importance of this information each time we meet someone and immediately draw inferences about that person based on a quick assessment of his or her membership in particular social groups. We learn—from others, from past experiences, from the media—the cultural significance in this society of being male or female, Asian or African American, upper class or working class, gay or straight. For instance, if all you know about someone you meet for the first time is that she's female, you might initially assume that she's probably more compassionate, more nurturing, and less aggressive than if she were male. Likewise, if all you knew about a person was that she is in her late 60s, you might conclude that she is close to retirement, enjoys the "oldies" radio station, goes to bed while it's still light out, and has no idea what Twitter or Pinterest is. Imagine learning that your college roommate is of a different race and comes from a different state or, for that matter, a different country. Think about all the inferences you'd make about this person even before you meet her or him. "She's Asian? I bet she'll be studying all the time." "He's from Texas? Well, I guess that means I'm doomed to a steady dose of Tim McGraw on iTunes." "She's originally from France? She probably wears black, smokes cigarettes, and constantly complains about how awful American fast food is."

Of course, these sorts of conclusions can never (or should never) be final. Forming impressions and expectations of others on such a tiny amount of information can never be completely accurate. Certainly, we don't want to admit that our interchanges with others depend on that person's sex or race or religion. But, whether we like it or not and whether it's fair or not, we always begin social interactions with these kinds of culturally defined ideas about how people in certain social groups are likely to act, what their values might be, and what we think their tastes are. These initial assumptions save us the energy of having to start from scratch in forming impressions of every single person we meet.

VARIATION BETWEEN GROUPS, VARIATION WITHIN GROUPS

When thinking about the implications of race, class, gender, and sexual diversity for people's everyday experiences, there is a tendency to focus on the differences that exist between broad groups (for instance, between men and women, between working-class people and upper-class people, between heterosexuals and homosexuals, or between African Americans and Whites). This emphasis on between-group differences can obscure both the differences that exist among individuals within groups as well as the similarities that exist between individuals who belong to different groups. It may be fashionable to talk about men and women as being from different planets, but such a conclusion overshadows the fact that they are much more alike than they are different. Similarly, if you're white, it's tempting to view African Americans, Latino/as, Asians, and Native Americans as uniform (what sociologists call *homogeneous*) communities of "others," with similar values, interests, and behaviors, even though there is tremendous variation within each of these groups. In Chapter 3, we will examine how this tendency is reflected in our racial language—for instance, using the term "Asian" to lump together a variety of people with very different languages, cultures, and immigrant experiences.

At the individual level, the tendency to overlook within-group variation can have important consequences. Students of color at predominantly white universities, for example, report that their white fellow students and even their white professors often look to them in class to provide a "minority perspective" on particular issues (Feagin, Vera, & Imani, 2000). Similarly, the thoughts, beliefs, and actions of a lone female executive in a predominantly male company may be taken by her male coworkers as typical of all women (Kanter, 1987). The assumption underlying such experiences is that members of a particular race or gender are so similar that one individual can be a spokesperson for the entire group.

But when we think of our own group—be it based on race, ethnicity, gender, class, or sexual orientation—we're more inclined to highlight or at least pay heed to the diversity of individuals within it. We're less willing to make generalizations about our own group because we know, from firsthand experiences with fellow members, that we don't all believe the same things, act the same way, or speak with a singular voice.

I teach at a private liberal arts university in the Midwest. My students are predominantly white (though this is less true than it used to be), and many come from wealthy families. As a way of introducing the topic of race in the introductory course I teach, I sometimes ask my students to list the features that they think are typical of African Americans. When they're finished compiling that list, we do the same for Latino/as, and then for Asian Americans. I don't filter or modify their lists. I simply record on the board what they mention. Once they get beyond their initial discomfort, they have little trouble identifying these traits, even though they're always quick to point out that many of the items on the lists are stereotypes that they, themselves, don't believe. Some of the characteristics they mention are positive (for instance, Asian families are supportive and tight-knit); others are distinctly negative (for instance, African American families are weak and prone to instability).

I then ask them to list the traits that characterize Whites. Here the discussion usually grinds to a screeching halt. They have difficulty with this question. But I don't come to their rescue. I let them struggle. After a while, some version of the following conversation inevitably ensues:

Student: "What kind of Whites are you talking about?"
    Me: "What do you mean?"
Student: "Well, there are too many kinds of white people to generalize."
    Me: "OK, what kinds of white people are there?"
Student: "Some are poor and they're different from those who are rich."
    Me: "Uh-huh. Go on."
Student: "Some are very religious and others are atheists. Also they might be of different nationalities, live in different parts of the country. You know, they're all different. There's no way you can come up with common traits."
    Me: "You're absolutely right! [The student usually beams with pride at this point for being a good sociologist.] But why didn't you ask me what kind of African Americans or Latino/as or Asian Americans I had in mind when I asked you to characterize them? Surely there are rich Asians and poor Asians. There must be religious Latino/as and nonreligious Latino/as out there. Some African Americans live in big cities and others live on farms, right?"

My point in these discussions is not to reinforce stereotypes or to publicly humiliate my students. Instead, it is to illustrate how our relative perspectives determine our perceptions of between-group and within-group diversity. These mostly white students were flummoxed by the question because of the obvious variety they saw in the category "white." Being a member of a majority racial group conferred on them the privilege of thinking about their whiteness in terms of individuality and not in terms of common traits (Waters, 2010). Yet, when considering other groups, they were more inclined to fall back onto broad generalizations, even though there's just as much within-group diversity among African Americans, Latino/as, and Asian Americans as there is among Whites. They soon realize that it's misleading to try to ignore these within-group differences to talk about all African Americans, all Latino/as, all Asians, or all Whites as if they were homogeneous groups. For that matter, it would be misleading to discuss all heterosexuals, all poor people, or all men as if they all looked alike, acted alike, and believed the same things.

THE POWER OF "NORMAL": ALL DIFFERENCES ARE NOT CREATED EQUAL

To "vary" is to deviate or to depart from what is expected. Variations fall outside the typical. When musicians talk about variations on a theme, they imply that there is a main, core composition from which other works diverge. The same goes for human difference. A term like "diversity" means variety; but it also implies that there is a standard way of being from which others deviate. If your campus is like most, conversations about "diversity" have become increasingly common and heated in recent years. But chances are when most of people talk about "diversity," it's usually in terms of underrepresented groups (the "variations") rather than of the dominant group.

Let's look at this more closely. In a racially imbalanced society like ours, whiteness, in general, is the unlabeled yardstick against which "non-white" racial groups are evaluated (Dyer, 2012). Likewise, "middle-class," "heterosexual," and "male" are the taken-for-granted standards of class, sexuality, and gender. Each year, the U.S. Bureau of the Census makes available a compendium of population statistics covering all aspects of social life. The index of this massive document contains entries for "Women," "Poverty," "Black, African American population," "American Indian, Alaska Native population" "Asian and Pacific Islander population," and "Hispanic or Latino origin population," but none for "Men," "Middle class," or "White population."

Consider the legalization of same-sex marriage (see Chapter 7 for a lengthier discussion of this issue). When the state of Massachusetts began issuing marriage licenses to same-sex couples in 2004, it marked the first time in our history that a state granted gay and lesbian couples full legal recognition of their marriages. Over the next decade, 30-plus other states followed suit. In the summer of 2015, the U.S. Supreme Court ruled that same-sex marriage was legal in all states. More than just a symbolic gesture, such recognition came with many rights and privileges traditionally accorded only to heterosexual married couples, such as coverage on spousal insurance policies and inheritance rights. While many people view this change as a positive step forward in the movement for civil rights and same-sex married couples may soon become as unremarkable as straight married couples, notice how the movement for marriage rights reinforces the idea that the standard of intimacy toward which people are presumed to want to aspire is heterosexual marriage. In fact, some legal scholars have voiced concern that the legalization of same-sex marriage could result in the reduction or even abolition of certain benefits for unmarried gay partners (known as domestic partners).

Indeed, only until very recently, the cultural and media representation of every aspect of romance simply presumed a world in which men were sexually attracted to women and vice versa. Even today, mainstream ads that depict same-sex couples remain rare. Around Valentine's Day, you'd be hard pressed to find ads that *don't* depict men and women embracing, gazing longingly into each other's eyes, buying each other expensive jewelry, or enjoying the Sunday paper together in bed in their pajamas. Furthermore, the heterosexual standard is even apparent in academic scholarship. A mountain of space is devoted to articles on why people are homosexual, but few researchers bother to ask the question: Why are people heterosexual?

The fact that we make assumptions about what's "normal" and what's "diverse" may seem insignificant, but it is at the root of much social conflict. If different categories of people were arranged horizontally—that is, with all groups considered normal and all aligned on the same level—there'd be no problem. We'd all simply be part of a "vast cultural smorgasbord" (Anderson, 2001). However, in all societies, such distinctions tend to be arranged vertically, resulting in a ranking of groups. In every society, some people make the rules and others must live by those rules; some are granted the right to make important decisions and others must endure the consequences of those decisions; some enjoy everyday privileges that provide comfort and stability and others lack such privileges and experience constant struggles in their lives as a result. It's no surprise then, that given the historical arrangement of power relations in this society the standard of social comparison continues to be white, heterosexual, middle-class, and male. These differences determine access to resources, future goals and aspirations, and overall life chances. Systems of difference are always associated with systems of power and privilege (O'Brien, 1999).

Indeed, groups with significant social power typically have the luxury of remaining unexamined. For people who identify themselves as African American, Latino/a, Asian, and Native American in this society, race may be the pivot around which the rest of their lives circles. For Whites, race is something they rarely have to think about. It's a characteristic that other groups have. In Chapter 5, we'll see how such racial "invisibility" creates and reinforces positions of authority and dominance. Similarly, men have the luxury of living in a society where gender inequality is typically seen as a "women's issue." Like most people in dominant positions, men are largely unaware of the small and large advantages the social structure provides them. The same can be said for middle- and upper-class individuals and for heterosexuals.

In examining the roles that race, class, gender, and sexuality play in determining an individual's position of privilege or disadvantage in society, it's important to note that these factors can often conflict, even within the same person. The complex intersections of privilege are apparent in this sociologist's memoir:

> As the first and, for a while, only child of upper-middle-class, Orthodox Jewish parents growing up in New York City, race and class privilege came easily to me, but it was gender that has always been problematic. I understood in some vague way that it would have been preferable had I been born a boy. . . . At another time and in another place, perhaps, my parents would have found the birth of a girl child so burdensome that they would have simply abandoned me or sold me into marriage as an infant. . . . But I was fortunate; I was born into a family that did not have to choose which of its children to feed and clothe, or which would receive medical treatment and which would die from neglect. In this respect, a potential fate for others of my gender was mitigated by my class. (Rothenberg, 2000, pp. 9–10)

Similarly, a white lesbian enjoys social advantages because of her race but disadvantages because of her gender and sexuality. Black lesbians face disadvantage on three levels. As one author puts it, "Heterosexual privilege is usually the only privilege that black women have. None of us have racial or sexual privilege, almost none of us have class privilege, maintaining 'straightness' is our last resort" (quoted in Collins, 1990, pp. 195–196).

STRATIFICATION, POWER, AND PRIVILEGE

It doesn't take being on the wrong end of "normal" to know that people categorize others in comparison with themselves, make judgments about those others, and then act toward them on the basis of those judgments. From there, it's just a short step to understanding that inequality is woven into the fabric of all societies through a structured system of **stratification,** the ranking of entire groups of people that perpetuates unequal rewards and life chances. Just as geologists talk about strata of rock that are layered one on top of another, the "social strata" of people are arranged from low to high.

Stratification systems can be based on a variety of different dimensions and statuses. Sometimes groups of people are ranked on the basis of what sociologists call ascribed statuses. An **ascribed status** is a social identity or position that we obtain at birth or develop into involuntarily as we get older. Race, sex, ethnicity, religion, and family status (that is, the identity as someone's child or grandchild) are all usually considered ascribed statuses. As we age, we enter an ascribed identity called "teenager," followed by "middle-aged person," and ultimately "elderly." We can try to hide our "membership" in these positions (by wearing a toupee or buying a more youthful wardrobe), and sometimes people go to great lengths to change their ascribed status (as when individuals have sex-reassignment surgeries), but for the most part, ascribed statuses aren't positions we choose to occupy. An **achieved status,** in contrast, is a social position or identity we take on voluntarily or earn through our own efforts or accomplishments, like being a student, an entrepreneur, a spouse, or a sociologist.

Of course, the distinction between an ascribed and an achieved status is not always obvious. Some people become college students not because of their own efforts but because of their parents' influence. In theory, you can choose to identify with any religion you want, but chances are that the religion with which you identify is the one your parents belong to. But some people decide to change their religious membership later in life. More importantly, sex, race, ethnicity, and age may be ascribed statuses, but they have a direct effect on our access to desirable or affluent achieved identities.

All societies past and present use ascribed and achieved statuses to create some form of stratification, although they may vary in the degree of inequality between strata. Most Western societies today rely on socioeconomic status as the primary criteria by which individuals and groups are stratified. **Socioeconomic status** refers to the prestige, honor, respect, and power associated with different social class positions in society (Weber, 1970). Socioeconomic status is obviously influenced by wealth and income, but it can also be derived from achieved characteristics, such as educational attainment and occupational prestige, and from ascribed characteristics, such as race, ethnicity, gender, and family pedigree. For instance, high school teachers have much higher occupational prestige than carpenters, plumbers, or mechanics (Davis & Smith, 1986), even though teachers usually earn substantially less. Organized criminals may be multi-millionaires and live in large estates, but they lack prestige and honor—and therefore socioeconomic status—in mainstream society.

THEORIES OF INEQUALITY

For well over a century, sociologists have been trying to figure out why societies are unequal and stratified. Let's take a brief look at the two main groups of theories regarding stratification: structural-functionalism and conflict theories. These groups of theories differ dramatically in their conclusions about the role of stratification in human societies.

Structural-Functionalism According to **structural-functionalism,** society is a complex system composed of various parts, much like a living organism. Just as the heart, lungs, and liver work together to keep an animal alive, so, too, do all the elements of a society's structure work together to keep society alive. From this perspective, if an aspect of social life does not contribute to social order and ultimately to society's survival— that is, if it is dysfunctional—it will eventually disappear. Things that persist, even if they seem to be harmful, unfair, or disruptive, must persist because they contribute somehow to the continued existence of society (Newman, 2017).

So how can society benefit in the long run from inequality? Societies are made up of a variety of different roles that people must fill in order for society to function. In complex, modern societies, these roles are allocated through a strictly defined division of labor. If the tasks associated with all social positions in a society were equally pleasant, were equally important, and required the same skills, who got into which position would make no difference. But structural-functionalists argue that it does make a difference. Some occupations, such as teaching and medicine, are more important to a society than others and require greater ability and training. Society's dilemma is to make sure that the most competent people perform the most important tasks. One way to ensure this distribution of tasks is to assign higher rewards—better pay, greater prestige, more social privileges—to some positions in society so that they will be attractive to the people with the necessary talents and abilities. Those who rise to the top are seen as the most worthy and deserving because they're the ones who can do the most good for society (Davis & Moore, 1945).

The functional importance of a position is not enough to warrant a high place in the stratification system, however. If a position is easily filled—even if it is vital for society's survival—it need not be heavily rewarded (Davis & Moore, 1945). For instance, there is perhaps no more important occupation in a society than trash collection. Imagine what our society would be like without people who remove our trash. Not only would our streets be clogged with litter, but disease would be rampant and our collective health and longevity would suffer in the long run. But garbage collection is neither prestigious nor considered worthy of high salary. Why not? According to the structural-functionalist perspective, it is because we have no shortage of people with the skills needed to collect garbage. And it doesn't take much training to learn how to dump people's trash. Physicians also serve the collective health needs of a society. But because of the intricate skills and extensive training needed to be a doctor, society must offer rewards high enough to ensure that qualified people will want to become one.

According to structural-functionalism, then, inequality is inevitable and necessary. Societies have to assign different levels of importance to different positions. They can't all be equal. And we all benefit in the long run when our most qualified members fill our most important positions. So, it's appropriate that certain "important" people earn a lot and accumulate a lot. If we take the functionalist argument to its logical conclusion, then there should be a direct correlation between the average salaries of a given occupation and its importance in society.

But a quick look at the salary structure in our society reveals obvious instances of highly rewarded positions that are not as functionally important as positions that receive smaller rewards. Our best-known actors, filmmakers, comedians, rock stars, reality TV celebrities, and professional athletes are among the highest-paid people in U.S. society, earning tens of millions of dollars each year to entertain us. You might say that boxers, singers, movie stars, and baseball players serve important social functions by providing the rest of us with a recreational release from the demands of ordinary life. However, society probably can do without another hip hop album, adventure movie, or pay-per-view prizefight more easily than it can do without competent physicians, scientists, computer programmers, teachers, or even trash collectors.

Furthermore, what this perspective overlooks is the fact that stratification can be unjust and divisive, a source of social disorder (Tumin, 1953). The argument that only a limited number of talented people are able to occupy important social positions is probably overstated. Many people have the talent to become doctors. What they lack is access to training. And why are some people—women and racial and ethnic minorities—paid less for or excluded entirely from certain jobs (see Chapter 6)? Finally, when functionalists claim that inequality and stratification serve the needs of society, we must ask, Whose needs? A system of slavery obviously meets the needs of one group at the expense of another, but that doesn't make it tolerable.

In a class-stratified society, those individuals who receive the greatest rewards have the resources to make sure they continue receiving such rewards. Over time, the competition for the most desirable positions will become less open and less competitive—less a function of achievement than ascription. In such circumstances, the offspring of "talented"—that is, high-status—parents will always have an advantage over equally talented people who had the bad sense to be born into less successful families.

Conflict Theories   Structural-functionalism has been criticized for accepting existing social arrangements without examining how they might exploit or otherwise disadvantage certain groups or individuals within the society. The **conflict perspective** addresses this deficiency by viewing the structure of society as a source of inequality, which always benefits some groups at the expense of other groups. Social inequality is neither a necessity nor a source of social order. Instead, it is a reflection of the unequal distribution of power in society and is a primary source of conflict, coercion, and unhappiness.

According to perhaps the most famous conflict theorists, Karl Marx and Friedrich Engels (1848/1982), stratification ultimately rests on the unequal distribution of resources—some people have them, others don't. Important resources include money, land, information, education, health care, safety, and adequate housing. The "haves" in such an arrangement can control the lives of the "have nots" because they control these resources and are ultimately the ones who set the rules. According to this perspective, a system of stratification allows members of the dominant group to exploit those in subordinate positions as consumers, renters, employees, and so on, thereby reinforcing their own superiority over others. Hence, stratification virtually guarantees that some groups or classes of people (those who have less) will always be competing with other groups or classes (those who have more). The fundamental proposition of this perspective is that stratification systems will always serve the interests of those at the top and not the survival needs of the entire society.

Marx's original theory was, in essence, a wholesale critique of capitalism. **Capitalists**—those who own the means of producing the goods and services society needs, and to whom others must sell their labor in order to survive—have considerable influence over what will be produced, how much will be produced, who will get it, how much money people will be paid to produce it, and so forth. Such power allows them to control **workers**—who neither own the means of production nor have the ability to purchase the labor of others. Hence, capitalists control other people's livelihoods, the communities in which people live, and the economic decisions that affect the entire society. Marx and Engels supplemented this two-tiered conception of class by adding a third tier, the petite bourgeoisie, which is a transitional class of people who own the means of production but don't purchase the labor power of others. This class consists of self-employed skilled laborers and businesspeople who are economically self-sufficient but don't have a staff of subordinate workers.

Rich and politically powerful individuals—who not coincidentally tend to come from advantaged gender and ethnoracial groups—frequently work together to create or maintain privilege, often at the expense of the middle and lower classes (Hacker & Pierson, 2010). What the conflict perspective gives us that the structural-functionalist perspective doesn't is an acknowledgment of the interconnected roles that economic and political institutions play in creating and maintaining a stratified society (Newman, 2017). In such a structure, the rich inevitably tend to get richer, to use their wealth to create more wealth for themselves, and to act in ways that will protect their interests and positions in society.

You'd expect constant attempts by those at the bottom to transcend their lowly status and seek control over limited resources. But such revolutions rarely occur in human societies. Why not? Marx and Engels argued that those in power have access to the means necessary to create and promote a reality that justifies their exploitative actions. Their version of reality is so influential that even those who are disadvantaged by it come to accept it. They called this phenomenon **false consciousness.** False consciousness is crucial because it is the primary means by which the powerful classes in society prevent protest and revolution. As long as large numbers of poor people continue to believe that wealth and success are solely the products of individual hard work and effort rather than of structured inequalities in society—that is, believe what in the United States has been called the American Dream—resentment and animosity toward the rich will be minimized and people will perceive the inequalities as fair and deserved (Robinson & Bell, 1978).

Marx's theory was based on 19th-century economic systems. In his time, the heyday of industrial development, ownership of property and control of labor in a capitalist system were synonymous. Most jobs were either on farms or in factories. It made sense to lump into one class all those who didn't own productive resources and who depended on wages from others to survive, and into another class all those who owned property and paid wages. However, the nature of capitalism has changed a lot since then. Today a person with a novel idea for a product or service, a computer, and a telephone can go into business and make a lot of money. Corporations have become much larger and more bureaucratic, with a long, multilevel chain of command. Ownership of large companies lies in the hands of stockholders (foreign as well as domestic), who often have distant connections or even no connections at all to the everyday workings of the business. Thus, ownership and management are separated. The powerful people who run large businesses and control workers on a day-to-day basis are frequently not the same people who own the businesses.

With these changes in mind, some sociologists have revised Marx's original argument. For instance, sociologist Erik Olin Wright and his colleagues (Wright, 1976; Wright, Costello, Hachen, & Sprague, 1982; Wright & Perrone, 1977) have developed a model that incorporates both the ownership of means of production and the exercise of authority over others. The capitalist and petite bourgeoisie classes in this scheme are identical to Marx and Engels's. What is different is that the classes of people who do not own society's productive resources (Marx and Engels's worker class) are divided into two classes: managers and workers.

Wright's approach emphasizes that class conflict is more than just a clash between rich people and poor people. Societies have, in fact, multiple lines of conflict—economic, political, administrative, and social. Some positions, or what Wright calls *contradictory class locations*, fall between two major classes. Individuals in these positions have trouble identifying with one side or the other. Managers and supervisors, for instance, can ally with workers because both are subordinates of capitalist owners. Yet, because managers and supervisors can exercise authority over some people, they also share the interests and concerns of owners. During labor disputes in professional sports, for example, coaches often struggle with the dilemma of whether they represent the interests of the owners or the players (Newman, 2017).

Other sociologists have criticized Marx's exclusive reliance on economic factors to explain inequality. The early 20th-century sociologist Max Weber (1970) identified two other sources of inequality—prestige and power—in addition to the control of property, wealth, and income. **Prestige** is the amount of honor and respect people receive from others. Class position certainly influences prestige, but so can family background, physical appearance, intelligence, political clout, and so on. **Power** is the ability to influence others and to pursue and achieve one's own goals. Wealth, prestige, and power usually coincide, but not always. Sometimes groups with little if any wealth have managed to have their voices heard and have exerted a powerful influence on more advantaged groups. In 2004, for example, cooks, housekeepers, and bellboys went on strike at four San Francisco hotels. Two days later, workers were locked out of 10 other hotels. The strike eventually spread to nearby Monterey. The actions of these low-wage laborers discouraged visitors from coming to the Bay Area and had an enormous effect on the local economy. Imagine what would happen if the trash collectors in your town went on strike?

Recently, the conflict approach to social inequality has expanded even further by incorporating race, ethnicity, and gender. For instance, workers of color may share a class location with Whites, but as you'll see in Chapter 6, the lower wages that working-class ethnoracial minorities earn as well as their concentration in particular low-paying occupations double their vulnerability to exploitation (Feagin & Feagin, 2004). Furthermore, as long as workers see their primary adversaries as other workers who are competing with them for scarce jobs (such as immigrants or members of other ethnoracial minorities), their anger will be directed toward one another and not upward against those in positions of power. Indeed, research has shown that downward mobility (Silberstein & Seeman, 1959) and the rapid influx of new ethnic groups into a community (Bergesen & Herman, 1998) are associated with higher levels of ethnic hostility, conflict, and backlash violence. One might conclude that it is in capitalists' best interest to foster ethnoracial divisions among workers, thereby preventing them from unifying and taking advantage of their numbers to seek a more equitable division of resources.

Another variety of the conflict perspective that has become particularly popular among sociologists in the last several decades is the **feminist perspective.** Feminist sociologists focus on gender, more so than class or socioeconomic status, as the most important source of conflict and inequality in social life. They argue that in nearly every contemporary society, important social institutions—education, economy, politics, religion, family—are controlled and dominated by men. Men use a variety of methods—including violence, exploitation, and other forms of discrimination—to reinforce their dominance. Consequently, women have less power, influence, and opportunity than men do. In families, for instance, women have traditionally been encouraged to perform unpaid household labor and child care duties, whereas men have been free to devote their energy and attention to earning money and power in the economic marketplace. Women's lower wages when they do work outside the home are often justified by the assumption that their paid labor is secondary to that of their husbands. But as women in many societies seek equality in education, politics, careers, marriage, and other areas of social life, their activities inevitably affect the broader structure of society.

Early forms of feminist thinking were often criticized for ignoring race and class and trivializing the experiences of poor women and women of color. So, more recent feminists (sometimes called "gender rebellion feminists" [Lorber, 1998]) focus on the complex connections between inequalities based on sex and gender and inequalities based on race, ethnicity, social class, and sexuality. By looking at the intersections among these varieties of difference, we can see what all disadvantaged segments of society have in common and how they're unique (Collins, 2004).

CULTURAL CAPITAL

Racial, gender, class, and sexual differences and similarities are an enormously powerful component of stratification systems because they determine life chances and access to important social resources. Sociologists use the term **cultural capital** to refer to the status characteristics that can influence a person's social and economic opportunities. For instance, many top universities reserve a certain number of positions for "legacies," applicants whose parents are alumni of that institution. Family name, in this case, can serve as a form of cultural capital. In a society that values physical appearance, beauty is also cultural capital that can be exchanged for economic advantage. Economists have coined the term *beauty premium* to refer to the economic advantages attractive people enjoy:

> Handsome men earn, on average, 5% more than their less-attractive counterparts (good-looking women earn 4% more); pretty people get more attention from teachers, bosses, and mentors. . . . Fifty seven percent of hiring managers [in a recent survey indicated that] qualified but unattractive candidates are likely to have a harder time landing a job, while more than half advised spending as much time and money on "making sure they look attractive" as on perfecting a résumé. (J. Bennett, 2010, p. 47)

Likewise, membership in advantaged gender, ethnoracial, and sexuality-based groups can serve as cultural capital as well, as illustrated by the historical preference for white, male, heterosexual employees over women, people of color, and homosexual or transgendered individuals.

Cultural capital can also provide advantage in the form of access to social connections and networks. In 2005, Hurricane Katrina decimated the Gulf Coast of the United States. The storm did not affect all residents equally, however. The vast majority of the evacuees who suffered for days in the sweltering darkness of the Superdome and convention center in New Orleans were poor people of color who came from the most vulnerable parts of the city. Certainly, these were individuals who didn't have the necessary resources to evacuate prior to the hurricane and didn't have the money to stay in hotels even if they could have gotten out (see Chapter 8 for more detail). But they also lacked cultural capital in the form of social connections—people who could have given them rides, negotiated discounted hotel rates for them, or provided lodging in their own homes (Sander, 2005).

The more privileged one's status, the larger one's endowment of cultural capital. In Chapters 5 through 8, I will examine the biological, political, educational, and economic imbalances that result from the cultural capital that people amass by virtue of their membership in certain groups.

CONCLUSION

This introductory chapter hints at several key themes that will percolate through the remainder of this book. In what ways are we different from one another? How are we the same? Is similarity or difference more important in our everyday lives? Are all differences inevitably associated with inequality? How is inequality constructed and reinforced in our everyday lives? How is it embedded in our language, our culture, and our social institutions? In addressing these general questions, I will pay particular attention to the key social characteristics that we use to differentiate ourselves from others: race (and ethnicity), gender (and sex), sexuality, and social class. No characteristics are as influential as these in determining our identities, our life chances, and the shape of our social institutions.

In any book that focuses on identities and inequalities, the use of particular terminology to refer to dimensions of social identity carries significant cultural and political weight. People often choose words carefully when referring to themselves and others. However, there is no consensus about the acceptability or unacceptability of particular terms. Nor is there agreement about the clarity of boundaries between groups or even how permanent they are. And the term of choice in one decade may fall out of favor in the next. Thus, my choice of words in this book inevitably runs the risk of offending at least some readers some of the time. But in the interests of consistency, I will use the terms *sex* and *gender* when referring to dimensions like girls/boys, women/men, and femininity/masculinity. I will use the terms *sexuality* or *sexual orientation* when discussing people's erotic identities (homosexual, heterosexual, bisexual, and so on). I will use the terms *race*, *ethnicity*, and *ethnoracial* when examining the lives of people who identify themselves as Asian American, Native American, Latino/a, African American, and White. When I talk about *minority groups*, I will be referring not to statistically underrepresented groups but to those that have historically been disadvantaged in this society. Indeed, a purely statistical definition of minority may soon be obsolete. According to the U.S. Census Bureau, for instance, about 1 in 3 residents is of a race other than White (ProQuest Statistical Abstract, 2014); by 2050, it's projected to be more than 1 in 2 (Martin & Midgley, 2010).

In addition, I will make the argument that race, class, gender, and sexuality are not biological givens but are, to a large degree, social constructions. Hence, when I refer to members of particular groups (for example, heterosexuals, lesbians, transgender, Whites, Asian Americans, and so on), I am talking about those people who identify themselves as members of these groups. The first step in exploring the intersections of race, class, gender, and sexuality is respecting the way that individuals define themselves.

[INVESTIGATING IDENTITIES AND INEQUALITIES]
Identity inheritance: Climbing up (or down) your family tree

The concept of cultural capital is important because it shows that social advantage and disadvantage do not emerge from differences in material wealth alone. Indeed, cultural capital consists of all the social assets that lead to differences in material wealth. Any characteristic, possession, or identifier that can be exchanged for economic gain can be considered a form of cultural capital. Often, people are unaware that they even have these non-economic forms of capital. Take, for instance, a person's family heritage. Wealthy parents often endow their children with reputations, connections, and cultured knowledge that will aid them as they grow up. Sometimes simply inheriting a family name is enough to provide economic, educational, and political advantages. Poor parents are less able to pass on such cultural capital to their children and instead are likely to leave their children a legacy of disadvantage that they must fight to overcome.

To understand how cultural capital is handed down from generation to generation, construct your own family tree. Go as far back into the past as you can. You may need to ask your parents, grandparents, and other older relatives about long-deceased ancestors. Face-to-face interviews are best, but you may have to conduct your interviews over the phone or via email, Facebook, Skype, or FaceTime. If family artifacts are available (for example, old letters, diaries, photographs, home movies/videos, heirlooms), use them for insight into the identities and lives of your ancestors.

You may focus on one side of your family or both sides. If there have been remarriages in your family's past, try to obtain information on the various familial branches.

For each person in the tree, identify the primary occupation and the highest level of education she or he achieved. Look for patterns in family members' experiences that are linked to race, ethnicity, culture, gender, social class, and religion. It would be helpful to determine how your family first came to the United States. If some of your ancestors lived their whole lives in another country, you can examine how their experiences and achievements differed from those of your ancestors who immigrated to the United States or those who lived here their entire lives.

Can you detect a pattern of upward or downward socioeconomic movement in your family? Did relatives from previous generations graduate from college? Did any attend the college you presently attend? Has some career legacy been handed down from generation to generation? For instance, has a family business, dwelling, or tract of property stayed in the family across generations? How do the occupational and educational paths of men and women differ in your family?

Now examine how your family history has influenced *your life*. What sorts of ideals, values, beliefs, and traditions do you think you've inherited from members in previous generations? How do your own career aspirations compare with those of your ancestors? If you have or expect to have children, what are your career and educational aspirations for them?

After a thorough examination of your family experience, ask yourself this question: Does your family tree support the contention that cultural capital is hereditary?

CHAPTER 2

Manufacturing Identities
The Social Construction of Race, Class, Gender, and Sexuality

Donald McCloskey received a Ph.D. in Economics from Harvard in 1970. He's been a professor of economics at several prestigious universities, including the University of Rotterdam, the University of Chicago, and the University of Iowa. In his career, McCloskey has written numerous influential books and articles; he is an internationally renowned economic historian. Married, with two children, his life appeared to be the great American success story. What his friends and colleagues didn't know, though, was that from age 11, Donald had been a part-time cross-dresser, outfitting himself in women's clothing a couple of times each week.

In 1994, at the age of 52 and after 30 years of marriage, Donald came to the conclusion that wearing women's clothing wasn't enough. He wanted to *be* a woman. So, over the span of the next three years, he underwent hormone replacement treatments, electrolysis to remove facial hair, facial plastic surgery, and ultimately genital surgery to transform his male body into a female one. Today, Donald McCloskey is Deirdre McCloskey, Distinguished Professor of Economics, History, English, and Communication at the University of Illinois–Chicago, Professor of Economic History at Gothenburg University in Sweden, and Extraordinary Professor at the University of the Free State, Bloemfontein, South Africa.

Deirdre's story is important not because it's rare or bizarre but because of what it says about how we all view, define, and take for granted the nature of sex and gender. Even though she knew she could never be like other women, her female identity solidified as others began to take her feminine appearance for granted:

> After [three years], I found to my delight that I had crossed. Look by look, smile by smile, I was accepted. That doesn't make me a 100 percent, essential woman—I'll never have XX chromosomes, never have had the life of a girl and woman up to age fifty-two. But the world does not demand 100 percents and essences, thank God. . . . Gender is not in every way "natural." "Feminine" gestures, for example, are not God's own creation. . . . The social construction of gender is, after all, something a gender crosser comes to know with unusual vividness. She does it for a living. (McCloskey, 1999, pp. xiv–xv)

Gregory Williams has earned five degrees (including a law degree) and holds three honorary degrees. Until his resignation in 2012, he was the president of the University of Cincinnati. Like Deirdre, he crossed an identity boundary—only his was not voluntarily.

Gregory was born in Virginia in the late 1940s, a time when racial segregation was a reality in the United States. He spent his days in Whites-only schools, movie theaters, and swimming pools. Then, when he was 10 years old, his parents divorced. His father was awarded custody and decided to move back to his hometown of Muncie, Indiana. On the way there, Mr. Williams gave Gregory and his other son, Mike, some startling news: Once they reached Indiana, they could no longer be white. The father explained to his bewildered sons that his mother—their paternal grandmother—was black and that this fact made them black too. "Life is going to be different from now on," he told them. "In Virginia you were white boys. In Indiana you're going to be colored boys. I want you to remember that you're the same today that you were yesterday. But people in Indiana will treat you differently" (Williams, 1995, p. 33).

At first, Gregory refused to believe his father's startling revelation, but his perceptions quickly began to shift:

> [F]or the first time, I had to admit Dad didn't exactly look white. His deeply tanned skin puzzled me as I sat there trying to classify [him]. Goose bumps covered my arms as I realized that whatever he was, I was. I took a deep breath. I couldn't make any mistakes. I looked closer. His heavy lips and dark brown eyes didn't make him colored, I concluded. His black, wavy hair was different from Negroes' hair, but it was different from most white folks' hair, too. He was darker than most Whites, but Mom said he was Italian. . . . [But when] I glanced across the aisle to where he sat . . . I saw my father as I never had seen him before. . . . Before my eyes he was transformed from a swarthy Italian to his true self—a high-yellow mulatto. My father was a Negro! We were colored! After ten years in Virginia on the white side of the color line, I knew what that meant. (Williams, 1995, pp. 33–34)

From that moment on, Gregory's life was a difficult struggle to learn to be black. He was rejected by black and white children alike. Members of his own extended family—aunts, uncles, and cousins—resented him because he looked white. And each day brought a new predicament about his proper place. As he got older, dating became especially difficult. Because he was identified as black, he wasn't supposed to date white girls. But because he looked white, the community couldn't tolerate seeing him with black girls. Despite all the obstacles, however, Gregory went on to a successful career as a lawyer and a professor and came to accept and embrace his multiracial identity. In the process of his "crossing," he learned the importance of racial constructions in everyday life.

Both Deirdre and Gregory experienced transformations despite enormous obstacles that few of us will ever have to face. But what makes their stories important is what they tell us about what are widely believed to be two of the most fundamental, biological, and permanent elements of personhood: our sex and our race. Deirdre made a conscious decision to alter her physical body so that it would align with an inner sense of femaleness that she had harbored for decades. Gregory's transformation was different. His body didn't change at all, but the way others perceived, defined, and treated him did. And that was enough to make him question and ultimately change a racial identity he had taken for granted for as long as he could remember. Their stories challenge some of our deepest assumptions about self, identity, and the way the social world is ordered.

In this chapter, I will examine the key sources of our personal identities— not only race, ethnicity, sex, and gender, but also social class and sexuality. Which, if any, of these identifiers exist as objective entities in nature? Which are human creations that emerge within particular cultural and historical contexts? Do the boundaries that separate different sexes, classes, races, or sexualities ever change? And how do our identities reflect the intersections of race, ethnicity, class, gender, and sexuality?

PERSPECTIVES ON IDENTITY

Identities are the definitional categories we use to specify, both to ourselves and to others, who we are. They are social locations that determine our position in the world relative to other people. They are, as one sociologist put it, "where the self meets society" (Markus, 2013, p. 180). At times, we purposely call attention to them, through how we dress, walk, and speak, whom we choose to associate with; perhaps even where we live. At other times, though, people ascribe importance to certain of our identities, whether we want them to or not. If you're openly gay, for example, others may react to your sexuality as the primary—perhaps only—definer of who you are, rendering other circumstances of your life and other components of your identity less relevant. In an early episode of the television show, *Nurse Jackie*, a gay male character is sadly tending to his hospitalized, terminally ill husband. A gay male nurse approaches him in the hallway and thanks him for "paving the way" on the issue of same-sex marriage. The man, grief-stricken and focused only on the deteriorating health of his partner, angrily replies, "Can I not be gay right now? Can I just be a guy whose spouse is dying?"

We all possess multiple identities, be they based on race, ethnicity, religion, gender, class, sexuality, occupation, education, family, age, geography, or some other aspect of our background. At any given moment, some of these identities can eclipse the others. For instance, if you suddenly find yourself in a crowd of people of a different race than yours, that feature of your identity will no doubt become quite prominent to you. When situational or life circumstances change, though, a different characteristic is likely to emerge as the most noticeable determinant of who you are. Students preparing for their first year of college can anticipate the confirmation of some old familiar identities, the creation of new ones, and the discovery of some they never knew existed (Holmstrom, Karp, & Gray, 2002).

Few of us spend much time thinking about how we acquire these identities. They are simply who we are. But people like Deirdre McCloskey and

Gregory Williams force us to question things that usually remain unquestioned. For instance, what makes a person male or female? Is it only their genitals and outward physical appearance? Deirdre's story raises the possibility that our sex is ultimately a matter of self-perception and self-definition. For most of her adult life, her body was genetically, anatomically, and physiologically male. Her outward appearance was male too. But in her mind, she was a woman. So, she had her body changed—first hormonally and then surgically. She couldn't change her chromosomes, though, so could she ever *really* be female? She may now look female and be visually classified by others as female, but can she be a complete woman without having experienced childhood, adolescence, puberty, and early adulthood as a female?

Likewise, what determines if you're black or brown or white? Is skin color all there is to it? A few years ago, my wife was Christmas shopping in a department store and noticed a display of 3-foot-tall singing Santa Claus dolls lined up in a row. They were all identical except for one, whose face was black. But because none of its other facial features were different from the rest of the dolls, this doll looked less like an African American Santa and more like a white Santa with its face painted black. As we'll see in this chapter, skin color itself is never the sole determinant of racial identity. So, if color isn't enough, what determines race? Is it the size and shape of one's eyes, nose, lips that determine racial identity? Hair texture? How about speech patterns or mannerisms? Does race reside permanently in our genes, or is it something so tenuous that it can be changed simply because others begin to label and treat us differently? If Gregory had moved back to Virginia while he was still young, would he have changed back into a white person?

Let's not stop there. What makes a person heterosexual or bisexual or homosexual? Is erotic activity with someone of the same sex, the opposite sex, or both sufficient to determine sexual identity? Perhaps not. In Mexico, there is a group of men who refer to themselves as HSHs, which stands for *hombres que tienen sexo con hombres* [translation: men who have sex with men]. Many of these men swear up and down that they are not gay. In Senegal, 88% of men who report having sex with men claim they are not gay because they also have sex with women (cited in Lacey, 2008b). Moreover, can a person be homosexual or heterosexual without ever having sexual contact with another person? Can sexual orientation change, like Gregory's race, when a person's social situation changes or is there something more permanent to it? Suppose Donald McCloskey was involved romantically with the same man both before and after he transitioned into Deirdre. You might characterize them as a homosexual couple before, but would they still be afterward? Or would they now be a heterosexual couple, with all the same rights, privileges, and cultural recognition that other heterosexual couples enjoy?

Finally, how do you know if you're *upper class*, *middle-class*, or *working class*? Is the size of your paycheck or savings account all that matters? What about your occupation? Your educational attainment? Do less measurable things like taste, sophistication, the restaurants you frequent, the music you listen to, or your family name matter? Is class standing linked to other identifiers like race or ethnicity? Is it easier or more difficult for members of certain ethnoracial groups to claim membership in the upper class? Are we quicker to assume some ethnoracial groups are of the lower classes?

All these questions are hard to ask and even harder to answer. How you respond to them depends in part on the basic perspective that influences your view of individual differences. It's common to see individuals as having a fundamental essence that may, at times, be disguised, hidden, or misinterpreted but never actually changed. But if you look hard enough, you will see instances in which the social environment has indeed changed an individual's true identity.

ESSENTIALISM

To most people, the boundaries that divide us into different sex, race, class, and sexual orientation groups are obvious and reflect who we truly are. A person *is* a female, *is* a Native American, *is* a heterosexual, *is* middle-class. This way of thinking, known as **essentialism,** focuses on what are believed to be universal, inherent, and unambiguous "essences" that clearly distinguish one group from another. It doesn't matter what people call these categories or how they react to them; the categories have a concrete truth that exists independently of people's judgments or definitions. From an essentialist perspective, people's definitions and labels can change, but an individual's essence is permanent.

Let me provide an analogy. When I was a little kid, I loved a TV show called *Flipper*. It was about the adventures of a boy and his pet dolphin (I know, it was a weird premise, but bear with me). I just assumed—as most kids my age would have—that Flipper, the dolphin, was a fish. I admit I don't know much about the history of biology, but I'd venture to guess that for centuries, other people must have thought the same thing. Dolphins look like fish, move like fish, and smell like fish. Eventually, some smart aquatic zoologist discovered their "true" essence: Dolphins weren't fish at all; they, like whales, sea lions, and walruses, were marine mammals. This conclusion eventually became part of the taken-for-granted truth of science. It wasn't that dolphins underwent some anatomical alteration that abruptly changed them from fish to mammals. Instead, we humans had mistakenly labeled them in the first place. Dolphins' essential "mammalness" had always resided and will always reside in their nature, whether people call them fish or rodents or cucumbers.

Is essentialism similarly at work when it comes to the ways that humans are classified? Consider sexual orientation. An essentialist view of sexual orientation might argue that people *are* homosexuals or heterosexuals, just as people have a certain blood type or eye color. But what would an essentialist say about the heterosexual who becomes homosexual later in life? To the essentialist, this person has always been in actual fact homosexual. She or he may have lived the life of a heterosexual, but one is either inherently heterosexual or inherently homosexual, and the act of coming out as a homosexual can negate an entire life of heterosexual activity up to that point (Fausto-Sterling, 2000).

Believing in the essential reality of these categories has important implications. When race, class, gender, and sexuality are seen as innate, individual characteristics rather than social locations in larger systems of inequality, group differences in behaviors or traits tend to be explained by group members' essential natures (Hollander, Renfrow, & Howard, 2011). And once these differences are assumed to be inherent and natural, they can then be used to justify unequal treatment and perhaps even the subordination of one group by another. For instance, men and women are biologically different in some obvious ways. But if you believe that those innate differences determine other differences (for instance, that men are more assertive and less nurturing than women simply because they're men), then it becomes justifiable to encourage or even require men to occupy the social positions for which they are "naturally" best suited (such as management and decision-making positions) and exclude them from domestic work and child care, activities for which they are "ill-suited" by nature.

CONSTRUCTIONISM

An alternative to essentialism is **constructionism** (also known as the social construction of reality perspective), which argues that what we know to be real and essential is always a product of the culture and historical period in which we live. Categorical distinctions based on race, class, gender, and sexuality are human creations and don't exist independently of our ideas about them and responses to them. We may be quite sure that an objective reality independent of us exists out there, but constructionists argue that what we believe to be real (and what we call that reality) is always a matter of human definition and collective agreement.

Let's return to our friend Flipper. From a constructivist perspective, *mammals* as a named class of creatures don't exist in nature. Scientists determined that certain organisms that meet a particular set of criteria (including nourishing their young with milk, having skin that is more or less covered with hair, breathing with lungs rather than gills, and being warm-blooded) could be grouped together and called mammals. Organisms that meet some but not all the criteria may be mistakenly classified. Dolphins are hairless creatures that live in the ocean (usually that means the creatures are fish). But they are also warm-blooded, breathe with lungs, and nourish their young with milk. So, we've decided to call them mammals. If zoologists ever decided to change the criteria of "mammalness," dolphins might once again fall into a different category.

Understanding race, class, gender, and sexuality as socially constructed human identifiers requires that we take into consideration the following points (Weber, 1998):

- *Identifiers depend on context.* Although race, class, gender, and sexuality have existed throughout most of history as ways to differentiate among individuals, their social meanings constantly change as a result of economic, political, and ideological trends and events. Their meanings vary not only across time but across different societies and even different regions within the same society. The significance of race, gender, class, and sexuality, therefore, is fluid, socially or politically determined, and historically or culturally specific.

- *Identifiers tend to make us think in terms of opposites.* We have a tendency to identify people in either/or terms—as white or black, rich or poor, man or woman, heterosexual or homosexual. It is a short step from these dichotomies to identifying one member of each pair as good and the other as bad, one moral and the other immoral, one worthy and the other unworthy. Thinking in terms of either/or dichotomies also reinforces the view that these identifiers are permanent fixtures in all human societies, a biological imperative.

- *Identifiers reflect social rankings and power relations.* Race, class, gender, and sexuality are not simply individual traits. They are systems of dominance and power that determine where and how important resources like income, wealth, and access to education and health care

are distributed. The status of one group is always defined in terms of its relations to other groups:

> There can be no controlling males without women whose options are restricted; there can be no valued race without races that are defined as "other"; there can be no owners or managers without workers who produce the goods and services that the owners own and the managers control; there can be no heterosexual privilege without gays and lesbians who are defined as "abnormal". (Weber, 1998, p. 20)

■ *Identifiers have both psychological and structural meanings.* Race, class, gender, and sexuality have meaning at the level of individuals' lived experiences as well as the level of communities and social institutions. Sociologists often look at national trends and broad economic indicators to describe the relative status of particular groups. But these societal-level trends are always felt by individuals where they work, where they live, and where they form and maintain close, personal relationships (Newman, 2017).

Constructionism taken to its extreme might lead you to conclude that race, class, gender, and sexuality have no reality at all independent of our definitions. The famous sociologists William Thomas and Dorothy Thomas (1928) once wrote, "If [people] define situations as real, they are real in their consequences" (p. 572). What they meant was that we respond to situations and events in our lives on the basis of the meaning we attach to them. Their essential reality, if it exists at all, is irrelevant. If you were an American living in the 1950s, chances were pretty good that you would have defined the Soviet Union as the most dangerous threat to national security. Hence, it's likely that if you had the chance to actually meet a Soviet person, perhaps as a tourist, you might have responded to this person as the treacherous individual you anticipated he or she would be. You might have looked at her or him with suspicion, cut conversations short, withdrawn from social interaction, avoided eye contact, and so on. It wouldn't have mattered whether or not this person really was dangerous. The fact that you defined her or him that way would have been sufficient to affect your behavior—not to mention his or her reactions to you. Indeed, such perceptions of distrust—on both sides—characterized U.S.–Soviet relations for the better part of the 20th century.

At a societal level, then, the Thomases are right: Our collective definitions of reality are what matter. But what about the individual level? We live in a society built on the assumption that we can do what we want and be what we want as long as we don't hurt others or infringe on their rights. Such a cultural value implies that perhaps how we identify ourselves is solely a matter of individual determination. But you're probably well aware that for some aspects of our identity, those choices are restricted. You may have seen a delightful old movie from 1979 called *Breaking Away*. In it, an Indiana teenager who dreams of becoming a professional bicycle racer proudly announces to his parents one day that he is Italian (the family clearly isn't Italian). Pretty soon, he's singing along to recordings of Verdi and Puccini operas and saying things like *grazie, buon giorno, and ciao, genitori* to his chagrined parents. The humor of the film comes from our understanding that, although there's no law against it, one cannot ignore personal history, physical reality, and community ratification and simply declare oneself to be a different ethnicity— or, for that matter, a different gender, race, social class, or sexuality.

You may recall the firestorm that erupted in 2015 when it was revealed that Rachel Dolezal—a self-identified black woman who was president of the Spokane, Washington chapter of the NAACP and an instructor of African American Studies at Eastern Washington University—was actually white. She professed deep empathy and sympathy with black people from the time, as a teenager, her parents adopted four black children. She attended a historically black college, Howard University. She married a black man. Her art reflected the black experience. She curled her hair and even darkened her skin. She constructed a reputation as a powerful advocate for civil rights. One acquaintance she knew when she was younger said she seemed like "a black girl in a white body . . . but she was snow white, white-white, lily white" (quoted in Johnson, Pérez-Peña, & Eligon, 2015, p. A13). But she wasn't just immersed in black political issues, appearance, and lifestyle, she said she *was* black, even though her biological parents are both white. Many people simply couldn't accept her claim that race was a constructed self-definition. Critics accused her of "playing black," choosing to adopt an African American heritage and look and to cast off her white racial advantage when it suited her, something actual people of color cannot do (Pérez-Peña, 2015). Blacks have always had a harder time claiming another race. Said one black author, "Unlike Rachel Dolezal, I don't have the option of choosing my race" (Harris, 2015, p. A25).

Individuals may play an important role in coordinating and giving meaning to definitions of reality in their everyday lives, but their ability to define these classifications on their own is always limited. We're all born into a preexisting society in which the criteria for determining difference have already been constructed and have largely become a taken-for-granted part of social institutions and belief systems. For instance, according to tradition, Judaism is a *matrilineal* religion, meaning that every child of a

Jewish mother is automatically considered Jewish, regardless of how religious he or she is. However, U.S.-born Jews who live in Israel are sometimes shocked when their Jewish-ness is challenged by the Orthodox Rabbinate—a government bureaucracy that provides official determination of religious identity—because they haven't strictly adhered to Jewish behavioral rules (Gorenberg, 2008). Similarly, some African Americans visiting Ghana are taken aback when Ghanaians refer to them as *obruni*, or "white foreigner" (Polgreen, 2005).

It's important to emphasize that, although the social construction of difference is a collective enterprise, it can be enormously consequential for individuals. Placement into a racial, gender, class, or sexual category is a powerful predictor of life chances and access to important social resources, as the discussion of the concept of cultural capital in Chapter 1 explains. But keep in mind too that because these categories are socially constructed, they are changeable.

DEFINITIONS OF DIFFERENCES AND IDENTITIES

From the time we're small children, we're exposed to cultural messages that teach us that we, as individuals, determine our lot in life. In principle, we are all capable—as long as we have the requisite energy, drive, and ambition—to improve our situation. It's up to us to "be all we can be." A Pew Center poll of 38,000 people in 44 countries found that the United States had the lowest percentage of citizens (about one-third) who agreed with the statement "Success in life is pretty much determined by forces outside of our control" (Pew Research Center, 2012a).

And yet we receive other messages that seem to suggest quite the opposite. More often than not, our race/ethnicity, our gender, our sexual orientation—all powerful markers of our identity—are portrayed as exclusively or at the very least primarily a product of genetic or anatomical factors over which we have little if any control. Certainly there's some truth to this contention. Men and women *do* have different bodies. People who identify themselves as members of different racial groups *do* possess certain distinguishable physical characteristics. The perpetuation of the species *does* depend on reproductive imperatives linking males and females that appear to be universal, essential, and perhaps even instinctual. But these obvious biological realities are not sufficient to explain the means by which human societies construct and define social differences. Let's take a look at how sociologists define race, class, gender, and sexuality. Although one of the themes of this book is that in people's lived experiences these elements of identity work in combination and not independently, it is useful at this point to define these concepts separately.

RACIAL/ETHNIC IDENTITIES

To most people, **race** is a category of individuals who share common inborn biological traits, such as skin color; color and texture of hair; and shape of eyes, nose, or head. It is widely assumed that people who are placed in the same racial category share behavioral, psychological, and personality traits that are linked to their physical similarities. But sociologists typically use the term **ethnicity** to refer to the nonbiological traits—such as shared ancestry, culture, history, language, patterns of behavior, and beliefs—that provide members of a group with a sense of common identity. Whereas ethnicity is thought to be something that we learn from other people, race is commonly portrayed as an inherited and permanent biological characteristic that can easily be used to divide people into mutually exclusive groups.

But the concept of race is neither as natural nor as straightforward as this definition implies. Some people who consider themselves "white," for example, may have darker skin and kinkier hair than some people who consider themselves "black." In addition, some groups have features that do not neatly place them in one race or another. Australian Aboriginals, for instance, have dark skin and "Negroid" facial features but have blond, wavy hair. The black-skinned San (or !Kung) who live in several countries in southern Africa have epicanthic eye folds, a characteristic typical of East Asian peoples.

In addition, since the earliest humans appeared, they have had a remarkably consistent tendency to migrate and interbreed. For instance, a recent genetic study of 160,000 Americans found that, on average, European genes account for almost one-quarter of the DNA of those who identify as African American; Latino/as were, on average, 65% European. The researchers also estimate that over 6 million European Americans have some African ancestry (Bryc, Durand, Macpherson, Reich, & Mountain, 2015). The famous naturalist Charles Darwin (1871/1971) wrote that despite external differences, it is virtually impossible to identify clear, distinctive racial characteristics. Indeed, there is no gene for race—that is, no gene that is 100% of one form in one racial group and 100% of a different form in another racial group (Brown, 1998).

I'm not saying that race has absolutely no connection to biology. Geneticists have known for quite a while that some diseases are not evenly distributed across racial groups. The overwhelming majority of cases of sickle-cell anemia, for instance, are people of African descent; it is rare among non-Hispanic Whites (BlackHealthCare.com, 2003). In 2005, the Food and Drug Administration approved the cardiac drug BiDil, which is intended to be used exclusively by African Americans, who have shown to be genetically predisposed to heart disease. Hemochromatosis is a digestive disorder that causes the body to absorb too much iron. Among Whites of Northern European descent about five people out of 1,000—0.5%—carry two copies of the hemochromatosis gene and are susceptible to developing the disease. One out of every 8 to 12 Whites is a carrier of one abnormal gene. The disease is virtually non-existent among African Americans, Asian Americans, Latino/as, and American Indians (National Digestive Diseases Information Clearinghouse, 2011). But no disease is found exclusively in one racial group. Furthermore, it's unclear whether these differences are due solely to some inherited biological trait or to the life experiences and historical, geographic, and/or environmental location of certain groups.

Certainly there are physical differences between people who identify themselves as members of different races. But it's human societies that organize, attach meaning to, and perhaps alter the meanings of those differences (Omi & Winant, 1992). If we didn't think that differences between people of varying skin hues were socially relevant in some way, we probably wouldn't see those differences. When I began graduate school in the early 1980s at the University of Washington, I served as a teaching assistant for a large Introduction to Sociology course. One day a student in the class, who was born in Vietnam and spent the early part of her childhood there, came to my office to discuss the day's lecture on race. She had been a small child in Vietnam during the war and had come into contact with many American soldiers. When she came to this country, she was astonished to find that we make such a big deal about differences between black Americans and white Americans. "In Vietnam," she said to me, "we thought all Americans were the same race. Yeah, some had darker skin than others, but that didn't matter to us. Some were taller than others too. Some were fatter than others. It didn't matter. To us, they all looked alike. We saw them all as Americans."

The Social Construction of Race and Ethnicity   What ties people together in a particular racial group, then, is not a set of shared physical characteristics—because there aren't any physical characteristics shared by *all* members of a particular racial group—but the shared experience of being identified by others as members of that group (Piper, 1992). The power of this experience is reflected by the fact that people who identify as one race but are perceived by others as a member of another race suffer higher levels of depression and psychological distress than people who are "correctly" classified (Campbell & Troyer, 2007).

During the process of growing up and creating an identity for ourselves, we learn three important things: the boundaries that distinguish group members from nonmembers, the perceived position of our group within society, and whether membership in our group is something to take pride in or be ashamed of (Cornell & Hartmann, 1998). These lessons reflect what the prevailing culture defines as socially significant (American Sociological Association, 2002). We decide that particular physical traits will be the primary markers of boundaries between groups. We invent these categories and they become socially significant to the extent that they're used to organize experiences, to form social relations, to evaluate others, and to determine social rankings and access to important resources (Cornell & Hartmann, 1998).

Evidence of the socially constructed nature of ethnoracial identity appears in the shifting boundaries between racial categories. In South Africa during the 1970s and 1980s, for instance, wealthy potential investors or powerful government representatives visiting from China, Japan, and Korea presented a problem. At the time, South Africa was ruled by a white minority and operated under a system of *apartheid*, or legal racial segregation. The country desperately needed the investment of foreign money to fund its many construction projects. But Asians were considered "colored" according to South African racial rankings and therefore were of subordinate status and subject to severe residential, commercial, and behavioral restrictions. So, the government created a category of "honorary white" for rich, powerful Asians (Hu-DeHart, 1996). Less affluent Asians—such as immigrant laborers from China—weren't afforded this privilege and remained "colored."

Social class can determine how people racially categorize others as well as the racial categories they choose for themselves (Sanchez & Garcia, 2012). In Brazil, as people climb the class ladder through educational and economic achievement, their racial classification changes, as illustrated by popular Brazilian expressions such as "Money whitens." College educated nonwhite parents in Brazil are significantly more likely to classify their children as white than are less-educated nonwhite parents (Schwartzman, 2007). Similarly, in Ecuador, infertile women pursuing in-vitro fertilization assistance frequently seek white egg donors as a means of "improving" the racial identity of their baby (Roberts, 2012). Even though Puerto Rico is a U.S. territory, conceptions of race there are markedly more fluid than they are in the states. Race is seen as a continuum of categories, with different shades of color as the norm and as a classification that can change as one's socioeconomic circumstances change (Rodriguez & Cordero-Guzman, 2004).

The ways in which particular groups are racially classified in a given society can change over time too. For instance, in 18th-century U.S. society, some European immigrant groups were considered racially inferior. Benjamin Franklin once expressed fear that white Pennsylvanians would be "overwhelmed by swarms of swarthy Germans, who 'will soon so out number us, that all the advantages we have will not . . . be able to preserve our language, and even our government will become precarious'" (quoted in Roberts, 2008, p. 6). In the 19th century, undesirable immigrant groups were often considered "Negro." Newspaper cartoons, for instance, frequently depicted Chinese immigrants as having African features. Such portrayals were attempts to transfer anti-black prejudice to the Chinese, rendering their condemnation more tolerable (Pieterse, 1995).

See if you can tell what immigrant group these late 19th-century characterizations refer to:

■ This is a race . . . of utter savages. For not merely are they uncouth of garb, but they also let their hair and beards grow to outrageous length . . .

■ I am haunted by the human chimpanzees I saw along that hundred miles of horrible country.

■ [They are] more like tribes of squalid apes than human beings.

■ [They are] the sons and daughters of generations of beggars. . . . They themselves are the missing link between the gorilla and the Negro. (all quoted in Shanklin, 1994, pp. 3–4)

It might surprise you to learn that the group seen so negatively was the Irish. In the 19th- and early 20th-century United States, Europeans were divided into higher and lower grades of white (Cose, 2010). Certain groups—Italians, Jews, as well as Irish—were thought to be in the latter category: non-white and inferior (Barrett & Roediger, 2011). As recently as the mid-20th century, many restaurants, clubs, and hotels actively restricted Jews from entry. In the Southern United States, Italian children were sometimes forced to attend black schools (Lee, 1993). Irish, Jews, and Italians only came to be seen as "white" when their large-scale immigration from Europe ended in the 1920s, thereby diminishing fears about an overflow of allegedly racial inferiors (Lee & Bean, 2004). Once they were considered "white," they entered the mainstream culture and gained economic and political power (Brodkin, 2004; Bronner, 1998). Many sociologists are quick to point out, however, that these white ethnic groups were never subjected to the same type of systematic bigotry as nonwhite groups, making their eventual societal acceptance easier (Lieberson, 1980). Such treatment may explain why Asian Americans—whose economic and educational achievements today parallel the successes of these white ethnic groups in the early 20th century—have not yet experienced a similar collective "whitening" (Kim, 2007).

In short, racial categories are not natural, essential realities. Instead, they are created, inhabited, transformed, applied, and destroyed by people and social institutions (Omi & Winant, 1992; Saperstein, Penner, & Light, 2013). Moreover, they often emerge from political, economic, and ideological struggles. Many historians of race argue that racial classifications didn't exist until white European settlers began confronting people of different colors for the first time (Zuberi, 2001). For instance, the appearance of slavery as an economic institution in 17th-century Colonial America coincided with the emergence of specific racial identities. All Africans, no matter what their specific ethnicity, were now "black." Not only did this term mask the diversity of cultural backgrounds among people of African descent, it also maximized the perceived differences between "black" Africans from the "dark" continent and "white" enlightened Europeans. By the 18th century, the black-white distinction had become more important than the Christian-pagan distinction as the primary justification for seizing the land or controlling the labor of others (Shoemaker, 1997).

Racial identity isn't imposed only on vanquished or enslaved peoples by European conquerors, however. Evidence from slave narratives suggests that black slaves used the term "white" to refer to people who owned property, no matter what their color (Roediger, 1998). Some southeastern American Indian groups used the terms "red men" or "red people" before they had contact with European settlers. The Choctaw word for Indian is *hatak api homma*, a combination of *hatak* (man) and *homma* (red) (Shoemaker, 1997). However, they could not prevent Whites from co-opting "red" and using it as a derogatory label for all Indians. By the 19th century, "red man" and "redskin" had become dehumanizing racial slurs.

The fluid, socially constructed nature of race can be seen in historical changes in the categories used by the U.S. government in its decennial population censuses (Lee, 1993). In 1870, there were five races: White, Colored (Black), Mulatto (people with some black blood), Chinese, and Indian. White people's concern with race-mixing and racial purity led to changes in the social rules used for determining the status of mixed-race people, particularly in the South. This concern is reflected in the race categories of the 1890 census. Eight races were now listed, half of them applying to black or partly black populations: White, Colored (Black), Mulatto (people with three-eighths to five-eighths black blood), Quadroon (people who have one-fourth black blood), Octoroon (people with one-eighth black blood), Chinese, Japanese, and Indian. In 1900, Mulatto, Quadroon, and Octoroon were dropped, so that any amount of "black blood" meant a person had to be classified as black. In 1910 and 1920, Mulatto returned to the census form, only to disappear for good in 1930. Between 1930 and 2000, some racial classifications (such as Hindu, Eskimo, and Mexican) appeared and disappeared. Others (Filipino, Korean, Hawaiian) made an appearance and have stayed ever since. Individuals filling out the 2010 census form had a wide array of racial categories from which to choose: White, Black, American Indian or Alaska Native, Asian Indian, Chinese, Filipino, Japanese, Korean, Vietnamese, Native Hawaiian, Guamanian or Chamorro, Samoan or other Pacific Islander.

Racial/ethnic categories in the U.S. Census still exhibit a fair amount of arbitrariness. For instance, you may have noticed that there is no "Asian" category; instead, Asian Americans must choose a specific nationality. However, Blacks and Whites do not have the opportunity to indicate their nation of origin. There is also no clear racial option for Arab Americans. Prior to the 2010 census, Arab leaders in California launched a "Check it Right, You Ain't White" campaign, which called on Arab Americans to use the "other" category and write in their true ancestry (Martin, 2010).

You might have also noticed that Latino/a or Hispanic is not included in the list of races on the latest census form. With the exception of the inclusion of Mexican in 1930, Spanish-speaking people have routinely been classified as white. But because Latino/as can be members of any race, "Hispanic origin" appears in a separate question on the census form, not as a race but as an ethnicity. In fact, the 2010 form explicitly states that "Hispanic Origins are not races."

This way of thinking has not been received well by all Latino/as. Recent census data show that 87% of Americans born in Cuba and 53% born in Mexico identify themselves as white; but a majority of those born in the Dominican Republic and El Salvador refused to identify themselves by any of the racial categories on the census form (cited in Roberts, 2010b). In the 2010 census, many Latino/as chose to use "American Indian or Alaska Native" to identify their race (cited in Decker, 2011). To overcome these problems, the U.S. Census Bureau is currently considering a combined "race or origin" question for the 2020 census that would include "Hispanic, Latino, or Spanish Origin" as a category along with "White," "Black, African American, or Negro," "American Indian or Alaskan Native," "Asian," and "Native Hawaiian or Other Pacific Islander" (Haub, 2012).

The way the government decides to draw these color lines is not trivial. The appearance and disappearance of particular racial labels reflect the visibility and value of certain groups in this society. And on a practical level, a great deal depends on the official system of racial categorization: antidiscrimination statutes, property and voting rights laws, health and education statistics, legislative redistricting, and social policies such as affirmative action. Racial information from the census is used by a variety of federal agencies, including the Departments of Commerce, Education, Justice, Labor, and Health and Human Services. The issue can be so divisive that some jurisdictions have tried to do away with racial classifications altogether, arguing that they have become so imprecise that they've lost all meaning and utility.

Multiracial Identities   Definitions of race and the way those definitions are incorporated into people's individual identities are particularly complicated for people whose biological parents are of different races. President Barack Obama, as you well know, is biracial. He is the son of a black father from Kenya and a white mother from Kansas. Although he sometimes jokingly refers to himself as a "mutt," he, like so many before him, is identified as black. He is called the first black or African American president, usually not the first biracial president and certainly not the first half-white president. Why not?

Since the era of slavery, the United States has adhered to the "one-drop rule" regarding racial identity (Davis, 1991). The term dates back to a common law in the South that a "single drop of black blood" made a person black. Sociologists call this a *hypodescent* rule, meaning that racially mixed people are always assigned the status of the subordinate group (Davis, 1991). During World War II, biracial U.S. citizens were required to relocate to internment camps if one parent was Japanese (Doyle & Kao, 2007). As the biracial singer, Mariah Carey once said, "How many times do I have to tell you—my father was black. My mother's white. In this country that makes you black" (quoted in Day, 2010, p. 5).

Conversely, other groups must meet a hereditary threshold in order to claim a particular ethnoracial identity. For instance, some Native Americans carry a card, known as the C.D.I.B. (Certificate of Degree of Indian Blood), that indicates whether they have enough Indian blood to be considered Indian

(Hitt, 2005). Entrants in San Francisco's Miss Chinatown USA contest must be at least 50% Chinese and must have a Chinese father (Orenstein, 2008).

As recently as 1990, mixed-race people who identified themselves on the census form as "black-white" were counted as black; those who wrote "white-black" were counted as white (Lee, 1993). Most multiracial people have experienced being arbitrarily assigned a racial identity by a school principal or an employer that may differ from the identity of other members of their families or may differ from their own identity in other settings. The dramatic growth in the number of multiracial children—the proportion of multiracial babies grew from 1% in 1970 to 10% in 2013 (Holmes, 2015)—has upset these traditional views of racial identity, however. And more and more people of mixed racial heritage are refusing to identify themselves as one race or another.

In the mid-1990s, these individuals began lobbying Congress and the Bureau of the Census to add a multiracial category to the 2000 census. They argued that such a change would add visibility and legitimacy to a racial identity that has heretofore been ignored. Some argued that a multiracial category might soften the racial lines that divide the country (Stephan & Stephan, 1989). When people blend several races and ethnicities within their own bodies, the divisiveness of race is reduced, thereby holding out the promise of a biological solution to the problem of racial injustice (White, 1997).

Not everyone thought such a change would be a good idea, though. Many civil rights organizations objected to the inclusion of a multiracial category (Farley, 2002). They worried that it would reduce the number of U.S. citizens claiming to belong to long-recognized minority groups, dilute the culture and political power of those groups, and make it more difficult to enforce civil rights laws (Mathews, 1996). Job discrimination lawsuits, affirmative action policies, and federal programs that assist minority businesses or that protect minority communities from environmental hazards all depend on official racial population data from the census. Even today there is concern with those who self-identify as multiracial. As one author put it, "mixed-race blacks have an ethical obligation to identify as black—and interracial couples share a similar moral imperative to inculcate certain ideas of black heritage and racial identity in their mixed-race children, regardless of how they look (T. C. Williams, 2012, p. 5). A recent survey found that 60% of multiracial adults are proud of their mixed race background and feel it makes them more tolerant of other cultures (Pew Research Center, 2015c). Interestingly, however, when asked how they identify themselves, only 40% of people with a mixed race background used the term "multiracial."

Exhibit 2.1: Multiracial Identification by Age

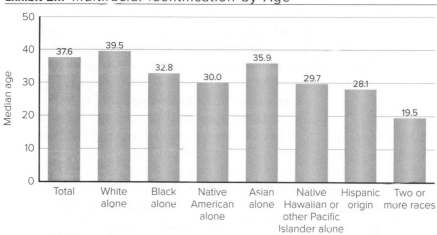

(Source: ProQuest Statistical Abstract, 2015, Table 10)

The rest identified with one race either because they look like one race or were raised as one race. And one in five said they felt pressure from others to identify as a single race.

In the end, the civil rights organizations won. For the 2000 census, the government decided not to add a multiracial category to official forms. Instead, it adopted a policy allowing people to identify themselves on the census form as members of more than one race. The new guidelines specify that those who check "white" and another category will be counted as members of the minority group (Holmes, 2000). In the 2010 Census, 9 million people– or about 3% of the population—identified themselves as belonging to more than one race (Humes, Jones, & Ramirez, 2011). As you might expect, most of the people choosing this option were young (see Exhibit 2.1). The changes in the census form illustrate that politics, not biology, is the determining factor when it comes to determining racial identity.

Some sociologists caution, however, that the Census Bureau's method of measuring multiracial identity—checking two or more race categories— does not adequately reflect the role that social context plays in how people personally experience race. For instance, middle- and upper-class multiracial people may distance themselves from their minority background and identify as "white" when they live in predominantly white, upper-class communities (Harris & Khanna, 2010). Similarly, the National Longitudinal Study of Adolescent Health, which contains information on the racial identity of a nationwide sample of over 11,000 adolescents, shows that almost twice as many adolescents identify themselves as multiracial when they're interviewed at school as when they're interviewed at home. Furthermore, nearly 15% expressed different racial identities across different settings (Harris & Sim, 2002). About three in ten adults with a multiracial background say that they have changed the way they describe their race over the years. Some say they once thought of themselves as only one race and now think of themselves as more than one race; others say just the opposite (Pew Research Center, 2015c). These findings are important because they show that the census data on multiracial identity don't necessarily account for the experiences of everyone who comes from a multiracial background.

In fact, despite growing numbers of people whose parents are of different races, there is evidence that not everyone is supportive of the idea of multiracial identities. Sizable numbers of multiracial adolescents change their racial identity—to that of a single race—as they enter adulthood (Doyle & Kao, 2007). In a 2010 poll, 55% of black respondents said President Obama is black and only 34% said he was mixed. Among white respondents, 53% said he was mixed, while 24% identified him as black (cited in Washington, 2010). Incidentally, when he filled out the 2010 census form, President Obama chose to identify himself only as "black."

CLASS IDENTITIES

Social class refers to a group of people who share a similar economic position in society based on their wealth and income (Newman, 2017). Class standing directly influences cultural capital and people's ability to attain higher education, their access to well-paying jobs, and the availability of adequate health care. Of the four principal components of identity and inequality addressed in this book—race/ethnicity, social class, sex/gender, and sexuality—class is no doubt the one that is least likely to be attributed to innate biological or anatomical traits. Few people would argue that social class is an essential identity we're born with. It would seem downright silly to talk about a "social class gene" or the biological underpinnings of income and wealth.

Nonetheless, in societies that stratify people on the basis of a **caste system,** socioeconomic status is determined at birth and considered unchangeable. Traditionally, in South Asia, for example, one's caste determines lifestyle, prestige, and occupational choices. Ancient Hindu scriptures identified a strict hierarchy consisting of elite priests, warriors, merchants, artisans, and untouchables who were so lowly they were actually considered to be outside the caste system. Untouchables were restricted to occupations dealing with the bodies of dead animals or unclaimed dead humans, tanning hides from such dead animals and manufacturing leather goods, and cleaning up the human and animal waste in traditional villages that have no sewer systems. In addition, they were once required by law to hide from or, if that wasn't possible, to bow in the presence of anyone from a higher caste. They were routinely denied the right to enter Hindu temples or to draw water from wells reserved for members of the higher castes, who feared they would suffer ritual pollution if they touched or otherwise came in contact with an untouchable (hence the term).

Things are changing somewhat. In India, for instance, where 16% of the population belongs to the untouchable caste (or *Dalits,* as they prefer to be called; Human Rights Watch, 2012), laws have been passed that prohibit caste-based discrimination. In fact, the benefits *Dalits* now receive—such as reserved spaces in universities and governmental jobs—have prompted members of the next highest caste of farmers and shepherds to lobby the government to have its caste status *downgraded* so as to be eligible for these benefits (Gentleman, 2007).

But the caste system still exists in practice and continues to serve as a powerful source of stratification and oppression. According to Human Rights Watch (2012), over 260 million people worldwide—including the *Dalits* in India, Nepal, Bangladesh, Sri Lanka, and Pakistan; the *Burakumin* in Japan; the *Osu* in Nigeria; the *Al-Akhdam* in Yemen—continue to suffer severe caste discrimination, exploitation, and violence. For instance, despite anti-discrimination laws in India, *Dalits* are sometimes forced to work as "manual scavengers," collecting human excrement and carrying it away in baskets for disposal. Women from this caste typically clean dry toilets in homes, while men do the more physically demanding cleaning of sewers and septic tanks. They face barriers when trying to leave such as threats of violence and eviction from local residents as well as harassment and unlawful withholding of wages by local officials (Human Rights Watch, 2014). Caste imposes massive obstacles to their full attainment of civil, political, economic, and cultural rights. Even Indians living in the United States find that cast sometimes colors their experiences with friends and business associates (Berger, 2004).

How Do Americans Determine Class Standing?   In U.S. society, we believe that the boundaries between class levels are more permeable than they are in a caste system. There are no legal barriers to **social mobility**— the movement of people or groups from one class level to another. Theoretically, anybody, no matter how humble their beginnings, can climb the class ladder. Yet even in an achievement-based class system like ours, where social standing is assumed to be a consequence of one's own actions and accomplishments, class standing is typically intertwined with and therefore inseparable from race and gender, which, as we've seen, are perceived by many people as fixed and biologically based.

Many contemporary American sociologists have a somewhat essentialist view of class, compiling information on measurable factors such as annual income, wealth, occupation, and educational attainment to determine class standing. The **upper class** (the highest-earning 5% of the U.S. population) is usually thought to include owners of vast amounts of property and other forms of wealth, major shareholders and owners of large corporations, top financiers, rich celebrities and politicians, and members of prestigious families. The **middle-class** (roughly 45% of the population) is likely to include college-educated managers, supervisors, executives, small-business owners, and professionals (for example, lawyers, doctors, teachers, and engineers). The **working class** (about 35% of the population) typically includes industrial and factory workers, office workers, clerks, and farm and manual laborers. Most working-class people don't own their own homes and don't attend college. Finally, the "poor" (about 15% of the population) consist of people who work for minimum wages or are chronically unemployed. They are sometimes referred to as the **lower class** or **underclass.** These are the people who do society's dirty work, often for very low wages (Newman, 2017).

Despite the apparent straightforwardness of these criteria, the boundaries between class levels tend to be unclear and highly subjective. Part of the reason for this lack of clarity is that in our everyday lives class is not so much a reflection of numbers and statistics but a matter of the way people talk about themselves and others. Indeed, there is often a disconnect between people's own class identity and that imposed on them by others. Consider the difficulties encountered by one researcher trying to study people's class identities:

> The vast majority of Americans think of themselves as "middle class." There is also the folk lexicon of subdivisions of this category—"upper middle," "lower middle," and just plain "middle." . . . The term "lower middle class" is very much disliked by those who might be so categorized, apparently because of the presence of the word "lower." . . . The plain "middle class" is the most slippery category. It is either used as the modest self-label for the upper middle class . . . or it is the covering label for the lower middle class. . . . Either way there is almost no "there" there; to be plain middle class is almost always to

be "really" something else, or on the way to somewhere else. At the same time, the "middle class" is the most inclusive social category; indeed almost a national category. . . . It is everybody except the very rich and the very poor. (Ortner, 1998, p. 8)

People usually think of their own social-class identity not just in economic terms but, more importantly, in moral and cultural terms (Lamont, 1995). Moral boundaries between the classes consist of assessments of such qualities as honesty, integrity, work ethic, and consideration for others. Cultural boundaries are identified on the basis of education, taste, and manners. In other words, class resides as much in how people talk, the way they dress, and the books, movies, and music they prefer as it does in how much money they make. For instance, when used in everyday conversation, "lower class" is more likely to be a synonym for lack of intelligence and taste than an assessment of one's income.

Class distinctions often go beyond upper-class snobbery and distaste for the lifestyles of "lower" classes. People at the top often blame those in the lower socioeconomic levels for their own condition (for example, "Poor people are lazy and just don't want to work and that's why they're in distress"). Such perceptions are an effective means of shifting responsibility away from the larger structural factors that contribute to class inequality — which can be tied to race, ethnicity, and gender— and toward individuals in the lower classes themselves. When seen this way, economic suffering is not a by-product of entrenched social circumstances but is instead a consequence of individual deficiency.

But perceptions of class differences don't always favor those at the top. In recent years, ostentatious displays of wealth have become the object of public anger and ridicule. In every election cycle, we watch all manner of very rich candidates go through the charade of altering their clothing, man- nerisms, tastes, and vocabulary to show voters that "they're less loftily removed from the so-called common man than they really are" (Bruni, 2012, p. 3). Privileged backgrounds simply don't provide the "up-from-nothing" life story every candidate these days seems to want (Leibovich, 2014). So, they'll talk about the struggles of their immigrant parents, highlight the dishwashing job they had when younger, or eat burgers and go bowling with blue-collar folk to convince voters that they're one of them.

The 2012 Republican presidential candidate, Mitt Romney, was one of the wealthiest people ever to run for president. Unfortunately for him, the election came at a time of growing complaints about income inequality and the wealthy "one percent." Most of his awkward attempts to present a "folksy" image—for instance, trying to relate to NASCAR fans by touting his friendships with race car *owners,* offering an off-the-cuff $10,000 bet to an opponent during one of the early televised debates, handing a $50 bill to an unemployed South Carolina woman who had just told him her hard luck story, or referring to his $375,000 income from speaking fees as "not very much"—merely called more attention to the gap between him and the vast majority of people who would be casting ballots.

Who Is Poor?   Although legislators and politicians are fond of talking about what they're doing or what they intend to do for the middle-class or the working class, the federal government has no official mechanism for determining class boundaries. The one exception is the identification of who is and who isn't poor. But the designation of the cut-off point between poverty and non-poverty is somewhat arbitrary and therefore quite controversial.

The official **poverty line** identifies the amount of yearly income a family requires to meet its basic needs. Those who fall below the line are considered officially poor; those above the line are not poor. In 2016, the poverty line for a family of four—two parents and two children—was an annual income of $24,036. The line is based on pretax money income only and does not include food stamps, Medicaid, public housing, and other non-cash benefits. The figure varies according to family size and is adjusted each year to account for inflation. But it doesn't take into account geographical differences in cost of living.

The poverty line is established by the U.S. Department of Agriculture and for decades has been computed from something called the Thrifty Food Plan (Newman, 2017). This plan, developed in the early 1960s, is used to calculate the cost of a subsistence diet, which is the bare nutritional minimum a family needs to survive. This cost is then multiplied by 3 because research at the time showed that the average family spent one-third of its income on food each year. The resulting amount was adopted in 1969 as the government's official poverty line. Even though the plan is modified periodically to account for changes in dietary recommendations, the formula itself and the basic definition of poverty have remained the same for over four decades.

Many policymakers, economists, sociologists, and concerned citizens question whether the current poverty line provides an accurate picture of basic needs in the United States. Several things have changed since the early 1960s. For instance, today food costs account for less than 13% of the average family's budget because the price of other things, such as housing, college tuition, childcare, and medical care, has increased over the past decade at much higher rates (U.S. Bureau of Labor Statistics, 2014a). In addition, there are more dual-earner and single-parent families than ever before, meaning that more families have to pay for childcare. In short, today's family has many more expenses and therefore probably spends a greater proportion of its total income on nonfood items. The consequence is that the official poverty line is probably set too low and therefore underestimates the hardships that struggling Americans experience (Swarns, 2008).

In 2011, the U.S. Census Bureau proposed a new way of determining the poverty line called *the supplemental poverty measure*. This new formula is based on an estimate of expenditures on food, clothing, shelter, and utilities. It also takes into consideration medical spending, taxes, commuting costs, and childcare (Short, 2012). More recently, some economists have proposed a measure, called the *Self-Sufficiency Standard*, that uses of the costs of *all* basic needs—housing, utilities, food, child care, health care, transportation, taxes, and so on—to compute a poverty threshold (Pearce, 2014). These costs are adjusted for geographic variation in cost of living. Using either of these alternative models would likely raise the poverty threshold for a family of four to an annual income of around $30,000.

Deciding who is and isn't officially poor is not just a matter of semantics. A needy family making slightly more than the poverty line may not qualify for a variety of public assistance programs, such as housing benefits, Head Start, Medicaid, or Temporary Assistance for Needy Families. As a result, their standard of living may not be as good as that of a family that earns less, thereby qualifying for these programs. Life slightly above the poverty line can be precarious (see Chapter 6 for more detail).

When nothing out of the ordinary happens, people can manage. But paying for an unexpected event—a sickness, an injury, the breakdown of a major appliance or automobile—can send them into poverty. Imagine being a poor single mother with a sick child. One trip to the doctor might cost an entire week's food budget or a month of rent. Dental work or an eye examination is easily forgone when other pressing bills need to be paid. If she depends on a car to get to work and it breaks down, a few hundred dollars to fix it might mean not paying the electric bill that month and having less money for other necessities. When gasoline prices exceed $4 a gallon—as they did in some places in early 2014—many poor families find that they have to cut down on food purchases so they can afford to drive to work.

Some economists suggest that the exclusive focus on income in setting the poverty line underestimates the harmful long-term effects of poverty. Obviously, when families don't have enough income, they can't buy what they need—adequate food, clothing, and shelter. But when families don't have any wealth or assets, such as savings and home equity, they lose economic security and their ability to plan, dream, and pass on opportunities to their children (Block, Korteweg, & Woodward, 2013).

GENDER IDENTITIES

When discussing gender in my Introduction to Sociology course, I often pose a question that invariably strikes my students as utterly stupid: "How do you know if a person is male or female?" After a few seconds of giggling and eye rolling, someone—usually a biology or pre-med major—will always mention the obvious: "Females have an XX chromosomal configuration while males are XY." I then reply, "Can you see a person's chromosomes? No? I didn't think so. So what observable information do you use to make this determination?" They then proceed to identify what they consider to be socially relevant markers of maleness and femaleness: Women have long hair, men have short hair; women have high voices, men have deep voices; women have wide hips and breasts, men have broad shoulders and facial hair; women wear dresses, men wear pants; and so on. I challenge every response: "Can a woman have a deep voice?" "Can a man wear a dress and still be a man?" "Can a man have breasts?" "What about women who have their breasts surgically removed? Do they stop being women at that point?" Eventually a bolder student will say something like "men have penises; women have vaginas." Setting aside the obvious problem (that is, unless we live in a nudist colony, we usually don't see people's naked crotches when we first meet them), I then ask, "Can a man not have a penis and still be a man? In 1993, a woman famously cut off her abusive husband's penis with a kitchen knife while he slept and threw it into a nearby field. Did he stop being a man at that moment?" The discussion typically evolves into a frustrating mess at this point.

Some of my students' anguish may be due to the fact that they, like most people, tend to confuse sex and gender. **Sex** is typically used to refer to the biological markers of maleness or femaleness. These indicators can be chromosomes (XX for female, XY for males), sex glands (ovaries for females, testes for males), hormones (more estrogen than testosterone for females, more testosterone than estrogen for males), internal sex organs (uterus for females, prostate gland for males), genitalia (vagina for females, penis for males), reproductive capabilities (pregnancy and lactation for females, impregnation for males), germ cells produced (eggs for females, sperm for males), or secondary physical characteristics (wide hips and breasts for females, facial hair and low-pitched voice for males).

Gender, on the other hand, designates the psychological, social, and cultural aspects of masculinity and femininity (Kessler & McKenna, 1978). People are not born with a gender; they cultivate it over time as they learn the cultural meanings and expectations associated with being a boy or a girl, a man or a woman. While conceptions of biological sex are fairly consistent (although, as we'll see, not universal), conceptions of gender vary enormously. How you're supposed to look, and the things you're expected to do by virtue of being labeled male or female are entirely dependent on the cultural, historical, and even the familial context in which you live. Sex may be a status ascribed to us at birth, but gender is something that we achieve through the process of conforming to (and reinforcing) broader cultural expectations.

Most of us assume that sex and gender, if not perfectly synonymous, are at least closely connected to one another. Based on a visual inspection— either of ultrasound images prior to birth or a quick glance at a newborn's genitals at the moment of birth—a baby is proclaimed as male or female and from that moment embarks on a lifetime journey within the confines of male or female cultural expectations. The official detection of a penis means that the baby will be labeled a "male." He'll be identified by others as male, be provided with male clothes, male toys, and so on. Ultimately, he'll come to think of himself as a male. Likewise, babies with vaginas will be designated as female and will be expected to look and act in the culturally acceptable ways we associate with the category "female."

People commonly see gender (the social) as an outgrowth of sex (the biological) (Epstein, 1988). Since sex is assumed to be rooted in biology, it's tempting to see it as natural, which is to say, given, fixed, and determined (Stanley, 2002). Behavioral or personality differences between males and females are therefore considered natural too. It would be silly to argue that there is absolutely no connection between sex and gender or that there are no biological or physical differences between males and females. But, like race, what's important is how we perceive and respond to the differences. Even biological predispositions aren't completely free from social influence. The members of a society can decide which sex differences ought to be amplified and which can and should be ignored.

Doing Gender   Early on, children begin to acquire knowledge about gender through socialization (see Chapter 4). What they learn are the gender rules that allow them to be perceived as masculine or feminine. Simply having knowledge of these rules does not in and of itself make a person feminine or masculine. To accomplish that, they must "do gender" appropriately and continuously through everyday social interaction (West & Zimmerman, 1987). That means behaving in ways that are considered gender appropriate. For girls and women in the United States, it means things like not burping in public, sitting in a "ladylike" fashion, paying attention to appearance, wearing makeup and jewelry. For boys and men, it usually means things like being assertive and physically active, not overtly displaying certain emotions, and not nurturing others, especially other adults.

It is impossible not to do gender. We might not do it well, or we might do it in culturally inappropriate ways, but if we try not to display or do gender at all, others will do it for us (Newman, 2017). For instance, sociologist Betsy Lucal (1999) describes what it's like to self-identify as a woman, but be mistaken for a man because she doesn't bear the traditional markers of femininity:

> I am six feet tall and large-boned. I have had short hair for most of my life. . . . I do not wear dresses, skirts, high heels, or makeup. My only jewelry is a class ring, a "men's" watch (my wrists are too large for a "women's" watch), two small earrings (gold hoops, both in my left ear), and (occasionally) a necklace. I wear jeans or shorts, T-shirts, sweaters, polo/golf shirts, button-down collar shirts, and tennis shoes or boots. . . . I prefer baggy clothes, so the fact that I have "womanly" breasts often is not obvious (pp. 786–787).
>
> Each day, I experience the consequences that our gender system has for my identity and interactions. I am a woman who has been called "Sir" so many times that I no longer even hesitate to assume that it is being directed at me. I am a woman whose use of public rest rooms regularly causes reactions ranging from confused stares to confrontations over what a man is doing in the women's room (p. 781).

According to Lucal, while she can choose not to do traditional femininity, she cannot choose not to do gender at all. Others will always place her in one or the other gender; it just so happens they often make a mistake. But for Lucal, as with most of us, gender is a significant part of her identity, and she is deeply embedded in the gender system:

> I am not to the point of personally abandoning gender. . . . I do not want people to see me as genderless as much as I want them to see me as a woman. . . . I would like to expand the category of "woman" to include people like me. . . . I do identify myself as a woman, not as a man or as someone outside of the two-and-only-two categories. (pp. 793–794)

Cultural and historical variation in the ways in which men and women are expected to appear and behave attests to the fact that gender is not innate. Genders are fluid. They can overlap (as when certain women are more aggressive or more skilled at math than certain men) and they can vary by degree (some men are extremely masculine, others mildly so).

The Sexual Dichotomy   Although most people acknowledge that gender is, to some degree, shaped by our social surroundings (we'll get to this in more detail in Chapter 4), the typical assumption is that sex isn't. Indeed, we live our lives under the taken-for-granted belief in the essential reality of the **sexual dichotomy**—the natural division of sex into two categories: male and female. These categories are considered to be biologically determined, permanent (you are what you're born with), universal (males are males and females are females whether one lives in Seattle, Seoul, or São Paulo; in the 15th century or the 21st century), exhaustive (everyone can be placed into one of the two categories), and mutually exclusive (you can only be one or the other sex; you can't be both). Casual references to the "opposite" sex reinforce the taken-for-grantedness of the sexual dichotomy. "Opposite" implies that there can be nothing in-between.

If you think about it, our entire culture is built around the belief in the sexual dichotomy. We have separate clothing sections for men and women, separate public bathrooms, separate hygienic products, separate sections in bookstores, separate sports leagues, and so on. The dichotomy, in short, is assumed to be in the nature of things. After all, don't we need two sexes in order for the species to procreate?

But on closer inspection, the essential reality of the sexual dichotomy begins to break down. More and more individuals now feel comfortable identifying as **transgender,** a broad label that describes individuals whose gender identity doesn't match their assigned sex or whose behavior does not conform to conventional gender expectations.

According to one author, "transgenderism" has become so common that it has replaced homosexuality as the newest civil rights frontier. To date, 17 states offer some form of legal protection for transgender people. Even therapists have begun affixing the label transgender to very young children (Talbot, 2013). In 2013, the Colorado state civil right division ruled that the Fountain-Fort Collins school district had discriminated against a transgender first grader—a biological boy who identifies as a girl—for not allowing her to use the girls' bathroom (Frosch, 2013). Today, over half a dozen states have policies that allow transgender students to compete on teams that correspond to their current expressed sex rather than the assigned sex listed on their school records (Lovett, 2013). Some of the top private women's colleges around the country, like Wellesley, Mills, Smith, and Mount Holyoke, face growing numbers of students who are admitted as women but who later transition into a male identity (Padawer, 2014). Six states—New York, California, Iowa, Oregon, Vermont, Washington—and the District of Columbia allow people to change the sex on their birth certificates, without evidence of surgery, if a qualified professional attests that the change accurately reflects the applicant's own sexual identity (Wong, 2014).

Transsexuals, like Deirdre McCloskey, not only identify with a different sex but sometimes undergo hormone treatment and surgery to physically change their sex, further challenging the idea that male and female are permanent biological characteristics. In the transformation process, transsexuals experience a transitional form of gender identity that momentarily blur boundaries. Consider the life of James Boylan, a successful professor and best-selling author. In the 1990s, James married and became the father of two boys. But Boylan didn't feel as if he was a man and by the early 2000s began to take steps to become a woman. She is now Jennifer Boylan. Obviously, her sons have known her as "Daddy" and "Mommy." But they were also around when neither term seemed to apply. As she was transitioning, her sons struggled with the impermanent gender of their parent:

> "We can't keep calling you 'Daddy," [her son] Zach said, shaking his head. "If you're going to be a girl. It's too weird . . . ." "I know . . . let's call you 'Maddy.' That's like, half Mommy, and half Daddy." (Boylan, 2013, p. 113)

The impermanence of sex received official recognition of sorts when the International Olympic Committee's executive board approved a proposal to allow transsexuals to compete in the 2004 Athens Olympic Games. Athletes who had undergone sex reassignment surgery were eligible to compete as long as they had been legally recognized as a member of the "new" sex and it had been at least two years since their surgery. Shortly afterward, the Ladies European Golf Tour enacted a similar policy, allowing a 37-year-old Danish male-to-female transsexual to play in one of their professional tournaments. In 2014, the U.S. government ruled that Medicare could no longer exclude sex reassignment surgery from its coverage (Rabin, 2014a). And shortly after Caitlyn Jenner (formerly Bruce Jenner) very publicly announced her sexual transformation, the Pentagon unveiled a plan that would allow transgender and transsexual people to openly serve in the military.

But the transsexual experience doesn't necessarily challenge other elements of the sexual dichotomy, chiefly its assumption that there are two and only two sexes. Deirdre McCloskey and Caitlin Jenner do not want to be considered a third, intermediate sex. They want to be women, in a very traditional, run-of-the-mill sense. For a limited time, Jenny Boylan may have been both a father and mother (and neither a father nor a mother), "like some parental version of the schnoodle, or the cockapoo" (Boylan, 2013, p. 9). But this was a transitory moment in the process of eventually becoming a woman.

Some features of the sexual dichotomy, however—namely mutual exclusivity, exhaustiveness, and universality—are challenged when we examine sex categories cross-culturally. Throughout human history and across all societies, certain people have transcended the two categories, male and female. They may be born with anatomical/genital configurations that are ambiguous. Or they may simply choose to live their lives in ways that don't conform to existing gender expectations associated with their sex. How societies respond to these individuals says a great deal about the cultural ideologies and values systems that underlie assumptions about sex and gender.

In traditional Navajo culture, for instance, one could be identified as male, female, or *nadle*—a third sex assigned to those whose sex-typed anatomical characteristics were ambiguous at birth (Lang, 1998). Physically normal individuals also had the opportunity to choose to become *nadle* if they so desired. The gender status of *nadle* is simultaneously masculine and feminine. They are allowed to perform the tasks and take up the occupations of both men and women. Far from being stigmatized, the Navajo regarded *nadle* as bringing luck and prosperity. They were said to "know everything"—a reference to the fact that they knew both the masculine and the feminine (Lang, 1998).

Similar institutionalized sex/gender variations have been documented in Tahiti (the *mahu*) and among the Lakota Sioux (the *wintke*). For the Chuckchi of Eastern Siberia, a biological male child with feminine traits gradually transforms into a "soft man." Although he keeps his masculine name, he is expected to live as a woman (Williams, 1992). In Samoa, *fa'afafines* are biological men who embody female traits and live their lives as women. In Afghanistan, sex/gender variation has nothing to do with biology. According to Afghan culture, inheritance is passed on through sons; families without sons are the objects of pity and contempt. So, families with only daughters will sometimes choose to raise one of them as a boy. Referred to not as "son" or "daughter" but as *bacha posh* (which translates to "dressed up as a boy"), these individuals have their hair cut and dress in traditional male clothing. The *bacha posh* can receive an education, work outside the home, and even escort their sisters in public, freedoms unheard of for girls. The parents then decide whether to return the child to womanhood when she reaches puberty (Nordberg, 2010).

As in most societies, in Hindu India, male/female and man/woman are viewed as natural categories whose essential characteristics set them in opposition to one another. Nonetheless, Indians also acknowledge sex/gender variants and changes. The most visible and culturally institutionalized variants are the *hijras*. *Hijras* are born as males, but by choice they have their genitals surgically removed (Reddy, 2005). Unlike male-to-female transsexuals in the United States, this surgery transforms them not into women but into *hijras*. By all appearances, they look like women. All aspects of their gender—their clothing, hairstyle, gestures, voice, facial expressions, manner of walking—are distinctly feminine. They take on feminine names and use female kinship terms—like sister, aunt, and grandmother—in their relationships with others. They only have sex with male partners. But although they are like women, they are not women. Their mannerisms are often exaggerated, and their sexual aggressiveness contrasts with the submissive demeanor of ordinary Indian women. They often use vulgar and abusive speech, which is likewise deviant for Indian women. But the main reason they're not considered women is that they don't have female reproductive organs and therefore cannot bear children. Though they have been a part of Indian culture since ancient times, it wasn't until 2014 that the Indian Supreme Court officially recognized the 5 to 6 million *hijras* living in India as an official—and legal—third gender category (Keck, 2014).

Because reproduction is seen as such a key determinant of sex in Hindu India, some biological females who voluntarily renounce reproduction are not considered women. Around puberty, a girl who rejects marriage (and thus sexuality and reproduction) can decide to become a *sādhin*. The decision is irreversible. *Sādhins* commit to celibacy for life. They cut their hair short and wear men's clothing. But like *hijras,* they are neither men nor women. Despite their male appearance, they remain socially women in many ways. They are allowed to engage in masculine tasks—like plowing, sowing crops, and herding sheep—but they also do women's work. They smoke water pipes and cigarettes—distinctly masculine behaviors—but don't attend funerals, something that is specifically a male prerogative (Nanda, 2003).

In these examples, we can see the tension between essentialism and constructionism. An essentialist would view these "intermediate" sexes as ways societies integrate biologically "abnormal" individuals into mainstream, everyday life. Note how such an approach still maintains that there are essentially only two sexes. Constructionists, on the other hand, would emphasize how these examples show that the reality of sex and gender is fluid, created and experienced differently in different societies. The existence

of third or fourth sexes/genders implies that they constitute part of a culturally constructed reality that recognizes statuses apart from "man" and
"woman" (Lang, 2003).

Intersexuality and Anatomical Ambiguity   When it comes to sex identification in U.S. society, physical ambiguity has historically been treated
from an essentialist perspective. For instance, consider the traditional reaction to **intersexuals** (or people with disorders of sexual development, as
many prefer to be known). These are individuals in whom anatomical sexual
differentiation is either incomplete or unclear. They may have the chromosomal pattern of one sex but the external genitals of another, or they may
have both ovaries and testicles. Experts estimate that between 1.5 and 2.0%
of all babies born have some form of intersexuality, meaning that they are
born with sexual organs that don't completely fit into standard sex categories
(Fausto-Sterling, 2000). However, intersexuality is usually defined by biolo-
gists as a combination of the two existing categories and not as a third,
fourth, or fifth category unto itself.

People born with genitals that are visually ambiguous are considered
victims of disorders of sex development. Moreover, the diagnosis of such
disorders is commonly framed as a tragedy that could doom a child to a life
of abnormality, persecution, and "freakhood" if not properly managed
(Fausto-Sterling, 2000). Advanced surgical, hormonal, and chemical technologies are deployed as soon after birth as possible to "fix" the anatomy
so as to establish consistency between it and the social label. About 2 babies
in 1,000 receive surgery to "normalize" their appearance (Intersex Society
of North America, 2008).

In recent years, some people with disorders of sexual development have
protested against the surgical techniques used to "fix" their genitals, claiming
such procedures are mutilating and potentially harmful. They cite cases of
people with ambiguous genitals being robbed of any sexual sensation in the
attempt to give them the outward physical appearance of either a male or a
female. An organization called Accord Alliance (2014) now recommends
that surgical intervention, if done at all, should not occur until puberty, when
the individual involved can be fully informed and included in all the
decision-making.

The medical profession has historically had difficulty postponing or
avoiding surgery in these cases because to do so would undermine our
culture's dichotomous and essentialist understanding of sex. Intersexuals
"exist on the margins and borders of society," forced to "pass" as normal
in order to remain hidden in the "official ideology and everyday commerce

of social life" (Herdt, 1994, p. 17). The drastic surgical intervention that ensues is undertaken not because the infant's life is threatened but because an entire social structure organized around having two and only two sexes is threatened. The sexual dichotomy in our culture is so crucial to our way of life that those who challenge it are considered either crazy people or cultural heretics who are being disloyal to the most fundamental of biological facts. To suggest that the labels "male" and "female" are not sufficient to categorize everyone is to challenge a basic organizing principle of social life. So pervasive is the sexual dichotomy that one doctor estimated her chances of persuading the parents of an intersexed child *not* to choose surgery at zero (Weil, 2006).

SEXUAL ORIENTATIONS

Related to sex and gender, of course, is **sexual orientation**—which indicates the sex for whom one feels erotic and romantic desire. Like all the elements of identity I've discussed so far, conceptions of sexual orientation (or **sexual identity**) are historically and culturally bound. Of course, the claim that sexual orientation is socially constructed does not necessarily mean that it is simply a learned behavior with no inherent genetic, hormonal, or physiological correlates. Instead, saying that sexual orientation is socially constructed means that our ideas about what sexual orientation is and how people are labeled and categorized are a matter of human definition influenced by cultural, historical, and political processes. Hence, it is impossible to understand the nature of sexual orientation and the means by which we classify ourselves and others without taking into consideration the broader sociocultural context in which sexuality in general exists.

The Complexities of Sexual Identity   Because of its connection to procreation, we tend to think of heterosexuality as a category of sexual orientation that has always existed. Certainly the earliest humans engaged in sexual intercourse with members of the other sex. If they didn't, none of us would be here today, right? But heterosexuality as a distinct and identifiable lifestyle and as an element of one's self concept didn't exist until quite recently in human history. People in the distant past named and organized their sexual activities in ways that are quite different from the ways we do today (Katz, 2003).

In the time of Plato, for instance, people didn't have a notion of two distinctly different sexual appetites allotted to different individuals. They simply saw various ways of experiencing sexual pleasure (Foucault, 1990). Although anal sex between two men was considered a punishable sin, colonial Americans had no concept of homosexuality or heterosexuality as a personal condition or identity. In the mid-19th century, same-sex romantic relationships among middle-class individuals—in which people expressed passionate longings for emotional and physical intimacy—were common and unremarkable. A man or a woman could write of desire for a loved one of the same sex without raising suspicions about sexual orientation (D'Emilio & Freedman, 1988).

The word "homosexuality" first appeared in print in 1869, when a German legal reformer sought to change existing anti-sodomy laws (Fausto-Sterling, 2000). The earliest use of the word "heterosexual" as a noun in the United States was in an 1892 medical journal that defined it as a person who was attracted to members of both the same sex and the opposite sex (Katz, 2003). Eventually, the word acquired its contemporary meaning: sexual attraction to members of a different sex. So those who had sexual relations with members of their own sex became "homosexuals." Medical writers eventually used this term to stigmatize same-sex relations as a form of sexual perversion. Men and women could no longer openly express affectionate desire for a loved one of the same gender without causing a stir, risking ridicule, or worse.

You'll notice in this brief history that, as we saw with sex and gender, sexual orientation is commonly viewed in dichotomous terms: One is either homosexual or heterosexual. Our culture's fondness for either-or sexual categories was challenged in the 1940s, when Alfred Kinsey published a report arguing that sexual orientation lies along a continuum, with "exclusively heterosexual" at one end of the scale and "exclusively homosexual" at the other. An "exclusive heterosexual," for example, is someone who has never had physical or psychosexual responses to individuals of his or her own sex. In between the two extremes are various gradations of sexuality, suggesting that people could be bisexual or predominantly heterosexual or homosexual.

Kinsey and his colleagues found that only 50% of the white males they studied identified themselves as exclusively heterosexual and only 4% identified themselves as exclusively homosexual (Kinsey, Pomeroy, & Martin, 1948). The rest fell somewhere between the two endpoints. When they focused on overt, physical sexual contact since adolescence, they found that 37% of men had had some homosexual experience that ended in orgasm. For women, the percentage was 13% (Kinsey, Pomeroy, Martin, & Gebhard, 1953). These percentages are significantly higher than the percentages of people who identified themselves as exclusively homosexual. In a more contemporary national survey, many more people reported homosexual desire and behavior than reported homosexuality or bisexuality as their sexual identity (Michael, Gagnon, Laumann, & Kolata, 1994). About 3% of the men surveyed identified themselves as gay—a figure that is pretty consistent with recent research, which estimates that about 3.4% of all Americans identify themselves as gay or bisexual (cited in Morello, 2011)—but 9% had had sex with a man since puberty. Among women, less than 2% identified as lesbian, but about 4% had had sex with another woman since puberty. Conversely, many college students who identify themselves as heterosexual have had some kind of homosexual experience (Hoburg, Konik, Williams, & Crawford, 2004).

Note that all these researchers recognized that sexual orientation cannot be measured solely in terms of sexual activity. An individual might be sexually aroused by homosexual fantasies but have had only heterosexual physical encounters. Such a person would fall somewhere in the middle of Kinsey's continuum. More recently, Fritz Klein (1990) has argued that sexual orientation is even more complex. Not only does it lie on a continuum, but it can change across time along several different dimensions: sexual attraction, sexual behavior, sexual fantasies, emotional preference, social preference, hetero/homosexual lifestyle, and self-identification. Sexual behavior and lifestyles, he argued, vary from day to day and year to year.

Indeed, being homosexual (or bisexual or heterosexual, for that matter) consists of more than simply physical attraction toward or sexual activity with members of a particular sex. People's desire to identify with a particular sexual orientation is always influenced to some degree by the costs and benefits of doing otherwise. Bisexuality, for instance, has until recently existed on the margins of the homosexual community, leading many bisexuals to hide their sexual identity:

> Being bi isn't a derogatory term at all . . . but that is not how I choose to identify. There are too many "queer" marches and events that only include lesbians and gays; bi and transgender people are peripheral. That's always the vibe I've gotten, and perhaps that is partly why it was so easy to say "I'm a lesbian. . . ." (quoted in Markowitz, 2000, p. 24)

The case of bisexuality raises an important sociological point about the social construction of sexuality. Categories of sexual orientation are not fixed, immutable, or mutually exclusive. People's sexuality can change during the course of their lives. Hence sexual identity can be fluid at some points and more stable at others (Howard, 2000). In the case of bisexuality, these changes could be a consequence not of a profound identity epiphany but of the fluctuating availability of male or female sexual partners during certain periods of one's life. Ironically, when a person's erotic attractions change—say, a lifelong lesbian marries a man and has children—others often invoke an essentialist frame, concluding perhaps that she was really straight all along. Conversely, people might contend that a woman who leaves her husband to begin a relationship with another woman was always a lesbian but is just now acknowledging that fact. To a constructionist, however, it may be just as correct to say that this person's sexual identity has changed along with the circumstances of her life.

Heteronormativity   Despite the growing acceptance and visibility of same-sex relationships, American culture can still be considered **heteronormative**—that is, a culture where heterosexuality is assumed to be the normal, taken-for-granted mode of sexual expression. Social institutions and social policies reinforce the belief that sexual relationships ought to exist between males and females. Cultural representations of virtually every aspect of intimate and family life—dating, sex, marriage, childbearing, erectile dysfunction, and so on—presumes a world in which men are sexually and affectionately attracted to women, and women are attracted to men (Macgillivray, 2000). In competitive figure skating, for example, the pairs competition always consists of women partnered with men (Wildman & Davis, 2002). The 2007 film *Blades of Glory* humorously lampooned this basic assumption by depicting two men as figure skating partners in the pairs event.

Adolescent women seeing a gynecologist for the first time can expect to be given information on birth control, highlighting the assumption that they will have sex with men, it's just a matter of when. A few years ago, I came across an issue of now-defunct *CosmoGirl* magazine in our campus fitness center. So I read it on the treadmill. A column giving sexual advice to teenage girls caught my eye. A 17-year-old from Kansas wrote in and asked, "I've never had an orgasm. Is something wrong with me?" The columnist replied:

> Absolutely not. Lots of women don't experience orgasm until they're in their twenties—after they have had more experience with guys and feel more comfortable with their bodies. ("Your most private," 2004, p. 111)

Another young woman, who worried about becoming sexually active, was given this advice:

> If you're scared to have sex, it might be because you're not emotionally ready or you haven't found the right guy yet. ("Your most private," 2004, p. 111)

Notice in both of these responses that the default assumption is that sexual concerns—as well as their solutions—are heterosexual in nature. The advice these young women are given to overcome their difficulties is to pursue relationships with men.

In a heteronormative culture, heterosexuals are socially privileged because their relationships and lifestyles are affirmed in every facet of the culture. Such privilege includes having positive media images of people with the same sexual orientation; not having to lie about who you are, what you do, and where you seek entertainment; not having to worry about losing a job because of your sexual orientation or receiving validation from your religious community.

"The Closet"   It would not be surprising, given such a cultural backdrop, that some people whose sexuality places them outside the heteronormative lines of acceptability would choose to keep this component of their identity hidden. Indeed, since the 1950s, the "closet" metaphor has played a prominent role in gay life in the United States. Traditionally, remaining in the closet has been a life-shaping strategy of concealing one's sexual identity to avoid interpersonal rejection and social discrimination. Historically, the closet has been a rational and understandable response to the typical treatment afforded gays and lesbians in the workplace, in the criminal justice system, in families, and in everyday encounters with others.

Typically people remain in the closet because they believe it will make their lives easier. Indeed, some therapists—who are gay themselves—at times advise their clients to stay in the closet in order to avoid psychological and interpersonal conflict (Swartz, 2011). However, such identity concealment can be extremely stressful and effortful, often evoking feelings of shame, guilt, and fear. It is not simply about denying and suppressing a potentially stigmatizing identity but instead involves close attention to every aspect of one's life in order to avoid detection:

> The closeted individual closely monitors his or her speech, emotional expression, and behavior in order to avoid unwanted suspicion. The sexual meaning of the things . . . and acts . . . of daily life must be carefully read in order to skillfully fashion a convincing heterosexual identity. (Seidman, 2004, p. 31)

The ever-present threat of being "outed," or forced to publicly acknowledge homosexuality, has long served as a means of social control, keeping homosexuals silent and invisible.

Over the past several decades, however, homosexuality in the United States has itself emerged from the cultural closet, leading some to argue that this metaphor is antiquated and no longer applicable. Indeed, as you'll see in more detail in Chapter 3, positive media and cultural images of homosexuality are more prevalent today than ever. Gay men and lesbians are freer to live outside the closet than at any other point in history. "Coming out" videos on *YouTube* have become increasingly common—and popular—in recent years.

However, gay men and lesbians still must navigate social institutions that maintain heterosexual privilege. In many areas of the labor force, for example, open homosexuality is still considered a liability. Despite corporate protections, over half of gay, lesbian, and bisexual employees nationwide hide their sexual orientation at work, and 35% lie about it. And 1 in 4 open LGBT employees feel that coworkers become uncomfortable when the topic of sexual orientation comes up or report hearing negative comments about LGBT people at work (Human Rights Campaign, 2014b).

Sociologist Steven Seidman (2004) interviewed 30 homosexuals of different races, classes, genders, and ages and found that, for the most part, they saw their homosexuality as natural and positive. They integrated it into their daily lives. Few of them seemed particularly concerned about sexual suspicion or outright exposure when making important decisions about love, work, friends, and other social activities. But they weren't completely open about their sexual identity either. They tended to conceal their homosexuality in specific situations or with specific people. To Seidman, this type of periodic closeting marks a noteworthy shift from the life-altering closet of the past. As he puts it, "there's a huge difference between concealing from an uncle or a client and marrying or avoiding certain occupations in order to pretend to be straight" (p. 8).

The experience of the closet and the consequences of coming out are influenced by other circumstances and components of social identity. For instance, gay men living in the South are far more likely to remain closeted than those living in the Northeast, even though the actual numbers of gay individuals living in these areas are comparable (Stephens-Davidowitz, 2013). Social class can also influence the likelihood of coming out of the closet. For instance, lesbians who are middle-class and white are more likely to come out, and be accepted by their families, than other lesbians (Mezey, 2013). Working-class individuals, no matter what their sexual orientation, expect to turn to aunts, uncles, cousins, or siblings for financial help at some point in their lives. They can never take material well-being for granted. So, for working-class gays and lesbians, being estranged from relatives as a result of exiting the closet carries the threat of losing an important source of economic and emotional support. In contrast, middle-class gays and lesbians usually have more options. Because of the high value placed on individual achievement, they can anticipate some degree of separation from their families and the communities in which they were raised. In addition, they have the economic wherewithal to support themselves if they become alienated from their families as a result of coming out.

Men and women also differ in the way they manage and conceal their sexual identities. For men who remain in the closet, simply appearing strong and masculine is usually enough to lead to the presumption that they're heterosexual and to confer the full measure of social authority and privilege given to men in our society. For lesbians, however, a traditionally feminine appearance may mark them as straight, but it also situates them as subordinates to men. The usual trappings of femininity do not carry the same status, authority, and economic advantage that traditional masculinity carries in this society. Closeted lesbians who wish to be strong, assertive, and authoritative risk exposure, and straight women who do likewise risk being labeled as lesbians. As Seidman writes:

> This is a dilemma that [homosexual] men don't experience. Men who claim masculine power are rewarded as men, and as presumptively straight; women who claim the same privileges associated with masculinity are gender rebels and risk stigma and social harm. (p. 50)

Decisions about concealing or publicly expressing homosexual identities are, of course, private matters that depend on the individual's circumstances. In a society that is built by, for, and around the interests of heterosexuals, however, such decisions are always influenced by larger structures of power and privilege, especially the willingness of employers and the legal system to accept homosexuality.

IDENTITIES ON THE BORDERLANDS

It would be tempting to see race, class, gender, and sexuality as four influential, but independent, characteristics that separately influence people's identities. But it's the intersections and interactions among these factors that are useful in explaining why people are the way they are and do the things they do. Race, class, gender, and sexuality operate concurrently in every social situation. At the societal level, they're embedded in every social institution. At the individual level, our location along the confluence of all these dimensions helps form our lives and our identities (Ocampo, 2012). For instance, one recent study found that living in poverty reduces the odds of being classified as white for men more than it does for women; and receiving welfare reduces the odds of being classified as white for women, but not at all for men (Penner & Saperstein, 2013). Similarly, among men in their

30s and 40s, Asians are more likely to identify as gay or bisexual than other groups; but Asian women in this age group are *less* likely than other women to do so (Gates & Newport, 2012).

The interconnectedness of these components of identity influences our social opportunities as well (Weber, 1998). On some dimensions, we may be dominant; on others, we may be subordinate. People might find themselves in positions of power sometimes (say, because they're male or white) but at other times find themselves in positions of disadvantage (because they're working class or homosexual). It's difficult, therefore, to argue that all disadvantages are the same or all victims of oppression are equally oppressed. Recognizing that every one of us benefits in some respects and suffers in others is important in fully understanding the impact of identities and inequalities in everyday life.

Some individuals face disadvantage on three or more dimensions. For instance, the intersections of race, class, and gender are particularly obvious to poor, black women. As far back as the late 19th century, black women argued that the concern with newly emancipated black men getting their rights eclipsed any concern for their rights (Weber, 1998). In addition, ideals of masculinity and femininity that emerged during the 19th century never included all men or women. The assumption that women were best suited to the domestic sphere where they would take care of the home and nurture children was an ideal that rarely extended to poor women of color, who have always participated in the paid labor force in higher numbers than white, middle-class women (see Chapter 6). Indeed, the feminist movement of the late 20th century was roundly criticized for excluding race and class in its attempts to shed light on the oppressive consequences of gender inequality alone.

Race, ethnicity, and class are so deeply interwoven in American culture that it may ultimately be impossible to pull them apart. For instance, "Jewishness" may be an ethnic or a religious category, but it is also conceptually inseparable from "middle classness" (Ortner, 1998). Nonetheless, many sociologists believe that it is important to examine the relative influence of race/ethnicity and social class on people's lives. Upwardly mobile people of color often find it difficult to leave their pasts behind and frequently feel caught between their poor ethnoracial communities of origin and the affluent communities where they now live (Feagin, 1991). They sometimes conclude that it's simply easier to keep these two facets of their lives separate. As one affluent black architect put it:

> It's like I have to be two different people. . . . It can just be easier to let my two parts stay apart. . . . I don't want people feeling uncomfortable around other people because they don't talk the same

71

language, or do the same things or anything like that, so I'd just as soon keep them apart. . . . I got my peers from work and that environment, business and professional, the movers and the shakers, and my peeps from way back when I used to run around in the streets like a wild man. (quoted in Jackson, 2004, p. 267)

Furthermore, middle-class and affluent African Americans still face discriminatory treatment in their everyday public encounters—ranging from closer scrutiny in stores to police harassment (see Chapter 5). As a result, even African Americans who've seen their socioeconomic standing improve have become discouraged about whether the "American Dream" applies to them (Hochschild, 1995). Other sociologists, like William Julius Wilson (1980), have long argued that class may be a more important determinant of social and political status than race. Wilson cites the fact that African Americans have become polarized into an educated, upwardly mobile middle-class and an economically destitute underclass. These two groups have very different ideologies, perceptions of social justice, and overall outlooks on life.

Intersections
Gay Men of Color on the *Down Low*

The ascription of sexual labels can be influenced by one's membership in other identifying categories. For white homosexuals, sexual orientation is the identifier that most distinguishes them from the dominant white population and culture. Their sexual orientation, therefore, may take on greater importance for them than it does for black, Latino/a, or Asian homosexuals, who live with an added layer of difference from the dominant group because of their race. For instance, gay Latino men have a strong sense of ethnic identity but are more ambivalent about their sexual identity because common depictions of gay identity and the larger gay community—as both feminine and white—don't align with their sense of self and Latino masculinity (Ocampo, 2012). In addition, gay men and lesbians of color often feel excluded both from their ethnoracial communities (because of their sexual orientation) and from the gay community (because of their minority status; Moore, 2011).

An examination of attitude surveys over the past 30 years reveals that African Americans are more disapproving of homosexuality than are other groups, particularly among black religious institutions (Moore, 2011). Not surprisingly, black homosexuals, especially men, are less likely than white homosexuals to be openly gay (Boykin, 1996). Certainly there are overtly gay black men and some high-profile black professional athletes—basketball's Jason Collins and football's Michael Sam, to name a few—have come out quite publicly in recent years. And there is some evidence that support of same-sex marriage may be increasing among African Americans (Demby, 2013). But because of the lingering stigma of homosexuality among African Americans, many gay black men still feel the need to lead secret lives (Lapinski, Braz, & Maloney, 2010). They are, as one author puts it, "products of a black culture that deems masculinity and fatherhood as a black man's primary responsibility—and homosexuality as a white man's perversion" (Denizet-Lewis, 2003, p. 30).

Faced with the sometimes volatile and destructive combination of racism and homophobia, many gay black men reject gay culture and live their lives on the "down low," or on the DL. Most of these men date or marry women and engage in sexual activity with men they meet anonymously at bathhouses, in parks, or online. While some of these men participate peripherally in mainstream gay culture, they are not known as gay by their colleagues or families. Even DL men who say they prefer sex with men are adamant that the gay label doesn't apply to them (Heath & Goggin, 2009). They identify themselves first and foremost as black, which is taken to be synonymous with being masculine. Indeed, masculine appearance is an effective defense against accusations of homosexuality because of widespread stereotypes that equate homosexuality with effeminate men.

The costs of being both black and gay can still be steep for some men. As one black man on the DL put it:

> If you're white, you can come out as an openly gay skier or actor or whatever. It might hurt you some, but it's not like if you're black and gay, because then it's like you've let down the whole black community, black women, black history, black pride. You don't hear black people say, "Oh yeah, he's gay, but he's still a real man. . . ." (quoted in Denizet-Lewis, 2003, p. 31)

Over the past several years, the DL culture has come to the attention of a worried public health community that attributes the high prevalence of HIV/AIDS among African Americans at least in part to these men, who have unprotected anonymous sex and then pass the virus to their unsuspecting wives and girlfriends. African Americans make up around 13% of the population in the United States, but according to the Centers for Disease Control and Prevention (2012a), they account for 44% of all diagnoses of HIV/AIDS. African American men who have sex with men (whether or not they identify as gay/bisexual) represent three-quarters of new infections among all African American men and 36% of new HIV infections among all gay and bisexual men. More new HIV infections occur among young African American gay and bisexual men (aged 13-24) than any other racial subgroup. And the death rate from HIV/AIDS among black men (16.5 per 100,000) is more than seven times higher than that of white men (2.3 per 100,000; ProQuest Statistical Abstract, 2014).

In short, the combinations of race, class, gender, and sexuality have complex effects on people's lives. We cannot understand the way people define themselves and others and the way different groups are situated in the larger society unless we look at the intersections among race, class, gender, and sexuality. Thus, throughout the remaining chapters of this book, I've highlighted some of these intersections.

CONCLUSION

We've seen in this chapter that cultural and historical ideas about race, class, gender, and sexuality can be just as influential in determining people's identities as biology. That is not to say that biology has no role. It simply means that our ideas about the contribution of genes, hormones, or anatomy ebb and flow with shifting political and cultural tides. What's important, for our purposes, is not so much whether race, class, gender, and sexual identities have biological underpinnings but how we, as a society, come to define and value the relative contributions of biology and culture. Biology needn't be destiny. We can choose to rely on skin color or genital configuration as the primary means by which we make "us-them" distinctions. Or we can choose to downplay these traits and treat them with the same nonchalance that we treat eye color, hair color, or the shape of a chin.

As long as people continue to believe that race differences or gender differences are rooted in nature, however, they will continue to accept social inequalities as natural. It's easier to justify women's lower wages in the workforce, for instance, if the cultural assumption is that they are innately less competitive and ambitious than men. It's easier to segregate members of particular racial or ethnic groups into occupations that involve tedious manual labor if the cultural assumption is that they are biologically built to tolerate such conditions.

In the following chapter, I will extend these ideas about the socially manufactured nature of difference to show how it is perpetuated through everyday language and represented through important media imagery.

[INVESTIGATING IDENTITIES AND INEQUALITIES]
A sociological treasure hunt: The artifacts of identity

Because we live in a society that is built on acquisition and consumption, components of identity are frequently reflected in the commercial objects of our physical environment. We tend to leave a visible trail of who we are for others to notice, whether it's in our fashions, our possessions, our Facebook or Pinterest profiles, or our homes. Messages about identity pervade everyday public space as well. If you look closely enough, you will notice that we are surrounded by visual images of gender, racial, ethnic, class, and sexual identity, even in those objects that are designed to symbolize other things.

For this exercise, you will go on a sort of sociological treasure hunt. Your task is to explore your campus and, if possible, the surrounding community noting and describing the consumer products, public objects, artwork, and other visual artifacts that present or reinforce images of race, ethnicity, religion, gender, sexuality, or social class. Some might be blatant (for instance, a store that sells National Coming Out Day t-shirts). But others may be much more subtle (for instance, the assumption of heterosexual romance that underlies advertisements for wedding rings or the gender assumptions behind detergent advertisements depicting women as the ones who do household laundry). The experience would work best if you use a digital camera or smart phone to immediately record the images you discover. Because this assignment is meant to focus your attention on the everyday visual objects of identities, avoid photographing other people. If possible, revisit areas that you think you know very well. One of the important features of the gender, class, race, and sexual messages that are expressed or assumed in cultural objects is that they become so commonplace that we rarely notice they're there.

For each of the images you collect, describe what you think it symbolizes about race, class, gender, or sexuality (or even better, the intersections of these identifiers). Do these images tend to support stereotypical conceptions? Are they designed to evoke feelings of pride or shame? Are they meant for group members or non-group members? At a societal level, why are these messages important? What influence do you think such images have on people's attitudes, perceptions, and behaviors?

CHAPTER 3

Portraying Identities
Race, Class, Gender, and Sexuality In Language and the Media

've spent the past 25 years living and teaching in a small town in rural west central Indiana. Apart from the university, it's not a very diverse community, and it's in a fairly poor county. So, cultural resources are limited. But living in a small town does have its advantages. It's relatively safe. Things are close enough to walk to. The cost of living is manageable. This town is probably no different from the thousands of other little-known small towns that dot the American countryside.

Because I had always lived in large cities, the lethargic pace of life and the howdy-neighbor demeanor of the residents took some getting used to. The first time a stranger said to me, "I saw you running out on Albin Pond Road last Thursday at 7:45 in the morning with a blue windbreaker on." I was taken aback. But by the tenth time you hear comments like that, it starts to feel a little less stalker-y. So, it shouldn't have surprised me when, on a mid-December shopping trip to the local supermarket shortly after we'd moved to town, a smiling clerk with a green and red felt elf hat leaned over the cash register, lowered her glasses, and asked my then-3-year-old son: "So, what are you going to ask Santa to bring you for Christmas?"

Now, you wouldn't think that such a friendly question during the holiday season would be particularly bothersome. From Thanksgiving to late December, such questions from retail employees to customers' children are as routine as flashy Christmas lights, piped-in renditions of "Jingle Bell Rock," and package-laden, glazed-eyed shoppers solemnly trudging through department stores. Every year around this time, "Merry Christmas!" replaces "Good-bye!" "Come back real soon!" or "Have a nice day!" as the courteous farewell of choice.

But I'm a sociologist. And that means I have an annoying tendency to pick things apart, searching for deeper meaning. So, of course, I just had to take a closer look at this friendly clerk's innocent but powerfully presumptuous question:

- The *asking for* part. First, she assumed that my son is in the habit of requesting specific gifts on holidays. Not a baseless assumption, to be sure, in a culture that instills a healthy dose of materialism in children from an early age. But for all she knew, my son could have come from a family where children are taught to be appreciative of any gift, making such a blatant demand for toys taboo. You know, "it's better to give than to receive" and all that. She also assumed that my son would know how to contact Santa: A prayer? A handwritten letter to the North Pole? A tweet to #JollyStNick?

- The *Santa* part. Second, she assumed that my son not only knew who Santa was (so much so that she only had to use his first name in her question), but that he also knew *what* Santa was: the chubby gatekeeper of goodies who breaks into children's homes once a year to bring them stuff. Apparently, the clerk was uninterested in finding out if I was one of the many parents who struggle to dispel the myth of Santa Claus from their children's minds at very early ages.

■ The *Christmas* part. Finally, the presumption that was the most obvious—but also the most disquieting—was simply that my son celebrated Christmas. When my children were young we didn't, in fact, celebrate Christmas. Although they have a mixed religious/ethnic heritage and they sometimes spent Christmas Day with their Christian relatives, we never had a tree, sang carols around the fireplace, or hung colorful lights in or on our house.

Even at age 3, my son had watched enough TV to know that Christmas had something to do with gifts and that a big guy with a white beard and a gaudy red jumpsuit was involved somehow. But beyond that, he was a little short on the specifics. I knew that his puzzled silence when the clerk asked her question wasn't going to cut it. I had a split-second decision to make: I could (a) correct her mistake and berate her for her ill-considered assumptions or (b) just smile, nod, and say something like, "Well, he hasn't asked for anything yet, but I'm sure he'll think of something. You know kids. Heh heh. And a Merry Christmas to you too." I opted for the latter strategy.

When I got home, I seethed. Mostly I was mad at myself for not calling out the clerk's blunder. As a sociologist interested in the role that language plays in constructing and reflecting social reality, I understood that even the smallest conversations can have deep implications. Although Christmas hasn't been a strictly religious holiday for some time, routine questions about Santa reflect the assumption that one is or should be Christian. Because my son and I apparently didn't seem religiously "exotic" in any way to the checker—no turbans, no yarmulkes, no safron-colored robes—it didn't even occur to her to ask, "Little boy, do you celebrate Christmas?" before proceeding to her Santa question.

The importance of language in creating and reinforcing perceptions of difference often lies more in what's not said than in what is. The fact that she didn't feel the necessity to ask him if he celebrated Christmas showed that Christianity—like whiteness or maleness or heterosexuality or middle-class status—has the privilege in everyday discourse not to be named. This privilege is not found only in small rural towns. It pervades society.

In this chapter, I will explore the cultural expression of images of difference. How are social differences—and ultimately, inequalities—portrayed in everyday communication? To answer this question, I will look first at the powerful role of language in highlighting identity and shaping social reality. I will then examine the equally powerful role of information and entertainment media in creating and reinforcing culturally dominant images of race, class, gender, and sexuality.

SYMBOLS AND LANGUAGE

We live in a social world in which our everyday interactions are mediated through symbols. A **symbol** is something used to represent or stand for something else (Charon, 1998). It can be a physical object (like an engagement ring standing for betrothal), a characteristic or property of objects (like a pink triangle standing for gay pride), a gesture (like a thumb pointed up standing for "everything's ok"), or a word (like the letters d-o-g standing for a particular type of household pet).

Symbols are powerful social constructions. They are created, modified, and used by people in their everyday contacts with others. We concoct them and learn to agree on what they should stand for. Our lives depend on such agreement. Imagine how chaotic car travel would be, for example, if we didn't all agree that green lights stand for "go" and red lights stand for "stop."

Symbols don't bear any necessary connection to nature. They're rather arbitrary human creations. There's nothing in the natural properties of greenness, for instance, that automatically determines that it means "go." We could have decided long ago that purple polka dots stand for "go." It wouldn't have mattered as long as we all learned and understood this symbol.

Even though symbols are arbitrary, they can evoke powerful emotional responses. All Americans know, for example, that a piece of cloth with red and white horizontal stripes and a blue square in the upper left corner containing 50 white stars symbolizes our nation. There's nothing particularly precious about the physical properties of the cloth itself. It's not as if it's woven of solid gold threads. It is simply a piece of cloth whose value comes from its symbolism, not from its material characteristics. In fact, the flag can even be made out of paper, plastic, or pixels on an iPad. When most Americans see the flag, they don't see the physical object; they see only the symbol. They respond to it as if it were the nation it represents. They may pledge their allegiance to it, treat it with ritualized reverence and respect, cry when it's raised after an Olympic victory, respond with anger when it is mistreated, and even risk their lives on the battlefield to protect it.

Not surprisingly, although symbols can evoke feelings of solidarity and unity, they can also separate, intimidate, and enrage. Take, for instance, a different piece of cloth: the Confederate battle flag. To some, it is a proud symbol of Southern heritage. But where they see celebrations of cultural pride, others see symbolic reminders of racial intimidation. To them, it is a painful reminder of slavery and segregation that has been appropriated by contemporary racist hate groups like the Ku Klux Klan (Coski, 2005). According to the Southern Poverty Law Center, hundreds of extremist groups use the Confederate battle flag as one of their symbols (cited in Brunner, 2004). In the past few decades, controversies—and lawsuits—have arisen over the policy in some Southern states of flying this flag along with the U.S. and state flags over their statehouses. In the aftermath of the 2015 racially motivated massacre at a church in Charleston, South Carolina, several states—not to mention some prominent organizations, such as NASCAR and WalMart—decided to remove or refuse to allow the public display of this volatile symbol. To be sure, it is more than just a piece of colored cloth.

Perhaps the most important kind of symbol is language. Words—whether spoken or written—form the basis for virtually all our experiences. We communicate with words. We form relationships with words. We think to ourselves with words. We imagine our futures and record our pasts with words. Indeed, cultures and civilizations would be impossible without symbols, of which language is the most important type. Just like physical objects that function as symbols (such as flags), language can evoke powerful emotions, even in the absence of the thing to which the words refer. I had a friend in college who would become visibly shaken and depressed when he heard or read his ex-girlfriend's name. Indeed, by simply vocalizing a string of certain words and putting them together in meaningful sentences, I can, if so inclined, make you happy, sad, frightened, angry, or sick to your stomach.

In Chapter 2, you learned about the differences between essentialist and constructionist perspectives. To an essentialist, what we call something is irrelevant. What is important is the inherent reality of that thing, which transcends human judgments and labels. But to a constructionist, what we choose to call something or someone is a crucial component of everyday life because these labels simultaneously shape and reflect social reality. The way we use words to define ourselves and others reveals broader cultural values and inequalities and also perpetuates them.

SLURS

The most obvious and personal way that words create and enforce social inequalities is through verbal slurs and affronts. Every conceivable racial, ethnic, national, religious, disability, body type, gender, or sexual group has at one time or another been subject to its own set of derogatory terms. A web site called the Racial Slur Database (www.rsdb.org) lists thousands of slurs applied to 160 different racial or ethnic groups.

Even if we don't use them, most of us learn slurs at fairly young ages, and we quickly come to understand the kinds of strong feelings that both motivate their usage and determine people's responses to them. The old playground retort to teasing, "Sticks and stones may break my bones, but names can never hurt me," sounds comforting and ego-affirming in the abstract, but it provides little solace in actual confrontations. The power of slurs stems from the realization that they are not simply personal insults. They always reflect broader cultural and political themes.

Often words become derogatory when they are applied to people who are not even members of the group identified by the term. Any male high school coach or military drill sergeant knows that the best way to whip his men into an aggressive frenzy is to call them *girls* or *ladies*. Likewise, among heterosexual adolescents, homophobic name calling (*queer, fag, dyke*) is one of the most common modes of bullying and coercion in school (Thurlow, 2001). But being called a *fag* has more to do with not meeting traditional standards of masculinity and revealing weakness than it does with sexual orientation (Pascoe, 2010). In 2013, the actor Alec Baldwin was caught on camera outside his Manhattan apartment calling a photographer a *cocksucking fag*. Baldwin wasn't disparaging the man's sexual orientation. Instead, he was enraged by the intrusion of paparazzi into his private life and no doubt thought using this term would be the most effective means of communicating his utter contempt for the practice.

The meaning of some slurs changes over time. Consider the word *bitch*. Originally a non-insulting term for a female dog, *bitch* eventually came to mean a malicious, spiteful, and domineering woman. It eventually expanded past its ties to femaleness and became a verb—meaning to complain or grouse about something. Later on, it acquired meaning as a term for any subordinate, male or female (as in "You're my *bitch* now"). It can be doubly insulting when used as an epithet against men ("Stop whining; you're acting like a little *bitch*!"). Not only is their identity being demeaned, but their masculinity is as well. The Jesse Pinkman character in the now-defunct TV show, *Breaking Bad,* became an online sensation for his consistent use of *bitch* to express any manner of anger, displeasure, or frustration.

In some circles, however, *bitch* is now embraced by women as empowering—for example, popular T-shirts for young women that say "100% Genuine American Bitch." An organization called BitchMedia publishes a magazine *Bitch: Feminist Response to Pop Culture.* Its website states that its "mission is to provide and encourage an engaged, thoughtful feminist response to mainstream media and popular culture" (BitchMedia, 2014, p. 1).

The meanings of slurs also change as society changes (Allen, 1990). Words may become more derogatory or less derogatory as the status of a particular group changes. The words *Negro* and *colored,* for example, were once common references used for and by African Americans. In time, the terms became pejorative and a variety of others rose to take their place— *black, Afro-American, African American.*

Interestingly, though, a sense of group identity can sometimes be derived from the retention of derogatory terms. One of the most powerful antidis- crimination organizations in the United States, the National Association for the Advancement of Colored People (NAACP), retains the word *Colored* in its title both as a reminder of past oppression and as a symbol of its com- mitment to the advancement of all people of color, not just Blacks. Similarly, other words, like *queer, redneck,* and *nigger,* have undergone a process of inversion whereby they have been in a sense repossessed by the groups that were originally targets of these hostile slurs. Today, they may be used either in a friendly fashion or as badges of honor and pride. In 2011, a Toronto police officer told a group of college women that if they wanted to avoid being sexually assaulted, they should stop dressing like *sluts.* In angry response, women in 70 cities around the world marched in bras and garter belts with the words *proud slut* written on their shirts and painted on their faces (Traister, 2011).

Of course, the desire to reclaim slurs varies along generational lines, with older members of certain groups less inclined to embrace a painful derogatory label of the past. The word *nigger* has been called the "nuclear bomb" of racial epithets because of its power to evoke such an enormous range of intense emotions. Young hip-hop artists defiantly claim their right to use the word whenever they wish. When pronounced differently— *niggah*—it becomes a term of endearment. For older people, however, who may recall a time when people fought and died over the word, it is likely to retain its sting (Waxman, 2004). The Reverend Al Sharpton, who is black, once said, "If you call yourself the n-word, you can't get mad when someone treats you like that" (quoted in Coates, 2013, p. 6). Indeed, an organization called "Ban the N Word" is dedicated to enhancing the image of African Americans by arguing that the use of this derogatory slur by Blacks is destructive. In 2014, the National Football League went so far as to consider banning players, no matter what their race or what the context, from using the word during a game.

Furthermore, any positive connotations derived from such terms are available only to those within the particular group in question. When uttered by outsiders, the words remain slurs:

> "Nigger" . . . is the signpost that reminds us that the old crimes don't disappear. It tells white people that for all their guns and all their gold, there will always be places they can never go (Coates, 2013, p. 6).

In 2013, the famous cooking show celebrity, Paula Deen, was fired by the Food Network after admitting that she had used the word *nigger,* even though she said she meant no harm. In an episode of the HBO sitcom *Curb Your Enthusiasm*, an African American hip-hop singer warmly refers to Larry David, the geeky, white, middle-aged star of the show, as "my *nigger.*" The term is meant not as an insult but as a sign of clubby friendship. The painfully unhip Larry beams with pride at the reference because it marks him, at least temporarily, as an "honorary" black person. Of course, the process of inversion is not applicable to terms that were never slurs in the first place. Larry's attempt to reciprocate by addressing his new African American friend as "my *Caucasian*" lacks the same in-group cachet and historical resonance.

THE LANGUAGE OF DIFFERENCE

The importance of understanding the relationship among language, definitions of difference, and inequality goes beyond blatant insults and slurs. Shifts in the usage of language as well as in reference terms and connotations often parallel changes in the social stature of particular groups. Let's take a look now at some of the linguistic issues relevant to gender, race, ethnicity, and sexual orientation.

Gendered Language   As you saw in Chapter 2, we live in a society built on dichotomous distinctions between boys and girls, men and women, and masculine and feminine. Such distinctions are particularly noteworthy in the content and usage of language. Although English is not grammatically gendered as, say, French or Spanish, gender pervades the language in obvious ways, such as the inclusive male pronoun *he*, the generic *man* in referring to humans of both genders, and other common terms, such as *chairman, ombudsman, brotherhood, freshman, penmanship, man-made,* and *man-to-man defense*. Such linguistic expressions either render females invisible or make them appear as exceptions. Indeed, only when referring to inanimate objects is the female pronoun *she* used in such a manner, as when applied to cars and boats.

In some societies, women are so devalued that the language lacks words that communicate female respect and authority. In China, for example, female scholars, authors, and opinion leaders are sometimes referred to in the press as men. In Twitter-like microblogs, one prominent woman was called *xiansheng* (the most common way to address a man in Mandarin) rather than the gender-free term *tongzhi*. A Chinese woman put it this way:

> Historically when a woman was called [*xiansheng*], it really elevated her to the status of a man. It meant a brilliant woman. . . . As a woman you have to be really outstanding to be called it, whereas if you are a man it can be anybody (quoted in Tatlow, 2013, p. A7).

In English, the priority of men is reinforced when female versions of certain words are created as extensions of existing male terms, either by adding an *ess* or *ette* (for example, hostess, stewardess, majorette) or by using the words *lady, female,* or *woman* as noun modifiers (for example, *woman* lawyer, *female* entrepreneur, the University of Tennessee *Lady* Volunteers). Even purposely non-gendered words like *congressperson, waitperson,* or *spokesperson* imply that the individual being described is female. The fact that these titles are modifications of traditional male terms buttresses the cultural belief that the occupations in question are still men's domain, with women being exceptions to the rule. There's no need to call a man a *male* engineer or a *male* doctor because the terms doctor and engineer already imply a male occupant. A 2010 *New York Times* article describing a terrorist attack in Russia carried the headline, "Female Suicide Bombers Strike at Moscow Subway." Clearly no one would have thought the attackers were women had the headline simply read "Suicide bombers."

Our gender-biased vocabulary also reflects and perpetuates underlying societal beliefs about the relative roles of men and women. To *mother* a child is to nurture, coddle, and protect that child; to *father* a child is simply to fertilize an egg. Similarly, a *governor* is an elected official who acts as the head of a state; a *governess* is one who cares for other people's children. In common usage, a *master* is one who rules over others; the female version, *mistress,* is a woman with whom a man has an extended extramarital affair (Richardson, 2004). The linguistic association of masculinity with toughness is especially pervasive, as when people—both men and women—are implored to *man up* when faced with situations that require courage or strength of character.

The movement for gender equality always includes battles over language. For instance, in the domain of politics, female lawmakers often face attacks on their suitability for office not in terms of their stands on important issues but through the strategic use of language (Parker, 2014b). Consider these cases:

- Patty Murray, a senator from Washington state, was disparaged early in her career by a state lawmaker who dismissed her "a mom in tennis shoes."
- An opponent of Missouri senator, Claire McCaskill, described her performance in one debate as "not particularly ladylike."
- Senator Amy Klobuchar of Minnesota was called "Miss Congeniality" and a "prom queen" by her male opponent in the 2012 campaign.

As you know, there is now greater sensitivity to the power of gender-biased terms than ever before. The state of Washington recently passed a law requiring all future legislation to include gender-neutral terms. In 2014, Facebook chief executive, Sheryl Sandberg, began a campaign called "Ban Bossy" to discourage use of the word *bossy* that she says is meant to put down assertive girls. The organization's web site (banbossy.com) states that when a boy asserts himself, he's called a "leader;" but when a girl does so, she's branded as "bossy." As a consequence, girls are less interested in leading than boys, a trend that continues well into adulthood.

Ethnoracial Language As we just saw in the discussion of slurs, language is especially volatile in the area of race and ethnicity. Here, words always reflect the relative cultural value of particular groups. Consider the connotations of the words *black* and *white*. *White lies* are small, insignificant, and harmless. *Black magic* is dark and ominous. *White knights* are heroes; *black hats represent cinematic villains*. A *black eye* and a *black mark* are symbols of shame. The *black sheep* of the family is an embarrassment to his or her relatives. Among the definitions of *black* in *Webster's New Universal Unabridged Dictionary* are "soiled and dirty," "thoroughly evil," "wicked," "gloomy," "hopeless," "marked by disaster," "hostile," and "disgraceful." The definition of *white*, in contrast, includes "fairness of complexion," "innocent," "favorable," "fortunate," "pure," and "spotless." The pervasive "goodness" of white and "badness" of black affects children at a very young age and can provide white children with a false sense of superiority (Moore, 1992).

The everyday use of ethnoracial labels carries important political significance too. For instance, there is little agreement among Spanish-speaking peoples as to whether they want to be called *Spanish-surnamed, Hispanic, Latino/a, Latin@,* or something else entirely. The stand up comedian, Carlos Mencia once described the hostility he faced from college students who objected to the way he tried to identify them:

I said "Latinos" and they said, "We're not Latin!" And then I said "Chicano," and they said, "We're not . . . Mexican." So I said "I don't know what to say – Hispanic?" And they said, "There's no such country as Hispania!" How am I supposed to describe us? (quoted in Bates, 2014, p. 2).

Terms like *American Indians, tribal nations, Indian tribes, indigenous nations, Fourth World peoples, Native American peoples, Aboriginal peoples, First Nations,* and *Native Nations* refer to native people living in North America (Wilkins, 2004). Officially, the U.S. government still uses the term *Indian.* What constitutes an Indian tribe, though, is a matter of some contention. The extension of federal recognition to a tribal nation is the formal acknowledgment of the tribe's legal sovereign status. The U.S. Department of the Interior's Bureau of Indian Affairs (2014) recognizes 566 tribal governments. In the distant past, "recognition" simply meant an acknowledgment that a tribe existed. But by the 1870s, "recognition" began to be used in a more formal sense to describe a political relationship between a tribe and the U.S. government. In this sense, recognition means that a tribe is entitled to some privileges (for instance, documented tribal nations are exempt from most state tax laws) but also certain limitations and obligations (Wilkins, 2004). In the 1950s and 1960s, more than a hundred tribes and bands had their "recognized" status terminated, rendering their members ineligible for the benefits and exemptions they had enjoyed up to that point.

On an individual level, the determination of who is an *Indian* is also linguistically complicated. Congress uses a variety of criteria for determining whether one can be labeled an *Indian,* including having a certain percentage of "Indian blood," belonging to a federally recognized indigenous community, living on or near a reservation, and being a descendant of a tribal member.

In addition to words that are direct identifiers of particular groups, some words that seem not to be ethnoracial at all are, at times, used as code words for particular groups. For instance, in some circles, *New Yorker* is still used as a code word for Jew. Likewise, euphemisms, such as *culturally deprived, economically disadvantaged, inner city, urban,* and *underprivileged* sound race-neutral, but they are commonly used to refer to poor black and Latino/a Americans (Krugman, 2014b). An examination of the 1995 Louisiana gubernatorial election revealed that the white candidate's discussion of the crime problems in particular inner-city neighborhoods (by which everyone knew he meant minority neighborhoods) subtly symbolized his racial attitudes, appealed to many white voters, and thereby contributed to his victory over a black candidate (Knuckey & Orey, 2000).

Sexual Language   The politics of language is especially important for people whose sexual practices and identities fall outside what is considered normative sexuality. Terms used to refer to people outside the sexual mainstream have throughout history expressed moral, spiritual, legal, or psychiatric condemnation.

Self-labeling at the individual level can also be seen as a political act of sorts. The distinction, for example, between *gay* and *lesbian* emerged from concerns among women that the word *gay*, despite common usage, technically applied only to men. Within the past 25 years, the word *queer* first became a reclaimed epithet and since has become a term applied not only to homosexuals but to any marginalized sexual minority (Zwicky, 1997). Indeed, Queer Studies is now a legitimate area of academic inquiry and is even listed in many college catalogs as a program in which students can major or minor.

As sexual categories expand in the interests of inclusion and social recognition, terms can become unwieldy and must be shortened either to abbreviations (such as *lesbigay*) or to acronyms: LGBT (lesbian, gay, bisexual, and transgendered) and, more recently, LGBTQIA (lesbian, gay, bisexual, transgendered, queer/questioning, interested/intersexed, ally/asexual; Schulman, 2013). Notice that the shifting terminology has nothing to do with essential changes in the nature and configuration of the group and everything to do with political and social pressures from subgroups seeking to expand conceptions of gender and sexual identity beyond dichotomous categories.

As much as we come to think of self-labels as crucial monikers of identity, they are always context- and audience-specific. Whether someone refers to herself or himself as *gay, homosexual, bisexual,* or *queer* may very much depend on the person to whom that individual is speaking and the nature of the interaction:

> Even when I was . . . by inclination and behavior bisexual, I spoke of myself as gay in most public contexts, preferring to ally myself with those whose orientation was entirely toward members of their own sex rather than risk being seen as some sort of straight person. (Zwicky, 1997, p. 25)

On the other hand, labels for heterosexuals in our heteronormative society bear little of the political weight and delicacy that labels for sexual minorities bear. In fact, the term *straight* emerged not as a result of some activist movement in the "heterosexual community" to establish a collective identity and political presence, but as a catch-all antonym to all labels for people with a different sexual orientation (Murphy, 1997).

THE USE OF LANGUAGE TO CONCEAL VARIATION

While linguistic terminology—whether imposed from the outside or embraced from the inside—marks groups as different, it can also be used to gloss over relevant internal variation, thereby lumping together disparate groups with different languages, cultures, religious beliefs, and histories. **Panethnic labels**—broad terms applied to diverse subgroups that are assumed to have something in common—have historically been used by people outside those groups for the sake of convenience. For instance, the 566 Native nations collectively recognized by the government as "Indian" have widely divergent cultures, languages, and histories. "Latino/as" may speak the same language, but Mexicans, Puerto Ricans, Cubans, Nicaraguans, Venezuelans, and others have dramatically different histories, dialects, immigration patterns, and citizenship experiences. People of Asian descent have rarely thought of themselves as a single racial group. Korean, Japanese, Chinese, Indian, Sri Lankan, Indonesian, and Filipino Americans may all be considered "Asian," but each group has its own language, religious beliefs, and history (Espiritu, 2004). To some, even the term "African American," which is widely considered to be a positive racial label, glosses over the thousands of ethnic groups, class interests, and indigenous religions that exist on the continent of Africa. And of course, terms like "White," "Caucasian," and "Anglo" also conceal enormous cultural, geographic, religious, and economic diversity.

Panethnic labels may be used to simplify, but they also have the effect of perpetuating the notion that the dominant group matters most. When I was in college, I remember watching television coverage of the Olympic marathon race and being struck by the announcer's consistent reference to the runners in the lead pack as "the Africans." These runners hailed from such diverse countries as Tanzania, Ethiopia, and Kenya. Yet referring to them as "the Africans" reduced them to a single entity and gave the impression that since they were all African, they were conspiring to compete against the non-African runners. Hence it didn't really matter which African country was victorious.

It's important to note, though, that panethnic labels aren't always negative nor always imposed by outsiders. I happened to be in Botswana during the 2010 World Cup soccer tournament, which was held in neighboring South Africa. Themes like "We are all Africans" and "Africa United" pervaded advertisements and promotional materials. Indeed, the whole continent celebrated when Ghana became the first African country in history to win a World Cup game.

In fact, some people argue that political power may emerge from adopting a panethnic identity and creating a common heritage among diverse groups. In this sense, the imposition of the label "Asian," for instance, becomes a symbol of the collective experience of discrimination, intolerance, exploitation, and perhaps even violence at the hands of non-Asians in the larger society (Espiritu, 2004). A study of Chinese American and Korean American college students found that the shared experience of being stereotyped as "nerdy" and being made to feel like outsiders led most of them to seek comforting friendships with other Asian students, no matter what their specific ethnic heritage (Kibria, 2004).

Group identity and political power are also reflected in the tendency toward hyphenation, especially among ethnoracial minorities (Japanese-American, Mexican-American, Italian-American, and so on). The use of a hyphenated label is a function of a group's degree of or desire for **assimilation,** the process by which members of minority groups alter their ways to conform to those of the dominant culture. One of the fundamental goals of U.S. society has always been the ultimate absorption of groups into mainstream society. Yet the goal of a fully assimilated society has never been realized. Many people are forced to or choose to retain connections to their ethnic or racial heritage. Indeed, **multiculturalism,** unlike assimilation, emphasizes the importance of maintaining those cultural elements that give us variety and make us different from one another. For many groups, moving away from assimilation and toward multiculturalism means adopting a hyphenated ethnoracial identity. Some have argued, for instance, that the movement from "Negro" to "Black" and then to "African American" as the racial label of choice marked a rejection of the idea of assimilation—symbolized by the middle-class "Negro" aspiring to assimilate into mainstream white culture—in favor of pride in the differences from mainstream culture (Spencer, 1994). But the notion of ethnic hyphenation doesn't mean that all ethnoracial qualities are valued equally (Alexander, 2001). For groups that are socially marginalized, subordinated, or repressed, it can be a stigmatizing reminder of difference.

THE DIFFERENCES OF LANGUAGE

Given the strong human desire to emphasize difference over similarity, it is not surprising that one of the chief interests of linguists is whether or not particular groups have their own distinct language, dialect, or vocabulary. You've probably learned that you can use a person's accent to determine whether she or he is from Brooklyn, Chicago, Boston, or Atlanta. If certain groups are considered cultures unto themselves and maintaining identifiable boundaries between "us" and "them" is a key concern, then it would make sense that they too would have a unique way of communicating with fellow members—in addition to a unique lifestyle and unique norms and values.

For instance, do you think you could tell the difference between someone defined as upper class and someone defined as working class simply by listening to they way they talk?

One object of this sort of sociological inquiry has been to determine whether or not certain language patterns are common to historically disadvantaged groups. For example, over 70 years ago, the folklorist Gershon Legman (1941) published a glossary of terms that he purported were used exclusively by male homosexuals. Some words disappeared; others, like *drag* and *straight*, entered the mainstream vocabulary. In the 1960s, sociologist Rose Giallombardo (1966) published a glossary of close to 300 terms used by lesbians in prison. In it, she describes an elaborate system of named kin and sexual relationships among the inmates.

Today, linguists talk about a "code," known variously by such terms as "gayspeak," "lgb talk," "queerspeak," "gay English," and "lavender language" (Kulick, 2000). For over 20 years, American University in Washington, D.C., has hosted a "Lavender Languages and Linguistics Conference.". One author describes communication patterns among homosexuals as the "language of risk," meaning that because of continuing fears about condemnation or discrimination, closeted gays and lesbians often develop ways of speaking that camouflage their identities (Leap, 1996). For example, they may use genderless pronouns to describe a partner or strategically maintain silence on certain issues to allow people to maintain default assumptions about heterosexuality. However, others (for example, Queen, 1997) argue that gay men and lesbians do not represent a single unified group and therefore cannot have a common language.

Gender differences in language use have occupied even more scholarly attention. In the 1990s, Deborah Tannen (1990) popularized the idea that men and women have dramatically different linguistic styles. She likened male-female differences in conversation and the use of language to cultural differences. She went so far as to argue that women and men frequently experience miscommunication with one another on a par with the sorts of miscommunications that can sometimes hinder interactions between people of different nationalities.

But some researchers (for example, Kollock, Blumstein, & Schwartz, 1985) have argued that certain gender-typed conversational styles actually reflect power differences rather than gender differences. Linguistic tendencies typically attributed to men—like interrupting, being nonresponsive, and controlling topics of conversation—are best understood not as essential differences between men and women but as a consequence of power imbalances. Each of these tactics is a way of preventing others from contributing to the conversation. To be silenced in such a way is to be rendered invisible (Lakoff, 1995). Similarly, the common belief that women's speech tends to be more revealing and emotionally expressive than men's reflects the deeper cultural belief that women are the ones who are supposed to tend to relationships (Lakoff, 1973). Unfortunately, one of the consequences of disclosing a great deal of information about yourself or openly showing your emotions is that it makes you less powerful (P. M. Blau, 1964). By linguistically overexposing themselves—something they are taught to do as a way to build and tend to relationships—women perpetuate the preexisting power differences between them and men.

Some ethnoracial groups, of course, literally speak a different language. The issue for them is not so much whether their unique language exists but where and when it should be spoken. Americans for whom English is a second language have historically faced pressure within the larger society to abandon their native tongue. A Mexican American woman recalls such pressure from her childhood:

> I remember being caught speaking Spanish at recess—that was good for three licks on the knuckles with a sharp ruler. I remember being sent to the corner of the classroom for "talking back" to the Anglo teacher when all I was trying to do was tell her how to pronounce my name. "If you want to be American, speak 'American.' If you don't like it, go back to Mexico where you belong." (Anzaldúa, 2003, p. 450)

To some people, the desire on the part of certain groups to retain their native languages poses a threat to U.S. society. Today, over 38 million U.S. residents speak Spanish as their first language (ProQuest Statistical Abstract, 2015). Immigrants are actually making the transition to speaking English more quickly than in the past, and over 90% of residents with a foreign born parent prefer to speak only English at home (Kent & Lalasz, 2006). Indeed, over three quarters of the children who speak Spanish as their first language also speak English "very well" (ProQuest Statistical Abstract, 2015). Nevertheless, many U.S. citizens fret about the primacy of English when they see street signs, billboards, election ballots, and automated teller machines in Spanish. Up until a few years ago, the state of Arizona sent government observers into classrooms to make sure that teachers didn't have heavy Spanish accents. Those who did were cited for violations and required, with the help of their school districts, to improve their English (Lacey, 2011). Indeed, 31 states have declared English as their official language (R. Brown, 2009; U.S. English Foundation, 2014).

THE BATTLE OVER "POLITICAL CORRECTNESS"

Few terms in the English language these days are as polarizing as "political correctness." It is commonly used to denigrate efforts to rectify—through the use of language—real or alleged discrimination. Sometimes, these efforts take the form of euphemistic terms for members of particular ethnic, racial, religious, gender, sexual, and ability groups. Other times, it is a more grammatical matter, as in the avoidance of gender- or sexually-exclusive language. In addition, it might also be exhibited in the refusal to point out that particular groups are overrepresented in certain undesirable activities, such as crime and unemployment ("Political correctness," 2004).

Since language is the vehicle through which groups are separated and stratified, so-called political correctness actually represents an attempt to give voice to or increase the visibility of groups that have been marginalized in society. Consider the flare-up over the use of Native American names and images as sports mascots (Braves, Chiefs, Indians, Redmen, Blackhawks, Warriors, Redskins, Aztecs, and so on). Some people argue that such names and mascots flatter indigenous people because they emphasize strength and bravery. They claim that the use of these terms is no different than the use of other ethnically inspired team names—Vikings, Canucks, Fighting Irish, Celtics—and therefore shouldn't be interpreted as derogatory (Eitzen & Baca Zinn, 2003). Nonetheless, caricatures of Native Americans that would not be tolerated if they portrayed other racial or ethnic groups are institutionalized in school, university, and professional sport teams and then distributed by local, national, and global media outlets (Strong, 2004). As one author put it:

> Can you imagine if they called them the Washington Jews and the team mascot was a rabbi leading them in [the song] "Hava Nagila," fans in the stands wearing yarmulkes and waving little sponge torahs? (quoted in Eitzen & Baca Zinn, 2003, p. 462)

Does such imagery act as an obstacle to equal cultural recognition and full societal participation, or is it trivial and inconsequential because it's "just a name"? The words *Indian* or *Chief* or *Seminole* or *Brave* aren't necessarily insulting or derogatory. But when the words are accompanied by simplistic and stereotypical symbols of the group's culture—rubber tomahawks, feather headdresses, war paint, dances and chants—and used in the context of a sporting event, their meaning becomes trivialized. Furthermore, "honoring" these groups by emphasizing aggression and violence overshadows other cultural features, such as cooperative social relations, democratic tribal structures, and environmental sensitivity and protection. In 2013, a law went into effect in Wisconsin that allows the state to ban race-based mascots and logos. In 2012, the state of North Dakota ruled that the University of North Dakota had to abandon its nickname, the Fighting Sioux. (Klugh, 2014). They are now known as the Fighting Hawks. In 2015, a federal court ruled that Washington, D.C.'s professional football team could not trademark its team name, the Redskins, because it disparaged Native Americans. Critics, however, often frame actions like these as misguided "politically correct" attempts to sanitize the language.

In some countries, derogatory language is more closely monitored and more severely punished than in the United States. England, France, Germany, the Netherlands, South Africa, India, and Australia all have laws banning hate speech. Israel and France forbid the sale of items that bear the Nazi swastika. In Canada, it is a crime to deny that the Holocaust occurred (Liptak, 2008). The United Nations' International Convention on the Elimination of All Forms of Racial Discrimination requires its members to outlaw all forms of hate speech.

In the United States, people—not to mention magazines and newspapers—can usually say what they like about members of other racial, ethinic, religious, or sexual groups without legal penalty. But such rights are not absolute. For instance, the government can ban speech that incites terrorism or increases the likelihood of imminent violence. The issue is murkier when a group's right to free speech clashes with an individual's right to be protected from harassment and defamatory remarks. In 2010, the U.S. Supreme Court agreed to review whether or not the Westboro Baptist Church, an anti-gay church based in Kansas, had the right to conduct demonstrations at the funerals of American soldiers. The church's pastor contended that the deaths of American soldiers were God's punishment for the country's tolerance of homosexuality and so he instructed church members to show up at military funerals carrying signs like "God Hates Fags," "Thank God for Dead Soldiers," and "God Hates the USA/Thank God for 9/11." The church had organized nearly 43,000 such protests between 1991 and 2010 (Barnes, 2010). In 2011, the Court ruled that these protests were expressions of free speech and therefore protected by the Constitution.

Concern over the potentially harmful impact of words is especially visible these days on college campuses that have enacted policies that ban things like "offensive or uncivil speech," "intolerant expression," or "hostile viewpoints" (Silverglate & Lukianoff, 2003). Some universities require professors to provide their students with "trigger warnings" in their syllabi, preemptive alerts indicating that material presented in class might be upsetting or traumatizing to some (Jarvie, 2014). Policies like these typically attempt to prevent and, if need be, punish speech that directly denigrates or threatens members of certain groups or creates a hostile environment. My university, for example, prohibits the inappropriate treatment of members of the campus community based on race, ethnicity, sex, religion, sexual orientation, veteran status, gender identity, or disability. Inappropriate treatment could mean slurs, epithets, abusive language, derogatory nicknames, taunts about cultural observances, or threatening or offensive texts, e-mail, or voice-mail messages.

An organization called the Foundation for Individual Rights in Education (FIRE) is committed to abolishing all such speech codes on college campuses. To this and other similar organizations, any attempt to limit the speech of anyone, no matter how offensive, is an attack on the Bill of Rights and the doctrine of free speech, which is traditionally a core value in universities.

The debate over policies meant to reduce the stigmatizing and alienating consequences of particular forms of speech will not be settled here. No one wants to have all their thoughts and utterances tightly monitored. The free exchange of ideas does require that everyone be willing to at least hear what others have to say, no matter how distasteful. Some well-meaning professors say they're reluctant to raise controversial issues or use humor in their classes for fear of being tagged as racist, sexist, or homophobic.

In the end, though, the issue of "political correctness" is less about the appropriate use of particular words than it is about the socially constructed nature of reality and the relationship between language and social inequality. It pits the rights of people to speak their minds no matter what against the rights of people who are the direct or indirect targets of such remarks. It's not a simple issue. However, when only the most extreme examples are presented to the public under the blanket accusation of "political incorrectness," actual instances of assaultive speech, threatening e-mails, degrading images, and verbal harassment directed toward marginalized groups are belittled. Those who are subjected to such verbal aggression experience real consequences, ranging from fear, humiliation, and discouragement to difficulty breathing, nightmares, hypertension, and, in rare cases, suicide (Matsuda, 1993). When some students must operate under the burden of painful or exclusionary symbols or words, their opportunities to learn and their ability to compete fairly are constrained.

MEDIA REPRESENTATIONS OF IDENTITIES

As you're well aware, people develop and communicate images of and attitudes toward race, class, gender, and sexuality through language and their interactions with others. But messages of difference don't emerge solely from interpersonal conversations. One of the chief sources of information about difference is the media. Boundaries between "us" and "them" are often constructed or reinforced through literature, television, film, video games, and the Internet.

Although whiteness, maleness, heterosexuality, and middle-class status pervade the entertainment media, they are rarely the subject of specific attention. One of the luxuries of taken-for-grantedness is that these categories don't require positive media depictions for their advantaged positions in society to be reinforced. So, the media portrayals that have received the most scholarly attention are of groups typically defined as "other": people of color, homosexuals, women, and, to a lesser degree, the lower and working classes. These depictions have historically been one-dimensional, as when media portrayals of ethnoracial minorities focus only on working-class and poor people.

GENDER IN THE MEDIA

By and large, media outlets are dominated by men. When it comes to reporting the news, for instance, women are on-camera 32% of the time, report 37% of stories in newspapers, and write 42% of features online (The Women's Media Center, 2015). The imbalance is particularly noteworthy in the entertainment industry. Among Academy Award nominated roles in 2014, lead actors averaged 85 minutes on screen compared to 57 minutes for lead actresses (Lee, 2014). On television, male writers, creators, and executive producers outnumber women four to one and male directors outnumber female directors eight to one. Furthermore, men accounted for 83% of all directors, executive producers, producers, writers, cinematographers and editors for the 250 most profitable feature films made in the United States in 2014 (The Women's Media Center, 2015). Such imbalances in productive and creative control mean that what we see in theaters and on television is likely to reflect men's perspectives.

The media are an important purveyor of information about gender. They promote stereotypes of masculinity and femininity, not only by choosing which kinds of men and women to portray but also by choosing which kinds of stories and programs to run. For example, television networks like Lifetime, Oxygen, OWN (the Oprah Winfrey Network), and WeTv (Women's Entertainment) openly and proudly devote most of their programming to women and women's "issues. In theaters, so-called women's movies (or "chick flicks") are designed to appeal to traditionally female interests, such as deep communication, emotional bonding, romance, and motherhood. On the other hand, television networks for men, such as Spike, offer shows, such as *Deadliest Warrior, Impact Wrestling, Urban Tarzan, Powerblock, Fight Master,* and *Savage Family Diggers.* And you can bet that films identified as men's movies" will contain little emotional introspection and plenty of scantily-clad women, gore, fast cars, high tech weaponry, and explosions.

Children's Gender Exposure   Media representations of gender reach children very early in their lives. Children's books, for instance, teach youngsters what is expected of girls or boys in their culture. In the early 1970s, Lenore Weitzman and her colleagues studied the portrayal of gender in popular U.S. preschool books (Weitzman, Eifler, Hodada, & Ross, 1972). They found that boys played a more significant role in the stories than girls by a ratio of 11 to 1. Boys were more likely to be portrayed in adventurous pursuits or activities that required independence and strength; girls were likely to be confined to indoor activities and portrayed as passive and dependent. Despite some improvement in the number and characterization of female characters (Williams, Vernon, Williams, & Malecha, 1987), gender stereotypes remain prevalent in children's books (Peterson & Lach, 1990). Furthermore, in spite of publishers' guidelines, elementary school reading textbooks still primarily portray males as aggressive, argumentative, and competitive (Evans & Davies, 2000). In fact, even children's books that are characterized as "nonsexist" portray gender-stereotypical personalities, domestic chores, and leisure activities. What's particularly striking about "nonsexist" books is that their response to gender inequality usually involves female characters taking on characteristics and roles typically associated with males. They rarely, if ever, portray male characters adopting female traits (Diekman & Murnen, 2004).

Media depictions of gender have a strong influence on children's perceptions and behaviors (Good, Porter, & Dillon, 2002). For instance, children who watch a lot of television are more likely to hold stereotypical attitudes toward gender, exhibit gender-stereotyped characteristics, and engage in gender-stereotyped activities than are children who watch little television (M. Morgan, 1987; Signorielli, 1990). In one study, girls who did not have stereotypical conceptions of gender to begin with showed a significant increase in such attitudes after 2 years of heavy television watching (M. Morgan, 1982). The more high school students watch talk shows and prime time programs that depict a lot of sexual activity, the more likely they are to hold traditional sexual stereotypes (Ward & Friedman, 2006).

As video games have grown in popularity among young people, they've attracted increasing attention for their demeaning portrayal of women. Most video games are designed by males for other males. Female characters in games with titles like *Bayonetta, Rapelay, Dead or Alive: Xtreme Beach Volleyball,* and *Lollipop Chainsaw* are provocatively sexual, and voluptuous. *Grand Theft Auto* has no shortage of prostitutes, strippers, and rape jokes. In the online game *Boneless Girl*, players poke, pull, and throw a bikini-wearing girl across the screen to get her through a maze of bubbles. *Duke Nukem Forever* allows players to slap semi-naked women if they don't coop-erate. To promote this game, 2K Games launched an accompanying web site that contained a flash game in which female targets take off a piece of cloth-ing for every successful shot until they are topless. The gender messages in such games may have a detrimental effect both on boys' attitudes toward girls and women and on their conceptions of appropriate male behavior.

Media advertising may also perpetuate gender stereotypes. A study of 467 TV commercials shown between children's cartoons found that, as in the shows themselves, male characters are more likely than female characters to be in a major role, to be active rather than passive, and to be depicted in an occupational setting (Davis, 2003). Similarly, an analysis of over 500 U.S. and Australian commercials targeting children found that girls were much more likely than boys to be portrayed as shy, giggly, and passive (Browne, 1998). The differences were less pronounced in Australia, however, where activists have had more success in countering gender stereotypes in the media than in the United States. Such images are not trivial, given that U.S. children watch over 40,000 TV commercials a year (Committee on Com-munication, 2006).

Media-Reinforced Femininity Even the most casual glimpse at the por-trayal of modern women in U.S. advertising, fashion, television, music vid-eos, and films reveals a dual stereotype (Sidel, 1990). On the one hand, we see images of the successful woman of the 21st century: the perfect wife and mother, the triumphant career woman. Like the high-powered female politicians, lawyers, and doctors we're likely to see on television these days, she is outgoing, bright, attractive, and assertive.

On the other hand, though, we continue to see the stereotypical image of the exhibited woman: the seductive sex object displayed in beer and fast food commercials, magazine advertisements, feature films, prime-time sit-coms, and soap operas. Film and television continue to present stereotypes that show women as shallow, vain, and materialistic characters whose looks overshadow all else. In feature films, females are almost four times as likely as males to be shown in sexy attire. From 2006 to 2009, not one female character in a G-rated family film was depicted in the field of medical science, as a business leader, in law, or in politics. In these films, 8 out of

10 working characters were male, which is a contrast to real world statistics, where women comprise over 50% of the workforce (Geena Davis Institute on Gender in Media, 2012).

Aside from occasional powerful female characters—like Daenerys Targaryen from *Game of Thrones,* Michonne from *The Walking Dead,* Olivia Pope from *Scandal,* or Temperance Brennan from *Bones*—when it comes to occupational depiction on television, traditional gender stereotypes remain. On prime-time shows, female characters comprise 14% of corporate executives, 28% of high-level politicians, 29% of doctors, and 21% of scientists/engineers (Smith, Choueiti, Prescott, & Pieper, 2012). Popular dating-themed reality shows like *The Bachelor* reinforce the belief that sexual charm and physical attractiveness are lures that women can use to attract men.

Even the media coverage of female sports events tends to focus on the physical appearance and sexual attractiveness of the athletes and not just their competitive accomplishments (Billings, Angelini, & Eastman, 2005; Shugart, 2003). Not surprisingly, one of the most popular televised events in the Summer Olympics is women's beach volleyball, where athletes' uniforms consist of revealing bathing suits. Not to be outdone, the Badminton World Federation issued an edict prior to the 2012 games requiring all female players to wear short skirts to create a more "attractive presentation" and thereby revive flagging interest in the sport (Longman, 2011).

Unfortunately, the image of beauty presented by the exhibited woman is artificial and largely unattainable. The average American woman is 5'4" tall and weighs 140 pounds. The average American fashion model is 5'11" tall and weighs 117 pounds and thus is thinner than 98% of adult American women (National Eating Disorders Association, 2011). Researchers at Johns Hopkins University compiled data on the heights and weights of Miss America pageant winners between 1922 and 1999. They found that the weights of these women has steadily decreased, reaffirming the cultural value of thinness (Rubinstein & Caballero, 2000). Recent winners have had a height-to-weight ratio that places them in a range of what the World Health Organization considers undernourished.

So, it's not surprising that women who regularly view these images spend a great deal of time and energy trying to emulate them through extreme dieting and other disordered eating patterns (Wilson, Peebles, Hardy, & Litt, 2006). Consider the following statistics compiled by the National Eating Disorders Association (2011):

■ Forty-two percent of first- to third-grade girls want to be thinner, 51% of 9- to 10-year-old girls feel better about themselves when they're on a diet, and 81% of 10-year-olds are afraid of being fat.

- Ninety-one percent of college women attempt to control their weight through dieting.
- On any given day, about half of American women are on a diet, even though 95% of them will likely regain the weight they've lost within one to five years.
- About 91% of the 11 million Americans diagnosed with eating disorders (anorexia, bulimia, binge eating) are girls or women.

Although many people view such figures with alarm, others see them as benign or even positive. An Internet movement, called "pro-ana" (for pro-anorexia) or "pro-mia" (for pro-bulimia), encourages young women to view eating disorders not as dangerous medical conditions but as positive lifestyle choices. Hundreds of pro-ana web sites and blogs provide young women with dieting challenges, discussion groups, and inspirational messages or "pep talks" about the desirability of limiting food intake and the appeal of extreme thinness. Some contain declarations, such as "Food is Poison." Pro-anas also post their messages and pictures celebrating extreme thinness on social network sites like Facebook, Twitter, Pinterest, and Tumblr. Other sites, like YouTube, provide "thinspiration" (or "thinspo") videos, visual celebrations of skeletal women, including some celebrities and models. Soundtracks to these videos include songs with messages like "Skeleton, you are my friend" and "Bones are beautiful" (Heffernan, 2008).

Supporters of this media movement argue that they are simply providing young anorexic and bulimic women a place to go where they can get support and not be judged. However, critics worry that the movement glorifies dangerous and potentially life-threatening conditions. Research seems to support this position. A study of 10- to 22-year-olds with diagnosed eating disorders found that those who frequented pro-ana web sites remained sicker for longer periods than those who visited pro-recovery sites. About 96% said they'd learned new tips for purging and weight loss from the pro-ana sites, and two thirds used these methods (Wilson, Peebles, Hardy, & Litt, 2006). Another study found that 84% of college women reduced their caloric intake within 90 minutes of being exposed to pro-ana sites (Jett, LaPorte, & Wanchisn, 2010). The potential for harm is so great that the Academy for Eating Disorders (2006) called on government officials and Internet service providers to require warning screens for pro-ana web sites much like the warning labels found on cigarette packs.

Media-Reinforced Masculinity   The overall portrayal of men in film and on television is much harder to pinpoint and has been the topic of considerably less research than the portrayal of women. Because of men's advantaged position in society, they needn't be named. When they are named, accurate portrayals of masculinity are virtually nonexistent. Instead, we're likely to find highly traditional stereotypes or negative portrayals in the form of gross caricatures. For decades, the quintessential Hollywood leading man was square-jawed, rugged, not particularly chatty, violent when necessary, and unemotional (think of Bruce Willis, Vin Diesel, Sylvester Stallone, and Arnold Schwarzenegger in their prime). That type hasn't disappeared completely. But today it exists side by side with a new generation of leading men who play characters that are considerably more thoughtful, sensitive, and emotionally available (for instance, Brad Pitt, George Clooney, Ryan Gosling, Bradley Cooper).

The traditional tough guy image has also given way to a less complimentary image: that of men as dumb and clueless. But far from being demeaning and destructive, these images have the luxury of being harmlessly humorous, even endearing (think of Phil Dunphy on *Modern Family*). Making fun of men—like making fun of heterosexuals or of white people—bears little, if any, of the cultural and historical weight that accompanies stereotypical portrayals of women and other disadvantaged groups. "As long as men are in power, they are the one group that television can ridicule without fear of reprisal" (Gates, 2000, p. 35).

It shouldn't shock us, then, that the media portrayal of boorish male behavior can sometimes become fashionable. One of the most popular and critically acclaimed television shows in recent years was *Mad Men*, which chronicled the escapades of men working in an early 1960s ad agency. Because the show took place half a century ago, its male characters could unabashedly express attitudes that would not be tolerated in a more contemporary setting: "We see sexist jokes, chronic philandering, and office parties in which executives tackle secretaries in order to see what color their panties are" (Doyle, 2010, p. 1). Supporters of the show argued that these sorts of activities were so obviously unacceptable in the 2010s that they actually afforded viewers an opportunity to conclude that we've come along way as a society. Critics, however, pointed out that such depictions created a sort of nostalgic desire to return to a time when "political correctness" didn't exist and "men could be men" (Kelner, 2010).

RACE AND ETHNICITY IN THE MEDIA

As you saw in Chapter 2, race is a social construction. Hence, it's not surprising that one of the most influential sources of information about race in this society is the media. Nor should it be surprising that the dominant white culture prevails and is taken for granted. Films, TV shows, and other entertainment products tend to reflect white sensibilities and assumptions. Ethnoracial minorities continue to be underrepresented in television, film, popular magazines, and advertising (Croteau & Hoynes, 2000).

Yet minority ethnoracial images are immensely popular with young people around the world. For instance, youth in Europe and Asia can be seen trying to emulate rap and hip-hop fashion, music, and demeanor. Latino/a musicians enjoy tremendous crossover appeal. Because of their global reach, American media images of African American and Latino/a pop culture have greatly increased the visibility of these ethnoracial groups worldwide.

As in the case of gender, media images play a significant role in the creation and maintenance of ethnoracial stereotypes. Consider the biased images of certain ethnic groups that have historically been served up on television: the savage Indian, the Italian Mafioso, the fanatical Arab terrorist, and so on. Asians are frequently depicted as camera-wielding tourists, scholastic overachievers, sinister warlords, or skilled martial artists. Latino/as have historically been cast as "hot-blooded lovers," "banditos," or "lazy good-for-nothings" (Reyes & Rubie, 1994). Popular contemporary characters like Han Lee on *Broke Girls,* Rajesh Koothrappali on *The Big Bang Theory,* and Gloria Delgado-Pritchett on *Modern Family* continue to present Chinese, Indian, and Latina characters in a stereotypical manner.

Common media stereotypes often reflect the intersections of race, ethnicity, class, and gender, as in the depiction of poor, black women as "welfare queens," wealthy Jewish women as "princesses," and poor Latino men as drug pushers. Recent reality shows, like *The Apprentice* and *Survivor* often portray black female participants as arrogant, pushy, or overly aggressive.

Stereotypical depictions are not limited to the entertainment media. For instance, an analysis of a random sample of television news shows aired in Los Angeles and Orange Counties in California revealed that Whites are more likely than African Americans and Latino/as to be portrayed on television news as victims of crime. Conversely, African Americans and Latino/as are more likely to be portrayed as lawbreakers than as crime victims (Dixon & Linz, 2000). Another study found that although people of color appear regularly in prime-time TV commercials, they usually appear as secondary characters. Furthermore, the nature of their depiction differs compared with that of Whites. Whites are more likely to appear in ads for upscale products, beauty products, and home products. People of color, in contrast, are more likely to appear in ads for low-cost, low-nutrition products (like fast foods and soft drinks) and in athletic or sports equipment ads (Henderson & Baldasty, 2003).

When people of color appeared in early Hollywood films, the language of race was apparent in such images as the familiar servant/slave figure: dependable and loving in a simple childlike way, like the devoted "Mammy" character in such films as *Gone with the Wind* (S. Hall, 1995). Chinese servants and Native American sidekicks in old westerns could fall into this category as well. But while devoted and naïve, the stereotypical servant/slave was also unpredictable and unreliable, susceptible to turning nasty at any moment. Another common early image was the clown. As an entertainer, the clown's job was to put on a show for others. While sometimes depicted as being physically graceful, the darker side of the clown image was that he or she need not be taken seriously.

Early television images didn't fare much better. Shows of the 1950s, like *Amos 'n Andy* and *The Beulah Show*, depicted Blacks as lazy buffoons, opportunistic crooks, or happy, docile servants. But by the 1970s, *Sanford and Son, Good Times, What's Happening*, and the other so-called ghetto sitcoms were trying to represent African Americans more positively. They showed slums and housing projects as places where people could lead happy, loving, even humorous lives.

When U.S. society itself could not achieve social reform through civil rights, television solved the problem by inventing symbols of black success and racial harmony (Gates, 1992). Shows such as *Julia* or *I Spy* in the 1960s; *Roots* and *The Jeffersons* in the 1970s; *Benson, A Different World*, and *The Cosby Show* in the 1980s; *The Fresh Prince of Bel-Air, Family Matters, Moesha*, and *Sister, Sister* in the 1990s; *Girlfriends, The Bernie Mac Show, The Parkers, My Wife and Kids, House of Payne, Meet the Browns* in the 2000s; *Empire* and *Black-ish* in the 2010s, seemingly overcame these harmful racial stereotypes by depicting Blacks as strong, smart, and successful.

In addition, popular shows with predominantly white casts, such as *CSI, Law & Order, Scandal*, and *The New Normal* began portraying successful black characters. These shows have played an unmistakable role in showing that Blacks and Whites often share the core values of U.S. culture.

Most researchers of race and the media argue that, in general, images of ethnoracial minorities have improved over time. However, although representation of ethnoracial minorities increased throughout the 1980s and 1990s, it has since leveled off or even dropped slightly. According to the Screen Actors Guild (2007), in 2006, 24.4% of all television and movie roles went to African American, Latino/a, Asian, or Native American performers, roughly the same as it was in 2000. For Latino/as, the number of primary or recurring television roles dropped by a third (Children Now, 2001).

The 2016 Academy Awards marked the second year in a row that not a single actor of color was nominated for an Oscar.

Furthermore, controversial depictions continue to exist. For instance, at the height of its popularity, the reality show *Jersey Shore*, came under attack for its portrayal of Italian-American stereotypes. Similarly, critics have charged that many of the recent portrayals of African Americans on television, in video games, and in film continue to reflect some of the negative stereotypes of the 1950s. For instance, the critically acclaimed 2009 film, *Precious,* generated a great deal of controversy for its depiction of illiteracy, out-of-wedlock birth, welfare dependence, drug use, and sexual abuse in an inner-city black single-parent family. To some, the main character's ability to overcome brutality, illiteracy, and obesity was an inspiring story of strength and determination. To others, however, it was a dangerous and demeaning film filled with racist clichés.

SEXUALITY IN THE MEDIA

To the casual outside observer, it might appear that U.S. society is becoming "homosexualized." Consider the popularity of television shows like *The L Word, Modern Family, The Fosters, Looking,* or the now-defunct *Will & Grace* and *Queer Eye for the Straight Guy.* Gay couples now appear on mainstream television commercials for products ranging from e-readers to painkillers. Major cruise lines, tour companies, and hotel chains openly advertise vacation packages for gay, lesbian, bisexual, and transgender travelers. Marketing researchers estimate that the annual economic impact of L.G.B.T. travelers is around $70 billion a year (Rosenbloom, 2014). Although homosexuality may have become somewhat trendy, debate continues to rage over their media depiction.

Not surprisingly, when it comes to media portrayals of sexual orientation, one would be hard pressed to think of a movie or a TV show that explicitly emphasizes or purposely draws attention to representations of "heterosexual lifestyles" or "the heterosexual community." There's no need. The plots of practically every movie and TV show routinely revolve around taken-for-granted heterosexuality in one form or another. As with other forms of power, those shows and films that do consciously call attention to heterosexuality often portray it in ways that are so excessive as to be harmless. For example, in virtually every teen-oriented film, youthful male heterosexuality is depicted for laughs as lustful, insatiable, and uncontrollable.

Although the portrayal of openly gay characters has been intermittent, American television has featured a wide array of gay characters over the years ("American Television," 2004). Early on, such characters were depicted as unstable villains or suspects in crime shows (Hantzis & Lehr, 1994). In sitcoms, they were usually minor characters. In the 1970s, openly gay and bisexual characters began appearing on popular sitcoms like *All in the Family, The Mary Tyler Moore Show, Barney Miller,* and *Soap.* But more commonly, homosexuality was presented as an implied—and stigmatized—identity. A continuing theme on the popular 1970s show *Three's Company,* in which a man pretended to be gay in order to share an apartment with two women, was dialogue between the man, Jack Tripper, and his homophobic landlord that relied on references to Jack's purported gay tendencies and on epithets like "Tinkerbell."

When not depicted as stereotypically effeminate, gay characters were often presented as victims. The film and television portrayal of homosexuality in the late 1980s and early 1990s often went hand in hand with depictions of or thinly veiled political statements about HIV/AIDS (Gross, 1994). In 1993, the film *Philadelphia* won acclaim for its portrayal of the discrimination faced by a sympathetic lead character with AIDS, played by Tom Hanks. Indeed, the first television documentaries and movies that dealt with HIV/AIDS shaped the way the public perceived the disease and its victims. In so doing, the media helped foster the impression that HIV/AIDS was a "gay disease" (Netzhammer & Shamp, 1994).

The 1990s brought unprecedented openness regarding homosexuality, although most depictions of homosexual people were one-dimensional caricatures. In 1994, PBS aired the controversial gay-themed miniseries *Tales of the City,* which featured frank language, nudity, and sexual situations. In the mid-1990s, same-sex weddings appeared on shows like *Northern Exposure, Roseanne,* and *Friends.* The Carter Heywood character on the sitcom *Spin City* was one of the first regularly appearing "normal queers," a gay man who was not mincing and flamboyant ("American Television," 2004).

Perhaps the watershed moment for gays and lesbians on television was the April 1997 coming out of Ellen DeGeneres's character on her show, *Ellen.* After months of media speculation as to the actress's own sexual orientation, her character's coming out was met with praise from the gay and lesbian community. Ironically, much of the humor and appeal of this show up to this point derived from the subtle references and "Is she or isn't she?" atmosphere surrounding Ellen's character. Hence, after this monumental declaration, the show's popularity waned, and it was soon canceled.

In the 2000s and 2010s, the number of gay-themed television shows and openly gay characters on other shows reached an all-time high. According to the Gay & Lesbian Alliance Against Defamation (GLAAD, 2014), 4.4%

of regular characters on television series in 2013 were gay, lesbian, bisexual, or transgender, up from 2.9% in 2012.

But despite their growing media presence and influence, one subtle but powerfully stereotypical theme remains: that gays and lesbians are either extremely or at least moderately preoccupied with sex. David and Keith, the openly gay, interracial couple on the early 2000s HBO show *Six Feet Under*, had professions and everyday lives that weren't about sex, but many of the plot lines that included these characters focused on their sexual appetites, activities, and problems. The openly gay character Elijah Krantz on *Girls* seems to be able to talk only about sex and the physical attractiveness of men. Such portrayals reinforce the perception that homosexuality is first and foremost about sex. Heterosexual couples on TV and in film typically are granted a wider array of interests, concerns, and life experiences that needn't be linked to eroticism.

Ironically, while media portrayals of homosexuality are populated by sexually obsessed effeminate men and butch women (Itzkoff, 2014), the actual public expression of gay intimacy is still rare (Bruni, 2014). Cam and Mitchell, the popular gay couple on *Modern Family*, may be sassy and spout sexual double entendres, but they are rarely seen kissing or in a romantic embrace. Indeed, social network sites blazed with criticism and consternation when Michael Sam, the first openly gay active professional football player, was recorded kissing his boyfriend after being drafted by the St. Louis Rams in 2014.

Moreover, in an era when web sites and blogs freely discuss the biographical details and sexual orientations of celebrities, the portrayal of gay and straight characters can easily be linked to the "gayness" or "straightness" of the actor him or herself. Darren Criss, who played the openly gay character, Blaine Anderson in *Glee,* routinely fielded reporters' questions about his sexuality (he's straight). While it is accepted practice for openly heterosexual actors to play gay characters, the reverse is not nearly as common (the gay actor, Neil Patrick Harris's portrayal of the womanizing Barney Stinson on the show *How I Met Your Mother* is a notable exception). Here's how one columnist described a Sean Hayes, a gay actor, playing a straight character named Chuck in the Broadway play, *Promises, Promises*:

> Frankly, it's weird seeing Hayes play straight. He comes off as wooden and insincere, as if he's trying to hide something, which of course he is. Even the play's most hilarious scene, when Chuck tries to pick up a drunk woman at a bar, devolves into unintentional

camp. Is it funny because of all the '60s-era one liners, or because the woman is so drunk (and clueless) that she agrees to go home with a guy we all know is gay? (Setoodeh, 2010, p. 50)

Gay men and lesbians are especially vulnerable to the power of images, perhaps even more than ethnoracial minorities and women are. The producers of TV shows and films have, over the years, become more sensitive to the blatant stereotyping of these groups. But the traditional stereotyping of homosexuality—effeminate gay men, masculine lesbians—is more likely to be tolerated than the stereotyping of other groups. As one author put it, gays and lesbians "are . . . the only group . . . whose enemies are generally uninhibited by the consensus of 'good taste,' which protects most minorities from the more public displays of bigotry" (Gross, 1995, pp. 63–64). Furthermore, while the media are increasingly likely to include diverse portrayals of other minority groups (for instance, not depicting all African Americans as poor), images of homosexuality remain rather narrow. Most gay and lesbian characters are white, and virtually all of them are comfortably middle class.

SOCIAL CLASS IN THE MEDIA

Social class pervades the media. The for-profit nature of the commercial media guarantees that class concerns will link advertisers, producers, and audiences. Consider, for example, the tendency for newspapers to reduce circulation in order to increase profits:

> Newspapers receive about two-thirds of their revenue from advertisers, not readers; therefore, they must be sensitive to advertiser needs in order to stay in business. In turn . . . advertisers want to reach only readers with enough disposable income to buy their products. . . . To sell advertising space at a premium, newspapers want to improve the demographic profile (in terms of average household income) of their readership. They can do this in two ways: Attract more affluent readers, and/or get rid of poorer readers. (Croteau & Hoynes, 2000, p. 215)

The comfortable middle classes and the affluent upper classes have always been a mainstay in the popular media as well. Indeed, the society that is usually portrayed on television is considerably wealthier than the society in which we actually live. Whether their lives are depicted with a hint of desirous envy (as in *Downton Abbey*) or playfully caricatured as snooty blue bloods, the very wealthy have been a surefire hit among television viewers for decades. Recent reality shows like *My Super Sweet 16* and

The Real Housewives of (Orange County, New York, Atlanta, Beverly Hills, or *New Jersey)* have jumped on the "If they're wealthy, people will watch" bandwagon. The E! Network's *Keeping Up with the Kardashians* celebrates the lives of Hollywood socialites whose allure is derived simply from the fact that they're famous and wealthy. A & E's *Duck Dynasty* portrays the "earthy" Robertson family that, despite appearances, has made a fortune in the duck hunting business.

On occasion, the working class is depicted with some admiration. Reality shows like *Deadliest Catch, Ice Road Truckers,* and *Dirty Jobs* provide a glimpse into the lives of the people whose jobs require constant toughness and courage. But for the most part, when working-class or poor people are shown, the portrayal is often either unflattering or pitying. The blue-collar heads of households who have been a fixture on prime-time television throughout the years are typically portrayed as dumb, immature, or irresponsible buffoons. *The Honeymooners, All in the Family, Married with Children, The Simpsons, Roseanne, King of Queens,* and *Mike and Molly* are the most famous examples. Films, such as *Saturday Night Fever, Working Girl, Good Will Hunting,* and *8 Mile,* portrayed working-class men as macho exhibitionists (Ehrenreich, 1995). On confrontational television talk shows, such as *Jerry Springer* or disorder-themed reality shows like *Hoarders,* the odd personal problems of working-class people are displayed for the condescending amusement of viewers. More sympathetic reality shows like the now-defunct *Extreme Makeover: Home Edition* often depicted desperately needy families being "saved" with a new house designed and built by the show's upscale cast.

It's difficult, if not impossible, to separate the images of working-class people from the images of gender or race/ethnicity. For instance, many of the earliest sitcoms on American television were constructed around working-class ethnic communities (Cornell & Hartmann, 1998). *The Goldbergs* was a 1950s comedy about a working-class Jewish family in the Bronx; *Mama* was about Norwegian immigrants in San Francisco; *Life with Luigi* was about Italian immigrants in Chicago. Later on, shows like *Sanford and Son* (a black father and son living in the Watts section of Los Angeles) and *Chico and the Man* (Mexicans living in Los Angeles) continued this tradition.

One enduring media image that reveals a great deal about attitudes toward both class and race is the "white trash" stereotype. White trash culture began as the maligned lifestyle of poor and working-class rural Southern Whites but soon became a metaphor for all that is tacky, unsophisticated, ignorant, or excessive—"from the darker aspects of racial politics and the

Ku Klux Klan, feuding, incest, and the cult of the Rebel, to country music, faith-healing and snake-handling, and the phenomenon of Elvis veneration" (Sweeney, 2001, p. 144). The white trash aesthetic has been featured in factual as well as fictional media. For instance, the news media's depiction of former President Bill Clinton—who was commonly referred to as "Bubba" even while in office—often focused on his Arkansas roots, good ol' boy carousing, love of junk food, and his turbulent childhood that included protecting his mother from his drunken and abusive stepfather. The filmmaker John Waters once said that white trash is "the last racist thing you can say and get away with" (quoted in Friend, 1994, p. 24).

The white trash culture is often portrayed through condescending humor. Movies like *Joe Dirt* and *Dukes of Hazzard,* and television shows like *Here Comes Honey Boo Boo* depict the low-brow lifestyles of working-class white folk as consisting of comedic preoccupations with hunting, beer-drinking, child beauty pageants, and NASCAR.

In the news media, stories about poor people tend to be quite rare. When the news media do turn their attention to the poor, the portrayals are often negative or stereotypical, as when local TV stations run the usual human interest stories about the "less fortunate" in soup kitchens and homeless shelters during Thanksgiving and Christmas. More detailed stories about poor people tend to focus on welfare cheats, drug addicts, negligent parents, street criminals, and aggressive panhandlers.

A reversal of the tendency to denigrate the poor and working class (but one that may be equally inaccurate) is the portrayal of poverty as righteous and wealth as inherently corrupt. Wily servants turning the tables and outwitting their complacent and pompous bosses has been a theme in comedic books and films for decades. Movies like *Down to Earth, Maid in Manhattan, Sweet Home Alabama, The Campaign,* and *The Hunger Games* franchise depict working-class characters as heroic, a counterpoint to the depiction of wealthy characters who are greedy, mean, and small-minded.

Usually, however, the media tend to focus much of their favorable attention on the concerns of the wealthy and the privileged. Television air time is filled with advertisements for luxury cars, cruise vacations, diamond jewelry, and other things that only the well-to-do can afford. If you take a peek at the "Style" section of a large metropolitan newspaper, you'll likely find a focus on high-priced fashion, designer home furnishings, costly vacation spots, investment opportunities in foreign real estate, expensive restaurants, and etiquette for lavish, formal dinner parties. The news media also devote a significant amount of broadcast time and print space to daily business news and stock market quotations (Mantsios, 1995), even though only about 50%

of U.S. families own any stock at all (ProQuest Statistical Abstract, 2015). Some cable television networks report exclusively on stock market issues. International news and trade agreements are reported in terms of their impact on the business world, not on ordinary working people.

The media also regularly provide information on individuals who have achieved extraordinary success. We receive regular reports about the multi-million-dollar contracts of professional athletes, film stars, and TV person-alities. *People* magazine devotes an entire issue each year to a detailed description of the expensive gowns and tuxedos celebrities wear on Oscar night. Society pages and gossip columns keep those in the upper class informed of one another's doings and entice the rest of us to admire their achievements.

The mass media clearly shape how people think about one another and about the nature of society. By celebrating the lifestyles of the upper and middle classes, the media create the impression that the interests and worries of the well-off are, or should be, important to everyone. Consequently, class differences and conflicts are concealed or rendered irrelevant.

CONCLUSION

This chapter has been about naming groups of people in order to highlight difference, both in language and in media portrayals. Our ideas about race and ethnicity, class, gender, and sexuality are both created and reinforced in everyday discourse and in the media.

Reconsider the supermarket clerk I described at the outset of this chap-ter. She is not an anomaly. Her question to my son about what he wanted to ask Santa to bring him for Christmas is repeated thousands of times throughout our society every December. Similarly presumptuous questions are asked at many other times and in many other situations. The supermar-ket clerk represents the way that our deepest routine beliefs drive our daily interactions with other people.

Linguistic conventions and media images that contain such default assumptions reinforce the differentness of people whose membership puts them on the religious, ethnic, racial, or sexual periphery. In short, the act of naming is never socially neutral. The extent to which certain identities can or must be named—both in everyday conversation and in media depictions—is inversely related to power in this society. Those who need not be named or represented—who need no modifying adjective or who need no film or television show to inform viewers of their way of life—are those who wield the authority to define themselves and others.

[INVESTIGATING IDENTITIES AND INEQUALITIES]
But I play one on TV: Media portraits of race, gender, and sexuality

A disturbing feature of racial, ethnic, gender, sexual, and class identity is that many of our beliefs and attitudes about people from other groups are formed without any direct contact with members of those groups. The media—most notably, television—play a significant role in providing the public with often inaccurate and oversimplified information that indirectly shapes attitudes. As you've seen in this chapter, the stereotypical media depictions of people who have historically been the least powerful in society—namely, women, homosexuals, and ethnoracial minorities—have received a lot of attention. But even though men, heterosexuals, and Whites dominate television and movies, their presence remains taken for granted and unexamined.

To compensate for this lack of attention to the dominant groups, your assignment in this exercise is to observe over the span of a week several prime-time television shows whose prominent recurring characters are from the following groups: Whites, men, and heterosexuals. Try to include both comedies and dramas. Avoid reality shows. For each show you watch, record the proportion of regular characters who are white, who are heterosexual, or who are male out of the total number of regular roles. Is the ethnicity or religion of these characters ever made clear on the show? If so, how? You may also want to note the proportion of white, heterosexual men on these shows.

Pay particular attention to the way these characters are portrayed. Examine their mannerisms, their occupations (if applicable), their apparent socioeconomic status, their dialogue, and their appearance (hairstyle, clothing, and so on).

Do these characters conform to common stereotypes associated with Whites, men, and heterosexuals? How frequently do these characters refer to their own whiteness, maleness, or heterosexuality? Do the plots of the shows revolve around what you might consider racial, gender, or sexual themes? That is, how often does the issue of race, ethnicity, or sexual orientation come up during the course of the show?

Did you notice any characters who act or appear in ways, or are employed in occupations, you'd consider nontraditional (for instance, a man working as a nurse or a white person working as a domestic servant)? Describe how these nontraditional portrayals deviate from more stereotypical characterizations. Are they treated positively or negatively on the show? Do characters make references to these depictions? Are they the source of conflict or humor? How might this type of depiction ultimately affect public perceptions of race, gender, and sexuality?

Interpret your observations sociologically. What are the implicit messages communicated by the portrayal of whiteness, maleness, and heterosexuality? Would this assignment have been easier or more difficult if you were asked to analyze the portrayals of women, homosexuals, and ethnoracial minorities? Explain. Based on your observations, what can you conclude about the relationship among power, invisibility, and media imagery?

CHAPTER 4

Learning Identities
Families, Schools, and Socialization

When I was in my first year of graduate school, I met a young couple who were the parents of twins—a boy and a girl. Although they were self-described feminists, they understood that they couldn't raise their children in a completely genderless fashion. Nevertheless, they did everything they could to try to minimize gender-specific child rearing so that both kids had the same opportunities, were exposed to the same expectations, and received the same type of parental encouragement.

For the twins' fourth-birthday party (an event to which I was inexplicably invited), the parents decided to buy each child the same gender-neutral gift: a big box of multicolored, soft rubber geometric shapes and blocks. The objects were safe, easily manipulable for little hands, and could be used for creating just about anything a kid's imagination could concoct.

The day of the birthday party arrived. I wasn't yet a parent myself at the time, so I watched the proceedings with detached objectivity, like an anthropologist's first visit to an unknown culture. After playing a few games with their little guests, the birthday boy and girl began tearing open their presents. Legos. Stuffed replicas of Bert and Ernie from *Sesame Street*. More Legos. A VHS tape of *101 Dalmatians*. Apparently, the other parents had gotten the message and had managed to avoid traditional gender-specific gifts. There wasn't a Barbie doll, a toy stove, a plastic automatic weapon, or a football helmet to be found anywhere near that party. When the twins opened their parents' gift, they seemed genuinely pleased, fondling the vibrant, multihued cones, spheres, cubes, and pyramids with glee.

As the party wound down, the adults decompressed with wine in the back-yard while a few of the remaining kids went off to play some more. All seemed well. After a while, some kind of mental alarm clock seemed to go off in the twins' mother's head and she got up to check on the kids. She returned a few minutes later, visibly shaken. "I can't believe it! They've divided themselves up!" she cried. "The boys are in one room and the girls are in another." That didn't seem so bad to the rest of us. "Well . . . there's more," she said, in a tone that was equal parts grief, exasperation, and embarrassment.

She mustered up the courage to tell us the "terrible" sight she had wit-nessed: When she went to check on the children, she first went to her son's room. As she approached, she could hear the sounds of little boys in full battle mode, making machine gun and explosion noises with their mouths. Horrified, she walked in and found her son "aiming" a purple rubber rectangle at another boy and "shooting" him. "I killed you! You're dead!" he screamed. The other boy, unshaken by the news, replied, "If I'm dead, I'm gonna bomb you so you're dead too!" as he threw his red rubber cone at the birthday boy.

Deflated by the sight of 4-year-old boys using this non-gendered gift as macho artillery, she ventured over to the room where the girls were. She heard no shooting or killing sounds. Instead, she found her daughter and another little girl sitting quietly in separate corners of the room, caressing, cooing to, and rocking their geometric shapes to sleep. "Time for baby's nap," she heard her daughter whisper to the yellow sphere she had wrapped in a blanket and was now cradling in her arms.

I lost track of this couple soon after the birthday party, so I don't know how the "trauma" affected either the parents or the children. My guess is that the parents recovered and the twins turned out just fine. Yet this incident reveals a great deal about the process by which children learn who they are. As much as parents would like to believe that they can completely control how their children turn out, their influence is, in fact, limited. On the developmental path to their social identities, children acquire information from a variety of sources—books, television, video games, the Internet, toys, teachers, other children, other children's parents, strangers they see on the street, and so on. Sometimes, this information aligns with the messages conveyed by parents; other times, however, this outside information contradicts and maybe even eclipses parents' messages.

What my grad school friends didn't want to acknowledge was that "becoming" a girl or a boy—or a white person, an African American, a Latino/a, a heterosexual, a homosexual, a member of the middle class, or whatever—never occurs in a social vacuum. The development of gender, ethnoracial, class, and sexual identities is always a joint social production that includes intimates as well as others outside the immediate family. It is always influenced by broader economic, political, and religious concerns. My well-meaning friends thought they could "create" their children in an image of their choosing. They didn't stand a chance.

Although learning about one's race, ethnicity, class, sexuality, or gender takes place throughout our lives and in a variety of settings, this chapter will focus on the lessons we learn in our families and those we learn in schools, through interactions both with teachers and with peers. In addition, since we don't live our lives just as a member of a particular race, gender, class, or sexual orientation, this chapter will examine how the intersection of these phenomena affects the way we learn our identities.

IDENTITY SOCIALIZATION IN FAMILIES

In previous chapters, you've seen that social reality is not an inherent feature of the natural world but is instead a human creation, established in a process of ongoing social interaction. We create, re-create, confirm, or change our social identities every time our actions, appearances, thoughts, perceptions, and values are taken as reflective of or opposed to what others expect of us. Just as our ideas about the nature of difference and the meanings of race, ethnicity, sex, gender, social class, and sexuality are socially constructed, so too are the individuals who constitute these groups.

One of the fundamental tasks facing any society is to create members whose values, behaviors, attitudes, and perceptions correspond to those deemed by that society as appropriate. This task is accomplished through the process of **socialization,** the way that people learn to act and think in accordance with the rules and expectations of a particular society (Newman, 2017). It's the means by which people acquire important skills and knowledge. One of the most crucial outcomes of the socialization process is the development of a sense of self. How does one become a male or a female; a white person or a Native American; a working class individual or a member of the upper classes; a heterosexual or a homosexual? I'm not talking here simply about inheriting a particular biological/anatomical/genetic identity or earning a certain amount of money that objectively puts one over—or under—some socioeconomic threshold. Instead, I want to focus on how we learn to think, act, and perceive ourselves as members of particular groups and how we incorporate those perceptions into our personal identity.

LEARNING GENDERS

Distinctions along sex/gender lines are the cultural, institutional, even architectural foundations of everyday life. Its importance as a shaper of our social experiences is beyond debate. What is debatable, though, is where gendered traits and behaviors come from.

Biological Predispositions?   Certainly, at a basic level, our genetic configuration and sexual anatomy have something to do with our gender identity. Sociologist Richard Udry (2000) studied 351 adult women whose pregnant mothers had been entered in the Child Health and Development Study between 1960 and 1969. Regular specimens of amniotic fluid were taken from these women and recorded. Hence, Udry could determine the levels of hormones his sample of women were exposed to before they were born. He found that those women who were exposed to higher levels of testosterone as fetuses exhibited more "masculine" traits and behaviors as adults than women who were exposed to lower levels of testosterone. He found these differences even in women whose own mothers had strongly encouraged them to be "feminine" as children. He concluded from this finding that biological predispositions can limit the effects of gender socialization.

Other researchers have attempted to uncover the biological underpinnings of gender by examining differences in the behaviors of male and female newborns and infants. For instance, one study found that consistent sex differences in the achievement of fundamental developmental milestones (smiling, sitting up on one's own, crawling, walking, and so on) appear within the first year of life, early enough to make cultural or environmental influence unlikely (Reinisch, Rosenblum, Rubin, & Schulsinger, 1997). The researchers argue that boys tend to reach these milestones earlier than girls, biologically predisposing them to be more independent later on and predisposing girls to be more warm, nurturing, and interested in relationships with others. They acknowledge that some of these differences may result from factors in the child's social environment. But because the differences appear so early, they attribute most of the effect to genetic, hormonal, or prenatal influences.

Others, however, have argued that even at so early an age, a wide variety of factors other than biology can affect physical development, such as how much parents encourage the child and how much opportunity a child has to learn these activities (Carli, 1997). For example, in some African cultures where mothers actively teach their babies to crawl, children reach this milestone significantly earlier than children raised in cultures where crawling is not taught (Super, 1976). Likewise, in the United States, giving infants practice in sitting or stepping can accelerate the age at which they learn these abilities. In fact, children who enter the crawling stage of development when the weather is cold tend to begin crawling later than children who enter this stage during the warmer months (Benson, 1993).

Using biology to explain gender differences later in life is also the subject of much disagreement. For instance, sociologist Steven Goldberg (1999) argues that because male rule and male dominance seem to characterize the vast majority of human societies, this gender difference must be rooted in evolutionary biology. However, anthropologists have identified noteworthy exceptions. The famous anthropologist Margaret Mead (1963) studied three cultures in New Guinea in the 1930s:

- Among the mountain-dwelling Arapesh, both men and women displayed traits we in the West would commonly associate with femininity: cooperation, passivity, sensitivity to others. Mead described both men and women as being "maternal." These characteristics were linked to broader cultural beliefs about people's relationship to the environment. The Arapesh didn't have any conception of "ownership" of land, so they never had aggressive conflicts over possession of property.
- South of the Arapesh were the Mundugumor, a group of cannibals and headhunters. Here, both men and women displayed traits that we in the West would associate with masculinity: assertiveness, emotional inexpressiveness, insensitivity to others. Mundugumor women, according to Mead, were just as violent, just as aggressive, and just as jealous as men. Both were equally virile, without any of the "soft" characteristics we associate with femininity.

■ The Tchambuli, the third culture Mead observed, did distinguish between male and female traits. However, their gender expectations were the opposite of what we expect in Western societies. Women were dominant, shrewd, assertive, and managerial; men were submissive and emotional and were seen as inherently delicate.

Mead's work is important because it shows that definitions of the "natural" tendencies of men and women aren't universal. The vast majority of societies may be dominated by men, but the fact that there are exceptions, no matter how rare, shows at the very least that biological predispositions, if they exist at all, can actually be modified or overcome by culture.

Furthermore, although media pundits and behavioral scientists are fond of emphasizing fundamental gender differences (you know, men are from Mars and women are from Venus and all that), decades of research indicate that boys and girls/ men and women are far more similar than different (Hyde, 2006). Within a particular culture, the distribution of males and females on most personality and behavioral characteristics generally overlaps (Carothers, 2013). For instance, men as a group do tend to be more aggressive than women as a group. But these differences are a matter of degree, not kind. Hence some women are much more aggressive than the average man, and some men are much less aggressive than the average woman. Indeed, social circumstances may have a greater impact on aggressive behavior than any innate, biological traits (Archer, 2004). Similarly, people tend to tune their gender-expressive behavior to what they perceive to be the expectations of others. For example, when women in one study were led to believe that they were interacting with a man who benevolently thought women should be protected, they behaved in far more stereotypically feminine ways (that is, weak and vulnerable) than those who thought they were interacting with men who believed otherwise (Sinclair, Huntsinger, Skorinko, & Hardin, 2005).

Gender Guidance Because beliefs about "natural" differences between males and females are so deeply ingrained—what one psychologist refers to as a cultural tendency toward *neurosexism* (Fine, 2010)—parents are often unaware that they are treating their children in accordance with these gender-typed expectations (Goldberg & Lewis, 1969; Will, Self, & Datan, 1976). A colleague of mine gave birth to a daughter a while back. When I saw her a few days after the baby was born, she described her daughter as looking like a "little China doll." A few years later, she gave birth to another child—a boy this time—whom she immediately described as "handsome." Such responses are common. In one study, 30 first-time parents were asked to describe their recently born infants (less than 24 hours old). Those with daughters used words like "tiny," "soft," "fine-featured," and "delicate" to describe them. Sons were seen as "strong," "alert," "hardy," and "coordinated" (Rubin, Provenzano, & Luria, 1974). A replication of this study two decades later found that U.S. parents continued to perceive their infants in gender-stereotyped ways, although to a lesser degree than in the 1970s (Karraker, Vogel, & Lake, 1995).

Researchers have also found subtle differences in the ways parents communicate with their sons and daughters. For instance, parents are more likely to talk about sadness with daughters than with sons; they're more likely to talk about anger with sons than with daughters (Adams, Kuebli, Boyle, & Fivush, 1995). Parents also tend to engage in rougher and more interactive physical play with infant sons than with infant daughters and use different pet names, such as "Sweetie" versus "Tiger" (MacDonald & Parke, 1986; Tauber, 1979). In one study, all mothers—whether they eschewed traditional gender expectations or embraced them—were more likely to verbally teach and direct their sons than their daughters. In addition, they were more likely to use action verbs, numbers, and explicit language with their sons (Weitzman, Birns, & Friend, 1985).

Such differences are also reflected in the kinds of information parents seek *about* their children. A recent analysis of data from Google searches found that parents with daughters are significantly more likely to submit queries about their child's weight and physical attractiveness while parents with sons are more likely to search for information about whether their child has above average intelligence or is a leader (Stephens-Davidowitz, 2014).

Parents also gender-socialize their children through the things they routinely provide for them. Clothes, for example, not only inform others about the sex of an individual, they also send messages about how that child ought to be treated and direct behavior along traditional gender lines (Shakin, Shakin, & Sternglanz, 1985). Frilly dresses do not lend themselves easily to rough and dirty play. Clothes for boys rarely restrict physical movement in this way and are usually manufactured to withstand vigorous activity.

Toys and games are another influential source of gender information. Research indicates that children usually prefer toys that are associated with their own sex (Martin, Eisenbud, & Rose, 1995). "Girls' toys" still revolve around themes of domesticity, fashion, and motherhood and "boys' toys" emphasize action and adventure (Renzetti & Curran, 2003). In one study, there was significant agreement among adults as to what were the most male toys (guns, toy soldiers, boxing gloves, G.I. Joe, and football gear) and the most female toys (makeup kit, Barbie, jewelry box, bracelet, doll clothes) (Campenni, 1999).

Even among 6- to 12-month old babies, boys had more of what one study called "toys of the world" (vehicles, machines, etc.) while girls had more "toys of the home" (housekeeping toys, dolls, etc.; cited in Fine, 2010).

A quick glance at toy store shelves, or toy company web sites reveals that toys and games remain segregated along gender lines. For instance, the web site of the retail giant Toys "R" Us gives online shoppers the option of selecting "girls' toys" or "boys' toys." The featured categories for boys include "Action Figures," while the featured categories for girls include "Dolls" and "Bath, Beauty Accessories." And although both boys' and girls' toys have a category called "Building Sets," the boys' sets include a "Star Wars Jedi Interceptor," a "Call of Duty Half Track Troop Transporter," and "Monster Fighter Vampire Castle"; the girls' sets, on the other hand, include "Cinderella's Romantic Castle," "Hello Kitty Beach House," and "Barbie's Glam House."

Mattel's "Little Mommy" doll is a soft, cuddly baby that drinks from a bottle and comes with a potty seat for toilet training. The product's web site states, in no uncertain terms, that "every little girl loves to pretend that she's a real mommy." The company also markets a pregnant version of Barbie's friend Midge (called "Happy Family Midge"). She comes with a distended tummy that, when removed, reveals a 1¾-inch baby nestled in the doll's plastic uterus. The doll comes with everything a girl needs to play out the birth and care of the new baby, including diapers (pink if it's a girl, blue if it's a boy), birth certificate, bottles, rattles, changing table, tub, and crib. All these dolls clearly teach young girls the cultural value of motherhood, a role most girls are encouraged and expected to enter later in life. You'd be hard pressed to find a comparable toy, popular among boys, that prepares them for future roles as fathers.

Gender differences in toy and recreational preferences can, however, change with age. One study of children between the ages of 5 and 13 found that boys' leisure preferences become slightly more masculine as they get older while girls' preferences become less stereotypical, turning to more neutral or even masculine toys, sports and computer games (Cherney & London, 2006).

Parents and other family members also provide children with direct instructions on proper gender behavior, such as "Big boys don't cry" or "Act like a young lady." For instance, one study found that mothers expect more risky behavior from their sons and tend to focus more on disciplinary issues with them than with daughters. Conversely, mothers tend to be more concerned about injuries and safety issues with their daughters than with sons (Morrongiello & Hogg, 2004).

And it's not just mothers, by the way. One day many years ago, when my older son was about 11 months old and just beginning to walk, he crawled into the kitchen, opened several drawers, and hoisted himself up to a standing position. With little hesitation, he let go and for a brief instant proudly stood on his own. His moment of glory lasted less than a second, though, for as he turned to receive congratulations from those in the room, he lost his balance and fell face-first into one of the open drawers. Through his hysterical crying, I could see that his lower lip was cut and bleeding. He was clearly in pain and obviously wanted some parental comfort. But as he crawled toward me, blood dripping on the carpet, I blurted out, "This is great!! He just got his first fat lip!!" Somewhere in the deep recesses of my brain, I saw this event as a normal male rite of passage. After all, boys are supposed to fall down and sometimes even get hurt. Instead of consoling him, I celebrated his injury. I've never lived this incident down.

As a consequence of this sort of differential treatment, both boys and girls learn to adopt gender as an organizing principle for themselves and the social world in which they live (Hollander, Renfrow, & Howard, 2011). Sometime between 18 and 24 months of age, most children develop the ability to label gender groups, use gender in their speech, and identify themselves as boys or girls (Martin & Ruble, 2009). But to a young child, being a boy or a girl means no more than being named Lee instead of Julie. It is simply another characteristic, like having brown eyes or curly hair. The child at this age lacks the full understanding that gender is a category into which every human can be placed (Kessler & McKenna, 1978). By the age of five or so, most children have developed a fairly extensive repertoire of gender stereotypes (often incorrect) that they then apply to themselves (Martin & Ruble, 2004). They also use these stereotypes to form impressions of others and to guide their own perceptions and activities. A boy, for instance, may avoid approaching a new girl who has just moved into the neighborhood because he assumes that she will only be interested in "girl" things. Acting on this assumption serves to reinforce the original belief that boys and girls are different. Indeed, gender, to children at this age, is typically seen as a characteristic that is fixed and permanent. A few years later, though, their attitudes toward gender are likely to become considerably more flexible, although such flexibility may not be reflected in their actual behaviors (Martin & Ruble, 2004).

It's important to note that the process by which children learn their own gender identity is not a passive one in which they simply absorb the information that bombards them. As part of the process of finding meaning in their social worlds, children actively construct gender as a social category. From an early age, they are like "gender detectives," searching for cues about gender, such as who should and shouldn't engage in certain activities, who can play with whom, and why girls and boys differ (Martin & Ruble, 2004, p. 67).

Intersections
The Influence of Race and Ethnicity on Gender Socialization

Most of the research on the role that parents play in the gender socialization of their children is based on samples of white, middle-class, two-parent families. Hence, the broad conclusions one draws about family influence on gender development must be made with caution. Some researchers have been trying to identify the nuances of gender socialization among different ethnoracial groups to give us a better understanding of the process. For instance, Marcella Raffaelli and Lenno Ontai (2004) have identified a set of unique cultural ideals that are relevant to gender socialization among many Latino/a groups:

- *Familismo*—cultural emphasis on family relations and child-bearing as an integral part of femininity.
- *Respeto*—cultural emphasis on respect and hierarchy in social relations.
- Strong gender role divisions that contain expectations that women be submissive, chaste, and dependent and men be dominant, virile, and independent.

Often, these values are reflected in the different ways that Latino/a parents attempt to regulate the sexual activity of their children. For example, they place much more importance on virginity until marriage for daughters than for sons. More generally, parents place stricter rules and more limits on girls than on boys in such matters as involvement in after-school activities and the age at which they allow their children to get jobs or drivers' licenses. In addition, Latina mothers tend to be more involved in the gender socialization of daughters and fathers more involved in the gender socialization of sons (Raffaelli & Ontai, 2004).

In a study that compared African American and white parents, the researchers found that white parents are significantly more likely to place a high value on their children's happiness and to see teaching as their most important parenting role. Black parents were more likely to value doing well and being obedient in school and to see being a disciplinarian and a provider as their most important parenting roles (Hill & Sprague, 1999).

The sex of the child can interact with race to further influence these tendencies. For example, white parents are more likely than black parents to emphasize obedience for sons more than for daughters. Withdrawing privileges is more commonly used to discipline boys rather than girls in black families (Hill & Sprague, 1999).

Although the socialization of young African American males and females is not entirely the same, parents tend to emphasize the importance of hard work, independence, and self-reliance equally among sons and daughters (Hale-Benson, 1986). The emphasis on gender equality seems to be more common in African American families than in other types of American families. Several historical trends—the high proportion of African American women in the paid labor force, the presence of female-centered households, and a history of racial discrimination and exclusion—can't help but influence notions of gender and the way African American parents teach it to their children. Some have gone so far as to say that age and competency—and not gender—are the chief determinants of children's roles in African American families (Peters, 1988).

Some sociologists have argued that apparent race differences in gender socialization may actually be an artifact of the way race and class intersect in this society (Hill, 2001). Among working class white parents, traditional gender socialization is more common than among working class black parents. Indeed, low-income African American parents often have higher expectations for their daughters than for their sons (Hill & Sprague, 1999). However, upper-middle-class black parents are more likely to socialize their sons and daughters into traditional gender roles than upper-middle-class white parents are (Hill, 1999).

Gender Neutrality   To diminish the heavy societal emphasis on gender distinctions, some parents and child development experts advocate **gender-neutral socialization**—bringing up boys and girls to have both male and female traits and behaviors (Bem, 1974). Advocates for gender-neutral socialization see no biological reason, except for a few anatomical and reproductive differences, to distinguish between what males and females can do.

Modern parents are probably more likely than their predecessors to attempt to overcome gender stereotypes in the raising of their children. For instance, a small but growing number of parents have begun to advocate a gender-fluid approach to child rearing by allowing their sons to wear dresses and high heels if that's what they choose. They refer to their children as "pink boys"—males with a strong interest in traditionally female presentation who still identify as boys (Padawer, 2012). These parents want their children to occupy the middle space between traditional boyhood and traditional girlhood. Although they are fully aware of the problems these boys will face when they display their appearance preferences in public (both from other children as well as adults), they argue that nobody fits the dichotomous gender categories perfectly anyway, so why should they crush their child's individuality by forcing them uncomfortably into a traditional gender group? But their battle is an uphill one as they fight against a community of others whose responses range from confused to hostile.

Likewise, a cultural backlash may also await parents who publicly advocate gender-neutral socialization. A few years ago, the Discovery Health web site listed gender-neutral parenting as the most *radical* parenting method ahead of "diaperless parenting" (self-explanatory), "unparenting" (parents who intervene as little as possible in their child's life), and "teacup parenting" (parents who believe their children are fragile, like teacups, and need constant supervision; Law, 2014).

Furthermore, as you recall from the story at the beginning of this chapter, parents' ability to carry out gender-neutral socialization may be somewhat limited. Four- and 5-year-old children often engage in strongly gender-stereotypical play, regardless of the attitudes and beliefs expressed by their parents (O'Brien & Huston, 1985). Findings like these have led some researchers to argue that the effects of gender-neutral socialization are more likely to show up later in life rather than in childhood, after individuals have developed the cognitive maturity and the confidence to incorporate nontraditional gender attitudes and beliefs into their everyday lives (Risman & Myers, 1997). Some researchers are even more pessimistic. Psychologist, Steven Pinker, once put it this way:

> It is said that there is a technical term for people who believe that little boys and little girls are born indistinguishable and are molded into their natures by parental socialization. The term is "childless" (quoted in Fine, 2010, p. 190).

But completely gender-neutral socialization is not difficult only because it runs up against some unbreachable biological walls. Instead, parental gender expectations—both before and after a child is born—can make it exceedingly difficult (Kane, 2009). Here's how one father put it, "I always wanted a son . . . I wanted to teach [him] to play basketball . . . baseball, and so forth." Daughters, by contrast, yield very different expectations: "I wanted [a girl] . . . to dress her up and to buy the dolls . . . A girl was someone that you could do all the things that you like to do with more than you could a boy" (Kane, 2009 p. 373).

Tomboys and Sissies   Furthermore, gender structures every organization and shapes every interaction in society, often in ways we're not consciously aware of. Hence, gender-neutral socialization always involves, at least to some degree, the violation of widely held gender norms. Unfortunately, children whose behavior doesn't conform to generally accepted standards of gender still risk ridicule or worse from their peers.

The social costs of violating gender norms are not felt evenly by girls and boys, or by women and men, however (Risman & Seale, 2010). Consider the different connotations and implications of the words *tomboy* and *sissy* (Schilt, 2009). The tomboy may fight, curse, play sports, and climb trees, but her entire sexual identity is not called into question by the label. In fact, in some situations, she is just as likely to be included by other children as shunned by them, as when, say, she is asked to play in informal games of football or basketball with neighborhood boys. Girls, in general, are given license to do "boy things" (Kimmel, 2004). Indeed, tomboy-ness, if considered negative at all, is typically seen as transitory, a stage that a girl will eventually grow out of. How many TV shows or movies have you seen in which a precocious tomboy reaches puberty, sprouts breasts, discovers boys, discards her rough-and-tumble ways, puts on makeup and a dress for the first time, and unveils to stunned friends and family her true feminine beauty?

For sissies, life on the other side of the gender fence is much more precarious. For boys, the chances to play girl games without ridicule are rare and the risks for doing so are steep. The sissy is not simply a boy who enjoys female pursuits. He is suspiciously soft and effeminate. His sissy-ness is likely to be seen as reflective of his sexual essence, a sign of his imminent homosexuality.

I remember an old television commercial for men's cologne that opened with a woman lying by herself in bed with a cup of coffee. She has a mischievous smile on her face as if recalling a recent satisfying sexual encounter. She gets up, goes to the closet, removes a man's dress shirt from a hanger, and puts it on. She puts on a tie and then grabs a man's hat off of a chair and dons it. Finally, she picks up a bottle of the cologne, looks at it for a second, and dabs some on her neck. At that moment, the phone rings. She answers it and coyly says, "Honey. I was just thinking about you." The ad works, of course, because putting on her partner's clothes and cologne is taken as a sexy way for her to feel close to him. But imagine if an ad for women's perfume used a similar approach: The scene opens with a man alone in a bedroom putting on his lover's bra and lacy sundress. He spritzes some of her perfume on his neck and wrists. When the phone rings, he picks up the receiver and in a deep, husky voice says to the woman on the other end, "Honey, I was just thinking about you." Would you consider this ad sexy? Doubtful.

Part of the reason for this asymmetrical response to gender-crossing behavior is the connection between the gender differences and gender inequalities that exists in society. Simply put, in a society structured around and for the interests of men, stereotypically masculine traits (strength, assertiveness, confidence, and so on) are likely to be valued culturally and interpersonally. For instance, most bureaucracies in institutional areas, such as business, politics, and the military, operate according to taken-for-granted masculine principles. Successful leaders and organizations are usually portrayed as aggressive, goal oriented, competitive, and efficient—all characteristics associated with masculinity in this society. Rarely are strong governments, prosperous businesses, or efficient military units described as supportive, nurturing, cooperative, kind, and caring (Acker, 1992). When institutions are gendered in these ways, everyday inequalities become apparent. Hence, many women conclude that their own success requires such traits. Even young children learn that "boy" traits are valued more highly than stereotypically "girl" traits:

> Boys and girls both understand the inequality between women and men, and understand, too, that their less-than-equal status gives girls a bit more latitude in the types of cross-sex (gender-inappropriate) behavior they may exhibit. Girls think they'd be better off as boys, and many of them declare that they would rather be boys than girls. By contrast, boys tend to see being girls as a fate worse than death. . . . [A little boy comes] to understand that his status in the world depends upon his ability to distance himself from femininity. By exaggerating gender difference, he both assures and reassures himself of his higher status. (Kimmel, 2004, pp. 132–133)

LEARNING RACES

Some research shows that children as young as three—no matter what their racial background—recognize skin color differences and hold a wide array of racial attitudes, assumptions, and behaviors (Van Ausdale & Feagin, 2001). But how do they incorporate these perceptions into their own sense of self?

Although everyone has a racial identity, different groups assign different degrees of priority to the role of race in their lives. For some, racial identity organizes virtually every aspect of their daily experiences; for others, it is for all intents and purposes irrelevant. Whether racial identity is all-encompassing or minimal depends on the group's historical position in the racial stratification system. The more advantaged a group's position, the less important racial identity is for the effective socialization of children within that group.

It's not surprising, then, that few sociologists have attempted to explain how white children come to understand and see themselves as white people, even though whiteness, like any other racial identity, must be learned, developed, and performed (Van Ausdale & Feagin, 2001). Those who do study the development of white racial identity typically focus on how white children move through various stages of prejudice—from early phases in which they acquire common racial stereotypes and beliefs in white superiority to later stages where a nonracist identity and a commitment to racial equality emerge (Helms, 1993). White parents may attempt to instill pride in their children's religious identity or hyphenated ethnicity (for instance, Greek-Americans, Italian-Americans, Irish-Americans), but they rarely have to teach their children about the conflicts and dilemmas that their race will create for them. In fact, Whites have the luxury of choosing whether or not to even include their specific ancestry in descriptions of their identity (Waters, 2010). In this sense, ethnicity is optional, voluntary, and perhaps even recreational.

Hence, learning to be white is less about defining one's race as it is about learning how to handle privileges and behaviors associated with whiteness in society (Van Ausdale & Feagin, 2001). Chances are good that schools and religious organizations will reinforce the socialization messages expressed to white children in their families—for example, that "a good education will pay off in the long run" or "you can be anything you want as long as you work hard." Because the messages that white children receive about race are likely to focus on the race of others, not their own race, the assumption that race is an insignificant component of their identity is perpetuated.

For children of color, however, racial socialization occurs within a different and much more complex social environment (Hughes & Chen, 1997). These children must live simultaneously in two different worlds: their family and ethnoracial community, which value them, and the "mainstream" (that is, white) society, which may not (Lesane-Brown, 2006). Hence, they're likely to be exposed to three different types of socialization experiences while growing up: that which includes information about the mainstream culture, that which focuses on their minority status in society, and that which focuses on the history and cultural heritage of their ethnoracial group (Scott, 2003; Thornton, 1997). In ethnoracial groups that have been able to overcome discrimination and achieve at high levels—such as some Asian American groups—ethnic socialization can focus simply on the values of their culture of origin. But among groups that, by and large, remain disadvantaged, such as African Americans, Native Americans, and Latino/as, parents' discussion of race and ethnicity is more likely to focus on preparing their children for the possibility of prejudice and mistreatment in a society set up to ignore or actively exclude them (McLoyd, Cauce, Takeuchi, & Wilson, 2000; Staples, 1992). For instance, these children may be taught that "hard work" alone might not be enough to get ahead in this society. Even children of color from affluent homes in racially integrated neighborhoods need reassurances about the racial conflicts they will inevitably encounter. Faced with a steady stream of cases in which police have used deadly force against unarmed people of color, former Attorney General, Eric Holder (who is black), talked publicly of a conversation he had with his teenage son about how he should interact with the police, what to say, and how to conduct himself if he was ever stopped or confronted in a way he thought was unwarranted (Franke-Ruta, 2013). Some black and Latino/a parents tell their children not to wear hoodies or baggy pants, fearing the lethal assumptions police might make (Eligon, 2013).

But even within a particular group, there can be tremendous variation in the content of racial socialization. For some parents of color, race is one of the central concerns in raising their children. They may believe that they are not simply raising an "American" but an American with a particular ethnoracial background. Some parents who anticipate that their children will face a hostile environment teach them to be comfortable with and proud of their own ethnicity. For other minority parents, however, race may play only a minor role in the socialization process. They may feel reluctant to discuss race or racism because they fear that such a discussion might make their children bitter, resentful, and prejudiced against others (Thornton, Chatters, Taylor, & Allen, 1990). Some critics argue that such parents cannot instill a positive racial identity in their children.

Ethnoracial socialization can be especially problematic when racial identity itself is complicated. Take, for instance, children who are adopted by parents of a different race. Since passage of the Multiethnic Placement Act of 1994, federally funded agencies have been prohibited from considering race, culture, and ethnicity in their placement decisions, making it easier for couples to adopt children of different racial backgrounds. According to the U.S. Department of Health and Human Services (2009), four out of ten adopted children are in transracial adoptions—that is, both adoptive parents are (or the single adoptive parent is) of a different race, culture, or ethnicity than the child. The majority of these adoptions—whether domestic or international—take place between non-Hispanic white parents and children of color.

Today, approximately 59% of American children awaiting adoption are members of ethnoracial minorities (ProQuest Statistical Abstract, 2015). Many adoption agencies take the position that a permanent home is more important than racial matching of parents and children. Advocates of transracial adoption also argue that the child, who likely comes from a financially depressed and deprived background, will have better opportunities in a more "advantaged" environment. In addition, they point out that transracial adoption has the potential to transform a racially divided society into a racially integrated one by creating such integration within individual families.

Transracial adoption has not been without its critics, however. In 1972, the National Association of Black Social Workers (2003) passed a resolution, still in effect today, against the adoption of black children by white parents unless all other placement efforts have been exhausted. The group argued that transracial adoptions are harmful to black heritage and threaten the preservation of black families and the integrity of black culture. They pointed out that a black child growing up in a white family will never learn about his or her own culture and will, therefore, never develop a positive racial identity. Hence, white parents can never provide a black child with sufficient information about what it is like to be black in a predominantly white society.

Considering the larger historical and political context, we can understand why some groups fear that transracial adoption weakens their racial identity and culture. In the 1960s and 1970s, for example, nearly 30% of all Native American children were removed from their families and put up for adoption in non–Native American homes (Egan, 1993). Social workers at the time deemed thousands of Native American parents unfit because of poverty, alcoholism, and other problems. So devastating to tribal cultures was the removal of these children that the Indian Child Welfare Act was passed in 1978, giving tribes special preference in adopting children of Native American heritage (Egan, 1993). However, this law has come under attack after reports of tribes contesting the adoption by white parents of children with only a minute trace of Indian ancestry. In 2009, a white couple from South Carolina adopted a Native American baby, called "Baby Veronica" in the media. The girl's biological father, who was on record as being 2.4% Cherokee, contested the adoption on the grounds that he didn't consent to it. Under the Indian Child Welfare Act, he sued for, and was granted, custody of the child. The case made it all the way to the U.S. Supreme Court, which in 2013 ruled that the father had no rights to custody because Baby Veronica had never lived with him; she was eventually returned to her adoptive parents.

In terms of their general adjustment, children of color placed in white homes seem to do just as well as other adopted children. However, when it comes to issues of self-esteem, ethnoracial identity, and strategies for living in a racist society, children who are adopted by parents of the same race or ethnicity tend to do better. Furthermore, the vast majority of white families that adopt children of color live in predominantly white neighborhoods and send their children to predominantly white schools. Although these parents are aware of the importance of exposing their children to other people of color, they tend to minimize the importance of race in their children's lives and downplay incidents that involve racial slurs or acts of discrimination (Vidal de Haymes & Simon, 2003).

Intersections
The Effects of Gender and Class on Racial Identities

The intersection of race, class, and gender is especially apparent during adolescence, when concerns about identity and self-definition may be central features of everyday life (Dion & Dion, 2004). Being a girl or boy, poor or nonpoor, and white, black, or Latino/a have varying implications for well-being depending on how these factors are combined. Poor children from an oppressed racial or ethnic group are especially vulnerable to an accumulation of disadvantage that can influence their psychological well-being over time (McLeod & Owens, 2004).

Consider the research of sociologist Mary Pattillo-McCoy (1999), who spent 3 1/2 years in a middle-class black Chicago neighborhood she called "Groveland," interviewing residents of all ages. In many respects, the Groveland families were just like families in any other middle-class neighborhood. Parents saw their children's development into self sufficient adults as their primary goal. And most of them had the wherewithal to pay for private schools, sports equipment, dance lessons, and so on. The black children in Groveland had access to computers and other resources that black children in poor neighborhoods did not.

But the black middle-class families in Groveland had to deal with markedly different problems than their white counterparts. For example, at the time of this study, 79% of middle-class Blacks in Chicago lived within a few blocks of a neighborhood where at least one-third of the residents were poor; only 36% of white, middle-class Chicago dwellers lived so close to a poor neighborhood (cited in Pattillo-McCoy, 1999). Thus, Groveland parents had to spend a lot of time trying to protect their children from the negative influences found in the neighboring poor, inner-city areas. In doing so, they faced some challenges other middle-class parents were unlikely to face:

> Groveland parents . . . set limits on where their children can travel. They choose activities—church youth groups, magnet schools or accelerated programs in the local school, and the Boy Scouts and Girl Scouts—to increase the likelihood that their children will learn positive values and associate with youth from similar families. . . . On their way to the grocery store or to school or to music lessons, Groveland's youth pass other young people whose parents are not as strict, who stay outside later, who have joined the local gang, or who earn enough money being a lookout at a drug house to buy new

gym shoes. They also meet these peers in school and at the park. . . . For some teenagers, the fast life looks much more exciting than what their parents have to offer them, and they are drawn to it. The simple fact of living in a neighborhood where not all families have sufficient resources to direct their children away from deviance makes it difficult for parents to ensure positive outcomes for their children and their neighborhood. (pp. 211–212)

Another sociologist, Mary Romero (2010), has been studying the intersections of race, class, and gender in her research on the lives of Latina and African American domestic workers. In one article, she provides a lengthy life history of "Teresa," the daughter of a Latina live-in maid working in a predominantly white, upper class neighborhood in Los Angeles. Teresa's entire childhood is spent in somebody else's house. At times, she is treated by her mother's employer and the employer's family as an ethnoracial outsider, a poor Latina whose appearance, language, and demeanor mark her, even to children her own age, as subordinate. At other times though—and often with little warning—she is treated as "one of the family," as when, for example, she is spontaneously invited to eat Thanksgiving dinner with the employer's family. The problem for Teresa is that such inclusive treatment is largely arbitrary and unpredictable. So, she must learn to be sensitive to "signs" in order to determine her position in each social setting and ultimately select the appropriate actions. Teresa's racial identity is complicated by the different socioeconomic environments she straddles:

Teresa and her mother maintained another life—one that was guarded and protected against any employer intrusion. Their other life was Mexican, not white, was Spanish speaking, not English speaking, was female dominated rather than male dominated, and was poor and working class, not upper middle-class. (p. 93)

It's easy to see how the development of Teresa's ethnoracial identity is inseparable from her socioeconomic standing. Imagine how different Teresa's sense of being "Latina" would have been if her parents had been wealthy Latino/a professionals. For that matter, consider how different her socialization experiences might have been if she had been the son of a maid rather than the daughter or had been white rather than Latina.

LEARNING SEXUALITIES

We're preoccupied with sex in the United States. It's everywhere: in our magazines, our novels, our television shows, our movies, our music videos, our video games, our text messages, our advertisements, our social network sites, and our politics. The impact of all this sexual imagery is not trivial. A study of American teens, for instance, found that frequent exposure to sexually oriented television shows like soap operas and music videos is associated with casual attitudes toward sex, higher expectations about the prevalence of sexual activity, and sometimes greater levels of actual sexual experience (Ward, 2003).

For all our cultural obsessions with sex, we really don't talk frankly or openly about it all that much. Communities across the country have fought against things like contraceptive ads on television and sex education in schools. Although most parents can be quite proactive when it comes to teaching their children how to ride a bike, how to read, or how to use the stove, they can be rather tight-lipped when it comes to teaching their children how to be sexual. They are more likely to act as inadvertent models for their children—as when an unsuspecting child barges into the parents' bedroom during when they're having sex—or to articulate what children shouldn't do rather than what they should. Straightforward, direct sexual socialization is relatively uncommon.

Consequently, the information that children do receive tends to be largely informal, piecemeal, and peer-driven. When older siblings are present, they, and not parents, are typically the ones who provide information on intercourse and contraceptive use (Kornreich, Hearn, Rodriguez, & O'Sullivan, 2003). Moreover, given the heteronormative nature of our society, it's a good bet that early sexual lessons young people receive from others are heterosexual. Hence, sexual socialization can be especially difficult for people developing non-heterosexual identities (Savin-Williams, 2007).

Born This Way? "Becoming" heterosexual in most cultures is neither problematic nor abnormal. When parents say things to their young daughters like, "Wait until you get married and have kids of your own someday; then you'll see how aggravating it is to be a parent!" they are implicitly reinforcing the "normality" of a heterosexual identity. So not surprisingly, media and scientific attention has largely been devoted to discovering the origins of homosexuality, not heterosexuality.

Interpretations of the origins of homosexuality have changed considerably. In the late 19th century, psychiatrists and other medical professionals developed a view of homosexuality as a form of mental illness—a disease that could somehow be cured through medical means. In fact, as recently as

1973, the *Diagnostic and Statistical Manual* of the American Psychiatric Association listed homosexuality as a mental illness associated with psychopathic personality disorders.

In the 1950s and 1960s, most experts believed that homosexuality was a pathological choice, which was influenced by interpersonal experiences and not by a person's biological inheritance. Psychological and sociological theories of the time focused on such factors as domineering mothers, submissive fathers, early childhood trauma, "recruitment" by gay school teachers, "failure" at heterosexuality, and a variety of emotional disturbances as the reasons why an individual would become homosexual. If homosexuality was acquired, the thinking went, it could perhaps be un-acquired.

So, psychiatrists at the time wrote extensively about how, with the appropriate therapy, homosexuals could "learn" to be heterosexual. Even today, debate rages over the efficacy of such therapy. In 2015, a New Jersey court ruled that groups offering "gay conversion therapy"—an intervention program designed to "cure" men of their homosexual urges—violated the state's Consumer Fraud Act and could no longer be practiced (Eckholm, 2015). However, attempts at similar bans in other states have failed to gain traction, paving the way for the issue to eventually reach the Supreme Court in the not-too-distant future.

Nonetheless, a growing body of literature today provides evidence that sexual orientation is not simply a lifestyle choice. Attention has been paid to such factors as brain structure, genes, hormones, pheromones, and the prenatal uterine environment both in humans as well as other animals. For instance, various forms of same-sex pairings have been found in over 450 animal species, including bison, dolphins, and flamingoes. In 1995, two scientists at the National Institutes of Health transplanted a single gene into the bodies of male fruit flies that caused them to display "courtship" behaviors with other male fruit flies (Zhang & Odenwald, 1995). Some female-female pairs of albatrosses nesting on the northwestern tip of Oahu are stable and monogamous, having been together for 4, 8, even 19 years (cited in Mooallem, 2010). Granted, the notion that a fruit fly or an albatross could be homosexual in the same sense that a human could be is an overstatement. You'll recall from Chapter 2 that sexual orientation is a human construction that includes not only physical desires but also psychological imagery and self-identity. Nevertheless, this research has added to the mounting body of evidence that sexual orientation is rooted in biology.

In 1991, a California neuroscientist performed autopsies on the brains of men and women of known sexual orientation (LeVay, 1991). He found that the hypothalamus region in the center of the brain was substantially smaller among the gay men he examined than among the heterosexual men. Despite the researcher's plea for caution in drawing quick conclusions from his limited findings, this study became a catalyst for scholarly and not-so-scholarly debate on the origins of human sexual orientation (Ordover, 1996).

Another study found that the male relatives of known gay men were substantially more likely to be homosexual themselves (13.5%) than was the entire sample studied (2%). Indeed, the researcher discovered more gay relatives on the maternal side, fueling the contention that homosexuality is passed from generation to generation through women (Hamer & Coupland, 1994). Some researchers even contend that studies like this one point toward a "gay gene."

As compelling as these findings may be, we must interpret them with caution. For instance, other researchers point out that genetic or hormonal influences, if they exist at all, do not function independent of social context (Bearman & Brückner, 2002). Furthermore, a single gene is unlikely to be responsible for *any* complex human trait. We know, for instance, that genes are responsible for the development of our lungs, larynx, mouth, and the areas of the brain associated with speech. But such complexity can't be collapsed into a single "talking" gene. Similarly, genes determine the development of our penises, vaginas, and brains. But that's a far step from the contention that a single gene determines sexual desires, feelings of attraction, fantasies, and patterns of arousal.

Moreover, these studies really aren't examining the origins of sexual orientation. They're examining the origins of one type of sexual orientation: homosexuality. None of these researchers seems interested in explaining the origins of heterosexuality or bisexuality or asexuality. For instance, if a certain structure in the brain is small in homosexual men and large in heterosexual men, is it somewhere in between among bisexual men? Is it completely absent in people who have no sexual attraction to anyone?

Although the debate over the origins of sexual orientation is far from settled, let's suppose for the moment that sexual orientation is, in fact, biologically determined. What would be the social implications of such a conclusion? Some people argue that understanding sexual orientation as an innate characteristic beyond personal control, like hair or eye color, will make people more open minded about equality and more protective of the civil rights of gay and lesbian individuals. The long-standing concern that homosexuals shouldn't work in occupations involving children (Boy Scout leader, elementary school teacher, child care worker, and so on) because of their potentially corrupting influence would disappear because environmental influence would no longer be considered a factor in the development of a child's sexual orientation.

On the other hand, information about the genetic origins of sexual orientation might be used to perpetuate the belief that homosexuality is a "defect" that needs to be fixed, thereby further stigmatizing gays and lesbians. Ideas about biological determinism inevitably carry the threat of encouraging us to try manipulating genes, the brain, hormones, or whatever the purported biological cause in order to adapt to prevailing social norms. For instance, some scientists have argued that exposure to certain levels of testosterone at certain times in fetal development is a crucial factor in the development of "sex centers" in the brain. If so, prenatal tests like amniocentesis could, perhaps, predict homosexuality. And if this "condition" can be predicted, prevention is but a short step away.

Intersections
Gendered Sexualities

Because of general differences in the ways that girls and boys are socialized in this society, the paths to sexual orientation are different too. For instance, gay men tend to become aware of same-sex attractions, act on those attractions, and identify themselves as gay earlier than lesbians. On the other hand, lesbians tend to create ongoing love relationships with members of the same sex earlier than gay men. Furthermore, they're more likely to commit to a lesbian identity in the context of an emotional relationship; men tend to commit to a gay identity within the context of their sexual experiences. In other words, as with women in general, lesbians tend to associate their sexual identity with relationships and not so much with erotic activity (Levine & Evans, 2003).

Some researchers also argue that lesbians are more likely to view the acknowledgment of their sexual identity as a choice, whereas men tend to see it as a discovery (cited in Levine & Evans, 2003). In part, this difference may derive from the fact that the declaration of a lesbian identity is sometimes more of a political/philosophical statement than a statement about one's physical desires. In fact, one early study suggested that there are actually three types of lesbians: "ideological lesbians" (women for whom a lesbian identity is highly political), "personal lesbians" (women who want to establish an independent identity and see lesbianism as supportive of this goal), and "interpersonal lesbians" (women who find themselves involved with another woman and who experience this involvement as a discovery and not a purposeful choice) (Henderson, 1979).

Sociologist Valerie Jenness (2002) has argued that for women who fall into this latter category, becoming a lesbian involves a redefinition of the term lesbian so that it becomes less stigmatizing. Often, a lesbian identity develops long after women begin engaging in erotic activity with other women. Initially, their understanding of the social category "lesbian" is vague and derives not from personal experiences but typically from the media. Because these initial ideas about lesbians are likely to be stereotypically negative or at best neutral, women at this stage see their own identities as incongruous with a lesbian identity. This woman lived with another woman for five years, and even felt that they were "married," but still didn't define herself as a lesbian:

> We considered ourselves married, although of course it was unofficial: we were both women. Never did I attach the label "lesbian" to either of us. I rarely thought of the term, and when I did I simply assumed that lesbians were women "out there" who were probably sick or deranged and at any rate were trying to be men. (quoted in Jenness, 2002, p. 138)

Before such a woman can define herself as lesbian, the meaning of the word to her has to change. As the connotations become more positive, the imagery associated with what it means to be a lesbian is likely to be seen as congruent with the individual's lived experiences, thereby making it easier to categorize herself as lesbian. Jenness warns, however, that the redefinition of what it means to be a lesbian is necessary, but not sufficient, for a woman to adopt a lesbian identity. Women can take a variety of different paths to defining themselves as lesbian.

Bisexualities   In a society built around a dichotomy in which people are likely to be categorized as either heterosexual or homosexual, developing a bisexual identity can be difficult. Even researchers have struggled to find evidence that bisexuality actually exists (Denizet-Lewis, 2014). Consider the opening paragraph of an article that appeared in a national newspaper a few years ago:

> In an unusual scientific about-face, researchers at Northwestern University have found evidence that at least some men who identify themselves as bisexual are, in fact, sexually aroused by both men and women (Tuller, 2011, p. 1).

It's hard to imagine such an evidence-based "conclusion" being so prominently expressed about people who identify themselves as heterosexual . . . or homosexual, for that matter.

So it shouldn't surprise us when researchers like sociologist Martin Weinberg and his associates (Weinberg, Williams, & Pryor, 2003) note that people who claim a bisexual identity face significantly more hostility than

even homosexuals because their identity involves the rejection of two recognized categories of sexual identity:

> While the heterosexual world was said to be completely intolerant
> of any degree of homosexuality, the reaction of the homosexual
> world mattered more. Many bisexuals referred to the persistent pres-
> sures they experienced to relabel themselves "gay" or "lesbian" and
> to engage in sexual activity exclusively with the same sex. It was
> asserted that no one was really bisexual, and that calling oneself
> "bisexual" was a politically incorrect and unauthentic identity.
> (Weinberg, Williams, & Pryor, 2003, p. 230)

Weinberg, Williams, and Pryor found that settling into a bisexual identity often occurs many years after one experiences strong sexual attraction
toward both men and women. Self-proclaimed bisexuals initially face a
period of confusion and doubt as they struggle with an identity that doesn't
fit into the two preexisting categories. This period can span years. Eventually, though, they come to see bisexuality as a plausible option and begin
to apply the label to themselves.

What makes bisexuality especially interesting is its lack of social confirmation. Homosexuals and heterosexuals alike often consider bisexuality
to be a transitional identity or worse an immature phase of development.
Indeed, the desire to form a permanent, monogamous relationship with
someone requires that an individual choose one or the other. Some popular
online dating sites—like Match.com, eHarmony, Chemistry.com—even prevent a person from retrieving information about *both* men and women.
Hence, bisexuality continues to be a fluid identity long after its first application. Although most of Weinberg, Williams, and Pryor's subjects indicated
that they didn't think they were in transition from homosexual to heterosexual (or vice versa), they did acknowledge that it was possible that some
time in the future they might identify themselves as either homosexual or
heterosexual. These expectations may simply reflect the power of a cultural
ideology that defines sexual orientation in either/or terms.

LEARNING SOCIAL CLASSES

Conflict and functionalist sociologists alike tend to conceive of social class
as more of a structural position than a component of personal identity. But
just as we must learn to understand the intersections of our race, ethnicity,
gender, and sexuality—and the values, tastes, styles, and behaviors that
derive from those identities—so too must we learn to self-consciously place

ourselves within the broader social stratification system. Aside from those in the upper class, though, who may receive rather specific lessons about their roles in society, the class identity lessons the rest of us learn are usually subtler and more indirect than the lessons we receive for other social identities. Nevertheless, class identity provides us with an important lens through which we see the world and our relative position in it.

The relationship between social class and socialization might appear obvious. For instance, social class begins to affect a child's development even before he or she is born. Poor pregnant women are less likely to receive quality prenatal care and more likely to be exposed to environmental toxins that can harm fetal development than wealthier women (Furstenberg, 2011). As kids grow, some families have greater access than others to the economic resources that are associated with a comfortable childhood: lots of the latest toys and athletic equipment, a nice house, access to a good school, parental support for "appropriate" activities. Children raised in such an environment are likely to reap the benefits that these material advantages create. But access to resources does not, in and of itself, ensure a smooth childhood. In contrast, children who live in unstable or substandard housing or in unsafe neighborhoods and whose parents work long hours but still can't afford the amenities of a healthy life face special burdens—not only in terms of their physical needs but also in terms of the identities they develop. Wealthy and middle-class children come to understand their "place" in society in far different ways than poor children do.

Consider the plight of children who spend some of their early years in homeless shelters. For these children, the expectations most of us take for granted—that we'll have enough food to eat, a place to sleep, and appropriate clothing—are unpredictable. The lack of a permanent home robs them of a comforting daily routine and the opportunity to acquire a strong sense of self-worth (Arrighi, 2002). The sight of a mother or father losing control over the basic needs of life can damage the child's sense of trust and stability. Furthermore, children in homeless shelters don't have the luxury of learning about abstract concepts and ideas—something they're expected to know by the schools they sporadically attend.

Less obvious is the way that class can influence broader cultural ideologies about the socialization of children. Since the beginning of the 20th century, millions of anxious new parents have turned to child rearing books—and later, web sites and blogs—for guidance and reassurance. Parents who tend to use these sources of information have always tended to be at least middle class (Hulbert, 2004). So, when so-called childrearing experts change their advice—from, say, bottle-feeding to breast-feeding or from disciplinary spanking to time-outs—middle-class parents are more likely than poor or working class parents to shift their practices accordingly (Rich, 2011). Middle-class parents also have the cultural and economic resources, as well as the time, to talk with their children, develop their educational interests, and play an active role in their schooling. The outcome is that middle-class parenting styles are more likely to coincide with professional philosophies about appropriate child care and that the parenting approaches available to poor and working class parents will inevitably be seen as inadequate.

Perhaps the most important way that class influences socialization is through its effects on the values held by parents, who pass these values along to their children. Sociologist Melvin Kohn (1979) interviewed 200 American working class and 200 middle-class couples who had at least one child of fifth-grade age. He found that working class parents want their children to be neat and clean and to follow the rules, habits that will help them succeed in blue-collar jobs later on. Conversely, middle-class parents are more likely to promote such values as self-direction, independence, and curiosity. More recent studies have found that middle-class parents are more likely than working class parents to spend more time cultivating their children's language development (Hart & Risley, 1995) and to foster their children's talents through organized leisure activities and logical reasoning (Lareau, 2003). Other researchers have found this tendency especially strong among middle-class mothers (Xiao, 2000).

Obviously, not all middle-class parents or all working class parents raise their children the same way, and many factors other than social class influence parental values and child rearing approaches. Nevertheless, these general tendencies have been found regardless of the sex of the child, the size and composition of the family (Kohn, 1979), or the parents' race (Lareau, 2003). Moreover, others have found that despite cultural differences, this relationship between social class standing and socialization of values exists in Western European societies, namely Germany (Williamson, 1984), non-Western societies, like Japan, and formerly noncapitalist countries, namely, Poland (Schooler, 1996).

Class differences in socialization have important implications for children's futures. Working class parents tend to believe that eventual occupational success, even survival, depends on their children's ability to conform to and obey authority (Kohn, 1979). Middle-class parents believe their children's future success will result from assertiveness and initiative. Hence, middle-class children's feelings of control over their own destiny are likely to be much stronger than those of working class children. In a study of African American women, those from middle-class backgrounds reported that their parents had had higher expectations for them and were more involved in their education than women from working class backgrounds reported (Hill, 1997).

Different parenting values and approaches to child rearing transmit different cultural advantages to children. Take, for instance, how children learn to interact with others. Sociologist Annette Lareau (2003) conducted intensive interviews with 12 families of different racial and class backgrounds. She and her associates visited each family about 20 times over the span of a month. She found subtle, but important, class differences:

> There was quite a bit more talking in middle-class homes than in working-class and poor homes, leading to the development of greater verbal agility, larger vocabularies, more comfort with authority figures, and more familiarity with abstract concepts. Importantly, children also developed skill differences in interacting with authority figures in institutions and at home. Middle-class children . . . learn, as young boys, to shake the hands of adults and look them in the eye. . . . Researchers stress the importance of eye contact, firm handshakes, and displaying comfort with bosses during [job interviews]. In poor families . . . however, family members usually do not look each other in the eye when conversing. . . . They [may] live in neighborhoods where it can be dangerous to look people in the eye too long. (p. 5)

As families climb the class ladder, children's sense of entitlement based on their class identity tends to increase as well. Middle-class children take for granted the right to be involved in activities like organized sports and music lessons, to attend summer school, and to go on class trips. Many of these activities replicate key aspects of the workplace, like meeting new people and learning to work effectively with them. Their travel experiences will give them a level of comfort when, as adults, they're called on to take a trip for business or interact with people from different regions (Lareau, 2003). All of these experiences and the skills that are developed in them will provide a smooth fit with the behaviors and expectations of other social institutions these children will encounter later in their lives.

In upper class families, an even greater sense of entitlement is likely to be transmitted from parents to children. Wealthy parents endow their children with varying amounts of cultural capital (family pedigree, reputations, skills, knowledge, social networks and connections, and so on). Even when not lavished with money and other financial resources, children of affluent parents may inherit other useful resources, such as a recognized family name and the respect, privilege, and personal contacts that go along with it. Upper class children are often taught to value their position and understand the responsibilities that come with it. Other children come to understand the responsibilities of their class position too, but they often absorb messages about their place in society that limit their aspirations.

Intersections
Class, Race, and Motherwork

According to sociologist Patricia Hill Collins (2001), socioeconomic status has long worked in tandem with a history of racial domination and gender inequality to shape the socialization of children. The relative economic security enjoyed by white middle-class mothers means they can devote much of their "motherwork" to tending to the emotional needs of their children. For poor mothers of color, however, child rearing revolves around three different themes:

- *Physical Survival*. Statistically, poor children of color face heightened rates of infant mortality and poverty (if they survive to childhood). In addition, they're more likely than advantaged children to live in environments where drugs, crime, industrial pollutants, and violence pose daily risks. Thus, for poor mothers of color, much of child rearing involves making sacrifices—of time, of their own physical well-being, of self-esteem—simply to ensure that their children are relatively safe and have enough to eat. Ironically, the concern with physical survival may actually mean spending less time with children because of the long hours of work that are necessary.
- *Power*. Poor mothers of color often feel powerless to control their own lives. They face the burden of overcoming the disillusionment and hopelessness that are likely to accumulate over years of interacting with dominant cultural, economic, educational, and political institutions. Furthermore, these institutions place poor mothers of color in positions that make them appear less powerful to their children. For instance, the current welfare system frequently forces poor mothers to choose between working for a wage and spending time with their children. For some groups—namely, African American and Native American women—the struggle for maternal empowerment is made more difficult by their ethnoracial histories of conquest.
- *Identity*. Maintaining a sense of self-worth in their children is a constant struggle for poor mothers of color. They fight to foster

a meaningful racial identity for their children within a society that tends to malign people of color and to teach their children to survive in systems that are not structured to provide them with long-term advantages. This dimension of motherhood is unnecessary among white, middle-class mothers whose children face no such identity challenges. White children may be taught by their parents to fight against racial oppression, but the intactness of their own identity doesn't depend on the outcome of that battle.

The messages children receive about their class standing are, of course, most painful for those at the lower economic rungs of society. When combined with racial and gender disadvantage, class stratification creates special pressures for some parents that other parents are able to avoid.

IDENTITY SOCIALIZATION OUTSIDE FAMILIES

As we saw in the little story at the beginning of this chapter, parents know—or quickly learn—that their ability to mold their children's identities as they see fit is limited. Indeed one of the developmental hallmarks of life in large, complex, industrialized societies is that many forces outside a family's control can influence children. Chief among these external socializing agents are other children (that is, peers) and schools.

PEER INFLUENCE

In everyday interactions, peers—close friends, acquaintances, neighbors, classmates—provide us with extensive information about our social identities. This influence is especially powerful among young people. As much as adults would like to think otherwise, peers have more access to children's everyday lives than just about anyone else. Parents don't usually see their kids at school. Teachers don't usually see their students at home. But peers interact with one another everywhere: in school, at home, on the street, at malls, on sports teams, online, and in a variety of other locations. It's not surprising, then, that as children reach adolescence and struggle to establish an identity distinct from their families, they turn more and more to peers as both a source of information about who they are and a reference point against which they measure themselves.

In many ways, peer groups reinforce the lessons about social identity learned at home, in part because neighborhoods and schools tend to be relatively uniform in social class and ethnoracial makeup. However, peer groups also help young people actively resist the efforts of families to socialize them (Adler & Adler, 1998). For instance, feminist sociologists have found that even children raised in households where they are taught by their parents to believe that men and women are equal and that no activity needs to be sex-linked act in ways that are quite gender stereotypical when they're away from home with their friends and schoolmates (Risman & Myers, 1997).

Similarly, because parental influence with regard to sexual behavior is often weak or nonexistent the development of sexuality tends to be peer-driven. Pressure on teens to become sexually active—and therefore to announce one's sexual identity—is sometimes direct and specific, as when one individual tries to persuade another to have sex. But more commonly, the pressure resides in the charged sexual atmosphere that pervades teen life: fashion, language, music, sexting, computer games, and daily conversation. This sort of environment has enormous influence over adolescent sexual decision making (Rubin, 1990)—from prepubescent chasing and teasing to post-pubescent sexting, sexual contact, dating, and romance. Moreover, this atmosphere is almost exclusively heterosexual. The identity costs of veering from heterosexuality can be especially steep in the teen subculture. As we saw in chapter 3, homosexual slurs and insults on the schoolyard are quite common. They effectively convey the message that non-heterosexual identities are unacceptable and impose heteronormative behavioral expectations and demands.

Peer groups have the power to simultaneously unite and divide. On the one hand, conformity—in terms of appearances, beliefs, and behaviors—is the preeminent characteristic of peer groups. Young people quickly learn the culturally acceptable guidelines and the consequences for violating them (Adler & Adler, 1998). In so doing, they gain a sense of belonging and come to see the commonality between themselves and fellow members who claim similar identities.

On the other hand, peer relations can be relentlessly critical and cruelly stratified, pitting individuals against one another. Attractiveness, prestige, and desirability are relentlessly and meticulously assessed. Groups create elaborate criteria for inclusion and exclusion. Sometimes, these criteria reflect those that divide groups in the larger society, chiefly, gender, race, ethnicity, social class, and sexual orientation. Other times, the criteria are vague, arbitrary, and fluid—the right logo to wear on clothing, for example, which can change in an instant. Although the standards of popularity may vary from neighborhood to neighborhood or even from clique to clique, all peer groups have ways of determining who's in and who's not. Acceptance leads to power and status. But rejection is a sort of social death sentence, especially in adolescence, and has been linked to poor school performance, depression, physical illness, disruptive behavior, and impaired adult relationships (Sunwolf & Leets, 2004).

GENDERED LESSON PLANS

Peer influence over identity socialization is undeniable. But in contemporary industrial societies, the most powerful *institutional* agent of identity socialization—perhaps even more powerful than families—is the educational system. Indeed, the primary reason schools exist is to socialize young people. Children enter the system at about age 5 (or sooner if you count day care and preschool), and most will spend at least the next 13 years of their lives in it. No other institution has such prolonged contact with the bodies and minds of individuals as the educational system.

Schools, of course, don't simply teach students basic educational skills like reading, writing, arithmetic, and science. More subtly, they teach them who they are and what they can expect from themselves and others in the future. In this way, schools can often solidify the identities that children initially developed within their families.

In societies where girls and women are either segregated or formally excluded from educational institutions—such as many fundamentalist Muslim countries—the gender lessons students receive are stark. In U.S. society, female students are no longer prevented or discouraged from receiving an education. Since 1980, more U.S. women than men have enrolled in college and women now earn over 57% of bachelor's degrees (National Center for Education Statistics, 2014a). Moreover, college women study more and have higher grade point averages than men. They're also more likely to complete their bachelor's degrees in 4 or 5 years (cited in Lewin, 2006).

Yet schools at all levels contain an abundance of subtle and not-so-subtle "lessons" about what is considered appropriate and inappropriate behavior for female and male members of our society. In earlier grades, teachers sometimes draw on sex as a basis for sorting students and organizing their activities or casually pit girls against boys for spelling or math competitions (Thorne, 1995). But the differential treatment needn't be so purposeful. As sociologists Myra and David Sadker (2002) point out, "Sitting in the same classroom, reading the same textbook, listening to the same teacher, boys and girls receive very different educations" (p. 583). Research over the past several decades has revealed patterns of differential treatment that create, for girls, a powerfully disabling educational climate:

- Girls receive less teacher attention and less useful feedback than boys.
- Girls talk significantly less in class than boys, and when they do speak up, they are more likely than boys to be reminded to raise their hands.

- Girls rarely see mention of the contributions of women in their text-books, which continue to emphasize male accomplishments.
- Girls are more likely than boys to be the focus of unwanted sexual attention in school. (Sadker, Sadker, Fox, & Salata, 2004)

The consequences of such socialization experiences are neither harmless nor trivial. Take, for instance, the common belief that boys are naturally better at mathematics than girls. Several years ago, a former Harvard University president publicly stated that the reason there are so few female mathematicians is that girls and women lack an "intrinsic aptitude" for math. Cross-cultural evidence, however, shows that many Asian and Eastern European countries consistently produce girls with superior mathematical abilities, while other countries (chiefly the United States) do not (Andreescu, Gallian, Kane, & Mertz, 2008). In fact, girls in developing countries are far more likely than girls in industrialized countries to indicate that they like math and science and would like to work in those fields (Charles, 2011). Even in countries we typically consider repressive when it comes to women's rights—like Iran, Saudi Arabia, and Malaysia—women earn the majority of science degrees (Charles, 2011).

In the United States, girls who excel in national and international math-ematical competitions are likely to be the daughters of immigrants. Research-ers locate the reason for this discrepancy in a culture that doesn't value, actively discourages, or even socially penalizes mathematical excellence in girls. Ironically, research indicates that when given the opportunity girls perform just as well as boys in math (and also science) classes (Hill, Corbett, & St. Rose, 2010; Hyde, Lindberg, Linn, Ellis, & Williams, 2008).

So, it's not surprising that even though as many girls as boys leave high school prepared for coursework in science and mathematics, fewer female than male students actually pursue these majors in college. Just 18.5% of high school students who take the AP exam in computer science are girls and women earn only 12% of college degrees in the field (cited in Miller, 2015). By graduation, men outnumber women in nearly every science and engineer-ing field. For instance, men earn 87% of degrees in engineering fields and two-thirds of degrees in the physical sciences, computer science, mathemat-ics, and statistics (Siebens & Ryan, 2012). The discrepancy increases at the graduate level and ultimately in the workplace. Consequently, men continue to far outnumber women as workers in the fields of science, technology, engineering, and mathematics (Hill, Corbett, & St. Rose, 2010). At compa-nies like Apple, Google, and Facebook, fewer than 20% of the technical employees are women (Miller, 2015). In fact, there are 6% fewer women working in technology today than there were in 1998 (cited in Kantor, 2014).

Segregating the Sexes?   Because boys and girls continue to have different school experiences, some educators have come to the conclusion that mixing them together in school settings may work to the disadvantage of students, especially girls, by reinforcing rather than reducing gender stereotypes. They argue for the establishment of single-sex schools and the inclusion of single-sex classrooms in public schools. They point out that girls who go to single-sex schools are more assertive, more confident, and more likely to take classes in math, computer science, and physics than girls in coeducational schools. Boys in single-sex environments are less likely to get into trouble and more likely to pursue interests in art, music, and drama than their coeducational counterparts (National Association for Single-Sex Public Education, 2013). Furthermore, graduates of single-sex schools—both girls and boys—are more likely to go to prestigious colleges and more likely to attend graduate or professional school than graduates of coeducational high schools (Lee & Marks, 1990).

Same-sex educational environments in public schools have become increasingly popular over the last decade. The Department of Education estimates that there are approximately 750 public schools around the country that offer at least one single-sex class and 850 entirely single-sex public schools (cited in Rich, 2014). Some private schools are now opting for a blend of mixed-sex and single-sex education, with boys and girls learning together in elementary school and high school but being taught separately during the turbulent middle-school years. As one prominent educator put it, "Girls who are 'confident at 11 and confused at 16' will more likely be creative thinkers and risk-takers as adults if educated apart from boys in middle school" (quoted in Gross, 2004, p. A16).

However, not everyone thinks that single-sex education is the answer (Fine, 2010). The American Council for CoEducational Schooling (2011) issued a report showing that girls don't learn any better or faster in a single-sex educational environment than they do in a coeducational setting. Furthermore, critics point out that separating girls and boys based on an assumption that girls can't learn effectively when in the presence of boys may actually promote rather than diminish gender stereotypes.

Intersections
Gender, Race, and Bullying

As I'm sure you're well aware, schools can be hostile places, especially in the teen years when kids are at their mean-spirited best and identities are most fragile. When we think of the torment and harassment that take place within U.S. schools, what tends to come to mind are boys intimidating other boys or harassing girls. Let's face it . . . aggression is the cultural hallmark of masculinity, from childhood to adulthood.

Parents and teachers tend to discourage direct physical aggression in girls (Fagot & Hagan, 1985). So, it might be surprising to learn that young women, particularly in distressed inner-city neighborhoods, can be just as violent as young men and live by the same code that recognizes the importance of a tough reputation and the willingness to retaliate when wronged (Jones, 2010). Indeed, a subculture of girls' aggression and bullying—whether face to face or, more recently, via social network sites and text messaging—is pervasive from elementary school to high school and may be just as harmful as boys' aggression. About 31% of teenage girls are bullied at school and another 11.2% report being cyber-bullied (ProQuest Statistical Abstract, 2015), most of it at the hands of other girls.

Rachel Simmons (2002) interviewed girls between the ages of 10 and 14 in 10 different schools over the span of a year. Some schools were private; others public. Some were predominantly white; others had a majority of black or Latino/a students. Some were coeducational; others were all-girls schools. She talked to students, parents, teachers, and staff in group meetings, one-on-one interviews, over the phone, and by e-mail. She found across all settings that female bullying is commonplace. But it is not the sort of direct physical intimidation that characterizes male bullying. Female bullying frequently focuses on relationships (such as excluding someone socially for revenge, ignoring a person as a form of punishment, sabotaging a friendship, spreading rumors, and so on). The object is not to inflict physical pain but to humiliate the victim socially, destroying the person's reputation, and undermining her self-esteem. As Simmons describes it:

> Girls use backbiting, exclusion, rumors, name-calling, and manipulation to inflict psychological pain on targeted victims. Unlike boys, who tend to bully acquaintances or strangers, girls frequently attack within tightly knit networks of friends, making aggression harder to identify and intensifying the damage to the victims. . . . Girls fight with body language and relationships instead of fists and knives. . . . In this world, friendship is a weapon, and the sting of a shout pales in comparison to a day of someone's silence. There is no gesture more devastating than the back turning away. (Simmons, 2002, p. 3)

Simmons attributes the use of these alternative forms of aggression to the persistent social norms of feminine restraint. However, girls from all races and classes do not feel the power of these norms uniformly. She points out, for instance, that among African Americans, Latinas, and working class white girls, there is a tradition of direct conflict and outspoken "truth telling." Many of the African American and Latina girls she interviewed indicated that they were socialized by their parents to use independence, confidence, and assertiveness to resist the discrimination that they would inevitably face. These girls—from both working class and middle-class backgrounds—made clear distinctions between committed "friends," whom they trusted, and "associates" or acquaintances, whom they didn't trust. The reason given for not trusting them was often that they were "two-faced," meaning that these girls had a tendency to talk behind their backs. But whereas white girls might just accept the behind-the-back whispering that goes on, African American and Latina girls saw such talk as grounds for confrontation. As one African American first-year high school student put it, "You've got to learn how to stick up for yourself. You can't let people push you down." Another said that when she hears that someone is talking about her, she says to that person "If you have something to say, say it to my face" (quoted on p. 187).

Simmons is quick to point out that such general racial tendencies do not apply universally. Not all girls of color were willing to be confrontational when they were harassed or belittled; not all white girls responded passively. One middle-class white student, for instance, recounted an incident in which she and her two sisters were confronted by two other girls: "We did not tolerate any crap, we knocked the shit out of these girls. Don't get me wrong, though, I never looked for, or wanted to fight" (quoted on pp. 179–180).

The intersections of race and class can make girls' responses to bullying particularly difficult. The middle-class African American girls Simmons interviewed consistently reported frustration over the fact that their assertive attempts at bringing out the truth were often rebuffed or punished. The very characteristics they had been taught were signs of strength were likely to be interpreted as "mean" or "bitchy" by others. Although they felt it was important to stand up for themselves, they also felt some reluctance to risk raising the ire of other middle-class students who might then stereotype them as "loud" and "disruptive."

Coaching Masculinities   The vast majority of research on the institutional context of gender socialization (schools, media, and so forth) tends to focus on girls and the structural and interpersonal disadvantages they face growing up in a relatively sexist society. Only recently has academic attention turned to understanding the process by which boys develop gender identities in this society. Although schools provide powerful gender lessons to both boys and girls, masculinity among boys is more likely to develop on the athletic fields than in the classroom. Even though some boys don't like sports and choose not to participate, it is still the case that most boys, to a greater or lesser degree, are judged according to their ability (or lack of ability) in competitive sports.

Sociologist Michael Messner (2002) conducted extensive interviews with 30 adult men from different ethnoracial and class groups who were athletes in their youth. For most of the men Messner interviewed, becoming involved in sports when they were young was not much of a decision. They said they did it simply because "it's just what everybody did." They recounted their earliest experiences with sports as an exclusively male world of fathers, older brothers, uncles, classmates, and coaches who served as athletic role models. Mothers who are present, typically occupy the role of chauffeur or team mom (Messner & Bozada-Deas, 2010). Even fathers who were otherwise absent or emotionally distant tended to be involved in their sons' athletic lives.

Despite the increasing participation of girls in organized sports, the athletic world remains the primary location for the development of traditionally masculine identities because of the heavy emphasis on competition and conquest. It is a hierarchical world where, despite the "it's not whether you win or lose but how you play the game" rhetoric, importance is placed on winning. Just being out there and participating is certainly presented to boys as a good thing, but being better than others is the key to prestige and approval.

Indeed, in most high schools, student culture revolves around sports, especially football. In such an environment, privilege and power are conferred on successful male athletes. Some sociologists and educators fear that high schools are now being pressured to apply an equally aggressive, competitive, masculinized approach to the curriculum as well, through emphases on academic rigor, high-stakes test taking, zero-tolerance discipline policies, and increased efforts in math, science, and technology (Lesko, 2008).

It's especially important to consider the role of race and social class in the relationship between sports and masculinity. For boys from all class levels, family members and peers respond positively to early indicators that they have athletic skills. However, males from ethnoracial minorities or from lower-status backgrounds are more likely than white middle- and upper-class males to see athletic prowess as a survival strategy—a way to improve their economic lot in life. In a middle-class or upper-class environment, boys have more options. By the time they reach high school and beyond, many decide to shift their focus away from sports toward the development of their careers. For them, organized sports are just one of several ways in which they can establish a positive and masculine identity. For lower-status boys, though, the broader social context—education, economy, the community—narrows rather than expands their options later in life. They come to perceive sports as their only option. Sports are the place, rather than a place, within which to construct their masculine identities.

The irony of this emphasis on athletic success in the development of masculinity is that almost all boys who participate in competitive sports will fail at some point in their lives. Only a tiny fraction of athletes ever make it to the top levels of their sports. For instance, about 3% of all graduating seniors who played basketball in high school will play in college; and only half of them will receive some kind of athletic scholarship (Rhoden, 2006). Only three in one thousand high school basketball players are ever *drafted* by an NBA team, let alone become a high-paid star (NCAA, 2013). As one sociologist once remarked, "You have a better chance of getting hit with a meteorite in the next 10 years than getting work as a professional athlete" (quoted in Sage, 2001, p. 283). Disadvantage, despair, and threats to masculinity can multiply in communities where athletic success is presented as the only way to "make it" but where so few actually do.

CLASS AND RACE LESSONS

Schools play an important role in class socialization. In public schools, for instance, working class and poor kids are subtly taught their place through authority relationships with teachers and principals so that they will be prepared for the subordinate work positions they will probably occupy in the future (Bowles & Gintis, 1976). In such environments, students are likely to be closely monitored for behavioral conformity and expected to follow a laundry list of formal and detailed rules. Discipline and compliance with teachers' and administrators' directions are primary goals (Brint, 1998). Furthermore, working class and poor parents may care just as deeply about their child's education as wealthier parents, but because they tend to have limited knowledge about the schooling process and are often unaware of how to approach teachers, they are less likely to intervene on their child's behalf (Lareau & Calarco, 2012). More advantaged students not only have more resources at their disposal, they are likely to speak, dress, and comport themselves in ways that teachers associate with "good students" (Brint, 1998). Consequently, they may receive preferential treatment even from teachers who could be described as fair and open-minded.

Socialization experiences in school are particularly important in the formation of identities for students who come from the highest reaches of the upper class. They frequently spend their childhood in exclusive private schools, their adolescence in boarding schools, and their college years in heavily endowed private universities (Domhoff, 1998). Tuition for elite boarding schools like Andover, Exeter, and Groton can approach or even exceed $50,000 a year. A study of more than 60 such schools in the United States and Great Britain showed how the philosophies, programs, and life-styles of boarding schools help transmit power and privilege (Cookson & Persell, 1985). In addition to the standard curriculum, these schools teach things not likely to be found in public schools, such as conversational etiquette, styles of dress, aesthetic tastes, values, and manners. Required attendance at school functions; participation in esoteric sports, such as lacrosse, squash, and crew; the wearing of school blazers or ties; and other "character-building" activities are designed to teach young people the expected lifestyle of the ruling class into which they were born.

The class identity that emerges from this school experience forms an everlasting social, political, and economic bond among all graduates. In adulthood, graduates connect with one another at the highest levels in the worlds of business, finance, and government. In this way, the privileged social status that is produced and maintained through the elite educational system practically guarantees that the people who occupy key political and economic positions will form a like-minded, cohesive group with little resemblance to the majority whose lives depend on their decisions.

Race is also an integral part of the school experience. In 1954, the U.S. Supreme Court ruled in *Brown v. Board of Education of Topeka* that racially segregated schools were unconstitutional because they were inherently unequal. School districts around the country were placed under court order to desegregate, often through forced busing. But within the past 10 years, courts have lifted desegregation orders in at least three dozen school districts around the country. In 2007, the Supreme Court reversed itself and ruled that public school systems could not try to achieve or maintain integra-tion through actions that take explicit account of students' race. At the time of the ruling, such programs were in place in hundreds of school districts around the country (Greenhouse, 2007). Some districts, recognizing the intersections of race and class, have resorted to using integration plans based on children's socioeconomic disadvantage, rather than race, to skirt these restrictions (Bazelon, 2008).

You might assume that the court took this action because desegregation plans based on students' race were no longer needed. However, African American and Latino/a students are actually more isolated from white stu-dents today than they were 30 years ago. The average black student attends a school in which 73% of students are not white and the average Latino/a student attends a school in which at least 75% of the students are not white (Orfield, Frankenberg, Ee, & Kuscera, 2014). In contrast, the average white student attends a school in which almost 72.5% of the students *are* white (Orfield, et al., 2014).

And it's not just students who are segregated. According to government estimates, 82% of public school teachers and 88% of private school teachers nationwide are white (National Center for Education Statistics, 2013). In general, white teachers have very little experience with racial diversity. They are likely to teach in schools where almost 90% of their faculty colleagues and over 70% of the students are white (Frankenberg, 2006).

Schools where the majority of students are not white are likely to be schools where poverty is concentrated. Almost 86% of schools in which black and Latino/a students represent more than 90% of the enrollment are also schools in which more than half the students came from poor families. This is not the case with majority-white schools, which almost always enroll high proportions of middle-class students. Just 12% of schools with less than 10% black and Latino/a students are schools where a majority of students are poor (Frankenberg, 2006).

The racial and class mix of schools has important implications for the quality of the education students receive. Racial segregation has long been associated with lower academic performance and lack of preparation for the interracial world that awaits students of color after graduation (Kleinfield, 2012). Schools in poor communities of color lack the financial and therefore educational resources that schools in more affluent communities have. For instance, 81% of Asian-American students and 71% of white students attend high schools that offer the full range of math and science courses (Algebra I, geometry, Algebra II, calculus, biology, chemistry, physics). However, less than half of Native American students, 57% of black students and 67% of Latino/a students have access to these courses. Furthermore, black, Latino, and Native American students are three times as likely as white students to attend schools that have high concentrations of first year teachers; they're also significantly likely to take classes from teachers with credentials in the subjects they're teaching (U.S. Department of Education, 2014). Such schools have more unstable enrollments, higher dropout rates, and more students with untreated health problems. Despite attempts to rectify the problem, black and Latino/a students still lag behind white and Asian students at all levels of the educational system (ProQuest Statistical Abstract, 2015).

Even when students perform well in school, social class and race can influence future outcomes. High school seniors who score between 1200 and

1600 on the SAT test *and* who come from families with incomes in the wealthiest 25% of households have an 82% chance of graduating from college. However students who score that well but who come from families in the poorest 25% have only a 44% chance of graduating. In fact, these students are actually less likely to get a college degree than wealthy students who score between 800 and 999 on the SAT (52%; Carnevale & Strohl, 2010).

Lack of money isn't the only problem, however. Common institutional assumptions and practices within the educational system can also lead to unequal outcomes. For instance, nationwide, black students are significantly more likely than other students to be subjected to disciplinary practices in school. According to 2012 data from the U.S. Department of Education, black students made up 18% of those enrolled in the schools that were studied, yet they accounted for 35% of one-time suspensions, 46% of multiple suspensions, and 39% of expulsions. Twelve percent of black girls in elementary and secondary schools are suspended, compared to 2% of white girls (cited in Vega, 2014). Black and Latino/a students, particularly those with disabilities, are also more likely to be subjected to seclusion and physical restraints than Whites who exhibit similar behavioral problems (cited in Lewin, 2012). And because of the growing popularity of get-tough, zero tolerance policies, students who exhibit behavioral problems are increasingly likely to wind up in the criminal justice system. Here too, race plays a role. Nationwide, 70% students who are arrested for misdemeanor offenses at school or referred to the courts are black or Latino/a (cited in Alvarez, 2013).

Consider also the widespread use of standardized tests, which are often used as the basis for *tracking* students—that is, assigning them to different educational programs based on their intellectual abilities. Standardized tests supposedly measure innate intelligence. Many educational experts agree, however, that these tests are culture bound, tapping an individual's familiarity with a specific range of white, middle-class experiences rather than indicating innate intelligence (Hout & Lucas, 2001). Hence, members of ethnoracial minorities consistently score lower on these tests than Whites (C. Jencks & Phillips, 1998).

Despite the potential for bias, more and more states across the country require high school students to pass a standardized test to graduate. At the same time, though, many universities and other educational organizations have begun seeking alternative ways to determine eligibility for admission. For instance, some universities now use a "strivers" approach, whereby college applicants whose SAT scores fall in the borderline range for many selective colleges but who manage to exceed the historical average for students from similar backgrounds are deemed "strivers" and given special consideration (Kahlenberg, 2013). The Texas legislature went a step further, ordering the University of Texas system to accept all students who graduate in the top 10% of their class, regardless of their SAT scores. In 1999, a U.S. district court judge ruled that the NCAA (National Collegiate Athletic Association) could no longer use SAT scores to determine athletic eligibility. The court concluded that the test is culturally biased and therefore discriminates against underprivileged students.

CONCLUSION

One of the things that I hope you take from this chapter is the knowledge that the very essence of who we are—our gender, our racial and class identity, our sexuality—is not private property. All of us in one way or another are a reflection of larger cultural values, historical processes, and the attitudes and expectations of other people in our lives. This realization can be humbling and frightening. It would be more comforting to think that who we become is solely a product of our own doing—either in the form of our genetic predispositions or as a result of our personal hopes, dreams, and desires. If this were the case, we would have a great deal of control over what and who we become.

But social life is never that simple. Broader values surrounding gender, sexuality, race, and class will always determine how we incorporate those features of our identity into our own self-concept. If we're lucky enough to occupy the most advantaged locations on all these dimensions, chances are our lives will be comfortable, our self-concepts will be positive, and our prospects for a successful future will be bright. However, if we happen to occupy a devalued category, we face an uphill struggle. We can—and hopefully would—take pride in our gender, our race and ethnicity, and our sexuality and extract from these components a strong sense of self-esteem. But if that esteem is undermined at the cultural and institutional levels, our pride will not automatically translate into greater social, economic, educational, and political opportunities.

[**INVESTIGATING IDENTITIES AND INEQUALITIES**]
Go to your room! Race, gender, and childhood discipline

You've seen in this chapter that early ethnoracial, gender, sexual, and class identities are usually formed in families. Children receive implicit and explicit instruction from parents and other relatives in meeting the cultural expectations associated with these features of their identity.

This exercise involves brief interviews with fellow students. Try to interview at least five to eight people. Select a variety of individuals so that you have a mix of genders, races, and ethnicities. Ask them a series of questions about their experiences growing up. The following questions are some examples. You needn't use all of them, and you can alter the wording to fit the circumstances of particular respondents. You may also add other questions that you think would work better.

- From the time you were born to the time you entered college, in which of the following living arrangements did you spend most of your childhood?

  - living with both biological parents
  - living with one biological parent and a stepparent
  - living with one parent
  - living with another adult caretaker (for instance, grandparents)

- How many siblings do you have? How many lived with you while growing up (that is, until you entered college)?
- Can you recall your parent(s) or adult caretaker(s) ever talking to you about your race or your ethnicity? What is your earliest memory of such a conversation? What did it entail?
- Can you recall your parent(s) or adult caretaker(s) ever talking to you about being female (or male)? Can you recall them ever providing explicit instructions on how to act as a girl (or boy)? Describe.
- Can you recall your parent(s) or adult caretaker(s) ever talking to you about sexuality? If so, what assumptions do you recall them making about the sexual orientation of your future partners?
- In general, how would you describe your relationship with your parent(s) or adult caretaker(s)?

  - very warm and close
  - warm and close
  - somewhat distant
  - very distant

- All children get into trouble from time to time. How did your parent(s) or adult caretaker(s) discipline you when you engaged in behavior they didn't like?

You can either record or write down responses you get. Another option would be to have respondents send their answers to you via e-mail.

Once you've gathered your answers, look for patterns in people's responses. Are there any systematic differences in the way that men and women answered the questions? Were women more likely than men to receive "traditional" gender socialization messages or was it the other way around? What about racial/ethnic differences? Were certain ethnoracial groups more or less likely to be subjected to harsh physical discipline? What about the "race messages" they received? Can you determine if your respondents' sense of inferiority or superiority (based on either race or gender) was cultivated by their parents or caretakers? You should always be cautious about drawing general conclusions from information provided by a small group of people. But based on the responses to your questions, see if you can gain some insight into the role that families play in young people's racial and gender socialization.

Note: All colleges and universities require that a campus or departmental review committee approve any student research project involving human subjects—even if it just entails asking people some questions. For instance, you will probably be required to show that your interviewees have consented to participate and that you've guaranteed that their identities will not be divulged. Make sure you talk to your instructor before proceeding with this exercise to see what steps you have to take in order to have it approved by the appropriate campus committee.

Inequalities

Race, class, gender, and sexuality are more than just note-worthy features of our social identities. If that's all they were, differences between groups would be nothing more than . . . well . . . differences between groups. But social identities are always related to unequal access to life chances.

Part 2 examines how the intersections of race, class, gender, and sexuality contribute to advantages and disadvantages in our dealings with others and in our institutional opportunities for financial well-being, legal protection, and a healthy life. ■

CHAPTER 5

Inflicting Inequalities
Prejudice and Discrimination in Everyday Life

When I was 9 years old, my family moved from a suburb just outside of New York City to a suburb just outside Los Angeles. The move represented many changes for us. My father's company had gone out of business and he was going to start a new job in California, managing a dry-cleaning store that one of his brothers owned. We went from living in a nice house in a middle-class subdivision to living in a small, cramped, nondescript apartment right across the street from the perpetually busy Ventura Freeway.

On the first day of school (I was just starting fourth grade), I immediately realized that I was different from the other kids. In New York, everyone I knew—my relatives, my friends, my schoolmates, and my neighbors—was like me, racially and religiously. My family is Jewish, though not particularly religious. In the New York community where I had lived, public schools closed on the Jewish holidays in October. Back there, I didn't know anyone close to me who wasn't white or Jewish.

In California, I was an outsider. I'd never gone to school with kids who wore crosses or St. Christopher medals around their necks. Many of my fellow students were Latino/a. They had names that sounded different from any I'd heard before. They spoke with unusual accents. Going to a new school is always a somewhat traumatic experience. But I felt like I had landed in a completely different world. The first few days, I ate lunch alone. I found myself wishing we'd never moved. But I figured sooner or later it had to get better.

When the 3:00 bell rang that first Friday, I was gleeful. The first week of school was mercifully over, and a weekend of rest and relaxation awaited. My escape was thwarted, however, by another fourth-grader who stopped me as I approached the schoolyard gate. Aside from brief kickball-related encounters during recess, I hadn't ever spoken to this kid. He was much bigger than me, which was not all that surprising since at that time I was pretty small for my age. He looked like every bully I'd ever seen on TV. It wouldn't have surprised me if his name was Butch or Rocky or Spike.

He asked me what my name was and I told him. "Hey, you're a *new . . . man* around here! Get it?" He laughed at his own joke, apparently convinced that combining my last name with my status in the school was hilarious.

"Yeah, I am," I replied, "Good one."

He squinted at me and asked, "So what are you, *New Man?*"

At first, I didn't know what he was getting at and flashed a "What do you mean?" look.

"You know, what church does your family go to?"

I paused. "I don't think we go to a church."

In retrospect, this equivocal response was pretty stupid, I know. Either you go or you don't go. But I was surprised by the question so I choked a bit.

"Everybody goes to church!" he shouted in disbelief. At this point, a few other kids—his henchmen, I surmised—began to mill around. "So which one do you go to?" For some reason, he decided that pressing me with the same question, only louder, would produce the response he was looking for.

"I told you, we don't go to church," I said with all the sternness I could muster.

He looked at me as if I'd just spoken in tongues and pivoted away, no doubt baffled by what to him was an incomprehensible response. Maybe he thought I came from a family of atheists and would leave. I could live with that.

But after a few steps, he spun around with a "Hey-wait-a-minute!" kind of look on his face. "Are you a Jew, New Man?! Are you a *Jew Man?!*" More evil laughs from his entourage.

In retrospect, I wish I had said something a movie tough guy would say, like "Yeah. What's it to you, punk!? You wanna make something of it!?" Instead, I just nodded feebly, vainly trying not to call attention to what I was quickly realizing was my seriously spoiled identity.

He paused for a second as if to weigh the magnitude of this new information. Then he punched me in the face and walked away.

It's been over 45 years since this incident occurred, and it still makes my stomach flip to think about it. I've wondered a lot about why exactly it happened and what I could have done to stop it. The physical sting of his blow (which harmlessly landed on my cheekbone) wasn't nearly as painful as the humiliation I felt. Why was being Jewish such a punishable offense? How could he work up such hostility without knowing anything about me, other than my religion? There were hardly any Jews in this area. So it was unlikely that I reminded him of other kids in school he already despised. Maybe his parents were neo-Nazi sympathizers who taught him to hate Jews and other people of different religions. In the end, I resigned myself to the discomforting fact that I got punched in the face by someone who probably had no clue as to why he was doing it.

While his motivation has always remained a mystery to me, what was distinctly not mysterious was that I had been tagged as an outsider. Like most kids that age, all I wanted was to blend in. Being the new kid in school was bad enough. Being the new kid who was different from everyone else was childhood hell.

As fate would have it, a few days later, I was standing in line at an ice cream truck after school. A girl standing in front of me turned around and out of the blue asked, "What religion are you?" This time I was ready. I had learned my lesson. I didn't hesitate. "I'm Catholic," I lied.

Perhaps the most insidious aspect of being targeted on the basis of some aspect of social identity—be it race, ethnicity, class, gender, sexuality, or religion—is the effect it has on one's self-concept. From that day on— through the rest of elementary school and well into high school—I tried mightily to hide my ethnic/religious identity. I became ashamed of who I was. Of course, my closest friends knew and accepted me (though I did get annoyed by their constant attempts to fix me up with the one Jewish girl in our high school). But for everyone else, I denied, I evaded, and I concealed. I became quite adept at anticipating the trajectory of conversations, and if I sensed that talk was veering toward religion or some other topic that might reveal my identity, I'd deftly shift it to something safer. It was a stressful existence, to be sure. Although what happened to me from fourth grade through high school may not match the intensity of the deep personal hatred and institutional disadvantage felt by racial, ethnic, gender, and sexual minorities, it did show me the external hostility and internal self-loathing that can arise from day-to-day dealings with difference and inequality.

In this chapter, I will examine the personal experience of prejudice and discrimination. It will serve as an introduction to the remaining chapters of this part of the book, which will examine in more detail the inequalities that exist in a variety of institutional areas of human life, including the economy and work, law and justice, and health and illness. With all due respect to the crafters of the Declaration of Independence, opportunities to achieve life and liberty and to pursue happiness have never been distributed equally in this country. Although some groups have been able to transcend the status of "despised minority," others continue to suffer. The disadvantages some groups must cope with exist on several levels, ranging from the very personal level of individual perceptions, feelings, and face-to-face interactions to their contacts with the long-standing institutional structure of society itself.

STEREOTYPES: THE BUILDING BLOCKS OF BIGOTRY

The early 20th-century political commentator Walter Lippmann (1922) was one of the first writers to use the word **stereotype,** which he defined as an oversimplified picture of the world, one that satisfies our need to see our social environment as a more understandable and manageable place than it really is. It is the overgeneralized belief that a certain trait, behavior, or attitude characterizes all members of some identifiable group. Stereotypes usually take the form "All _____ are _____."

While ethnoracial, religious, gender, and sexual stereotypes are the most familiar, other social groups can easily be the object of cultural stereotyping. Take, for instance, the blue-collar and service workers who occupy the "undignified," low-paying jobs that keep society going. Often referred to as "unskilled" workers, these individuals are consistently marginalized either by more affluent people who treat them as if they are invisible or by widely held cultural stereotypes that they are unintelligent and unrefined. Because there's a perception that the work itself is mindless, there's a belief that those who do it aren't that bright. Asked why the public is so disdainful of the working-class women who are hired to clean other people's homes, two maids replied, "They think we're stupid. They think we have nothing better to do with our time. We're nothing to these people. We're just maids" (quoted in Ehrenreich, 2001, p. 100).

Although there may be a kernel of truth to stereotypes, they are never completely accurate. For instance, low-wage "unskilled" occupations often require an enormous amount of knowledge, judgment, and talent (Rose, 2004). Hairstylists, for example, must show an astounding amount of aesthetic and mental agility when they turn vague requests ("I want something light and summery") into an actual hairstyle pleasing to the customer. They must also have command of a remarkable range of knowledge—nutrition, hair growth patterns, the biology of skin, chemicals, and popular culture images of beauty—in order to provide their customers not only with a look they want but with advice on how to maintain a stylish appearance.

Casual observations easily refute the accuracy of even the most common stereotypes. Not all African Americans are poor and on welfare. Not all Italians belong to the Mafia. Not all Asian Americans excel in mathematics. Not all Muslims are terrorists. Not all men are emotionally inaccessible. Not all homosexuals are fastidious. Not all wealthy people exploit the less advantaged. Overgeneralizations such as these can never be true for every member of that group.

THE NORMALITY OF STEREOTYPES

Our brains have a tendency to divide the world into distinct categories: good and bad, strong and weak, them and us (Rothenberg, 1992). Thus, we could say that stereotyping is a universal feature of human thought (Hamilton, 1981). By allowing us to focus on traits people have in common and to group them into easily identifiable categories, stereotypes make the processing of information and the formation of impressions more efficient. We can (and frequently do) construct stereotypes for every conceivable group into which we can place people. We stereotype people on the basis of the region of the country they come from, the type of car they drive, their clothing, or their hair color/style. As a college student, you have no doubt learned an entire repertoire of stereotypes that refer to different segments of your campus population: students who major in certain subjects, participate in certain sports or clubs, or live in certain dorms or Greek houses. Likewise, you've probably identified the appearances and behaviors that characterize professors. You might even make fine character distinctions, say, between sociology professors and physics professors.

Stereotypes can be quite resistant to change. They set expectations even in the absence of any confirmatory evidence and persist even in the face of contradictory evidence. If you believe that all professors are dull eggheads who wear unfashionable clothing and are totally out of touch with modern culture then you'll probably be reluctant to seek out a professor for advice on problems you're having with your friends. Knowing one professor who is hip, insightful about such matters, and has an active Twitter account is probably not going to be enough to abandon the more general stereotype entirely, and that person will likely be dismissed as an exception to the rule.

While such occupational stereotypes may influence—and even impede—interactions between individuals, they lack the broader societal significance of ethnic, religious, racial, class, gender, or sexual stereotypes. We learn these stereotypes at young ages, from our families, from the media, and from peers. Consequently, they have become fixtures on the social landscape, working their way into our thoughts and conversations, cultural imagery, and the everyday workings of larger organizations and institutions in society.

THE NEGATIVITY OF POSITIVE STEREOTYPES

Ironically, even apparently positive stereotypes can work to a group's disadvantage. Although positive stereotypes may seem harmless or humorous, they may actually be more likely than unfavorable stereotypes to go unquestioned and to trigger beliefs in the biological or "natural" foundations of group differences (Kay, Day, Zanna, & Nussbaum, 2013). Take, for instance, the characterization of Asian Americans as a "model minority" and the belief that women are naturally kind and nurturing. On the surface, these stereotypes seem complimentary. But a closer look shows how they can create damaging expectations and limit people's freedom to be unique individuals.

A "Model Minority"   The irony of race and ethnicity for Chinese, Japanese, Koreans, Vietnamese, Cambodians, Laotians, Indians, and other Asian groups is that they are often perceived as "model minorities" or "America's greatest success story." For instance, the average total SAT scores for Asian American high school seniors is 1656, compared with 1576 for Whites and 1486 for the general population (National Center for Fair & Open Testing, 2014). Fifty-three percent of Asian Americans complete college, compared to 32% of Whites, and their average household income is actually higher than that of the population as a whole (ProQuest Statistical Abstract, 2015).

But the expectations and resentment associated with being the "model minority" can be as confining and oppressive as those created by more negative stereotypes. Here's how one Asian American college student describes her experience:

> I feel as though I, along with others, am boxed in by this stereotype because even though it's easy to just ignore assumptions that I'm as smart as I'm "supposed" to be, it's hard to ignore that I'm regarded as smart only because I am Asian. And it's even harder to ignore that I'm not "Asian enough" if I struggle academically. Stereotypes are inevitable, but something like intelligence can be so important to a person's life that attributing it merely to race and disguising it as a compliment is more than a stereotype—it's an outright insult (Yook, 2014, p. 1).

By characterizing Asian American success as natural and expected, the model minority stereotype downplays the problems Asian Americans continue to face in all areas of public and private life. Recall, for example, that the term *Asian American* encompasses dozens of groups—from Japanese and Chinese to Pakistani and Indian to Hmong, Sri Lankan, Nepalese, and Laotian. While some members of some of these groups may be educationally or economically successful, others aren't. For instance, between 2007 and 2011, only 5.8% of Filipino-Americans lived below the poverty line; however, 15% of Vietnamese and Korean-Americans were poor (Macartney, Bishaw, & Fontenot, 2013). In Minnesota and Alaska, at least 50% of Asian elementary school students are below basic reading levels (Lepkowska, 2004). Most Indian and Pakistani adults have earned bachelor's degrees; but most Cambodian adults never finish high school (The College Board, 2008). Furthermore, the model minority stereotype portrays Asian American success as proof that the United States provides equal opportunities for those who conform and work hard, even though many ethnoracial groups continue to suffer.

Asian American stereotypes are part of a broad continuum of no-win attitudes toward people of color in this society:

> When Blacks don't make it, it's because . . . their culture doesn't teach respect for family; because they're hedonistic, lazy, stupid, and/or criminally inclined. But when Asians demonstrate their ability to overcome the obstacles of an alien language and culture, when the Asian family seems to be the repository of our most highly regarded traditional values, white hostility doesn't disappear. . . . [Instead,] the accomplishments of Asians . . . [are] credited . . . to the fact that they're "single minded," "untrustworthy," "clannish drones," "narrow people" who raise children who are insufficiently "well rounded." (Rubin, 1994, p. 188)

The model minority image can also turn ugly when equated with perceptions that Asians are over-studious loners who can't be trusted. These stereotypes bubbled to the surface in the immediate aftermath of the 2007 massacre at Virginia Tech University, in which a Korean American student went on a rampage and killed 32 people. Although it turned out that the gunman suffered from serious mental problems and the feared anti-Korean backlash never materialized, media portrayals continued to highlight both his ethnicity and his lack of social skills, perpetuating the idea that shy, bookish Asian American college students might be ticking time bombs.

The Lady and the Good Mother   A book on inequalities, like this one, inevitably focuses on the groups in the racial, ethnic, gender, and class stratification systems that face disadvantage. Surely compared with men, women face more economic, educational, physical, and cultural obstacles. But while all that is true, it's also the case that some stereotypes seem to exalt women. For instance, it's commonly believed that women are kinder, gentler, more nurturing, and more refined than men. Often women are compared favorably with nasty, brutish, aggressive, slovenly men. So when women act in ways that are distinctly unkind or brutal, the response can be harsh. In 2009, a female soccer player at the University of New Mexico was caught on tape yanking an opposing player to the ground by her ponytail during a game. Media pundits seemed fixated on trying to figure out how *a woman* could do such a thing. She was immediately kicked off the team but not before she became the poster child for all that is wrong with college athletics. A British commentator called her the "dirtiest soccer player ever." But had she been a man, I doubt there would have been such a reaction. Indeed, a few months earlier, on national television, a football player at the University of Oregon walked across the field after a game and punched an opposing player square in the face. He was initially suspended, but was eventually reinstated. He now makes $865,000 a year playing in the NFL. Somehow his violence didn't seem as inexplicable or problematic as hers. After all, he's a man and men do this sort of thing.

The more serious problem with the "women are nice and polite" stereotype is that these positive characteristics do not serve women's economic interests. Professional women who are perceived as "soft and cuddly" aren't considered tough enough to be competitive in the business world or decisive enough to be effective organizational leaders (Deveny, 2009).

When it comes to positive gender stereotypes, though, few have more collective support than the belief that women are anatomically and hormonally predisposed to be better parents than men. Although this "good mother" stereotype only rose to prominence in the late 19th and early 20th centuries (Gillis, 1996), most people today simply take for granted that women are built to be mothers and that they possess some kind of maternal instinct that is an unalterable and universal fact of nature. As such, women tend to be guided and judged by a different set of parenting expectations than men.

Given the lofty status that family and parenthood enjoy in this society, the belief that women naturally make better parents than men should translate into elevated cultural approval for mothers. But the belief that women are innately inclined to be parents means that some people see female child-bearing and childrearing as rather unremarkable. While people still may marvel at the sight of a father pushing a stroller in a park or changing a diaper in a shopping mall bathroom, mothers engaging in such activities rarely elicit such a response. Their actions are far from praiseworthy; they're simply what mothers are meant to do.

Not surprisingly, the women who are most culturally noticeable in this society are those who don't become mothers in the first place—whether by choice or not—or who are less-than-perfect parents when they do have children. These women are especially likely to be pitied, maligned, or looked on with suspicion (Hays, 1996). The criminal prosecution of women who drink alcohol or take other drugs while pregnant, the desire on the part of some lawmakers to limit women's access to legal abortion, and public concern over the negative consequences on children of mothers working outside the home illustrate the power and the paradox of stereotypical expectations regarding women and motherhood.

Ironically, at the same time women are expected or at least encouraged to become mothers, they often suffer financially from parenthood (Crittenden, 2001). According to the Organization for Economic Co-operation and Development, employed mothers—in most developed countries, not just the United States—earn, on average, 14% less than employed women without children (cited in Kornbluh, 2012). One study that charted the work experiences of about 5,000 American women over a 10-year period found that on average mothers see their wages reduced by 7% per child (Budig & England, 2001). The penalties are actually larger for married mothers than for unmarried mothers. The researchers concluded that only about one-third of this penalty is attributable to deficiencies in past work experience or lack of seniority. They suggest that the bulk of the reduction in wages results either from the long-term effects of motherhood on productivity or from employer discrimination. Hence, we can see that what appear on the surface to be positive stereotypes about women and motherhood are actually linked to the broader gender inequalities that exist in society.

Intersections

The Strong Black Woman

Black women have more trouble paying their bills and getting loans than white women and many worry that they lack the necessary skills and education to compete for jobs (Mui & Jenkins, 2014). Yet one of the defining characteristics of black women in the United States is strength. A nationwide poll conducted by the *Washington Post* reveals a portrait of contemporary black women as confident, resilient, empowered, and self-assured. As one woman put it, "I can go to school. I can be successful. I can make money. I can have a career. That is in my power to control (quoted in Thompson, 2012, p. 1).

Historically, the cultural image of the "Strong Black Woman" has been one of a tireless, stoic, deeply caring, invulnerable woman who perseveres through all sorts of adversity (Beauboeuf-Lafontant, 2009). Prominent social activists like Harriet Tubman, Fannie Lou Hamer, and Rosa Parks are exemplars of this image; the embodiment of courage and self-less devotion to helping those in need.

This stereotype has actually been around, in one form or another, for centuries. Dating back to the time of slavery, the "Mammy" image presented poor black women as stout, diligent, and hard working. But the ability to endure in harsh conditions was attributed not to some kind of superior or noble quality, but to their subhuman, animal-like nature. Physical strength allegedly provided black women with extraordinary stamina. But like the beasts of burden they were likened to, physical strength rendered them intellectually and morally inferior. Such an image contrasted sharply with another popular image of femininity at the time: the delicate, but morally superior upper class white woman, whose physical frailty was a by-product of a refined and civilized lifestyle (Ehrenreich & English, 1989).

After slavery and well into the 20th century, the "Strong Black Woman" solidified her position at the center of African American families. Continuing social, legal, and economic exclusion made it difficult for black men to find employment adequate enough to support their families or to maintain their dominance in them. Survival dictated that black women enter the labor force, which they did in large numbers. In 1900, 41% of black women were in the paid labor force, compared with 16% of white women (cited in Staples, 1992). Hence, black families often coalesced around a strong maternal presence. By the 1950s and 1960s, the domineering and controlling matriarch became a popular stereotype of black family structure.

However, like any stereotype, the image of the "Strong Black Woman" has its limitations, inaccuracies, and painful consequences. Because the idea of strength appears to celebrate accomplishments made in the face of unfavorable or even hostile social conditions, the concept seems to be an honorable, respectful recognition of the unforgiving reality of their lives. However, the characterization of black female strength is a double-edged sword that, while admirable, defends the current stratified social order by obscuring black women's continuing experiences of suffering, desperation, and anger. As we'll see in Chapter 6, black women still find themselves at the bottom of the U.S. pay scale. Sociologist Tamara Beauboeuf-Lafontant interviewed 58 black women ranging in age from 19 to 67. She found that behind the image of strength, lurked a darker reality, one marked by unexpressed vulnerability, anxiety, and depression. Living up to the expectation of strength can take its toll. As one of her interviewees put it,

> A lot of people tell me that [I'm strong]. Like when my mom passed, I didn't cry. . . . And one of my brothers said that, "I've never seen her cry." . . . I lost my husband . . . ten years ago. I haven't been married [since]. . . . My family . . . [thinks] that I'm keeping everything under control, so I'm a strong person, despite whatever. Even though deep down inside, you don't be feeling that way. You be feeling like life is just biting you up or something. (p. 4)

Another woman talked about trying to juggle the perception that she is a strong, capable person who is always available to tend to others' needs with the reality that she has needs of her own:

> I hide my emotions a lot. So I think when people see you doing good from the outside, they think you're a strong person. . . . I think I like the idea when people see me as a strong person. . . . I want people to look at me as a person [they can go to] . . ., but at the same, I really want them to leave me the hell alone. (p. 5)

Such is the dilemma of this seemingly positive "Strong Black Woman" stereotype. If she lives up to the image of strength, her problems, needs, fears, and vulnerabilities remain unknown to others and she is left on her own to deal with them. If she admits to weakness, she risks being dismissed or disregarded by others for not living up to the very powerful cultural expectation of self-reliance.

PREJUDICE: PERCEIVING INEQUALITIES

Stereotypes, in and of themselves, are merely cognitive mechanisms we all use to find commonalities among groups and to simplify our perceptual worlds. Hence, they can be positive or negative or even neutral. When they become the basis for a set of rigidly held, unfavorable judgments, beliefs, and feelings about members of another ethnoracial, gender, class, or sexual group, however, they constitute **prejudice**, an attitude with an emotional, evaluative bias (Allport, 1954).

Prejudice tends to ebb and flow as social conditions change. When people's self-interest, sense of cultural integrity, and economic livelihood are threatened—by either the real or the perceived infiltration of others—prejudicial attitudes tend to become more open and hostile. For instance, widespread anti-Catholic sentiment became especially virulent in the late 19th and early 20th centuries as waves of Catholic immigrants entered the country looking for a better life. Native Protestants characterized Catholics—especially those from Ireland and Italy—as drunken, lower-class louts who would destroy the sanctity of the country. The passage in 1919 of the 18th Amendment prohibiting the use of alcohol marked, in part, a cultural victory of traditional, rural, middle-class Protestants over urban, lower-class Catholics (Gusfield, 1963). Financial stress can exacerbate such prejudices. As one out-of-work white auto mechanic put it, it's bad enough to have to compete with a white man for a job. "But a black guy? It would mean you lost a job to someone that everybody knows is lower than you" (quoted in Feagin, Vera, & Batur, 2000, p. 40).

Specific historical events can also shape prejudices. The equation of Muslims with violent terrorism has been a common attitude for decades, dating back to the murder of 11 Israeli athletes during the 1972 Summer Olympics in Munich. But the September 11, 2001 attacks—as well as more recent incidents in Paris, Brussels, and San Bernardino, California—have served to bolster anti-Muslim prejudice. In one study of teachers' attitudes shortly after the attacks, relatively few of the respondents knew much about Islam. Nonetheless, one-third of them associated the word Islam with terms like terrorists, enemy, trouble, and war (Mastrilli & Sardo-Brown, 2002). Another study found that a high level of anti-Islamic imagery in the media supported the negative portrayal of Muslims and helped to fuel the belief that all Muslims are terrorists (Khalema & Wannas-Jones, 2003). Indeed, these prejudices have become so common that the mere suggestion that someone is a Muslim can sometimes be enough to disparage that person. False rumors that Barack Obama is a Muslim dogged him throughout the 2008 election and continued during the 2012 election. A 2012 poll found that after four years in the White House less than half of Americans accurately identified Obama as Christian

(Bingham, 2012). The fact that he and his representatives felt this allegation had to be denied reinforced its negative status in the culture.

A recent poll found that favorability toward Muslim-Americans actually declined from 36% to 27% between 2010 and 2014 (cited in Siddiqui, 2014). And the situation is not limited to this country. A similar anti-Muslim backlash occurred in England following the 2005 subway bombings in London and in Paris following the December 2015 bombings there. In a recent election in Switzerland, the tiny Swiss People's Party sponsored ads in which three white sheep push one black sheep off the Swiss flag. They won almost 30% of the vote (Feldman, 2008). Hatred of Muslims is growing so rapidly in Europe that one columnist drew parallels to the prejudices of Nazi Germany in the 1930s and 1940s by stating that, "Muslims are the new Jews of Europe" (Cengiz, 2009, p. 15).

There is some evidence that blatant and highly publicized expressions of prejudice in the U.S. are becoming increasingly likely to be denounced by the general public. In 2014 alone, several high profile incidents of outright bigotry brought swift condemnation online and in the news media:

- The police commissioner of Wolfeboro, New Hampshire publicly called President Obama a *nigger.* Initially he remained steadfast and unapologetic. However, after a cascade of complaints from around the country, he relented and resigned (Seelye & Bidgood, 2014).
- Cliven Bundy, a Nevada cattle rancher who made headlines for his public confrontation with the government over grazing fees on federal land, said the following:

  > I want to tell you one more thing I know about the Negro . . . they abort their young children, they put their young men in jail, because they never learned how to pick cotton. And I've often wondered, are they better off as slaves, picking cotton and having a family life and doing things, or are they better off under government subsidy? They didn't get more freedom. They got less freedom (quoted in Coscarelli, 2014, p. 1).

  His remarks went viral and were roundly criticized and lampooned. Legislators who had previously sided with Bundy quickly distanced themselves from him.

- The billionaire owner of the NBA's Los Angeles Clippers, Donald Sterling, was banned for life from the league, fined $2.5 million, and forced to sell the team after these secretly recorded comments he made to his girlfriend were posted on TMZ:

> It bothers me a lot that you want to broadcast that you're associating with black people . . . You can sleep with [black people]. You can bring them in, you can do whatever you want, [but] the little I ask you is . . . not to bring them to my games (TMZ.com, 2014, p. 1).

■ The newly appointed CEO of the software firm, Mozilla, was forced to resign when his strong anti-homosexual views were publicized and publicly condemned.

These incidents might indicate a collective movement toward an "intolerance of intolerance." However, we are far from a moment in our collective history when we can accurately say that prejudice no longer exists.

THE POLITICS OF RACIAL PREJUDICE: OBAMA EFFECT OR OBAMA BACKLASH?

A case in point: the election and re-election of Barack Obama. It remains to be seen what impact these events will have on future racial prejudice and race relations. Like millions of other Americans, I sat transfixed in front of my television on the night of November 4, 2008, watching the presidential election results trickle in. At about 11:00 p.m. Eastern time, the networks made the astounding projection: Barack Obama would be the 44th president of the United States. I sat in semi-disbelief. Had this country, one with such a difficult, painful, and deadly racial history, really just elected a black man to the highest office in the land? A development that would have been unthinkable 50, 25, or even 10 years ago had just happened. People of all colors and classes here and abroad danced in the streets.

Sociologists, columnists, and pundits of all political persuasions struggled to find the most memorable and most articulate way to capture the historical significance of the moment. Some speculated that it might mark the end of racial prejudice and inequality in this country; others wondered if we had become a "postracial" society, where traditional racial categories no longer matter. In a national poll shortly after the election, more than two-thirds of African Americans said they believed that Martin Luther King's famous 1963 dream (of a country where race and ethnicity are losing their status as major criteria for judging the content of a person's character) had finally been fulfilled (CNN.com, 2009). Psychologists talked about how having a black president would serve as a positive role model for all people of color and lead to unprecedented levels of academic and perhaps even financial achievement (Marx, Ko, & Friedman, 2009).

This sort of optimism wasn't confined to the United States. Social observers in Europe began to speculate on how Barack Obama's ascendency to the highest office in the land would influence race relations there. As an editor of a French blog put it, "They always said, 'You think race relations are bad here in France, check out the U.S.' But that argument can no longer stand" (quoted in Erlanger, 2008, p. 1). France's defense minister pondered how Obama's victory might serve as a lesson to the French on dealing with issues of immigration and integration. In many African countries, Obama's election created a palpable affection for the United States that veteran travelers to the region told me was nonexistent in the past. As my wife, who was working in Botswana at the time of his first election, put it, "In Africa, they think Obama is *their* president."

But other signs suggest that the election and reelection of the country's first black president has also stirred up nasty feelings of racial prejudice and animosity. As one retired black congressman put it, "I've lived too much history, and . . . seen too much discrimination, to see [Election Day, 2008] as a new world" (quoted in Fineman, 2010, p. 24). There is some evidence that racial prejudice is significantly correlated with opposition to the president and to his policies (Knowles, Lowery, & Schaumberg, 2010). At a more virulent level, racially offensive online images of Barack and Michelle Obama were so widespread the first year of his presidency that Google was forced to run an apologetic ad when it presented results of image searches of the first couple. Six years later, moments after President Obama sent his first Twitter post from the Oval Office, profanity-laced racial slurs and hate-filled posts poured into his account. One had an image of the president with a noose around his neck; another called him a black monkey (Hirschfeld Davis, 2015).

GENDER AND SEXUAL PREJUDICE

While some forms of prejudice fluctuate as social conditions change, others are remarkably persistent over time. Research on U.S. gender stereotypes and prejudice, for instance, has shown that they haven't changed all that much over the years (D. L. Berger & Williams, 1991; Eagly & Karau, 2002; Fine, 2010; Rudman & Glick, 1999). Despite breakthroughs in various sectors of social life, women have been consistently perceived as more passive, emotional, easily influenced, and dependent than men (Broverman, Vogel, Broverman, Clarkson, & Rosenkrantz, 1972; Deaux & Kite, 1987; Tavris & Offir, 1984).

What often seems to be universal prejudice against certain devalued groups is usually more nuanced. Consider anti-homosexual prejudice (known variably as **heterosexism** or **sexual prejudice**). For many decades, gays and lesbians worldwide have been rejected, ridiculed, and condemned on moral, religious, criminal, or even psychiatric grounds. According to the International Lesbian and Gay Association, 2.7 billion people today live in countries where homosexuality is a crime punishable by imprisonment, beatings, or even death (cited in Ball, 2014). Consider these examples:

- Legislators in the Ukraine introduced a bill a few years back that made it a crime punishable by imprisonment for producers of television shows and movies to sympathetically depict homosexuals ("Ukraine Bill Proposes Prison," 2012).
- In Nigeria, people who "directly or indirectly" make a "public show" of same-sex relationships, participate in gay clubs, societies, and organizations, or who simply support those organizations can be thrown into prison for as long as 10 years (Nossiter, 2014).
- Iran, Mauritania, Saudi Arabia, Sudan, and Yemen have a statutory death penalty for homosexuality (Ball, 2014). The Sultan of Brunei recently signed into law a new penal code that prescribes death by stoning for gay sex (Garcia, 2014).

Attitudes in the United States seem to have become more favorable in recent years. For instance, in the 1970s, three-quarters of respondents to an annual nationwide survey considered homosexual behavior to be "always wrong" or "almost always wrong." By 2010, that figure had dropped to 47% (Smith, 2011). Yet anti-gay prejudice persists:

- Now that same-sex marriage is legal, gay couples who obtain a public marriage license in a state that doesn't provide non-discrimination protection could still be at risk in other aspects of their lives, like losing their job or being denied credit or housing (Bernard, 2015). In 16 states, gays and lesbians lack virtually any explicit legal protections (Stolberg, 2014).
- Twenty states have laws (called "Religious Restoration Acts") that allow business owners to deny service to gays and lesbians if such actions impose a "substantial burden" on their religious beliefs. As one Oklahoma state senator put it, "[Homosexuals] don't have the right to be served in every single store. People need to have the ability to refuse service if it violates their religious convictions" (quoted in Fausset & Blinder, 2015, p. A18).
- Gay and lesbian travelers are still advised to prepare for trips by consulting with travel agents or websites about tolerance and safety issues associated with particular destinations. Said one columnist, "the last

thing you want to do [on a vacation] is lie awake at night feeling unwanted or even afraid (McElroy, 2014, p. 5).

- In December of 2015, the Food and Drug Administration lifted its lifetime ban on blood donations from all gay and bisexual men. This policy was instituted in 1983 in the early days of the AIDS crisis, before tests for HIV in donated blood, which could easily identify the presence of the virus, became standard. However, the FDA will continue to prohibit donation of blood from gay and bisexual men who have had sex with another man within the past 12 months. Hence, an HIV-negative, married, monogamous, gay man would have to abstain from sex with his spouse for one year to be eligible to donate blood.

What is perhaps more interesting from a sociological perspective is that anti-gay prejudice is not uniform throughout society. For instance, it is highest among individuals who know no gays and lesbians personally and who are older, less educated, and living in rural parts of the U.S. South or Midwest (Finlay & Walther, 2003; Herek, 2000). Despite the existence of pro–gay rights churches, most religions condemn or at least oppose homosexuality. Indeed, many churches, especially conservative and evangelical Protestant denominations, have added anti-homosexual statements to their official policies (Finlay & Walther, 2003).

PREJUDICE, PRIVILEGE, AND IDEOLOGIES OF INFERIORITY

One of the unfortunate by-products of living in a diverse society is that we have perhaps as many types of prejudice as there are types of groups living here. The forms that prejudice can take are infinite: anti-Semitic, anti-Muslim, anti-Black, anti-gay, anti-female, anti-male, anti-rich, anti-poor, anti-Republican, anti-Democrat, anti-Latino/a, anti-White, anti-Catholic, anti-Asian, and so on. If there's a group of people that is distinctive and identifiable, it's inevitable that someone will find these people unfit, unapproachable, or undesirable. When it comes to intolerance and hatred, we are truly an equal opportunity society.

But although anybody can hold stereotypes of others, judge them negatively, and disparage them as a result, it's important to remember that not all prejudice is created equally. To say, for instance, that a lesbian who hates heterosexuals is "just as prejudiced" as a straight person who hates homosexuals ignores the historical and cultural underpinnings of prejudice, the differences in power and privilege between these groups, and the different consequences that depend on who is expressing prejudice toward whom.

Furthermore, calling someone a racist or a bigot—no matter what group they happen to belong to—individualizes the behavior and obscures the group-level prejudice that is culturally, economically, legally, and socially supported (Wildman & Davis, 2002). Similarly, the suffix –phobic (homophobic, Islamophobic, transphobic, and so on) turns societal-level prejudice into individual-level fear and irrationality (Hess, 2016). Hence the blame for unequal treatment rests on the individual and not on the broad systematic forces that are required for large-scale inequality to take hold and become a common feature of society.

For decades, sociologists have been examining how prejudice makes the jump from an individual attitude to a structural phenomenon. It appears that several factors are involved. Two of these factors are beliefs of innate differences ("those people aren't like me") and feelings of superiority ("those people are not as good as me"). In this sense, prejudice exists not just in a set of feelings that individuals in one group have toward individuals in another group but in a perception of relative group position. The combination of feeling distinctive and feeling superior can easily give rise to expressions of hostility and social exclusion. The bully who punched me in the face in fourth grade clearly zeroed in on what he thought were my inherent (and inferior) differences from him and those like him.

Feeling different and feeling superior aren't in themselves sufficient to create group-level prejudice, however, because they could conceivably apply to the feelings one individual harbors toward another individual, regardless of each person's group membership. Sociologist Herbert Blumer (1958/2004) introduced two other beliefs—entitlement and suspicion—that can transform individual-level prejudice into group-level prejudice. First consider entitlement, the belief that one's group has a rightful claim to certain privileges and advantages. Historically, this feeling has translated into exclusive claims to resources such as upscale residential neighborhoods; financial benefits; prestigious occupations or professions; positions of control and authority in the government; inclusion in privileged schools, churches, and recreational facilities; positions of social prestige and the symbols of these positions; and certain areas of intimacy and privacy.

Arguably, this feeling of entitlement can exist in the absence of prejudice. In a feudal system, for example, a lord may feel his position of entitlement is simply a reflection of the natural order of things; in a tribal culture, a chief may feel the same way toward commoners. If these claims are accepted by everyone as legitimate, they wouldn't constitute prejudice.

But when feelings of entitlement combine with a suspicion that the subordinate group covets the privileges of the dominant group, prejudice results. In other words, the subordinate group is perceived to be threatening or is feared to threaten the advantaged position of the dominant group.

Acts that are suspected to be attacks on the "natural" superiority of the dominant group or intrusions into their sphere of privilege—as when women enter traditionally male occupations or organizations—are crucial in arousing group prejudice.

What's important about all these feelings—difference, superiority, entitlement, and suspicion—is that they combine to reflect the hierarchical positioning of groups in society. Feelings of superiority by definition place others below one's own group, and feelings of differentness place them beyond it. And the feeling of entitlement excludes others from the privileges of group position. Consequently, prejudice can rise and fall in response to the threat of changes in one group's social position relative to another group's.

Ideologies of inferiority and perceptions of entitlement and threat have long been used to explain why certain groups lag behind others in such areas as educational achievement, financial success, and even morality. These belief systems often provide "scientific" justification and a seemingly intellectual climate for the perpetuation of prejudice and inequality. Usually, such ideologies revolve around the notion of biological predisposition and "natural" differences between groups.

Race and Innate Weakness   In the 18th and 19th centuries, few white people doubted the "truth" of natural racial rankings: Indians below Whites, and Blacks below everyone else. Even idols of Western culture and advocates for human liberty—George Washington, Thomas Jefferson, Abraham Lincoln, Charles Darwin—believed in the natural inferiority of some races. These beliefs were commonly accepted knowledge at the time but would be considered bigoted or at the very least racially insensitive today.

The acceptance of these conventional racial rankings arose not from objective data and careful research but from a shared worldview and a belief that racial stratification was natural, inevitable, and proper (Gould, 1981). Such beliefs easily morphed into independent support when framed in the language of science. Scientists, like everybody else, have attitudes and values that shape what they see. Such thinking need not be the result of outright dishonesty or hypocrisy; rather, it is the combination of the way human minds work and the generally accepted knowledge of the day.

Despite historical and contemporary efforts to find a link between "inferior" race-based genes and intelligence, creativity, or other valued abilities, none has been found (Hacker, 1992). For one thing, comparing racial groups on something like intelligence overlooks the range of differences within as well as between groups. Many Latino/as are more intelligent than the average White; many Whites are less intelligent than the average Native American. Variations such as these are difficult to explain in terms of the genetic superiority of one race over another. Moreover, such comparisons ignore a problem I described in Chapter 2: that race itself is a meaningless biological category. How can we attribute racial differences in intelligence to genetic differences when there is no single gene associated with race?

Despite the lack of scientific support, beliefs about racial inferiority—be they genetic, anatomical, or cultural—always serve to privilege dominant groups. When these beliefs become part of the cultural stock of knowledge, they discourage subordinate groups from challenging their disadvantaged status. In addition, they provide moral justification for maintaining a society in which some groups are routinely deprived of their rights and privileges. Whites could justify the enslavement of Blacks or the conquest of Native Americans, and Nazis could justify the extermination of Jews and other "undesirables," by promoting the belief that those groups were fundamentally inferior (even subhuman) and deserved their fate.

In its less extreme forms, the idea that racial inferiority is innate remains appealing to those alleged to be superior. If observable physical differences among races are inherited, why not differences in social behavior, moral character, occupational placement, leadership ability, and so on? The belief in innate racial inferiority places the blame for suffering and economic failure on the individual rather than on the society in which that individual lives.

Gender and Biological Inevitability   Like racial prejudice, the supporting ideology for gender prejudice is often biologically based. The belief that men and women are biologically, naturally different has historically served to maintain women's subordinate position in society.

For instance, in 19th and early 20th century medical practice, few claims had wider acceptance and appeal than the contention that women were the products and prisoners of their reproductive anatomy (Scull & Favreau, 1986). Everything supposedly known about women that made them different from men—their subordinate place in society, the predominance of the emotional over the rational, their capacity for affection, their love of children and aptitude for child rearing, their "preference" for domestic work, and so on—could be explained by the existence and functioning of their uteruses and ovaries (Ehrenreich & English, 1989; Scull & Favreau, 1986). Scholars and physicians at the time warned that young women who studied too much were fighting against nature, would badly damage their reproductive organs, and would perhaps even go insane in the process (Astbury, 1996; Fausto-Sterling, 1985).

So the official exclusion of women from colleges and universities was not only justifiable but necessary for health reasons and for the long-term good of society.

Some functionalist sociologists have also cited biological differences between men and women as an explanation for the persistence of gender inequality in society (e.g., Parsons & Bales, 1955). They often cite sex-linked behaviors in nonhuman animals as evidence of the biological underpinnings of male-female behavioral differences among humans (Sperling, 1991). They argue that the fact that males tend to be physically stronger and that females bear and nurse offspring has created many recognized and necessary sex-segregated roles. Among humans, this specialization of roles at work and in the family is purported to be the most effective way to maintain societal stability. By giving birth to new members, by socializing very young children, and by providing affection and nurturing, women make invaluable contributions to the reproduction of society. The common occupations that women have traditionally had outside the home—teacher, nurse, day care provider, maid, social worker, and so on—tend simply to be extensions of their "natural" tendencies (for more on gender inequality in the labor force, see Chapter 6). Similarly, men's physical characteristics have been presumed to better suit them for the roles of economic provider and protector of the family. If it's true that men are naturally endowed with such traits as strength, assertiveness, competitiveness, and rationality, then they are best qualified to enter the serious and competitive world of work and politics (Kokopeli & Lakey, 1992). Such beliefs remain entrenched.

At the cultural level, the qualities we consider naturally feminine are often degraded and seen as less socially valuable than those considered masculine. As you will recall from Chapter 4, girls do suffer sometimes when their behavior is considered tomboyish. But when a boy is accused of acting like a girl, it implies weakness, frailty, and lack of ability. Even today, many men consider accusations of femininity the ultimate insult. In a recent TV commercial for Miller Lite a man at a bar orders a beer from the female bartender. When she asks him if he cares how it tastes, he says no. She then says, "When you start caring, put down your purse and I'll give you a Miller Lite."

The problem with depicting masculinity and femininity as natural, biological phenomena is that it confuses sex with gender (see Chapter 2). Things besides genes, hormones, and anatomy always shape social behavior. Even the sex-linked activities of nonhuman animals, from rodents to baboons, are not inevitable and can be influenced by environmental conditions (Sperling, 1991). Furthermore, the ideology of biological inevitability overlooks extensive similarities between the sexes and extensive variation within each sex. For instance, men as a group do tend to be more aggressive than women as a group. Yet some women are much more aggressive than the average man, and some men are much less aggressive than the average woman. Indeed, social circumstances may have a greater impact on aggression than any innate, biological traits. Some studies show that when women are rewarded for behaving aggressively, they can be just as violent as men (Hyde, 1984).

THE HIDDEN (AND NOT SO-HIDDEN) PRIVILEGES OF SOCIAL DOMINANCE

People who are members of dominant racial, sexual, gender, or class groups often have trouble appreciating the humiliating effects of everyday encounters with prejudice and lack of access to opportunities that other groups experience. For instance, we tend to think that marriage is an intimate relationship that is available to people of all classes. But according to some sociologists, marriage in the 21st century has become an increasingly inaccessible option for poor and working-class people. Middle- and upper-class individuals have the educational background and finances necessary to "purchase" what is needed to establish and maintain stable relationships (sufficient resources for everyday expenses, couples therapy, regular vacations, health club memberships, etc.). Poorer people, by contrast, are too concerned with their own survival to provide for others financially and emotionally and may come to view marriage as a luxury item they can't afford (Corse & Silva, 2014).

Often, the desire on the part of people from disadvantaged groups to stick with others like themselves is perceived as "separatism" rather than as a reasonable response to consistent expressions of prejudice. This dynamic is clearest with regard to race and ethnicity. Whenever discussions of race relations arise at my university for example, white students inevitably identify the tendency of students of color to socialize only with other students of color as one of the main reasons for interracial difficulties and misunderstandings. "If they want to be fully integrated into campus life, they should eat lunch with white students or join predominantly white fraternities and sororities. But they don't make the effort." What these white students fail to realize is that such voluntary isolation is typically a reaction to a long chain of interpersonal experiences that can make students of color feel like outsiders. Predictably, many Whites in the United States think people of color are obsessed with race and ethnicity and find it difficult to understand the emotional and intellectual energy that minorities devote to the subject (Haney López, 1996).

In a society in which they are the statistical and cultural majority, U.S. Whites rarely have to define their identity in terms of race. As I mentioned in Chapters 1 and 4, whiteness is unremarkable and unexamined. It is so obvious and normative that white people's racial identity is, for all intents and purposes, invisible. Whites enjoy the luxury of **racial transparency** or "having no color" (Haney López, 1996). Many Whites become conscious of their racial identity only when they find themselves in the company of large numbers of people of a different race. Sociologist Edward Morris (2006) studied the lives of minority white students at an inner city Texas middle school that was predominantly African American and Latino/a. Although more aware of their whiteness than students at predominantly white schools, these students didn't see their race as an unexamined source of strength and pride. In order to gain acceptance, they tended to distance themselves from their whiteness by adopting the dress, hairstyle, and language of black culture. However, both black and white teachers continued to draw on broader stereotypes, casting white students—especially those from middle-class backgrounds—as better behaved and more academically gifted.

The invisibility of whiteness as a racial position doesn't mean that white people are never discussed. On the contrary, they're spoken about all the time. You can't turn on the television or pick up a newspaper without seeing white people. But when white people talk about other white people, the discussion is couched in terms of, simply, "people." Whites need not be bigots nor feel racially superior or more deserving than others to enjoy the privileges that their racial transparency brings. The power of whiteness reproduces itself regardless of people's intentions, because it is seen not as whiteness but as normal (Dyer, 2012).

Sociologists Joyce Bell and Douglas Hartmann (2007) examined how the unseen privileges and normative presumptions of whiteness affect the way people talk about issues of racial equality and diversity. They drew data from interviews with 166 people, two-thirds of whom were white. They found that although respondents initially voiced positive attitudes toward diversity, in general—for instance, by talking about how diversity makes life "more interesting" and "more exciting"—they had difficulty describing specific benefits. In fact, many went on to talk about problems and frustrations of racial diversity, such as the threat to national unity. This sort of view is illustrated by responses of this white woman:

> I think . . . overall . . . it's a good thing, but it's a kind of delicate balance because . . . we're . . . at a place in this country where . . . [we] still need to keep our American identity and nationalisms.

> We . . . necd to respect one another's differences and backgrounds and all that, and be tolerant of one another. But by the same token, you know, there has to be a defining thread somewhere. (p. 900)

Clearly her ideas about "national unity" and a "common thread" were synonyms for mainstream culture, a system dominated and defined by Whites. Diversity, then, is seen not as the true coexistence of different-but-equal groups, but as the encroachment of nonwhite add-ons into dominant white culture. "American" norms and cultural practices equal "white" norms and cultural practices. As one respondent summed it up, "Whites are the hosts and people of color are the guests" (p. 908).

If whiteness is "normal" and "invisible," then what are the stereotypes used to describe—and perhaps even stigmatize—it? Sociologist Ruth Frankenberg (2002) interviewed 30 white women of various nationalities, sexualities, and political orientations to determine how they perceived their own whiteness. To many of these women, being white meant being cultureless. Whiteness was difficult if not impossible for them to describe, especially when not modified by specific ethnicities, regions, or classes. Many shared the habit of turning to elements of white culture as an unspoken norm, such as when comparing Latin music with "regular" music (when regular meant "white"). When these subjects did describe whiteness, they depicted it as "bland" or "blah." White culture, they seemed to suggest, lacked the vibrancy and "color" that other ethnicities seemed to have. But again, such a seemingly negative portrayal paradoxically conveys power. Other cultures are more interesting than white culture only because their elements fall outside the mainstream, outside the "normal." In addition, whiteness is often signified by commodities and brand names—Wonder bread, Kleenex, mayonnaise, and so on—thereby linking it to the broader economy in ways that other ethnicities aren't.

The curious combination of invisibility and ubiquity is also apparent in white people's sense of their own ethnicity, which for most is an optional component of their identity (Waters, 2010). Sociologist Charles Gallagher (1997) asked white college students to describe themselves in ethnic or racial terms. Few chose to consider their ethnicity at all. The majority labeled themselves simply as "white" or "Caucasian," ignoring hyphenated ethnicities such as "Italian-American" or "Irish-American." So complete was their extraction from any ethnic identity that some called themselves "plain old American" or "nothing." Even the handful of students who did acknowledge their ethnicity recognized that it was in name only, implying that the label bore little importance for how they lived their lives on a daily basis.

They couldn't speak the language of their European ancestors and didn't feel compelled to date or marry someone from within their ethnic group. So although whiteness remains largely indescribable, it has also become a proxy for ethnicity among young Whites.

The connections between the invisibility of whiteness and broader social inequalities cannot be ignored:

> Each thing with which "they" have to contend as they navigate the waters of American life is one less thing Whites have to sweat: and that makes everything easier, from finding jobs, to getting loans, to attending college. . . . The virtual invisibility that whiteness affords those of us who have it is like psychological money in the bank, the proceeds of which we cash in every day while others are in a perpetual state of overdraft. (Wise, 2002, pp. 107–108)

One white author (McIntosh, 2001) cataloged all the everyday privileges she enjoyed (and often didn't notice) simply because she was white. They included such advantages as the ability to shop alone in a department store without being followed by suspicious salespeople, to buy greeting cards or children's picture books featuring people of her race, and to find bandages that match her skin color. The privilege of not having to think about race provides advantages to Whites whether or not they approve of the way they have acquired those advantages.

Intersections
Wealthy White Men and Perceptions of Race

One of the great ironies of inequality in American society is that perceptions of those who are the most powerful and influential are often the least understood. For instance, the views and perspectives of wealthy white men with regard to race have received virtually no academic attention. To overcome this deficiency, sociologists Joe Feagin and Eileen O'Brien (2003) interviewed about 100 affluent white male executives, managers, administrators, and professionals about a range of racial issues. Understanding the perceptions of these men is important because many of them have the ability to influence local and national views on race matters. They have the power to shape policies, laws, and actions involving ethnoracial minorities and majorities.

Because of their socioeconomic status, these men lived most of their lives in segregated well-to-do neighborhoods. As children and teenagers, most of them attended schools that had few, if any, ethnoracial minorities.

Only a handful of the interviewees reported long-term friendships with people of other races.

Hence their initial and sometimes most significant encounters with ethnoracial minorities were often with domestic and other service workers, usually female maids or male servants:

> Although I don't remember my first experience of meeting a black person, I would assume it was . . . my grandfather's chauffeur when I was five years old. So to me, Blacks at that point were people that waited on you.

> My very first contact with a black person was with a black maid who essentially raised my sister and [me].

> Honestly, the first black person I ever met was probably a household employee at my parents' house a long time ago. (all quoted in Feagin & O'Brien, 2003, pp. 34–35)

Recollections of these initial contacts tended to be fond. Many men spoke lovingly of these household servants because these people played a significant role in raising them (some respondents referred to their black maids and nannies as "second mothers"). However, they also were taught, early on, that there was a social distance between their families and "the help" that had to be maintained. Furthermore, it's clear that the men didn't see these individuals as real people with real lives. For instance, most were unaware of the impact that being a domestic servant had on these individuals' relationships with their own families.

Feagin and O'Brien found that in many ways these men are not that different from "ordinary" white Americans when it comes to racial attitudes. They often share the same negative images of Americans of color. Furthermore, they often indicate a desire to maintain many white privileges in society as well as their control over major social institutions. But since they are generally highly educated, they are well aware that they should not be too explicit in expressing their racial attitudes.

Interestingly, while most white people in this society don't think much about their race and profess "not to see" race, these men seemed quite aware of the fact that as society becomes increasingly more multiracial, whiteness—and more specifically, white maleness—may no longer be the certain boost for success that it once was. Their understanding of "whiteness" included both the knowledge that it works in their favor and the perception that they are now "victims" in a multiracial society that is slowly taking away their advantage:

> I feel that I am definitely becoming discriminated against because I am white. . . . [It's] harder for me to get a job in a governmental agency than for a Latino or an African American or any other ethnic. It's harder for me than any other group. . . . If you just watch the news . . . , just look at the news anchors themselves. They always try to have a woman, a black, a Latino, Asians. They never have white males. (quoted in Feagin & O'Brien, 2003, p. 85)

Not all the men interviewed by Feagin and O'Brien felt this way. A minority of them expressed positive attitudes toward race relations. These individuals often voiced dismay over racial and class inequality and spoke of the need for a significant shift in the balance of economic and political power in the United States. The factor that seemed to separate these men from the others who held more traditional (and negative) attitudes toward race is the nature of the relationships they've had with Americans of color. Those who had long-term friendships or extended regular contact with members of other races were the ones who showed a willingness to consider dismantling the structures that perpetuate racial inequality.

WITHIN-GROUP PREJUDICE

When most people think of prejudice and bigotry, they think of negative feelings that cross broad racial, ethnic, religious, gender, or sexual lines, especially in the direction of most powerful toward least powerful groups. However, because definitions of race are social constructions, people often make finer, within-group distinctions between fellow members that are largely invisible or irrelevant to outsiders but nonetheless constitute an additional layer of prejudice. Take, for example, the skin color prejudice that exists among African Americans.

Skin color prejudice (also known as **colorism**) originated during the period of slavery when whiteness was equated with all things refined and beautiful and blackness represented the sinister and the ugly (Hill, 2002). In such an environment, skin color (along with other race-related physical features like hair texture, nose shape, and lip prominence) became the paramount indicator of social status. Both Whites and light-skinned black slaves came to consider darker-skinned black slaves to be less civilized and intellectually inferior (Graham, 1999). Light-skinned slaves were often allowed to work in the main house; dark-skinned slaves were usually relegated to the fields.

During the early to mid 20th century, many African American churches, social clubs, fraternities, and other organizations still used skin lightness tests to determine the suitability of candidates for membership. The so-called brown bag test restricted membership to those whose skin was lighter than the color of a brown paper bag. Here's how one author describes growing up in such an environment:

> I recall summertime visits from my maternal great-grandmother, a well-educated, light complexioned, straight-haired black southern woman who discouraged me and my brother from associating with darker-skinned children or from standing or playing for long periods in the July sunlight, which threatened to blacken our already too-dark skin. . . . At age six, I already understood the importance of achieving a better shade of black. (Graham, 1999, pp. 1, 4)

Such a preference exists today among African Americans of all ages—especially children and college students from affluent families:

> It is hard to find an upper-class black American family that has been well-to-do since before the 1950s that has not endured family conversations on the virtues of "good hair, sharp features, and a nice complexion." These code words for having less Negroid features have been exchanged over time for more politically correct ones, but it is a fact that the black upper class thinks about these things more than most. This is not to say that affluent Blacks want to be white, but it certainly suggests that they have seen the benefits accorded to lighter-skinned Blacks with "whiter features"—who are hired more often, given better jobs, and perceived as less threatening. (Graham, 1999, p. 377)

Studies have indeed found that lighter-skinned Blacks have higher educational attainment, more prestigious occupations, greater likelihood of holding elected office, less contact with the criminal justice system, and higher annual incomes than darker-skinned Blacks, regardless of their parents' socioeconomic status, sex, region of residence, age, or marital status (Hill, 2002; Hochschild & Weaver, 2007; Keith & Herring, 1991). Recent data show that dark-skinned black girls in elementary and secondary public schools are three times more likely to be suspended than lighter-skinned black girls (cited in Vega, 2014).

Skin-color distinctions within an ethnoracial group reflect the broader racial values of the culture at large. Many scholars argue that this sort of stratification comes from a deeply embedded racial ideology that equates character, prestige, and merit with skin tone. Hence, in the United States, individuals and institutions distribute rewards to those who most closely approximate white, European standards.

A fair amount of research suggests that skin-color distinctions are more important for African American women than for African American men. One African American woman recalls the pain of being told frequently, "You're pretty attractive for someone so dark" (Graham, 1999, p. 37). In the interests of being perceived by others as attractive, black women are often compelled to imitate whiteness through the use of skin bleaches and hair dyes and straighteners. Indeed, most beauty products marketed toward black women are designed to make them look more like white women.

Not surprisingly, evidence suggests that African American men find lighter-skinned women more sexually desirable and marriageable (Hamilton, Goldsmith, & Darity, 2008). And African American celebrities who are considered "sex symbols" (Halle Berry, Beyoncé, Vanessa Williams, Alicia Keys, Kerry Washington) typically approximate white beauty standards. Using data from the National Survey of Black Americans, sociologist Mark Hill (2002) found a strong preference for women with lighter skin. Interestingly, female respondents were just as likely as male respondents to express a preference for lighter-skinned women.

Using the same survey data, sociologists Maxine Thompson and Verna Keith (2004) examined how black men and women internalize these cultural messages. They were particularly interested in how people felt about themselves (self-esteem) and their perceived ability to master situations, control their own lives, and achieve success (efficacy). They found that light skin color was associated with higher levels of efficacy for black men, but not for black women. Traditional notions of masculinity demand that men achieve outside the home and exhibit competence. The researchers found that dark-skinned men often feel powerless, whereas light-skinned men often feel better able to improve their socioeconomic status. Conversely, color is closely associated with self-esteem for black women, but not for black men. Light-skinned black women showed the highest feelings of self-worth and confidence. These findings reflect the wider cultural tendency for women, of all races and ethnicities, to be judged on the basis of their physical appearance and not necessarily their social achievements.

Colorism is not limited to Blacks in the United States. A few years ago, I met a woman from India at a small dinner party. During the course of our conversation, I mentioned to her that I work with a female Indian colleague from the state of Kashmir, in the northern part of the country. Her immediate response was, "Oh, she must be beautiful." At the time, it struck me as a peculiar reaction. So when I got home I did some searching online and found many blog threads in which people talk about Kashmiris being lighter skinned than other Indians. The equation of light skin with beauty (and status) is well known in India. For decades the cosmetics industry there has made millions of dollars selling skin-lightening products to Indian women. The desire for a "fair" skin complexion is intertwined with long-standing Indian hierarchy where light skin is associated with higher status. As one writer put it, light skin "indicates to someone who's meeting you for the first time that you are born into a family where you haven't had to do any outdoor work, and that your status is higher as you haven't had to be in the fields" (quoted in National Public Radio, 2009, p. 2).

Similarly, the darkness of one's skin, has long determined a person's status in Mexico. Most Mexicans are of mixed lineage, so that nearly everyone could be considered at least part indigenous Indian. Nevertheless, Mexicans who are considered Indians are the object of severe discrimination. More than 80% of Mexico's Indian communities suffer high levels of poverty. Nearly half of all Mexican Indians are illiterate, and only 14% complete sixth grade. Many Mexicans, especially in the larger cities, use hair dyes, skin lighteners, and blue or green contact lenses to appear more European (DePalma, 1995).

In the United States, after controlling for all other relevant factors, dark-skinned Mexican Americans who have a Native American physical appearance have fewer years of education than light-skinned Mexican Americans who appear more European (Murguia & Telles, 1996). In addition, they are more likely to live in segregated, low-income neighborhoods (Relethford, Stern, Caskill, & Hazuda, 1983) and consistently earn lower wages (Telles & Murguia, 1990).

Beyond skin tone, cultural background also sometimes forms the basis of within-group prejudice. Many black immigrants from the West Indies, for example, refuse to call themselves "black" when they come to this country. West Indian immigrants generally make substantially more money than U.S.-born Blacks and live in better neighborhoods (Gladwell, 1996). They often try to distance themselves as much as possible from U.S.-born Blacks, whom they feel are socially, culturally, and financially inferior. Not having experienced the debilitating effects of discrimination, West Indian immigrants often have difficulty, as do some Whites, understanding why American Blacks have such a tough time "making it" in U.S. society.

Some African immigrants and their children also seek to distinguish themselves from downtrodden black Americans by calling themselves "African" or using some form of hyphenation that incorporates their country of origin, like "Nigerian-American" or "Ethiopian-American." At the same time, though, there is some debate over whether foreign-born black citizens who want to call themselves "African American" can legitimately claim the label. Some black Americans argue that the term "African American" should refer only to the descendants of slaves brought to this country centuries ago and not to new immigrants from Africa who do not have a heritage of bondage, segregation, and discrimination. Many fear that immigrants and their children will co-opt the hard-won opportunities acquired as a result of the civil rights movement. Says one man who traces his ancestry back to slavery:

> We've suffered so much that we're a bit weary and immigration seems like one more hurdle we will have to climb. . . . These are very aggressive people who are coming here. I don't berate immigrants for that; they have given up a lot to get here. But we're going to be in competition with them. We have to be honest about it. That is one of the dividing lines." (quoted in Swarns, 2004, p. A14)

Indeed, there is some evidence that black immigrants and their children have more education and higher median incomes than native-born Blacks (cited in Swarns, 2004).

DISCRIMINATION: INEQUALITY IN ACTION

As you can see from this discussion so far, the mental formation of stereotypes and prejudices in and of itself would be of little significance if it didn't sometimes motivate people to take actions against others. **Discrimination** refers to the unfair treatment of people based on some identifiable social characteristic such as race, ethnicity, gender, sexuality, or class. From forced enslavement and employment restrictions to segregation and interpersonal violence, discrimination has historically been one of the defining characteristics of U.S. society. In the past half century, however, some historically disadvantaged groups have made tremendous progress, largely because of the 1964 Civil Rights Act, which prohibits discrimination or segregation on the grounds of sex, race, color, religion, and national origin.

Nevertheless, discrimination still exists, operating simultaneously at several levels. Sometimes, it resides in the actions of individuals. At other times, however, it is embedded in the everyday workings of larger systems and institutions.

PERSONAL DISCRIMINATION

When we think of racism, sexism, classism, heterosexism, or any other "ism," what usually comes to mind are examples of **personal discrimination,** unfair treatment of certain groups by individual people. This type of discrimination includes biased treatment during face-to-face encounters, avoidance, exclusion, and threats or acts of violence. It's personal discrimination that receives the most media attention, especially when it is violent and brutal, such as racially motivated hate crimes:

- In 2012, four East Haven, Connecticut, police officers were accused of systematically mistreating Latino/as in the community by conducting unreasonable searches of residents; slapping, hitting, and kicking suspects when in custody; and regularly harassing customers as they emerged from Latino/a-owned businesses (Barron, 2012).
- That same year, a Wisconsin man murdered six congregants and wounded a police officer at a Sikh temple, probably because he thought the Sikhs were Muslim. A day later, a mosque in Joplin, Missouri, was burned to the ground (Beinart, 2012).
- In 2015, two white Mississippi men pled guilty to violations of federal hate crime laws for a string of attacks in which they threw beer bottles and shot metal ball bearings at random black pedestrians from moving vehicles. In one incident, they beat up a 47-year old black factory worker and then fatally struck him with their pick up truck (Fausset, 2015).
- In the summer of 2015, a 21-year old avowed white supremacist opened fire in an African Methodist Episcopalian church in Charleston, South Carolina, killing nine people who were there for a bible study meeting. Witnesses said that before he began shooting, he shouted out a series of racial epithets. In the week following the massacre, fires destroyed six black churches in five southern states.

Consider also personal discrimination directed at sexual minorities. People with homosexual or bisexual orientations—as well as people merely assumed to be or accused of being gay—routinely experience personal discrimination in the form of violence and interpersonal rejection (Herek, 2000). In a nationwide study of gay, lesbian, and bisexual college students, 32% had experienced some form of harassment, ranging from derogatory remarks to outright violence, and close to 20% feared for their physical safety because of their sexual orientation (Rankin, 2003). More results of the college study are shown in Exhibit 5.1. These students are not only more likely than heterosexuals to be harassed by fellow students, they're also at greater risk of being harassed by teachers and school employees (Hill & Silva, 2006).

This sort of harassment can sometimes be fatal. According to one researcher, gay, lesbian, and bisexual youth are about five times as likely as heterosexuals to attempt suicide (Hatzenbuehler, 2011); transgender and

Exhibit 5.1:   Anti-Gay Harassment

Percentage of gay, lesbian, bisexual or transgender college students (n = 1,669) who within the past year . . .

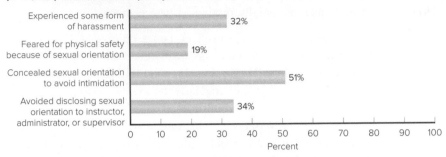

Percentage of gay, lesbian, bisexual or transgender students who experienced . . .

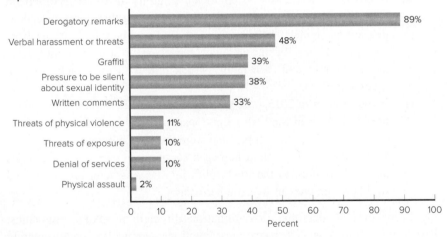

Percentage of gay, lesbian, bisexual or transgender students who experienced some form of harassment . . .

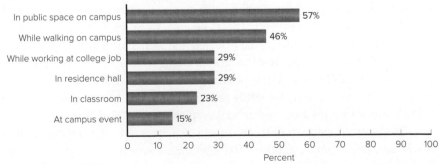

(Source: Rankin, 2003)

gender non-conforming individuals are nine times more likely (Haas, Rodgers, & Herman, 2014). A few years ago, a rash of suicides among harassed and bullied gay teenagers in New Jersey, California, Texas, and Indiana focused national attention on the problem. In one Minnesota school district alone, four gay and lesbian teenagers committed suicide in one school year (Erdely, 2012).

Quiet Bias Some forms of personal discrimination can be subtler and more difficult to detect than the overt acts that most often come to our attention. In reference to the Donald Sterling situation discussed earlier, former Attorney General, Eric Holder, said this in a 2014 speech:

> These outbursts of bigotry, while deplorable, are not the true markers of the struggle that still must be waged, or the work that still needs to be done—because the greatest threats do not announce themselves in screaming headlines. They are more subtle. They cut deeper (quoted in Reuters, 2014, p. 1)

Where blatant discrimination can be "hot, close, and direct," subtle discrimination can be "cool, distant, and indirect" (Meertens & Pettigrew, 1997, p. 54). Such quiet bias might take forms that, at first blush, don't appear discriminatory at all. Take, for instance, the high school guidance counselor who sympathetically steers poor and working-class students away from "hard" subjects and toward vocational courses. Similarly, in the workplace, women are sometimes subjected to superficially courteous or chivalrous behavior that is meant to be protective but ends up reinforcing women's subordinate position. Whether the motivation is malevolent or benevolent, such actions reinforce inequality. Women treated as non-adults by their male coworkers may find it hard convincing others that they have what it takes to be in high-paying positions of authority. Such treatment is far more common than more noticeable acts of personal discrimination and can, over time, be just as harmful.

Some people may subscribe to conventional stereotypes of other groups and feel hostility toward them but not engage in acts of discrimination because of laws or customs that discourage open discrimination. These individuals may interact with members of the despised group on a regular basis but suppress the expression of their underlying negative feelings and remain silent when others express such feelings (Trepagnier, 2013). In short, the only reason such a person—what one sociologist calls the "timid bigot"— doesn't openly discriminate is because she or he is not allowed to do so (Merton, 1949). What's troublesome about such individuals is that if such restrictions are ever lifted, discriminatory activity would likely be unleashed.

The underlying feelings that accompany quiet bias don't need to be hate or hostility. Instead, discomfort, uneasiness, and sometimes fear, can motivate a less obvious type of discrimination. Hence, the person who subtly discriminates might support ethnoracial equality in principle but justify opposition to government programs for ethnoracial minorities on the seemingly nonprejudiced grounds that everyone's taxes would have to go up or that an individual's rewards should be based exclusively on personal achievements and not race or that enough has been done already.

Quiet bias has several features that distinguish it from the blatantly discriminatory ideologies (Ansell, 2000):

- *Sanitized, coded language that adheres to nondiscriminatory values but is nonetheless prejudicial in its effect.* For example, words like "welfare," "inner city," and "crime" often tap into racial anxieties.
- *Avid disavowals of discriminatory intent.* The benign-sounding language provides only superficial evidence that the person is unbiased, however.
- *Co-opting of classical antidiscrimination arguments.* For example, a popular slogan from the civil rights movement—"Judge people not by the color of their skin but by the content of their character"—is adopted by those who argue that affirmative action is largely to blame for the continued oppression of people of color. Anti-racist "bureaucrats" rather than discriminators become the new villains.
- *Shift from explaining inequality as an innate, biological matter to explaining it as a matter of cultural differences and national identity.* For example, discussions of the so-called "culture of poverty" avoid attributing a group's failures to their genes—as is the argument of more traditional forms of racial prejudice—but attribute them instead to the group members' antisocial behavior, pathological family structures, and immoral value systems.

Alterations in the manner in which underlying prejudice is expressed and communicated have serious societal consequences. When bias remains camouflaged, people are tempted to assume that discrimination has disappeared, making it unnecessary to help groups that have traditionally been the objects of discrimination (Bonilla-Silva, 2003). It is easier in some ways to confront overt bigotry and hatred based on assumptions that differences between groups of people arise from their essential nature.

The Enduring Importance of Race   Some social observers have noticed the decline of overt racial discrimination and concluded that it is dead. In fact, some sociologists have been among those arguing that racial discrimination is actually based on differences in social class rather than race. If this belief were accurate, however, the lives of middle- and upper-class women and members of ethnoracial minorities, both part of the hypothetically privileged social class, should be relatively free of discrimination. Yet they are not. For instance, many highly successful professionals of color report that even they experience a lack of respect, faint praise, low expectations, the presumption of failure, pigeonholing, exclusion, and even outright harassment. An African American woman who happens to be a Georgetown University law professor recounts an interaction with a colleague, a middle-aged white man, who explained to her that she should not be offended at being called a "jungle bunny" because "you are cute and so are bunnies" (quoted in Cose, 1993, p. 23). Another colleague told her she reminded him of his family's former maid.

More generally, minority professionals often bemoan the tendency of others to assume they bring to every interaction the perspective of their entire group. A successful law professor, who happens to be Chinese American, once said, "I suspect . . . that at every appearance . . . my audience continues to see and hear me as a spokesperson on behalf of Asian Americans" (Wu, 2002, p. 37).

Sociologists Joe Feagin and Karyn McKinney (2003) analyzed data from focus group and individual interviews with several hundred middle-class U.S. Blacks to determine the consequences of the discrimination they experienced at work. These individuals, all of whom were college educated and held professional or managerial jobs, were in agreement that the work-related stresses they felt did not come from the demands of the job itself but from racially hostile workplace environments that often include the mistrust of colleagues, unfair promotion practices, or outright mistreatment through the use of racial epithets and derogatory names.

Everyday life can be trying as well. Wealthy black residents of affluent neighborhoods all over the country sometimes complain that they are watched closely when shopping in upscale stores or that the police view them with suspicion simply because their skin color doesn't match the neighborhood. Situations like these are disturbing and frustrating not only because of the racist attitudes that lay behind them but also because the people who experience them had come to believe that their upward social mobility protected them from such treatment. A respondent in Feagin and McKinney's (2003) study put it this way:

> I'm always in the process of trying to develop a better and healthier way of working through the inevitable anger about this situation. There's a price you pay in being sensitive and conscious. . . .

Have you ever seen a dog really being angry about his condition? If you really were a beast, it wouldn't bother you. The problem is that . . . this treatment bothers you most, because you definitely and clearly aren't what the world thinks you are. (p. 45)

Less obviously, the belief on the part of these individuals that their class status ought to shield them from discriminatory treatment is yet another way of drawing us-them distinctions. Their frustration implies that socioeconomic achievement and advantage should have enabled them to transcend the ethnoracial prejudice and discrimination that more understandably adheres to people of lesser means. Notice what this black, female college professor's description of her experiences implies about the "other" Blacks she seeks to distance herself from:

Because I'm a large black woman, and I don't wear whatever class status I have, or whatever professional status [I have] in my appearance when I'm in the grocery store, I'm part of the mass of large black women shopping. For most Whites, and even for some Blacks, that translates into negative status. That means that they are free to treat me the way they treat most poor black people, because they can't tell by looking at me that I differ from that. (quoted in Feagin, 1991, p. 109)

Such an attitude is also reflected in the tendency for middle-class people of color to use their middle-class appearance as a resource when necessary. For instance, when making transactions over the phone, some African Americans use a "white voice" to ensure that they get fair treatment (Feagin, 1991). The heartbreak of such a strategy is twofold. First, it acknowledges that race is so important in this society that knowledge of one's race would inevitably prompt unfair treatment. Second, it shows that poorer members of ethnoracial minorities who lack the signifiers of class stature are doomed to a life of discrimination.

Intersections
Race, Class, and Gender in Everyday Social Encounters

Although encounters with personal discrimination can be disheartening for middle- and upper-class members of ethnoracial minorities, poor or working-class men are perhaps most susceptible to the preconceptions and prejudices of others in social interactions. Sociologist Elijah Anderson (1990) observed everyday public encounters in a racially, ethnically, and economically diverse area of Philadelphia. This community was home to two neighborhoods: one black and poor, the other middle- to upper-income and predominantly white. Anderson was particularly interested in how young black men—the overwhelming majority of whom were civil and law-abiding—dealt with residents' biased assumption that they are dangerous criminals.

What Anderson discovered was that residents of both neighbor-hoods were incapable of making distinctions between law-abiding young black men and criminally-involved young black men. So they relied on broad stereotypes: Whites are middle-class, law-abiding, and trustworthy; young black men are poor, crime-prone, and dangerous. Black residents, as well as white residents, were likely to defer to and avoid contact with unknown black men on the street. Women—particularly white women—clutched their purses and edged up closer to their companions as they walked down the street. Many pedestrians crossed the street or averted their eyes from young black men whom they perceived as unpredictable and menacing.

In response, some of these men developed strategies to overcome the immediate assumption that they were dangerous. For instance, in hopes of deflecting any negative prejudgments, some conspicuously car-ried props with them in public that they felt both symbolized higher class status and represented law-abiding behavior (for instance, a briefcase, a shirt and tie, a college identification card). In addition, they often used friendly or courteous greetings as a kind of preemptive peace offering, designed to signal to others their civil intentions. Or they went to great lengths to behave in ways contrary to what they presumed were others' stereotypes of them:

> I find myself being extra nice to Whites. A lot of times I be walk-ing down the streets . . . and I see somebody white. . . . I know they are afraid of me. They don't know me, but they intimi-dated. . . . So I might smile, just to reassure them. . . . At other times I find myself opening doors, you know. Holding the eleva-tor. Putting myself in a certain light, you know, to change what-ever doubts they may have. (Anderson, 1990, pp. 185–186)

Such interactional strategies require an enormous amount of effort and place responsibility for ensuring social order on these men. They feel compelled to put strangers at ease so they can go about their own busi-ness. Such actions indicate an understanding that their mere presence makes others nervous and uncomfortable. They understand that they must work hard to be perceived as trustworthy in public interactions.

Power and Personal Discrimination   In theory, personal discrimination can be practiced by anyone against any other group. Even members of the least powerful, most disadvantaged segments of society can harbor personal animosity toward others. Native Americans sometimes lash out against Whites; poor people may express openly hostile feelings toward the wealthy.

Certainly some women dislike men, judge them on the basis of stereotypes, hold prejudiced attitudes toward them, consider them inferior, and even discriminate against them socially or professionally. And sometimes, those in dominant positions can feel the effects of societal disadvantage. For instance, some people have argued that men are disadvantaged by the long history of social and legal pressures on them to fight in war, thereby risking their lives and their bodily and psychological health. Others have highlighted judges' alleged preference for maternal child custody after a divorce as another example of men being victimized by discrimination (Benatar, 2003). We must keep in mind, though, that the historical balance of power in most societies has allowed men as a group to subordinate women socially and sometimes legally in order to protect male interests and privileges. Because men tend to dominate major social institutions, their discriminatory actions have more cultural legitimacy and more serious consequences than women's discrimination.

Indeed, when groups lack societal power, their discrimination is of little significance within the larger social structure. Take, for instance, the growing objectification of men in advertising, what one columnist calls "hunkvertising" (Gianatasio, 2013). In one television commercial for Diet Coke some years back, a group of wide-eyed women stare out of an office window during their work break at a muscular construction worker who has just taken off his shirt. As the sweaty worker downs his Diet Coke, the ogling women fantasize all sorts of things. The commercial grabbed attention by reversing the more common situation in which men sexually objectify women. But the two types of sexual objectification don't carry the same meaning. Such sexual attention may be an enjoyable experience for men because it doesn't have the weight of a long tradition of subordination or the threat of violence behind it. A man who is being ogled isn't being socially or economically reduced to his physical attractiveness. He doesn't have to fear for his physical safety. One female distance runner, describing the inevitable lewd cat calls she gets from men when she runs, put it this way: "Men are in danger of, at worst, being laughed at by a woman. Women are in danger of being *killed* by men" (quoted in Sagal, 2015, p. 30).

So for women, who continue to fight to be taken seriously in their social and professional lives, sexual objectification is a reminder that their value in this society is judged primarily, or even exclusively, on their looks. Therefore, such treatment serves to reinforce, rather than reduce, gender inequalities.

Global Ethnic Violence   Given this chapter's focus on U.S. society so far, it would be tempting to conclude that the sorts of discrimination I've described are uniquely American phenomena. But around the world, discrimination—especially violent ethnoracial discrimination—is the rule, not the exception. For instance, in Eastern European countries such as Bulgaria, Romania, Hungary, Slovakia, and the Czech Republic, personal discrimination against the Roma—or Gypsies—is the norm. They have been despised for centuries and characterized as thieving subhumans with no respect for the law. They are stereotyped as loud, dirty, indecent, and sloppy. According to a poll of Czech attitudes, 39% of the population feel that "only force is effective" in dealing with Romas (cited in Erlanger, 2000). Another survey found that 70% of respondents would object to having Romas as neighbors (cited in Bilefsky, 2010). As a result of such attitudes, Romas suffer disproportionately from violence, poverty, illiteracy, and disease. Vicious, sometimes deadly, incidents against Romas have occurred throughout Eastern Europe. Unemployment among Romas is about 70% (cited in Perlez, 1998). In Sofia, the capital of Bulgaria, the unemployment rate among Romas is 94%. In some Roma neighborhoods, 80% of residents have only an elementary school education (Wood, 2005). In Ostrovany, Slovakia, a 500-foot-long, 7-foot-high concrete wall separates a Roma ghetto from a handsome *gadzo* or white neighborhood on the other side (Bilefsky, 2010). Ironically, two-thirds of the population in Ostrovany is Roma. Such treatment is not confined to countries where Romas have long resided. In 2010, France embarked on a major push to reduce crime and illegal immigration by forcibly expelling some Romas, even though such mass expulsion based on ethnicity violates European Union law (Erlanger, 2010).

At a time when people from every corner of the globe are linked technologically, economically, and ecologically and when mass migrations mix people from different races, religions, and cultures in unprecedented numbers, racial and ethnic hostilities are at an all-time high. Look at any online news service and you'll see stories of ethnic, religious, or racial conflict: Jews and Palestinians in Israel and Gaza, Buddhists and Muslims in Myanmar, Chechens and Russians in the former Soviet Union, Janjaweed and Darfurians or Sudanese and Nubans in Sudan, Hindus and Muslims or Bengalis and Gurkhas in India, the Han and Uighurs in western China, Lendus and Hemas in the Democratic Republic of the Congo, Georgians and Ossetians in Georgia, Sunni and Shiite Muslims in Iraq and Syria, Orma and Pokomo in Kenya, Tajiks and Pashtuns in Afghanistan, the Kyrgyz and Uzbeks in Kyrgyzstan, and the Ijaw and Itsckiri in Nigeria. Racial and ethnic hatred costs the lives of millions of people around the world each year.

It's tempting to view this sort of violence as the pent-up expression of age-old ethnic loyalties and cultural differences. However, in many areas of the world, the origins of conflict can be traced to the lingering effects of colonialism and the manipulation of political leaders. Consider, for instance, the ethnic violence that occurred between Hutus and Tutsis in Rwanda in the mid-1990s. The way the conflict was presented in the media led many outside observers to assume that these two groups had some deep-seated, centuries-old ethnic hatred of one another that had reached its boiling point. It turns out, though, that prior to German colonization in the 19th century and Belgian colonization in the early 20th century, Rwandans didn't consider themselves Hutu or Tutsi. They saw themselves as one group. People drew their identity from where they were born or by how much wealth they had (Bowen, 1996). It was the colonizers who decreed that each person had to have an "ethnic identity" that determined their place in society. By pitting one group against another, colonial rulers, whose numbers were always quite small, could seek out allies among certain ethnic groups. Belgian rulers formed such an alliance with the Tutsis. Their suppression of the Hutus created a sense of collective Hutu identity and outrage. In the 1950s, Hutus successfully rebelled against Tutsis. Eventually, Tutsi resentment led to the creation of their own rebel army. The conflict reached its bloody conclusion in the civil war of 1994, in which hundreds of thousands of Tutsis and moderate Hutus were killed.

INSTITUTIONAL DISCRIMINATION

Institutional discrimination—established laws, customs, policies, and practices that systematically reflect and produce inequalities in society, whether or not the individuals maintaining these practices have discriminatory intentions—can only work to the advantage of those who already wield power and control major social institutions. Because women, poor people, African Americans, Latino/as, Asian Americans, Native Americans, sexual minorities, and other groups have historically been excluded from key positions of authority in dominant social institutions, they often find themselves victimized by the routine workings of such structures. Chapters 6, 7, and 8 will examine in more detail the broader institutional causes and consequences of this sort of discrimination.

On occasion, institutional discrimination is obvious and codified into the law. Until the early 1990s, for example, South Africa operated under an official system of apartheid whereby non-white groups were legally segregated and subjected to sanctioned forms of political and economic discrimination. In the United States, the forceful relocation of Native Americans in the 19th century, repressive Jim Crow laws in the 20th-century South, and the internment of Japanese Americans during World War II are all examples of legislated policies that purposely worked to the disadvantage of already disadvantaged groups.

But most of the time, institutional discrimination is even less easily recognized than the quiet, subtle forms of personal discrimination I described earlier and therefore is more difficult to address. Because institutional discrimination is a built-in feature of social arrangements, it is often camouflaged by organizational policy and other institutional concerns. For example, the U.S. Army has a grooming policy, known as AR670-1, that describes, among many other things, acceptable hairstyles for military personnel. The policy makes no mention of race or ethnicity, but it specifically forbids cornrows, braids, twists, and dreadlocks (Byrd & Tharps, 2014). Since these hairstyles are most likely to be worn by African American women the *consequence* of the policy is that it systematically imposes appearance limitations on one racial/gender group and not others and therefore may be institutionally discriminatory.

Sometimes, institutional discrimination is cloaked in claims that seem quite reasonable on their face, as when taxi companies or home delivery businesses protect the safety of their drivers by enacting policies that prohibit service to neighborhoods they consider to be dangerous. Although such practices may be considered good business policy and are not intentionally discriminatory, their consequences very well may be. High-risk neighborhoods tend to be inhabited primarily by people of color. Several years ago, Domino's Pizza got into a public controversy when it was revealed that the company was distributing software to its outlets to let them mark addresses on computers as green (deliver), yellow (curbside delivery only), or red (no delivery). The red and yellow addresses were considered dangerous to Domino's easy-to-spot delivery people but also happened to be highly concentrated in minority neighborhoods. The delivery policy was subsequently changed.

As a consequence of institutional practices and policies, housing discrimination based on class and race pervades the American landscape. Nearly fifty years ago, the Fair Housing Act prohibited discrimination based on race, color, religion, or national origin. There is some evidence that residential segregation based on race has dropped in recent years (Glaeser & Vigdor, 2012). However, segregation—especially when it comes to Whites—still exists (Crowder, Pais, & South, 2012). For instance, 41% of Blacks live in majority-black neighborhoods and 43% of Latino/as live in majority-Latino/a neighborhoods. Indeed, the average white person lives in a neighborhood that is 77% white (National Fair Housing Alliance, 2015).

Residential segregation is not just about people living near others of the same race. Research indicates that for members of ethnoracial minorities it can be associated with a variety of problems, such as lower income, wealth, homeownership, school performance, and educational attainment; less access to healthy food; greater exposure to environmental hazards; and shorter life expectancy (National Fair Housing Alliance, 2015). In fact, among white and black families with similar incomes, white families are more likely to live in neighborhoods with better schools, more day-care options, nicer parks and playgrounds, and more transportation options (Reardon, Fox, & Townsend, 2015). Racially segregated neighborhoods are also the ones where daily humiliations are a way of life: trash is collected less frequently, streets remain unpaved, and water, power, and sewage services are less reliable (Rothstein, 2014).

The National Fair Housing Alliance (2015) conservatively estimates that there are approximately 4 million fair-housing violations every year in the rental market alone. Apart from incidents of landlords discriminating against families with small children or against people with disabilities, most of these cases involve ethnoracial minorities. On occasion, such housing discrimination is personal, the result of individuals' blatant "we don't want you people here" attitudes. More commonly, though, it's institutional, politely and subtly driven by company policies (D. Pearce, 1979). Discriminatory policies include making fewer houses or rental units available to minorities, limiting their access to financial assistance, and steering them toward particular neighborhoods. Because these policies restrict their opportunities, people of color are much more likely than white families to live in neighborhoods that have a shortage of important commercial, educational, and financial resources (National Fair Housing Alliance, 2015).

One study found that African Americans were twice as likely as Whites, and Latino/as one and a half times as likely as Whites to be denied a conventional 30-year home loan (cited in Kilborn, 1999). When they do receive home loans, African Americans and Latino/as are twice as likely as Whites to have to pay substantially higher "subprime" interest rates (cited in Bajaj & Fessenden, 2007). Some argue that the discrepancy in rates is justified because borrowers who have poor credit histories are higher risks or because Blacks and Latino/as have fewer assets and therefore have less money for down payments than white borrowers (Blanton, 2007). But the discrepancy is even found between minority and white borrowers with similar credit scores (Bocian, Ernst, & Li, 2006). In 2009, the city of Baltimore sued Wells Fargo Bank for systematically steering Blacks into subprime mortgages, which sent hundreds of homeowners into foreclosure and cost the city tens of millions of dollars (Powell, 2009).

In sum, the distinction between personal and institutional discrimination is crucial. Privileged groups can protect or even enhance their advantaged positions through institutional practices and policies that often appear to have little, if anything, to do with race, ethnicity, class, sexuality, or gender. Indeed, what distinguishes personal from institutional discrimination is often the ability to pinpoint blame for the resulting disadvantage. If someone refuses to admit me to a club or serve me in a restaurant because she or he despises people of my race, the blameworthy party is fairly obvious. But who's responsible for nationwide residential segregation? Who's responsible for the low SAT scores of inner-city high school students? Who's responsible for relatively high rates of unemployment, low rates of health insurance coverage, and low rates of personal computer ownership among ethnoracial minorities? If all personal hatred, prejudice, and discrimination were to end today, entrenched systematic arrangements that benefit some at the expense of others—be they in hospitals, retail businesses, workplaces, courthouses, schools, or any other institutional location—would continue.

CONCLUSION

In his novel, *The Painted Bird* (1965), Jerzy Kosinski tells the tale of an unnamed boy in an unnamed Eastern European country caught in the confusion of the beginnings of World War II. When he is six, his middle-class parents, like thousands of others, send him to the countryside in the hope that he will be spared the brunt of the war. He is entrusted to the care of a peasant woman who dies shortly after he arrives. He has no way of contacting his parents and so must fend for himself. His problems are multiplied because he has dark hair, dark eyes, and speaks an educated dialect while those amongst whom he lives are blond, blue-eyed, and speak a peasant dialect. Because he is dark and different, he is assumed to be either "a Gypsy or a

Jewish stray," neither of which is a good thing to be, considering that the Germans at the time are rounding up both to be sent to the death camps. Hence, it is very dangerous for the peasants in the area to protect him, and he is treated with suspicion, cruelty, and almost constant violence.

For a while, the boy lives under the protection of Lekh, a huge man who makes a living as a bird catcher. When Lekh would become angry, which happened frequently, he would calm his rage by torturing one of his captured birds:

> After prolonged scrutiny, he would choose the strongest bird. . . .
> Lekh would turn the bird over and paint its wings, head, and breast in rainbow hues until it became more dappled and vivid than a bouquet of wildflowers. . . . When a sufficient number of birds gathered above our heads, Lekh would give me a sign to release the prisoner. It would soar, happy and free, a spot of rainbow against the backdrop of clouds, and then plunge into the waiting brown flock. For an instant the birds were confounded. The painted bird circled from one end of the flock to the other, vainly trying to convince its kin that it was one of them. . . . But dazzled by its brilliant colors, they flew around it unconvinced. . . . We saw soon . . . how one bird after another would peel off in a fierce attack. Shortly the many-hued shape lost its place in the sky and dropped to the ground. (Kosinsky, 1965, pp. 43–44)

In this scene, we can see the key theme of this chapter—the interface between social difference and unequal treatment. What is especially poignant about this story is that the differences that elicit such treatment needn't be "real"—in the sense of being biological, essential, and inevitable. We, ourselves, create the boundaries that separate groups and then respond to "outsiders" as if their outside status is natural. Just as Lekh knew, such a process is a set-up because rarely do individuals embrace those who appear different, whether it's a painted bird, a sexual or ethnoracial minority, or a 9-year-old kid coming to grips with his differentness in a new school.

I would have preferred to end this chapter on a positive note, claiming that prejudice and discrimination are relics of the past and that differences based on skin color, ethnicity, religion, social class, gender, and sexuality have become irrelevant, carrying as much social significance as, say, differences based on eye color or hair color. But I can't. Not yet, anyway. Prejudice and discrimination still exist, though not as automatically and obviously as they did half a century ago. But even when prejudice and discrimination seemingly disappear, it is often because they have given way to quiet, almost imperceptible forms that reside not in hatred, bloodshed, and legal exclusion but in quiet distrust, polite avoidance, microaggression, and the impersonal day-to-day workings of our major social institutions.

In the story of the painted bird, however, there is some hope. You see, if we are the ones who create the differences that result in harmful, discriminatory treatment, then we have the power to change them. The people of any society decide which differences are irrelevant and which differences are legitimate for making crucial social and legal distinctions between groups of people. We can change perceptions, alter behaviors, and even modify social institutions if we decide it's worth our while to do so.

[**INVESTIGATING IDENTITIES AND INEQUALITIES**]
Race and retail: Personal and institutional
discrimination in everyday life

Often, social inequality is felt most forcefully in the interpersonal indignities that people of particular ethnoracial, gender, class, or sexual groups must contend with in their day-to-day lives. To the outside observer who has never had to deal with the humiliation, these experiences might seem trivial and insignificant, mere annoyances rather than crises. However, to those who face this sort of treatment, the cumulative effect can be demoralizing and have long-term consequences for their self-esteem, state of mind, and even physical health.

This exercise requires that you enlist the assistance of three close friends: a person who is of the same race as you but of a different sex, and a man and a woman who are both of a race different from yours. If you have trouble finding people to help you, consider working with students who are in your sociology class. Once you've selected your accomplices, identify at least two retail businesses—perhaps in a nearby shopping mall—in which salespeople typically approach customers as they enter the store to ask if they need assistance. Examples of such businesses include clothing stores, jewelry stores, electronics stores, and so forth. One of the stores you choose should sell fairly expensive items, like jewelry, computers, or upscale clothing. The other should sell moderately priced products, such as sporting goods or bath and body products. Avoid stores where it is likely that the salespeople will recognize you or your accomplices.

At different times, each of you individually will go to each store acting as if you were a customer interested in buying a gift for someone. It's important that you and your accomplices decide ahead of time what sort of product you will be "shopping" for and the price range you have in mind so that each of you is looking for the same thing. Try to dress in casual clothing, neither sloppy nor formal. Although you won't actually end up buying anything, try to appear as if you are a serious shopper. Be as polite as you can be. Try to ask relevant questions about the products in question.

While in the store, pay close attention so you can answer the following questions (or variations on them or even additional questions that you devise on your own):

- Was the store busy or quiet? About how many other customers were in the store when you arrived? About how many people were working?
- How long did it take for a salesperson to approach you? What was this person's race? His or her approximate age?
- Did she or he ask you any questions that seemed designed to determine your ability to pay (such as "will this be cash or charge?" or "what were you thinking in terms of price?")? Did the salesperson seem to steer you in the direction of particular products?
- Did she or he ask friendly sorts of questions that seemed to have nothing to do with the products being sold there, such as where you were from, if you were a student or not, and so forth? Did she or he make any comments about your appearance?
- Did the salesperson stay with you the entire time you were in the store, or did she or he shift attention to other customers or coworkers?
- Did you feel pressured to buy something?
- How would you characterize the salesperson's assistance? Helpful? Courteous? Uninterested? Rude?

When you've completed your shopping excursions, immediately record your observations. The longer you wait, the harder it will be to remember specific details. Provide as much specific evidence from the encounter as you can to support your characterization.

Compile the experiences of each person in your group. Use the material on personal and institutional discrimination in this chapter to interpret your findings. Although you need to be cautious when generalizing from such a small number of individual perceptions and experiences, try to identify any noticeable differences in the way store employees treat customers of different races or sexes. If there were differences, describe them in detail. Who seemed to be treated more favorably? Did the salespeople seem to be making assumptions about your socioeconomic status? Did the differences seem more pronounced in the expensive store or in the moderately priced store? Do you think the differential treatment was a result of the personal proclivities of the salesperson or a result of company policy? Why do you think so? If you noticed no differences along racial or sex lines, how do you account for *that* experience? Try to draw some general conclusions about the effects of race and sex on public encounters.

CHAPTER 6

Inequalities in Economics and Work

When my older son turned 18 about a decade ago he received a letter in the mail from the Selective Service System reminding him in chirpy, upbeat language that he was now eligible to register with the service. The letter pointed out that, for his "convenience," he could register online and that within seconds he'd receive his selective service number! They made it sound like he was about to win some cool prize.

What he was winning, as you may know, was the "right" to be called into military service. The mission of the Selective Service System is to provide manpower for the U.S. armed forces should Congress and the president decide, in the event of a national emergency, that a return to a military draft is necessary. Eighteen-year-old men are required by law to register. Failure to do so is a serious crime, punishable by a fine of up to $250,000 and imprisonment for up to 5 years. In addition, registration with the service is a requirement for such things as federal student financial aid, job training, and government employment. (And yes, I did say *man*power. At the time I was writing this chapter, women—more specifically, genetic females—don't yet have to register. Hence female-to-male transsexuals are *not* required to register, but male-to-female transsexuals are.)

Despite repeated statements ten years ago from the president, some cabinet members, and various senators and congressional representatives that there would be no draft, I was worried. Like many people in the early 2000s, I closely followed the military situation in the Middle East. Back then, the United States was struggling to find enough enlisted personnel to fight the wars in Iraq and Afghanistan. The military had been forced to resort to drastic measures such as "stop loss," which barred soldiers from retiring or resigning and compelled them to continue assignments after their tours ended. This policy had the potential to force thousands of soldiers to remain in uniform for a year or more after their contracts expired. I worried about how long it would be until the military situation was defined as a "national emergency" and the draft was reinstated.

To calm myself, I tried to think about the situation from a more sociological (and less parental) perspective. But that only succeeded in reminding me of the inherent inequalities of conscripted military service. Historically, the U.S. military has rarely accurately reflected the population at large. As far back as the Civil War, for instance, if an able-bodied man had enough money he could hire a substitute to fight in his place. On the Confederate side, plantation owners were entirely exempt from the draft. Today—or more accurately, since the early 1970s when the military became all voluntary—those who are members of ethnoracial minority groups and who come from the lower socioeconomic reaches of society have been overrepresented, especially during times of high unemployment (Kelty, Kleykamp, & Segal, 2010). To people with limited educational and occupational opportunities, military service has long held out the promise of stable employment, comprehensive insurance coverage, a living wage, free schooling, and the development of marketable skills they can use after being discharged.

During the wars in Iraq and Afghanistan, African Americans made up 22% of enlisted personnel, even though they constituted about 13% of the same-age civilian population. The figures were even more disparate for women. More than 35% of enlisted women were African American. And African American women outnumbered African American men in the military two-to-one (Kelty, Kleykamp, & Segal, 2010). Aside from high-ranking officers, it was all but impossible to find U.S. soldiers from very wealthy families serving in these wars (Halbfinger & Holmes, 2003).

Furthermore, military service was, and continues to be, an attractive option for working-class immigrants, many of whom are not yet U.S. citizens. In 2004, the U.S. Congress enacted a law that shortens the waiting period for immigrants seeking citizenship if they volunteer to serve in the armed forces. And the military now allows immigrants on short-term visas to enlist. In the past, they would have been ineligible without legal permanent resident status. Hence, many immigrants have joined—and hundreds have died—simply because military service provides them with an opportunity to improve their lives. As one professor put it, "The bottom line, whatever the casualties, is that [immigrants] are going to continue to join because they have to. They want to live better" (quoted in Davey, 2004, p. A21).

Those in decision-making positions—in the White House and in Congress—remain almost exclusively middle-class and above and therefore have the political and economic wherewithal to keep their children out of harm's way. The fierce political debates that always rage over when American troops should be deployed (in Syria, the Ukraine, or some other global hot spot) or when they should be withdrawn (from Iraq and Afghanistan, for example) continue to be carried out, for the most part, by people who have no personal, familial stake in military action. When my son received his letter from the Selective Service System, only one member of Congress had a child serving on the front lines of the war (Kiely, 2007).

The controversy over forced versus voluntary military service in wartime represents, in microcosm, the unbalanced economic structure that exists in society today. Access to life chances is not equally distributed across all identity groups. In this chapter, I will focus on economic inequalities, both globally and locally, paying close attention to the intersections of race, class, gender, and sexuality in determining people's chances of living a comfortable life. Since most people must earn a living by working for a salary or a wage, I will also spend quite a bit of time exploring the intersections of these identities in the workplace.

UNDERPRIVILEGE AND OVERPRIVILEGE: FINANCIAL IMBALANCES IN EVERYDAY LIFE

Economic institutions are the most fundamental source of inequality in society today. Subsequent chapters will focus on imbalances in the justice and health care systems. But we can't understand people's unequal access to legal protections and healthy lives without first taking financial imbalances into account.

GLOBAL INEQUALITIES

Globally, economic imbalance is the rule, not the exception. The average per-capita yearly income in Western Europe, the United States, Canada, Japan, and other developed countries is $37,470; in the less developed countries of the world, it's $8,920 (Population Reference Bureau, 2014b). By conservative estimates, more than 1.3 billion people in the less developed world live on the equivalent of less than $1.25 a day (World Hunger Education Service, 2012). At the other end of the spectrum, almost half the world's wealth is owned by just 1% of the global population. Indeed, the richest 85 *individuals* in the world own as much as the combined wealth of the entire bottom half of humanity (close to 4 billion people; Oxfam, 2014).

Even though economic growth in developing countries has been increasing over the past several years and the number of people living in extreme poverty has dropped in the past 20 years (Population Reference Bureau, 2014a), global imbalances will continue to exist for the foreseeable future. Such a depressing conclusion is less a statement about the natural inevitability of inequality as it is a reflection of the kinds of choices countries tend to make (Piketty, 2014). Wealthy nations seek to retain their favored positions while keeping other nations in their place. In a global economy, such dominance is accomplished not by force but through financial pressure—as when powerful industrialized countries set world prices on certain goods (Chase-Dunn & Rubinson, 1977). Because their economic base is weak, poor countries often have to borrow money or buy manufactured goods on credit from wealthy countries. The huge debt they build up locks them into a downward spiral of exploitation and poverty. As a result, they have difficulty developing independent economies of their own and thus remain dependent on wealthy nations for their very survival.

ECONOMIC INEQUALITIES MADE IN AMERICA

Even if economic inequality *between* societies were to decline, inequalities *within* societies would probably persist. It's ironic that a society like ours, which extols the virtues of "equality" and "justice," is also one of the most stratified in the industrialized world. According to the U.S. Bureau of the Census (ProQuest Statistical Abstract, 2015), the average annual income of the top 5% of U.S. households is around $196,000 while the average annual income of the bottom 20% of households is under $21,000.

There's nothing particularly remarkable about that. All societies have wealthy people and poor people. However, this wide income gap between the richest and poorest segments of the U.S. population has been growing steadily over the past few decades (see Exhibit 6.1). Between the 1940s and the 1970s, incomes for all American households, whether rich or poor, grew at fairly similar rates. But since then, things have changed dramatically (Phillips, 2002). The income gap between those at the top and those at the bottom is the highest it's been since 1967 (Mather & Jarosz, 2014). Over the last several decades, incomes of the richest 1% have grown 275% while incomes for the poorest 20% have grown only 18% (Congressional Budget Office, 2014). As the country recovers from the recent recession, the wealthy have done better than anyone else. Some economists estimate that 95% of gains in income since 2009 have gone to the richest 1% of the population (Oxfam, 2014). By comparison, the wealthiest 1% accounted for only 45% of the nation's income growth following the economic downturn of the early 1990s (Saez, 2012).

Exhibit 6.1: Growing Gap Between Rich and Poor Americans

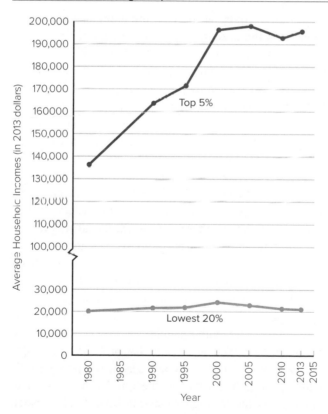

(Source: ProQuest Statistical Abstract, 2015, Table 716)

Overcoming this trend is not easy. Consider, for instance, periodic efforts to pay low-wage employees higher wages for the work they do. In 2007, after 10 years of debate, Congress finally approved a measure to increase the federal minimum wage from $5.15 an hour to $7.25 an hour, where it remains today. In 2014, the International Monetary Fund (2014) issued a report calling on the United States to raise its minimum wage in order to boost the economy. President Obama has proposed increasing it to $10.10. But it's unlikely that Congress will approve of such a step anytime soon. It's worth noting though that about three-quarters of Americans now support raising the federal minimum wage to over $12 an hour (National Employment Law Project, 2015). To date, 29 states and the District of Columbia, as well as 21 cities and counties, have set their minimum wages above the federal rate. The Fight for $15 campaign has encouraged workers across the country to demand a living wage from their employers. As a result, cities such as Seattle and San Francisco have raised their minimum wages to $15.

Meanwhile, compensation for those at the very top continues to soar. In 1964, the average income for a top executive in an American company was about $822,000 a year. In 2014, chief executives at the S&P 500 companies averaged $13.5 million in total compensation. In the early 1980s, corporate executives earned $42 for every $1 earned by the average production worker; by 2014, that figure had increased to $373 (AFL-CIO, 2015). We may want to believe that personal effort and hard work solely determine our success, but it's hard to imagine that a CEO of, say, an automobile company works 373 times harder than a person who actually assembles the cars.

Moreover, income deficiencies tend to persist over time. Recent economic studies have found that it takes five or six generations to erase the advantages or disadvantages of a person's economic origins (Clark, 2014). Within the span of a single generation, there isn't much social mobility—wealthy parents tend to have wealthy children; poor parents tend to have poor children. More than 40% of Americans born into the poorest fifth of households remain there as adults (cited in "Upper Bound," 2010).

Inequalities in income (what people earn) lead to even more striking inequalities in wealth (what people have): property; durable consumer goods such as cars, houses, and furniture; and financial assets such as stocks, bonds, savings, and life insurance. The wealthiest 1% of U.S. households controls 35% of all the country's wealth. By comparison, the poorest 90% controls only 23% of all the wealth. Moreover, the top 1% has a median net worth 288 times as large as the average American household (Mishel, Bivens, Gould, & Shierholz, 2013). In fact, the wealth gap between upper- and middle-income households is the widest on record (Fry & Koch-har, 2014). The Walton family (owners of Walmart) have as much wealth as the poorest 134 million Americans *combined* (Bittman, 2014).

Furthermore, because wealth accumulates over generations, a history of ethnoracial discrimination in lending, housing, and employment can solidify the wealth deficiencies for families of color. Thirty-one percent of Latino/a households, 35% of black households, but only 15% of white households had zero or negative net worth in 2009 (Kochhar, Fry, & Taylor, 2011). Even those whose income is comparable to that of Whites tend to have less wealth (Shapiro, 2010). The recession took a toll on just about everyone, but the already-wide wealth gap between white and non-white households (see Exhibit 6.2) has widened over the past several years (Kochhar & Fry, 2014).

We will never live in a society with a perfectly equal distribution of income and wealth. Some people will always earn more, have more, and maybe even deserve more than others. But the fact that the gap between rich

Exhibit 6.2: Median Household Net Worth by Race and Ethnicity (in 2013 dollars)

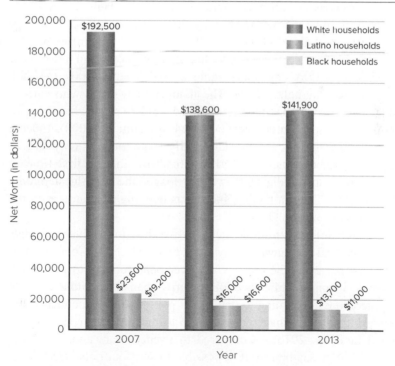

(Source: Kochhar & Fry, 2014)

and poor in the United States continues to grow challenges the notion that we live in a society where everyone is valued equally. As disparities in income and wealth expand, so too does the gap in quality of life and access to opportunities between those at the top of society and those at the bottom.

SQUEEZING THE MIDDLE

The middle-class—as an abstract ideal as much as a specific group of people—has historically occupied a lofty position in this society. Its moods, political leanings, values, habits, lifestyles, and tastes tend to define U.S. culture. It's an identity to which many people aspire, and it's the standard against which other classes are measured and judged. It is also perhaps the most coveted constituency in politics. But if we look at the actual economic lives of people who are literally in the middle class—that is, whose income places them right in the center of the population—we see some troubling recent trends.

Median household incomes rose steadily throughout the 1980s and 1990s but have stagnated ever since. In 1980, the median household income (in current dollars) across all ethnoracial groups in the United States was $44,059. In 2007, it was $50,303. But by 2014, it had only increased to $53,657 (DeNavas-Walt & Proctor, 2015). Hourly earnings, weekly earnings, and employer-provided benefits like pensions and retirement accounts all have either stayed the same or fallen since 2007 (Mishel, Bivens, Gould, & Shierholz, 2013). The number of workers who earn at least $20 an hour (a wage that once symbolized "middle class") has dropped nearly 60% over the past three decades (cited in Uchitelle, 2008). Indeed, after adjusting for inflation, the median hourly wage today is only $16.71 (U.S. Bureau of Labor Statistics, 2013b). In 2014, for the first time in history, the American middle class was no longer the wealthiest middle class in the world: Canada's median income is now higher than that in the U.S. (Leonhardt & Quealy, 2014).

Today, even families with stable incomes live close to the financial edge, one layoff or medical emergency away from financial crisis. Consequently, Americans now see a middle class with fewer opportunities to get ahead, less disposable income, and lower job security than the middle class of previous generations. According to one recent poll, 85% of respondents said it was more difficult now than a decade ago to maintain their standard of living (cited in Blow, 2013a). Compared to twenty years ago, a smaller percentage of Americans believe it is possible to start out poor, work hard, and get rich (Sorkin & Thee-Brenan, 2014).

As you might expect, race and ethnicity factor into the increasingly precarious financial state of middle-class households. As Exhibit 6.3 shows, decreases in median income vary across ethnoracial lines.

Not only do middle-class jobs pay less than they used to, but there are fewer of them to go around. Many people who have followed the traditional path to success—getting college degrees, developing marketable skills, building impressive résumés—are finding themselves out of work as companies cut costs or turn to automation to stay afloat. For instance, there were 74% fewer word processor/typist jobs, 70% fewer computer operators, 46% fewer travel agents, and 29% fewer accountants and bookkeepers in 2013 compared to 2000 (Rattner, 2014).

And with 7.8 million Americans officially unemployed (an unemployment rate of about 5.0%), many people who were once middle class are either marginally attached to the labor force or completely discouraged over their job prospects. Incidentally, the official unemployment rate only includes people who have been actively looking for a job for the past month. Hence it doesn't include people who have given up trying to find a job, have other factors in their lives, like family obligations, that prevent them from looking

Exhibit 6.3: Recent Trends in Median Household Income by Race & Ethnicity, 2005–2013

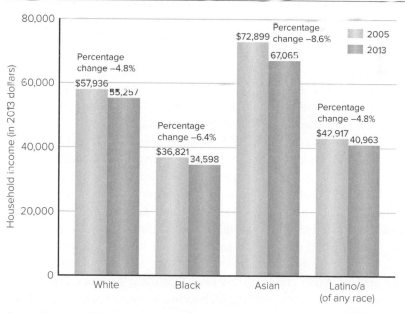

(Source: ProQuest Statistical Abstract, 2015, Table 713)

for work, or are disabled (U.S. Bureau of Labor Statistics, 2014b). Overall, 30 million adults of prime working age (25 to 54) are not presently employed, constituting 13% of the U.S. population (Hamel, Firth, & Brodie, 2014).

THE FACE OF AMERICAN POVERTY: IN THE SHADOW OF PLENTY

The poverty rate—the percentage of residents whose income falls below the official poverty threshold (see Chapter 2)—is one of the measures the U.S. government uses to assess the financial state of the country. In 2014 (the most recent year available at the time of this writing), 14.8% of the population—or 46.6 million Americans—fell below the poverty line (DeNavas-Walt & Proctor, 2015). Between 2009 and 2011, 31.6% of the U.S. population experienced poverty for at least 2 months, up from 27% over the period of 2005–2007 (Edwards, 2014).

When used to describe national trends in poverty, this overall poverty figure can obscure important differences among subgroups of the population. In 2014, 10.1% of people who identify themselves as non-Hispanic Whites and 12% of Asian Americans fell below the poverty line. That same year, 26.2% of Blacks and 23.6% of Latino/as (who could be of any race) were considered poor. The poverty rate in the South (16.5%) and West (15.2%) is higher than the rate in the Midwest (13%) and Northeast (12.6%). Finally, poverty is higher in rural areas (16.5%) than in metropolitan areas (14.5%), although it's highest in inner cities (18.9%; DeNavas-Walt & Proctor, 2015).

Although racial and ethnic minorities have consistently been rated among the poorest Americans, other groups have seen their status change over time. Before Social Security was instituted in 1935, many of the most destitute were elderly. As recently as 1970, 25% of U.S. residents over the age of 65 fell below the poverty line. Today, only 10% of the people in this age group are poor (DeNavas-Walt & Proctor, 2015).

Children's fortunes have gone in the reverse direction. About 15.5 million American children under the age of 18 (21.1%) live in households that are officially poor. This is a disproportionate share of the people in poverty. Children make up about 23.3% of the total population yet account for 33.3% of all poor people in this country (DeNavas-Walt & Proctor, 2015). As you would suspect, poverty figures for children vary dramatically along ethnoracial lines. About 38% of African American and 30% of Latino/a children under 18 live in poverty—compared with 16% of non-Hispanic white children and 10% of Asian children (ProQuest Statistical Abstract, 2015).

Getting out of poverty is not simple, because it is a complicated condition with multiple causes and multiple consequences. A job alone may not be enough if a family has huge debt. Good housing might not be enough if the house is far away from where the jobs are and the family lacks transportation. One costly incident can create a cycle of economic despair that lasts for years:

> A run-down apartment can exacerbate a child's asthma, which leads to a call for an ambulance, which generates a medical bill that cannot be paid, which ruins a credit record, which hikes the interest rate on an auto loan, which forces the purchase of an unreliable used car, which jeopardizes a mother's punctuality at work, which limits her promotions and earning capacity, which confines her to poor housing. (Shipler, 2004, p. 11)

Sleepless on the Street   The most publicly visible consequence of poverty is homelessness. No one knows for sure exactly how many homeless people live in the United States but the National Alliance to End Homelessness (2015) estimates that on any given night there are about 578,000 homeless people, 31% of whom are completely unsheltered. But because individuals tend to move in and out of homelessness, it's estimated that somewhere between 2.3 and 3.5 million people experience some type of homelessness for some period of time over the course of a year. According to a 2014 survey of 25 major American cities, 63% of homeless people are single adults, 37% are persons in families, and a little less than 1% are children on their own (U.S. Conference of Mayors, 2014).

Homeless people exist on the margins of society. In rural areas, they are largely invisible; in urban areas, they are faceless public annoyances whom most people try to avoid or ignore. The homeless are walking evidence of economic failure and unfulfilled promise. Thus, community tolerance of homeless people wears thin in many places, leading some cities to impose harsh restrictions on them in an attempt to reduce their visibility. A 2014 survey of 187 U.S. cities found that 53% of them ban sitting and lying down in public places, 57% prohibit camping in public places, 43% prohibit sleeping in vehicles, and 76% outlaw begging in certain places (National Law Center on Homelessness and Poverty, 2014). Some cities have removed park benches, closed all public bathrooms, and banned sleeping in cars (cited in Wollan, 2012). The mayor of Honolulu, which has seen a surge in its homeless population over the past 5 years, recently stated, "It's time to declare a war on homelessness . . . we cannot let [it] ruin our economy and take over our city." (quoted in Nagourney, 2014, p. A1).

The homeless as a group tend to be so stigmatized that any racial or even gender disadvantage would not add that much to their already destitute state. It's hard to imagine homeless people being treated any worse than they already are just because they happen to be Latino/a or Asian or African American. However, race and ethnicity do appear to matter with regard to people's chances of becoming homeless in the first place. In Great Britain, for example, ethnic minorities compose about 8% of the population, yet they account for 22% of those considered homeless ("Probe into race link," 2002). In U.S. society, Blacks are two to three times as likely as others to use homeless shelters (Culhane & Metraux, 1999).

The causes of homelessness in the United States are typically institutional ones: stagnating wages, deficiencies in government assistance programs, and, perhaps most important, lack of affordable housing. Nearly three quarters of homeless families cite lack of affordable housing as the principal cause of their situation (United States Conference of Mayors, 2014). When rising wealth at the top end of society drives up housing prices, the poor are left unable to afford decent housing.

According to the federal government, housing is considered "affordable" if it costs 30% or less of a family's income. The poorest fifth of the American population spend about 78% of their wages on housing. By comparison, the wealthiest fifth of the population spend less than 20% of their income on housing (cited in Swartz, 2007). In 2015, the nationwide median housing wage—the minimum amount of money a person would have to make to afford a modest two-bedroom apartment—was $19.35 an hour (or an annual income of over $40,000, assuming full-time, year-round employment). That's two and a half times the federal minimum wage ($7.25 an hour) and four dollars more than the average wage earned by renters nationwide ($15.16 an hour). Nowhere in the United States does a full-time, minimum-wage job provide enough income to afford adequate housing, and in some states—New York, California, Connecticut, New Jersey, and Massachusetts to name a few—a household would need the income of at least three minimum-wage jobs. In Hawaii, *four* minimum-wage jobs wouldn't be enough (National Low Income Housing Coalition, 2015).

Poverty's Border   You will recall from Chapter 2 that the official poverty line for a family of four is an income of a little over $24,000 a year. But because this figure is computed using outdated assumptions about people's spending patterns, it is likely set too low. Thus, it overestimates the number of families that earn an income high enough to be financially secure (rendering them ineligible for certain forms of governmental assistance) while underestimating the amount of money families actually need for economic stability and well-being.

Even if the method of computing the poverty line were revised to account for contemporary spending patterns, it would still be inadequate, because it is determined by current income alone. Economic factors that reflect a family's past, like assets and debts, are ignored. So, for example, a person who has racked up debt while unemployed or even in college but who has now found a job and is earning enough to rise out of poverty may discover that paying off past debts eats up so much income that he or she is actually worse off than before.

Thus, official poverty statistics conceal the people who live on the upper fringe of poverty. The U.S. Bureau of the Census defines the 14.7 million people who earn up to 25% above the official poverty line amount as the "near-poor" or "working poor" (DeNavas-Walt & Proctor, 2015). These are the people who earn more than the poverty threshold, but who face difficulties making ends meet. And because of the recent recession, they tend to be older and better educated than the near-poor were 30 years ago (cited in Greenhouse, 2014).

The everyday lives of near-poor families are fraught with irony. Because they fall above the poverty line, they escape most academic attention and tend not to be the focal point of large-scale governmental assistance programs. In fact, many states have been forced to balance their budgets by cutting child care subsidies for low-income parents. For many of these families, child care costs suck up nearly a third of their household budgets. So losing this form of government assistance has made it even more difficult for them to stay above the poverty line (Goodman, 2010).

While they seem to be a low policy priority (Povich, Roberts, & Mather, 2014), the working poor are everywhere, doing the tasks with which others come into contact and on which they depend on a daily basis:

> They serve you Big Macs and help you find merchandise at Wal Mart. They harvest your food, clean your offices, and sew your clothes. In a California factory, they package lights for your kids' bikes. In a New Hampshire plant, they assemble books of wall-paper samples to help you redecorate. (Shipler, 2004, p. 3)

Dubious Fault Lines   One of the enduring myths that surrounds economic disadvantage in this society—whether we're talking about the poor or the working poor—is that people suffer simply because they don't work hard enough, lack the skills and abilities to get ahead, or have become lazy because they receive too much government assistance. When people were asked in a recent poll what factor was most responsible for the continuing problem of poverty in this country, the most common response was "Too much welfare that prevents initiative" (Blow, 2013b). Such an ideology works to justify social inequalities. In 2010, for instance, some U.S. senators tried to block a bill that would have extended unemployment insurance benefits for the 15 million or so Americans who had lost their jobs that year. One of the senators said, "You can make more money on unemployment than you can going down and getting one of those jobs that is an honest job but it doesn't pay as much. We've put in so much entitlement into our government that we really have spoiled our citizenry" (quoted in Krugman, 2010, p. 17). In 2012, the chair of the House Budget Committee echoed these sentiments when he proposed a sharp reduction in government assistance programs: "We don't want to turn the safety net into a hammock that lulls able-bodied people to lives of dependency and complacency, that drains them of their will and their incentive to make the most of their lives" (quoted in McAuliff, 2012, p. 1).

If we, as a society, conclude that people suffer because of something they themselves have done (or have failed to do), then there's no reason to question the fairness of the economic system itself and therefore no motivation to rectify the situation at the structural level by providing more economic opportunities. The irony is that more than two-thirds of low-income people work (Lalasz, 2005). These individuals frequently work long hours, sometimes in more than one job, often sacrificing other aspects of their lives (such as family, education, and recreation) as a means of economic survival. After years of disappointment and working hard just to barely get by, they either give up on the dream of economic comfort or slip back into poverty and government assistance.

Indeed, some prominent economists argue that the reason so many Americans remain mired in poverty is not that they receive too much government assistance, but that they receive too little (Krugman, 2014a). One international charity organization, called GiveDirectly, gives money to poor people around the world without any conditions on how they spend it. Assessments of this program have found that children from families that receive these payments are more likely to stay in school and less likely to get sick. Contrary to popular stereotypes, recipients tend not to blow the money on alcohol or tobacco. Furthermore, the payments have no effect on the number of hours recipients work and some studies even show an increase in working hours as household members use the cash to obtain better jobs (GiveDirectly, 2014; Goldstein, 2013).

THE ECONOMIES OF RACE AND ETHNICITY

The economic outlook for ethnoracial minorities has shown some improvement over the last several decades. Asian Americans, in particular, continue to be better off financially than any other ethnoracial group, including non-Hispanic

Whites. According to the U.S. Bureau of the Census (DeNavas-Walt & Proctor, 2015), the median household income for families of Asian descent is $74,297 compared with $60,256 for non-Hispanic Whites. In addition, 53.2% of Asian Americans attain a bachelor's or higher compared with 32% of non-Hispanic Whites, 21.8% of African Americans, and 15.1% of Latino/as (ProQuest Statistical Abstract, 2015). Nonetheless, over the past 30 years, the proportion of all college undergraduates who are African American or Latino/a has grown from 14% to 26% (National Center for Education Statistics, 2010).

But this rosy economic picture has its share of thorns. African Americans, Latino/as, and Native Americans remain, on average, the poorest and most disadvantaged of all groups in the United States; their average annual income is still substantially below the national median. With the exception of Asian Americans, the rate of unemployment for people of color is regularly higher than that of Whites (ProQuest Statistical Abstract, 2015). In 2015, the unemployment rate for Blacks was 9.6%, compared with 6.9% for Latino/as, 4.7% for Whites, and 4.4% for Asians (ProQuest Statistical Abstract, 2015). About 15% of Latino/a students drop out of high school, compared with about 10% of black students and 7.2% of white students (ProQuest Statistical Abstract, 2015). And despite recent advances, workers from ethnoracial minorities tend to be concentrated in lower-paying jobs (see Exhibit 6.4). Fifteen percent of American workers who earn minimum wage are African American and 19.5% are Latino/a. African Americans make up 11.2% of the entire civilian U.S. workforce but only 4.2% of lawyers, 6.4% of physicians,

Exhibit 6.4: Ethnoracial Occupational Concentration, 2013

Occupations that are at least 25% African American	Occupations that are at least 25% Latino/a
• Bus driver	• Private household cleaner/servant
• Postal service mail sorter	• Maid/janitor
• Security guard	• Gardener
• Nurses' aide/orderly/home health aide	• Farmworker
• Barber	• Sewing machine operator
	• Construction laborer
	• Cook/dishwasher

(Source: ProQuest Statistical Abstract, 2014, Table 642)

and 5.5% of architects and engineers. Similarly, Latino/as make up 15.6% of the labor force but are underrepresented in the fields of law (5.1%), medicine (3.8%), and architecture/engineering (7.5%; ProQuest Statistical Abstract, 2015).

Ethnoracial minorities are particularly vulnerable to economically motivated business changes, such as plant shutdowns, the automation of lower-level production jobs, and corporate relocations. For example, when a factory in a predominantly black or Latino section of a city moves to an all-white suburb, minority employees tend to face greater problems than white employees in securing housing in the new location or experience higher transportation costs in commuting to the job if they want to keep it.

The disappearance of blue-collar jobs has devastated many inner-city neighborhoods. As sociologist William Julius Wilson (2003) puts it:

> A neighborhood in which people are poor, but employed, is much different from a neighborhood in which people are poor and jobless. Many of today's problems in the inner-city . . . neighborhoods— crime, family dissolution, welfare, low levels of social organization, and so on—are fundamentally a consequence of the disappearance of work. (p. 301)

As populations drop and the proportion of nonworking adults rises, basic neighborhood institutions—stores, banks, restaurants, gas stations, and so on—become more difficult to maintain. Churches experience dwindling numbers and shrinking resources; clubs and community groups also suffer. As a consequence, formal and informal social controls in these neighborhoods become weaker. At such times, crime and violence are likely to increase, further deteriorating already troubled neighborhoods.

It's worth noting that the disappearance of work in inner-city ethnoracial enclaves is not just a matter of race, even though those most affected are members of ethnoracial minorities. It is a structural consequence of broad trends, namely deindustrialization and economic globalization, which lie largely beyond the control of the individuals who suffer the most. These trends are unlikely to change in the foreseeable future. Potential employers see deteriorating inner-city neighborhoods full of undesirable workers and decide that it is unwise to locate businesses or manufacturing facilities there. Even special federal tax credits that are provided as an economic incentive do little to draw new businesses to these areas. The concerns of these businesses are economic, not racial. But the result is that these neighborhoods have no opportunities for recovery, thereby compounding their destitution.

Intersections
Race, Class, and Immigration

Immigrants have always occupied a rather curious and ambivalent place in U.S. society. In prosperous times, when workers are typically in short supply, they have been welcomed into this country as essential contributors to the economy. In the early 20th century, their labor helped build roads and the U.S. rail system. They have historically filled unwanted jobs (such as landscaping suburban gardens, harvesting crops, toiling over hot restaurant stoves, or sewing clothes), opened businesses, and improved the lives of many U.S. residents.

But when times are lean or when political winds shift, they may become victims of exploitation, exclusion, hostility, and sometimes violence. During these periods, people often describe the influx of immigrants, especially undocumented immigrants, as a "flood," subtly equating their arrival with disaster. In 2006, Congress passed the Secure Fence Act, allocating $2.7 billion for the construction of a 700-mile reinforced wall along the Mexican border. In 2010, Arizona attracted national attention when it enacted a law that makes the failure to carry immigration documents a crime and gives police broad powers to detain anyone who "appears" to be in the country illegally. The following year, five more states—Alabama, Georgia, Indiana, South Carolina, and Utah—passed similar laws. In fact, in the span of two years, 164 anti-immigration bills were passed around the country (Gordon & Raja, 2012). Alabama's law is particularly rigorous. It cuts off *all* state and local services to undocumented immigrants, makes it a crime to hire, rent property to, or "harbor" unauthorized immigrants, and deputizes local police officers to initiate deportation proceedings if they encounter someone suspected of being here illegally (Symmes, 2012).

In general, however, the American public tends to have mixed feelings about immigration. For instance, in a recent poll, 72% of respondents said that undocumented immigrants currently living in the United States should be allowed to stay in the country legally, if they meet certain requirements. And while roughly half (51%) said immigrants strengthen the country because of their hard work and talents, 41% felt that immigrants are a burden because they take jobs, housing and health care. In addition, more people felt that legal immigration should be decreased (31%) than felt it should be increased (24%; Pew Research Center, 2015b).

The immigrants who bear the brunt of antagonism and resentment tend to be people of color from Latin America, Asia, the Middle East, or Africa. In the late 19th century, 90% of the documented immigrants who came to the United States were from northern and southern Europe. But in 2012, only 7.9% were from Europe. The majority came from Asia (41.6%) and Latin America and the Caribbean (31.8%; ProQuest Statistical Abstract, 2015). In addition, 59% of unauthorized immigrants come from Mexico alone. This shifting configuration has changed the ethnoracial composition of the United States. In 1900, one out of every eight U.S. residents was of a race other than white; in 2010, the ratio is one in three; and by 2050, it is projected to be one in two (Martin & Midgley, 2010).

To the extent that expanded immigration means greater competition for unskilled jobs, working-class U.S. citizens of color are affected most. The issue of competition for jobs is especially volatile when it comes to undocumented immigration. Over 8 million unauthorized immigrants are employed, or about 5.2% of the entire U.S. labor force (Passel & Cohn, 2011). Nationwide, one out of every four low-wage workers in farming, fishing, construction, housekeeping, and forestry is an unauthorized immigrant (Broder, 2006; "Laboring in the U.S.," 2006). It's estimated that 90% of California's farmworkers are undocumented (cited in Welch, 2007). As one journalist put it, without such workers,

> fruit and vegetables would rot in fields. Toddlers in Manhattan would be without nannies. Towels at hotels in states like Florida, Texas, and California would go unlaundered. Commuters at airports from Miami to Newark would be stranded as taxi cabs sat driverless. Home improvement projects across the Sun Belt would grind to a halt. And bedpans and lunch trays at nursing homes in Chicago, New York, Houston, and Los Angeles would go uncollected. (Murphy, 2004, p. 1)

In addition, some economists argue that immigrant workers boost states' economies. Fifteen percent of U.S. workers are born outside the United States (Martin & Midgley, 2010). One study found that a 1% increase in employment in a state due to immigration produces an income increase of 0.5% in that state (Peri, 2009). Others point out that Social Security would go broke without the $7 billion or so in annual payments from undocumented workers, many of whom—contrary to popular perceptions—pay their share of income taxes (Murphy, 2004; Porter, 2005).

The flow of undocumented immigrants from Latin America into the United States has slowed in recent years. After peaking at 12.2 million in 2007, the number dropped following the economic recession and has stabilized at around 11.3 million a year since (Passel, Cohn, Krogstad, & Gonzalez-Barrera, 2014). The drop has been particularly steep among undocumented Mexican immigrants (Passel, Cohn, & Gonzalez-Barrera, 2012). Between 2000 and 2004, there were more than 500,000 illegal border crossings per year; in 2010, the figure dropped to 100,000 (cited in Cave, 2011). Experts attribute the decrease not only to economic slow-downs and immigration crackdowns in the United States but also to expanding economic and educational opportunities and declining birth-rates in Mexico.

The immigration issue illustrates a clash of political and economic forces. To politicians of all stripes, immigration is a crucial and sometimes volatile issue. But as long as powerful business interests see the need for a pool of cheap, mobile labor that is willing to work outside union and regulatory constraints, attempts to crack down on illegal immigration will remain ineffective. As long as jobs are available, poor foreigners will continue to come here seeking a better life.

THE ECONOMIES OF GENDER

In most countries around the world, women have much less earning power in the labor market than men. In the United States, the 1963 Equal Pay Act guaranteed equal pay for equal work and Title VII of the 1964 Civil Rights Act banned job discrimination on the basis of sex (as well as race, religion, and national origin). In 2010, for the first time in our history, women out-numbered men in the paid labor force—though this shift had as much to do with larger numbers of men losing their jobs than with larger numbers of women entering the labor force (cited in Rampell, 2010). Yet a significant gender gap in earnings remains. The median annual earnings for all U.S. men working full-time, year-round, is $50,033; the figure for women is $39,197. Thus, even among the fully employed, a woman still earns only about 79 cents for every dollar a man earns (DeNavas-Walt & Proctor, 2015). Although women have been closing the wage gap over the past sev-eral decades, progress has been rather slow. At the current rate, they won't achieve full pay equity with men until the year 2057 (Institute for Women's Policy Research, 2013a). It's even been estimated that one out of every three American women lives on the verge of poverty (Conley, 2014).

The gendered earnings gap widens with age. Women between 18 and 24 working full-time, year round earn about 87% of what male counterparts earn. But by the time they reach the years leading up to retirement (between the ages of 45 and 64), they earn only 68% of what men earn (ProQuest Statistical Abstract, 2015). That means that over a 40-year career, the aver-age working woman will earn $499,000 less than the average working man

(Gault, 2013). In addition, women over 50 who leave the workforce permanently to care for an elderly parent can expect to lose an additional $325,000 in wages and benefits (cited in Searcey, 2014). And because they earn less when employed, women's retirement pensions are also significantly smaller than men's (National Women's Law Center, 2006).

Moreover, the wage gap is especially pronounced for women of color. In 2012, the weekly earnings for African American women were 65% of men's earnings. Latinas earned 54% of men's pay. Asian American women were more successful, earning 88% of men's pay (Institute for Women's Policy Research, 2015b).

Why is the wage gap so persistent? One reason, of course, is occupational segregation and the types of jobs women are most likely to have. For five of the "most female" jobs (that is, those that are around 95% female)—namely, preschool teacher, teacher's assistant, housekeeper, child care worker, and dental assistant—the overall average weekly salary is $502. For five of the "most male" jobs (those around 95% male)—namely, airplane pilot, firefighter, aircraft engine mechanic, plumber, and construction worker—the overall average weekly salary is $1,117 (U.S. Bureau of Labor Statistics, 2015b).

Some economists and policymakers argue that the wage gap is essentially an institutional by-product that exists because men on the whole have more work experience and training, work more hours per year, and are more likely to work a full-time schedule than women (Dey & Hill, 2007). Thanks to the recent economic recession, large numbers of both men and women have been forced to work part-time because their employers have had to cut labor costs. But women are particularly susceptible to this trend. According to the U.S. Bureau of Labor Statistics (2015d), 14% of employed men work part time, compared with 34% of employed women. Not only do part-time workers earn less and have fewer benefits, but during hard times, they are usually the first ones pushed out of employment—not because they're women but because their jobs are the most expendable.

However, even when controlling for differences in experience, age, and education—factors that might justify discrepancies in salary—the wage gap between men and women remains (Weinberg, 2007). Women with bachelor's degrees can expect to earn less than men with a two-year associate's degree (mean annual earnings of $47,209 compared with $50,059). Similarly, women with doctoral degrees (with mean annual earnings of $80,501) earn much less than men with only master's degrees (with mean annual earnings of $97,365; ProQuest Statistical Abstract, 2015). Women with professional degrees (law, medicine, etc.) can expect to earn $51,000 *less* a year than their male counterparts.

Intersections
Race, Gender, and the Poverty of Single Parenthood

Obviously, economic disadvantage isn't equally distributed among differ-ent races or genders. But the intersection of race and gender, especially when coupled with marital status, creates a recipe for financial disaster. The poor people who receive government assistance in this society are predominantly women (and their children), disproportionately non-white, and almost exclusively single parents. In this country, women are more likely than men to be the sole caregivers of children born out of wedlock and more likely to have custody of children after a divorce (Hays, 2003). As a result, one out of every four children in the United States lives with only their mother. Forty-five percent of these families are poor compared to 20% of single-father families (Vespa, Lewis, & Kreider, 2013). Single working mothers and their children also make up a disproportionate num-ber of near-poor households too. While these families account for 22% of all working families, they make up 39% of all low-income families. The proportion is particularly high among African American single mothers (65%; Povich, Roberts, & Mather, 2014).

The reason so many single mothers are poor is that they suffer from what some sociologists have called the "triple whammy." First, like all women, they are paid lower wages than men when they work. Second, like all mothers who work outside the home, they must juggle paid and unpaid work. Taking care of children when employed requires the time and flexibility that few low-paying or part-time jobs provide. And third, unlike married mothers, single mothers must perform this feat without the consistent help of another adult (Albelda & Tilly, 2001). Child-rearing responsibilities restrict single mothers' economic opportunities by limiting their work schedules and job locations, their availability to work overtime, and their ability to travel, attend conferences, take off-hour training work-shops, and take advantage of other chances for advancement.

Race compounds the problem. People of color have consistently been less likely than Whites to have the economic resources to get them through tough times. Because of lower marriage rates, women of color are also more likely than their white (and male) counterparts to become single parents. Consequently, the chances of a child living in a single-mother family being poor vary along ethnoracial lines (see Exhibit 6.5).

The current welfare system further complicates the situation for sin-gle mothers. In the interests of reducing the welfare rolls, the government enacted massive reforms in 1996. As a result, financial assistance to the

Exhibit 6.5: Distribution of Children in Single-Mother Families by Race and Income, 2012

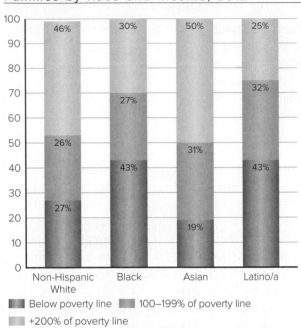

Below poverty line ■ 100–199% of poverty line
■ +200% of poverty line

(Source: Vespa, Lewis, & Kreider, 2013, Table 6)

poor is no longer a federal entitlement. Instead, each state receives a block grant and decides for itself how best to distribute the money to needy individuals. Contrary to popular belief, this financial assistance is usually not enough to sustain a life that is remotely comfortable. According to the Center on Budget and Policy Priorities, welfare benefit levels are so low that they don't provide family income above half of the poverty line in *any* state. And since 1996, the value of cash assistance benefits has declined by 20% or more in 37 states. In six states, it's dropped by over 40% (Floyd & Schott, 2013). In 2013, Congress cut Food Stamp benefits by over $400 a year for a family of four (Severson & Hu, 2013).

In addition, unemployed recipients are required to seek employment after 2 years of receiving benefits, and there is a 5-year lifetime limit on benefits. The idea behind such restrictions is that mandatory work requirements will teach welfare recipients important work values and make poor single mothers models for their children. The irony is that the prototype of the "good mother" in this society has always been the devoted stay-at-home mother. Yet, for poor single women on public assistance, such a goal is not only unattainable but discouraged. Even though raising children can provide far more satisfaction for many poor women than the drudgery of a low-paying, dead-end job, they are forced to place their work roles above their parent roles. They must often work long hours, and because these jobs frequently lack sick leave or paid vacation, poor working single mothers may have trouble taking time off to care for sick children.

Even though single parenthood is so closely related to poverty, it doesn't necessarily follow that marriage is an easy escape. Marriages are best for children only when the family is financially stable and physically safe (Shoener, 2014). Most women end up marrying men of their same social class, which in this case means either poor or working-class men. So the family is still subject to financial stress. Although married couples, on average, may be wealthier than single mothers, marriage in and of itself cannot lift single mothers out of poverty (Ehrenreich, 2004).

Many poor single mothers themselves don't see marriage as the solution to their economic problems. Sociologist Kathryn Edin (2003) interviewed 130 poor black, white, and Puerto Rican single mothers in Philadelphia. She found that most of them want to marry but only if they can marry men who are upwardly mobile and who are not abusive. Such men, they point out, are in short supply in the neighborhoods in which they tend to live. Mothers whose boyfriends live with them often impose a "pay and stay" rule, kicking the men out if they aren't employed and are not contributing toward household expenses. As one Puerto Rican mother put it:

> I didn't want to be mean or anything, [but when he didn't work], I didn't let him eat my food. I would tell him, "If you can't put any food here, you can't eat here. These are your kids, and you should want to help your kids, so if you come here, you can't eat their food." Finally, I told him he couldn't stay here either. (quoted in Edin, 2003, p. 164)

These mothers are all too aware that any additional threat to their precarious financial situation, even when it involves someone they care deeply for, can be tragic for them and for their children.

Edin's research is important because it shows that very few women avoid marriage simply to maintain their welfare eligibility, as many critics claim. In fact, marriage is often a marker of respect in ethnoracial minority communities. They remain unmarried because they have come to the rational conclusion that marriage would actually make their lives more difficult. If they can't enjoy economic stability and respectability from marriage, they see little reason to expose themselves or their children to men's unreliability, economic dependence, and perhaps even violence.

ON THE JOB: RACE, CLASS, GENDER, AND SEXUALITY IN THE WORKPLACE

Work is a key component of the identity and the self-esteem of most American adults. Upon meeting someone for the first time, we typically ask, "So, what do you do?" This question is not so much about how you spend your time but about who you are.

Unfortunately, we are not always free to choose any occupation that appeals to us. Large-scale economic trends, which may make certain jobs scarce or even obsolete, are only part of the picture. Race, class, gender, and to some degree sexuality can also influence the way people prepare for occupations, whether or not they get hired in the first place, how they're treated on the job once they get there, and their prospects for promotion. Consequently, discrimination can affect not only economic stability but how people ultimately identify themselves and others.

PROFESSIONAL TRAINING

The influence of race, class, gender, and sexuality on people's everyday work experiences begins early. For instance, a study of third-year medical school students reveals that although the proportions of women, people of color, and openly identified gay, lesbian, and bisexual students enrolled in North American medical schools have all increased over the past 50 years, subtle forms of bias still create a climate that can marginalize and alienate them (Beagan, 2001). Women report being mistaken for nurses, being called "girls," and being ignored by instructors. Students of color report high degrees of racial segregation in extracurricular activities. Students from poor and working-class families describe their struggle to construct the "right look," the professional appearance they feel is expected in medicine. Students from upper- and upper-middle-class backgrounds seem to have an easier time "fitting in." Such subtle inequities may appear normal, natural, and acceptable. However, they convey unmistakable information about who does and who doesn't belong.

In pursuit of a better understanding of identity-based inequities in professional training, sociologist Robert Granfield (2005) conducted in-depth interviews and surveys with students attending a prestigious East Coast law school. He was especially interested in the experiences of students who came from poor or working-class backgrounds. Initially, the working-class students saw their class background as a badge of honor, indicating how far they had come and what they were able to overcome. Many of them entered the legal profession in the first place because they wanted to help the downtrodden. But these students quickly came to see their working-class backgrounds as a burden. For instance, they became self-conscious of the way they spoke and noticed that their instructors assumed all students came from the same privileged class background. Their feelings of "differentness" added a layer of stress to the already stressful experience of being a law school student. They worried that, despite their solid academic records, they wouldn't make it.

Rather than simply dealing with their feelings of alienation, many working-class students attempted to distance themselves from their background. They often tried to mimic the more privileged students in terms of dress, speech, and demeanor. Some students in Granfield's study reported that their ultimate success in the legal profession came from their ability to appear privileged.

But the costs of such success can be steep, and not just because the strategy may ultimately fail. Many working-class students of color were unable to shed the stigma of their class background or the suspicions of others about their credentials and continued to feel like outsiders. Furthermore, law school—like medical school and other professional and graduate schools—takes a tremendous amount of work. Success often comes to those who can invest enormous amounts of time and energy in their studies. Spending time perfecting the accoutrements of an upper-class lifestyle necessarily takes time away from one's coursework, putting these students at a competitive disadvantage in the classroom. Finally, many of these students ended up feeling deceptive and experienced the added burden of believing that they had "sold out" and let their group down.

THE CORPORATE CLOSET

The Civil Rights Act of 1964 says that a person cannot be denied a job or fired from existing employment because of his or her gender, race, religion, or ethnicity. Sexual orientation, however, doesn't currently enjoy such explicit federal protection. There are some safeguards against unfair treatment at the state and local levels. Numerous counties and municipalities—not to mention 21 states and the District of Columbia—have enacted legislation banning workplace discrimination based on sexual orientation (Human Rights

Campaign, 2014b). In 2014, President Obama signed an executive order explicitly protecting gay, lesbian, bisexual, and transgender employees from discrimination by companies that have contracts with the federal government (Davis, 2014). However, at the time of this writing, gay people still lack virtually any legal protections in 16 states (especially in the South and Mountain West; Stolberg, 2014),

Meanwhile, corporate America appears to be at the forefront of workplace protections for LGBT workers. According to the Human Rights Campaign (2014a), 91% of Fortune 500 companies provide explicit non-discrimination protections based on sexual orientation and 67% offer same-sex partner benefits.

But corporate policies don't always translate into individual behavior. In many areas of the labor force, open homosexuality is still a liability. Despite the corporate protections, over half of gay, lesbian, and bisexual employees nationwide hide their sexual orientation at work and 35% lie about it. And 1 in 4 open LGBT employees feel that coworkers become uncomfortable when the topic of sexual orientation comes up or report hearing negative comments about LGBT people at work (Human Rights Campaign, 2014b). Indeed, some gay and lesbian workers believe that discrimination actually increases as they climb through the corporate hierarchy. There are only a handful of openly gay CEOs among the top companies in the country, and those who are gay are often reluctant to discuss their sexuality publicly (Miller, 2014).

RACIAL DISCRIMINATION IN THE WORKPLACE

Members of ethnoracial minorities have historically faced enormous formal and informal impediments in the business world, both as employees and as customers. In recent years, such top companies as Merrill Lynch, Comcast, Wells Fargo, Bank of America, and Macy's have paid tens of millions of dollars to settle racial discrimination cases brought by employees. A few years ago, three former managers at Wet Seal, a nationwide clothing store, successfully sued the company, asserting that it had a policy of firing and denying raises and promotions to African American employees because they didn't fit its "brand image" (Greenhouse, 2012). Sixteen employees at Coca Cola bottling plants in New York sued the company over its policy of subjecting its black and Latino/a employees to unfair and dangerous work assignments, limiting the hours of minority truck drivers, preventing them from working overtime, and systematically retaliating against them when they complained (Greenwald, 2012).

Ethnoracial discrimination is also apparent in the way some businesses treat their customers. Consider these examples:

- The Adam's Mark Hotel in Daytona Beach, Florida, was charged with discriminating against African Americans who had gathered for the annual Black College Reunion. The lawsuit asserted that the hotel required black guests to wear orange wristbands to enter the hotel and pay a $100 damage deposit, a $25 deposit to have the room telephone turned on, and a $300 deposit for access to minibars. None of these policies applied to Whites staying in the hotel (Holmes, 1999).
- The Cracker Barrel restaurant chain agreed to overhaul its training and management practices after the U.S. Department of Justice accused it of widespread discrimination against African American diners in 50 locations. Black customers were routinely given tables apart from Whites, seated after white customers who had arrived later, and given inferior service. Rather than being isolated incidents committed by bigoted servers, the practices were a consequence of organizational policies to which managers directly contributed (Lichtblau, 2004).
- Several black customers accused the upscale Manhattan retail store, Barneys, of discrimination when they were wrongly charged with fraud by undercover police officers after purchasing expensive items (Washington, 2013).
- CVS Pharmacies uses undercover teams of market investigators (MIs) to track and arrest shoplifters in many of its stores. In 2015, four former MIs sued the company, charging that its managers directed these teams to intentionally target black and Latino/a shoppers, even when there was no evidence of them stealing (Saul, 2015).

Think back to the distinction between personal and institutional discrimination discussed in the previous chapter. It is unlikely that cases like these occur because individual bigoted business owners harbor intense hatred of certain racial groups and treat them accordingly. Instead what often happens is that managers and senior executives, convinced that minority customers are costing their companies money, issue policy directives that are widely interpreted by employees to mean they have to discriminate on racial grounds (Kohn, 1994). In the CVS case, for example, these incidents occurred in several stores in the New York City area alone, indicating that it wasn't just individual bigotry; it came from company-issued instructions.

Typically, companies claim that their actions are motivated by business concerns. Hence, they do not perceive them as racist but as a function of the competitive, profit-driven nature of the economic marketplace. For instance, loan companies usually demand a credit history, some form of collateral, and evidence of the likelihood of success before they will lend money to prospective businesses. These are standard business practices, but they can perpetuate racial inequality because members of groups that have been mistreated in the past tend to be poorer to begin with and thus have poor credit ratings and no collateral. Admittedly, poor people are greater credit risks than those with economic resources, and businesses in poorer communities must pay more for insurance because of the greater likelihood of theft or property damage. But of course, the higher costs of doing business in a poor community usually make small-business loans to minority group members even more essential.

The important point here is that racial and ethnic discrimination in business settings is sometimes difficult to overcome precisely because it may occur for reasons other than overt racial or ethnic hatred. It is part of the taken-for-granted rules about doing business.

AFFIRMATIVE ACTION: OVERCOMING INSTITUTIONAL DISCRIMINATION

If tomorrow everybody in the United States were to wake up completely free of any hatred, prejudice, and animosity toward other groups, institutional discrimination would still exist. As Chapter 5 explains, because it is a problem that often lies at the structural level, it requires a structural solution.

The most far-reaching structural attempt to solve the problem of institutional discrimination has been a loosely defined governmental policy developed in the 1960s referred to as **affirmative action.** Affirmative action is a set of programs and policies that seeks out or provides equal opportunities to members of ethnoracial minority groups and women for educational or occupational positions to which they had previously been denied access. The assumption is that past discrimination has left certain people ill equipped to compete as equals today. Another assumption is that organizations will not change discriminatory practices unless they are forced to do so.

The protections and remedies embedded in affirmative action policies have been used successfully in several areas of social life. Cities have bused children to schools outside their neighborhoods to reduce school segregation. Businesses, unions, universities, and local governments accused of discrimination in hiring or admission have been sued under the 1964 Civil Rights Act, fostering widespread attempts to increase diversity. In part because of such action, more than 40% of U.S. colleges and universities reported enrollment gains among African Americans and Latino/as during the mid-1990s (cited in Worsnop, 1996). People of color now hold a greater percentage of management, white-collar, and upper-level blue-collar jobs than ever before. Wages and salaries relative to those of Whites have also improved somewhat. The American Civil Liberties Union (2000) has called affirmative action "one of the most effective tools for redressing the injustices caused by our nation's historic discrimination against people of color and women" (p. 1).

But today, affirmative action has also become a lightning rod for deeply held feelings about race, gender, and justice. Some politically liberal critics argue that the lives of people for whom affirmative action policies were originally designed—the poorest and most disadvantaged—remain largely unchanged. It's certainly true that top U.S. colleges accept more students of color than ever before. But these students tend to come from middle-class or upper-class backgrounds. About 8% of Harvard's undergraduates are African American. But the vast majority of these students are West Indian or African immigrants, children of immigrants from these regions, or children of biracial couples. Only a few are from families in which all four grandparents were born in this country and were descendants of slaves (Rimer & Arenson, 2004). Yet it's these students who were supposed to be the beneficiaries of affirmative action. They are the ones most disadvantaged by decades of racial discrimination, poverty, and inferior educations.

In addition, universities are typically more concerned with improving admission rates than with students' success once they're enrolled. The 6-year college graduation rate for Latino/a students is about 50%; for Native American and African Americans it's below 40%. By comparison, 62% of white students and 70% of Asian students graduate within six years (National Center for Education Statistics, 2014b). Because a college degree is associated with success later in life (bachelor's degree holders earn about twice as much a year as those with high school diplomas), such educational disappointment can have far-reaching effects on the education system, the economy, and society at large.

Other critics consider affirmative action demeaning to the people it is supposed to help and unfair to everybody else. They say it undermines standards by favoring the unqualified. Some conservative critics call it a form of "reverse discrimination." They argue that preferential treatment of any group, even one whose rights have been historically unrecognized, amounts to a form of discrimination. According to one study, such an assessment reflects an attitude held by many Whites that racism is a "zero-sum game," meaning that any *decrease* in bias against members of ethnoracial minorities must be associated with an *increase* in perceived bias against Whites (Norton & Sommers, 2011).

Contrary to popular belief, however, college admissions officers and employers are not compelled to institute quotas or to compromise their standards to meet affirmative action goals. They are simply required to make sure historically underrepresented groups have access to application information, to gather all relevant information on all qualified applicants, and to offer both minority and majority candidates the same opportunities for interviews and the like (Cherry, 1989). Quotas have been only a last resort, reserved for situations in which organizations are not making good-faith efforts to seek out qualified minority candidates. For example, if a firm announces a job opening in newspapers that reach only the white community or uses discriminatory procedures to eliminate minorities from employment, the government can then impose quotas.

Ironically, those who are most likely to be treated preferentially when it comes to college admissions are largely white, affluent "legacies," or children of alumni. Playing favorites with alumni children is openly practiced at almost all private colleges and many public institutions as well (Kahlenberg, 2010). At some highly selective universities, like Harvard and Princeton, legacies are five times as likely to be accepted as unconnected applicants with similar or better credentials (cited in Manderey, 2014). Some schools even reserve a certain number of spaces for legacies. In one recent year at Harvard, marginally qualified legacies outnumbered all African American, Mexican American, Puerto Rican, and Native American students combined.

People in the United States strongly disagree about whether past discrimination justifies preferential treatment of ethnoracial minorities in education or hiring. When asked if they thought affirmative action programs designed to increase the number of minorities on college campuses was a good thing, 63% of respondents to a recent survey said yes (Drake, 2014). However, members of different ethnoracial groups disagree on such issues as whether affirmative action itself is discriminatory, whether people should be compensated for past discrimination, and whether black and white children have the same chance to get a good education ("Attitudes toward affirmative action," 2003). According to the Pew Research Center (2009), 58% of Blacks—but only 22% of Whites—agree that the government should make every effort to improve the position of ethnoracial minorities, even if it means giving preferential treatment.

In 2014, the U.S. Supreme Court ruled that states have the right to ban affirmative action in college admissions decisions. To date, eight have done so: Oklahoma, New Hampshire, Arizona, Colorado, Nebraska, Michigan, Florida, Washington, and California. Overall, since the mid-1990s, the percentage of four-year public colleges that use race or ethnicity in admissions decisions has fallen from 60% to 35% (Cashin, 2014).

Affirmative action remains a controversial solution to institutional racism. Even if economic opportunities have been equalized, it doesn't mean that the accumulated disadvantages of the past have been entirely erased. For a long time to come, members of certain ethnoracial minorities will continue to be underrepresented in traditionally white positions. Can U.S. citizens achieve complete equality without forcing those who have benefited historically to give up some of their advantages? The answer to this question is complex, controversial, and emotionally charged and will have a great impact on the nature of ethnoracial relations in the United States in the coming years.

GENDER AND WORK

Like members of ethnoracial and sexual minorities, women have a long history of discriminatory treatment in the workplace. Thus, before we talk about the relative positions of men and women in the paid labor force today, we have to trace a bit of history. As we'll see, the differential treatment of women in the workplace has, for centuries, been supported by a somewhat biologically based ideology that the different genders are naturally suited to different economic and occupational pursuits.

Separate Spheres   Until the early to mid 19th century, the economies of most societies in the world were primarily agricultural. In the United States, people's lives centered around farms, where husbands and wives were interdependent partners in making a living; women provided for families along with men (Bernard, 1981). Although the relationship between husbands and wives on the farm was never entirely equal—wives still did most if not all of the housekeeping and family care—complete male dominance was offset by women's important contributions to the household economy (Vanek, 1980).

With industrialization, things began to change. New forms of technology and the promise of new financial opportunities and a good living drew people (mostly men) away from the farms and into cities and factories. For the first time in history, the family economy was based on money earned outside the household. Women no longer found themselves involved in the day-to-day supervision of the family's business as they had once been. Instead, they were consigned to the only domestic responsibilities that remained necessary in the growing industrial economy: the care and nurturing of children and the maintenance of the household.

The result was the development of a **separate spheres ideology,** beliefs that promoted the notion that women's natural place is in the home (the private sphere) and men's is in the work world outside the home (the public sphere). This ideal, in turn, fostered the belief that men and women are innately predisposed to different pursuits. Women were assumed to be inherently nurturing, demure, and sacrificial—a perfect fit for their restricted domestic roles. Their "natural" weakness and frailty were assumed to make them ill suited to the dog-eat-dog life of the competitive labor force and to justify their limited job opportunities. The ideal for men, on the other hand, was rugged self-reliance, power, and mastery of job and family. Men were thought to be naturally aggressive, calculating, rational, and bold—a perfect fit for the competitive demands of the marketplace. As long as men controlled the public sphere, they could wield greater economic and political power within society and translate that power into authority at home. The ideology of separate spheres was used to justify restrictions on women's involvement in economic, political, and educational activity and men's lack of involvement in family and community.

In truth, the reality of American family life has never quite fit the image painted by the ideology of separate spheres. Even in the late 19th century, many women were in the industrial labor force. By 1900, one-fifth of American women worked outside the home (Staggenborg, 1998). But the experiences of working women varied along class and race lines. For middle- and upper-class white women, few professions other than teaching and nursing were available, and these jobs paid poorly. Most of the women from these advantaged groups who did work entered and exited the labor force in response to family demands or took up volunteer work to fill their free time. In contrast, poor women worked mostly in unskilled jobs in clothing factories, canning plants, or other industries. Working conditions were often dangerous and exploitative. The one thing they shared with middle- and upper-class women was low pay compared with men doing the same jobs.

The conditions for women of color were especially bad. Black domestic servants, for instance, frequently left their own families to live in their employers' homes, where they were expected to work around the clock. Throughout history, poor African American women have rarely had the luxury of being stay-at-home spouses and parents. In 1880, 73% of black single women and 35% of black married women reported holding paid jobs. Only 23% of white single women and 7% of white married women reported being in the paid labor force at that time (cited in Kessler-Harris, 1982). Ironically, the privileged, upper-class white women who could afford to embrace the notion of separate spheres were able to do so only because they depended on other women—their servants—to do much of the household labor (Boydston, 2001).

The years following World War II represented the heyday of the separate spheres ideology. Media messages emphasized women's obligations to take their rightful position on the domestic front. Men pursued advanced educational opportunities during this period, but few women entered college. Of those who did, two out of three dropped out before graduating. Most women left because they feared that a college education would hurt their marriage chances (Mintz & Kellogg, 1988) or because they had already married and chose to abandon their educational pursuits to turn their attention to raising their families (Weiss, 2000).

Since the 1950s, though, the boundary separating men's and women's spheres has steadily eroded. Exhibit 6.6 depicts these trends, in both higher education and labor force participation. In 1960, about a third of female high

Exhibit 6.6: Historical Trends in Male and Female Preparation for and Involvement in the Economic Sphere

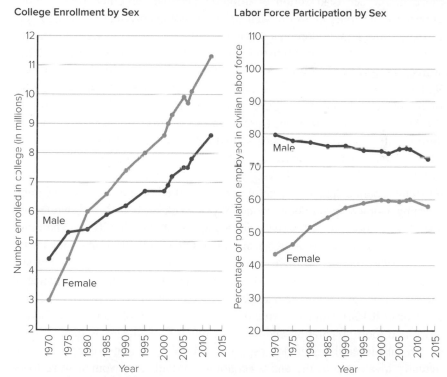

College Enrollment by Sex

Labor Force Participation by Sex

(Sources: ProQuest Statistical Abstract, 2014, Table 240, Table 620; U.S. Bureau of Labor Statistics, 2004; U.S. Bureau of the Census, 2011)

school graduates enrolled in college (compared with over 50% of male high school graduates); today, more U.S. women than men are enrolled in college (ProQuest Statistical Abstract, 2015). Since 1991, the proportion of women between the ages of 25 and 29 with a bachelor's degree or higher has exceeded that of men, a trend found across all racial and ethnic groups (Pollard, 2011). In 1950, a little over 30% of adult women were employed in the paid labor force; today, that figure is almost 60%, and it increases to 68.1% for married mothers, 71.3% for single mothers, and 79.7% for widowed, separated, and divorced mothers (ProQuest Statistical Abstract, 2015). The increase in female labor force participation has been particularly dramatic in some traditionally male-dominated fields such as medicine and law. For instance, in 1983, 15% of lawyers and 16% of physicians in the United States were women; by 2013, those figures had more than doubled (ProQuest Statistical Abstract, 2015).

Yet despite these trends, occupational segregation on the basis of sex is still the rule and not the exception. Most of the changes that have taken place in the sex distribution of different occupations come from women entering male lines of work. Men have not noticeably increased their representation in female-dominated occupations. For instance, according to the U.S. Bureau of Labor Statistics (ProQuest Statistical Abstract, 2015), women constitute 94.4% of all secretaries, 90.1% of all registered nurses, 94.8% of all childcare workers, 98.3% of all dental hygienists, and 97.8% of all preschool and kindergarten teachers (ProQuest Statistical Abstract, 2015). Despite their increased presence in traditionally male occupations, women still tend to be underrepresented among dentists (30.8%), physicians (35.5%), engineers and architects (14.1%), lawyers (33.1%), police officers (13.4%), and firefighters (3.5%).

The separate spheres ideology persists in the home as well. On average, working women spend about 19 hours per week on housework, while men spend only about 10 hours (Bianchi, Robinson, & Milkie, 2006). The hours that women spend on housework are down from 35 hours in the mid 1960s, and men have increased their contribution from 4 hours per week, but still men contribute only half as much time as women do to the maintenance of the household. According to a survey conducted by the U.S. Bureau of Labor Statistics (2013a), women devote three times as much of their day to housework and food preparation and twice as much to childcare as men.

What makes this situation especially troubling is that domestic work is actually invaluable to the entire economic system. If a woman were to be paid the minimum going rate for all her labor as mother and housekeeper, including child care, transportation, housecleaning, laundry, cooking, bill paying, and grocery shopping, her annual salary would be larger than the average salary of full-time male workers. One study found that if we apply average hourly wage rates to the typical daily amounts of child care mothers of children under 12 provide, a low-end estimate of the monetary value of this work is about $33,000 a year (Folbre & Yoon, 2006). But because societal and family power is a function of who brings home the cash, such unpaid work does not afford women the prestige it might if it were paid labor.

Gender Discrimination in the Workplace   The standard assumptions that drive the typical workplace often subtly work against women. Think of the things an employee generally has to do in order to be considered a valuable worker by a boss: Work extra hours, travel to faraway business meetings, go to professional conferences, attend training programs, be willing to work unpopular shifts, entertain out-of-town clients. Notice how these activities assume that people will have the time and the freedom from familial obligations to do them. Because women, especially mothers, still tend to have the lion's share of responsibility at home, they have more difficulty making time for these activities than male employees do and therefore are less able to "prove" to their bosses and coworkers that they are committed, enthusiastic employees.

The deep-seated nature of assumptions about what one needs to do to get ahead is reflected in the experiences of men and women who cross traditional gender lines in their jobs. Women in traditionally male occupations (like law, medicine, and engineering) carry extra burdens as they try to adjust to the workplace expectations and overcome the prejudices of others. When college students were asked to evaluate two highly qualified candidates for a job in engineering—one had more education; the other had more work experience—they preferred the more educated candidate 75% of the time. But when the more educated candidate had a female name, she was picked only 48% of the time (cited in Angier & Chang, 2005).

In addition, women's wages don't measure up to men's in traditionally male occupations, and women are more likely than men to face subtle obstacles to promotion to a management position, a phenomenon sometimes called the **glass ceiling** (Padavic & Reskin, 2004). For instance, the median weekly income for male lawyers is $1,986, but female lawyers earn only $1,566 a week. Likewise, female physicians and surgeons make, on average, $600 a week less than male physicians and surgeons (U.S. Bureau of Labor Statistics, 2013d).

Female lawyers report that they are often given low-status projects to work on, which are not only less interesting but also a professional dead end. Consequently, their rate of promotion is lower than that of their male counterparts, and they remain underrepresented in private practice, law firm partnerships, and in such high positions as judges on the federal courts, district courts, and circuit courts of appeals. In addition, women are more likely than men to enter the legal profession in relatively low-paying positions in the government or in public interest firms, hampering the trajectory of their careers (Hull & Nelson, 2000).

Similarly, although it is much easier for women to become physicians today than it once was, they still face pressures and problems that their male counterparts rarely face. Not only are they paid less relative to men at similar career stages; they also tend to be segregated into particular specialties that reflect common gender expectations. As I mentioned, women make up about a third of all practicing physicians. But they account for over 60% of pediatricians and around 50% of child psychiatrists, geriatric doctors, obstetricians/gynecologists, and neonatal doctors. By contrast, less than 10% of neurological, vascular, orthopedic, heart, and thoracic surgeons are women (Association of American Medical Colleges, 2014). In addition, female physicians who want to alter their work schedules to fulfill parental roles sometimes face unsympathetic male colleagues. Male doctors may feel that their female counterparts will not perform their fair share of unappealing tasks, such as being on-call around the clock (Lowes, 2002).

The relatively few men who do cross gendered occupational boundaries tend to have entirely different experiences. Male nurses, librarians, or elementary school teachers may confront some prejudices and discrimination from people outside the profession, particularly assumptions regarding their sexuality. But with the exception of fashion modeling and prostitution, men in traditionally female occupations consistently out earn women (Williams, 2004). For instance, male secretaries and male nurses can expect to make about $125 a week more than their female counterparts (Institute for Women's Policy Research, 2015a). In fact, men who want to be librarians or nurses or secretaries discover that there is actually a preference for hiring them. And the more women there are in an occupation, the greater men's chances of being promoted into supervisory positions (Maume, 1999). These men sometimes ride a **glass escalator**—invisible pressures to move up in their professions, often regardless of their desire to move up (Williams, 2004). For instance, a male nurse who just wants to take care of patients might be encouraged, even expected, to become a floor supervisor or pursue a position in hospital administration; male kindergarten teachers may be urged to pursue positions as principals (Williams, 2004).

But it's important to note that the glass escalator does not operate equally for all men. African American male nurses, for example, do not enjoy the sorts of benefits white male nurses enjoy (Wingfield, 2013). They are often subjected to common racial stereotypes that emphasize danger and threat. Therefore, they are less likely than white male nurses to receive a warm reception from female colleagues or patients. Here's how one man describes an encounter with a white female patient:

> I said good evening, my name's Chris, and I'm going to be your nurse. She says to me, "Are you from housekeeping? . . . I've had other cases. I've walked in and had a lady look at me and ask if I'm the janitor (Wingfield, 2013, p. 487).

Furthermore, the lingering perception that they are better suited to lower-level service work means that they are rarely, if ever, mistaken for doctors; nor are they encouraged by supervisors to pursue more prestigious positions in the hospital.

Intersections
Gendered Racism in the Workplace

Sociologists Yannick St. Jean and Joe Feagin (1998) were also interested in the double burden of gender and race on people's work-related identities. They conducted in-depth interviews with middle-class African American men and women to understand how the distinctive combinations of race and gender affect their everyday work lives.

The researchers conclude that discrimination against African American women is pervasive in workplaces. They may face stereotyping, excessive demands, and exclusion from friendship groups. Frequently, black women carry the stigma that comes with the assumption that they were hired because of their race and gender and not because of their qualifications for the job. Hence, the question of their ability is raised over and over. Sometimes, such questions are camouflaged, as when ordinary competence is seen as remarkable and worthy of praise. Here's how a school counselor described this experience:

> What I resent is, a lot of times that if I do something and do it well, it's like "Oh my God," like they are so surprised. "Oh, you write really well. You speak really well." . . . They thought they were complimenting me. But, actually, I was a little offended. . . . I got the feeling it was like, ". . . You are black and I did not know you could really talk like that." (quoted in St. Jean & Feagin, 1998, p. 42)

However, St. Jean and Feagin note that black women are often more acceptable to white male managers, supervisors, and coworkers than black men. From a white male manager's perspective, black women can be controlled and managed more easily than men. As one white male accountant noted:

> If there's a choice between a black woman and black man, all things being equal, the black woman will be given the benefit of the doubt. . . . I'm not saying that black women are necessarily less aggressive, or anything like that, but it's sometimes too intimidating. . . . Corporate America would probably rather deal with a black woman than a black man. (quoted on p. 57)

There is a long tradition, dating back to Reconstruction, of black women being the sole or primary breadwinners in their families. Today, black women have actually seen their opportunities increase relative to black men's. According to the U.S. Bureau of the Census (ProQuest Statistical Abstract, 2015), more black women than men go to and graduate from college and more work as professionals. In addition, college-educated black women generally hold better-paying jobs than black men.

You can see that combining race and gender reveals subtle nuances in the way discrimination functions in employment situations. Hiring a black woman may provide a company with "evidence" that it is "diversifying" its workforce. However, the gendered nature of hiring practices obscures the underlying biases that still exist.

CONCLUSION

I've spent a lot of time and space in this chapter assessing economic and occupational inequalities based on race, ethnicity, gender, class, and sexuality. The progress that has been made in overcoming the blatant and massive inequalities of the past is real and commendable. But the progress is incomplete. And even though things aren't as bad as they once were, the dogged persistence of economic inequality—borne out by official statistics as well as people's everyday lived experiences—is troubling.

So as I conclude this chapter, I'm left with a perplexing sociological question. Given the undeniable economic inequality that exists both locally and globally today, why aren't we more bothered by it? Why aren't we distressed by the misery and hardships of others? Why aren't there more massive demonstrations over the growing gap between the very rich and the very poor than the ones that crop up every now and then? Do we see poverty, unemployment, and homelessness simply as unfortunate but inevitable side effects of an economic system that works the way it's supposed to by rewarding those who are successful? I think the answers to these questions lie less in the factual reality of economic inequality than in our own perceptions of it. Just because inequalities exist doesn't necessarily mean that people will perceive them as unfair.

If that sounds confusing, let me explain. *Equality* means that people get the same things and are treated the same way. *Fairness*, on the other hand, refers to a situation in which people's outcomes are proportional to their inputs. In other words, fairness means that everybody gets what he or she deserves. Imagine two people investing in a particular stock. Person A invests $1,000; Person B invests $100,000. If they both get the same rate of return on their investments, you'd expect that Person B's profit would be 100 times greater than Person A's, right? Their objective payoffs would be extremely unequal, but most people would consider the situation to be perfectly fair. Why? Because Person B invested more and therefore deserves more in return. By separating equality from fairness, we can see that a situation that appears unequal can still be considered fair

In a situation where the investments and payoffs are obvious, the difference between equality and fairness is easy to see. But can we apply this kind of thinking to the sorts of inequalities discussed in this chapter? If we define an investment as anything that entitles someone to certain outcomes, then personal traits and even elements of one's social identity can count as an investment. If you believe, for example, that men have more to offer in the paid labor force than women (because you think they're stronger, more rational, more competitive, and so on), then you probably wouldn't think it's unfair to pay them more than women, even if they're in the same occupation. Similarly, if you believe, as some retail chains have argued, that white people or heterosexuals in sales positions bring certain financial advantages into a situation (for instance, that customers feel more comfortable around them), then you might conclude that they deserve to be given more visible and more lucrative positions than members of ethnoracial or sexual minorities do. It's only when we can convince ourselves that people are getting what they deserve that we can ultimately accept, and maybe even justify, their suffering.

All social movements that attempt to overcome past injustices—the Civil Rights Movement, the Women's Movement, the Gay Rights Movement, the Living Wage Movement—are about the same thing: human investments and the calculation of fairness. All have tried to make the claim that the unequal distribution of rewards in society (access to higher education, good-paying jobs, political participation, legal protection, effective medical care, and so on) is unjust. Showing that inequalities exist is the easy part.

Reams of statistical evidence can back up claims that some people aren't getting as much as others. We can show that men and women get different salaries for the same job or that members of ethnoracial minorities are confined to certain occupations or that openly gay employees lose their jobs more frequently than heterosexuals.

The hard part is to prove, argue, or maybe simply assert that these inequalities are unfair. If differences in race, gender, class, or sexual orientation are accepted as unequal investments, then there is no unfairness, no injustice. When people claim that gays and lesbians don't deserve equal protection under the law because their behavior is immoral, they are essentially making an argument that homosexuality is not as high an investment as heterosexuality and therefore doesn't necessitate the same treatment under the law. Only when inequality is seen as unfair—when it becomes impossible to justify the different outcomes for certain racial, gender, class, or sexual groups on the grounds that some are more deserving than others—can meaningful social change occur.

[**INVESTIGATING IDENTITIES AND INEQUALITIES**]
Living on the outskirts of poverty: A balanced budget

This chapter has provided a lot of information on the lives of people who are economically disadvantaged and face discrimination in the workplace. We've seen that even people who are employed and whose income is above the official poverty line can sometimes find it difficult to make ends meet. Let's take a closer look at what that looks like.

Imagine a family of four living in your hometown: a mother, a father, and two children ages 3 and 7. Suppose that both parents work full-time outside the home. They each earn the federal minimum wage: $7.25 an hour. If they both worked 40 hours a week, 52 weeks a year, they'd each earn roughly $15,080 for a total pretax household income of $30,160. Using the 2015 tax rate schedule, they would pay about $3,604 in income taxes, making their annual take-home pay $26,556. The parents' pretax income is over $6,000 above the official poverty line for a family of four, which is $24,036 before taxes, so they are not "officially" poor.

Make a list of all the goods and services this family needs to function at a minimum subsistence level—that is, at the poverty line. Be as complete as possible. Assume that the 7-year-old attends school all day but the 3-year-old must be cared for by someone during the day. Consider food, clothing, rent for an unfurnished two-bedroom apartment, household amenities, utilities (gas, electricity, water, sewage, trash, if applicable), transportation, medical care, child care, entertainment, and so on.

Now estimate the minimum monthly cost of each item. If you currently live on your own and must pay these expenses yourself, use those figures as a starting point (but remember that you must estimate for a family of four). If you live in a dorm or at home, ask your parents (or anyone else who regularly pays bills) what their expenses are for household goods and services. Call a local day care center to see what it charges for child care. Call local utilities companies to see what the average gas, electric, cable/Wi-Fi, and water bills are in your community. Go to the local supermarket and compute the family food budget. Don't forget, you have to feed four people three meals a day, every day. For those items that aren't usually purchased on a monthly basis (for example, clothing and household appliances), estimate the yearly cost as best you can and divide by 12.

Once you have estimated the total monthly expenses, multiply by 12 to get the annual subsistence budget for the family of four. If your estimate is higher than the family's take-home pay, what sorts of items could you reduce or cut out entirely to make ends meet? Justify your choices about what categories of expenses can be reduced or cut. Did you have to make any tough choices (for instance, between money for food and paying the electric or gas bill)?

Try to describe the quality of life of this hypothetical family. What sorts of things are they forced to do without that a more affluent family might simply take for granted (for example, annual vacations, pocket money, a second car, eating out once a week)? What would be the impact of poverty on the lives of the children? How will the family's difficulty in meeting its basic subsistence needs translate into access to opportunities (education, jobs, health care) for the children later in life?

CHAPTER 7

Inequalities in Law and Justice

Several years ago, when my younger son was still in high school, he and I watched a television about "the 100 scariest movie moments of all time." The scenes—taken from the grainy, classic horror films of the 1920s as well as the high-tech, multimillion-dollar blockbusters of today—ranged from creepily suspenseful to graphically gruesome. Although many of the clips were truly terrifying or disgusting, we both went to bed that night comfortable in the knowledge that everything we saw was phony. These movies were meant to entertain. Evil villains, reptilian monsters, space aliens, cyborgs, and demons were nothing more than actors, animatronic beasts, or computer-generated freaks. The blood, gore, and decapitations were merely makeup, camera, and CGI tricks. The frightening surprises were simply the products of skillful moviemaking and tension-building musical soundtracks. Had these films been documentaries about real evil, we might have been scared out of our wits.

But even the most ingenious Hollywood effects seem amateurish compared with the actual tales of cruelty and mayhem that litter the historical record. The Torture Museum in San Gimignano, Italy, houses one of the world's most extensive collections of ghastly devices invented for inflicting agony on and ultimately destroying people. Among them are the "Inquisition Chairs," upholstered with flesh-piercing metal spikes that were common instruments of torture in Europe until the 1800s. Another device, the "Wooden Horse," consisted of a wooden saddle in an upside-down V-shape. The victim would be forced to straddle the saddle. Weights would then be placed on his or her feet one by one. The mounting pressure would eventually split the body in half ("Crime and too much punishment," 1997). It seems as if humans are at their creative best when thinking up ways to inflict pain on one another.

Such devices may be curiosities of the past, but as a species humans are no less brutal nowadays than 500 years ago. Consider Ariel Castro, the middle-aged Cleveland man who kidnapped three teenage girls between 2002 and 2004. He raped, tortured, and held them captive until their escape in 2013. Accounts of his cruelty sounded like they had come off the pages of a Hollywood script.

As troubling as such incidents are, what is especially upsetting is that the majority of pain and mayhem we impose on one another today is rarely this random and arbitrary. When it comes to violence, some people—because of their race, class, gender, religion, or sexuality—have a greater chance of being victimized than others. Consider this brief sampling of events that have occurred in the recent past:

- A gay college student in Wyoming is pistol-whipped, tied to a fence, and left to die. At his funeral, protesters from a church in Topeka, Kansas, hold up signs reading "God Hates Fags!" The church's web site has a picture of the man depicted burning in hell. The same web site has a similar photo of a lesbian who was mauled to death by two dogs several years earlier. Above her picture, it reads "God used literal dogs to kill a figurative dog."

- A few years later, an 18-year old Colorado woman is beaten to death with a fire extinguisher. The man accused of killing her tells the police that he attacked her when he found out that she was biologically a man, after the two met online and had a sexual encounter.

- A 21-year old man shouting racial epithets opens fire in an African Methodist Episcopalian church in Charleston, South Carolina, killing 9 people who were there for a bible study meeting. In the weeks following the massacre, fires destroy 6 black churches in 5 southern states.
- A 22-year old California man kills six people and injures 13 at the University of California, Santa Barbara. In a YouTube video posted before the massacre, he describes his hatred of women and his contempt for racial minorities.

According to the FBI (ProQuest Statistical Abstract, 2015), in 2012, there were over 4,000 racially or ethnically motivated violent offenses (mostly against African Americans), nearly 1,100 religiously motivated crimes (mostly against Jews), and about 1,200 sexually motivated crimes (mostly against gay men and lesbians). In the last 15 years, there have been nearly 1,500 assaults committed against homeless people resulting in close to 400 deaths (National Coalition for the Homeless, 2014). Forty-five states plus the District of Columbia have found it necessary to amend their criminal codes to deal with bias-motivated or hate crime. In each case, the law carries either additional or heightened penalties for these crimes.

Not only do different groups face different likelihoods of being assaulted, they have vastly different experiences with the people, governing bodies, agencies, and institutions that supposedly exist to protect us from wrongdoing. Some people can "get away with" more when they cause harm to others. And those in positions of authority seem to respond to some people more harshly than to others when acts of violence—or any crime, for that matter—occur.

In this chapter, I will look at the complex relationship among law, justice, crime, and social inequality. Just how fair is our justice system? For instance, whose interests are represented in the ways that laws are written? Who suffers? How do race, class, gender, and sexuality affect the likelihood of criminal victimization? Criminal commission? How are people's interactions with police, courts, and prisons influenced by personal and institutional discrimination?

THE SOCIAL CONSTRUCTION OF LAWS

We live in a society of laws. Laws dictate the actions of companies that produce the innumerable goods and services we use in our daily lives. Laws direct the behavior of the government and other social institutions. Virtually everything we do—driving cars, paying taxes, ingesting particular substances, getting married, solving disagreements with others—occurs under some set of legal rights and restrictions. We may disagree with some laws from time to time or complain when we feel they are too restrictive or vague, but it's hard to imagine living in a society without them. Most of us come to trust that the people in our legal institutions who define and uphold these laws—legislators, judges, police, and so on—will always act to protect the common good. In short, laws presumably protect good people from the actions of bad people.

POWER, POLITICS, AND LEGAL DEFINITIONS

It seems obvious that societies define certain acts as crimes because they threaten or offend a majority of people. But according to some conflict sociologists (for example, Quinney, 1970), the law is better seen as a political instrument used by specific groups to further their own interests, often at the expense of others. The law, they argue, is typically created by economic elites who control the production and distribution of major resources in society.

For instance, aside from toxic poisons, tobacco is probably the single most lethal substance we can consume. According to the World Health Organization (2015), nearly 6 million people around the world die each year from tobacco-related causes. In the United States, the death rate among smokers is 2 to 3 times higher than that of non-smokers (Carter, et al., 2015). Cigarette smoking is responsible for one in five deaths annually, or about 480,000 deaths a year (Centers for Disease Control and Prevention, 2014). That means that more people die from smoking-related causes than from HIV/AIDS, illegal drug use, alcohol use, motor vehicle injuries, suicides, and murders *combined*. Ten times as many U.S. citizens have died prematurely from cigarettes than have died in all the wars fought by the U.S. during its history. Tobacco significantly increases the risk of respiratory disease, cataracts, stroke, low birth weight babies, six categories of cardiovascular disease, and roughly twelve different types of cancer. The costs of smoking are financial as well as physical. It's estimated that smoking and exposure to tobacco smoke cost nearly $130 billion in direct medical costs and $150 billion in lost productivity each year (U.S. Surgeon General, 2014).

Yet tobacco—whether smoked or chewed—remains legal, with only age restrictions on its purchase and usage. The tobacco industry is powerful, both economically and politically. Despite its link to death and illness, it has one of the most influential lobbies in Washington. The economies of several states depend on tobacco. Even the United States Chamber of Commerce supports the American tobacco industry by fighting anti-smoking laws in places like Australia, Jamaica, Nepal, and Uruguay (Hakim, 2015). With such powerful friends, it's highly unlikely that the possession and use of tobacco would ever be criminalized.

Laws, of course, are determined by the actions of elected legislators—who often bear little resemblance to the constituents they serve. Politicians may present themselves as just regular folks or claim to be able to "feel our pain," but in truth lawmakers tend to come from lives of privilege. The median net worth of a member of Congress is about $1,008,767, 14 times more than that of a typical American household. Indeed, the average per capita net worth of the 10 wealthiest members of Congress is about $192 million (Center for Responsive Politics, 2014a, 2014b).

All this shouldn't be a surprise. Running for public office, especially at the national level, takes millions of dollars. Even if they're not independently wealthy themselves (like, say, Donald Trump), successful candidates are often bankrolled by wealthy donors and patrons who pump money into campaigns because they see a particular candidate as the one most likely to support their economic interests (Knott, 2004). The U.S. Supreme Court opened the door for even deeper financial influence when it ruled recently that limits on the amount of money individuals and groups can contribute to campaigns are unconstitutional, equating the right to financially support a candidate to the freedom of speech.

Legislators, of course, can also be greatly influenced by powerful segments of society through lobbying groups, political action committees, individual campaign contributions, and so on. As a consequence, the higher a group's political and economic position in society, the greater the likelihood that its values and interests will be reflected in and protected by the law.

THE LAWS OF INTIMACY

Laws that control our private, intimate choices also serve the interests of some at the expense of others. Take, for instance, the formation of romantic relationships. No one tells you with whom you can fall in love, right? By and large, we don't live in a society in which our families arrange our relationships. But our intimate experiences are always subject to societal—and sometimes state—control. Marriages, for example, are legal contracts. Each state determines the lawful age at which people can marry as well as health requirements, inheritance rules, property division in case of divorce, and so on. Laws also prohibit being married to more than one person at a time and marrying certain blood relatives.

In some societies, where intimacy falls under tighter community control, the violation of normative restrictions can be lethal:

■ In 2003, two young lovers from a small town in the Indian state of Uttar Pradesh were beaten to death by members of their own families for breaching a village taboo (Waldman, 2003). In several rural areas of India, it is considered incest if two people from the same village fall in love. Similarly, a few years later, a 22-year-old upper-caste Indian woman was found dead in her bedroom after she had told her family that she was secretly engaged to a man from a lower caste. Said a lawyer involved in the case, "Her family was trying their level best to prevent her from marrying that boy. The pressure was such that either she was driven to suicide or she was killed" (quoted in Yardley, 2010, p. 1).

■ In 2010, a young couple in northern Afghanistan were stoned to death for trying to elope (Worth, 2010). The Afghan Women's Network estimates that there are 150 such "honor killings" in the country each year (cited in Nordland, 2014).

■ In 2014, a pregnant Pakistani woman was beaten to death by her family because she had defied their wishes to marry a cousin and instead married the man of her choice. Police investigators said she was killed on a busy street as a crowd of about 30 men watched but did nothing (Gillani & Walsh, 2014).

■ In Syria, relatives sometimes kill girls who bring dishonor to their families by having premarital sex. Under Syrian law, these killings, called *ghasalat al arr* ("washing away the shame"), are not considered murder. If the killer is convicted of anything it is usually the lesser charge of "crime of honor," resulting in a prison sentence that can be as short as a few months (Zoepf, 2007).

But even in the United States, where we assume that the formation of relationships is based solely on the desires and attractions of the individuals involved, the law has historically restricted certain types of intimate contact. Sometimes, as in the case of race, legal prohibitions have applied to intimacy that crossed an identity boundary; other times, as with same-sex marriage, the prohibitions have applied to intimacy that doesn't cross such a boundary.

Miscegenation   Fear and condemnation of interracial intimacy have been a part of American culture, politics, and law since the first European settlers arrived here close to 400 years ago. The first law against **miscegenation**— sexual contact and marriage between people of different races—was enacted in Maryland in 1661, prohibiting Whites from marrying Native Americans or African slaves. According to this law, a white woman who married a black slave became a slave herself (Bardaglio, 1999). Over the next 300 years or so, 38 more states put miscegenation laws on the books, expanding their coverage to include Chinese, Japanese, Koreans, Indians, and Filipino Americans. These laws were enacted to prevent a mixing of the races (referred to as *mongrelization*) that would destroy the racial purity (and assumed superiority) of Whites (Lemire, 2002).

Because of the "one-drop rule" for determining who was black that was in effect at the time (remember from Chapter 2 that in the past a single drop of "Negro blood" in one's ancestry made a person a "Negro"), white men were largely exempt from anti-miscegenation laws. This conception of race meant that a white woman impregnated by a black man gave birth to a black child, but a black woman impregnated by a white man also gave birth to a black child. So white men could "roam sexually among women of any color without threatening the color line" (Bardaglio, 1999, p. 115).

For black women, interracial sexual contact was more likely to be a punishment in itself rather than the reason for punishment. Sexual access of white men to black women was the cornerstone of male power from the beginning of the country, much of it through rape and other forms of coercive sexuality (J. D. Hall, 1995). Any assertion of a woman's will could be met with sexual violence. In early America, enslaved women were especially vulnerable since their rape could lead to pregnancy and thus could increase a slave owner's "holdings." White men had a powerful economic incentive to engage in interracial sex. The incentive became even stronger in the early 19th century when the importation but not the reproduction of slaves was outlawed in the United States. In addition, lighter-skinned, mixed-race slaves typically fetched a higher price at market. The ability to afford light-skinned slaves symbolized the owner's social status (Nagel, 2003).

The fact that white men could force themselves on black women with impunity didn't end with slavery. A decade ago, an elderly black woman named Essie Mae Washington revealed that she was the daughter of the late Senator Strom Thurmond. Thurmond was a powerful white senator from South Carolina who was an energetic supporter of racial segregation in the mid-20th century. Not only did Thurmond contradict his segregationist leanings back in 1925 when he impregnated his family's teenage black maid, he also violated the law against statutory rape and miscegenation. Yet he received no punishment (Crenshaw, 2004b).

Black men have not experienced the same level of tolerance when it comes to interracial sexual relations. During slavery, Whites worried that the same strength and virility they exploited in their black male slaves for economic gain could be wielded as a weapon of vengeance through the sexual assault of white women. After slavery was abolished, fears of black male sexuality—combined with the fear that freed Blacks would penetrate the economic and cultural worlds of Whites—served to justify Jim Crow laws. In 1896, the U.S. Supreme Court ruled that racial segregation was constitutional, and it continued to be legal until the middle of the 20th century.

Fears of black male sexuality spawned much violence against black men, especially in the South. Well into the 20th century, lynching and the threat of lynching were effective tools of terrorism and vigilante justice, typically rationalized in terms of the protection of white womanhood. There is documented evidence of 4,000 lynchings of Blacks in 12 southern states between 1877 and 1950 (Equal Justice Initiative, 2015). The Ku Klux Klan's original charter was to protect white women's chastity after the emancipation of slaves (Baldauf, 2000). Unlike official justice agencies, like the police, a lynch mob could operate with no limits and sometimes without an actual crime. In fact, less than a quarter of lynch victims were actually accused of rape or attempted rape (J. D. Hall, 1995). Lynching was, most of all, a tool of psychological intimidation, "an instrument of coercion intended to impress not only the immediate victim but all who saw or heard about the event" (J. D. Hall, 1995, p. 436).

Violent disapproval of interracial sexual contact continued well into the 20th century. It reached a highly publicized turning point in the summer of 1955. That year, a 14-year-old African American boy from Chicago named Emmett Till traveled by train to visit his relatives in Mississippi. He boasted to his cousins there that, back in Chicago, he had many friendships with white girls. On a dare from one of his cousins, Emmett went into a candy store and talked to the white woman who worked there, Carolyn Bryant. Ms. Bryant interpreted the conversation as a flirtation. Not long after that, two white men—one of them Carolyn's husband, Roy—showed up at Emmett's uncle's house, abducted Emmett, and drove off. A few days later, Emmett's body was found floating in the Tallahatchie River, with a bullet hole in his head, a 75-pound fan tied around his neck, and a horribly battered face. Mr. Bryant and another man were arrested and charged with murder. At the trial, the defendants testified that they didn't mean to kill Emmett but wanted to teach him a lesson. It took the all-white jury 75 minutes to find the defendants not guilty.

A legal response to anti-miscegenation sentiment came over a decade later. It began in 1958 when a Virginia couple, Richard and Mildred Loving, were awakened in the middle of the night by the local sheriff and two assistants and immediately arrested for violating Virginia's law prohibiting interracial marriage. Richard was white and Mildred was "colored." The Lovings were sentenced to 1 year in jail but then learned that the judge would suspend the sentence if they left the state and promised not to return for 25 years. At the time, the majority of states, including California, Oregon, Indiana, all the mountain states, and every state in the South, legally prohibited interracial marriage (Liptak, 2004). The Lovings found a home in Washington, D.C., where interracial marriage was not prohibited, and had three children. While there, they embarked on an appeal of their conviction. In 1967, the Supreme Court ruled in favor of the Lovings, concluding that using racial classifications to restrict freedom to marry was unconstitutional.

Since the Loving case, law and public opinion regarding interracial marriage has shifted. The year after that decision, Americans still disapproved of interracial marriage by a margin of three to one. Fifty years later, however, the majority of Americans approve of it. Four in ten Americans say that growing rates of intermarriage is a change for the better in society; only one in ten think it is for the worse (Wang, 2012).

In light of these more positive attitudes, it is not surprising that the number of interracial marriages in the United States has grown, from 3.2% of all existing marriages in 1980 to 8.9% today (ProQuest Statistical Abstract, 2015). In addition, marriages between Latino/as and non-Latino/as (regardless of race) increased from less than 2% of all marriages in 1980 to more than 4% today (ProQuest Statistical Abstract, 2014). These figures grow each year.

Yet interracial intimacy still lacks complete acceptance in some areas of the country. A few years ago, a poll of Mississippi Republicans found that 47% believed that interracial marriage should be illegal; only 40% thought it should be legal (Public Policy Polling, 2011). In 2009, newspapers reported that a Louisiana Justice of the Peace regularly refused to issue marriage licenses to interracial couples, claiming that he was doing it to protect children because of the instability of such marriages. He was eventually forced to resign.

In addition, many Americans, especially those in black-white relationships, still experience some social disapproval. About half of the black-white couples in one study felt that biracial marriage makes things harder for them, and about two-thirds reported that their parents had a problem with the relationship, at least initially (Fears & Deane, 2001). As one woman in an interracial marriage put it, "In a perfect world, race wouldn't matter, but that day's a while off" (quoted in Saulny, 2011, p. 4).

Same-Sex Marriage   The issue of legal restrictions on intimacy has become especially prominent recently with the heated controversy over the legalization of same-sex marriage. At the time of this writing, 20 other countries—Argentina, Belgium, Brazil, Canada, Denmark, England/Wales, Finland, France, Iceland, Ireland, Luxembourg, the Netherlands, New Zealand, Norway, Portugal, Scotland, South Africa, Spain, Sweden, and Uruguay—grant gay men and lesbians the right to legally marry. Australia, Germany, Austria, Switzerland, and many other European countries allow same-sex couples to enter "civil unions" (sometimes called "domestic partnerships" or "registered partnerships"), which grant them many of the legal protections and economic benefits and responsibilities of heterosexual marriage. Israel and Mexico recognize marriages between same-sex couples, but only if they are performed in other countries (Freedom to Marry, 2014).

The matter was only recently resolved in the United States. Twenty years ago, the federal Defense of Marriage Act—written at a time when three-quarters of Americans disapproved of same-sex marriage and *no* state allowed it—formally defined marriage as the union of one man and one woman; authorized all states to refuse to accept same-sex marriages from other states where it could become legal; and denied federal benefits such as Social Security survival payments and spousal burials in national military cemeteries to same-sex couples. But between 2004 and 2014, 36 individual states legalized same-sex marriage, creating a confusing patchwork of recognized legal status. In 2013, the U.S. Supreme Court ruled that the Defense of Marriage Act was unconstitutional, meaning that gay and lesbian couples who lived in states where same-sex marriage was legal were entitled to all the federal marriage benefits that heterosexual couples were entitled to. Two years later, the U.S. Supreme Court ruled once and for all that state bans on same-sex marriage were unconstitutional.

The 2015 Supreme Court decision legalizing same-sex marriage nationwide reflected a massive historical shift in public opinion. In 1996, 27% of the population favored legalizing same-sex marriage; by 2015, that figure was 60% (Pew Research Center, 2015d). In fact, over the last decade, support for legalizing same-sex marriage increased in *every* state by an average of 13.6% (Flores & Barclay, 2013). Younger people are especially inclined to support it. In one survey, 73% of people younger than 34 support same-sex marriage rights, compared with 39% of people over 70 (Pew Research Center, 2015d).

Favorable attitudes toward marital equality can even be found in segments of society that one would consider more traditional in their attitudes toward marriage, such as the military, religion, and conservative politics.

In 1993, the U.S. Department of Defense enacted the "Don't ask, don't tell" policy. According to this rule, military personnel could not be asked about their sexual orientation. However, openly professing one's homosexuality or engaging in sexual conduct with a member of the same sex could still constitute grounds for discharge. In 2010, President Obama signed a law repealing the "Don't ask, don't tell" policy. Three years later, the Undersecretary of Defense (2013) issued a memorandum stating, "The Department will work to make the same benefits available to all spouses, regardless of whether they are in same-sex or opposite sex marriages, and will recognize all marriages that are valid in the place of celebration" (p. 1).

It's certainly the case that the overwhelming majority of Evangelical Christians oppose the legalization of same-sex marriage (Pew Research Center, 2015d). However, a majority of mainline Protestants and Catholics are in favor of it. In fact, 75% of self-identified Catholics between the ages of 18 and 29 support legalization (Lipka, 2014). In 2014, the Presbyterian Church (U.S.A.) voted in its General Assembly to change the definition of marriage from "a man and a woman" to "two people" and to allow its ministers to perform same-sex marriage ceremonies in those states where it is legal (Goodstein, 2014). Other religions—the United Church of Christ, the Quakers, the Unitarian Universalist Association of Congregations, and the Reform and Conservative movements in Judaism—have taken similar actions.

Even in the realm of conservative politics, the public expression of support for or at least tolerance of legal same-sex marriage is growing. While it's true that people who identify as politically liberal are still more likely to approve of legal same-sex marriage than those who identify as politically conservative (Cohn, 2013), the gap is shrinking. And even prior to the Supreme Court's decision, equal numbers of Republicans and Democrats (about 72%) felt that legalization was inevitable (Pew Research Center, 2015d). In 2014, a prominent Republican senator said in a speech that if his party wanted to win elections in the future it had to abandon opposition to same-sex marriage as a campaign issue. That same year, three Republican Congressional candidates running for Congress featured their same-sex spouses prominently in their campaign literature (Parker, 2014a).

There is some concern, however, that the legalization of same-sex marriage will reinforce the idea that the only legitimate intimate relationship is marriage and therefore may actually limit the diversity of "acceptable" relationships rather than expand it. Some fear that now that same-sex marriage is legal all gay couples will be expected to want it. Those who prefer to cohabit could find themselves marginalized and stigmatized. Some legislators have already expressed a desire to get rid of domestic partnership benefits for same-sex cohabiting couples. The logic is that when marriage is available, domestic partnerships become unnecessary and irrelevant. Marriage would be formally privileged above any other type of relationship, and discrimination based on sexual orientation would be supplanted by discrimination based on marital status. Even before the Supreme Court ruling, several large companies—Verizon, Delta Airlines, and IBM, to name a few—had already rescinded health care coverage for cohabiting partners of employees in states that had legalized same-sex marriage and replaced it with spousal coverage. These companies told their employees that they had to marry within a certain period of time—usually one year—or lose the benefit (Bernard, 2015).

The merits of these debates notwithstanding, the legalization of same-sex marriage will have practical, everyday significance for couples. Marriage conveys protected legal status. Legally married couples are eligible for about 1,100 benefits, such as inheritance rights, pension and Social Security benefits, insurance coverage on a spouse's policy, eligibility to live in certain apartment complexes, savings from joint tax returns, the ability to make medical decisions for a partner in an emergency, and visitation rights in prisons and hospital intensive care units (Marriage Equality USA, 2014). People in non-marital relationships are not legally entitled to such benefits.

Furthermore, when states did not legally recognize same-sex marriages, gay couples of color, who already faced both racial and anti-gay bias, suffered the most. Nearly a quarter of same-sex couples in the United States are nonwhite (Gates, 2010). Their households are about twice as likely as white same-sex households to include children. But they also report lower median household incomes and lower home ownership than both black heterosexual couples and white same-sex couples (Gates, 2010). Hence, their inability to gain access to the legal and financial benefits of marriage created additional disadvantage by hurting their ability to provide for children, buy houses, and prepare for retirement (Dang & Frazer, 2004).

RACE, CLASS, AND JUSTICE

> "There can be no equal justice where the kind of trial a [person] gets depends on the amount of money he [or she] has." (Justice Hugo Black quoted in Cole, 1999, p. 3)

The relationship between social inequalities and the law is nowhere more apparent than in the way people are processed through the massive criminal justice system once they are suspected or accused of breaking the law.

And perhaps no other criminal case in the past two decades brought the matter of legal imbalances to the forefront of American consciousness (and frenzied media attention) as much as the O. J. Simpson trial in 1995. Simpson—an African American, former star football player, and international celebrity—was tried for and acquitted of the murder of his white wife, Nicole, and her white companion, Ron Goldman. Before, during, and after the trial, about three-quarters of African Americans maintained that Simpson was innocent; at the same time, about three-quarters of white Americans thought he was guilty (Cole, 1999).

Many Blacks considered Simpson's acquittal a reversal of centuries of injustice in which the mere accusation that a black man had murdered two Whites would have been sufficient to see him lynched. They pointed to the suspicious actions of police officers who handled the evidence in this case and the racist remarks of one of the prosecution's key police witnesses. To them, the verdict showed that perhaps the system was no longer set up to disadvantage people of color. They felt they had every reason to cheer (Cole, 1999).

To many Whites, however, the case was a bewildering travesty of justice. The evidence against Simpson, they believed, was overwhelming. His blood was found at the scene of the murder; the victims' blood was in his car and on his clothes; one of Simpson's gloves had hair from the two victims, fibers from their clothes, and their blood on it. To many Whites, it seemed like the predominantly black jury in the case had blatantly ignored the evidence and voted for one of their own.

The Simpson case is important, however, precisely because of what these polarized reactions overlooked: It wasn't just about his race. Simply put, Simpson wasn't like any other black murder defendant. He had substantial financial resources and celebrity status. Most defendants of color can't afford private attorneys let alone a high-powered, high-profile "dream team" of lawyers. Ironically, the features of the case that worked to Simpson's advantage, and that led to such outrage among Whites, are the same features that have historically benefited Whites in court—the ability to buy a good defense, a face not stereotypically associated with crime, a jury composed of members of one's own race. It's safe to say that had Simpson been unknown and destitute—as many defendants of color are—the case would have turned out quite differently.

We don't have to travel back 20 years to see examples of such judicial imbalance. In 2013, a juvenile court judge in Texas sentenced a 16-year old boy from a wealthy family to 10 years probation after he killed four pedestrians in a drunk driving crash. His blood-alcohol level was three times the legal limit for an adult when he lost control of his truck and plowed into a group of people helping a woman whose car had stalled. The judge decided on this sentence, instead of the 20-year prison term sought by the prosecutors, in part because a psychologist during the trial testified that the young man suffered from psychological problems (like an undeveloped sense of responsibility) that sometimes afflict children who are coddled by extremely wealthy parents. Dylann Roof, the white gunman who massacred 9 black parishioners in a Charleston, South Carolina church in 2015, was not only captured alive, he was treated to a meal by arresting officers and assigned a judge who expressed concern for his family (Sehgal, 2015).

In contrast, over the last few years, we have all witnessed a steady stream of incidents in which unarmed people of color end up dead in confrontations with police officers. Among the most publicized are:

- Trayvon Martin, the black teenager gunned down in 2012 by the neighborhood watch coordinator in the gated community where Trayvon was staying.
- Timothy Russell and Malissa Williams, the Cleveland couple killed in a hail of police bullets after their car backfired. Police fired 137 shots into the car, hitting both Russell and Williams 2 dozen times.
- Michael Brown, the black teenager and robbery suspect shot to death in the street by a police officer in Ferguson, Missouri in 2014.
- Eric Garner, the 44-year old black man from Staten Island, New York killed in 2014 as a result of an illegal chokehold used by police officers to subdue him.
- Tamir Rice, a 12-year old black boy shot and killed by police in 2014 after they'd received a dispatch call describing a "young, black male" brandishing a gun (the gun was a toy).
- Walter Scott, a 50-year old black man shot from behind in 2015 by a police officer in North Charleston, South Carolina as he fled on foot following a traffic stop for a nonfunctioning brake light.
- Freddie Gray, a 25-year old black man in Baltimore who died in 2015 from spinal injuries sustained while he was being transported in a police van after being arrested.

No matter what your feelings are about these cases, one thing that they illustrate is clear: Justice is not now, nor has it ever been, blind. In theory, under the U.S. Constitution, every American is entitled to the same legal protections. In practice, however—from the way laws are written to the way people are treated by police, processed through the courts, and punished— equal protection and equal treatment have always been an illusion.

RACIAL PROFILING

To many observers, the killings I just described reflect the depth of beliefs people have about "dangerous" black males. As one columnist put it, "It's an open secret among African-American men and boys that people are often afraid of them" (Martin, 2015, p. 1). Such fears are less about individual bigotry as they are about the influence race has on the way people define others. Officers involved in such incidents routinely explain that they used lethal force because they had a "reasonable fear of imminent threat" (Wines & Robles, 2014). So as long as people automatically assume that young black men are a physical menace, deadly reactions will be seen not only as understandable but as justified:

> Poor, young, urban, (disproportionately) black males make up the core of the enemy forces in the crime war. They are the heart of a vicious, unorganized guerrilla army, threatening the lives, limbs, and possessions of the law-abiding members of society, necessitating recourse to the ultimate weapons of force and detention in our common defense (Reiman & Leighton, 2013, p. 69).

A quick glance at statistical information on the relationship between race, crime, and law enforcement confirms what these incidents illustrate: that the justice system is dramatically imbalanced. A recent examination conducted by *The New York Times* revealed that in hundreds of police departments across the country, the percentage of white officers on the force is more than 30 points higher than the percentage of whites in the communities they serve. And in some cases, the gap is 60 or 70 points. For instance, in Ferguson, Missouri, Whites make up 29% of the city's population; however, 83% of police officers there are white. In Stone Park, Illinois—a suburb of Chicago—8% of residents are white but 83% of police officers are white (Ashkenas & Park, 2015).

The picture is equally skewed on the side of those who are the focus of law enforcement attention. For instance, African Americans make up about 13% of the general population, but they account for 38% of all arrests for violent crime, 29% of arrests for property crimes, and 32% of arrests for drug violations. Blacks are nearly four times more likely than Whites to be arrested on charges of marijuana possession, even though the two groups use the drug at comparable rates; in some places like Iowa, Minnesota, Illinois, and the District of Columbia, Blacks are eight times more likely than Whites to be arrested (American Civil Liberties Union, 2013). In addition, African Americans account for 39% of convictions for violent crimes, 34% of convictions for property crimes, and 46% of convictions for drug crimes (U.S. Bureau of Justice Statistics, 2012).

These sorts of official statistics paint a grim picture of the relationship between crime and race, but they may mislead us into thinking that Blacks are simply more criminally inclined than members of other ethnoracial groups. In the 2008 National Crime Victimization Survey, 23% of violent crime victims reported that their assailants were black. That same year, however, 32% of arrests for rape, 56% of robbery arrests, and 34% of arrests for aggravated assault were of Blacks. Similarly, Blacks constitute 13% of all monthly drug users, but make up 35% of those arrested, 55% of those convicted, and 74% of those sentenced for drug possession. Such figures suggest that police are especially likely to use race as one of the factors in making an arrest (Reiman & Leighton, 2013).

Oversimplified images of criminals always fall short of applying to all individuals. The vast majority of African Americans do not commit crimes, just as the vast majority of Muslims are not terrorists, and the vast majority of Italians are not involved in organized crime. Nevertheless, the degree to which such images are assumed to characterize an entire group is important because it can influence the reactions of individuals and the criminal justice system itself. For instance, after the attacks of September 11, 2001, federal, state, and local governments faced the difficult dilemma of trying to balance security concerns with individual freedom. The use of race—in particular, "looking Middle Eastern"—as a factor in stopping suspected terrorists became a widely accepted law enforcement practice. Not only has the profiling of Arabs and Muslims been tolerated to a large degree, but some citizens and even some legislators have actually demanded it on the grounds that these individuals are statistically more likely to be terrorists (Beinart, 2003).

From the 1930s to the 1960s, many Blacks in this country wouldn't embark on a long-distance automobile trip without a guidebook called The Negro Motorist Green Book. The book provided blacks with city-by-city information about where they could drive, sleep, eat, buy gas, or shop without being harassed, humiliated, or attacked (McGee, 2010). Although such blatant discrimination is much less common today, travel may still be a perilous venture for people of color. According to the U.S. Bureau of Justice Statistics, white, black, and Latino/a drivers are equally likely to be stopped by police; however, black and Latino/a drivers are significantly more likely to be searched by police once they are stopped (see Exhibit 7.1). The odds are even higher for young men in these ethnoracial groups (Engel & Calnon, 2004).

Police often argue that, like it or not, race in some cases constitutes "reasonable suspicion," something the U.S. Supreme Court has ruled is justifiable grounds for investigatory stops. They further defend their use of race in deciding which travelers or pedestrians to stop by pointing to the statistics showing that African Americans and Latino/as are more likely than Whites to be

Exhibit 7.1: The Effect of Race on Contact with Police

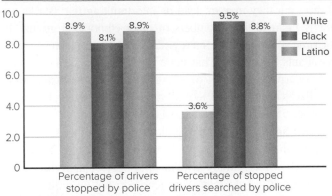

(Source: Durose, Smith, & Langan, 2007)

arrested and convicted of the most common street crimes. According to the former police chief of Los Angeles, who happened to be African American, "In my mind it is not a great revelation that if officers are looking for criminal activity, they're going to look at the kind of people who are listed on crime reports" (quoted in J. Goldberg, 1999, pp. 53–54). This line of thinking is pervasive among civilians as well. Reverend Jesse Jackson once said, "There is nothing more painful to me at this stage in my life than to walk down the street and hear footsteps and start thinking about robbery—then look around and see somebody white and feel relieved" (quoted in Cole, 1999, p. 41).

Is racial profiling as a crime control tactic effective? When law enforcement agents stop and interrogate people of color, are those individuals more likely than Whites to be carrying illegal drugs, weapons, or other forms of contraband? A study of over 1 million cases found that close to 17% of white drivers who were searched were actually carrying drugs or weapons, compared with only 9% of Latino/a drivers, 7% of black drivers, and 0% of drivers of other races/ethnicities (Engel & Calnon, 2004).

In light of these sorts of statistics, local, state, and federal law enforcement agencies around the country have come under attack in recent years for their racial profiling policies. Consider New York City's controversial "stop and frisk" policy, which gave police the power to stop and detain someone based on "reasonable suspicion" of involvement in criminal activity. Although not defined in racial terms, many civil rights groups alleged that the policy was applied overwhelmingly to young black and Latino men (Harris-Perry, 2012). Between 2004 and 2012, 83% of those stopped and interrogated were black or Latino/a (Bergner, 2014). In 2013, a federal judge ruled that these tactics violated the constitutional rights of people of color.

To date, however, 26 states allow law enforcement officials to use racial profiling. Forty-six states allow profiling based on religion or religious appearance (Amnesty International, 2010). A bill called the "End Racial Profiling Act," which would prohibit the use of profiling on the basis of race, ethnicity, national origin or religion by police, was introduced in Congress in 2007 and re-introduced in 2013, but has not yet passed. In 2014, the Obama Administration issued new rules that prohibit racial profiling in some law enforcement contexts but still allow federal agents to consider race and ethnicity when stopping people at airports, border crossings, and immigration check points (Apuzzo & Schmidt, 2014).

CLASS AND CRIME

When politicians talk about fighting crime, or when news outlets report fluctuations in crime rates, they are usually referring to crimes associated with the people at the lower end of the socioeconomic spectrum (illegal drug use, robbery, burglary, murder, assault, and so on) rather than corporate crimes, governmental crimes, or crimes more likely to be committed by privileged people in influential positions. On occasion—such as when it was revealed in 2014 that General Motors knew about and failed to inform government regulators of an ignition switch defect that was responsible for the deaths of at least 17 Americans—the public directs its collective anger toward a large powerful corporation responsible for some wrongdoing. But in general we easily accept the "fact" that the individual street criminals highlighted in the media are our biggest enemies and the most serious threat to our personal well-being and the well-being of the entire society.

Ironically, however, ordinary lower-class street crime is actually less of a constant and imminent physical danger to us than things like unsafe work conditions; dangerous chemicals in our air, water, and food; faulty consumer products; unnecessary surgery; and shoddy emergency medical services. Approximately 12,765 Americans were murdered in 2012 (ProQuest Statistical Abstract, 2015). Yet, at the same time:

- About 4,400 Americans died on the job in 2013 (U.S. Bureau of Labor Statistics, 2015a).
- It's estimated that 4% to 10% of all cancer cases in the U.S. (48,000 annually) are caused by occupational exposure (Centers for Disease Control and Prevention, 2012c).
- Approximately 1.7 million healthcare-associated infections occur in U.S. hospitals each year, resulting in 99,000 deaths (Centers for Disease Control and Prevention, 2015).

Add in the 3.7 million Americans who suffer from nonfatal workplace injuries and illnesses each year (U.S. Bureau of Labor Statistics, 2015c) and you can see that street crime is not the biggest threat to our health and safety.

Corporate and white-collar misbehavior also pose greater economic threats to Americans than street crime does. The FBI estimates that burglary and robbery cost the United States $3.8 billion a year. Unnecessary medical treatments alone, such as unwarranted scans, blood tests, and surgical procedures, cost at least $210 billion annually (cited in Parker-Pope, 2012). And the total cost of white-collar crimes like corporate fraud, bribery, embezzlement, insurance fraud, cell phone fraud, internet-related crimes, and securities fraud amounts to over $680 billion a year (Reiman & Leighton, 2013).

To be fair, some people actually do view certain types of corporate malfeasance as a more serious form of deviance than street crime (Huff, Desilets, & Kane, 2010). Indeed, the financial crisis that first gripped the nation in 2008 created a firestorm of public anger that cast unprecedented scrutiny on white-collar misconduct. President Obama vowed to crack down on Wall Street bankers for their reckless practices (P. Baker & Herszenhorn, 2010). In a few high-profile cases, executives convicted of corporate crimes have received harsh prison sentences:

- In 2006, Jeffrey Skilling, former CEO of Enron, received a 24-year sentence for securities fraud and other crimes.
- In 2009, a wealthy stockbroker and financial adviser named Bernard Madoff pled guilty to charges of securities fraud, investment fraud, mail fraud, wire fraud, money laundering, and theft from an employee benefit plan, to name a few. Prosecutors estimated that these schemes cost his clients about $65 billion. The judge called Madoff's actions "extraordinarily evil" and sentenced him to 150 years in prison, an act that was largely symbolic since Madoff was 71 years old at the time (Henriques, 2009).
- In 2011, billionaire hedge fund manager Raj Rajaratnam was found guilty of securities fraud and conspiracy. He was sentenced to 11 years in prison (though the government recommended a sentence twice that long).

But by and large responses like these have been directed at *individual* white-collar criminals. Corporations themselves rarely receive heavy criminal punishment when their dangerous actions violate the law. In 2015, Turing Pharmaceuticals raised the price of the antiparasitic drug, Daraprim 5,556%—from $13.50 a tablet to $750 a tablet. But public outrage and legal action were not directed toward the company; instead they were focused on the company's highly visible founder, Martin Shkreli, who quickly acquired the title of "the most hated man in America."

Indeed, to ease the inconvenience of prosecution for corporate wrongdoers, the U.S. Justice Department has instituted a form of corporate probation called *deferred prosecution*. Several major companies that have been charged with billions of dollars worth of accounting fraud, bid rigging, and other illegal financial schemes—including American International Group, PNC Financial Services Group, Merrill Lynch, AOL-Time Warner, Toyota, and American Express—have agreed to deferred prosecutions, in which they accept responsibility for wrongdoing, agree not to fight the charges, agree to cooperate with investigators, pay a fine, and implement changes in their corporate structure to prevent future criminal wrongdoing. If the company abides by the agreement for a specified period of time—usually 12 months—prosecutors will drop all charges (Mokhiber & Weissman, 2004). Since 2007, the Department of Justice has made over 150 deferred prosecution agreements with companies accused of criminal activity (Henning, 2012).

Such arrangements are meant to avoid more drastic punishment, which could destroy these companies and cost thousands of innocent lower-level employees their jobs. For instance, when the government aggressively prosecuted the Arthur Andersen accounting firm in 2002 for its criminal role in the famous Enron scandal, 28,000 employees lost their jobs (Lichtblau, 2008). But the penalties companies do receive are relatively minor and don't do much to deter their future law violations. In 2009, UBS AG, Switzerland's largest bank, entered a deferred prosecution agreement on charges that it had helped U.S. taxpayers hide accounts from the IRS. In exchange for a dismissal of the charges, the bank agreed to pay $780 million in fines, penalties, interest, and restitution; acknowledge responsibility for its actions and omissions; and continue cooperating with Justice Department officials (U.S. Department of Justice, 2009). It's no wonder that many large corporations consider the punishments they receive for wrongdoing simply a cost of doing business.

Why aren't these costly corporate acts considered as dangerous as face-to-face street crime? According to conflict sociologist Jeffrey Reiman (Reiman & Leighton, 2013), the answer resides in the circumstances surrounding these acts. People typically perceive the injuries caused by wealthy corporations as unintentional, indirect, and a consequence of an endeavor defined in this culture as legitimate or socially productive: making a profit. In most people's minds, someone who tries to harm someone else is usually considered more evil than someone who harms without intending to. Moreover, being harmed by a street criminal is a more terrifying experience than being harmed indirectly by a white-collar criminal. Finally, harm that results from illegitimate activities is usually considered more serious than harm that is a by-product of standard business activities.

PRISONS

In recent years, governments at the state and federal levels have implemented tougher policies—cracking down on drug users and dealers, scaling back parole eligibility, lengthening prison sentences, building more prisons, and rescinding legal protections for people suspected of being linked to terrorism. Many states now have "three-strike" laws that impose lengthy mandatory prison sentences for three-time offenders.

Not surprisingly, the inmate population has swelled. In 1970, there were fewer than 200,000 people in state and federal prisons; today that figure is about 1.6 million (Carson & Sabol, 2012). Another 4.8 million Americans are under community supervision, probation, and parole (ProQuest Statistical Abstract, 2014), meaning that almost 6.5 million people, or about 2% of the population experience some sort of criminal justice supervision. This situation is less a function of some staggeringly high number of evil people in this country than it is of the "tough on crime" policies that have taken hold in the last few decades. In 2013 the U.S. incarceration rate was 716 prisoners per 100,000 people (Walmsley, 2013). No other industrialized country comes close to this figure. For instance, Canada's rate is 118 per 100,000; in Japan it's 51 per 100,000.

These statistics are distressing enough. What is even more disturbing is that the population of prisoners does not accurately reflect the general population. For one thing, prisoners are overwhelmingly male. Men account for over 93% of all prisoners and are 14 times more likely than women to be incarcerated (ProQuest Statistical Abstract, 2014).

The ethnoracial identities of prisoners are also out of balance. Latino/as and African Americans make up over 70% of the U.S. inmate population even though they compose only about 27% of the general population (U.S. Sentencing Commission, 2011). Black men have a 32% chance of spending time in prison, compared to 17% for Latinos and 6% for white men (The Sentencing Project, 2014).

Furthermore, the risk of imprisonment rises steeply as level of education drops. For instance, on any given day, young black men without a high school diploma are more likely to be behind bars (37%) than to be employed (26%; Pettit, 2012). Sadly, imprisonment can actually deepen the inequalities that gave rise to disproportionate incarceration in the first place. Early incarceration is associated with low wages, unemployment, family instability, further criminal activity and incarceration, and restrictions of political and social rights (Pettit & Western, 2004).

The highly publicized "War on Drugs" that began in the 1980s worsened ethnoracial disparities in incarceration. Close to half of all federal prisoners are behind bars on drug offenses (The Sentencing Project, 2014). It seems that heightened media and political attention and increased budgets for law enforcement led to more police resources being used to ferret out drug offenders. This escalation of incarceration for drug offenses has created significant ethnoracial imbalances. Police agencies frequently target low-income, minority communities for enforcement operations. Hence, although there is some evidence that the racial composition of imprisoned drug offenders is beginning to balance out (Mauer, 2009), Blacks and Latino/as still make up over two-thirds of people in prison on drug charges (U.S. Sentencing Commission, 2009).

Another reason for this disparity may reside on how particular drugs are defined in the first place. Consider the legal punishments for the possession of crack cocaine versus powdered cocaine. Although the two types of cocaine cause similar physical reactions, the sentences for those convicted of selling them are vastly different. The average length of a sentence for selling crack cocaine is over 2 years longer than the average sentence for selling powdered cocaine (96 months vs. 79 months; United States Sentencing Commission, 2014a, 2014b). According to federal law, possession of 28 grams of crack cocaine yields a five-year mandatory minimum sentence for a first offense; it takes 500 grams of powder cocaine to prompt the same sentence (Drug Enforcement Administration, 2015).

Some law enforcement officials argue that the disparity is justified because crack cocaine is more closely associated with violence than powdered cocaine, is more dangerous to the user, and is more likely to cause birth defects in babies whose mothers use it while pregnant. However, studies of the two forms of cocaine indicate that their effects are in fact quite similar. In addition, the effects of maternal crack use on fetuses are no different from those of tobacco or alcohol use (cited in Coyle, 2003). Many sociologists have concluded that crack laws have as much to do with race, poverty, unemployment, and homelessness as with the properties of the drugs themselves (Duster, 1997). The common perception is that the typical user of powdered cocaine is a white suburbanite and that the typical crack user is young, urban, and a member of an ethnoracial minority. Official crime statistics support this perception, although the discrepancy has grown smaller in the past decade. In 2013, 93% of those convicted of crack possession were black and Latino/a; less than 6% were white. By contrast, 31.2% of those convicted of powdered cocaine possession were black, 10% were white, and 58% were Latino/a (though most of these individuals are white; U.S. Sentencing Commission, 2013). In 2010, President Obama signed into law the Fair Sentencing Act, which aims to reduce these sentencing disparities. In 2011, the U.S. Sentencing Commission voted unanimously to reduce the unfairly long sentences for crack offenders already in prison so that they are more in line with shorter terms given powder cocaine offenders (Serrano, 2011).

Prisons are also skewed with regard to class. In some countries—including up until the 1830s, the United States—people could be thrown into jail for not paying their debts. Only recently did the U.S. Supreme Court rule that a judge can't add prison time on an inmate because of his or her inability to pay fines or court costs. But while poverty isn't a crime anymore, contemporary prisons operate for all intents and purposes as the nation's poorhouses. In some places, people who can't afford to pay fines—say, for speeding tickets—often end up in jail (Bronner, 2012). Furthermore, although the accused have a constitutional right to an attorney even if they can't afford one, many poor people still face the legal system alone. It turns out that this constitutional provision only applies to criminal cases, not civil ones. Hence in civil matters like home foreclosures, job loss, and child support, poor people often end up representing themselves, which usually means they lose because they don't present necessary evidence, commit procedural mistakes, and fail to examine witnesses thoroughly. It's estimated that 80% of the legal needs of the poor in the United States go unmet (Bronner, 2013).

In and of itself, the statistical fact that the poor and ethnoracial minorities are overrepresented among those who spend time in prison for committing crimes needn't be evidence of discrimination or injustice. After all, if people from these groups commit more imprisonable crimes, then the fact that more of them ultimately wind up behind bars is simply an accurate reflection of reality (Tonry, 1995). Indeed, one of the most consistent findings in criminal research is the correlation between unemployment (a factor closely associated with economic disadvantage) and violent crime, property crime, and illegal drug use (Hagan, 2000). Furthermore, economic and educational disparities may also relate to differences in crime patterns and the way people are processed through the system. Certainly, those with little or no income and little schooling experience frustration at blocked opportunities and therefore may be pushed into criminal activities (Merton, 1957).

Nevertheless, other evidence shows that poor individuals from ethnoracial minorities are policed, prosecuted, and sentenced more punitively than wealthier Whites because law enforcement officials perceive them to be more threatening and dangerous (Reiman & Leighton, 2013; Tittle, 1994). Even when they commit the same crime, poor Blacks and Latino/as are sentenced to longer prison terms than other offenders (Reiman & Leighton, 2013).

Incarceration can also influence the way people racially identify themselves. Sociologists Aliya Saperstein and Andrew Penner (2010) analyzed data from the National Longitudinal Survey of Youth, a survey administered to over 13,000 young men and women over the span 2 decades. Among the questions respondents were asked was how they identify themselves with regard to race. The researchers found that those who identified as white during the first year of the survey were significantly more likely to identify as black during the last year of the survey if they had spent time behind bars, compared to those who had not been incarcerated. Not only does this finding illustrate that racial identity is influenced by social context (see Chapter 2), it also shows the power of imprisonment in reaffirming racial stereotypes even to the point of "coloring" people's self-concepts.

The overrepresentation of the poor and ethnoracial minorities in prisons is not just a personal tragedy for individuals. It can create further inequalities that span generations. For instance, children of prisoners are more likely to live in poverty, to end up on welfare, and to suffer the sorts of serious emotional problems that tend to make holding down jobs more difficult (Western & Pettit, 2010).

It also has implications at the community level. For instance, increasing rates of incarceration tend to be accompanied by heightened police surveillance and supervision in poor, urban, minority communities. Video cameras mounted on street lights and hovering police helicopters have become the ubiquitous markers of these neighborhoods, bringing with them a climate of fear and suspicion. In such an environment, life for everyone is anxious and unsettled: "Family members and friends are pressured to inform on one another and young men live as suspects and fugitives, with the daily fear of confinement" (Goffman, 2009, p. 353).

RACE, CLASS, AND DEATH

The most extreme state-supported punishment for crime is the death penalty. While debate over the deterrent effects of capital punishment continues to rage, another issue has garnered attention over the past several decades: bias in its administration. Since the death penalty was reinstated in the United States in 1977, the evidence clearly indicates that Whites and people of color—especially African Americans—have been treated differently. Since that time, 42% of defendants who have been executed have been Latino/a or African American, and 54% of the current death row population is Latino/a or African American (Death Penalty Information Center, 2014).

The race of the victim may actually have as much to do with the decision to pursue a death sentence as the race of the defendant. According to Amnesty International (2013), the single most reliable predictor of whether a defendant will be sentenced to death is the race of the victim. For instance, African Americans account for almost half of all homicide victims (Fox & Zawitz, 2010). But the overwhelming majority of people put to death since 1976 (76%) were convicted of killing white victims. In contrast, only 15% of those executed were convicted of killing Blacks, and 6.5% involved Latino/a victims (Death Penalty Information Center, 2014).

One of the hallmarks of the American criminal justice system is that defendants are entitled to be judged by a jury of their peers. In theory, such an arrangement is designed to overcome the individual bias and arbitrariness of having a single person, namely the judge, render all verdicts. However, racial discrimination in jury selection is a persistent problem. Attorneys are entitled to *peremptory challenges,* the ability to strike a potential juror from the jury without offering any explanation. In 1986, the U.S. Supreme Court ruled that race-based peremptory challenges were unconstitutional. But they still occur. In a study of 100 criminal trials in Dallas County, Texas, over a 1-year period, prosecutors challenged 405 of 467 eligible black jurors, five times the number of potential white jurors who were dismissed (cited in Cole, 1999). In 2008, the U.S. Supreme Court overturned the murder conviction of a black defendant citing racial bias in the selection of an all-white jury (Greenhouse, 2008). The prosecutor in this case had used peremptory challenges to remove all five potential black jurors.

Racial bias can also influence juries' decisions. Even though jurors in capital murder cases make life-or-death decisions, they are ordinary people. They inevitably come to the courtroom with their own set of prejudgments. For instance, black jurors may be more sympathetic than white jurors to mitigating evidence presented by a black defendant, whose background and experiences they may feel they understand. A study of capital cases in Philadelphia found that death sentences for black defendants are less likely when black jurors are more numerous (cited in Bowers, Steiner, & Sandys, 2001).

Sociologist Benjamin Fleury-Steiner (2002) examined transcripts of interviews with 66 black and white jurors who had served on capital murder cases involving black defendants. Some white jurors voiced overt racism and contempt for the defendant they had sentenced to death ("If [he'd] been white . . . , I would've had a different attitude"). But others painted a more subtle picture of racial inferiority. Here's how one white interviewee recounted her impressions of a black defendant during the trial:

> I saw the defendant as a very typical product of the lower socio-economic, black group who grew up with no values, no ideals, no authority, no morals, no leadership, and this has come down from

> generation to generation. . . . I just saw him as a loser from day
> one, as soon as he was born into that environment, and into that set
> of people who basically were into drugs, alcohol, illegitimacy,
> AIDS, the whole nine yards. This kid didn't have a chance. That's
> how I saw the defendant. And there are 10,000 others like him out
> there, which is very tragic. (quoted in Fleury-Steiner, 2002, p. 562)

You can see that even though she considers the defendant's life tragic, she nonetheless draws on some extensive stereotypes about his presumably inferior racial environment. His actions confirmed what she "already knew" about Blacks.

Among other interviewees, such "inferiority" was often couched in race-neutral terms like the defendant's "menacing" appearance (one black defendant was described as a "chained gorilla"), governmental programs ("the welfare system makes these people"), or displeasure with a defendant's attempt to use his life of racial disadvantage as an excuse. The anger of some jurors stemmed from their feelings about not only the defendant's actions but also the circumstances represented by the defendant and his family.

On the other hand, many of the black jurors who were interviewed felt more hostility and alienation toward their fellow white jurors than they did toward the defendant:

> They wanted to fry those black boys. I'm serious, that's the feeling
> I got. I felt that they didn't give a shit one way or the other. . . .
> They felt like these two black boys took a white man's life: We're
> going to burn them. That's the impression I got. (quoted in Fleury-
> Steiner, 2002, p. 570)

Others became frustrated by their thwarted attempts to educate the white jurors who they felt were unfamiliar with poor Blacks' lifestyles and therefore were basing their death sentence decisions on unfair racial stereotypes.

Three decades ago, the U.S. Supreme Court acknowledged the danger that racial attitudes might influence jurors' sentencing decisions in capital cases, especially when the defendant is black and the victim is white. In the 1986 case of *Turner v. Murray*, the court ruled that a capital defendant accused of an interracial crime is entitled to have prospective jurors informed of the race of the victim and questioned on the issue of racial bias (Bowers, Steiner, & Sandys, 2001).

However, even when race doesn't seem to be a factor, socioeconomic status usually is. When wealthy or powerful individuals face a possible death sentence (an occurrence that, in and of itself, is rare), they can usually afford effective legal representation. In contrast, poor defendants in such cases are often represented by public defenders, who have fewer resources available for investigative work and who may have little, if any, experience in such matters. Supreme Court Justice Ruth Bader Ginsburg summed up the situation this way:

> People who are well represented at trial do not get the death penalty. . . . I have yet to see a death case among the dozens coming to the Supreme Court on eve-of-execution stay applications in which the defendant was well represented at trial. (quoted in Death Penalty Information Center, 2013, p. 1)

Legislative attempts to address race and class biases in death penalty cases, have had mixed results. In 1998, Kentucky became the first state to pass a "Racial Justice Act," a law that allows defendants in capital cases to use statistical evidence of racial bias to show that their race influenced the decision to seek the death penalty. North Carolina seemingly followed suit in 2009. But in 2013, the state legislature, with the backing of the governor, repealed the law arguing that so many inmates on death row were appealing their sentences on racial bias grounds that it effectively banned capital punishment in the state (Smith, 2013).

GENDERED JUSTICE

Although legal inequalities are especially vivid with regard to race, ethnicity, and class, they also exist along gender lines. Although some men may claim legal disadvantage these days in areas like post-divorce child custody decisions, women have struggled for years to achieve equal legal protection in all areas of life.

GENDER AND THE LAW

Throughout history, women have been denied many of the legal rights that men take for granted. For instance, in the 18th century, when women got married, they lost many of the rights they enjoyed as single women, such as legal title to their property and the right to execute contracts. A married woman's legal identity was submerged into that of her husband; she literally didn't exist as an independent citizen (Crittenden, 2001). Husbands were allowed by law to punish their wives, force them to stay at home, and even force sex on them without legal sanction.

To counteract a long history of legal inequality, the U.S. Congress has passed many important laws over the years aimed at improving the situation of women:

- In addition to its central focus on eliminating racial segregation, the 1964 Civil Rights Act contained provisions forbidding sex discrimination in employment.
- The 1972 Educational Amendments Act included a section forbidding sex discrimination in all federally funded institutions of education. This law includes Title IX, which requires schools receiving federal money to fund male and female athletic programs equitably.
- The 1993 Family and Medical Leave Act guarantees some working mothers (as well as fathers) up to 12 weeks of unpaid sick leave per year to care for a new child or a sick relative.

Courts in the United States have also made several noteworthy decisions that specifically address women's concerns. In 1993, the U.S. Supreme Court ruled that victims of workplace harassment could win lawsuits without having to prove that the offensive behavior left them psychologically damaged—which in the past meant either a documented nervous breakdown or psychiatric hospitalization—or unable to do their jobs. Now, workers need prove only that as a result of harassment, the workplace environment "would reasonably be perceived as hostile or abusive" (Greenhouse, 1993). In 1996, the Court ruled that all-male public colleges and universities have to admit women.

These laws and court rulings haven't been completely effective in rooting out sex discrimination. Supreme Court Justice Ruth Bader Ginsburg recently stated that when it comes to issues like equal pay, medical/family leave, contraception, and abortion the nation's highest court has never fully embraced "the ability of women to decide for themselves what their destiny will be" (quoted in Liptak, 2014, p. A1). In fact, she argues that there have been greater advances over the past decade in gay and lesbian legal rights then in women's legal rights.

Even laws ostensibly designed to protect women's rights have created unforeseen disadvantages. Divorce laws in the United States, which were revised in the 1970s to make the termination of marriages less adversarial and more fair, have actually increased the number of women who become poor after a divorce (Arendell, 1984). Divorced husbands typically experience an increase in their standard of living, but divorced wives—who usually maintain physical custody of children after the divorce—suffer a decrease (Peterson, 1996). In California, for instance, after no-fault divorce laws were enacted only 13% of mothers with preschool children received financial support from their ex-husbands (cited in Tavris, 1992).

SEXUAL HARASSMENT

Two decades after the Supreme Court affirmed women's right to work in environments free of sexual hostility or abuse, sexual harassment remains a common experience for girls and women. In a variety of institutional settings—from schools to workplaces to military bases—women are routinely exposed to unwelcome leers, comments, requests for sexual favors, and unwanted physical contact. The U.S. Equal Employment Opportunity Commission (2013) resolves about 12,000 cases of workplace sexual harassment each year, though these figures obviously don't include episodes that are never reported. According to one national poll, close to one-third of female workers report being sexually harassed on the job (cited in Sexual Harassment Support, 2009). In addition, According to the American Association of University Women (2013), 56% of all girls in grades 7 to 12 experience verbal, physical, or electronic sexual harassment in a given year and 87% say it had a negative effect on them (American Association of University Women, 2013). In addition, about one-third of teenage girls are bullied at school and another 11% report being cyber-bullied (ProQuest Statistical Abstract, 2015). And nearly two thirds of female college students experience sexual harassment at some point during their college careers, though fewer than 10% tell a university official and an even smaller number file an official complaint (C. Hill & Silva, 2006).

Most feminist sociologists interpret sexual harassment as an attempt to reinforce positions of power (Uggen & Blackstone, 2004). For instance, 70% of women who are sexually harassed on the job are harassed by a supervisor or senior colleague (American Association of University Women, 2014). Because harassment is about power, men can also be victims. Although images of either an overbearing, sexually aggressive female boss (consider the film, *Horrible Bosses*) or a gay superior coming on to a male subordinate may come to mind, cases of men being sexually harassed more commonly involve heterosexual men creating a hostile environment for other heterosexual men. According to the U.S. Equal Employment Opportunity Commission (2015), sexual harassment charges filed by men increased from 11.6% of all cases to 17.5% of all cases between 1997 and 2014. These claims often involve "bullying," "hazing," "goosing," a variety of sexual insults, and other boorish behaviors. In 1998, the U.S. Supreme Court ruled that in cases of men harassing other men, a plaintiff could win a suit if the alleged harasser was homosexual and therefore motivated by sexual desire, if the harasser was motivated by a general hostility toward all men, or if men were systematically treated differently from women in the workplace (Talbot, 2002). By the logic of this final criterion, an alleged harasser who demonstrated equal contempt for both men and women would be innocent. Indeed, this defense was used successfully in 2000 in a case involving a bisexual male supervisor who had punished a female employee for not sleeping with him and threw away a male employee's belongings when he didn't give in to the supervisor's advances.

GENDER AND VIOLENCE

Definitions of male power have traditionally encompassed sexual aggression and physical violence as their primary features. The statistics support this observation. Men account for 87% of robberies, 77% of aggravated assaults, 88% of homicides, and 93% of rapes and sexual assaults in the United States (ProQuest Statistical Abstract, 2014). Men are also more likely than women to be *victims* of violence, including not only assaults, robberies, and homicides but suicides, deaths in military combat, and even accidental deaths from working in hazardous occupations and participating in other high-risk activities (Gilligan, 2004). A look at Exhibit 7.2, which presents some of the data on gender and homicides, confirms this imbalance. Except for intimate and sex-related violence, men predominate as both offenders and victims.

Exhibit 7.2: Type of Homicide by Gender

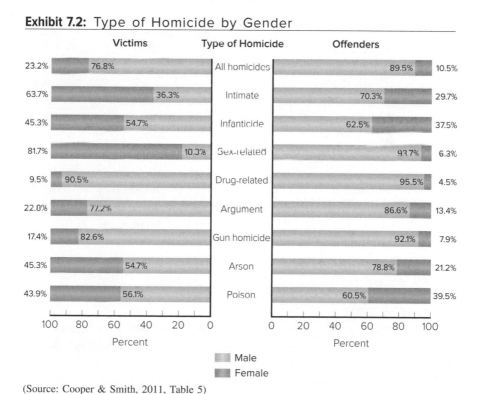

(Source: Cooper & Smith, 2011, Table 5)

Intersections
Poverty, Gender, and Human Trafficking

Violent gender victimization often crosses national boundaries. One of the most pernicious international forms of such violence is human trafficking. The International Labor Organization estimates that 20.9 million adults and children are bought, sold, transported, or kept against their will in the world today (U.S. Department of State, 2012). Women and girls account for 55% of forced labor victims and 98% of sex trafficking victims.

They may be forced to labor in sweat shops or become domestic servants. They might also be sold into prostitution, sex tourism, or even forced marriage. In China, where males significantly outnumber females, young women and girls may be kidnapped by or sold to potential bridegrooms by their impoverished families. Between 1991 and 1996, Chinese police freed about 88,000 women and girls who had been kidnapped for this purpose (Goodwin, 2003). The growth of trafficking in humans has reached crisis proportions in the countries where the trade originates, through which the captives are transported, and where they end up (Clark, 2003).

Human trafficking is not solely a foreign problem either. According to the U.S. State Department (cited in Ribando, 2007), as many as 17,500 people are trafficked to this country each year. They are forced to work as prostitutes, laborers, or servants. In 2002, police in Plainfield, New Jersey, raided a house expecting to find a brothel. Instead, they found a group of teenage girls from Mexico who were being held captive as sex slaves in squalid conditions (Landesman, 2004). In 2007, a couple who ran a multimillion-dollar perfume business in a wealthy New York suburb were charged with violating a federal antislavery law after it was discovered that they had kept two Indonesian women as sex slaves for years, paying them virtually nothing and forcing them to sleep on mats and to hide when visitors came ("Slaves of New York," 2007). The National Center for Missing and Exploited Children estimates that at least 100,000 American children are the victims of commercial sexual trafficking and prostitution each year (Allen, 2010). About 1 in 6 child runaways is a victim of sex trafficking (National Center for Missing and Exploited Children, 2014).

Traffickers find victims in several ways. Frequently, they take out ads in local newspapers offering good jobs at high pay in exciting cities. In politically unstable countries with high rates of poverty and unemployment, destitute women may see these offers as opportunities to help their families financially. Traffickers often use fraudulent modeling, matchmaking, or travel agencies to lure unsuspecting victims. They may even visit families in local villages, assuring them that their daughters will be taught a useful trade or skill or even promising parents that they themselves will marry the daughters. Traffickers deftly target the weakest and most vulnerable populations to victimize. Seventy percent of the world's poor are girls and women. Their low cultural status in many countries makes their victimization all that much easier. And they are increasingly at risk in precisely those environments that are usually considered safe: their communities and their families (Clark, 2003).

Traffickers use threats, intimidation, and violence to force poor victims to engage in sex acts or to work as slaves for the traffickers' financial gain. The vulnerability of trafficking victims is reflected in this Mexican woman's account of her ordeal. She was hoping to go to the United States and earn enough money to support her daughter and parents in Mexico. She was told that there were plenty of good jobs available in restaurants:

> I was transported to Florida and there, one of the bosses told me I would be working in a brothel as a prostitute. I told him he was mistaken and that I was going to be working in a restaurant, not a brothel. He said I owed him a smuggling debt and the sooner I paid it off the sooner I could leave. I was eighteen years old and had never been far from home and had no money or way to return. I was constantly guarded and abused. If any of the girls refused to be with a customer, we were beaten. . . . We worked six days a week, 12 hours a day. Our bodies were sore and swollen. If anyone became pregnant we were forced to have abortions. The cost of the abortion was added to the smuggling debt. The bosses carried weapons. . . . I never knew where I was. We were transported every fifteen days to different cities. I knew if I tried to escape I would not get far because everything was unfamiliar. The bosses said that if we escaped they would get their money from our families. ("Survivor stories," 2001, p. 1)

As this woman's account suggests, by moving their victims away from their homes, often to other countries, traffickers isolate them and render them helpless. The victims may be unable to speak the language of the place where they are held or may be unfamiliar with the culture. They also lose contact with friends and family, making them even more vulnerable to the traffickers' threats.

THE VIOLENCE OF INTIMACY

Aside from trafficking, the areas in which women's rates of violent victimization outpace men's—incest, rape/sexual assault, and domestic assault—are closely related to their familial or sexual disadvantage. Because they tend to be tied to intimacy, such violent acts have often fallen outside the criminal justice system or have been treated less seriously.

These crimes have existed for as long as humans have lived in societies; they exist throughout the world, in the most democratic societies as well as in the most repressive. Such violence against women continues despite—or perhaps because of—some economic, educational, and political advances for women.

Rape and Sexual Assault   In the United States, rape is the most frequently committed but least reported violent crime. According to the Centers for Disease Control and Prevention, about 19.3% of American women have been raped in their lifetimes and another 27% have been subjected to some other form of unwanted sexual contact (Breiding, 2014). But less than 40% of these crimes ever come to the attention of the police—compared with 68% of robberies and 58% of aggravated assaults (Planty, Langton, Krebs, Berzofsky, & Smiley-McDonald, 2013; Truman & Rand, 2010). Among college students, only 20% of these crimes are ever reported (Sinozich & Langton, 2014). According to the National Crime Victimization Survey—an annual assessment of crime carried out by the U.S. Bureau of Justice Statistics—more than 300,000 women over the age of 12 said they'd been raped or sexually assaulted in 2013, about triple the 104,000 cases that were officially reported to the police that year.

No doubt one of the reasons for this reluctance to report is the perception that any action taken will either be ineffective, disbelieved, or lead to further victimization. For instance, research indicates that prosecutors are most likely to file charges when there is evidence of violence (such as physical injury) and when the *victim's* character and behavior are not questionable. Consequently, two-thirds of victims who do report the crime have their cases dismissed (The White House Council on Women and Girls, 2014).

This issue has been particularly problematic in the military. Over the past few years, we've heard many stories about the threatening actions and sex discrimination that female cadets, soldiers, sailors, and pilots have had to endure. A survey conducted by the U.S. Department of Defense (2013) found that about 6% of active female service members said they had experienced sexual assault at least once in the past year. Perhaps as many as one in three female soldiers has been sexually assaulted at some point during her military career (cited in Risen, 2012). To put it another way, female soldiers are statistically more likely to be assaulted by a fellow soldier than killed in combat (Ellison, 2011). And such figures don't even include the countless number of female soldiers who regularly face degradation, hostility, and loneliness instead of the camaraderie every soldier depends on for comfort and survival. Many female military personnel end up waging what amounts to two wars—one against the enemy and one against their fellow soldiers (Benedict, 2009). But the Pentagon estimates that less than 20% of sexual assaults are ever reported (cited in Cooper, 2014).

As far back as 2004, the Department of Defense concluded that the root cause of the problem was failure on the part of commanding officers to acknowledge its severity (cited in Shanker, 2004). Things got so bad that in 2005, the department rewrote its rules so that female soldiers could report sexual assaults confidentially and gain access to counseling and medical services without setting off an official investigation.

However, the military chain of command and the way alleged victims are treated during investigative proceedings continues to deter victims from filing formal charges. Article 32 of the *Uniform Code of Military Justice* allows defense lawyers to ask aggressive questions of alleged victims that would not be permitted in civilian courts. For example, in 2013 a female Navy midshipman who accused three Naval Academy football players of rape was asked whether she wore a bra, how wide she opened her mouth during oral sex, and whether she'd apologized to another midshipman with whom she'd had sex for "being a ho" (Steinhauer, 2013). And under Article 60 of the *Code*, the convening authority in a sexual assault case has the power to reduce or even dismiss sentences entirely regardless of a jury's decision. In many situations, this authority is the commanding officer of or works closely with the defendant (Draper, 2014).

To address these problems, President Obama signed into law a modification of Article 60 that takes away a commander's power to overturn jury verdicts. However, a bill, which would have allowed victims to bypass the military chain of command and go straight to military prosecutors when reporting sexual assaults, was defeated in the Senate.

In civilian life, the fact that rape is the most personal of violent crimes furthers inhibits victims from reporting the incident. Fifty-one percent of female victims are raped by a current or former intimate partner; 41% are raped by an acquaintance (The White House Council on Women and Girls, 2014). The problem has gotten so bad on college campuses that in 2014 the White House published the names of 55 colleges that were under investigation for their insensitive handling of sexual assault complaints and released guidelines to all colleges and universities on how to more aggressively combat sexual assaults on their campuses (Steinhauer & Joachim, 2014).

Rape is a reflection of broader patterns of gender inequality. Throughout history, women have been viewed socially and legally as the property of men, first their fathers and later their husbands. Thus, in the past—not to mention many traditional societies today—rape was considered a crime against men or, more accurately, against men's property (Siegel, 2004). Any interest a husband took in a rape or sexual assault on his wife probably reflected a concern with his own status, the loss of his male honor, and the devaluation of his sexual property.

Feminist sociologists have argued that through most of human history, men have used rape, the threat of rape, and the fear of rape to exert control over women (Brownmiller, 1975). Fear of crime in general—and rape in particular—can be a dominant force in women's lives. The mere existence of rape limits women's freedom of social interaction, denies them the right of self-determination, makes them dependent on men for "protection," and ultimately subordinates them (Griffin, 1986).

Worldwide, cultural beliefs about gender, power, control, and sexuality strongly influence societal and legal responses to rape and rape victims. Consider these examples:

- In Peru and Colombia a man who rapes a woman—whether he knows her or not—can be absolved of all charges if he offers to marry her (Morgan, 1996).
- In Morocco, rape is defined as a crime against family order and public morality, not against individual women. The punishment—5 to 10 years in prison—is doubled if the victim is a virgin (Morgan, 1996).
- In Senegal, single women who are rape victims may be killed by their families because as nonvirgins they can no longer command a high dowry; a married woman who's been raped may be killed by her "dishonored" husband (Morgan, 1996).
- In Iran, because Islamic tradition forbids the execution of virgins, any woman condemned to die for a crime she's committed must first lose her virginity through forced temporary marriage or rape (Morgan, 1996).
- About 60% of Pakistani women who file rape charges—which require two witnesses for a conviction—are later criminally charged themselves for having sex outside of marriage (cited in Fisher, 2002).

Globally, rape is a time-tested wartime tactic of terror, revenge, and intimidation, not only against female victims but also against husbands, sons, and fathers whose idea of honor is connected to their ability to protect "their" women (Amnesty International, 2004; Enloe, 1993; Sengupta, 2004). For instance,

- In Somalia, the militant group Al-Shabab routinely seizes and gang rapes women and girls as a way of supporting its reign of terror in the southern part of the country (Gettleman, 2011).
- In the Democratic Republic of the Congo, bands of soldiers have been "waging a war of rape and destruction against women" since the 1980s (Herbert, 2009, p. A17). Congolese girls and women of all ages have been publicly gang raped, had their reproductive organs deliberately destroyed, and been violated with loaded guns. In one four-day stretch during 2010, gangs of marauding Congolese soldiers raped at least 200 women in one village, despite the fact that United Nations peacekeepers were based just up the road (Gettleman, 2010).
- In Syria and Iraq, thousands of young girls—some as young as 9—have been raped and tortured by ISIS terrorists since 2014 (Raven, 2015).
- In Nigeria, hundreds of women and girls kidnapped by Boko Haram, a radical Islamist sect, have been repeatedly raped as part of a deliberate strategy to dominate and intimidate rural residents (Nossiter, 2015).

Even when women are not seen as men's property, their lives can be controlled by the fear of rape and sexual assault. Men in South Africa sometimes rape lesbians (or suspected lesbians) because they believe it will "cure" them of their sexual orientation. These violent acts are known as "corrective rapes." South African lesbians are sexually assaulted twice as often as heterosexual women (Hunter-Gault, 2012). As one woman put it,

> We get insults every day, beatings if we walk alone, you are constantly reminded that . . . you deserve to be raped, they yell, "if I rape you then you will go straight . . . you will buy skirts and start to cook because you will have learned how to be a real woman." (quoted in ActionAid, 2009, p. 15)

Arguably, the United States has a more sympathetic and supportive response to rape victims than what we see in these examples. But the American legal system still tends to favor men's interests by focusing on women's complicity or blameworthiness. In rape cases, unlike any other crime, victims typically must prove their innocence (that is, lack of consent). Theft victims aren't asked if they wanted their house broken into or whether they were ever in a relationship with the thief; physical assault victims aren't asked if they enticed someone to beat them up and steal their wallet. Yet if women cannot prove that they resisted a sexual assault (either physically or verbally), lack of consent becomes that much more difficult to prove in court (Siegel, 2004). In one study of college students, about 17% of women believed a man has a right to assume consent if a woman allows him to touch her in a sexual way; 25% believed that if a woman touches a man in a sexual way, he has a right to assume consent; and 33% believed a man has a right to assume consent if a woman has had an oral sexual encounter with him (Johnson, Kuck, & Schander, 1997).

The common courtroom practice of introducing evidence about the circumstances of the act and about the relationship between the people involved indicates that the victim's complicity remains a matter of legal contention. Often the assertion that a rape victim "moaned" during the assault is an effective means of persuading police, attorneys, judges, and jurors that the sex was consensual, even though people moan in fear and pain, not just pleasure. In 2014, Jameis Winston, then the Heisman Trophy-winning quarterback of the Florida State Seminoles, was accused of raping a fellow student. When asked in a student conduct hearing what led him to believe she had given consent, he claimed she provided consent by "moaning." He was cleared of the charge (Krakauer, 2015).

Depending on where you live, consent may be seen as negotiable or even time-sensitive. In most states a woman may withdraw her consent to have sex at any time, even after initial penetration; if the man continues, he is committing rape. But in North Carolina once a woman gives consent, she cannot rescind it. Such an understanding of consent rests on the belief that at a certain point during arousal, a man loses the ability to stop (Lee-St. John, 2007).

Things may be changing, however. Recently, the U.S. Department of Justice (2012) revised its definition of rape to include instances in which the victim is incapable of giving consent because of temporary or permanent mental or physical incapacity (including being under the influence of drugs or alcohol) or because of age. The purpose of this redefinition was to increase legal support for victims. And in 2014, California became the first state to address this matter when its legislature enacted an "affirmative consent" policy (referred to as "the Yes Means Yes" law) for all college campuses in the state. The policy specifies that consent can no longer be inferred from failure or ambiguity about saying "no." Instead consent must be conscious, clear, and voluntary. Silence or lack of protest no longer constitutes consent (California Legislative Information, 2014).

It's worth noting too that race and class differences may come into play when rape cases go to trial. Working-class women, for example, are often seen as less respectable and therefore less credible plaintiffs in court cases because of perceptions that sexual violence is a common part of their social experiences and that they have higher sex drives than women of other classes (Phipps, 2009). As a result, prosecutors must weigh the wisdom of proceeding with a rape case:

> I had to think about what the jury would think. They are from other areas, they are white and wealthy. Most of the defendants and victims are black and Latino. . . . The jurors don't understand why she went out at midnight. That was probably when she got her kids down to sleep and finally had free time to go out and party. But the people in Mission Hills don't think that way. (quoted in Frohmann, 1997, p. 540)

Despite the massive amount of attention that has been devoted to rape and sexual assault in recent years, public perceptions remain resistant to change. Many people are unsympathetic toward rape victims if they put themselves at risk—by hitchhiking, attending a wild party, acting seductively, drinking with strangers, wearing "provocative" clothing, and so forth. In one study, male and female high school students were given a list of statements and asked to indicate the extent to which they agreed with them (Kershner, 1996). Of the male and female subjects, 52% agreed that most women fantasize about being raped by a man, 46% felt that women encourage rape by the way they dress, and 53% said they felt that some women provoke men into raping them. Moreover, 31% agreed that many women falsely report rapes, and 35% felt that the victim should be required to prove her innocence during a rape trial. Research has linked such attitudes to the heightened risk of rape and sexual assault on college campuses (Ching & Burke, 1999).

The important sociological point in studies like these is that many men and even some women don't always define violent sexual assault as a form of victimization. They think it is what men are expected to do under certain circumstances. These views have become so entrenched that many women have internalized the message, blaming themselves to some degree when they are assaulted.

Intimate Partner Violence   According to the World Health Organization, the greatest threat of violence to women worldwide is in their own homes (Garcia-Moreno, Jansen, Ellsberg, Heise, & Watts, 2006). Consider these examples:

- In 2013, over 8,000 Indian women—an average of 22 a day—were killed by their husbands for not providing adequate dowries (National Crime Records Bureau, 2014). Even though India officially banned dowry (gifts that a woman receives from her parents on marriage) in

1961, it is still an essential part of premarital negotiations and now encompasses the wealth that the bride's family pays the groom. Young brides, who by custom live with their new husbands' parents, are commonly subjected to severe abuse if the promised money is not paid. Sometimes dowry harassment ends in suicide or murder.

■ In Afghanistan, women can be killed by their husbands for having sex outside the marriage or for not bearing a son (Bowley, 2012).

■ In Egypt, a third of all married women—and 41% of poor married women—are physically abused by their husbands. Such abuse is associated with more sexually transmitted diseases, higher rates of unintended pregnancies, and limited or nonexistent access to prenatal and postnatal medical care (Monazea & Abdel Khalek, 2010).

■ In Spain, intimate violence against women became so severe and so common that in 2004 the new prime minister, upon taking office, made it his first order of business to stamp out what he called "criminal machismo." He proposed legislation that would criminalize violent threats against women, provide more money to protect battered women, and create work-training programs for victims (Sciolino, 2004).

In the United States, the home is also one of the most dangerous locations for women. Exact statistics about the prevalence of intimate partner violence are difficult to collect because it is usually concealed and private, occurring in seclusion, beyond the watchful eyes of relatives, neighbors, and strangers. Even with the more stringent rules for police reporting of domestic calls that have been instituted by police departments across the country in the past decade or two, most incidents are never reported; others are dismissed as accidents. To complicate matters, definitions of abuse and reporting practices vary from state to state.

The statistics on intimate partner violence that do exist indicate that it is a widespread problem, although it has declined somewhat in recent years. More than one in three women—and 1 in 4 men—in the United States have experienced violence and/or stalking by a current or former spouse, boyfriend, girlfriend in their lifetimes, and nearly half of all men and women have experienced psychological abuse (Centers for Disease Control and Prevention, 2011). About 85% of victims were women; and 76% of these women were previously victimized by the same offender (Catalano, 2012). In general, women are far more likely than men to be beaten by someone they know (see Exhibit 7.3).

Other studies place the prevalence rate for intimate partner violence even higher. For instance, the National Violence Against Women Survey of

Exhibit 7.3: Victim/Offender Relationship in Serious Violent Victimizations

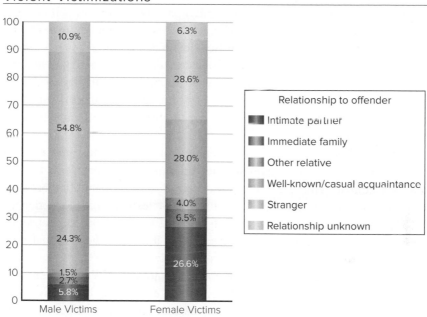

(Source: Truman & Morgan, 2014, Table 3)

16,000 women and men nationwide found that nearly 25% of surveyed women and 7.6% of men said they'd been raped or physically assaulted by a spouse, partner, or date at some point in their lifetimes (Tjaden & Thoennes, 2000). Within the previous 12 months, 1.5% of women and 0.9% of men reported being raped or physically assaulted. According to these estimates, that means about 1.5 million women and over 800,000 men are assaulted by an intimate partner annually in the United States.

Given the shame and stigma associated with reporting such violence, we can probably assume that all these figures are underestimates of the actual incidence of violence between intimates. Some researchers estimate that only about half of the cases of non-lethal violence against women are reported to the police (Rennison & Welchans, 2000).

The effects of intimate violence can be deadly. Close to 2,000 women are killed by an intimate partner each year (Catalano, Smith, Snyder, & Rand, 2009). One study found that almost half the women murdered by their intimate partners had visited the emergency room within the 2 years before they were killed (Crandall, Nathens, Kernic, Holt, & Rivara, 2004).

But women don't just suffer disproportionate physical consequences. Female victims of intimate violence are also more likely than male victims to suffer psychologically (e.g., from depression, anxiety, or low self-esteem) and socially (such as isolation from friends). The economic costs can be steep too. It's estimated that intimate violence costs the country about $6 billion a year in direct costs (medical and mental health care) and indirect costs (lost productivity due to time away from work; cited in Harjani, 2013). Women who experience severe forms of abuse are also more likely than women who experience less serious forms of abuse to lose their jobs or to go on public assistance.

Although intimate violence between heterosexual partners gets most of the attention, same-sex couples are not immune to the problem. Indeed, same-sex intimate violence is fairly widespread. It's estimated that between 42% and 79% of gay men and 25% to 50% of lesbians have experienced some type of intimate violence (cited in Burke & Owen, 2006). In fact, some researchers claim that more violence occurs in long-term homosexual relationships than in heterosexual relationships (Cameron, 2003).

Power and perceived threats to dominance and authority underlie almost all acts of intimate partner violence (Gelles & Straus, 1988). In male-dominated heterosexual households, for instance, husbands sometimes turn to violence to intimidate their wives. But it's also true that in an achievement-oriented society like ours, husbands who lack the financial, occupational, and educational resources necessary to establish household dominance may turn to violence or coercion (Yllo & Straus, 1990). The effect of men's employment on violence was demonstrated in a study of 12,000 Canadian women over the age of 18 (MacMillan & Gartner, 1999). The researchers found that wives' exposure to spousal violence had little to do with whether or not they were employed. But when their husbands were unemployed, employed wives' risk of victimization increased significantly. Experts noted that rates of intimate violence increased as a result of the recent economic recession (Lauby & Else, 2008).

Although we've long since abandoned the belief that abuse victims should stay with their violent partners to try to "work things out," getting out of abusive relationships can be difficult, if not impossible. Nevertheless, we no longer expect victims to put up with being abused.

Ironically, because of this expectation, there's often a perception that women who don't leave are passive and weak-willed, even though the available evidence seems to suggest otherwise. One study of 1,000 battered and formerly battered women nationwide found that the vast majority tried a number of active strategies to end the violence directed against them

(Bowker, 1993). They attempted to talk men out of beating them, extracted promises that the men wouldn't batter them anymore, avoided their abusers physically or avoided certain volatile topics, hid or ran away, and even fought back physically. Many of these individual strategies had limited effectiveness, however, and so most of these battered women eventually turned to people outside the relationship for informal support, advice, and sheltering. From these informal sources, the women generally progressed to organizations in the community, such as police, social service and counseling agencies, women's groups, and battered women's shelters. Some of these women were able, eventually, to end the violence; others weren't.

Women often leave their partners on multiple occasions before completely severing ties. One study of battered women who were in a shelter in the Midwest found that close to 80% of them had temporarily left their partners at least once prior to the current attempt, and 19% had left at least 10 times (Sullivan, Tan, Basta, Rumptz, & Davidson, 1992). Many women who return cite the lack of opportunities and resources outside the relationship, such as overcrowded shelters and no one to care for the children while they search for jobs.

Escaping abuse is made more difficult by the fact that women may actually be in greater danger after they leave. Approximately 25% of women killed by male partners were divorced or separated from the men who killed them. And 70% of reported injuries due to domestic violence occur after the couple has separated (Fine & Weis, 2000).

Furthermore, not all victims have equal chances of escaping abuse and receiving help. For instance, within certain communities of color, there are prohibitions against publicizing or seeking protection against domestic violence out of fear that doing so would reinforce racial stereotypes of minority men as violent (Crenshaw, 2004a). Services designed to help these battered women, like shelters, are often unattractive because of language barriers or the lack of other women of color in leadership positions.

Battered gay men and lesbians have an especially difficult time escaping the violence and getting help because of the animosity directed toward homosexuals in the larger society and the gay community's failure to acknowledge domestic violence as a serious problem. As a result, battered homosexual partners are even less likely than battered heterosexual wives to tell anyone about the abuse and seek help, putting themselves at risk for more severe and more frequent violence (Letellier, 1996).

Women with limited financial means also face daunting obstacles in leaving abusive relationships. Hundreds of cities around the country have what are called "nuisance property" ordinances. These laws are designed to protect neighborhoods from seriously disruptive households. However, police can invoke these laws and pressure landlords to evict a renter if they have been called to the apartment on domestic violence complaints too often. One study found that rental properties in poor black neighborhoods were most likely to be singled out (Eckholm, 2013). Hence victims of intimate violence may be reluctant to contact the police for fear of being kicked out of their apartments.

Moreover, poor women often live in neighborhoods that have few resources for victims. In poor rural areas with no public transportation, the shelters that do exist may be inaccessible to women who live miles away and don't own cars. To make matters worse, governmental programs that may have helped these women leave in the past have been dismantled in recent years. Prior to the highly publicized welfare reforms of the mid-1990s, as many as two-thirds of women who received welfare payments had abuse in their backgrounds, suggesting that welfare may have been a way out for many battered women with children (Gordon, 1997). Today, however, fewer poor women are on the welfare rolls, and the unpredictability of the system may force many of them to stay in abusive situations in order to survive financially.

CONCLUSION

When children pledge their allegiance to the American flag each morning in school, they conclude with the phrase, ". . . and justice for all." The concept behind "justice for all" seems fairly straightforward, even to little kids: Everyone should have the same opportunities for a safe life, should be entitled to the same legal protections, and should be treated the same when accused of breaking the law. But we've seen in this chapter that this rather clear, simple standard has always eluded U.S. society. Inequalities based on race, ethnicity, gender, class, and sexuality are woven into the fabric of our entire legal system. The discrepancies that I've touched on in this chapter are even more troubling when we weigh them against the key values of equality and fairness on which this country was founded.

If you look up the word *justice* in the dictionary, you'll come across terms like *fairness, impartiality, integrity,* and *even-handedness.* But when we assess the information presented in this chapter, it's hard to avoid the conclusion that, for some of us, justice remains elusive. For the most fortunate among us, our race, our gender, our class standing, and our sexual orientation shield us from being unfairly treated. But for many others, those traits offer little protection when it comes to the legal standing of our actions, our chances of being victimized, and our experiences with the justice process itself.

It's true that things are getting better, however. We have moved away from the days in which injustices and inequalities were actually codified in the law; when certain members of this society were not afforded the luxury of being treated like full citizens and some were even defined as less than full human beings. But the Pledge of Allegiance may still ring hollow to many of those children who have to recite its lines each day. Complete "justice for all" remains a goal not fully reached.

[## INVESTIGATING IDENTITIES AND INEQUALITIES]

Safe havens: Race, class, gender, and

the fear of crime

Certainly there are police officers, attorneys, judges, and jury members who dislike, resent, or hate members of certain groups and bring those feelings with them when they make crucial decisions on whom to interrogate, whom to arrest, whom to charge, whom to find guilty, whom to sentence, and so on. And we've seen in this chapter that those people with the economic means can purchase better treatment within the system. But just how does this system look from the perspective of citizens that it is supposed to protect?

To answer that question, interview a variety of people about their experiences with and attitudes toward the criminal justice system. Try to select people from different ethnoracial groups, different socioeconomic backgrounds, different genders, and different sexual orientations. You may ask your respondents questions face-to-face, via a paper-and-pencil questionnaire, or through an online survey. Here are some possible questions to ask (though you should feel free to design your own set of questions):

- Have you ever been the victim of a crime? If so, was it a violent crime? Property crime? Fraud? Identity theft? For each instance of victimization:

  - What was your initial response after the victimization? Whom did you contact first? Police? Friends or neighbors? Family?
  - If you contacted the police, how long did it take for them to respond? Were they helpful?
  - To your knowledge, was the perpetrator ever caught? If so, were charges brought against him or her? Was there a trial? How did that end?

- If you've never been a crime victim, describe other direct contacts that you have had with police or security personnel (such as TSA agents in airports or officers at the scene of an accident, during a traffic stop, or when controlling a crowd). How would you characterize the treatment you received during these contacts?

- Describe your feelings about your campus police or the local police in the town where you attend college.

  - Do you consider them fair? Trustworthy? Helpful? Protective? Do they make you feel safe? If you answer no to any of these questions, how would you characterize them?
  - On a scale of 1 to 10, with 1 being very biased and 10 being very fair, how would you rate your local/campus police?
  - Do you know of any specific instances (involving you or people you know) in which local/campus police acted unfairly?

- On a scale of 1 to 10, with 1 being very fearful and 10 being not at all fearful, how would you rank your fear of being a crime victim where you live right now?
- What kinds of precautions do you *currently* take to avoid being victimized? List as many as you can think of.

Based on your results, analyze whether certain groups (ethnic, class, racial, and gender, or sexual) are significantly less confident than others in their local police. Are there differences in people's fear of crime? Use your findings to address the question of whether the criminal justice system is really "just."

(*Note:* If you are unable to interview people for this assignment, you can modify it by examining national racial, gender, and class trends in crime and criminal victimization with data from the Bureau of Justice Statistics [www.ojp. usdoj.gov/bjs/] or the Federal Bureau of Investigation [www.fbi.gov/stats-services/crimestats]).

CHAPTER 8

Inequalities in Health and Illness

Several years ago, I had the opportunity to travel through Asia. About 5 days into the trip, in the city of Xian in central China, I seriously injured my lower back. The pain was unbearable. I spent several excruciating days trying to sightsee in China before flying to Bangkok, where some American friends lived. Noticing the misery etched on my face as I got off the plane, they decided to take me to a hospital near their apartment. I was told not to worry because it was a "Western" hospital, meaning that the style of medicine and the approach to treatment were similar to what you'd find in the United States and in most developed countries.

When I arrived at the hospital, I was stunned by the conditions of the place. Even though it was touted as one of the best hospitals in Bangkok, by U.S. standards it was run-down, dingy, and noisy. It seemed like every available space in the waiting area was occupied by some sick or injured person in need of medical attention. They were crammed into little alcoves or lined up in hallways. No one complained; no one looked aggravated. Many had staked out their little patch of floor as if it were a campground, setting up blankets for themselves and their children to sit on. By the looks of it, I surmised that most of them had come to the hospital knowing they'd be there for the long haul.

For a brief moment, I considered bolting for the door. But I wasn't going to get very far in my condition. I hobbled to the registration desk. The receptionist curtly told me in broken English to "have a seat and wait until your name is called." So I found an old plastic chair and slowly eased myself into it. I figured it could be hours before I'd see a doctor. Maybe even days.

After about 20 minutes, a young woman in a starched white dress and one of those old-timey nurse's hats ventured into the throng of waiting patients. By the way she was thumbing through the papers on her clipboard, it looked like she was about to announce some lucky person's name. I didn't pay too much attention though because by my estimate there were *at least* 50 people ahead of me.

"DAY-veed NYOO-mahn!"

"Huh? That can't be me," I thought to myself.

She waited about 10 seconds and shouted the name again. "DAY-veed NYOO-mahn!" It was me! Gleefully, I hoisted up my aching body and without giving a moment's thought to my inexplicable good fortune or making eye contact with the other patients-to-be who'd been skipped over, followed her out of the waiting area.

Now, if you've ever been to a hospital in the United States, you know that at this point in the script of events you'd be sent to another room to wait some more. But not here. Almost immediately, someone took my vital signs. Then two extremely friendly people escorted me to the x-ray room. From there, someone else took me to a therapy room, where I was placed on a bed with some kind of heating device pressed against the area of my back that was injured. An alarm rang after about 30 minutes, and another person instantly came in and walked me to a doctor's private office. The doctor soon entered and, in English better than mine, proceeded to describe to me in great detail the nature of my injury. Her presentation included visual aids—a bright color poster of the human spine and a life-size plastic skeleton. She gave me three prescriptions—pain pills, pills for potential stomach problems caused by the pain pills, and vitamin B complex. In addition, she Xeroxed several pages of a book of rehabilitation exercises that she said would help in my recovery. She also gave me a back brace that looked like a girdle. Finally, as I got up to leave, she handed me a business card with her office phone number on it. "Call me directly if you have any questions, okay?"

My injury didn't get much better right away, but all in all, it was a remarkably pleasant experience. I was amazed at the medical attention I received, which was far more courteous than any you'd see in a U.S, hospital. But something kept bugging me. Why didn't I have to wait like all those other people? And why did the doctor, who had scores of patients waiting to see her, spend so much time casually chatting with me? Surely a hospital with that volume of patients couldn't possibly treat everyone this way.

As we left, I asked my friend why I had received what I considered to be preferential treatment. Her response was quick and short. "Well, they knew you were an American, and they knew you'd be able to pay on the spot." Indeed, although I am a college professor (and therefore not wealthy by any stretch of the imagination), I was able to pay in cash because the services and prescriptions I received were very inexpensive.

Upon returning to the United States, I read a couple of stories about Thai citizens who died on their way to distant government-run hospitals after being turned away by private hospitals like the one I went to because they didn't have any money. And I've since learned that it's common practice in some Thai hospitals to make sure patients pay up front, before they receive any treatment. I felt lucky and guilty at the same time.

Even if you've never been to Thailand (or any other foreign country for that matter) and have never had a debilitating injury, my story should still sound a little familiar. This theme, "the more money you have, the better the health care you receive," is just as true here as it is in Thailand. As medical costs—insurance premiums, prescription drugs, hospital care, and so on—soar beyond the reach of more and more Americans, effective affordable health care is fast becoming a luxury for the few, not an inalienable right of the many.

Working-class and poor people receive less preventive health care than wealthy people and often must endure inadequate treatment in crowded city hospitals or public clinics. At the same time, those at the top of the socioeconomic ladder can afford the best, most personal care available. For instance, for an annual fee that can be as high as $20,000, wealthy individuals can buy "concierge" medical services, which include, among other things: same-day appointments with guaranteed waiting time of less than 15 minutes; 24/7 cell phone and text messaging access; smart phone accessibility; focus on preventive care; nutrition and exercise physiology exams at the patients' homes; doctors or nurses to accompany them when they go to see specialists; and routine physicals that are so thorough they can last up to 3 days (Belluck, 2002; Garfinkel, 2003; Government Accountability Office, 2005). For those well-off individuals who end up in the hospital, the pampering continues. New York-Presbyterian/Weill Cornell Hospital offers a luxury penthouse wing whose deluxe accommodations rival the world's best hotels: chef-prepared gourmet menus, the finest Italian bed linens, a marble bathroom, and a butler (Bernstein, 2012).

This chapter will explore the relationship between our ethnoracial, class, gender, and sexual identities and our physical and mental well-being. This relationship is a complex one that exists at several levels. First, how do social identities influence the social construction of health and illness? How do social inequalities affect our bodies, especially with regard to physical appearance and food-related conditions like hunger and obesity? Finally, how do race, class, gender, and sexuality—individually and in combination— influence susceptibility to illness and access to health care?

THE SOCIAL CONSTRUCTION OF HEALTH AND ILLNESS

Before examining the relationship between social identities and health-related inequalities, we must first look at the socially constructed nature of illness itself. "Healthy" and "sick" are not simply objective, physical states found universally. Instead they are social creations that can vary dramatically between groups and within the same group over time. A prominent doctor once said, "A disease does not exist until we name it" (quoted in Kolata, 2011, p. 3). Conditions that are considered problematic or life-threatening in one culture might be considered quite normal in another; diseases that are common in one society may be unknown in others. In Malaysia, a man may be diagnosed with *koro*, a sudden, intense anxiety that his sexual organs will recede into his body, causing death. In some Latin American countries, some people suffer from *susto*, an illness tied to a frightening event that makes the soul leave the body, causing unhappiness and sickness (American Psychiatric Association, 2013). Neither of these conditions exists as a medical diagnosis in other parts of the world. But they are not simply anthropological curiosities. They show that culture shapes everyday notions of health and illness.

Even cultures that are quite similar in other ways can have very different conceptions of health and illness. In the United States, people tend to see their bodies as machines that require basic upkeep and annual checkups for routine maintenance. In addition, diseases are considered enemies that need to be conquered. Not surprisingly, American doctors are much more likely than European doctors to take an aggressive approach to the treatment of illnesses, frequently prescribing drugs and resorting to surgery (Payer, 1988). Women in the United States have more radical mastectomies, deliveries by cesarean section, and routine hysterectomies while still in their 40s than women in Europe. To be considered a good doctor in the United States typically means doing something proactive and forceful, even when there is some doubt as to what the best course of action is.

In contrast, doctors in Great Britain tend not to recommend routine examinations, seldom prescribe drugs, and order about half as many x-rays as U.S. doctors do (Payer, 1988). British patients are also much less likely to have surgery. For British doctors, the guiding principle seems to be "when in doubt, do nothing." These attitudes also influence the perceptions of patients. People who are quiet and withdrawn—which U.S. doctors might consider symptoms of clinical depression in need of immediate attention—tend to be seen by British psychiatrists as perfectly normal.

Ironically, despite their more aggressive approach, Americans, on average, are actually sicker than their British counterparts, even though the U.S. spends more than twice as much on health care per person than Great Britain (Emanuel, 2011). They suffer higher rates of conditions like diabetes, heart disease, and obesity and have a lower life expectancy. These differences exist even when controlling for social class. According to one study, the richest one-third of U.S. citizens are in worse health than the poorest one-third of Britons (Banks, Marmot, Oldfield, & Smith, 2006). In fact, when compared to other wealthy, industrialized countries —not just Great Britain— Americans fare worse on such major health indicators as infant mortality, HIV/AIDS, drug-related deaths, obesity, diabetes, heart disease, chronic lung disease, and life expectancy (Institute of Medicine, 2013; National Academies, 2013). Of the 34 highest-income, industrialized nations in the world, the United States ranks 29th in terms of life expectancy for newborn girls (Woolf & Aron, 2013).

Definitions of health can change over time even within the same culture. Over the past decade the medical field has reversed its position on at least 146 standard medical practices (Prasad, 2013). We've seen a redefinition of autism and grief-induced depression (American Psychiatric Association, 2013); and challenges to the necessity of vitamin D and calcium supplements (Begley, 2011), routine mammograms and pelvic exams for healthy women (Bleyer & Welch, 2012; Rabin, 2014b), and regular blood tests for prostate cancer in healthy men (Harris, 2011). The frequency with which conceptions of health and illness emerge only to be reversed or debunked later on led one columnist to write, with a fair amount of exasperation, "Sometimes you really do want to tell the medical profession to just make up its mind" (Collins, 2011, p. A23).

In addition to determining the nature of illness, cultural and historical attitudes also influence what it means to be a sick person. Every society has a **sick role,** a widely understood set of expectations regarding how people are supposed to behave when sick (Parsons, 1951). The sick role entails certain obligations (things sick people are expected to do) as well as certain privileges (things sick people are entitled to):

- Because we tend to think of most illnesses as things that happen to a person, the individual may be exempted from responsibility for the condition itself. Nevertheless, she or he also has a moral obligation to recognize the condition as undesirable, as something that should be overcome as soon as possible.

- The individual who is allowed to occupy the sick role is excused from ordinary daily duties and expectations (Newman, 2017). National legislation, namely the Family & Medical Leave Act, and private workplace sick leave policies are the institutional manifestation of these expectations. Sick people are also entitled to ask for and receive care and sympathy from others and, depending on the magnitude of the malady, may even be given relief from the ordinary norms of etiquette and propriety. Think of the nasty moods, actions, or insults you're able to "get away with" when you're sick that people wouldn't tolerate from you if you were well.

- The person in the sick role is required to take the culturally prescribed actions that will aid in the process of recovery, including, if the condition is serious enough, seeking help from a culturally appropriate health care professional (Parsons, 1951). Sometimes, to obtain the privilege of exemption from normal social obligations, you must be documented as officially ill (Lorber, 2000). Without a "doctor's note" to validate an illness, your boss might not give you the day off or your instructor might not allow you to take a makeup exam. In the United States, such documentation is usually considered valid only if it comes from traditional medical doctors, not from holistic healers, chiropractors, homeopaths, osteopaths, or any other alternative practitioner outside the mainstream. In addition, being legally "disabled," securing insurance reimbursement, even being officially born or dead all require physician's documentation. These legal requirements keep people under the control of the medical system (Lorber, 2000).

Failure on the part of sick people either to exercise their rights or to fulfill the obligations of the sick role may elicit sanctions from others (Coe, 1978). For instance, those who do not appear to want to recover or who seem to enjoy being sick quickly lose certain privileges, such as sympathy. A person may also give up legal rights by not seeking or following expert advice. In some cases, parents who are members of religious groups that eschew medical intervention have been arrested and charged with child endangerment for not acquiring culturally approved medical assistance for their sick children (Newman, 2017).

While different cultures define the sick role differently, it can also vary considerably along social class and gender lines within the same culture (Freund & McGuire, 1991). In the 19th century, for example, the sick role was considered appropriate for middle- and upper-class women because it was thought to reflect their refinement and delicacy. It was expected, even stylish, for affluent women to faint frequently or spend days in bed for "nerves," "sick headaches," "neurasthenia," or "female troubles" (Ehrenreich & English, 1989). Lower-class women, by contrast, were considered stronger and heartier. Their purported physical strength simultaneously made them better able to withstand illness but less socially refined. In reality, because they depended on the wages they earned from employment, they simply couldn't afford to take days or weeks off from work to convalesce in bed. Hence, they weren't able to claim sick role privileges and exemptions from their ordinary responsibilities. Even giving birth did not relieve working-class mothers from their job duties.

Similar class differences in the sick role exist today. Someone might have a debilitating disease, but without health insurance she or he may not have the wherewithal to seek the care of health professionals (and receive an official diagnosis) or may not be able to take time off of work for fear of losing her or his job. In short, socioeconomic factors may preclude such people from claiming sick role status.

THE EMBODIMENT OF INEQUALITY

Social inequalities leave their mark on our bodies even before we enter a formally recognized sick role. Several years ago, a colleague returned from a trip to Hungary, where decades of economic and environmental devastation have worn people down, making them look 20 or 30 years older than they are. Hungarians consistently estimated that he was in his mid-20s (he was actually close to 50 at the time). One person said to him, "You Americans . . . you wear your affluence on your faces!"

People's physical appearance often reflects their level of economic comfort. Listen to the way one sociologist describes how poverty marked her as a child:

> What I recall most vividly about being a child in a profoundly poor family was that we were constantly hurt and ill, and because we could not afford medical care, small illnesses and accidents spiraled into more dangerous illnesses and complications that became both a part of who we were and written proof that we were of no value in the world. . . . At an early age my brothers and sister and I were stooped, bore scars that never healed properly, and limped with feet mangled by ill-fitting, used Salvation Army shoes. When my sister's forehead was split open by a door slammed in frustration, my mother "pasted" the angry wound together on her own, leaving a mark of our inability to afford medical attention . . . on her forehead. (Adair, 2004, p. 195)

The cycle of poverty-generated physical markers is a vicious one for the working poor. Consider this description of a woman who has been turned down time and again for jobs and promotions:

> The people who received promotions tended to have something that Caroline did not. They had teeth. Caroline's teeth had succumbed to poverty, to the years when she could not afford a dentist. . . . Where showing teeth was an unwritten part of the job description, she did not excel. . . . If she were not poor, she would not have lost her teeth, and if she had not lost her teeth, perhaps she would not have remained poor. (Shipler, 2004, pp. 52–53)

The marks left on our bodies by social inequalities may come from the day-to-day physical toll of economic insecurity, from not eating enough, or from eating too much unhealthful food. Some people have the economic wherewithal to correct bodily flaws they find undesirable; others must bear the stigma of their socioeconomic status as if it is a "brand of infamy" (Adair, 2004).

TO EAT OR NOT TO EAT

Food isn't just something we need to keep us alive. It's a key component of some of our most important life events—the first time a baby eats solid food or uses utensils properly, family-affirming holiday traditions like Thanksgiving and Christmas, and even personally important moments like bar mitzvahs, wedding receptions, and even wakes.

But some of our greatest collective anxieties revolve around food as well. For those who don't have enough to eat, each day brings a life-and-death struggle to secure the next meal. For those who have more than enough to eat, life is a daily battle to avoid weight gain. As we'll see, these ends of the anxiety continuum are correlated quite closely with economic security, socioeconomic standing, race, and gender.

Hunger   For the vast majority of Americans, who are pre-occupied with weighing too much, the reality of not having enough to eat is a distant one. But "in a world where the rich spend millions on ways to avoid carbohydrates and the United Nations declares obesity a global health threat, the cruel reality is that far more people struggle each day just to get enough calories" (McNeil, 2004, p. 4:1).

When most Americans hear the word hunger, they are likely to conjure images of famine-ravaged countries in sub-Saharan Africa or destitute villages in Latin America or Southeast Asia, where naked, dusty children, stomachs bloated with the telltale signs of malnutrition, plead for scraps of food. According to the United Nations, there are approximately 842 million undernourished people in the world today, meaning that about 1 in 8 people don't have enough food to be healthy and lead an active life. (World Food Programme, 2014).

A common misconception about hunger is that food supplies are inadequate to feed every human being because of natural factors, such as droughts, crop or livestock infestation, and soil erosion. But abundance, not scarcity, best describes the world's food supply. Even the "hungriest" countries have enough food to feed all their people (Boucher, 1999). Shortages of food are usually human, not natural, phenomena. Even in the most destitute countries, nourishment is always available to those who can afford it. Social institutions and human policies usually determine who eats and who doesn't. For instance, women's education and status are associated with the quality of their children's nutrition; where women suffer deep discrimination, more children go hungry. Inadequate transportation routinely makes it difficult for food to reach the people who need it most.

Politics and economics play a role too. Many developing countries export huge amounts of food while millions of their people go hungry or malnourished. Thailand, for example, produces 10 million more tons of rice annually than it consumes; however, Thai supermarkets post signs limiting the amount of rice local shoppers can buy (Lacey, 2008a). In an attempt to modernize and improve their international reputations, countries often spend a disproportionate amount of money on building cities, industrializing their economies, or hosting glittering world events like the Olympics or World Cup. As a result, farmers in rural areas don't receive the incentives to grow as much food as they could. Driven by global economic uncertainty, food prices have also hit record levels in recent years, fueling anger toward governments in the world's poorest areas (MacFarquhar, 2011). According to the World Bank, since 2007, rising food prices have caused 51 food riots in 37 countries (including Tunisia, South Africa, Cameroon, India, and Venezuela; cited in Adams, 2014). In other societies, civil wars and border disputes also take up a significant proportion of revenue that might otherwise go to domestic food production and distribution. Corrupt governments and warring factions may also disrupt food production and distribution and prevent food supplies from reaching the neediest people.

Whatever hunger's cause, as long as it is defined as a faraway problem, Americans can continue to convince themselves that it can comfortably be addressed with benefit concerts, online fundraising, and high-profile charity events. But sooner or later, we will be forced to acknowledge the magnitude of the problem in our own country. Approximately 14.3% of American households are *food insecure*—meaning that some members don't have enough to eat or the family uses strategies like eating less varied diets, participating in food assistance programs, or getting emergency food from community food pantries (ProQuest Statistical Abstract, 2015). That means that about 33 million adults and 16 million children live in households that experience hunger or the risk of hunger.

Even when poor families aren't food insecure, they may find their healthy food choices limited. As I was writing this chapter, I heard a talk show on the radio in which nutritionists were discussing "the Dirty Dozen"— 12 fruits and vegetables (among them, strawberries, grapes, and apples) that contain high, and maybe even toxic, levels of pesticides. When asked how to avoid this potential health problem, one of the panelists said that if people wanted to continue eating these foods they simply have to buy (more expensive) organic produce. Those who don't have the money are left with two choices: they can continue to eat non-organic (potentially dangerous) produce or cut these foods out of their diet altogether.

Obesity At present, the problem of American hunger and malnutrition continues to go largely unnoticed. Instead, food-related bodily concerns in the United States are more likely to focus on the opposite end of the scale: people who eat—and perhaps weigh—too much. And with good reason. Overall, roughly 32% of children and 68% of adults in this country are overweight or obese (The State of Obesity, 2014). As these numbers grow, other areas of society are forced to adapt. Consider these recent developments (Taubes, 2012):

- In 2012, the Coast Guard increased its assumption about the average weight of a boat passenger from 160 pounds to 185 pounds.
- Around 25% of Americans between 17 and 24 are unqualified for military service because of their weight.
- Compared to 1960, airlines spend about $5 billion more each year in jet fuel because of the extra power needed to fly heavier Americans.

Obesity has been linked to several critical health problems, including heart disease, atherosclerosis, and diabetes. But the interpersonal and economic consequences of being overweight can be just as devastating as its health effects. In U.S. society, and in most industrialized societies, people are likely to judge an overweight person as lacking in willpower and as being self-indulgent, personally offensive, and even morally and socially unfit (Millman, 1980). "Being fat" is the most common reason kids get bullied and picked on in this country, above such traits as race, ethnicity, religion, and physical disability (Bradshaw, Waasdorp, O'Brennan, & Gulemetova, 2011). In one study, physicians showed more warmth and empathy in their conversations with normal weight patients than with obese patients. Furthermore, overweight patients often complain that doctors criticize them for their weight even when the health problem that brought them to the doctor in the first place (say, a broken toe or an ear infection) is unrelated to their size. These are not insignificant findings since patients are far more likely to follow doctors' advice and to have a better health outcome when they feel the doctor empathizes with their situation (cited in Parker Pope, 2013).

Research has found significant discrimination against obese people at every stage of the employment cycle as well, including hiring, placement, compensation, promotion, discipline, and discharge (Roehling, 1999). In high-visibility occupations, such as public relations and sales, overweight people might be regarded as unemployable because it is feared that they would project a negative image of the company they are working for. One study found that heavy and very heavy women earn between $9,000 and $19,000 a year less than their average weight counterparts (Judge & Cable, 2011). Obese customers, too, may find themselves the target of discrimination. The CEO of Abercrombie & Fitch got into some hot water a few years ago when he stated that he didn't want fat people wearing any of the company's clothes. The stores don't stock any sizes larger than "L" for women (Lutz, 2013). Some people have even suggested that because of high cost of treating obesity-related illnesses—it's estimated that almost 10% of medical costs in the United States are obesity-related—overweight people ought to pay a "fat tax," higher premiums for health insurance not unlike the higher rates smokers must pay (Leonhardt, 2009).

The devaluation of overweight people is not universal, however. In Mexico, for instance, people are significantly less concerned about their own weight and are more accepting of overweight people than individuals in the United States are (Crandall & Martinez, 1996). In many countries, fatness is equated with fertility, especially among women, and is therefore a positive sign of one's marriageability. In Botswana, large women are considered sexually desirable because they have "fat eggs" and are therefore fit to bear children (Upton, 2010). In Niger, being overweight is considered such an essential part of female beauty that women sometimes take steroids to gain bulk or even ingest feed and vitamins that are meant to be consumed by livestock (Onishi, 2001).

Rates of obesity have been on the rise worldwide, due principally to the increased production of more processed and affordable food than ever before (Swinburn, Sacks, Hall, McPherson, Finegood, Moodie, & Gortmaker, 2011). But because of advances in global communication technology, western images of thinness—and perhaps the stigmatization of obesity as well—have infiltrated places that once had different ideals of body size, like Mexico, Tanzania, and Puerto Rico (Brewis, Wutich, Falletta-Cowden, & Rodriguez-Soto, 2011). An Indian businesswoman recently stated, "I think all around the ideal of beauty is skinny thin. I had a highly educated friend confess that she would prefer for her children to be anorexic rather than overweight" (quoted in Parker-Pope, 2011, p. A3).

In the United States, the relationship between obesity and inequality has shifted over the years. In the past, being stout was considered a sign of good health, which is not surprising since most of the illnesses that concerned people at the time were wasting diseases like tuberculosis. Being fat was also associated with good, cheerful character (Gilman, 2004). In addition, up until the 20th century, plumpness was associated with prosperity because only wealthy people could afford to eat enough food to make them overweight. In studying excavations in New York City, anthropologist Nan Rothschild (1990) found that wealthy areas in the 18th century could be identified by the remains of heavy meat bones; poorer neighborhoods were indicated by cheaper vegetables and fish. By the 1980s, however, that pattern had completely reversed.

Today, the lighter the food one eats, the higher one's status. Diet, counting calories, weight loss, exercise, and health are more likely to be concerns among affluent rather than among poor Americans. In fact, one of the clearest indicators of the economic status of a community is the presence of well-kept jogging trails, private health clubs, and large, gleaming health food supermarkets.

Conversely, obesity in the United States today tends to be equated with poverty (Gilman, 2004). Eight of the ten fattest states in the U.S. are also among the ten poorest (Christie, 2010; Goldman & Lubin, 2011). It may seem contradictory that both hunger and obesity are associated with poverty. But, as the director of New York City's Coalition Against Hunger put it, "hunger and obesity are often flip sides of the same malnutrition coin" (quoted in Dolnick, 2010). Because of inadequate grocery distribution in low-income neighborhoods, fresh fruits and vegetables are actually more expensive than in suburban stores. Poor black and racially mixed neighborhoods have significantly fewer large chain supermarkets, natural food stores, fruit and vegetable markets, and bakeries than wealthier white neighborhoods. What they have more of are local grocery stores and convenience stores—both of which tend to charge higher prices for healthier food (Lee, 2006)—and fast food restaurants, which offer high-calorie, high-fat food. These areas are sometimes referred to as *food deserts* because of their nutritional isolation and the lack of mainstream, high-quality grocery stores. One study found that the most economically disadvantaged school districts have the highest percentage of the population living in *food deserts* (neighborhoods where healthy food is difficult, if not impossible to obtain). These districts, in turn, also have higher rates of children who are overweight and obese (Schafft, Jensen, & Hinrichs, 2009).

Not surprisingly, fast-food companies have grown more aggressive in targeting poor, minority communities. One out of every four McDonald's hamburgers sold is purchased by consumers in inner cities (Critser, 2000). Such a situation is not inconsequential. Researchers have found that obesity rates among ninth graders increase by an average of 5% when their school is located within one-tenth of a mile of a fast-food restaurant (Currie, DellaVigna, Moretti, & Pathania, 2009). Another study found that lower-income black adults who live closer to fast food restaurants have higher body mass indexes than those who live farther away (Reitzel, Regan, Nguyen, Cromley, Strong, Wetter, & McNeill, 2014).

The link between obesity and poverty disproportionately affects ethnoracial minorities, particularly Latino/as and African Americans. For example, Starr County, Texas, is one of the poorest counties in the nation and is 98% Mexican American. By age 4, 24% of children in this county are overweight or obese. By the time they enter elementary school, 50% of boys and 35% of girls are overweight or obese. In addition, over half of the adults have

Exhibit 8.1: Obesity by Age, Gender, Race/Ethnicity

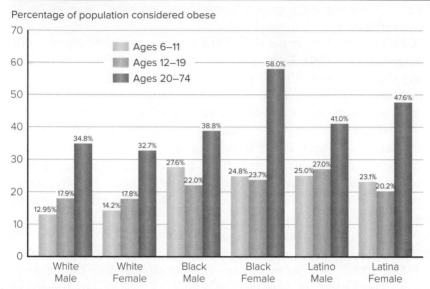

Percentage of population considered obese

(Source: National Center for Health Statistics, 2014, Tables 69 & 70)

Type 2 diabetes, an affliction closely associated with obesity (Weil, 2005). Exhibit 8.1 presents the obesity statistics for the American population by age, race, and gender.

The association between obesity, class, and race is often tinged with prejudice, combining the stigma of fat with the stigma of poverty and non-whiteness:

> The fact that African, Native American, and Latin cultural traditions [define] large bodies as beautiful—and that, in general, poor people of all colors are heavier and eat fattier diets than the well-to-do—allows an ugly stew of hatreds to come together in the abhorrence with which we regard fleshy bodies, especially if they are dark-skinned, ineptly groomed, or cheaply dressed. (Weismantel, 2005, p. 51)

Many cases have been reported of fat children being removed from their homes because their obesity is taken as a sign of abuse and neglect. These cases almost always involve people of color and the poor or working class. Their blameworthiness, as perceived by the state, stems from a combination of unacceptable cultural traditions and their own alleged ignorance (LeBesco, 2004).

Intersections
Race, Class, Gender, and Weight

Although the American distaste for obesity applies to both sexes, it is felt particularly strongly by women, who are more likely than men to evaluate their self-worth in terms of their physical appearance. Not surprisingly, they're also more likely than men to be dissatisfied with their bodies, a dissatisfaction that is frequently framed in terms of weight (Renzetti & Curran, 2003) and one that is often unwittingly reinforced by parents. One study found that mothers were three times as likely to notice excess weight in daughters than in sons, even though boys are larger than girls (cited in Orenstein, 2010).

But weight concern is not felt equally by all women. As you can see if you refer back to Exhibit 8.1, almost 58% of African American women and 48% of Latina women are obese compared with less than 33% of white women (National Center for Health Statistics, 2014). Yet white women are significantly more likely than women of color to be concerned about their weight and to exhibit disordered eating behaviors (Abrams, Allen, & Gray, 1993). In one study, 90% of white junior high and high school girls voiced dissatisfaction with their bodies compared with 30% of black teens (Parker, Nichter, Nichter, Vuckovic, Sims, & Ritenbaugh, 1995). Indeed, black adolescents tend to perceive themselves as thinner than they actually are, whereas white adolescents tend to perceive themselves as heavier than they actually are.

Historically, African American women, especially poor and working-class African American women, worried less than women of other races about dieting or about being thin (Molloy & Herzberger, 1998). They tended to be less dissatisfied than white women with their body weight and therefore had higher self-esteem, had a more positive body image, and suffered from fewer eating disorders. Indeed, when African American women do diet, their efforts to lose weight are usually more realistic and less extreme than white women's attempts.

However, researchers have recently begun to challenge the suggestion that women of color are somehow immune to disordered eating (e.g., Beauboeuf-Lafontant, 2009). Some evidence indicates similar levels of body dissatisfaction and weight loss attempts among Asian, black, Latina, and white girls (National Eating Disorders Association, 2011). Other studies have found that black women are often just as likely as white women to report binge eating or vomiting and were more likely to report fasting and the abuse of laxatives (National Eating Disorders Association, 2014).

Some have suggested that women of color have always suffered from body dissatisfaction and disordered eating but have largely been overlooked by researchers because they are less likely than white women to seek treatment (Brodey, 2005). Others speculate that disordered eating among women of color has actually increased recently because they are more likely than their predecessors to be exposed to and adopt for themselves dominant white preferences, attitudes, and ideals about beauty and weight. One study found that the risk of disordered eating increases for African American women who have a strong desire to assimilate into the dominant white culture (Abrams, Allen, & Gray, 1993). Another study discovered that the more acculturated Mexican-American women are to dominant white standards of weight and physical appearance, the more likely they are to exhibit disordered eating patterns (Chamorro & Flores-Ortiz, 2000).

Whatever the reason, the relationship between race, class, and weight remains complicated. On the one hand, the life circumstances of poor people and people from ethnoracial minorities increase the risk of obesity. To some observers, women who don't see their weight as problematic and therefore aren't motivated to improve the healthiness of their lifestyle face serious health risks. On the other hand, excessive concern with weight and body image in the culture creates other potentially serious problems, like disordered eating habits, which can be equally dangerous.

IT'S NOT HOW YOU FEEL, IT'S HOW YOU LOOK

Concerns with bodily appearance go beyond weight anxiety. For centuries, people around the world have caused themselves serious pain and injury in their attempts to conform their bodies to cultural definitions of attractiveness. In traditional China, for example, young girls had their feet tightly bound to prevent them from growing and to thus produce the tiny feet that were considered attractive. Today, hundreds of Chinese women each year, convinced that being taller will improve their job and marriage prospects, subject themselves to a procedure in which their leg bones are broken, separated, and stretched. Metal pins and screws pull the bones apart a little less than a millimeter a day, sometimes for close to 2 years. Many women undergoing this treatment have lost the ability to walk; others have suffered permanent, disfiguring bone damage (Smith, 2002).

In the United States, women once wore tight, suffocating, organ-injuring corsets to achieve a desirable "hourglass" figure. Today, American women do all kinds of things, from ripping out their facial and body hair through tweezing or waxing to wearing spine-altering high heels in order to reach a particular beauty ideal. A growing number of affluent American women have engaged in a modern form of footbinding in recent years: the so-called "Cinderella surgery," which alters the shape and size of feet to fit more easily into designer shoes (Ross, 2014).

Physical attractiveness is typically equated with economic advantage, what economists call the "beauty premium." Handsome men earn about 5% more than less attractive men and good-looking women earn 4% more. In one study, 61% of hiring managers said it would be an advantage for a woman to show off her figure in the workplace and 57% said that unattractive job candidates have a harder time getting hired (cited in Bennett, 2010).

Not surprisingly, physical attractiveness is also big business. Even in economic hard times, people are willing to spend huge sums of money to alter their looks. Beauty shops generate over $19 billion in revenue each year (ProQuest Statistical Abstract, 2014). According to the American Society of Plastic Surgeons (2014), there were 1.6 million cosmetic surgery procedures and 13.4 million minimally invasive, nonsurgical procedures (such as Botox injections, cellulite treatments, and chemical peels) in the United States in 2014. Ninety-one percent of patients are women. The overall cost for these procedures was about $12.6 billion.

It's tempting to see concerns with physical appearance and the desire to cosmetically alter one's face or body as exclusively the province of white, wealthy women. But that's not entirely the case. People of color account for about 22% of all cosmetic procedures (American Society for Aesthetic Plastic Surgery, 2014). For instance, the number of African American men and women seeking cosmetic facial or reconstructive surgery more than tripled between 1997 and 2002. For years, the African American community has frowned on cosmetic surgery and supported larger body types, wider noses, and not-so-perfect features. Some still see cosmetic surgery as an insult to "one's ancestors and to the culture" (Samuels, 2004, p. 48). But some social observers say that this increase in plastic surgery is simply an extension of other social trends, including concern with appearance and the growing affluence of African Americans. African Americans have become the biggest consumers of beauty products in the United States. Black hair care products alone—hair extensions, weaves, hair relaxer chemicals, and so on—are a multibillion dollar a year industry.

Asian American women are more likely than any other ethnoracial group to pursue cosmetic surgery (Kaw, 2002). But the specific procedures they seek are different from those preferred by other groups. White women might opt for liposuction or breast augmentation and African American women for lip or nasal reduction surgeries, but Asian American women are more likely to undergo surgeries to make their eyes appear wider and "less Asian." Their desire for such a procedure reflects the fact that they've internalized the larger society's negative appraisal and stereotyping of "Asian" features. A 21-year-old Chinese American woman who had the surgery said, "When I look at other Asians who have no folds and their eyes are slanted and closed, I think of how they would look . . . more awake [if they had eye surgery]." Another said she had the surgery so she could "avoid the stereotype of the 'oriental bookworm' who is dull and doesn't know how to have fun" (both quoted in Kaw, 2002, p. 358). Incidentally, the cultural attitudes underlying this procedure have even migrated to China, where surgical eye-widening has become the most popular cosmetic operations in the country (LaFraniere, 2011).

Although the vast majority of people who are concerned about their appearance are women—they account for 91% of all cosmetic procedures (American Society of Plastic Surgeons, 2014)—men are not entirely immune to concerns over body image. Cultural constructions of masculinity are changing. Men are paying more attention to their looks than ever before. Male grooming products now account for a significant piece of the cosmetics market. Indeed, men are now being encouraged to see the relationship between their physical appearance and economic advantage. As one cosmetic surgeon put it, "A youthful look gives the appearance of a more dynamic, charging individual who will go out and get the business" (quoted in Bordo, 1999, pp. 195–196). Since 2000, the number of men having cheek implants, thigh lifts, and tummy tucks has grown by nearly 100%; buttock lifts have grown 283%; and lip augmentation procedures have increased 371% (American Society of Plastic Surgeons, 2014).

We can see in these trends that the cultural value placed on appearance is so strong in this society that it has begun to overcome traditional gender, ethnoracial, and class differences in how people view their bodies and the extent to which they'll go to alter them.

UNEQUAL AND UNWELL: THE STRATIFICATION OF HEALTH AND HEALTH CARE

To people whose lives are a daily struggle for survival, weight-loss programs and expensive elective surgeries to alter physical appearance are luxuries they will never enjoy. But they, like everyone else, will almost certainly get sick at some point in their lives and will eventually die. Unfortunately, the chances of getting sick and getting well are not equally distributed. Imbalances in susceptibility to illness and access to effective health care are unquestionably one of the hallmarks of human civilization worldwide. In the United States, health and health care are also stratified along class, ethnoracial, gender, and sexual lines.

GLOBAL GAPS IN HEALTH

According to the World Health Organization (1995), poverty is the single greatest cause of ill health in the world today:

> Poverty is the main reason why babies are not vaccinated, why clean water and sanitation are not provided, why . . . drugs and other treatments are unavailable and why mothers die in childbirth. It is the underlying cause of reduced life expectancy, handicap, disability, stress, suicide, family disintegration, and substance abuse. (p. 1)

For the over 1 billion people worldwide who live on less than one U.S. dollar per day, basic health services and medicines are virtually nonexistent. People living in extreme poverty lack every conceivable correlate of good health: safe drinking water, decent housing, adequate sanitation, sufficient food, health education, effective birth control, professional health care, transportation, and secure employment. The 2014 Ebola virus outbreak in several West African countries was fueled to some degree by underfunded and outdated health care systems that lacked the necessary resources to contain the spread of the disease. Likewise, overcrowding, poor housing, lack of clean water were linked to the 2016 transmission of the mosquito borne Zika virus in Latin America.

At the level of global economics, poor and middle-income countries are home to more than 80% of the world's population and carry 90% of the world's disease burden but only account for 11% of worldwide health care spending (Carr, 2004). As a result, poor countries in the developing world lag behind wealthier developed countries on almost every social indicator of health: infant and child mortality, stunted growth, malnutrition, childhood vaccinations, prenatal and postnatal care, and life expectancy (Population Reference Bureau, 2014b; UNICEF, 2009). Millions of people die prematurely each year from diseases that, in more prosperous countries, are preventable, curable, or nonexistent. In the United States and the developed countries of Western Europe about 5% of child deaths are attributable to infectious diseases. In Southeast Asia, infectious diseases account for 57% of child deaths, and in Africa the figure increases to 77% (Kent & Yin, 2006).

People in wealthy countries experience less pain as well. Six countries—the United States, Canada, France, Germany, Britain, and Australia—consume 79% of the world's medical narcotics, principally morphine. In contrast, poor and middle-income countries consume only 6% of pain-reducing drugs (cited in McNeil, 2007). Exhibit 8.2 illustrates the relationship between health spending and health outcomes like infant mortality and life expectancy.

HIV/AIDS presents one of the most troubling global health imbalances. Although significant progress has been made in the past few years with rates of new infections on the decline worldwide (UNAIDS, 2014), the vast majority of HIV-infected people around the world remain those who live in the least developed regions. Seventy percent of people living with HIV/AIDS worldwide live in sub-Saharan Africa and three-quarters of people who die from AIDS-related causes come from this region (UNAIDS, 2014).

The effect that HIV/AIDS has had on overall life expectancy is staggering. In the developed regions of North America and Europe, people born today can expect to live until they are close to 80. In the poorest, least developed countries in the world, life expectancy is just over 60. In African countries with high rates of HIV infection life expectancy is under 50 (Population Reference Bureau, 2014b). Such startling figures will have severe long-term consequences as millions of the world's poorest children become orphaned and face a lifetime of despair.

The news is not all bad though. Over the last few years, AIDS patients' access to effective treatment in the form of ant-retroviral drugs (ARVs) has expanded dramatically worldwide, tripling between 2009 and 2015. In 2015, over 15 million people in low- and middle-income countries—and over 9 million in Africa alone—received this treatment, thereby exceeding the number of people who were eligible for it, but who lacked access (World Health Organization, 2014). In the sub–Saharan African countries that continue to have the world's highest rates of HIV infection—Botswana, Swaziland, Zambia, Namibia, and South Africa—over 80% of people in need now have access to ARVs (Avert, 2013). Globally, the rate of new HIV infections has been dropping over the last several years (UNAIDS, 2014).

What remains the case, however, is that HIV/AIDS is in many ways a "feminized" global health problem. Women in sub-Saharan Africa make up close to 57% of all HIV-infected adults in the world and 92% of all HIV-infected pregnant women (Avert, 2014). In this region, girls and young women make up 75% of those between 15 and 24 who are HIV-positive (Lalasz, 2004). To experts, one of the most important reasons for the increase

Exhibit 8.2: Global Imbalances in Health

Total annual spending on health per person (in U.S. dollars)

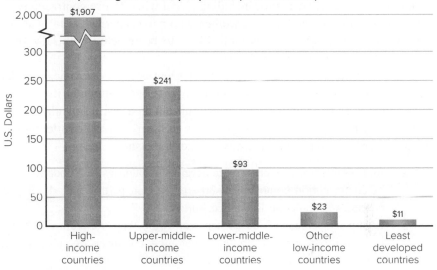

Infant mortality, 2013*

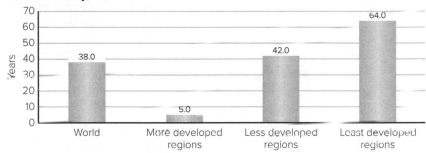

* # of deaths of infants under the age of 1 per 1,000 live births

Life expectancy at birth for both sexes, 2013

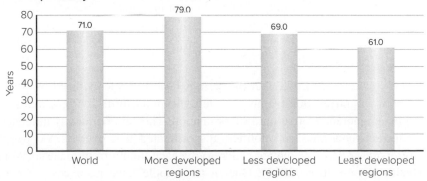

(Sources: Carr, 2004; Population Reference Bureau, 2014b)

of AIDS cases in women is that in many poor countries, particularly those in sub-Saharan Africa, is the lingering gendered power imbalance where men make all sexual decisions, including if and when to use contraceptives. According to the United Nations, women who have experienced intimate or sexual violence are three times more likely to be infected with HIV than other women (cited in Fustos, 2011).

Poor women around the world face persistent and pervasive health risks beyond HIV/AIDS. Because they occupy subordinate statuses in most societies and face extra economic and social burdens as a result of childbearing and child rearing, global health inequalities hit them and their children particularly hard (Ashford, 2005). Consider these statistics:

- Sixty percent of women in more developed countries use modern forms of contraception compared to 30% of women in the least developed countries (Population Reference Bureau, 2014b).
- Eighty-six percent of all women worldwide who die from childbirth complications come from the developing countries of sub-Saharan Africa and Southern Asia (UN Women, 2015).
- According to the organization, Save the Children (2014), when considering things like risk of maternal death, availability of modern contraception, access to a skilled attendant at delivery, female life expectancy, and maternal leave benefits, the top five places on earth to be a mother are Finland, Norway, Sweden, Iceland, and Denmark—all developed, wealthy countries. The five worst places to be a mother are Somalia, Democratic Republic of Congo, Niger, Mali, and Guinea-Bissau—all poor, underdeveloped countries.
- Children of poor mothers are three times more likely to be stunted in their growth and twice as likely to die as children of wealthy mothers (Population Reference Bureau, 2004). Malnutrition among poor women and girls around the world wreaks havoc on their health as well as the health of their children in numerous ways, such as low birth weight, impaired physical and mental development, and increased risk of maternal mortality and chronic disease in adulthood (Ransom & Elder, 2003).

It's important to note that the serious health problems faced by people in poor countries don't emerge solely from harmful living conditions, hygienic ignorance, or cultural subordination. They are frequently influenced by global economics and politics. It's estimated that over 52,000 people worldwide (77% of whom are children) die each month from malaria (World Health Organization, 2013). One in ten people have no access to clean drinking water (UNICEF/WHO, 2012). Wealthy countries could easily afford to provide regular vaccines, mosquito nets, soil nutrients, sufficient food, or clean water supplies to poor countries to address these treatable problems. In fact, in 2005, the United Nations declared that ending world hunger and disease was "utterly affordable" and would require only that wealthy countries commit one-half of 1% of their total incomes to aid poor countries. However, many of these nations have been notoriously reluctant to provide such assistance. The United States, for example, provides less than one-fifth of 1% of its total income, the smallest percentage among major donor countries (Dugger, 2005). Subsidizing the health care of people in poor countries tends to be politically unpopular in wealthy countries.

WEALTH AND HEALTH IN THE UNITED STATES

Socioeconomic inequalities in health and health care exist *within* countries as well. Even in relatively healthy places like the Netherlands, Finland, the United States, and Great Britain, poor people die 5 to 10 years sooner, on average, than wealthy people (Carr, 2004). Diseases, nutritional deficiencies, birth complications, injuries, substance abuse, and violence tend to be concentrated among the poorest people in any society. Such discrepancies are by no means new. As far back as the 16th and 17th centuries, records show a relationship between socioeconomic inequalities and health. In 17th-century Geneva, for instance, average life expectancy was 18 for the lowest socioeconomic group and 36 for the highest group (cited in Rogmans, 2001).

In the United States today, the overwhelming empirical evidence indicates that aside from those illnesses associated with outdoor leisure activities like skin cancer, in which wealthier, better-educated white individuals are at highest risk (Hausauer, Swetter, Cockburn, & Clarke, 2011), rates of illness increase and life expectancy decreases as one climbs down the socioeconomic ladder (Marmot, 2004). The poorer you are, the greater your risk of chronic headaches, varicose veins, respiratory infection, childhood asthma, hypertension, emotional distress, low-birth-weight babies, and heart disease (Perez-Peña, 2003; Shweder, 1997).

The states with high rates of poverty have maternal death rates 77 times higher than states with the low poverty rates (Chesler & Flynn, 2014). A data analysis organization affiliated with the *New York Times* examined every U.S. county in terms of various indicators of financial well being (such as, educational attainment, unemployment rate, and median household income) and health (such as, life expectancy, obesity rate, and disability rate).

Exhibit 8.3: Health and Wealth in Two U.S. Counties

	Clay County, KY (poorest county in the United States)	Los Alamos, NM (wealthiest county in the United States)
% of residents with college degree	7.4%	63.2%
median household income	$ 22,296	$ 106,462
unemployment rate	12.7%	3.5%
% of adults who smoke	36.7%	18.1%
Life expectancy	71.4	82.4
Obesity rate	44.5%	21.9%
% of adults who engage in sufficient physical activity	35.5%	68.1%

Sources: Institute for Health Metrics and Evaluation, 2014; Lowrey, 2014, p. 15).

The poorest counties invariably had the lowest life expectancy and the highest rates of obesity and disability (see Exhibit 8.3).

Moreover, less affluent people's living and work conditions are more likely to be unhealthy. They are exposed to more environmental toxins and have access to less effective medical care than more affluent Americans. Consider these other findings:

- Poor children in both urban and rural regions of the country have lead levels in their blood that far exceed national health standards. About 12% of children living in poor families have dangerous blood lead levels compared with about 2% of children in high-income families. In every income group, African American children are more likely than children of other ethnoracial groups to have elevated blood lead levels (Northridge, Stover, Rosenthal, & Sherard, 2003). Perhaps, therefore, it's not surprising that Flint, Michigan—the city that is currently enduring a tragic lead-poisoning crisis due to a contaminated water supply—has a poverty rate of nearly 42% (U.S. Bureau of the Census, 2016).

- Tobacco use is highest among people who have working-class jobs, have achieved a low level of education, and earn a low income (Barbeau,

Krieger, & Soobader, 2004). While health concerns have driven rates of tobacco use down nationwide over the past 15 years, the decline has been noticeably faster in wealthier regions of the country than in poor regions (Dwyer-Lindgren, Mokdad, Srebotnjak, Flaxman, Hansen, & Murray, 2014).

- Large agribusinesses expose their poor, itinerant, and largely minority employees to various health risks by spraying deadly pesticides and herbicides in the wind, sending workers into the fields too soon after the chemicals have been applied, and failing to provide sinks, showers, and laundries so the workers can wash off the harmful substances. The most obvious health effects are vomiting, nausea, dizziness, headaches, skin rashes, bronchitis, and asthma. Less immediate but more serious effects include brain tumors, leukemia, non-Hodgkin's lymphoma, and sarcoma. The incidence of birth defects is 3 to 14 times higher among farmworkers than among the general U.S. population (Shipler, 2004).

As in underdeveloped countries, illness and poverty interact in ways that are especially dangerous to children. Low-income families typically have problems paying rent, buying food, obtaining access to health services, providing transportation, and offering a safe and stress-free physical environment for their children. Even before birth, low-income mothers have less access to prenatal resources and a healthy diet and greater exposure to harmful substances like environmental toxins. All of these things can impair neurological growth and affect a child's later language development (Furstenberg, 2011). The most pervasive neurological harm due to low socioeconomic status occurs between the ages of 6 months and 3 years (cited in Cookson, 2008).

It might be tempting to attribute such class disparities to the unhealthy lifestyles of people on the bottom socioeconomic rungs of society. However, it is impossible to ignore the institutional activities that aggravate the problem. For instance, consider rules that determine eligibility for government programs for the needy (see Chapter 6). Poor children whose Supplemental Nutrition Assistance Program benefits are cut or reduced when their parents' income rises slightly above the eligibility threshold, are significantly more likely to be in poor health, be at risk for developmental delays, and experience child food insecurity than those whose families remain eligible to receive benefits (Children's Health Watch, 2013).

What's even more striking, perhaps, is what happens to poor children who beat the odds and overcome the obstacles poverty puts in their way. One study (Brody, Yu, Chen, Miller, Kogan, & Beach, 2013) followed a group of about 500 poor black children from rural Georgia between ages 11 and 19. Those students who, at age 11, were rated by their teachers as diligent, focused, and academically successful were more obese, had higher blood pressure, and experienced more stress at age 19 than those kids who were rated aggressive, difficult, and isolated when they were younger. In fact, when "resilient" kids made it to college, their health was much worse than students who grew up in affluent, educated neighborhoods. The researchers concluded that overcoming initial poverty sometimes creates tremendous pressure to not fail, resulting in increasing risk of various stress-related ailments.

Not only do people without sufficient economic means face greater health risks than others, they may also lack the ability to get effective treatment when they need it. According to recent data from the U.S. Department of Health and Human Services (Cohen & Martinez, 2015), 11.5% of the U.S. population was uninsured in 2014. While this represents a 25% decrease compared to 2013 (Sanger-Katz, 2014) and the lowest level since 2008 (principally due to subsidies provided by the Affordable Care Act), it means that about 36 million Americans (including about 4 million children) still have no health insurance.

Poor, uninsured parents face decisions that more affluent parents never do, such as choosing between buying a child a birthday gift and paying to have his or her cavity filled. Without insurance, one sickness or one accident can destroy a family financially. A nationwide study found that uninsured people and those covered by Medicaid are significantly less likely than people covered by private insurance to receive cancer diagnoses in early stages, diminishing their chances of survival (Halpern, Ward, Pavluck, Schrag, Bian, & Chen, 2008).

The effects of being able to afford health insurance can't be overstated. When the state of Massachusetts adopted mandatory health care coverage in 2006, the death rate in the state dropped significantly. The decline was steepest in those counties that had the highest proportion of poor and uninsured people prior to the adoption of the law (Sommers, Long, & Baicker, 2014).

To make matters worse, despite advances in medicine and technology, the health gap between people at the lowest and highest ends of the socioeconomic spectrum seems to be getting worse. For instance, for American men born in 1920, there was a six-year difference in life expectancy between the richest 10% of wage earners and the poorest 10%. But for men born in 1950, the difference has more than doubled to 14 years. The gap in life expectancy between wealthy and poor women likewise grew from about 5 years for those born in 1920 to 13 years for those born in 1950 (cited in Tavernise, 2016).

Intersections

Race, Class, and Social Vulnerability—The (Un)Natural Disaster of Hurricane Katrina

Across the globe, disasters—natural or otherwise—take their greatest toll on the least powerful segments of society. Whether it's an earthquake in Haiti, a typhoon in the Philippines, or a heat wave in Pakistan, poor people have always been particularly vulnerable to death, disability, and displacement. The same can be said for the U.S. Hurricane Katrina hit the Gulf Coast region of the United States in 2005, killing over 1,000 people in Louisiana, Mississippi, and Alabama. It might be tempting to think that these people died in an unfortunate and unavoidable natural disaster. However, most died not because of the hurricane's torrential rains and high winds but because of the flooding that occurred when the levees that ordinarily protect the low-lying areas of New Orleans (which were in desperate need of repair to begin with) were breached. In addition to the fatalities, hundreds of thousands of people lost everything they owned and were forced to relocate. Many never returned.

The storm and its aftermath did not affect all residents equally. The neighborhoods that experienced the most significant flooding had a lower median income, a higher poverty rate, and a higher percentage of households without a vehicle than the areas that experienced little or no flooding (Schwartz, Revkin, & Wald, 2005). Those of us watching the tragedy unfold on television could not help but notice the obvious fact that the vast majority of the evacuees who suffered for days in the sweltering darkness of the Superdome and convention center in New Orleans were poor people of color who came from the most vulnerable parts of the city. These individuals either didn't have the necessary transportation to evacuate prior to the hurricane or stayed behind to tend to sick and elderly relatives who couldn't be moved:

> With no welfare check (the hurricane struck near the end of the month), little food, and no help from city, state, or federal officials, the poor were forced to ride out the storm in their homes or move to shelters of last resort. This is the enduring face of Hurricane Katrina—poor, black, single mothers, young, and old—struggling just to survive; options limited by the ineffectiveness of preparedness and the inadequacy of response. (Cutter, 2006, p. 3)

The social vulnerability of poor citizens of color continued long after the waters receded. For instance, in the aftermath of the hurricane, states were required to spend half of the federal grant money they received on low-income citizens. However, two years after Katrina hit, Mississippi had spent only 10% of the federal money on programs dedicated to helping the poor; the rest went to relatively affluent citizens and big businesses (Eaton, 2007). Even three years later poor, displaced children who were forced to live in ramshackle government trailer parks after the hurricane continue to suffer from various ailments including anemia, respiratory infections, and depression (Carmichael, 2008). Again we see how the lack of economic resources can have direct, physical consequences in people's lives.

THE COLOR OF HEALTH

As with other outcomes of inequality, it's often impossible to separate the health effects of race from those of class. Nevertheless, a substantial body of research points to wide ethnic and racial disparities in health care and health insurance coverage (Kirby & Kaneda, 2010). Blacks and Latino/as remain the ethnoracial groups most likely to be uninsured. Though their numbers have gone down since the implementation of the Affordable Care Act, 13.5% of Blacks and over 25% of Latino/as lack health insurance. By comparison, less than 10% of Whites are uninsured (Cohen & Martinez, 2015). In addition, Blacks and Latino/as are significantly less likely than Whites to have a regular doctor (cited in Wilson, 2009).

Not surprisingly, members of ethnoracial minorities continue to face long-term disadvantages in health. For instance, African Americans make up about 13% of the population in this country but account for 41% of all new HIV/AIDS diagnoses (ProQuest Statistical Abstract, 2015). The rate of new infections is 20 times higher among black women than white women (Centers for Disease Control and Prevention, 2012b). According to the National Institutes of Health the overall 5-year cancer survival rate for African Americans is 61.5%; the survival rate for white cancer patients is almost 70% (ProQuest Statistical Abstract, 2014). White women with breast cancer live, on average, three years longer than black women with breast cancer (Silber, Rosenbaum, Clark, Giantonio, Ross, Teng, Wang, Niknam, Ludwig, Wang, Even-Shoshan, & Fox, 2013). And even when they have similar insurance coverage, black women with abnormal mammograms wait longer to begin treatment than white women (cited in Freeman, 2014). Blacks now die at a rate comparable to the death rate of Whites *over 30 years ago* (Blitstein, 2009).

Exhibit 8.4 shows other discrepancies in the relationship between race/ethnicity and the cause of death. For most causes, death rates for Blacks are

Exhibit 8.4: Age-Adjusted Death Rates for Selected Causes by Gender, Race, and Ethnicity (Deaths per 100,000)

Cause of death	Male	Female	Non-Hispanic White	Black	American Indian	Asian	Latino/a
All causes	887.1	634.9	755.0	898.2	628.3	424.3	558.6
Heart disease	225.1	143.3	179.9	224.9	128.6	100.9	132.8
Cancers	209.9	146.7	176.5	203.8	122.4	108.9	119.7
Accidental Injuries	51.5	25.6	42.4	31.3	46.9	15.0	25.8
Diabetes Mellitus	24.9	17.6	18.2	38.7	36.4	15.5	25.8
Suicide	19.8	5.0	15.0	5.2	10.8	6.2	5.9
Cirrhosis of the liver	12.9	6.2	9.4	6.7	22.8	3.2	13.7
Homicide	8.4	2.3	2.5	17.7	5.7	1.8	5.3
HIV infection	3.8	1.4	1.1	11.6	1.6	0.4	2.8

(Source: National Center for Health Statistics, 2014. Table 20)

far above those of any other ethnoracial group, largely because of socioeconomic status, health-risk behavior, psychosocial factors (for example, stress), access to and quality of health care, culture, genetic factors, and environmental and occupational dangers (Kaneda & Adams, 2008). The exceptions are accidents, suicide, and cirrhosis of the liver, for which Native Americans rank at or near the top. Here, too, social structural factors are likely respon sible. The hopelessness of life on destitute reservations, where economic and educational opportunities are virtually nonexistent, can create a level of despair so great that it may lead to suicide or be lessened only through alcohol, which can be linked to liver disease and accidental deaths.

Even when insurance coverage, incomes, and severity of illness are the same, members of ethnoracial minorities in the United States do not receive the same quality of health care as do white Americans (Institute of Medicine, 2003). People of color are less likely than Whites to be given appropriate medication for heart ailments, undergo coronary bypass surgery, and receive kidney dialysis or transplants. Other studies have found that African American cancer patients receive fewer effective surgeries and get less adequate pain medication than white patients with similar characteristics (cited in Mayberry, Mili, & Ofili, 2000). On the other hand, patients of color are more likely than Whites to receive less sophisticated treatments like arm and leg amputations. One study found that African American patients with circulatory problems were more than twice as likely as comparable Whites to have a leg amputated. In addition, African American men with prostate cancer were far more likely than other men to have their testicles removed (cited in Feagin & McKinney, 2003). So problematic are racial and ethnic discrepancies in health and well-being that the American Medical Association established a permanent Commission to End Health Care Disparities in 2005.

Whether differences in medical care and health outcomes are a result of conscious individual bigotry or something more systemic is a matter of some debate. It seems unlikely that doctors would purposely give patients of particular ethnoracial groups substandard care. What's more likely—and in some ways more insidious—is that subtle stereotypes influence the way doctors perceive their patients. For instance, one study found that doctors view white patients as more intelligent and more likely to abide by medical instructions than patients of color (cited in Feagin & McKinney, 2003). In another study, doctors described African American patients—no matter what their education and income levels—as less intelligent, less likely to follow medical advice, less likely to participate in rehabilitation, and more likely to abuse alcohol and drugs than white patients (Van Ryn & Burke, 2000). Other research has found that doctors often stereotype Asian patients as compliant and "problem free" (cited in American Sociological Association, 2005). When time and medical resources are limited, such beliefs can influence the treatment decisions doctors make.

Beyond deeply entrenched stereotypes, the differential treatment of certain groups is often motivated by financial concerns. Consider, for instance, racial differences in organ transplants. According to the Organ Procurement and Transplantation Network (2015), the 2015 national kidney transplant waiting list consisted of 36.6% whites and 34% African Americans. (This figure in and of itself is telling: African Americans make up only about 13% of the population yet account for over one third of people in need of kidney transplants.) However, that same year, Whites received 54.5% of all kidney transplants, while African Americans received only 22%. Such a discrepancy is likely linked to hospitals' determination of a candidate's ability to pay before approving an expensive procedure. These policies are sometimes referred to as "green screens" or "wallet biopsies." For example, the total cost of a kidney transplant—including preoperative and postoperative care—is about $334,000. A liver transplant can run over $739,000, and a heart transplant costs over $1.2 million (Bentley, 2014). So it's not surprising that most hospitals would screen potential recipients for some kind of evidence up front that their insurance will cover the procedure. Because ethnoracial minorities are less likely than Whites to have medical insurance, they are less likely to receive a referral for transplant surgery (Stolberg, 1998). Financial concerns, not outright racial prejudice, lie at the heart of these policies.

Environmental Discrimination   Health disparities along ethnoracial lines are sometimes not so obvious. For instance, people in neighborhoods where hazardous waste treatment facilities or other sources of industrial pollution exist are disproportionately exposed to the unhealthful effects of air pollution, water pollution, and pesticides. In the interests of economic expansion, companies—often with the support of local governments and labor groups—decide on the location of such facilities based on factors that, on the surface, have nothing to do with the ethnoracial configuration of communities: the cost of land, population density, and geological conditions. But because the more desirable industrial areas tend to be the areas where existing houses can be purchased and demolished cheaply, industrial facilities are disproportionately likely to be built in areas populated by poor members of ethnoracial minorities.

Furthermore, if a community is poor and inhabited largely by people of color, there's a good chance that environmental protections help it less than a community that is affluent or white (Bullard, 2001). For instance, because Native American reservations have less stringent environmental regulations than other areas, they have been targeted by the U.S. military for the location of stockpiles of nuclear, chemical, and biological weapons and by private companies seeking to build solid waste landfills, hazardous waste incinerators, and nuclear waste storage facilities (Hooks & Smith, 2004). In addition, when it comes to the federal government cleaning up polluted areas, predominantly white communities see faster action, better results, and stiffer penalties for polluters than communities where ethnoracial minorities predominate (Bullard, 2001).

People of color make up the majority of residents who live in neighborhoods within two miles of the nation's hazardous waste treatment facilities (Dosomething.org, 2007). The predominantly Latino/a neighborhoods south of Tucson, for instance, are exposed to twenty times the acceptable levels of the carcinogenic solvent trichloroethylene. Rates of cancer, birth defects, and genetic mutations in those neighborhoods far outpace national averages (Velázquez, 2002).

Poor African American communities are often the hardest hit. Blacks are 79% more likely than Whites to live in areas where air pollution levels constitute serious health risks (cited in Little, 2007). In Port Arthur, Texas roughly two-thirds of the population is non-white and median household income is about a third lower than that of the rest of the state. Over the years, several companies—including some based in Mexico—have received exemptions from the Environmental Protection Agency to transport the banned carcinogenic substance polychlorinated biphenyls (PCBs) to incinerators in the Port Arthur area (Ellick, 2008). Similarly, a 100-mile, predominantly African American, stretch of towns between New Orleans and Baton Rouge is known as "Cancer Alley" because it is the polluted home to over 150 petrochemical plants and 17 oil refineries (Flaherty, 2014).

But before we simply blame callous companies for maliciously endangering the health of poor people of color in the interests of maximizing their profits, we must realize that the phenomenon of environmental discrimination is complicated by financial need. Often, a destitute community welcomes a hazardous facility as a much-needed source of employment. For instance, in 1998 the Louisiana chapter of the National Association for the Advancement of Colored People (NAACP) supported the construction of a $700 million plastics plant in St. James Parish that it knew could pose dangerous health risks to the neighborhoods nearby. African Americans made up 81% of the residents within 4 miles of the proposed site (Hines, 2001). At the time, the region suffered an unemployment rate of 12% and a poverty rate of 44%. The average income among its black residents was less than $5,000 a year. So the opportunity to bring in a steady source of employment, no matter how dangerous, was too attractive to pass up. Nobody wants an ugly garbage dump, landfill, toxic waste incinerator, or polluting factory in their neighborhood. But if these are the only ventures that will provide steady employment for residents, poor communities are left with little choice but to support them. The president of the NAACP once said, "Poverty has been the No. 1 crippler of poor people, not chemical plants" (quoted in Cooper, 1998, p. 532).

Medical Suspicions   As we've seen, the undeniable fact about the American health care system is that the poorer you are and the darker your skin, the worse the health care you'll receive. So it's not all that surprising that Whites, the wealthy, and the well-educated report that they are more trusting of the health care system than their darker, poorer, and less educated counterparts are (Schnittker, 2004).

Mistrust is especially pervasive among African Americans. Much of their anxiety is sharpened by memories of the federal government's infamous Tuskegee experiment. In 1932, the U.S. Public Health Service began a study in Tuskegee, Alabama, to learn about the natural course of untreated syphilis. In exchange for their participation, 400 black men—all poor and most illiterate—received free meals, free medical exams, and burial insurance. The researchers and health care workers never told the men that they had syphilis. Instead, they were told that they had "bad blood," for which they would receive treatment. In reality, they received no treatment. Even when penicillin—the most effective treatment for syphilis—became available in the early 1950s, the men were not treated. In fact, the Public Health Service went to great lengths to prevent the men from receiving penicillin. Even as they began to die or to go blind or insane, treatment was withheld. When the experiment was made public in 1972—four decades after its inception— it was finally stopped. Since then, the federal government has paid out more than $9 million in damages to victims and their families and heirs.

It's not only the Tuskegee study that created a pervasive distrust of medical research among many African Americans. During World War II, the U.S. government used black soldiers as experimental subjects to examine the effects of mustard gas and other chemical agents on American troops. They wanted to see if black skin influenced the effects of the chemical. White soldiers were used too, but they served as scientific control groups (and hence weren't exposed to the mustard gas). Experimenters used the white soldiers' reactions to establish what was "normal," and then compared them to the minority soldiers. All of the experiments were done in secret and weren't recorded on the subjects' official military records so there is no proof of what they went through. They received no follow-up health care at all. And they were sworn to secrecy about the tests and were threatened with dishonorable discharge and military prison time if they told anyone. So they were not able to receive adequate medical treatment for their injuries because they couldn't tell doctors what had been done to them (Dickerson, 2015).

A few years ago, the Kennedy Krieger Institute in Baltimore was accused of intentionally exposing black children—some as young as a year old—to high levels of dangerous lead dust in their homes as part of a study exploring the hazards of lead paint. The Institute, which provided no medical treatment for lead poisoning, had assured families that the homes were "lead safe" (T. C. Williams, 2011).

Today, many African Americans—as well as Latino/as and Native Americans—avoid participating in medical research because of their fear of being used as guinea pigs and suspicions of malicious attempts to intentionally cause illness (cited in Alvidrez & Areán, 2002). Furthermore, members of ethnoracial minorities are often skeptical that their participation in clinical studies would be a benefit either to them personally or to their communities. One survey of African Americans about their attitudes toward research on cancer treatments found that only 43% felt medical research in the United States is conducted ethically (cited in Alvidrez & Areán, 2002). It's no surprise, therefore, that ethnoracial minorities are underrepresented in medical research across all health fields.

Mistrust has also been cited as one of the reasons why African American and other patients of color have been slow to seek medical care and testing for diseases like HIV/AIDS (Richardson, 1997), are less inclined to submit to breast cancer screenings (Thompson, Valdimarsdottir, Winkel, Jandorf, & Redd, 2004), and are less likely than Whites to get surgery for early stages of deadly diseases like lung cancer (Bach, Cramer, Warren, & Begg, 1999). Because of their mistrust, members of ethnoracial minorities may obtain health care only when their problems become severe or even beyond help, leading to the perception that the treatments themselves may be not only ineffective but perhaps even harmful.

Whether these deeply ingrained suspicions are warranted or not is in some sense irrelevant. Medical mistrust needn't derive from specific historical events or even be based on factual data in order for it to have significant effects on people's lives. There only needs to be a cultural ideology of mistrust for it to perpetuate itself among the members of any group (Cort, 2004).

GENDERED HEALTH

Because of their different anatomies, women and men face many different health-related issues. Men don't get ovarian cysts; women don't get prostate cancer. But beyond these disparities, the reasons behind gender differences in health and illness are less anatomically inevitable. For instance, men tend to occupy more physically demanding jobs and engage in riskier physical activity than women. Hence they've historically been at greater risk for various bodily injuries and stress-related ailments. According to the National Center for Health Statistics (2014), men have higher rates of cancer (excluding breast, cervical, and ovarian types) and lower overall life expectancy than women.

Women may be healthier, in general, than men. But, historically, women have been more susceptible than men to being labeled "ill" or "sick" by medical professionals (Rothman, 1984). Women are far more likely than men to undergo surgical and diagnostic procedures. Indeed, the three most common short-stay surgical procedures for women—cesarean section, repair of lacerations during childbirth, and hysterectomy—all deal with exclusively female anatomy and physiology. The three most common short-stay procedures for men—cardiac catheterization, coronary bypass, and reduction of fracture—are not sex-specific (ProQuest Statistical Abstract, 2015).

Normal biological events in women's lives—menstruation, pregnancy, childbirth, and menopause—have long been "**medicalized**" or "**pathologized**," meaning that they are considered problematic or risky conditions in need of medical attention. The social message has always been clear: Women, biologically frail and emotionally erratic because of their anatomy and physiology, cannot be allowed to work too hard or be trusted in positions of authority (Fausto-Sterling, 1985).

According to anthropologist Sherry Ortner (1996), the pathologization of women's normal functioning is due, in part, to the fact that many areas and processes of women's bodies serve a procreative function but no apparent function for the health or stability of the individual. As these body parts perform their specific reproductive functions, they can be the source of discomfort, pain, even danger. Breasts, for example, serve no organic purpose for a woman and can be removed at any time in her life if they become diseased. Ovarian secretions function for the benefit of the egg, promoting its maturation, but they can cause disequilibrium in the woman. Menstruation can be painful and is stigmatized in many cultures. When she is pregnant, a woman's intake of vitamins and minerals is channeled into nourishing the fetus, thereby depleting her strength and energy. And, of course, childbirth itself is a painful and potentially hazardous experience. In short, compared with a man, more of a woman's body space and more of her lifetime are taken up with natural processes involved in reproducing the species, sometimes at great risk to personal health.

Prior to the Affordable Care Act, it was legal in most states for insurance companies selling individual policies—those for people who don't have group insurance coverage through their employers—to charge women higher premiums than men for the same medical coverage . . . a practice known as *gender rating*. The difference in price ranged from 4% to 48% and collectively cost women about $1 billion annually. The obvious justification for this practice was the belief that women used the health care system more than men because of all the medical procedures associated with pregnancy and childbirth. The Department of Health and Human Services ended the practice of *gender rating* when health care reforms went into effect in 2014.

Premenstrual Syndrome   Perhaps the female body process that has received the most medical attention—and caused men the most bewilderment—is premenstrual syndrome (PMS). A woman once wrote in to *Shape* magazine concerned about the fact that her emotions fluctuate. The columnist advised her that although mild mood swings can be normal, it would be wise for her to first rule out premenstrual syndrome as the possible cause (Paul, 2004). The fact that PMS was automatically suspected to be the culprit attests to the level of acceptance the diagnosis has reached in this society. People inside and outside the medical profession so readily believe in the essential reality of PMS that it has become the default explanation for any emotional inconsistencies women may have. We once had a secretary in our department who had a sign over her desk that read, "I have PMS and a gun. Any questions?"

Yet, despite the current popularity of PMS as a catch-all diagnosis, it's not altogether clear exactly what the condition is. Some women experience premenstrual bodily changes; others report emotional changes; and some have a combination of both. Over 100 symptoms have been identified as characteristic of PMS, including (but not limited to):

- physical complaints (muscle stiffness, headache, cramps, backache, fatigue, insomnia, chest pains, ringing in the ears, fuzzy vision, numbness)
- impairments of concentration (confusion, distractibility, lowered judgment)
- dizziness (faintness, cold sweats, nausea, hot flashes)
- water retention (weight gain, skin disorders, painful breasts)
- emotional problems (crying, anxiety, anger, irritability, mood swings, depression, tension) (American Psychiatric Association, 2013)

Premenstrual syndrome as a diagnosable ailment is a relatively recent social construction. It first began to receive widespread public notoriety in the 1980s. A criminal case in Great Britain had a lot to do with popularizing PMS. A woman who ran over her boyfriend with her car was convicted of manslaughter, not murder, after her attorney successfully argued that she was suffering from PMS at the time of the crime, a condition that made her irrational and uncontrollably violent. As a condition of her probation, the woman was required to receive monthly hormone injections to control her symptoms (Renzetti & Curran, 2003).

The value of identifying PMS as a "real" malady is disputable. Some feminists in the 1970s and 1980s pressed for research money and scientific attention to be given to bodily processes, such as premenstrual syndrome, that only women experience. But the focus on PMS masks the fact that menstrual processes do not affect healthy women's ability to function, that some women actually experience positive changes prior to their periods, or that men experience periodic hormonal fluctuations that affect their mood, as much as women do, if not more (Tavris, 1992). The pervasiveness of PMS as a diagnosable disorder also means that women who may experience normal mood changes during their menstrual cycles are encouraged, indeed expected, to consider them abnormal. As one author puts it, "Biomedical researchers have taken a set of bodily changes that are normal to women over the menstrual cycle, packaged them into a 'Premenstrual Syndrome,' and sold them back to women as a disorder, a problem that needs treatment and attention" (Tavris, 1992, p. 133). PMS has thus become a financial boon for medical researchers and drug companies.

The American Psychiatric Association (2013) designates *Premenstrual Dysphoric Disorder* as a legitimate mental illness. Certainly, women around the world experience varying degrees of grumpiness, irritability, and other symptoms related to hormone cycles. In many areas, these experiences are perceived as normal and expectable. The issue, then, is whether these "symptoms" ought to be labeled as a medical problem. To do so reinforces the belief that women's bodies are highly susceptible to disorders and are therefore always in need of medical attention.

From a sociological perspective, it seems highly likely that women's experiences with the "symptoms" surrounding menstruation are related to the place that menstruation occupies in the larger society. We live in a culture that, by and large, has tried either to ignore menstruation or to present it as shameful. Only relatively recently—as evidenced by the glut of commercials and advertisements for feminine hygiene products—has it come out of the closet. But, of course, the attention we as a culture devote to menstruation continues to be almost exclusively negative, focusing on overcoming bothersome premenstrual symptoms or camouflaging the unsightly or otherwise unappealing by-products of menstruation itself. A web site called beinggirl.com regularly posts advice for girls on the use of tampons. A few years ago, a blog on the site, called "Keeping it quick and quiet," reinforced the idea that menstruation is shameful by providing advice such as, "Be discreet when you're bringing a tampon into the girls' room . . . Anyone can bring a purse to the restroom (a classic hiding spot) but try tucking it in your waistband, bra, sock, or cell phone case. No one needs to suspect a thing" and "For better hiding potential, try compact tampons."

The Medicalization of Childbirth   Another area in which women's normal functioning has been medicalized is childbirth. Until the 19th century, doctors were almost completely absent from the birthing process. Female midwives and other women in the family or in the community commonly attended women during and after childbirth (Howell-White, 1999). Birth was considered a woman's affair. Every effort was made to keep men as far away as possible. Only in extremely wealthy families or when the mother's life was in danger was a male doctor consulted (Ulrich, 1990).

By the middle of the 20th century, the hospitalized birth became the delivery method of choice for middle- and upper-class white women, although poor, minority pregnant women still found hospitals largely out of their reach. In 1900, only 5% of American births took place in hospitals; by 1939, over 50% of all births and 75% of urban births occurred there. Today over 98% of American births happen in hospitals (MacDorman, Matthews, & Declercq, 2014).

The overwhelming consideration for hospitalized expectant mothers was the minimization of pain (Mitford, 1993). Obviously, pain has always been an element of childbirth. But with advances in medical technology, affluent women started to believe that they had a right to avoid pain if at all possible. Initially, expectant mothers were put to sleep with chloroform or ether throughout labor and delivery. Eventually, localized anesthetics—drugs that alleviated pain but allowed women to remain conscious throughout the delivery—became popular.

The medicalization and hospitalization of childbirth increased women's dependence on the medical profession. During typical deliveries, relatively little attention was paid to the mother's comfort, well-being, or self-esteem. Typically, she was placed in a position with her legs widespread in the air and her genitals totally exposed. Once labor began, doctors commonly resorted to invasive procedures, such as the use of forceps and suction. Episiotomies—incisions that increase the size of the vaginal opening to give the baby more room to emerge—became a common part of the birthing process. Clearly, a medicalized childbirth meant that the doctor, not the mother, delivered the baby.

But by the 1950s, concern was beginning to grow over the possibility that babies might be harmed in some way by the use of drugs and other common invasive procedures during delivery. And some women were starting to publicly voice their concerns about the dehumanizing conditions of hospital delivery wards. As one mother of three in the 1950s wrote:

> Women are herded like sheep through the obstetrical assembly line, are drugged and strapped on tables while their babies are forceps-delivered. Obstetricians today are businessmen who run baby factories. Modern painkillers and methods are used for the convenience of the doctor, not to spare the mother. (quoted in Gillis, 1996, p. 173)

As a result of such criticisms, "natural" childbirth—deliveries without the aid of anesthetics, suction, or forceps—became popular in the 1960s and 1970s. It restored women to a more central role in the birth process. The popularity of "natural" childbirth—less medical intervention, more maternal contact with the newborn right after birth, and so on—was accompanied by a nostalgic desire to return to a simpler, less technological childbirth experience. Expectant mothers, and their sometimes reluctant husbands, were encouraged to attend childbirth classes to learn special breathing techniques that could ease the delivery without resorting to drugs. Today, many hospitals have turned their cold and sterile delivery rooms into homelike, reassuring birthing suites. The goal is to re-create the benefits of the cozy home birth of the 19th century, but to do so within a safe hospital setting.

However, episiotomies are still used in 9 out of 10 American births, even though recent research has shown that these procedures have no benefits and actually cause more complications for women who receive them (Hartmann, Viswanathan, Palmieri, Gartlehner, Thorp, & Lohr, 2005). Cesarean sections are performed in one-third of U.S. births (Hamilton, Martin, & Ventura, 2011), and most mothers use some sort of pharmaceutical pain control (Davis-Floyd, 1996; Gillis, 1996).

The Gendering of Medical Practice and Research Because of the tendency in the medical profession to see the normal functioning of women's bodies as problems in need of control, doctors can specialize in women's health care—but usually not in men's. Obstetricians and gynecologists deal exclusively with the reproductive and sexual matters of female patients. There are no comparable specialties of medicine devoted solely to men's reproductive health.

Given the special attention women's health problems receive, it's ironic that research on women's general health needs has been rather limited and sometimes contradictory. Nearly thirty years ago, the United States Public Health Service reported that a lack of medical research on women limited our understanding of their health concerns (Rothman & Caschetta, 1999). The reason often given for their exclusion from medical studies was that their menstrual cycles complicated the interpretation of research findings. This way of thinking has been so pervasive that even female rats are commonly excluded from basic medical research. In addition, medical researchers have historically been reluctant to perform research on women of childbearing age because of fears that exposing them to experimental manipulations might harm their future reproductive capabilities. In fact, in the 1970s and 1980s, federal policies and guidelines actually called for the blanket exclusion of women with childbearing potential from certain types of drug research. That meant that any woman capable of becoming pregnant, regardless of her own desires to do or not to do so, could be excluded.

To alleviate the problem, Congress in 1993 passed a law stipulating that women must be included in clinical trials in numbers sufficient to provide evidence of the different ways men and women respond to drugs, surgical treatments, and changes in diet or behavior. Nevertheless, a 2000 study found that many researchers were not complying with the law, perpetuating a lack of understanding of how men and women respond (cited in Pear, 2000). In 2003, the Agency for Healthcare Research and Quality reported that research on coronary heart disease (CHD) still either excluded women entirely or included them only in limited numbers. Consequently, the therapies used to treat women with CHD—a disease that kills 250,000 women a year—were based on studies conducted primarily on middle-aged men (cited in "Research findings affirm," 2003). Because of lingering gender bias (Holdcroft, 2007), the National Institutes of Health (NIH) re-issued a set of policy guidelines in 2013 requiring all applicants for government grants to provide assurance that women (not to mention people of color) are being included in their study design. In 2014, the NIH went further, calling on all laboratories to take steps to include female mice, rats, pigs, and other animals in preliminary drug studies that use non-humans (Rabin, 2014d). That same year, the organization took the unprecedented step of distributing $10.1 million in grants to more than 80 medical researchers for the sole purpose of including more female participants in their studies (Rabin, 2014c).

Virility and Viagra　The one area in which men's health has received medical attention comparable to the focus on women's health is not heart disease or accidents—for which men far outnumber women—but rather the much less serious area of sexual performance. It's a good bet that in an evening of television viewing, you'll see a commercial for a drug that treats erectile dysfunction or low testosterone. While problems with sexual performance may be associated with some other illness or disorder, they are not, in and of themselves, life-threatening conditions. Instead, they can best be characterized as an embarrassment, disappointment, or inconvenience.

Still, a significant proportion of medical research today is devoted to drugs to treat these problems. Drugs for erectile dysfunction have become a $4.3 billion a year industry (Transparency Market Research, 2015). About 30 million American men suffer from erectile dysfunction and since 1998 when Viagra first appeared on the market, tens of millions have used it or similar drugs like Levitra and Cialis (Tuller, 2004).

As with the development of many drugs, Viagra's discovery as a treatment for erectile problems was accidental. Its generic form—sildenafil citrate—was initially designed in the late 1990s as a treatment for heart ailments. But the detection of the unanticipated side effect of creating erections led to a flurry of clinical trials and ultimately massive public demand. Originally, physicians recommended Viagra only to men who had lost sexual function as a result of injury or illness. However, it quickly came to be viewed as an appropriate aid for otherwise healthy men who are simply not satisfied with their sexual performance. The official definition of erectile dysfunction is no longer the "inability to get an erection" but is now the inability to get an erection that is adequate for "satisfactory sexual performance" (Bordo, 2003; Potts, Grace, Gavey, & Vares, 2004). Some healthy men actually go so far as to equip themselves with a Viagra pill before a night on the town as a form of "sexual insurance" to guard against the possibility of performance problems (Kirby, 2004).

In a culture where everyday life is framed as a series of competitions, it's not surprising that erectile dysfunction would be presented as one of the most horrible personal tragedies than can befall a man. According to promotional material from Viagra's manufacturer, Pfizer, erectile dysfunction inevitably affects confidence, self-esteem, health, and happiness. Hence, a deficiency in performance is not seen merely as a failure isolated in one region of the body; it implicates the whole man and is inseparable from his total personality (Bordo, 2003). It represents the very loss of manhood (Loe, 2001).

Furthermore, similar to the way in which PMS has become medicalized, so too has erectile dysfunction. Before drugs like Viagra, erectile changes were seen as a normal part of the aging process. As one man put it:

> I think you've got to recognize that . . , as you get older you've got less physical ability, you can't walk as far, as vigorously . . . and the same with sex, you've got to accept it. . . . I don't treat it as negative because I think . . . I just accept it as a fact. I think your drive diminishes as well, the need to have sex as frequently. (quoted in Potts, Grace, Gavey, & Vares, 2004, p. 492)

However, the publicity surrounding erectile dysfunction—and more recently, low testosterone—may produce a societal expectation that a healthy and normal life for older men requires the continuation of a "youthful" focus exclusively on penetrative intercourse (Potts, Grace, Gavey, & Vares, 2004).

In a more general sense, drugs like Viagra support the view that "normal" and "healthy" sexual functioning requires penile-vaginal sex with orgasms, particularly male orgasms. Ironically, the availability of these drugs highlights the fact that much of the sexual difficulty men experience is not necessarily physiological in origin but may be grounded in anxiety and insecurity brought about by the cultural emphasis on successful performance:

> The hype surrounding [erectile dysfunction drugs] encourages rather than deconstructs the expectation that men perform like power tools with only one switch—on or off. Until this expectation is replaced by a conception of manhood that permits men and their penises a full range of human feeling, we will not yet have the kind of "cure" we really need. (Bordo, 2003, p. 152)

In short, Viagra has been as much a cultural event as a biotechnological tool (Marshall, 2002). The drug has reshaped our views of gender and sexuality under the guise of technological progress (Loe, 2001) and has altered our sense of sexual normality as well as men's sense of personal efficacy. The availability of Viagra means that every man who experiences erectile problems is encouraged, even expected, to seek a pharmaceutical solution.

SEXUAL ORIENTATION AND HEALTH

Erectile dysfunction and low testosterone are presented in the media and in the culture at large as exclusively heterosexual conditions. They can affect any man, however, including homosexual men. For the most part, sexual minorities face the same health issues that heterosexuals face. But the way gay men, lesbians, and bisexuals experience the health care system can be quite different than the way heterosexuals do.

As we saw in Chapter 5, perceptions of homosexuals as sinful or sick have a long history. Since the late 19th century, some doctors have attempted to "cure" individuals of their desire for same-sex intimacy. Over the years, "curative treatments" have included castration, ovary removal, hypnosis, aversion therapy, radiation, psychoanalysis, and even lobotomy (Romesburg, 1997). Today some psychologists and psychiatrists still prescribe so-called conversion and reparative therapies in an attempt to restore gay and lesbian patients to "healthy" heterosexuality.

Social rejection, stigmatization, and discrimination can affect the physical health of lesbians, gay men, and bisexuals by increasing their levels of self-hatred and anxiety (Meyer, 1995). Living in a hostile social—and sometimes family—environment puts these individuals at high risk of drug abuse, depression, and stress-related ailments. As we saw in Chapter 5, a disproportionate number of suicides among young people in the United States each year are attributable to the emotional turmoil over sexual orientation issues and the cultural stigma surrounding same-sex relationships (Hillier & Harrison, 2004).

The presumption of heterosexuality that underlies most health care situations also creates problems for patients who are homosexual, bisexual, or transgendered (Dunham, 2014). For instance, most medical schools don't prepare doctors for dealing with transgender people in the midst of a sexual transition who may retain the reproductive organs of the sex assigned at birth (Ellin, 2016). Furthermore, medical examinations that involve health care personnel and patients of a different sex almost always presuppose sexual tension. Efforts to desexualize these encounters (say, for example, by having a female chaperone present when a male gynecologist gives a pelvic examination) may actually reinforce stereotypical expectations (Giuffre & Williams, 2000). But heteronormative presumptions in medical interactions don't just create interpersonal awkwardness. They can actually impede access to adequate health care. Consider this scenario:

> You are a 37-year-old lesbian who hasn't been to a gynecologist in 10 years. . . . You have what you think is a garden-variety infection. . . . The first thing you are asked to do is complete the patient history form. . . . For marital status you are only given four choices: married, single, widowed, or divorced. Since you have lived with the same woman for the past 12 years, you hardly qualify as single but there is no other option allowed that fits. . . . Next question: "Are you sexually active?" "Yes." . . . Next question: "What type of birth control do you use?" . . . Answering "none" means that you will have to explain why a sexually active single woman would not use some form of birth control. . . . Or you could tell the truth. . . . The choice to "come out" in vulnerable situations is never an easy one, and when the intake form does not include your reality that decision is even more stressful. (Fields & Scout, 2001, p. 182)

Put in such situations, many people decide that the stress is too much and avoid seeing physicians altogether.

In addition, health professionals sometimes bring negative feelings to bear on their treatment of gay, lesbian, and bisexual patients (Saulnier, 2002). In the mid-1980s for instance, as the AIDS epidemic took hold and people's fears were unleashed, many doctors and nurses around the country refused to treat gay male patients. Even though the American Medical Association makes clear that a doctor's right to religious refusal applies to certain procedures (for example, abortion), but not to particular groups of people (like homosexuals), discrimination persists in some settings and has, in fact, been institutionalized, becoming part of broad-based policies. For example, in 2004, the state of Michigan passed a law that allows health care providers to refuse to treat patients because of their sexual orientation if their objection is a matter of conscience based on ethical, moral, or religious grounds. Other states are currently considering similar bills.

Although incidents of outright medical discrimination are clearly not as common as they once were, developments like these, and the climate they foster, create additional burdens in the health care experiences of sexual minorities who already face difficult circumstances in their everyday lives.

CONCLUSION

In the summer of 1995, a weeklong heat wave killed over 700 people in Chicago, more than twice the number of people who died in that city's famous fire of 1871. Thousands of others were stricken by heat-related illnesses. Severe weather patterns alone could not fully account for the calamity. It was not as much a disaster of nature—like a hurricane or earthquake—as it was a disaster of inequality. The overwhelming majority of victims in Chicago were poor and elderly people who couldn't afford air conditioning or fans and who ended up suffocating in their sealed, stifling homes (Klinenberg, 2002). Some of them lived in dangerous neighborhoods and were afraid they'd be burglarized if they left their windows and doors open at night. Furthermore, insufficient government funding left poor, isolated seniors in stigmatized minority neighborhoods and housing projects, on the periphery of formal assistance networks that could have provided them with some heat relief.

Similar but even more devastating tragedies have occurred elsewhere. A three-day heat wave in Karachi, Pakistan in 2015 killed 650 people, mostly poor and old. As one observer there put it, "The first to die were the people on the streets—heroin addicts, beggars, the homeless" (quoted in Imtiaz & Walsh, 2015, p. A4). Twelve years earlier over 11,000 people died during a record-breaking heat wave in Paris. Like the Chicago and Karachi tragedies, the majority of victims in Paris were elderly people on fixed incomes—80% of those who died were over 75 (Crabbe, 2003)—who were left to cope with the heat on their own. By and large, these were not well-to-do people living out their golden years in comfort. August is holiday month in Paris. The population of Paris during August is overwhelmingly made up of poor, working-class people or immigrants. People who can afford to leave the city for vacation homes, mountain villas, or beach resorts do so in droves. When socioeconomic disadvantage was coupled with isolation—most of the elderly victims either lived alone or were left behind by families that went on vacation—catastrophe ensued. Government officials were apparently reluctant to cut short their own vacations to deal with the crisis. They waited until the temperatures began to fall to launch an emergency response, such as opening up hospitals that had closed for the August vacation season.

These heat wave catastrophes serve as metaphors for the main theme of this chapter: Our personal health and well-being cannot be understood without taking into consideration inequalities based on race, class, gender, and sexuality. That is not to say that particular races or classes or genders or sexual groups are genetically or biologically predisposed to be more or less healthy than other groups. Nor are race, class, gender, and sexual differences simply a matter of diverse lifestyles, cultures, and tastes. Instead, broader conceptions of difference—and the imbalances that derive from those conceptions—have very real consequences for the quality, comfort, and length of people's lives.

[**INVESTIGATING IDENTITIES AND INEQUALITIES**
Hospital stays: The unequal contours of American health care]

This chapter has highlighted imbalances in access to health care based on class, gender, race/ethnicity, and sexuality. One of the keys to a sociological understanding of such inequalities is that they are usually institutional, existing at a level above that of individuals who work in the system. In other words, differential treatment is not simply due to prejudiced doctors, nurses, and medical staff. Sometimes, the inequalities reside in the structure of health care facilities themselves.

For this exercise, locate several types of health care facilities in your area. It would be especially effective to visit some in both poor communities and more affluent communities. Try to visit a private hospital and a public/community hospital. If you have time, you can also go to a Veterans Administration (VA) hospital, an outpatient facility, or a community free clinic.

Your task is to observe and describe the *physical* characteristics of each facility in as much detail as possible. Limit your observations to the areas that are publicly accessible. It would be inappropriate, for instance, to go into patients' rooms, examination rooms, intensive care units, and other "off-limits" space. Pay particular attention to the following characteristics:

- *Physical layout/condition of the building.* Does it appear to be relatively new, or does it show signs of wear? Can you tell if there have been any recent renovations or additions to the building? How much attention is devoted to the decor of the facility? Is there any artwork (wall paintings, sculpture, and so on)? How would you describe its quality? Is there any music playing? Are the directional and departmental signs legible and easy to follow? Are they in languages other than English? Are the outside grounds landscaped attractively? Are the furnishings in the various waiting rooms comfortable? Are entertainment media available to people who are waiting (such as televisions, magazines, and so on)? In general, would you characterize the environment as comforting or sterile?

- *Amenities.* What sorts of nonmedical services are available to visitors? Cafeteria? Gift shop? Comfortable lounges? Free Wi-Fi? How would you describe the quality of these services?
- *Social identities of the patients, visitors, and staff.* Do the patients and visitors seem to be of a particular ethnic or racial group? Can you discern their socioeconomic status? Is there any noticeable ethnoracial diversity among the staff?
- *The way clients (patients and visitors) are treated.* Try to spend some time in the various public waiting areas of the facility (outpatient surgery, emergency room, and so on). Does the staff (nurses, orderlies, physicians, clerical administrators) treat clients in waiting areas with kindness and respect? Do they interact much with family members or friends of patients? Are some people treated differently than others? Does it seem that people are forced to wait for a long time before they get to see medical staff?

(*Note:* To save time, you may be able to gather some of this information on the hospital's or the clinic's web site. In addition, www.hospital-data.com is a useful web site that provides informative profiles of thousands of hospitals and medical clinics around the country.)

Once you've compiled information for a few different health care facilities, compare them to see if there are any obvious imbalances in the quality of care that patients receive and the settings within which they receive them. Provide detailed evidence from your observations to support the existence of the imbalances you identify. Use your conclusions as a starting point to discuss the current state of the American health care system. Assess whether different levels of care are available to different segments of the population.

CHAPTER 9

The Futures of Identities and Inequalities

Likc many young American kids, my early reading experiences included piles of colorful books by Dr. Seuss. Of course, being 6 years old and struggling with all those peculiar words and creatures, I didn't notice that there were deeper meanings- –sometimes even controversial sociopolitical messages about racism, environmental protection, rampant materialism, and so on—cleverly buried in these silly stories. I just liked the funny pictures and rhymes. I still do.

So I think it's completely appropriate to begin this final chapter by examining a Seuss short story called *The Sneetches*. In this tale there are two types of bird-like creatures called Sneetches, who are physically indistinguishable from each other except for one key characteristic: The Star-Belly Sneetches sport green stars on their bellies; the Plain-Belly Sneetches have bare bellies. The green stars are small and barely noticeable. Nonetheless, the Star-Belly Sneetches are elitist snobs who interpret the stars as indicators of their lofty status. And they spend most of their time figuring out ways to belittle, exclude, and discriminate against the Plain-Belly Sneetches. The Plain-Bellies are kept out of all sorts of social activities, including picnics, parties, and children's games.

The Plain-Bellies develop a massive inferiority complex, reflected in their perpetually mopey faces. They seem to spend all their time wallowing in envy, wishing they had stars on their bellies like their more advantaged counterparts.

Then one day, everything changes. A stranger arrives in town, promising that for $3 he can fix things for the Plain-Belly Sneetches. He has them walk into an odd-looking contraption, and miraculously they emerge from the other end with stars on their bellies. The formerly Plain-Belly Sneetches are ecstatic. They've successfully leveled the playing field, and they fully expect to be treated as equals from now on.

Though the original Star-Belly Sneetches are dismayed by the fact that it'll be hard for them to tell which Sneetch is which, they continue to believe in their own superiority. But they need some way to prove it. At that point, the stranger approaches the Star-Belly Sneetches and promises that he can easily return them to their place of privilege. He assures them that "Belly stars are no longer in style," and that for a mere $10 each, his machine can remove theirs. They gladly pay the money. Once they've all gone through the machine and are now star-less, they parade around singing the virtues of their own dominance, this time based on their plain appearance.

This is where things get a little messy. The Plain-Belly Sneetches have smelled the sweet aroma of equality and don't want to return to their inferior status. As is always the case when powerful groups feel their position is being threatened, the historically advantaged Star-Belly Sneetches will do anything to maintain their privilege. So each group pays more and more money to the stranger to either add or remove belly stars depending on whether they want to look like or distinguish themselves from the other group. Pretty soon, both groups go broke, and the stranger skips town.

The story ends on a high note as the Sneetches suddenly realize that they're all alike and all equal, regardless of whether they have belly stars or not. It's not clear why they start thinking this way; after all, they've lost all their money to a stranger who is nowhere to be found. But it's the sort of "happily ever after" ending that little kids can live with.

We see in this children's storybook, unmistakably and importantly, the socially constructed nature of difference and inequality. As is the case in human societies, positions of dominance and subordination do not automatically rise from natural and inherent characteristics but from socially created and sometimes arbitrary ones. Dr. Seuss's story provides a fitting prologue to this final chapter on the futures of social inequalities because it shows, albeit in a simplified and fanciful way, the malleability of social relations and the possibility of change.

What the story gets wrong, however (and, of course, we can't expect Dr. Seuss to touch all the right sociological bases), is that although the differences that foster inequalities may be socially created, they're rarely, if ever, so interchangeable or capricious as they are in this story. Those groups with little power seldom have the wherewithal to create social equality, let alone turn the tables of stratification, by altering the perceptions of more dominant groups. And within a given society, ideologies of inequality based on race, gender, class, and sexuality become embedded in the culture and in important social institutions to the point that they're difficult if not impossible to reverse.

The 19th-century British statesman William Gladstone once said, "You can't fight against the future" (quoted in Seldes, 1985, p. 161). Still, as you've seen in the first eight chapters of this book, definitions of difference are neither permanent nor universal. The criteria used to determine social inequalities can vary across time and from culture to culture. Thus, the future is not some inevitable destiny that looms ominously around the bend. Just like societies today, future societies will be molded and shaped by human action. I've chosen to use the word "futures" rather than "future" in the title of this chapter to reinforce this idea that our experiences with inequalities are not set in stone. We have the ability to determine the course of ethnoracial, class, gender, and sexual identities in the future. We can choose to live in a society that continues to be structured around vastly unequal privileges, or we can transform society into one marked by truly equitable relationships and opportunities. To put it simply: We can shape our own destinies.

POSSIBILITIES: MOVEMENTS FOR CHANGE

One of the inherent difficulties in creating equality—and one that should be fairly obvious by now—is that even though inequalities are created and maintained by people in their interactions with others, they eventually make their way into impersonal social institutions, where they become solidified and somewhat impervious to individual action. Institutions, by their very nature, are quite resistant to social change. Often, what are needed to influence institutional change are organized, large-scale, collective actions known as **social movements.** The Civil Rights Movement, the Women's Movement, the Labor Movement, the Living Wage Movement, the Gay Liberation Movement, the Tea Party Movement, the Pro-Life Movement, the Black Lives Matter Movement, and others have achieved some notable political and cultural successes over the years but have never completely altered the institutional landscape. So, as we've seen in Chapters 5 through 8, institutional inequalities based on race, gender, class, and sexuality remain the rule rather than the exception in our day-to-day lives.

Consequently, the task of transforming entire systems of privilege and disadvantage or even resisting their influence on a personal level seems daunting. Students in sociology courses commonly leave at the end of a semester feeling as if there's nothing they can do to change structures that systematically work to the advantage of some at the expense of others. "What's the use?" "The problem's too big!" "You can't fight City Hall!" "I give up!" Maybe you're feeling that way right now as you're coming to the end of this book. But many people underestimate their ability to influence the very social institutions they spend their lives in.

Even though the structure of society seems massive and often detached from the desires of ordinary people, it ultimately depends on human actions for its very survival. People can and frequently do change things. Whether through acts of support or defiance, we create and recreate the very social institutions under whose powerful influence we live. Our history is filled with stories of individuals and groups of individuals who—for better or worse, depending on your position—have altered the course of society.

Some of the most socially influential acts for change may at first blush appear pretty insignificant. One of my favorite examples concerns the activities in 1960 of four black students at North Carolina Agricultural & Technical State University in Greensboro. Ezell Blair, Franklin McCain, Joseph McNeil, and David Richmond spent a lot of time talking in their dormitory rooms about the state of the Civil Rights Movement. They knew about bus boycotts in Alabama and the desegregation of schools in Arkansas. But they didn't think that enough was being done to change things in the still-segregated South. They decided it was time for them to do something that would contribute to the effort.

What they decided to do on February 1, 1960, was to go to the lunch counter at the local Woolworth's department store and order coffee and doughnuts. That might not seem like such a big deal to people in the 2010s, but in the 1960s South, Blacks were forbidden by law to eat in facilities that weren't designated as being "for Blacks only." After buying some school supplies in another part of the store, they sat down at the lunch counter and placed their orders. As they expected, the stunned waitperson replied, "I'm sorry, we don't serve you here" (McCain, 1991, p. 115). They stayed seated there for 45 minutes, politely pointing out that they had made a purchase in another part of the store without any difficulty. Angry white customers gathered around, shouting racial slurs at them and even trying to forcibly remove them. The four students never responded and never fought back. They simply sat there waiting to be served until the lunch counter closed for the day.

Unlike speeches and boycotts, the actions of these four young men openly and directly defied the entrenched system of everyday segregation. They attracted the attention of religious leaders, community activists, and students from other area colleges, both black and white. Despite the abuse they knew would await them, the four men returned a few days later, only this time with more demonstrators. At one point, they and their fellow protestors occupied 63 of the 65 seats available at the lunch counter. Because this was the first social movement covered by television, word of their actions spread quickly. They received endorsements from religious organizations like the North Carolina Council of Churches. Within weeks, young African Americans and sympathetic Whites had engaged in similar acts in nine states and 54 cities in the South as well as several areas in the North, where stores were picketed. After several months of protests, Woolworth's integrated its lunch counter.

The "sit-ins," as they came to be called, eventually proved to be one of the most effective tactics of the Civil Rights Movement: "The students sat in. Went to jail, came out, sat in again. Marched. Picketed. Sat in again. And went to jail again. They simply would not stop" (Farmer, 2004, p. 1). Indeed, some sociologists have argued that many of the social movements for change that burst onto the scene in the 1960s—including the Women's Movement, the Antiwar Movement, and the Student Free Speech Movement—could trace their philosophical and tactical roots to the actions of these four students (Cluster, 1979). Today, American college students have staged sit-ins to protest the working conditions in clothing and footwear factories overseas, the construction of an oil pipeline from Canada, the high cost of college tuition, and incidents of racial injustice on their campuses. In addition, since the early 1960s, protesters have created several variations on the sit-in theme:

- "work-ins"—where employees who are about to be laid off or whose factory is about to be shut down resolve to remain on their jobs and continue producing without pay. The goal is to show that their place of work is still productive. This tactic was used by workers at a British shipbuilding facility and an Australian steel plant in the 1970s.

- "teach-ins"—where experts on a particular topic organize an extended open forum consisting of lectures and free discussions that is designed to create support for a particular movement. Teach-ins have become a popular means of creating awareness of and mobilizing political action over such issues as global climate change, environmental degradation, and economic globalization.
- "die-ins"—where protesters lie down and simulate death. This has become a common tactic among anti-tobacco, human rights, AIDS, anti-abortion activists. In the past two years, protestors of the police killings of unarmed Blacks have conducted Black Lives Matter die-ins in major cities around the country.

Admittedly, the participants in these movements might have developed these tactics on their own, even if those four Greensboro students had been served coffee and doughnuts at Woolworth's that day. The point is, though, that the widespread collective movements that arose from the actions of these individuals in 1960 had an enormous impact on the massive changes that occurred in the United States and beyond over the next 50 years.

But you'll also notice that these four young men couldn't change things all by themselves. It takes more than the actions of oppressed individuals for meaningful, long-term change to occur. The movements for social change that tend to be the most effective and long-lasting must successfully frame the unfairness of particular social phenomena to gain support from various segments of the population. They must also be well organized (often at the national or even international level), have a coherent set of beliefs, values, and goals, and make use of current technologies to spread the word and mobilize resources. What's especially important is the formation of coalitions, the bringing together of different groups in different structural positions. Consider these examples of the power of coalitions:

- The Civil Rights Movement has been effective because participants have come from all racial groups and all geographic areas. Many of the individuals who fought successfully for Blacks' voting rights in Alabama and Mississippi during the late 1950s and early 1960s were middle-class white students from the North. When Blacks boycotted segregated buses in Montgomery, Alabama, in 1955 and 1956, Virginia Foster Durr, a wealthy white Southern woman, drove black workers to and from work every day so they wouldn't lose their jobs. Today, people like Morris Dees, a white attorney who gave up a lucrative law practice to devote his life to bringing white supremacists to trial, continue the battle for racial equality and equity.

- The movement for gay rights has been bolstered by the participation and support of non-gay allies. PFLAG (Parents and Friends of Lesbians and Gays) is an organization of mostly heterosexuals who provide education and advocate on behalf of gays and lesbians. They speak at churches, schools, and community organizations, describing their commitment to protecting the rights of gays and lesbians. Their impact, which at times has been significant, arises from the fact that they are heterosexuals talking, for the most part, to other heterosexuals (Ayvazian, 2001).

- Living Wage Movement is made up of people who seek to require cities and counties to pay their low-wage workers an amount above the federal minimum wage. At first, the people who were seeking to increase wages were the low-wage workers themselves. They weren't particularly effective in gaining public support. Only when religious organizations, labor groups, and college students got involved did the movement achieve some notable successes. A recent off-shoot of this movement, called The Fight for $15 Movement, seeks a $15 an hour minimum wage for low-wage workers in places like fast food restaurants, aiports, and convenience stores. By 2013, over 4 million workers had received raises as a result of corporate policy changes and legislation at the state and local levels (National Employment Law Project, 2014).

In most cases, it's usually not enough simply for the people who are suffering the most from structural disadvantage to complain about their plight. The movements that are most effective in creating long-term institutional change are the ones that construct a broad coalition of supporters. These are the movements that may not only affect current social arrangements but also help shape future conceptions of race, class, gender, and sexuality.

PREDICTING UNPREDICTABLE FUTURES

I've always envied TV meteorologists. They can get their weather-related forecasts flat-out wrong most of the time and still keep their jobs. In fact, their popularity (and hence their job security) has more to do with their personal likability and the appeal of their catchphrases ("Here's what's happening in your neck of the woods!" "Here's a peek out your window!") than with how many predictions they actually get right.

Social scientists have no such luck. Arguably, there's more at stake when trying to forecast the future of the job market, race relations, and divorce rates, or trends in health care provision and legal justice than when trying to predict if it's going to rain by the end of the week. And yet, discussing the future of some key aspect of society—especially when inequality is part of it—may be even more difficult and dubious than forecasting the weather. Human behavior is notoriously erratic. So sociologists usually talk about projections rather than predictions, implicitly acknowledging the impossibility of foretelling the future with any certainty. At best, we can examine past and current patterns and say something about what social life might look like if these patterns continue. With that caveat in mind, let's take a peek at some possible trends regarding social identities and inequalities in the future.

ETHNORACIAL OUTLOOKS

In 1900, Americans lived, for the most part, in distinctly separate racial worlds. In the South, it had only been a little over three decades since slavery was abolished, and a system of official, legally sanctioned segregation maintained unmistakable partitions between races. In the North, the dividers were less formal but no less powerful in maintaining racial boundaries and racial injustice. Few white Americans 120 years ago thought about, let alone questioned, racial arrangements, and Americans of color lacked the power to mobilize social movements and make their concerns heard. It's safe to say that most Americans in 1900 simply took the divided racial landscape of the United States for granted (Wolfe, 2000).

But on other dimensions, Americans in 1900 were actually much less divided culturally than they are today. For instance, whatever differences existed between a black American and a white American, chances were pretty good that both were Christian. Furthermore, they probably spoke the same language. The huge influx of immigrants at that time didn't disrupt that assumption. Many of them, like the Irish and the British, came from countries that already spoke English; others, like Poles and Italians, believed that the only way they and their children would succeed in this country would be to assimilate as quickly as possible, shedding the language and customs of their old country for their new one (Wolfe, 2000).

To someone living in the 21st century, however, U.S. society looks much more diverse. For instance, the racial configuration of the U.S. population has changed dramatically in recent years. In 1900, one out of every eight U.S. residents was of an ethnoracial group other than non-Hispanic white; in 2010, the ratio was one in three; and by 2050, it is projected to be more than one in two (P. Martin & Midgley, 2010; U.S. Bureau of the Census, 2014).

Much of this growth can be attributed to the rapidly expanding size of the Latino/a population. Today, one in every six U.S. residents is Latino/a

(Humes, Jones, & Ramirez, 2011). While the general population increased by 9% between 2000 and 2010, the Latino/a population increased by 43% (Humes, Jones, & Ramirez, 2011). Since 2000, the proportion of people under the age of 20 who are *not* Latino/a decreased from 61% to 57% (Roberts, 2010a). Experts estimate that by the year 2060, close to one out of three U.S. residents will be Latino/a (U.S. Bureau of the Census, 2014). The continuing influx of Latino/a immigrants will virtually ensure that the Spanish language and elements of Latino/a culture will occupy an ever more prominent place in U.S. culture. Expect Latino/a groups to occupy more visible and powerful positions in the government, in the health care system, and in religious institutions as well.

It makes even less sense to talk about today's United States as a Christian country. Over the past few decades, membership in a variety of non-Christian religious groups has grown significantly, For instance, between 1990 and 2008, the number of Muslims and Buddhists in the United States increased from a little less than 1 million to more than 2.5 million (ProQuest Statistical Abstract, 2015). In fact, population experts project that over the next 20 years, the number of Muslims will grow at twice the rate of non–Muslims (Pew Forum on Religion and Public Life, 2011). Immigration has helped fuel this growth too. More than four times as many immigrants as native-born Americans report non–Christian religious affiliations (Pew Forum on Religion and Public Life, 2008).

At the same time, the percentage of Americans who identify with *no* religion (atheists, agnostics, and those who say they are spiritual but have no religious affiliation) grew from 16% in 2007 to 23% in 2014 (Pew Research Center, 2015a). The trend is especially pronounced among those younger than 30. Consequently, over the past decade, many of the most prominent religious groups have experienced a decline in membership. For instance, between 1990 and 2008, the Lutheran and the Presbyterian Churches suffered a 5% drop in membership. The United Methodist Church saw a 25% decrease and membership in the Episcopal Church dropped 26% (ProQuest Statistical Abstract, 2015). It's important to remember though that decline in membership does not necessarily mean that religion is losing its influence in U.S. society. Indeed, at the same time that membership in some Christian denominations has shrunk, that of so-called conservative churches (Roman Catholic Church, Church of Jesus Christ of Latter-Day Saints, Assemblies of God, United Church of Christ, and Southern Baptists) has increased (ProQuest Statistical Abstract, 2015).

Nevertheless, to people who believe that our national strength depends on a common system of spirituality and moral thought, such religious diversity signifies a weakening of society. To people who believe that the values of tolerance, equality, and respect for difference are what define us as a culture, this growing religious diversity instead symbolizes our strength.

What's especially interesting to me—both as a sociologist and as a citizen of this country—is not simply how many people will be counted as members of particular groups in the future, but how race and ethnicity will be defined and how those definitions will affect cultural values and ethnoracial diversity. It seems to me that the future of diversity can go in (at least) two possible directions. At one end of the continuum of possibilities is what some call a "post-ethnic" or "post-racial" society in which race and ethnicity no longer matter. At the other end is a society in which people make increasingly fine distinctions between and among ethnoracial groups, creating more boundaries than ever.

Evolving a Post-Racial, Post-Ethnic Society   One possibility for the future is a society in which traditional racial and ethnic definitions would become obsolete or at least irrelevant. Ethnoracial boundaries could simply melt away with increasing numbers of interracial marriages and children born with multiracial, multi-ethnic identities. As one optimistic supporter of such a view put it,

> It's only a matter of time before DNA testing persuades many "whites" that they are much more mixed than they ever imagined. So what does that mean for the future of America? . . . Race is not going to be quite as big a deal as it is now; in the America of tomorrow—whatever people decide to call themselves—race will not be synonymous with destiny. That's a future worth embracing. (Cose, 2010, p. 22)

The accuracy of this projection rests, in part, on broader attitudes toward multiracial backgrounds. People who have a multiracial heritage do feel less pressure today to claim a single, identifying race label than they once did. They might simply say, "my mother is white and my father is black" and leave it at that (McWhorter, 2004). Indeed, multiracial identities have been endorsed in some respects by the official definer and maintainer of racial and ethnic boundaries, the U.S. Bureau of the Census. Instead of simply reporting statistics for "Whites," "Blacks," "Asians," "American Indians or Alaska Natives," "Native Hawaiian or other Pacific Islander," and "Hispanics," the Census Bureau can now provide data for 63 possible racial categories including 6 categories for those who report they are members of exactly one race and 57 categories for those who report combinations of two or more races.

Consequently, the Census Bureau now urges caution in making historical comparisons among and between racial groupings on phenomena like median income and poverty. The change has other far-reaching implications as well. How can we have meaningful conversations about race relations and racial inequality if we have 63 different racial identity groups? Furthermore, as the number of people with some sort of combined identity increases, the mixtures will become more complex. Traditional ethnoracial boundaries may become fainter and less vivid, eventually disappearing entirely. The result could be a society in which race and ethnicity literally don't matter. Either they wouldn't be noticed or they wouldn't be associated with character assessments. They wouldn't be predictors of social and cultural achievement and access to opportunities. And they wouldn't determine the quality of people's lives.

If we were to look only at the visible trappings of American popular culture over the past decade or so, we might conclude that we already live in a "color-blind"—or at the very least, a color-vision-impaired—society:

It is quite unremarkable to observe Whites, Asians, or African Americans with dyed purple, blond, or red hair. White, black, and Asian students decorate their bodies with tattoos of Chinese characters and symbols. In cities and suburbs, young adults across the color line wear hip-hop clothing and listen to white rapper Eminem or black rapper Jay-Z. A north Georgia branch of the NAACP installs a white biology professor as its president. . . . Du-Rag kits, complete with bandana headscarf and elastic headband, are on sale for $2.95 at hip-hop clothing stores and family-centered theme parks like Six Flags. Salsa has replaced ketchup as the best selling condiment in the United States. Companies as diverse as Polo, McDonald's . . . , Walt Disney World, Master Card, Skechers . . . , [and] Giorgio Armani have each crafted advertisements that show a balanced, multiracial cast of characters interacting and consuming their products in a post-race, color-blind world. (Gallagher, 2004, pp. 575–576)

Nationwide surveys consistently show that the majority of Whites feel that members of other racial groups now have equal chances in getting jobs and are doing as well. As the thinking goes, if personal and institutional discrimination have now been replaced by equality of opportunity, then the path to upward mobility runs directly through one's individual qualifications, not one's color or ethnicity. To some, therefore, the life stories of people of color who have achieved noteworthy successes (like Barack Obama or Oprah Winfrey) reinforce the belief that race is losing its relevance.

But individual "success stories" feed the conclusion that certain groups' overall lack of achievement is not a result of any systemic discrimination or ethnoracial barriers. After all the people who have succeeded were able to overcome any obstacles they faced. Lack of success, as this thinking goes, must therefore be the fault of individuals who lack the ambition, initiative, or desire to make something of themselves. And those who cite continuing racial discrimination as an impediment to their educational or economic achievement are branded as "reverse racists" whose claims are illegitimate or they are accused of "playing the race card" to promote a political agenda. We must remember, however, that the ability to ignore race—both as a component of one's identity and as a primary source of discrimination—always reflects the power and privilege of dominant groups. Hence members of ethnoracial minority groups tend to be far less optimistic about the state of racial fairness than Whites (see Exhibit 9.1).

And so, I guess I'm a bit pessimistic about suggestions that race will ever be completely insignificant and that group boundaries will at some

Exhibit 9.1: Racial Disparities in Perceptions of Fairness

Percentage saying Blacks in their community are treated *less fairly* than Whites:	Blacks	Whites
...in dealing with police	70	37
...in courts	68	27
...at work	54	16
...in stores or restaurants	44	16
...in local public schools	51	15
...in getting health care	47	14
...when voting in elections	48	13
Number of social institutions seen as unfair:		
Four to seven	58	14
One to three	29	36
None	13	49

Source: Patten, 2013

point disappear fully. In the multi-hued future of the United States, there will still be some people who are considered more deserving (perhaps still on the basis of the lightness of their skin) than others (Cose, 2010). If today's news headlines are any indication, stubborn pockets of discrimination, not to mention violent racial hatreds, will always exist.

Furthermore, just like those Sneetches I described at the beginning of this chapter, humans have a strong tendency to seek out and find ways to make us–them distinctions. Even if race disappeared as a meaningful social marker, we'd inevitably draw influential boundaries on some other dimension. Maybe our distinctions will be based on what people have or earn rather than what they look like. Perhaps resident status—native born versus immigrant—rather than race or ethnicity will someday function as the key construct in distinguishing "us" from "them."

Intersections
Ethnoracial Discrimination Without Ethnoracial Difference—Japan's Burakumin

If we look to other cultures, we can see that even something as apparently irrelevant as the occupational status of distant ancestors can determine group distinctions and influence everyday life chances. Take, for example, the *burakumin*, the most disadvantaged minority group in Japan, who represent about 2% of the population. Their low socioeconomic status dates back to the 17th century, when their ancestors' role in society was to slaughter animals and dispose of the remains, tasks that although necessary for public health violated Buddhist principles (Kristof, 1995). The *burakumin* are biologically, religiously, and ethnically indistinguishable from other Japanese. Yet many Japanese people considered them a completely different race and innately inferior. They were forced to wear recognizable clothing and were restricted to living in special villages (the word *burakumin* literally means "people of the hamlet"). *Burakumin* were widely stereotyped as mentally weak, aggressive, impulsive, and dirty (Neary, 1986). Before marrying someone or hiring a new employee, some Japanese would have a detective check the background of a person for *burakumin* ancestors.

In fairness, the treatment and perception of the *burakumin* have improved somewhat in recent years. Today, almost two-thirds say they've never encountered blatant discrimination, although many parents never tell their children that they are *burakumin*. More than 70% now marry non-*burakumin,* and most believe they are treated fairly by the police

(Kristof, 1995). The Japanese government invested large sums of money to improve *burakumin* neighborhoods so they are no longer unlivable slums. It ended these projects in 2002, concluding that enough had been done.

But despite improvements, the *burakumin* still suffer compared with other Japanese citizens. They have the lowest income and educational attainment of any group in Japanese society and the highest rates of poverty, crime, alcoholism, single parenthood, and welfare dependency. And like some ethnoracial minority groups in the United States, their dependence on government assistance has created resentment from a public that believes they are getting special, undeserved help. Moreover, because many of them still tend to live in segregated ancestral villages, they are singled out for all manner of abuse and discrimination based on their addresses. Even today, families will abruptly terminate engagements if *burakumin* origins are uncovered. In 2004, a Japanese father threw his son's fiancée out of their home because she was found to be a descendent of the *burakumin*. The woman's father said he receives daily hate letters with messages like "You non-humans from the hamlets have blood that is vulgar and tainted" (quoted in Yamaguchi, 2004, p. A18).

In 2001, a *buraku* man named Hiromu Nonaka worked his way up Japan's political ladder by becoming the ruling party's number 2 official. The next logical step would be to become prime minister. But that never happened. Some have suggested that had Nonaka become Japan's top leader, it would have been just as significant as Barack Obama's election as the first black U.S. president. But many people in Japan, even top officials in his own party, weren't ready for him to become their candidate for prime minister. Some detractors spread rumors that perhaps his closest allies were also *burakumin* who were hiding their identities. The outgoing prime minister was overheard saying, "Are we really going to let those people take over the leadership of Japan?" (quoted in Onishi, 2009, p. 1).

Some younger *burakumin* advocate using the socially constructed nature of the stigma as a reason to actively reject it:

> Although we cannot choose our parents or birthplace, we can choose not to be fettered by them; and while not hiding the possibility that we might be labeled *burakumin*, we could positively reject it: I am not a *burakumin* if I say I am not. I might even recognize that my father was a *burakumin* but claim that I am not. (Neary, 2003, p. 285)

Just as arbitrary identities (in this case, the occupational status of bygone generations) can motivate discrimination, so too can they open the door to possible change. Perhaps someday in the United States, multiracial individuals will have the same opportunity to create a society in which ethnoracial identity, though still noticeable, loses its power to determine people's access to important life chances.

Subdividing Race and Ethnicity   Another future possibility regarding race—not entirely distinct from the first one—is that instead of a modern version of the "melting pot" in which race and ethnicity become obsolete, we will experience just the opposite: a growing number of more narrowly defined ethnic or national groups seeking cultural, social, and legal recognition. In this scenario, we'd have more, rather than fewer, ethnoracial boundaries.

I've been arguing throughout this book that although most scholars (myself included) use broad labels like "Black," "Asian," "Native American," "White," "Latino/a," and so on, there are numerous within-group subdivisions in each of these categories already—for example, Koreans and Laotians within the category "Asian." Perhaps in the interests of ethnic pride, each of those subgroups—as well as yet-to-be-defined new ones—will become a distinct social group in its own right. As a result, ethnic communities could become more isolated and insulated than those of the past. Some argue that such a trend has been evident for years:

> Their ethnic shopping malls, ethnic restaurants and groceries, in-language newspapers, one-country Rotary Clubs, community banks, ethnic movie theaters and other amenities often make it unnecessary to have much contact with the integrated mainstream. The more newcomers arrive from the old country, the larger and more all-encompassing these enclaves—both rich and poor—grow, reducing incentives to make the difficult transition to a mixed neighborhood. (Jacoby, 2004, p. 7)

Maybe it's not so far-fetched to suggest that racial distinctions will become more narrow, specific, and personally significant in the future. As an analogy, consider what has happened to the world of ethnic cuisine today. In our largest and most diverse cities, it's not enough for an eatery to simply advertise itself as a Chinese restaurant or an Italian restaurant anymore. Instead, it must specify its regional or culinary accent: Hunan, Cantonese, Szechuan, Mandarin; Northern versus Southern Italian. I once attended a dinner party where one of the guests, a young woman living in New York City, talked about how she only goes to *Korean* karaoke bars, which—unbeknownst to me—are apparently quite different from the Japanese or American karaoke bars that didn't meet her standards.

Will people in the future be content to identify themselves in terms of traditional broad pan-ethnic markers, or will they begin to search for finer distinctions, providing them with a sense of uniqueness that they find lacking now? For example, will it be enough to be Asian American or will it be necessary to identify a regional heritage or country of origin, such as Filipino-American, in order for one to feel a sense of psychological completeness? What will it mean for those who lack or eschew a specific ethnic identity? Will it be desirable to call oneself "plain old American"? The answers to all these questions rest not so much in the private desires of individual people but in the broader cultural attitudes toward race and the relative societal statuses of the groups involved.

A serious and perhaps dangerous downside accompanies the continued subdivision of race and ethnicity. If the economy remains tight or if we enter into another severe recession, competition for scarce economic resources could become even more heated and virulent ethnoracial prejudices could easily erupt. A campaign promoting "Americanization" could make all ethnic and racial distinctions grounds for discrimination. We need only examine what has happened in some parts of Europe to see what such a pessimistic vision might look like: "Barred from settling permanently, denied equal rights, largely without access to political power, unable to close the education gap and cut off from the job opportunities that only a college degree or better can open for them, migrants languish at the bottom of the social pyramid in many of the world's most civilized nations" (Jacoby, 2004, p. 9).

In just which direction our ethnoracial future lies is anybody's guess. It's certainly premature to talk about a completely color-blind society or the total elimination of race and ethnicity. Race-based segregation, poverty, and discrimination will never disappear fully. Indeed, given the growing proportion of Asian Americans and Latino/as in the general population and the continuing economic disadvantage of Blacks, some sociologists have begun to talk about a new racial split in the United States. Instead of the old black/white divide, the one that is now most likely to separate us is a black/nonblack divide (Lee & Bean, 2004).

According to sociologist Eduardo Bonilla-Silva (2004), the United States is already evolving into an even more complex tri-racial system similar to what is found in some Latin American countries with Whites at the top, an intermediate category of "honorary Whites" in the middle, and a non-white category he refers to as "collective Black" at the bottom. These categories are not merely racial but include elements of ethnicity and social class as well. For instance, Whites include assimilated white Latino/as, some multiracials, and urban Native Americans as well as Euro-Americans. "Honorary Whites" include groups that have achieved middle-class status, such as Japanese Americans, Korean Americans, Asian Indians, Chinese Americans, and Arab Americans. "Collective Blacks" comprise groups that languish at the bottom of the stratification system, including African Americans, dark-skinned and poor Latino/as, Filipinos, Southeast Asians, and reservation-bound Native Americans.

Yet it also may be overly gloomy to talk about a future society in which racial divisions become more polarizing than they are now. What we can safely project is that 10, 20, or 50 years from now, racial and ethnic identities and the color lines that divide us will not take the form they take today.

THE FUTURES OF GENDER AND THE SEXUAL DICHOTOMY

It seems a little strange to talk about the futures of sex and gender in the same way that I've been discussing the futures of race and ethnicity. We're not in the midst of a massive redefinition of sex as we are regarding race and ethnicity. The U.S. Bureau of the Census isn't currently debating ways to redefine sex categories on the census form or weighing the utility of allowing people to legally claim more than one sex. Surely no one would argue that there won't be a difference between men and women in the future or that dichotomous thinking about sex will disappear anytime soon. For that matter, I doubt that many people would maintain that we're headed toward an androgynous society in which gender is a meaningless social identifier.

Yet our ideas about sex and gender differences have changed in the recent past and will therefore no doubt continue to change in the coming decades. The recent trend toward searching for the biological underpinnings to gendered behavior suggests that we might someday rely more on anatomical and genetic explanations of gendered characteristics than we do now. At the same time, though, there is increasing awareness that sex and gender—both as a source of identity and as a set of cultural expectations—are not fixed and immutable.

In fact, we seem to be in the midst of a transformation in our thinking about female and male identifiers. As you may recall from Chapter 2, intersexual and transgendered people have become more visible and more vocal in their challenges to traditional dichotomous thinking about sex and gender.

High profile celebrities like Caitlyn Jenner, television shows like *Orange is the New Black* and *Transparent,* and even some children's books that focus on transgender characters have pushed the conversation into mainstream society. No less of a barometer of social trends than Facebook provided some cultural legitimacy to the questioning of dichotomous sex identifiers when, in 2014, it began allowing users to select from *over 50* sex/gender categories (with identifying terms like, *agender, transsexual, cisgender, gender fluid,* and *neither*) in creating their online profiles. Young people today seem far more comfortable with sex and gender ambiguity and complexity than older generations.

Changes taking place in what is expected of and accepted for males and females (that is, gender) are even more obvious. For a glimpse of the future of gender, one need look no further than the institution of family. Fifty years ago, the "normal" family was thought to be one with a female homemaker and a male breadwinner. Functionalist sociologists claimed that this family type was ideally suited to meet the needs of individuals and social institutions (Gerson, 2000). Today, though, fewer than one quarter of all married-couple families with children fit this pattern (ProQuest Statistical Abstract, 2015). Mothers are less likely to be the sole or even the primary caretakers of their children than they were 50 years ago, forcing them to depend on paid caregivers, friends, or teachers to fulfill the traditional maternal role. At the same time, they're more likely than ever to be the sole or primary breadwinners in their families. In short, gendered roles in today's American families bear little resemblance to the cultural ideal that existed just a generation ago.

Despite the growing acceptance of non-marital adult relationships, it's likely that the vast majority of the adult population will continue to marry. Only 10.9% of men and 9.0% of women between the ages of 55 and 64 have never married (ProQuest Statistical Abstract, 2015). Marriage, for all its problems and pitfalls, is here to stay. Indeed, now that same-sex couples can legally marry, the percentage of adults who choose to marry will no doubt continue to grow.

But when it comes to what people are actually doing in their marriages, we can see some dramatic changes. American men and women are slowly moving toward a blurring of gender expectations and away from traditional notions of wives and husbands, mothers and fathers (Cherlin, 2004). Each year, Americans show more accepting attitudes toward women's independence and influence at home and at work. Attitudes about men are changing too. Surveys of high school students over the years show that a growing proportion believe that husbands should take on more household and child care responsibilities. The vast majority believe that wives should expect their husbands to participate fully in these duties. Most adolescent boys expect that when they get married, their wives will work, and more and more of them indicate that they intend to take time off from work after becoming fathers (Coltrane, 1996).

As couples in which both partners work outside the home become the norm, employers will have more and more trouble ignoring employees' desire to achieve balance between their work and family lives. We are beginning to see the slow disappearance of the 9-to-5, Monday-through-Friday workweek (an acknowledgment of how employees' needs change through the life course). If this trend continues, we will likely witness the appearance of a more flexible and less gender-specific definition of what it means to be a good worker (and, by extension, a good spouse).

Furthermore, as working families become more common, fewer people will publicly condemn working mothers as negligent parents. Most people today already say that they believe, at least in principle, in the ideal of equal opportunities for men and women. If current trends continue, more people will endorse such a belief in the future.

With regard to the work that takes place *within* households, some sociologists argue that changes in the gender-based division of labor will help to propel us toward equality between men and women at home. Whenever men take on more of the mundane domestic tasks, the balance of power in the household begins to shift. When fathers take on more child care responsibilities, they begin to develop the sort of nurturing sensitivities traditionally associated with mothers. When parents share responsibilities, children thrive intellectually and emotionally and grow up holding less-rigid gender stereotypes. Of course, not everyone's attitudes will conform to this picture. Nevertheless, household tasks may become less tied to gender in the future.

These changes in the home and the workplace have the potential to transform the meaning of gender for future generations. But we have a long way to go yet, and the road toward true gender equity and equality is not completely free of potholes. As you will recall from Chapter 6, most jobs are still based on the assumption that an employee can and should work long hours without worrying about child care and other household needs. Most employed women continue to work in traditionally "female" occupations and still earn substantially lower wages than men. And the vast majority of women are still responsible for the bulk of the housework and child care.

Moreover, work still tends to be structured around a male career model: 20 years of schooling, followed by 40 years of employment and then retirement (Skolnick, 1996). This model doesn't work for many women, who still must search for ways to combine work and domestic responsibilities (see Chapter 6). They often have to step out of the paid labor force to raise a family and return to it later when the children are finally grown.

Most of the positive changes we've witnessed regarding gender have been a result of alterations in *women's* educational, occupational, and family lives. And so perhaps the most certain projection I can make regarding the future of gender is that men's position will remain, at least for a while, uncertain. The direction in which society will head rests on how men interpret and respond to the changes they face as a result of changes in women's lives. In the face of women's growing confidence—and broader economic trends toward greater balance—some men are beginning to feel threatened. Men may want to devote more of themselves to their relationships these days and, for those who become parents, more time and energy to the rearing of children. But as long as there continues to be a close relationship between paid work, occupational status, and male identity, they will have trouble abandoning the notion that in order to be a man, they must be the household breadwinner (Reeves, 2004).

Even if gender becomes less of a determinant of work achievement and family responsibilities than it is today, gender-motivated discrimination is unlikely to disappear entirely. For several decades, some sociologists have been arguing that family status rather than gender may become the most potent polarizing characteristic among workers in the future (e.g., Hunt & Hunt, 1990). These sociologists point out that the social and economic gap between "career-oriented" workers (those single people and couples who downplay family life in pursuit of career advancement) and "child-oriented" workers (those single parents and couples who downplay careers in the interests of their families) will inevitably widen. They fear that as long as employers remain concerned with productivity and profits, they will continue to favor career-oriented workers (whether male or female) over workers (whether male or female) who want to spend more time with their families.

Such thinking has already started to affect the lives of child-oriented couples. During the recent economic recession, for instance, some mortgage lenders became skittish about approving home loans for expectant parents. They feared that these couples would inevitably experience a temporary drop in income if one of the partners went on temporary parental leave—or perhaps a permanent loss of income if one partner decided to leave the workforce entirely—and therefore be unable to make their mortgage payments (Bernard, 2010). If future employers still assume that the most committed employees are those unfettered by family demands, both women and men who openly express a desire to balance work time with time away from work will risk falling behind occupationally.

THE FUTURES OF "[BLANK]SEXUALITY"

As with future definitions of race and ethnicity, the familiar dividing lines between homosexuality and heterosexuality may prove insufficient to capture the ways that many individuals "do" their sexual lives (Lawler, 2001). As we saw in Chapter 2, many people today reject rigid sexual categorization and instead consider their sexual orientation fluid rather than permanent, something that can change as their interpersonal circumstances change.

Yet it's nearly impossible to imagine a society in which some forms of sexual expression are not privileged over others. The line between the favored and the stigmatized may shift from time to time, pushing toward greater tolerance at one point and more restrictive and punitive definitions at another. But from a societal perspective, there will always be some forms of sexual orientation that are defined as good and "normal" and others defined as bad and "abnormal."

Nevertheless, the growing cultural acceptance of homosexuality is undeniable. According to a recent poll (Pew Research Center, 2014a), two-thirds of Americans now say that it wouldn't matter to them if a presidential candidate were gay. In fact, according to these respondents, a candidate's sexual orientation is less relevant than if he or she is old (over 70) or has had an extra marital affair.

In the end, the future place of sexuality or sexual orientation in the stratification system may have less to do with how and with whom people achieve sexual pleasure in their private lives and more to do with legal recognition of certain forms of intimacy. In recent years, we've seen attempts to expand the American definition of family beyond traditional parameters According to some, lingering opposition to legal same-sex marriage has become an untenable position to take, not unlike segregationists who continued to espouse the separation of races long after the culture—and the law—had moved in the opposite direction.

For compelling evidence of the growing acceptance of "nontraditional" intimacy, we can look to some unlikely places. For instance, gay and lesbian students at highly conservative Christian colleges are coming forward to demand the right to openly proclaim their identities, form campus clubs, and reject suggestions that they seek help to suppress their homosexual desires (Eckholm, 2011). And, as we saw in Chapter 6, ordinarily conservative corporate America was at the forefront of granting benefits to same-sex intimate partners and spouses long before the Supreme Court legalized such relationships. Huge multinational companies are in the business of making profits, not taking public stands on controversial political issues. They don't establish their policies frivolously. Many of these companies concluded years ago that implementing discrimination protection based on sexual orientation makes good financial sense because they increase workers' satisfaction and hence motivation, productivity, and loyalty. To the extent that an inclusive definition of family continues to make good business sense, the list of economically and socially "legitimate" types of families will continue to expand. Perhaps these companies will ultimately put pressure on local, state, and federal legislatures to create laws that parallel their policies and protect the rights of gay, lesbian, bisexual, and transgender employees. Such action will inevitably influence the manner in which sexual orientation is considered in the future.

STRATIFICATION OUTLOOKS: CLASS DISMISSED?

In 2015, Pope Francis issued a statement in which he referred to capitalist greed and the wanton pursuit of money as "the dung of the devil" (Squires, 2015, p. 1). But I don't think anyone—not even the most vociferous advocate of equality and social justice—would predict that we would ever live in a world, or even a society, where there were no distinctions between the very rich and the very poor. In fact, if recent figures are any indication of what's in store (see Chapter 6), we're actually moving in the opposite socioeconomic direction, as the income and wealth gaps between the richest and poorest Americans continue to grow wider.

Keep in mind, though, that economic inequality is not inevitable; it always depends on the choices we make as a society: how we regulate corporate and union activity, how we distribute the tax burden, how we choose to invest in education, how we set wages, how we choose to pay for health care, how we support children, the elderly, and the disabled, and so on (Hout & Lucas, 2001; Piketty, 2014). We can look to other industrialized countries (Sweden, Norway, the Netherlands) for evidence that societies can in fact reduce the gaps between rich and poor if they so desire. When we assume that class inequality is unchangeable, however, we free ourselves from any obligation to do something to reduce it.

Hence, socioeconomic boundaries may actually become more rather than less relevant in the future. Even today, some sociologists argue that class, and not race, is becoming the great divider in U.S. society in the 21st century. Of course, there's no way to project economic trends with any amount of certainty (just ask all the economists who didn't see the 2008 recession coming). What we can anticipate, though, is that as long as we continue both individually and culturally to subscribe to a political ideology and an economic system in which one's socioeconomic status derives from one's competitive achievements, we will always have some people who succeed and some people who fail. Because this ideology forms the basis of our very way of life in this society—from educational achievement to financial well-being—it seems unlikely to shrink in importance in the future.

FUTURE INTERSECTIONS

"The weakest link in the chain is indifference to the suffering of others." Harry Belafonte (speech given at DePauw University, 2002)

All of us, to one degree or another, are selfish. I don't mean that we're all greedy or that we never care about other people. I mean that we all can get so caught up in our own lives and what's happening to us personally that we fail to recognize how interconnected our lives are with the lives of others. We sometimes forget that our thoughts and our deeds have an impact on other people. If we happen to occupy a position of advantage and privilege in society, we sometimes don't see our daily ties to the countless unnamed and largely invisible people who provide us with the goods and services we need to sustain our own lives.

Even when we aren't especially advantaged, we sometimes fail to see the hardships that other people experience. Most of us have little difficulty seeing our own victimization within larger systems of inequality. What we have a harder time doing is seeing how our thoughts, beliefs, and actions lead to and support other people's subordination and disadvantage. People see the type of subjugation most closely associated with the group to which they belong as being most important and classify other types as less so. For example, many poor Whites during the Great Depression of the 1930s suffered enormous financial hardship, but their plight didn't compare to that of poor Blacks who couldn't vote and lacked access to public parks and school (Sehgal, 2015). According to sociologist Patricia Hill Collins (2003), some middle-class, white feminists are inclined to focus on their own disadvantage as women quite clearly but fail to see how their skin color or class standing privileges them.

Broadening our view to encompass the multiple dimensions of inequality helps us see that we're all dominant and all disadvantaged simultaneously:

I, for instance, am simultaneously dominant as a white person and targeted as a woman. A white able-bodied man may be dominant in those categories, but targeted as a Jew or Muslim or as a gay person.

> Some people are, at some point in their lives, entirely dominant; but if they are, they won't be forever. Even a white, able-bodied, heterosexual, Christian man will literally grow out of his total dominance if he reaches old age. (Ayvazian, 2001, p. 610)

Similarly, none of us are ever totally without virtue or vice (Collins, 2003). Meaningful social change can take place only when we realize that there are few pure victims or pure victimizers. All of us derive at some point varying amounts of penalty and privilege from the systems of inequality that frame our lives.

The key to undermining or overcoming disadvantage is to recognize the multiple intersecting dimensions of privilege: race, class, gender, and sexuality, as well as others not directly addressed in this book. Dichotomous, either/or thinking—for example, conceiving of race only in black/white terms or sexuality only as gay or straight—corners us into thinking about groups as opposing forces. This way of framing the world encourages us to see ourselves and others as oppressed/not oppressed or powerful/ powerless. If we acknowledge the simultaneity of all of the different social dimensions on which we are positioned, however, we can see ourselves and others as advantaged in some ways and disadvantaged in others (Collins, 2003).

Dichotomous thinking also encourages a ranking of differences and inequalities. Taking a "my oppression is more oppressive than your oppression" stance—what one sociologist called "the Oppression Olympics" (Martinez, 2003, p. 624)—dooms us to endless competition for attention and resources and forces us to ignore the similar experiences and similar strategic battles faced by all disadvantaged groups.

In order to move to a new vision of equality and inequality, we must begin to ask different questions. Rather than simply asking who is more disadvantaged than whom, we should first assume that race, class, gender, and sexuality are always present (even though one dimension of identity might be more prominent than others at any given point) and then ask how they interlock to shape relations of inequality. As an example of this inter-connected approach, the National Organization of Men Against Sexism (NOMAS) moves beyond the singular issue of gender inequality and defines itself as an organization that "advocates a perspective that is pro-feminist, gay affirmative, anti-racist, dedicated to enhancing men's lives, and commit-ted to justice on a broad range of social issues, including class, age, religion, and physical abilities" (NOMAS, 2014, p. 1). The NOMAS mission state-ment recognizes that, because race and sexual orientation (and class) are so tightly connected to gender in the social systems that create and reinforce inequality, gender inequality cannot be remedied without considering the multiple forms that racial and economic exploitation take.

FINAL THOUGHTS

Some historically disadvantaged groups—women, ethnoracial minorities, sexual minorities—have made amazing advances in the United States in recent years. The racial and ethnic landscape of contemporary society would have been unimaginable to even the most optimistic civil rights activist of the 1960s. Could she or he have possibly envisioned a black man being elected president...twice? Could anyone fighting for the rights of homosexuals in the 1970s ever have imagined a time when the United States Supreme Court would grant two people of the same sex the right to legally marry? Could a women's liberationist 50 years ago have ever foreseen a time when female legislators would be commonplace and female college students would outnumber male college students?

We can't ignore the fact, though, that real, significant, and debilitating imbalances continue to harm some segments of society while leaving others unscathed. People continue to be born into positions of advantage that they themselves had nothing to do with achieving or creating. We continue to live in a society where distrust of, avoidance of, and even hostility toward those perceived to be different is common. As I was writing an earlier edition of this book, my university erupted in a controversy over this "Cinco de Mayo party" invitation that a fraternity posted on Facebook:

> Cinco de Mayo has come to represent a celebration of the contributions that Mexican Americans . . . have made to America." Our grass is constantly cut, leaves blown, mulch spread, fences painted. . . . Not to mention they have contributed to the well being of every American by introducing the practice of a siesta. Who would have thought to take a 5 hour nap in the middle of the day if it weren't for Mexicans? . . . Taking all this into account, we have decided that it is necessary to drink ungodly amounts of tequilla and Dos Equis, and we would be happy to have you join in on the festivities. . . . Please don't forget your green cards, border patrol will be attending this event.

Students of all races and ethnicities on campus mobilized in protest and those responsible for the invitation quickly issued a public apology. But several of my colleagues incredulously asked a similar question: "What year is this? 1960?"

Well, it was over 50 years later, and despite all the progress that has been made over the past five decades, such incidents have not disappeared.

Truth be told, I wish I didn't have to write this book (now in its third edition). Or more accurately, I wish I could have written it as a history book rather than a contemporary sociological one. I wish that social inequality was extinct, a relic of bygone human societies, like the feudal system or traveling minstrel shows or rotary dial telephones. I wish I could have written that all these problems of inequality were in our past; that we've managed to overcome them and people don't suffer so much anymore. I wish that people truly were judged by who, rather than what, they are. But clearly, we aren't there yet.

So as I wrap up this book, I'm left with a weird empty feeling, as if I still may not have convinced you of the multidimensional nature of social inequality in everyday life. It would have been easier to take the more traditional approach and discuss race, class, gender, and sexuality as discrete dimensions of identity and inequality. I could have written a separate chapter on each. The result would have been clear, understandable, nicely organized, and informational. You might have had an easier time summarizing chapters and taking exams. But it would have painted an incomplete picture.

And herein lies the dilemma in writing a book about social identities and inequalities. At times, it's been necessary, just to be able to write coherently, to address race, class, gender, and sexuality separately. But that does not mean that they are experienced separately or even that they influence people's lives and the society as a whole separately. People don't live their lives solely as a man, solely as a working-class person, solely as a Latina, or solely as a heterosexual. People have identities on all of these dimensions—and more— at the same time. Add age, religion, nationality, educational achievement, occupation, political affiliation, physical ability, family status, level of attractiveness, height and weight, geographic area of residence, personality, and any other characteristic that distinguishes some people from others. Throughout the book, I've also tried to move beyond just talking about inequality only from the perspectives of those who are "different" (and therefore disadvantaged) to talking about those in the majority who are advantaged—which has traditionally meant men, white people, middle- and upper-class people, and heterosexuals. Now you have an even more complex picture of how identities form and how inequalities arise and function.

So, in the interests of trying to highlight the intersections of race, class, gender, and sexuality, I've ended up asking more questions than I've answered. Instead of simplifying things, I've complicated them. We've seen in this final chapter, for example, that social inequality is simultaneously resistant to and amenable to change. In the interests of understanding people's hostilities and anger toward "others," I may have inflamed them. There are no definitive, iron-clad answers here as to how or why race, ethnicity, class, gender, and sexuality combine to influence people's lives. But there are questions, lots of them, that I hope make you think about and perceive your life in relation to others differently now than you did before you read this book. If you now pay attention to your own race, class, gender, and sexuality and the intersections between them more than you did before—and if you now understand how tremendously fortunate you are in some ways, and how disadvantaged you are in others—then maybe I've succeeded after all.

[INVESTIGATING IDENTITIES AND INEQUALITIES]

Organizing for a change: Student groups on campus

Changes in the way we think about race, gender, class, and sexuality don't just materialize out of the blue. More often than not, they are the result of people's concerted efforts to alter conditions that they find unacceptable, unfair, and perhaps even harmful. Practically every college campus in the country has a variety of student organizations that seek to address the interests of historically marginalized groups. On my campus, for example, you can find organizations for African Americans; gay men, lesbians, bisexuals, and transgendered individuals; Latino/as; Asian Americans; and women.

For this exercise, identify all the student organizations on your campus that represent the interests of students from historically disadvantaged groups. Start by gathering some background information (usually available from the Office of Student Affairs or Student Services). Are they chapters of national organizations, or are they exclusively grassroots and local? How long have they existed on campus? Do they have a mission statement, a charter, a Facebook page, or a Twitter feed that describes their purpose and overall philosophy? What is their annual operating budget? Are there organizations that once existed on campus but no longer do? What happened to them? Is their disappearance a sign of failure or of success in meeting their goals?

Next, see if you can interview student leaders and faculty sponsors of some of these organizations. Why did they decide to take leadership roles in their organizations? What do they see as the organization's purpose? What do they think have been the organization's most noteworthy accomplishments? What have been the biggest disappointments?

In addition, talk to a few students who are members of some of these groups. Why did they join? What sorts of organizational activities do they participate in? It might also be interesting to talk to some students who are not members of these organizations to get a sense of "outsiders'" perceptions. Do non-members see these organizations as valuable or problematic?

For comparison, you might want to also identify the campus organizations that represent historically *advantaged* groups (such as College Republicans, Christian student groups, various men's clubs, and so on). How are these organizations similar to and different from the organizations representing historically disadvantaged groups?

Once you've gathered your information, try to draw some conclusions about the utility of such organizations at both local and national levels. Racially, ethnically, sexually, religiously, or politically exclusive groups give members a sense of pride and a feeling of solidarity. But at what point do they reinforce rather than overcome the features that divide us as a society?

REFERENCES

Abrams, K. K., Allen, L., & Gray, J. J. 1993. Disordered eating attitudes and behaviors, psychological adjustment and ethnic identity: A comparison of black and white female college students. *Journal of Eating Disorders, 14,* 49–57.

Academy for Eating Disorders. 2006. *Academy for Eating Disorders calls for warning labels on "pro-ana" Web sites.* newswise.com/articles/academy-calls-for-warning-labels-on-pro-anorexia-web-sites. Accessed February 15, 2016. www.aedweb.org/public/proana.cfm

Accord Alliance. 2014. *FAQs – What are major recent changes in terms of "standard of care" for various DSD?* www.accordalliance.org/learn-about-dsd/faqs/. Accessed July 16, 2014.

Acker, J. 1992. From sex roles to gendered institutions. *Contemporary Sociology, 21,* 565–569.

ActionAid. 2009. *Hate crimes: The rise of "corrective" rape in South Africa.* www.actionaid.org/assets/pdf/CorrectiveRapeRep_final.pdf. Accessed June 3, 2009.

Adair, V. 2004. Branded with infamy: Inscriptions of poverty and class in America. In D. M. Newman & J. O'Brien (Eds.), *Sociology: Exploring the architecture of everyday life (Readings).* Thousand Oaks, CA: Pine Forge Press.

Adams, M. 2014. World Bank warns of food riots as rising prices push world populations toward revolt. *Natural News.* May 30. www.naturalnews.com/045369_world_bank_food_riots_emergency_preparedness.html. Accessed July 1, 2014.

Adams, S., Kuebli, J., Boyle, P. A., & Fivush, R. 1995. Gender differences in parent-child conversations about past emotions: A longitudinal investigation. *Sex Roles, 33,* 309–323.

Adler, P. A., & Adler, P. 1998. *Peer power.* New Brunswick, NJ: Rutgers University Press.

AFL-CIO. 2015. *Executive pay watch.* www.aflcio.org/Corporate-Watch/Paywatch-2015. Accessed May 28, 2015.

Albelda, R., & Tilly, C. 2001. It's a family affair: Women, poverty, and welfare. In S. J. Ferguson (Ed.), *Shifting the center: Understanding contemporary families.* Mountain View, CA: Mayfield.

Alexander, J. C. 2001. Theorizing the "modes of incorporation": Assimilation, hyphenation, and multiculturalism as varieties of civil participation. *Sociological Theory, 19,* 237–249.

Allen, I. L. 1990. *Unkind words: Ethnic labeling from* Redskin *to* WASP. New York: Bergin & Garvey.

Allen, E. 2010. *Testimony for the Victims' Rights Caucus, U.S. House of Representatives, July 19.* www.missingkids.com/missingkids/servlet/News EventServlet?LanguageCountry=en_US&PageId=4312. Accessed February 15, 2013.

Allport, G. 1954. *The nature of prejudice.* Reading, MA: Addison-Wesley.

Alvarez, L. 2013. Seeing the toll, schools revisit zero tolerance. *The New York Times.* December 2.

Alvidrez, J., & Areán, P. A. 2002. Psychosocial treatment research with ethnic minority populations: Ethical considerations in conducting clinical trials. *Ethics and Behavior, 12,* 103–116.

American Association of University Women. 2013. *Crossing the line: Sexual harassment at school.* www.aauw.org/files/2013/02/crossing-the-line-sexual-harassment-at-school-executive-summary.pdf. Accessed June 19, 2013.

American Association of University Women. 2014. *Know your rights: Workplace sexual harassment.* www.aauw.org/what-we-do/legal-resources/know-your-rights-at-work/workplace-sexual-harassment/#reference. Accessed June 26, 2014.

American Civil Liberties Union. 2000. *Affirmative action.* www.aclu.org/sites/default/files/FilesPDFs/affirmative_action99.pdf. Accessed June 23, 2014.

American Civil Liberties Union. 2013. *The war on marijuana in black and white.* www.aclu.org/files/assets/1114413-mj-report-rfs-rel1.pdf. Accessed July 30, 2014.

American Council for CoEducational Schooling. 2011. *Evidence-based answers.* lives.clas.asu.edu/access/faq-schoolachievement.html. Accessed June 21, 2013.

American Psychiatric Association. 2013. *Diagnostic and statistical manual of mental disorders.* Fifth edition. Washington, DC: American Psychiatric Association.

American Society for Aesthetic Plastic Surgery. 2014. *Quick facts: Highlights of the ASAPS 2013 statistics on cosmetic surgery.* www.surgery.org/media/statistics. Accessed July 2, 2014.

American Society of Plastic Surgeons. 2014. *2013 plastic surgery statistics report.* www.plasticsurgery.org/Documents/news-resources/statistics/2013-statistics/plastic-surgery-full-report-2013.pdf. Accessed January 13, 2015.

American Sociological Association. 2002. *Statement of the American Sociological Association on the importance of collecting data and doing social scientific research on race.* www.asanet.org/governance/racestmt.htm. Accessed June 18, 2003.

American Sociological Association. 2005, *Race, ethnicity, and the health of Americans* (ASA Series on How Race and Ethnicity Matter). Washington, DC: Author.

American television, situation comedies. 2004. *glbtq: An encyclopedia of gay, lesbian, bisexual, transgender, and queer culture.* www.glbtq.com/arts/am_tv_sitcoms.html. Accessed June 17, 2004.

Amnesty International. 2004. *Rape as a tool of war: A fact sheet.* www.amnesty-usa.org/women/pdf/rapeinwartime.pdf. Accessed September 4, 2009.

Amnesty International. 2010. *Racial profiling.* www.amnestyusa.org/us-human-rights/racial-profiling/page.do?id=1106650. Accessed July 1, 2010.

Amnesty International. 2013. *Death penalty and race.* www.amnestyusa.org/our-work/issues/death-penalty/us-death-penalty-facts/death-penalty-and-race. Accessed June 25, 2014.

Anderson, E. 1990. Streetwise: Race, class and change in an urban community. Chicago: University of Chicago Press.

Anderson, M. L. 2001. Restructuring for whom? Race, class, gender, and the ideology of invisibility. *Sociological Focus, 16,* 181–201.

Andreescu, T., Gallian, J. A., Kane, J. M., & Mertz, J. E. 2008. Cross-cultural analysis of students with exceptional talent in mathematical problem solving. *Notices of the American Mathematical Society, 55,* 1248–1260.

Angier, N., & Chang, K. 2005. Gray matter and the sexes: Still a scientific gray area. *The New York Times,* January 24.

Ansell, A. E. 2000. The new face of race: The metamorphosis of racism in the post–civil rights era United States. In P. Kivisto & G. Rundblad (Eds.), *Multiculturalism in the United States.* Thousand Oaks, CA: Pine Forge Press.

Anzaldúa, G. 2003. How to tame a wild tongue. In T. E. Ore (Ed.), *The social construction of difference and inequality: Race, class, gender, and sexuality.* New York: McGraw-Hill.

Apuzzo, M., & Goldstein, J. 2014. New York drops unit that spied among Muslims. *The New York Times.* April 16.

Apuzzo, M., & Schmidt, M. S. 2014. U.S. to continue racial profiling in border policy. *The New York Times,* December 6.

Archer, J. 2004. Sex differences in aggression in real-world settings: A meta-analytic review. *Review of General Psychology, 8,* 291–322.

Arendell, T. 1984. Divorce: A woman's issue. *Feminist Issues, 4,* 41–61.

Arrighi, B. A. 2002. America's shame: Women and children in shelters. In R. H. Lauer & J. C. Lauer (Eds.), *Sociology: Windows on society.* Los Angeles: Roxbury.

Ashford, L. S. 2005. Good health still eludes the poorest women and children. *Population Reference Bureau Report.* www.prb.org. Accessed April 23, 2005.

Ashkenas, J., & Park, H. 2015. The race gap in America's police departments. *The New York Times Interactive.* April 8. www.nytimes.com/interactive/2014/09/03/us/the-race-gap-in-americas-police-departments.html?_r=0. Accessed July 23, 2015.

Association of American Medical Colleges. 2014. *2012 physician specialty data book.* www.members.aamc.org/eweb/upload/Physician_Specialty_Databook_2014. Accessed June 12, 2015.

Astbury, J. 1996. *Crazy for you: The making of women's madness.* Melbourne: Oxford University Press.

Attitudes toward affirmative action. 2003. *American Demographics,* May.

Avert. 2013. *Universal access to HIV/AIDS treatment.* www.avert.org/universal-access.htm#contentTable2. Accessed July 2, 2013.

Ayvazian, A. 2001. Interrupting the cycle of oppression: The role of allies as agents of change. In P. S. Rothenberg (Ed.), *Race, class, and gender in the United States.* New York: Worth.

Bach, P. B., Cramer, L. D., Warren, J. L., & Begg, C. B. 1999. Racial differences in the treatment of early-stage lung cancer. *New England Journal of Medicine, 341,* 119–205.

Bajaj, V., & Fessenden, F. 2007. What's behind the race gap? *The New York Times,* November 4.

Baker, P., & Herszenhorn, D. M. 2010. Obama chastises Wall St. in call to stiffen rules. *The New York Times.* April 23.

Baldauf, S. 2000. A hanging exposes views on race and dating. *Christian Science Monitor,* July 13.

Ball, J. 2014. More than 2.7 billion people live in countries where being gay is a crime. *The Guardian.* May 16.

Banks, J., Marmot, M., Oldfield, Z., & Smith, J. P. 2006. Disease and disadvantage in the United States and in England. *Journal of the American Medical Association, 295,* 2037–2045.

Barbeau, E. M., Krieger, N., & Soobader, M. J. 2004. Working class matters: Socioeconomic disadvantage, race/ethnicity, gender, and smoking in NHIS 2000. *American Journal of Public Health, 94,* 269–278.

Bardaglio, P. 1999. "Shameful matches": The regulation of interracial sex and marriage in the South before 1900. In M. Hodes (Ed.), *Sex, love, race: Crossing boundaries in North American history.* New York: NYU Press.

Barnes, R. 2010. Supreme Court to rule on anti-gay protests at military funerals. *Washington Post,* March 9.

Barrett, J. E., & Roediger, D. 2011. How white people became "white." In P. S. Rothenberg (Ed.), *White privilege: Essential readings on the other side of racism.* New York: Worth.

Barron, J. 2012. Connecticut police officers accused of mistreating Latinos. *The New York Times.* January 24.

Bates, K. G. 2014. "Hispanic" or "Latino"? Poll says it doesn't' matter—usually. National Public Radio. www.npr.org/blogs/codeswitch/2014/01/21/262768075/hispanic-or-latino-polls-say-it-doesnt-matter-usually. Accessed May 30, 2014.

Bazelon, E. 2008. The next kind of integration. *The New York Times Magazine,* July 20.

Beagan, B. 2001. Micro inequities and everyday inequalities: "Race," gender, sexuality, and class in medical school. *Canadian Journal of Sociology, 26,* 583–610.

Bearman, P. S., & Brückner, H. 2002. Opposite-sex twins and adolescent same sex attraction. *American Journal of Sociology, 107,* 1179–1205.

Beauboeuf-Lafontant, T. 2009. *Behind the mask of the strong black woman: Voice and the embodiment of a costly performance.* Philadelphia: Temple University Press.

Begley, S. 2011. Why almost everything you hear about medicine is wrong. *Newsweek.* January 31.

Beinart, P. 2003. Blind spot. *The New Republic,* February 3.

Beinart, P. 2012. The violence we don't see. *Newsweek.* August 27.

Beinggirl.com. 2010. *Keeping it quick and quiet.* www.beinggirl.com/en_US/articledetail.jsp?ContentId=ART11906. Accessed June 25, 2010.

Bell, J. M., & Hartmann, D. 2007. Diversity in everyday discourse: The cultural ambiguities and consequences of "happy talk." *American Sociological Review, 72,* 895–914.

Belluck, P. 2002. Doctors' new practices offer deluxe service for deluxe fee. *The New York Times,* January 15.

Bem, S. L. 1974. The measurement of psychological androgyny. *Journal of Consulting and Clinical Psychology, 42,* 155–162.

Benatar, D. 2003. The second sexism. *Social Theory and Practice, 29,* 177–210.

Benedict, H. 2009. *The lonely soldier: The private war of women serving in Iraq.* Boston: Beacon Press.

Bennett, J. 2010. The beauty advantage. *Newsweek,* July 26.

Bennett, J., Ellison, J., & Ball, S. 2010. Are we there yet? *Newsweek,* March 29.

Benson, J. B. 1993. Season of birth and onset of locomotion: Theoretical and methodological implications. *Infant Behavior and Development, 16,* 69–81.

Bentley, T. S. 2014. 2014 U.S. organ and tissue transplant cost estimates and discussion. *Milliman Research Report.* www.milliman.com/uploadedFiles/Insight/Research/health-rr/1938HDP_20141230.pdf. Accessed June 3, 2015.

Berger, D. L., & Williams, J. E. 1991. Sex stereotypes in the United States revisited: 1972–1988. *Sex Roles, 24,* 413–423.

Berger, J. 2004. Pressure to live by an outmoded tradition is still felt among Indian immigrants. *The New York Times.* October 24.

Bergesen, A., & Herman, M. 1998. Immigration, race, and riot: The 1992 Los Angeles uprising. *American Sociological Review, 63,* 39–54.

Bergner, D. 2014. Is stop-and-frisk worth it? *The Atlantic.* March 19.

Bernard, J. 1981. The good provider role: Its rise and fall. *American Psychologist, 36,* 1–12.

Bernard, T. S. 2010. Need a mortgage? Don't get pregnant. *The New York Times,* July 19.

Bernard, T. S. 2015. Fate of domestic partner benefits in question after marriage ruling. *The New York Times.* June 29.

Bernstein, N. 2012. Chefs, butlers, and marble baths: Not your average hospital room. *The New York Times.* November 22.

Bianchi, S. M., Robinson, J. P., & Milkie, M. A. 2006. *Changing rhythms of American family life.* New York: Russell Sage Foundation.

Bilefsky, D. 2006. How to avoid honor killing in Turkey? Honor suicide. *The New York Times,* July 16.

Bilefsky, D. 2010. Walls, real and imagined, surround the Roma in Slovakia. *The New York Times,* April 3.

Billings, A. C., Angelini, J. R., & Eastman, S. T. 2005. Diverging discourses: Gender differences in televised golf announcing. *Mass Communication and Society, 8,* 155–171.

Bingham, A. 2012. Half of Americans do not know the President's religion. *ABC News Online.* abcnews.go.com/blogs/politics/2012/07/half-of-americans-do-not-know-the-presidents-religion. Accessed June 13, 2013.

BitchMedia. 2014. *About us.* bitchmagazine.org/about-us. Accessed June 13, 2014.

Bittman, M. 2014. Is it bad enough yet? *The New York Times.* December 14.

BlackHealthCare.com. 2003. *Sickle-cell anemia—Description.* www.blackhealthcare.com/BHC/SickleCell/Description.asp. Accessed June 17, 2003.

Blanton, K. 2007. A "smoking gun" on race, subprime loans. *Boston Globe.* March 16.

Blau, P. M. 1964. *Exchange and power in social life.* New York: Wiley.

Bleyer, A., & Welch, G. 2012. Effect of three decades of screening mammography on breast cancer incidence. *New England Journal of Medicine, 367,* 1998–2005.

Blitstein, R. 2009. Weathering, the storm. *Miller-McCune,* July-August.

Block, F., Korteweg, A. C., & Woodward, K. 2013. The compassion gap in American poverty policy. In D. Newman & J. O'Brien (Eds.), *Sociology: Exploring the architecture of everyday life (Readings).* Thousand Oaks, CA: Sage.

Blow, C. M. 2008. Racism and the race. *The New York Times.* August 9.

Blow, C. M. 2013a. The morose middle class. *The New York Times.* April 27.

Blow, C. M. 2013b. A town without pity. *The New York Times.* August 10.

Blow, C. M. 2015, January 5. Privilege of "arrest without incident." *The New York Times.* January 5.

Blumer, H. 1958/2004. Race prejudice as a sense of group position. In C. A. Gallagher (Ed.), *Rethinking the color line: Readings in race and ethnicity.* New York: McGraw-Hill.

Bocian, D. G., Ernst, K. S., & Li, W. 2006. *Unfair lending: The effect of race and ethnicity on the price of subprime mortgages.* Durham, NC:

Center for Responsible Lending. www.responsiblelending.org. Accessed October 10, 2007.

Bonilla-Silva, E. 2003. *Racism without racists: Color-blind racism and the persistence of racial inequality in the United States.* Lanham, MD: Rowman & Littlefield.

Bonilla-Silva, E. 2004. From bi-racial to tri-racial: The emergence of a new racial stratification system in the United States. In C. Herring, V. M. Keith, & H. D. Horton (Eds.), *Skin deep: How race and complexion matter in the "color blind" era.* Urbana, IL: University of Illinois Press.

Bordo, S. 1999. *The male body: A new look at men in public and in private.* New York: Farrar, Straus, & Giroux.

Bordo, S. 2003. Pills and power tools. In T. E. Ore (Ed.), *The social construction of difference and inequality: Race, class, gender, and sexuality.* New York: McGraw-Hill.

Boucher, D. M. 1999. *The paradox of plenty: Hunger in a bountiful world.* Oakland: Food First Books.

Bowen, J. R. 1996. The myth of global ethnic conflict. *Journal of Democracy, 7,* 3–14.

Bowers, W. J., Steiner, B. D., & Sandys, M. 2001. Death sentencing in black and white: An empirical examination of juror race and jury racial composition in capital sentencing. *Penn Journal of Constitutional Law, 3,* 171–274.

Bowker, L. H. 1993. A battered woman's problems are social, not psychological. In R. J. Gelles & D. R. Loeske (Eds.), *Current controversies on family violence.* Newbury Park, CA: Sage.

Bowles, S., & Gintis, H. 1976. *Schooling in capitalist America: Educational reform and the contradictions of economic reform.* New York: Basic Books

Bowley, G. 2012. Afghan kin are accused of killing woman for not bearing a son. *The New York Times.* January 30.

Boydston, J. 2001. *Cult of true womanhood.* www.pbs.org/stantonanthony/resources/culthood.html. Accessed July 10, 2001.

Boykin, K. 1996. *One more river to cross: Black and gay in America.* New York: Anchor Books.

Boylan, J. F. 2013. *Stuck in the middle with you: A memoir of parenting in three genders.* New York: Crown.

Bradshaw, C. P., Waasdorp, T. E., O'Brennan, L. M., & Gulemetova, M. 2011. *Findings from the National Education Association's Nationwide Study of Bullying.* National Education Association. www.nea.org/assets/docs/Nationwide_Bullying_Research_Findings.pdf. Accessed July 15, 2015.

Bragg, R. 1999. Restaurant's added gratuity leads to discrimination claim. *The New York Times,* November 10.

Breiding, M. J. 2014. Prevalence and characteristics of sexual violence, stalking, and intimate partner victimization—National Intimate Partner and Sexual

Violence Survey, United States, 2011. *Morbidity and Mortality Weekly Report, 63,* 1–18.

Brewis, A. A., Wutich, A., Falletta-Cowden, A., & Rodriguez-Soto, I. 2011. Body norms and fat stigma in global perspective. *Current Anthropology, 52,* 269–276.

Brint, S. 1998. *Schools and societies.* Thousand Oaks, CA: Pine Forge Press.

Broder, J. M. 2006. Immigrants and the economics of hard work. *The New York Times.* April 2.

Broderick, R. 2013. A lot of people are very upset that an Indian-American woman won the Miss America Pageant. *Buzzfeed.* September 16. www.buzzfeed.com/ryanhatesthis/a-lot-of-people-are-very-upset-that-an-Indian-American-woman. Accessed May 31, 2014.

Brodey, D. 2005. Blacks join the eating-disorder mainstream. *The New York Times,* September 20.

Brodkin, K. 2004. How the Jews became white folk. In D. M. Newman & J. O'Brien (Eds.), *Sociology: Exploring the architecture of everyday life (Readings).* Thousand Oaks, CA: Pine Forge Press.

Brody, G. H., Yu, T., Chen, E., Miller, G. E., Kogan, S. M., & Beach, S. R. H., 2013. Is resilience only skin deep? Rural African Americans' socioeconomic status-related risk and competence in preadolescence and psychological adjustment and allostatic load at age 19. *Psychological Science, 24,* 1285–1293.

Bronner, E. 1998. Inventing the notion of race. *The New York Times,* January 10.

Bronner, E. 2012. Poor land in jail as companies add huge fees for probation. *The New York Times.* July 3.

Bronner, E. 2013. Right to lawyer can be empty promise for poor. *The New York Times.* March 16.

Broverman, I., Vogel, S., Broverman, D., Clarkson, F., & Rosenkrantz, P. 1972. Sex role stereotypes: A current appraisal. *Journal of Social Issues, 28,* 59–78.

Brown, P. 1998. Biology and the social construction of the "race" concept. In J. Ferrante & P. Brown (Eds.), *The social construction of race and ethnicity in the United States.* New York: Longman.

Brown, R. 2009. Nashville won't make English official language. The New York Times, January 23.

Browne, B. A. 1998. Gender stereotypes in advertising on children's television in the 1990s: A cross-national analysis. *Journal of Advertising, 27,* 8–7.

Brownmiller, S. 1975. *Against our will: Men, women and rape.* New York: Fawcett.

Bruni, F. 2012. Running from millions. *The New York Times.* January 15.

Brunner, B. 2004. *Confederate flag controversy.* www.infoplease.com/spot/confederate1.html Accessed June 23, 2004.

Bryc, K., Durand, E. Y., Macpherson, J. M., Reich, D., & Mountain, J. L. 2015. The genetic ancestry of African Americans, Latinos, and European Americans across the United States. *American Journal of Human Genetics, 96,* 37–53.

Budig, M. J., & England, P. 2001. The wage penalty for motherhood. *American Sociological Review, 66,* 204–225.

Bullard, R. D. 2001. Decision making. In L. Westra & B. E. Lawson (Eds.), *Faces of environmental racism: Confronting issues of global justice.* Lanham, MD: Rowman & Littlefield.

Burke, T. W., & Owen, S. S. 2006. Same-sex domestic violence: Is anyone listening? *Gay & Lesbian Review, 8,* 6–7.

Byrd, A., & Tharps, L. L. 2014. When black hair is against the rules. *The New York Times.* May 1.

California Legislative Information. 2014. *Senate Bill No. 967.* leginfo.legislature. ca.gov/faces/billNavClient.xhtml?bill_id=201320140SB967. Accessed September 7, 2014.

Cameron, P. 2003. Domestic violence among homosexual partners. *Psychological Reports, 93,* 410–416.

Campbell, M. E., & Troyer, L. 2007. The implications of racial misclassification by observers. *American Sociological Review, 72,* 750–765.

Campenni, C. E. 1999. Gender stereotyping of children's toys: A comparison of parents and nonparents. *Sex Roles, 40,* 121–138.

Carli, L. L. 1997. Biology does not create gender differences in personality. In M. R. Walsh (Ed.), *Women, men and gender: Ongoing debates.* New Haven: Yale University Press.

Carmichael, M. 2008. Katrina kids: Sickest ever. *Newsweek,* December 1.

Carnevale, A. P. & Strohl, J. 2010. How increasing college access is increasing inequality and what to do about it. In R. D. Kahlenberg (Ed.), *Rewarding strivers: Helping low-income students succeed in college.* New York: The Century Foundation Press.

Carothers, B. 2013. The tangle of the sexes. *The New York Times.* April 21.

Carr, D. 2004. Improving the health of the world's poorest people. *Health Bulletin #1.* Washington, DC: Population Reference Bureau.

Carson, E. A., & Sabol, W. J. 2012. *Prisoners in 2011.* U.S. Bureau of Justice Statistics. NCJ239808. bjs.ojp.usdoj.gov/content/pub/pdf/p11.pdf. Accessed January 21, 2013.

Carter, B. D., et al. 2015. Smoking and mortality—Beyond established causes. *New England Journal of Medicine, 372,* 631–640.

Cashin, S. 2014. *Place not race: A new vision of opportunity in America.* Boston: Beacon Press.

Catalano, S. 2012. *Intimate partner violence, 1993–2010.* U.S. Bureau of Justice Statistics, NCJ239203. bjs.ojp.usdoj.gov/content/pub/pdf/ipv9310.pdf. Accessed January 16, 2013.

Catalano, S., Smith, E., Snyder, H., & Rand, M. 2009. *Female victims of violence.* U.S. Bureau of Justice Statistics. NCJ228356. www.bjs.gov/content/pub/pdf/fvv.pdf. Accessed June 26, 2014.

Cave, D. 2011. Better lives for Mexicans cut allure of going north. *The New York Times.* July 6.

Cengiz, O. K. 2009. In Europe, Muslims are the "new Jews." *The Week.* September 11.

Center for Responsive Politics. 2014a. *Millionaires' club: For first time, most lawmakers are worth $1 million plus.* www.opensecrets.org/news/2014/01/millionaires-club-for-first-time-most-lawmakers-are-worth-1-million-plus/. Accessed June 25, 2014.

Center for Responsive Politics. 2014b. *Net worth, 2012.* www.opensecrets.org/pfds/overview.php?type=W&year=2012. Accessed June 25, 2014.

Centers for Disease Control and Prevention. 2011. *The national intimate partner and sexual violence survey.* www.cdc.gov/violenceprevention/pdf/nisvs_report2010-a.pdf. Accessed June 26, 2014.

Centers for Disease Control and Prevention. 2012a. *CDC Fact Sheet: New HIV infections in the United States.* www.cdc.gov/hiv/risk/racialethnic/aa/. Accessed June 1, 2014.

Centers for Disease Control and Prevention. 2012b. *HIV among African Americans.* www.cdc.gov/hiv/risk/racialethnic/aa/facts/index.html. Accessed July 3, 2014.

Centers for Disease Control and Prevention. 2012c. *Occupational cancer.* www.cdc.gov/niosh/topics/cancer/. Accessed January 21, 2015.

Centers for Disease Control and Prevention. 2014. *Tobacco-related mortality.* www.cdc.gov/tobacco/data_statistics/fact_sheets/health_effects/tobacco_related_mortality/index.htm#cigs. Accessed June 24, 2014.

Centers for Disease Control and Prevention. 2015. *Preventing healthcare-associated infections.* CDC at Work. www.cdc.gov/washington/~cdcatWork/pdf/infections.pdf. Accessed January 21, 2015.

Chamorro, R., & Flores-Ortiz, Y. 2000. Acculturation and disordered eating patterns among Mexican American women. *International Journal of Eating Disorders, 28,* 125–129.

Charles, M. 2011. What gender is science? *Contexts.* Spring. contexts.org/articles/spring2011/what-gender-is-science/. Accessed June 21, 2011.

Charon, J. 1998. *Symbolic interactionism.* Upper Saddle River, NJ: Prentice Hall.

Chase-Dunn, C., & Rubinson, R. 1977. Toward a structural perspective on the world system. *Politics and Society, 7,* 453–476.

Cherlin, A. 2004. The deinstitutionalization of American marriage. *Journal of Marriage and the Family, 66,* 848–861.

Cherney, I. D., & London, K. 2006. Gender-linked differences in the toys, television shows, computer games, and outdoor activities of 5- to 13-year-old children. *Sex Roles, 54,* 717–726.

Cherry, R. 1989. *Discrimination: Its economic impact on blacks, women and Jews.* Lexington, MA: Lexington Books.

Chesler, E., & Flynn, A. 2014. *Breaking the cycle of poverty: Expanding access to family planning.* Roosevelt Institute. www.rooseveltinstitute.org/sites/all/files/Chesler_and_Flynn_Family_Planning.pdf. Accessed July 4, 2014.

Children Now. 2001. *Prime time for Latinos. Report II: 2000–2001 prime time television season.* National Hispanic Foundation for the Arts. www.children-now.org/media/fc2001/latino2001.pdf. Accessed June 17, 2003.

Children's Health Watch. 2013. *Punishing hard work: The unintended consequences of cutting SNAP benefits.* Policy report. www.childrenshealthwatch.org/publication/punishing-hard-work-unintended-consequences-cutting-snap-benefits/. Accessed July 3, 2014.

Ching, C. L., & Burke, S. 1999. An assessment of college students' attitudes and empathy toward rape. *College Student Journal, 33,* 573–584.

Christie, L. 2010. America's wealthiest (and poorest) states. *CNN Money.* September 16. money.cnn.com/2010/09/16/news/economy/Americas_wealthiest_states/index.htm. Accessed July 2, 2014.

Clark, G. 2014. *The son also rises: Surnames and the history of social mobility.* Princeton: Princeton University Press.

Clark, M. A. 2003. Trafficking in persons: An issue of human security. *Journal of Human Development, 4,* 247–263.

Cluster, D. 1979. *They should have served that cup of coffee.* Boston: South End Press.

CNN.com. 2009. *Most blacks say MLK's vision fulfilled, poll finds.* http://edition.cnn.com/2009/POLITICS/01/19/king.poll/. Accessed August 13, 2009.

Coates, T-N. 2013. In defense of a loaded word. *The New York Times.* November 23.

Coe, R. M. 1978. *Sociology of medicine.* New York: McGraw-Hill.

Cohen, J., & Agiesta, J. 2008. 3 in 10 Americans admit to race bias. The *Washington Post,* June 22.

Cohen, R. A., & Martinez, M. E. 2015. *Health insurance coverage: Early release of estimates from the National Health Interview Survey, 2014.* Centers for Disease Control and Prevention. www.cdc.gov/nchs/data/nhis/earlyrelease/insur201506.pdf. Accessed June 24, 2015.

Cohn, N. 2013. As a long-term political issue, gay marriage will be more like abortion than integration. *New Republic.* June 27.

Cole, D. 1999. *No equal justice: Race and class in the American criminal justice system.* New York: The New Press.

The College Board. 2008. *Facts, not fiction: Setting the record straight.* http://professionals.collegeboard.com/profdownload/08-0608-AAPI.pdf. Accessed June 17, 2010.

Collins, G. 2011. Medicine on the move. *The New York Times.* April 7.

Collins, P. H. 1990. *Black feminist thought: Knowledge, consciousness, and the politics of empowerment.* New York: Routledge.

Collins, P. H. 2001. Shifting the center: Race, class, and feminist theorizing about motherhood. In S. Ferguson (Ed.), *Shifting the center: Understanding contemporary families.* Mountain View, CA: Mayfield.

Collins, P. H. 2003. Toward a new vision: Race, class, and gender as categories of analysis and connection. In T. E. Ore (Ed.), *The social construction of difference and inequality*. New York: McGraw-Hill.

Collins, P. H. 2004. Some group matters: Intersectionality, situated standpoints, and black Feminist thought. In L. Richardson, V. Taylor, & N. Whittier (Eds.), *Feminist frontiers*. New York: McGraw-Hill.

Coltrane, S. 1996. *Gender and families*. Thousand Oaks, CA: Pine Forge Press.

Committee on Communication. 2006. Children, adolescents, and advertising. *Pediatrics, 118,* 2563–2569.

Congressional Budget Office. 2014. *The distribution of household income and federal taxes, 2011.* www.cbo.gov/sites/default/files/cbofiles/attachments/49440-Distribution-of-Income-and-Taxes.pdf. Accessed May 28, 2015.

Conley, T. T. 2014. *1 in 3 women hover between poverty and the middle class.* Population Reference Bureau. www.prb.org/Publications/Articles/2014/shriver-report-poverty.aspx. Accessed June 18, 2014.

Cookson, C. 2008. Poverty mars formation of infant brains. *Financial Times,* February 16.

Cookson, P., & Persell, C. 1985. *Preparing for power.* New York: Basic Books.

Cooper, A., & Smith, E. L. 2011. *Homicide trends in the United States, 1980–2008.* U.S. Bureau of Justice Statistics. NCJ236018. www.bjs.gov/content/pub/pdf/htus8008.pdf. Accessed June 26, 2014.

Cooper, H. 2014. Pentagon study finds 50% increase in reports of military sexual assaults. *The New York Times.* May 2.

Cooper, M. H. 1998. Environmental justice. *CQ Researcher,* June 19.

Cornell, S., & Hartmann, D. 1998. *Ethnicity and race: Making identities in a changing world.* Thousand Oaks, CA: Pine Forge Press.

Corse, S., & Silva, J. 2013. Intimate inequalities: Love and work in a post-industrial landscape. Paper presented at Annual Meeting of the American Sociological Association. New York, NY. August 9.

Cort, M. A. 2004. Cultural mistrust and use of hospice care: Challenges and remedies. *Journal of Palliative Medicine, 7,* 63–72.

Coscarelli, J. 2014. Cliven Bundy's racist rant captured on video, obliterating claim he was misquoted, not racist. *New York Magazine.* April 24. nymag.com/daily/intelligencer/2014/04/cliven-bundy-racist-rant-video.html. Accessed June 12, 2014.

Cose, E. 1993. *The rage of a privileged class.* New York: HarperCollins.

Cose, E. 2010. Red, brown and blue: America's color lines are shifting. *Newsweek,* January 11.

Coski, J. M. 2005. *The confederate battle flag.* Cambridge, MA: Harvard University Press.

Coyle, M. 2003. Race and class penalties in crack cocaine sentencing. *The Sentencing Project Report #5077.* www.sentencingproject.org/policy/mc-crackcocaine.pdf. Accessed June 20, 2003.

Crabbe, C. 2003. France caught cold by heat wave. *Bulletin of the World Health Organization, 81,* 773–774.

Crandall, C. S., & Martinez, R. 1996. Culture, ideology, and antifat attitudes. *Personality and Social Psychology Bulletin, 22,* 1165–1176.

Crandall, M., Nathens, A. B., Kernic, M. A., Holt, V. L., & Rivara, F. P. 2004. Predicting future injury among women in abusive relationships. *Journal of Trauma: Injury, Infection, and Critical Care, 56,* 906–912.

Crenshaw, K. 2004a. Mapping the margins: Intersectionality, identity politics, and violence against women of color. In L. Richardson, V. Taylor, & N. Whittier (Eds.), *Feminist frontiers.* New York: McGraw-Hill.

Crenshaw, K. 2004b. Was Strom a rapist? *The Nation,* March 15.

Crime and too much punishment. 1997. *The New York Times,* August 3.

Critser, G. 2000. Let them eat fat: The heavy truths about American obesity. *Harper's Magazine,* March.

Crittenden, A. 2001. *The price of motherhood: Why the most important job in the world is still the least valued.* New York: Owl Books.

Croteau, D., & Hoynes, W. 2000. *Media/society: Industries, images, and audiences.* Thousand Oaks, CA: Pine Forge Press.

Crowder, K., Pais, J., & South, S. J. 2012. Neighborhood diversity, metropolitan constraints, and household migration. *American Sociological Review, 77,* 325–353.

Culhane, D., & Metraux, S. 1999. One year rates of public shelter utilization by race/ethnicity, age, sex, and poverty status for New York City (1990 and 1995) and Philadelphia (1995). *Population Research and Policy Review, 18,* 219–236.

Currie, J., DellaVigna, S., Moretti, E., & Pathania, V. 2009. *The effect of fast food restaurants on obesity (Working Paper No. 14721).* Cambridge, MA: National Bureau of Economic Research. www.nber.org/papers/w14721.pdf. Accessed May 15, 2009.

Cutter, S. 2006. *The geography of social vulnerability: Race, class, and catastrophe.* Social Sciences Research Council. http://understandingKatrina.ssrc.org/Cutter/. Accessed June 20, 2010.

Dang, A., & Frazer, S. 2004. *Black same-sex households in the United States: A report from the 2000 Census.* New York: National Gay and Lesbian Task Force Policy Institute and the National Black Justice Coalition.

Darwin, C. 1971. *The descent of man.* Adelaide, Australia: Griffin Press. (Original work published 1871)

Davey, M. 2004. For 1,000 troops, there is no going home. *The New York Times,* September 9.

Davis, F. J. 1991. *Who is black?* University Park: Pennsylvania State University Press.

Davis, J. A., & Smith, T. 1986. *General social survey cumulative file 1972–1982.* Ann Arbor, MI: Inter-University Consortium for Political and Social Research.

Davis, J. H. 2014. Obama set to bar contractors from anti-gay discrimination. *The New York Times.* July 19.

Davis, K., & Moore, W. 1945. Some principles of stratification. *American Sociological Review, 10,* 242–247.

Davis, S. 2003. Sex stereotypes in commercials targeted toward children: A content analysis. *Sociological Spectrum, 23,* 407–424.

Davis-Floyd, R. E. 1996. The technocratic body and the organic body: Hegemony and heresy in women's birth choices. In C. F. Sargent & C. B. Brettell (Eds.), *Gender and health: An international perspective.* Upper Saddle River, NJ: Prentice Hall.

Day, E. 2010. Mariah Carey: Who are you calling a diva? *The Observer.* www.guardian.co.uk/lifeandstyle/2010/jan/17/new-year-new-cool-mariah-carey/print. Accessed May 27, 2010.

Death Penalty Information Center. 2013. *Death penalty representation.* www.deathpenaltyinfo.org/death-penalty-representation. Accessed January 23, 2013.

Death Penalty Information Center. 2014. *National statistics on the death penalty and race.* www.deathpenaltyinfo.org/race-death-row-inmates-executed-1976. Accessed June 25, 2014.

Deaux, K., & Kite, M. E. 1987. Thinking about gender. In B. B. Hess & M. M. Ferree (Eds.), *Analyzing gender: A handbook of social science research.* Newbury Park, CA: Sage.

Decker, G. 2011. More Hispanics are identifying themselves as Indians. *The New York Times.* July 4.

Demby, G. 2013. *Crunching the numbers on Blacks' views on gays.* National Public Radio. www.npr.org/blogs/codeswitch/2013/05/02/180548388/crunch-the-numbers-on-blacks-views-on-gays. Accessed May 27, 2014.

D'Emilio, J., & Freedman, E. B. 1988. *Intimate matters: A history of sexuality in America.* New York: Harper & Row.

DeNavas-Walt, C., & Proctor, B. D. 2015. Income and Poverty in the United States: 2014. *Current Population Reports,* p. 60–252. www.census.gov/library/publications/2015/demo/p60-252.html. Accessed February 4, 2016.

Denizet-Lewis, B. 2003. Double lives on the down low. *The New York Times Magazine,* August 3.

Denizet-Lewis, B. 2014. The scientific quest to prove bisexuality exists. *The New York Times Magazine.* March 20.

DePalma, A. 1995. Racism? Mexico's in denial. *The New York Times,* June 11.

Deveny, K. 2009. Who you callin' a lady? *Newsweek.* November 30.

Dey, J. G., & Hill, C. 2007. *Behind the pay gap.* Washington, DC: American Association of University Women Educational Foundation. www.aauw.org. Accessed April 1, 2007.

Dickerson, C. 2015. *Secret World War II chemical experiments tested troops by race.* National Public Radio. June 22. www.npr.org/2015/6/22/415194765/

u-x-troop-tested-by-race-in-secret-world-war-ii-chemical-experiments. Accessed June 23, 2015.

Diekman, A. B., & Murnen, S. K. 2004. Learning to be little women and little men: The inequitable gender equality of nonsexist children's literature. *Sex Roles, 50,* 373–385.

Dion, K. K., & Dion, K. L. 2004. Gender, immigrant generation, and ethnocultural identity. *Sex Roles, 50,* 347–355.

Dixon, T. L., & Linz, D. 2000. Race and the misrepresentation of victimization on local television news. *Communication Research, 27,* 547–573.

Dolnick, S. 2010. The obesity-hunger paradox. *The New York Times,* March 14.

Domhoff, G. W. 1998. *Who rules America? Power and politics in the year 2000.* Mountain View, CA: Mayfield.

Dosomething.org. 2007. *11 facts about environmental racism.* www.dosomething.org/tipsandtools/11-facts-about-environmental-racism. Accessed June 19, 2011.

Doyle, J. M. & Kao, G. 2007. Are racial identities of multiracials stable? Changing self-identification among single and multiple race individuals. *Social Psychology Quarterly, 70,* 405–423.

Doyle, S. 2010. Mad Men's very modern sexism problem. *The Atlantic,* August 2. www.theatlantic.com/entertainment/archive/2010/08/mad-mens-very-modern-sexism-problem/60788/. Accessed April 12, 2011.

Drake, B. 2014. *Public strongly backs affirmative action programs on campus.* Pew Research Center. www.pewresearch.org/fact-tank/2014/04/22/public-strongly-backs-affirmative-action-programs-on-campus/. Accessed June 18, 2014.

Draper, R. 2014. In the company of men. *The New York Times Magazine.* November 30.

Drug Enforcement Administration. 2015. *Federal trafficking penalties for Schedules I, II, III, IV, and V (except marijuana).* www.dea.gov/druginfo/ftp_chart1.pdf. Accessed January 25, 2015.

Dugger, C. W. 2005. U.N. proposes doubling of aid to cut poverty. *The New York Times,* January 18.

Dunham, K. 2014. In the hospital, there's no such thing as a lesbian knee. *National Public Radio,* November 21.

Durose, M. R., Smith, E. L., & Langan, P. A. 2007. *Contacts between police and the public, 2005.* U.S. Bureau of Justice Statistics. http://bjs.ojp.usdoj.gov/content/pub/pdf/cpp05.pdf. Accessed June 30, 2010.

Duster, T. 1997. Pattern, purpose, and race in the drug war. In C. Reinarman & H. G. Levine (Eds.), *Crack in America.* Berkeley: University of California Press.

Dwyer-Lindgren, L., Mokdad, A. H., Srebotnjak, T., Flaxman, A. D., Hansen, G. M., & Murray, C. J. L. 2014. Cigarette smoking prevalence in US counties: 1996-2012. *Population Health Metrics, 12.* Online version. www.pophealthmetrics.com/content/12/1/5. Accessed July 3, 2014.

Dyer, R. 2012. The matter of whiteness. In P. S. Rothenberg (Ed.), *White privilege: Essential readings on the other side of racism.* New York: Worth.

Eagly, A. H., & Karau, S. J. 2002. Role congruity theory of prejudice toward female leaders. *Psychology Review, 109,* 573–598.

Eaton, L. 2007. In Mississippi, poor lag in hurricane aid. *The New York Times,* November 16.

Eckholm, E. 2011. Even on religious campuses, students fight for gay identity. *The New York Times,* April 19.

Eckholm, E. 2013. Victims' dilemma: 911 calls can bring eviction. *The New York Times.* August 16.

Eckholm, E. 2015. In a first, New Jersey jury says group selling gay cure committed fraud. *The New York Times.* June 26.

Edin, K. 2003. Few good men: Why poor mothers stay single. In A. S. Skolnick & J. H. Skolnick (Eds.), *Family in transition.* Boston: Allyn & Bacon.

Edwards, A. N. 2014. *Dynamics of economic well-being: Poverty, 2009–2011.* P70-137. U.S. Bureau of the Census. www.census.gov/prod/2014pubs/p70-137.pdf. Accessed January 21, 2014.

Egan, T. 1993. A cultural gap may swallow a child. *The New York Times,* October 12.

Ehrenreich, B. 1995. The silenced majority: Why the average working person has disappeared from American media and culture. In G. Dines & J. M. Humez (Eds.), *Gender, race, and class in media.* Thousand Oaks, CA: Sage.

Ehrenreich, B. 2001. *Nickled and dimed: On (not) getting by in America.* New York: Metropolitan.

Ehrenreich, B. 2004. Let them eat wedding cake. *The New York Times,* July 11.

Ehrenreich, B., & English, D. 1989. *For her own good: 150 years of the experts' advice to women.* Garden City, NY: Anchor.

Eitzen, S. D., & Baca Zinn, M. 2003. The dark side of sports symbols. In T. E. Ore (Ed.), *The social construction of difference and inequality: Race, class, gender, and sexuality.* New York: McGraw-Hill.

Eligon, J. 2013. Florida case spurs painful talks between black parents and children. *The New York Times.* July 17.

Ellick, A. B. 2008. Tons of PCBs may come calling at a down-at-the-heels Texas city. *The New York Times,* June 19.

Ellin, A. 2016. Patients facing barriers in care. *The New York Times.* February 16.

Ellison, J. 2011. The military's secret shame. *Newsweek.* April 11.

Emanuel, E. J. 2011. How much does health cost? *The New York Times.* October 30.

Engel, R. S., & Calnon, J. M. 2004. Examining the influence of drivers' characteristics during traffic stops with police: Results from a national survey. *Justice Quarterly, 21,* 49–90.

Enloe, C. 1993. *The morning after: Sexual politics at the end of the Cold War.* Berkeley: University of California Press.

Epstein, C. F. 1988. *Deceptive distinctions: Sex, gender, and the social order.* New Haven: Yale University Press.

Epstein, C. F. 1997. The multiple realities of sameness and difference: Ideology and practice. *Journal of Social Issues, 53,* 259–278.

Equal Justice Initiative. 2015. *Lynching in America: Confronting the legacy of racial terror.* www.eji.org/files/EJI%20Lynching%20in%20America%20 SUMMARY.pdf. Accessed July 23, 2015.

Erdely, S. R. 2012. One town's war on gay teens. *Reader Supported News.* February 4. readersupportednews.org/news-section2/328-121/9792-one-towns-war-on-gay-teens. Accessed February 5, 2012.

Erlanger, S. 2000. Across a new Europe, a people deemed unfit for tolerance. *The New York Times,* April 2.

Erlanger, S. 2008. After U.S. breakthrough, Europe looks in mirror. *The New York Times,* November 12.

Erlanger, S. 2009. Study says Blacks and Arabs face bias from Paris police. *The New York Times,* June 30.

Erlanger, S. 2010. France intensifies effort to expel Roma, raising questions. *The New York Times,* August 19.

Espiritu, Y. L. 2004. Asian American panethnicity: Bridging institutions and identities. In C. A. Gallagher (Ed.), *Rethinking the color line: Readings in race and ethnicity.* New York: McGraw-Hill.

Evans, L., & Davies, K. 2000. No sissy boys here: A content analysis of the representation of masculinity in elementary school reading textbooks. *Sex Roles, 42,* 255–270.

Fagot, B. I., & Hagan, R. 1985. Aggression in toddlers: Responses to the assertive acts of boys and girls. *Sex Roles, 12,* 341–351.

Farley, R. 2002. Identifying with multiple races: A social movement that succeeded but failed? *Population Studies Center Research Report #01 491.* Institute for Social Research, University of Michigan.

Farmer, J. 2004. *The story.* www.sitins.com/story.shtml. Accessed September 10, 2004.

Fausset, R. 2015. Two Mississippi men plead guilty in hate-crimes string. *The New York Times.* January 8.

Fausset, R., & Blinder, A. 2015. States weigh legislation to let businesses refuse to serve gay couples. *The New York Times.* March 6.

Fausto-Sterling, A. 1985. *Myths of gender: Biological theories about men and women.* New York: Basic Books.

Fausto-Sterling, A. 2000. *Sexing the body: Gender politics and the construction of sexuality.* New York: Basic Books.

Feagin, J. R. 1991. The continuing significance of race: Anti-black discrimination in public places. *American Sociological Review, 56,* 101–116.

Feagin, J. R., & Feagin, C. B. 2004. Theoretical perspectives in race and ethnic relations. In C. A. Gallagher (Ed.), *Rethinking the color line: Readings in race and ethnicity.* New York: McGraw-Hill.

Feagin, J. R., & McKinney, K. D. 2003. *The many costs of racism.* Lanham, MD: Rowman & Littlefield.

Feagin, J. R., & O'Brien, E. 2003. *White men on race: Power, privilege, and the shaping of cultural consciousness.* Boston: Beacon Press.

Feagin, J. R.,Vera, H., & Batur, P. 2000. *White racism.* New York: Routledge.

Feagin, J. R., Vera, H., & Imani, N. 2000. The agony of education: Black students at white colleges and universities. In D. M. Newman (Ed.), *Sociology: Exploring the architecture of everyday life (Readings).* Thousand Oaks, CA: Pine Forge Press.

Fears, D., & Deane, C. 2001. Biracial couples report tolerance. *Washington Post,* July 5.

Feldman, N. 2008. The new pariahs? *The New York Times Magazine,* June 22.

Fields, C. B., & Scout, 2001. Addressing the needs of lesbian patients. *Journal of Sex Education and Therapy, 26,* 182–188.

Fine, C. 2010. *Delusions of gender: How our minds, society, and neurosexism create difference.* New York: Norton.

Fine, M., & Weis, L. 2000. Disappearing acts: The state and violence against women in the twentieth century. *Signs, 25,* 1139–1146.

Fineman, H. 2010. Borderline dumb. *Newsweek,* August 23.

Finlay, B., & Walther, C. S. 2003. The relation of religious affiliation, service attendance, and other factors to homophobic attitudes among university students. *Review of Religious Research, 44,* 370–393.

Fisher, I. 2002. Seeing no justice, a rape victim chooses death. *The New York Times,* July 28.

Flaherty, J. 2014. In Louisiana's "cancer alley," growing sinkhole creates more concerns. *Al-Jazeera America.* January 15. america.aljazeera.com/watch/shows/america-tonight-blog/2013/9/12/in-Louisiana-s-canceralley/hugesinkholecreatesmoreconcerns.html. Accessed July 6, 2014.

Fleury-Steiner, B. 2002. Narratives of the death sentence: Toward a theory of legal narrativity. *Law & Society Review, 36,* 549–576.

Flores, A. R., & Barclay, S. 2013. *Public support for marriage for same-sex couples by state.* The Williams Institute. www.williamsinstitute.law.ucla.edu/research/marriage-and-couples-rights/public-support-for-marriage-for-same-sex-couples-by-state. Accessed June 25, 2014.

Floyd, I., & Schott, L. 2013. *TANF cash benefits continued to lose value in 2013.* Center on Budget Policy and Priorities. www.cbpp.org/research/family-income-support/tanf-cash-benefits-continued-to-lose-value-in-2013. Accessed May 29, 2015.

Folbre, N., & Yoon, J. 2006. The value of unpaid child care in the U.S. in 2003. Paper presented at the Meeting of the Allied Social Science Association, Boston (cited with permission of author). January 5.

Foucault, M. 1990. *The history of sexuality*. New York: Vintage.

Fox, J. A., & Zawitz, M. W. 2010. *Homicide trends in the U.S.* U.S. Bureau of Justice Statistics. http://bjs.ojp.usdoj.gov/content/homicide/homtrnd.cfm. Accessed June 30, 2010.

Franke-Ruta, G. 2013. Listening in on "the talk": What Eric Holder told his son about Trayvon. *The Atlantic*. July 16.

Frankenberg, E. 2006. *The segregation of American teachers*. Cambridge, MA: Civil Rights Project at Harvard University.

Frankenberg, R. 2002. Whiteness as an "unmarked" cultural category. In D. M. Newman & J. O'Brien (Eds.), *Sociology: Exploring the architecture of everyday life (Readings)*. Thousand Oaks, CA: Sage.

Freedom to Marry. 2014. *The freedom to marry internationally*. www.freedomtomarry.org/landscape/entry/c/international. Accessed June 24, 2014.

Freeman, H. P. 2014. Why black women die of cancer. *The New York Times*. March 14.

Freund, P. E. S., & McGuire, M. B. 1991. *Health, illness, and the social body: A cultural sociology*. Englewood Cliffs, NJ: Prentice Hall.

Friend, T. 1994. White trash nation: White hot trash and the white trashing of America. *New York Magazine*, August 22.

Frohmann, L. 1997. Convictability and discordant locales: Reproducing race, class, and gender ideologies in prosecutorial decision making. *Law & Society Review, 31*, 531–555.

Frosch, D. 2013. Rights unit finds bias against transgender student. *The New York Times*. June 24.

Fry, R., & Kochhar, R. 2014. *America's wealth gap between middle-income and upper-income families is widest on record*. Pew Research Center. www.pewresearch.org/fact-tank/2014/12/17/wealth-gap-upper-middle-income/. Accessed December 17, 2014.

Furstenberg, F. F. 2011. Diverging development: The not-so-invisible hand of social class in the United States. In S. Ferguson (Ed.), *Shifting the center*. New York: McGraw-Hill.

Fustos, K. 2011. *Gender-based violence increases risk of HIV/AIDS for women in sub-Saharan Africa*. Population Reference Bureau. www.prb.org/Articles/2011/gender-based-violence-hiv.aspx?p=1. Accessed April 26, 2011.

Gallagher, C. A. 1997. White racial formation: Into the twenty-first century. In R. Delgado & J. Stefancic (Eds.), *Critical white studies: Looking behind the mirror*. Philadelphia: Temple University Press.

Gallagher, C. A. 2004. Color-blind privilege: The social and political functions of erasing the color line. In C. A. Gallagher (Ed.), *Rethinking the color line: Readings in race and ethnicity*. New York: McGraw-Hill.

Garcia, M. 2014. Brunei phasing in antigay law; will soon allow death by stoning. *The Advocate*. April 30.

Garcia-Moreno, C., Jansen, H., Ellsberg, M., Heise, L., & Watts, C. H. 2006. Prevalence of intimate partner violence: Findings from the WHO multi-country study on women's health and domestic violence. *Lancet, 368,* 1260–1269.

Garfinkel, J. 2003. Boutique medical practices face legal, legislative foes. *Cincinnati Business Courier.* www.bizjournals.com/cincinnati/stories/2003/02/24/focus2.html. Accessed July 12, 2004.

Gates, A. 2000. Men on TV: Dumb as a post and proud of it. *The New York Times,* April 9.

Gates, G. 2010. Diversity among same-sex couples and their children. In D. Newman & J. O'Brien (Eds.), *Sociology: Exploring the architecture of everyday life (Readings).* Thousand Oaks, CA: Pine Forge Press.

Gates, G. J., & Newport, F. 2012. Special report: 3.4% of U.S. adults identify as LGBT. *Gallup Report.* www.gallup.com/poll/158066/special-report-adults-identify-lgbt.aspx. Accessed May 27, 2014.

Gates, H. L. 1992. TV's black world turns—but stays unreal. In M. L. Anderson & P. H. Collins (Eds.), *Race, class and gender: An anthology.* Belmont, CA: Wadsworth.

Gault, B. 2013. *The wage gap and occupational segregation.* Institute for Women's Policy Research. www.iwpr.org/initiatives/the-wage-gap-and-occupational-segregation. Accessed June 24, 2013.

Geena Davis Institute on Gender in Media. 2012. *Research facts.* www.seejane.org/research. Accessed January 9, 2013.

Gelles, R. J., & Straus, M. A. 1988. *Intimate violence.* New York: Touchstone.

Gentleman, A. 2007. Indian shepherds stoop to conquer caste system. *The New York Times.* June 3.

Gerson, K. 2000. Resolving family dilemmas and conflicts: Beyond utopia. *Contemporary Society, 29,* 180–187.

Gettleman, J. 2010. 4-day frenzy of rape in Congo reveals U.N. troops' weakness. *The New York Times,* October 4.

Gettleman, J. 2011. For Somali women, pain of being a spoil of war. *The New York Times.* December 28.

Giallombardo, R. 1966. *Society of women: A study of women's prison.* New York: Wiley.

Gianatasio, D. 2013. Hunkverttising: The objectification of men in advertising. *AD Week.* Octobert 7. www.adweek.com/news/advertising-branding/hunkvertising-objectification-men-advertising-152925. Accessed June 15, 2014.

Gillani, W., & Walsh, D. 2014. Pregnant Pakistani woman is beaten to death by her family. *The New York Times.* May 27.

Gilligan, J. 2004. Culture, gender, and violence: We are not women. In M. S. Kimmel (Ed.), *The gendered society reader.* New York: Oxford University Press.

Gillis, J. R. 1996. *A world of their own making: Myth, ritual, and the quest for family values.* New York: Basic Books.

Gilman, S. 2004. *Fat boys*. Lincoln: University of Nebraska Press.

Giuffre, P. A., & Williams, C. L. 2000. Not just bodies: Strategies for desexualizing the physical examination of patients. *Gender & Society, 14,* 457–482.

GiveDirectly. 2014. *Evidence.* www.givedirectly.org/evidence.php. Accessed June 18, 2014.

GLAAD. 2014. *Where we are on TV: 2012–2013 season.* www.glaad.org/publications/whereweareontv12. Accessed July 17, 2014.

Gladwell, M. 1996. Black like them. *The New Yorker,* April 29, May 6.

Glaeser, E., & Vigdor, J. 2012. *The end of the segregated century: Racial separation in America's neighborhoods, 1890–2010.* Manhattan Institute for Policy Research. Civic Report #66. www.manhattan-institute.org/html/cr_66.htm. Accessed June 14, 2013.

Goffman, A. 2009. On the run: Wanted men in a Philadelphia ghetto. *American Sociological Review, 74,* 339–357.

Goldberg, J. 1999. The color of suspicion. *The New York Times Magazine,* June 20.

Goldberg, S. 1999. The logic of patriarchy. *Gender Issues, 17,* 53–69.

Goldberg, S., & Lewis, M. 1969. Play behavior in the year-old infant: Early sex differences. *Child Development, 40,* 21–31.

Goldman, L., & Lubin, G. 2011. The 10 fattest states in America. *Business Insider.* July 7. www.businessinsider.com/fattest-states-in america-2011-7#. Accessed July 2, 2014.

Goldstein, J. 2013. The crazy cash-giveaway experiment. *The New York Times Magazine.* August 18.

Good, G. E., Porter, M. J., & Dillon, M. G. 2002. When men divulge: Portrayals of men's self-disclosure in prime time situation comedies. *Sex Roles, 46,* 419–427.

Goodman, P. S. 2010. Cuts to child care subsidy thwart more job seekers. *The New York Times,* May 24.

Goodstein, L. 2011. Omitting clergy at 9/11 ceremony prompts protest. *The New York Times,* September 9.

Goodstein, L. 2014. Presbyterians vote to allow same-sex marriages. *The New York Times.* June 20.

Goodwin, J. 2003. The ultimate growth industry: Trafficking in women and girls. In E. Disch (Ed.), *Reconstructing gender: A multicultural anthology.* New York: McGraw-Hill.

Gordon, I., & Raja, T. 2012. 164 anti-immigration laws passed since 2010? A MoJo analysis. *Mother Jones.* www.motherjones.com/politics/2012/03/anti-immigration-law-database#database. Accessed June 19, 2015.

Gordon, L. 1997. Killing in self-defense. *The Nation,* March 24, 25–28.

Gorenberg, G. 2008. How do you prove you're a Jew? *The New York Times Magazine,* March 2.

Gould, S. J. 1981. *The mismeasure of man.* New York: Norton.

Government Accountability Office. 2005. *Physician services: Concierge care characteristics and considerations for medicine.* www.gao.gov/new.items/d05929.pdf. Accessed June 24, 2010.

Graham, L. O. 1999. *Our kind of people: Inside America's black upper class.* New York: HarperCollins.

Granfield, R. 2005. Making it by faking it: Working-class students in an elite academic environment. In S. J. Ferguson (Ed.), *Mapping the social landscape.* New York: McGraw-Hill.

Greenhouse, L. 1993. Court, 9–0, makes sex harassment easier to prove. *The New York Times,* November 10.

Greenhouse, L. 2007. Justices, 5–4, limit use of race for school integration plans. *New York Times,* June 29.

Greenhouse, L. 2008. Court details opposition to bias in jury selection. *The New York Times,* March 20.

Greenhouse, S. 2012. Lawsuit claims race bias at Wet Seal retail chain. *The New York Times.* July 12.

Greenhouse. S. 2014. The walls close in. *The New York Times.* March 17.

Greenwald, J. 2012. Coca-cola unit sued for alleged racial discrimination. *Business Insurance.* March 19. www.businessinsurance.com/article/20120319/NEWS07/120319876/coca-cola-unit-sued-for-alleged-racial-discrimination. Accessed June 19, 2014.

Griffin, S. 1986. *Rape: The power of consciousness.* New York: Harper & Row.

Gross, J. 2004. Splitting up boys and girls, just for the tough years. *The New York Times,* May 31.

Gross, L. 1994. What is wrong with this picture? Lesbian women and gay men on television. In R. J. Ringer (Ed.), *Queer words, queer images.* New York: NYU Press.

Gross, L. 1995. Out of the mainstream: Sexual minorities and the mass media. In G. Dines & J. M. Humez (Eds.), *Gender, race and class in media.* Thousand Oaks, CA: Sage.

Gusfield, J. 1963. *Symbolic crusade.* Urbana, IL: University of Illinois Press.

Haas, A. P., Rodgers, P. L., & Herman, J. L. 2014. *Suicide attempts among transgender and gender non-conforming adults.* The Williams Institute. williamsinstitute.law.ucla.edu/wp-content/uploads/AFSP-Williams-Suicide-Report-Final.pdf. Accessed July 26, 2014.

Hacker, A. 1992. *Two nations: Black and white, separate, hostile, unequal.* New York: Scribner's.

Hacker, J. S., & Pierson, P. 2010. *Winner-take-all politics: How Washington made the rich richer—and turned its back on the middle class.* New York: Simon & Schuster.

Hagan, J. 2000. The poverty of a classless criminology: The American Society of Criminology 1991 presidential address. In R. D. Crutchfield, G. S. Bridges,

J. G. Weis, & C. Kubrin (Eds.), *Crime readings*. Thousand Oaks, CA: Pine Forge Press.

Hakim, D. 2015. U.S. chamber travels the world, fighting curbs on smoking. *The New York Times*. July 1.

Halbfinger, D. M., & Holmes, S. A. 2003. Military mirrors a working-class America. *The New York Times,* March 30.

Hale-Benson, J. E. 1986. *Black children: Their roots, culture, and learning styles*. Provo, UT: Brigham Young University Press.

Hall, J. D. 1995. "The mind that burns in each body": Women, rape, and racial violence. In M. L. Anderson & P. H. Collins (Eds.), *Race, class, and gender*. Belmont, CA: Wadsworth.

Hall, S. 1995. The whites of their eyes: Racist ideologies and the media. In G. Dines & J. M. Humez (Eds.), *Gender, race and class in media*. Thousand Oaks, CA: Sage.

Halpern, M. T., Ward, E. M., Pavluck, A. L., Schrag, N. M., Bian, J., & Chen, A. Y. 2008. Association of insruance status and ethnicity with cancer stage diagnosis for 12 cancer sites: A retrospective analysis. *Lancet Oncology, 9,* 222–231.

Hamel, L., Firth, J., & Brodie, M. 2014. *Kaiser Family Foundation/The New York Times/CBS News non-employed poll*. The Henry J. Kaiser Family Foundation. kff.org/other/poll-finding/kaiser-family-foundationnew-york-timescbs-news-non-employed-poll/. Accessed December 17, 2014.

Hamer, D., & Coupland, P. 1994. *The science of desire*. New York: Simon & Schuster.

Hamilton, B. E., Martin, J. A., & Ventura, S. J. 2011. Births: Preliminary data for 2010. *National Vital Statistics Report, 60,* 1–25.

Hamilton, D. L. 1981. *Cognitive processes in stereotyping and intergroup behavior*. Hillsdale, NJ: Erlbaum.

Hamilton, D., Goldsmith, A. H., & Darity, W. 2008. *Shedding "light" on marriage: The influence of skin shade on marriage for black females*. Globalisation and Development Centre Working Paper #16. epublications.bond.edu.au/cgi/viewcontent.cgi?artivle=1015&context=gdc. Accessed June 10, 2014.

Haney López, I. F. 1996. *White by law: The legal construction of race*. New York: NYU Press.

Hantzis, D. M., & Lehr, V. 1994. Whose desire? Lesbian (non) sexuality on television's perpetuation of hetero/sexism. In R. J. Ringer (Ed.), *Queer words, queer images*. New York: NYU Press.

Harjani, A. 2013. Domestic violence results in huge costs for economy. *CNBC Online*. November 24. www.cnbc.com/id/101224173#. Accessed June 26, 2014.

Harris, C. A., & Khanna, N. 2010. Black is, black ain't. Biracials, black middle-classers, and the social construction of blackness. *Sociological Spectrum, 30,* 639–670.

Harris, D. R., & Sim, J. J. 2002. Who is multiracial? Assessing the complexity of lived race. *American Sociological Review, 67*, 614–627.

Harris, G. 2011. U.S. panel says no to prostate test for healthy men. *The New York Times*. October 7.

Harris, T. W. 2015. Black like who? *The New York Times*. June 17.

Harris-Perry, M. 2012. What it's like to be a problem. *The Nation.* April 16.

Hart, B., & Risley, T. R. 1995. *Meaningful differences in the everyday experience of young American children.* Baltimore: Paul H. Brookes.

Hartmann, K., Viswanathan, M., Palmieri, R., Gartlehner, G., Thorp, J., & Lohr, K. N. 2005. Outcomes of routine episiotomies. *JAMA, 293*, 2141–2148.

Hatzenbuehler, M. L. 2011. The social environment and suicide attempts in lesbian, gay, and bisexual youth. *Pediatrics, 127*, 896–903.

Haub, C. 2012. *Changing the way U.S. Hispanics are counted.* Population Reference Bureau. www.prb.org/Articles/2012/us-census-and-hispanics.aspx?p=1. Accessed November 9, 2012.

Hausauer, A. K., Swetter, S. M., Cockburn, M. G., & Clarke, C. A. 2011. Increases in melanoma among adolescent girls and young women in California. *Archives of Dermatology,* March 21. http://archderm.ama-assn.org/cgi/content/short/archdermatol.2011.44. Accessed March 30, 2011.

Hays, S. 1996. *The cultural contradictions of motherhood.* New Haven, CT: Yale University Press.

Hays, S. 2003. *Flat broke with children: Women in the age of welfare reform.* New York: Oxford University Press.

Heath, J. & Goggin, K. 2009. Attitudes toward male homosexuality, bisexuality, and the Down Low lifestyle: Demographic differences and HIV implications. *Journal of Bisexuality, 9*, 17–31.

Heffernan, V. 2008. Narrow minded. *The New York Times Magazine,* May 25.

Helms, J. E. 1993. *Black and white racial identity: Theory, research, and practice.* Westport, CT: Praeger.

Henderson, A. F. 1979. College age lesbianism as a developmental phenomenon. *Journal of American College Health, 28*, 176–178.

Henderson, J. J., & Baldasty, G. J. 2003. Race, advertising, and prime-time television. *The Howard Journal of Communication, 14*, 97–112.

Henning, P. J. 2012. Deferred prosecution agreements and cookie-cutter justice. *Dealbook/The New York Times.* September 17. dealbook.nytimes.com/2012/09/17/deferred-prosecution-agreements-and-cookie-cutter-justice/. Accessed January 22, 2013.

Henriques, D. B. 2009. Madoff, apologizing, is given 150 years. *The New York Times,* June 30.

Herbert, B. 2009. The invisible war. *The New York Times,* February 21.

Herdt, G. 1994. *Third sex, third gender: Beyond sexual dimorphism in culture and history.* New York: Zone Books.

Herek, G. M. 2000. The psychology of sexual prejudice. *Current Directions in Psychological Science, 9,* 19–22.

Hess, A. 2016. Fear factor. *New York Times Magazine.* January 31.

Hill, C., & Silva, E. 2006. *Drawing the line: Sexual harassment on campus.* American Association of University Women. www.aauw.org/research/upload/DTLFinal.pdf. Accessed September 5, 2009.

Hill, C., Corbett, C., & St. Rose, A. 2010. *Why so few? Women in science, technology, engineering, and mathematics.* American Association of University Women. www.aauw.org/learn/research/upload/whysofew.pdf. Accessed June 16, 2010.

Hill, M. E. 2002. Skin color and the perception of attractiveness among African Americans. *Social Psychology Quarterly, 65,* 77–91.

Hill, N. E. 1997. Does parenting differ based on social class? African American women's perceived socialization for achievement. *American Journal of Community Psychology, 25,* 67–97.

Hill, S. A. 1999. *African American children: Socialization and development in families.* Thousand Oaks, CA: Sage.

Hill, S. 2001. Class, race, and gender dimensions of childrearing in African American families. *Journal of Black Studies, 31,* 494–508.

Hill, S. A., & Sprague, J. 1999. Parenting in black and white families: The interaction of gender with race and class. *Gender & Society, 13,* 480–502.

Hillier, L., & Harrison, L. 2004. Homophobia and the production of shame: Young people and same sex attraction. *Culture, Health, and Sexuality, 6,* 79–95.

Hines, R. I. 2001. African Americans' struggle for environmental justice and the case of the Shintech plant: Lessons learned from a war waged. *Journal of Black Studies, 31,* 777–789.

Hirschfeld Davis, J. 2015. Slurs hurled at president via Twitter. *The New York Times.* May 22.

Hitt, J. 2005. The new Indians. *The New York Times Magazine,* August 21.

Hoburg, R., Konik, J., Williams, M., & Crawford, M. 2004. Bisexuality among self-identified heterosexual college students. *Journal of Bisexuality, 4,* 25–36.

Hochschild, J. L. 1995. *Facing up to the American Dream: Race, class, and the soul of a nation.* Princeton: Princeton University Press.

Hochschild, J. L., & Weaver, V. 2007. The skin color paradox and the American racial order. *Social Forces, 86,* 643–670.

Hokayem, C. & Heggeness, M. L. 2014. Living in near poverty in the United States: 1966–2012. *Current Population Reports.* P60-248. www.census.gov/prod/2014pubs/p60-248.pdf. Accessed May 27, 2014.

Holdcroft, A. 2007. Gender bias in research: How does it affect evidence based medicine. *Journal of the Royal Society of Medicine, 100,* 2–3.

Hollander, J. A., Renfro, D. G., & Howard, J. A. 2011. *Gendered situations, gendered selves.* Lanham, MD: Rowan & Littlefield.

Holmes, A. 2015. Background checks. *The New York Times Sunday Magazine.* July 5.

Holmes, S. 1999. Blacks sue, saying hotel discriminated. *The New York Times,* May 21.

Holmes, S. 2000. New policy on census says those listed as white and minority will be counted as minority. *The New York Times,* March 11.

Holmstrom, L. L., Karp, D. A., & Gray, P. S. 2002. Why laundry, not Hegel? Social class, transition to college, and pathways to adulthood. *Symbolic Interaction, 25,* 437–462.

Hooks, G., & Smith, C. L. 2004. The treadmill of destruction: National sacrifice areas and Native Americans. *American Sociological Review, 69,* 558–575.

Hout, M., & Lucas, S. R. 2001. Narrowing the income gap between rich and poor. In P. S. Rothenberg (Ed.), *Race, class, and gender in the United States.* New York: Worth.

Howard, J. A. 2000. Social psychology of identites. *Annual Review of Sociology, 26,* 367–393.

Howell-White, S. 1999. *Birth alternatives: How women select childbirth care.* Westport, CT: Greenwood Press.

Hu-DeHart, E. 1996. *Beyond black and white: A conversation with Evelyn Hu-DeHart.* www.jhu.edu/~igscph/spr96ehd.htm. Accessed January 7, 2005.

Huff, R., Desilets, C, & Kane, J. 2010. *The 2010 National Public Survey on White Collar Crime.* National White Collar Crime Center. Crimesurvey. nw3c.org/docs/nw3c2010survey.pdf. Accessed January 22, 2013.

Hughes, D., & Chen, L. 1997. When and what parents tell children about race: An examination of race-related socialization among African American families. *Applied Developmental Science, 1,* 200–214.

Hulbert, A. 2004. *Raising America: Experts, parents, and a century of advice about children.* New York: Vintage Books.

Hull, K. E., & Nelson, R. L. 2000. Assimilation, choice, or constraint? Testing theories of gender differences in the careers of lawyers. *Social Forces, 79,* 229–264.

Human Rights Campaign. 2014a. *Corporate equality index 2014: Rating American workplaces on lesbian, gay, bisexual, and transgender equality.* www.hrc.org/campaigns/corporate-equality-index. Accessed June 18, 2014.

Human Rights Campaign. 2014b. *The cost of the closet and the rewards of inclusion.* www.hrc.org/resources/entry/the-cost-of-the-closet-and-the-rewards-of-inclusion. Accessed June 18, 2014.

Human Rights Watch. 2012. *India: UN members should act to end caste discrimination.* www.hrw.org/news/2012/05/14/india-un-members-should-act-end-caste-discrimination. Accessed May 29, 2014.

Human Rights Watch. 2014. *Cleaning human waste.* www.hrw.org/reports/2014/08/25/cleaning-human-waste-0. Accessed May 30, 2015.

Humes, K. R., Jones, N. A., & Ramirez, R. R. 2010. Overview of race and hispanic origin: 2010. *2010 Census Briefs C2010BR-02.* www.census.gov/prod/cen2010/briefs/c2010br-02.pdf. Accessed April 1, 2011.

Hunt, J. G., & Hunt, L. L. 1990. The dualities of careers and families: New integrations or new polarizations? In C. Carlson (Ed.), *Perspectives on the family: History, class, and feminism.* Belmont, CA: Wadsworth.

Hunter-Gault, C. 2012. Violated hopes. *The New Yorker.* May 28.

Hyde, J. S. 1984. How large are gender differences in aggression? A developmental meta-analysis. *Developmental Psychology, 20,* 722–736.

Hyde, J. S. 2006. The gender similarities hypothesis. *American Psychologist, 60,* 581–592.

Hyde, J. S., Lindberg, S. M., Linn, M. C., Ellis, A. B., & Williams, C. C. 2008. Gender similarities characterize math performance. *Science, 321,* 494–495.

Imtiaz, S., & Walsh, D. 2015. Heat wave's unlucky timing prompts a crisis in Pakistan. *The New York Times.* June 24.

Institute for Health Metrics and Evaluation. 2014. *US county profiles.* www.healthdata.org/us-county-profiles. Accessed July 3, 2014.

Institute for Women's Policy Research. 2013. *At current pace of progress, wage gap for women expected to close in 2057.* IWPR#Q004 updated. www.iwpr.org/publications/pubs/at-current-pace-of-progress-wage-gap-for-women-expected-to-close-in-2057/at_download/file. Accessed June 18, 2013.

Institute for Women's Policy Research. 2015a. *The gender wage gap by occupation 2014.* IWPR#c431. www.iwpr.org/publications/pubs/the-gender-wage-by-occupation-2014-and-by-race-and-ethnicity/at_download/file. Accessed June 14, 2015.

Institute for Women's Policy Research. 2015b. *The status of women in the United States: 2015—Employment and earnings.* www.statusofwomendata.org/app/uploads/2015/02/EE-CHAPTER-FINAL.pdf. Accessed June 15, 2015.

Institute of Medicine. 2003. *Unequal treatment: Confronting racial and ethnic disparities in health care.* National Academy Press. www.nap.edu/books/030908265x/html/. Accessed July 19, 2004.

Institute of Medicine. 2013. *U.S. health in international perspective: Shorter lives, poorer health.* Report Brief. www.iom.edu/~/Media/Files/Report%20files/2013/US-Health-International-Perspective/USHealth_Intl_PerspectiveRB.pdf. Accessed February 14, 2013.

International Monetary Fund. 2014. *2014 Article IV consultation with the United States of America concluding statement of the IMF mission.* www.imf.org/external/np/ms/2014/061614.htm. Accessed June 16, 2014.

Intersex Society of North America. 2008. How common is intersex? www.isna.org/faq/frequency. Accessed May 27, 2014.

Itzkoff, D. 2014. Oh you silly thing, of course he's gay. *The New York Times.* June 29.

Jackson, J. L. 2004. Birthdays, basketball, and breaking bread: Negotiating with class in contemporary black America. In L. D. Baker (Ed.), *Life in America: Identity and everyday experience.* Malden, MA: Blackwell.

Jacoby, T. 2004. Defining assimilation for the 21st century. In T. Jacoby (Ed.), *Reinventing the melting pot.* New York: Basic Books.

Jarvie, J. 2014. Trigger happy. *The New Republic.* March 3.

Jencks, C., & Phillips, M. 1998. *The black-white test score gap.* Washington, DC: Brookings Institute.

Jenness, V. 2002. Coming out: Lesbian identities and the categorization problem. In D. M. Newman & J. O'Brien (Eds.), *Sociology: Exploring the architecture of everyday life (Readings).* Thousand Oaks, CA: Pine Forge Press.

Jett, S., LaPorte, D. J., & Wanchisn, J. 2010. Impact of exposure to pro-eating disorder websites on eating behavior in college women. *European Eating Disorders Review, 18,* 410–416.

Johnson, B. E., Kuck, D. L., & Schander, P. R. 1997. Rape myth acceptance and sociodemographic characteristics: A multidimentional analysis. *Sex Roles, 36,* 693–707.

Johnson, K., Pérez-Peña, R., & Eligon, J. 2015. At center of storm, a defiant "identify as black." *The New York Times.* June 17.

Jones, N. 2010. Walking "the code": On girls, gender, and inner-city violence. In D. Newman & J. O'Brien (Eds.), *Sociology: Exploring the architecture of everyday life (Readings).* Thousand Oaks, CA: Pine Forge Press.

Judge, T. A., & Cable, D. M. 2011. When it comes to pay, do the thin win? *Journal of Applied Psychology, 96,* 95–112.

Kahlenberg, R. D. 2010. Elite colleges, or colleges for the elite? *The New York Times,* September 30.

Kahlenberg, R. D. 2013. The untapped pool of low-income strivers. *Chronicle of Higher Education.* March 19.

Kane, E. 2009. I wanted a soul mate: Gendered anticipation and frameworks of accountability in parents' preferences for sons and daughters. *Symbolic Interaction, 34,* 372–389.

Kaneda, T., & Adams, D. 2008. *Race, ethnicity, and where you live matters: Recent findings on health and mortality of U.S. elderly.* Population Reference Bureau. www.prb.org/Articles/2008/racialdisparities.aspx. Accessed June 24, 2010.

Kanter, R. M. 1987. Men and women of the corporation revisited: Interview with Rosabeth Moss Kanter. *Human Resource Management, 26,* 257–263.

Kantor, J. 2014. A gender gap more powerful than the Internet. *The New York Times.* December 23.

Karraker, K. H., Vogel, D. A., & Lake, M. A. 1995. Parents' gender stereotyped perceptions of newborns: The eye of the beholder revisited. *Sex Roles, 33,* 687–701.

Katz, J. N. 2003. The invention of heterosexuality. In T. E. Ore (Ed.), *The social construction of difference and inequality: Race, class, gender, and sexuality.* New York: McGraw-Hill.

Kaw, E. 2002. "Opening" faces: The politics of cosmetic surgery and Asian American women. In D. M. Newman & J. O'Brien (Eds.), *Sociology:*

Exploring the architecture of everyday life (Readings). Thousand Oaks, CA: Pine Forge Press.

Kay, A. C., Day, M. V., Zanna, M. P., & Nussbaum, A. D. 2013. The insidious (and ironic) effects of positive stereotypes. *Journal of Experimental Social Psychology, 49,* 287–291.

Keck, Z. 2014. Indian Supreme Court creates "third gender" category for transgenders. *The Diplomat.* April. thediplomat.com/2014/04/indian-supreme-court-creates-third-gender-category-for-transgenders/. Accessed May 23, 2014.

Keith, V. M., & Herring, C. 1991. Skin tone and stratification in the Black community. *American Journal of Sociology, 97,* 760–778.

Kelner, A. 2010. The "Mad Men" effect: Bringing back sexism with style. *Ms. Blog.* http://ms.magazine.com/blog/blog/2010/07/22/the-mad-men-effect-bringing-back-sexism-with-style. Accessed April 12, 2011.

Kelty, R., Kleykamp, M., & Segal, D. R. 2010. The military and the transition to adulthood. *The Future of Children, 20,* 181–207.

Kent, M., & Lalasz, R. 2006, June. *In the news: Speaking English in the United States.* Population Reference Bureau. www.prb.org. Accessed July 20, 2006.

Kent, M., & Yin, S. 2006. *Controlling infectious diseases.* Population Reference Bureau. www.prb.org. Accessed May 1, 2007.

Kershner, R. 1996. Adolescent attitudes about rape. *Adolescence, 31,* 29–33.

Kessler, S. J., & McKenna, W. 1978. *Gender: An ethnomethodological approach.* Chicago: University of Chicago Press.

Kessler-Harris, A. 1982. *Out to work: A history of wage-earning women in the United States.* New York: Oxford University Press.

Khalema, N. E., & Wannas-Jones, J. 2003. Under the prism of suspicion: Minority voices in Canada post–September 11. *Journal of Muslim Minority Affairs, 23,* 25–39.

Kibria, N. 2004. College and notions of "Asian American": Second-generation Chinese and Korean Americans negotiate race and identity. In L. D. Baker (Ed.), *Life in America: Identity and everyday experience.* Malden, MA: Blackwell.

Kiely, K. 2007. "Lawmakers have loved ones in combat zone. *USA Today,* January 23.

Kilborn, P. T. 1999. Bias worsens for minorities buying homes. *The New York Times,* September 16.

Kim, N. Y. 2007. "Critical thoughts on Asian American assimilation in the whitening literature. *Social Forces, 86,* 561–574.

Kimmel, M. 2004. *The gendered society.* New York: Oxford University Press.

Kinsey, A. C., Pomeroy, W. B., & Martin, C. E. 1948. *Sexual behavior in the human male.* Philadelphia: Saunders.

Kinsey, A. C., Pomeroy, W. B., Martin, C. E., & Gebhard, P. H. 1953. *Sexual behavior in the human female.* Philadelphia: Saunders.

Kirby, D. 2004. Party favors: Pill popping as insurance. *The New York Times,* June 21.

Kirby, J. B., & Kaneda, T. 2010. Unhealthy and uninsured: Exploring racial differences in health and health insurance coverage using a life table approach. *Demography, 47,* 1035–1051.

Kleinfield, N. R. 2012. Why don't we have any white kids? *The New York Times.* May 13.

Klinenberg, E. 2002. *Heat wave: A social autopsy of disaster in Chicago.* Chicago: University of Chicago Press.

Klugh, J. 2014. "Fighting Sioux" debate leaves University of North Dakota nameless in Frozen Four. *Philadelphia Inquirer.* www.philly.com. April 10. Accessed June 3, 2014.

Knott, A. 2004. *Lobbyists bankrolling politics.* Center for Public Integrity. www.publicintegrity.org/bop2004/report.aspx?aid=273. Accessed August 7, 2004.

Knowles, E. D., Lowery, B. S., & Schaumberg, R. L. 2010. Racial prejudice predicts opposition to Obama and his health care reform plan. *Journal of Experimental Social Psychology, 46,* 420–423.

Knuckey, J., & Orey, B. D. 2000. "Symbolic racism in the 1995 Louisiana gubernatorial election." *Social Science Quarterly, 81,* 1027–1035.

Kochhar, R., & Fry, R. 2014. *Wealth inequality has widened along racial, ethnic lines since end of Great Recession.* Pew Research Center. www.pewresearch.org/fact-tank/2014/12/12/racial-wealth-gaps-great-recession/. Accessed December 14, 2014.

Kochhar, R., Fry, R., & Taylor, P. 2011. *Hispanic household wealth fell by 66% from 2006 to 2009.* Pew Research Hispanic Trends Project. www.pewhispanic.org/2011/07/26/the-toll-of-the-great-recession. Accessed June 16, 2014.

Kohn, H. 1994. Service with a sneer. *The New York Times Magazine,* November 6.

Kohn, M. L. 1979. The effects of social class on parental values and practices. In D. Reiss & H. A. Hoffman (Eds.), *The American family: Dying or developing.* New York: Plenum.

Kokopeli, B., & Lakey, G. 1992. More power than we want: Masculine sexuality and violence. In M. L. Anderson & P. H. Collins (Eds.), *Race, class and gender: An anthology.* Belmont, CA: Wadsworth.

Kolata, G. 2011. Mysterious maladies. *The New York Times.* February 6.

Kollock, P., Blumstein, P., & Schwartz, P. 1985. Sex and power in interaction: Conversational privileges and duties. *American Sociological Review, 50,* 34–46.

Kornbluh, K. 2012. The international mommy tax. *The Atlantic.* November 30. www.theatlantic.com/sexes/archive/2012/11/the-international-mommy-tax/265754/. Accessed June 11, 2014.

Kornreich, J. L., Hearn, K. D., Rodriguez, G., & O'Sullivan, L. F. 2003. Sibling influence, gender roles, and the sexual socialization of urban early adolescent girls. *Journal of Sex Research, 40,* 101–110.

Kosinsky, J. 1965. *The painted bird*. Boston: Houghton Mifflin.

Krakauer, J. 2015. *Missoula: Rape and the justice system in a college town*. New York: Random House.

Kristof, N. D. 1995. Japanese outcasts better off than in past but still outcasts. *The New York Times,* November 30.

Krugman, P. 2010. Punishing the jobless. *The New York Times,* July 5.

Krugman, P. 2014a. The hammock fallacy. *The New York Times*. March 6.

Krugman, P. 2014b. That old-time whistle. *The New York Times*. March 17.

Kulik, D. 2000. Gay and lesbian language. *Annual Review of Anthropology, 29,* 243–285.

Laboring in the U.S. 2006. *The New York Times*. June 19.

Lacey, M. 2008a. Across globe, empty bellies bring rising anger. *The New York Times,* April 18.

Lacey, M. 2008b. Vulnerable to H.I.V., resistent to labels. *The New York Times,* August 7.

Lacey, M. 2011. In Arizona, complaints that an accent can hinder a teacher's career. *The New York Times*. September 25.

LaFraniere, S. 2011. For many Chinese, new wealth and a fresh face. *The New York Times,* April 24.

Lakoff, R. 1973. Language and women's place. *Language and Society, 2,* 45–80.

Lakoff, R. 1995. Cries and whispers: The shattering of the silence. In K. Hall & M. Bucholtz (Eds.), *Gender articulated: Language and the socially constructed self*. New York: Routledge.

Lalasz, R. 2004. World AIDS Day 2004: The vulnerability of women and girls. *Population Reference Bureau Report,* November. www.prb.org. Accessed December 1, 2004.

Lalasz, R. 2005. Full-time work no guarantee of livelihood for many U.S. families, *Population Reference Bureau Report,* January. www.prb.org. Accessed January 19, 2005.

Lamont, M. 1995. Money, morals, and manners. In D. M. Newman (Ed.), *Sociology: Exploring the architecture of everyday life (Readings)*. Thousand Oaks, CA: Pine Forge Press.

Landesman, P. 2004. The girls next door. *The New York Times,* January 25.

Lang, S. 1998. *Men as women, women as men: Changing gender in Native American cultures*. Austin: University of Texas Press.

Lang, S. 2003. Lesbians, men-women, and two-spirits: Homosexuality and gender in Native American cultures. In S. LaFont (Ed.), *Constructing sexualities: Readings in sexuality, gender, and culture*. Upper Saddle River, NJ: Prentice Hall.

Lapinski, M. K., Braz, M. E., & Maloney, E. K. 2010. The down low, social stigma, and risky sexual behaviors: Insights from African American men who have sex with men. *Journal of Homosexuality, 57,* 610–633.

Lareau, A. 2003. *Unequal childhoods: Class, race, and family life*. Berkeley: University of California Press.

Lareau, A., & Calarco, J. M. 2012. Class, cultural capital, and institutions: The case of families and schools. In S. T. Fiske & H. R. Markus (Eds.). *Facing social class: How societal rank influences interaction.* New York: Russell Sage.

Lauby, M. R., & Else, S. 2008. Recession can be deadly for domestic abuse victims. *Boston Globe,* December 25.

Law, B. M. 2014 Top 10 radical parenting methods. *How Stuff Works.* health. howstuffworks.com/pregnancy-and-parenting/10-radical-parenting-methods. htm#page=0. Accessed June 4, 2014.

Lawler, S. 2001. Introduction: The futures of gender and sexuality. *Social Epistomology, 15,* 71–76.

Leap, W. 1996. *Word's out. Gay men's English.* Minneapolis: University of Minnesota Press.

LeBesco, K. 2004. *Revolting bodies? The struggle to redefine fat identity.* Amherst, MA: University of Massachusetts Press.

Lee, J., & Bean, F. D. 2004. America's changing color lines: Immigration, race/ethnicity, and multiracial identification. *Annual Review of Sociology, 30,* 221–242.

Lee, K. B. 2014. The gender gap in screen time: Cinemetrics extracts statistical data from movies. *The New York Times.* March 2.

Lee, M. 2006. *The neglected link between food marketing and childhood obesity in poor neighborhoods.* Population Reference Bureau. www.prb.org/Articles/2006/TheNeglectedLinkFoodMarketingandChildhoodObesityinPoorNeighborhoods. aspx. Accessed June 20, 2010.

Lee, S. M. 1993. Racial classifications in the U.S. Census: 1890–1990. *Ethnic and Racial Studies, 16,* 75–94.

Lee, V., & Marks, H. M. 1990. Sustained effects of the single-sex secondary school experience on attitudes, behaviors and values in college. *Journal of Educational Psychology, 82,* 578–592.

Lee-St. John, J. 2007. A time limit on rape. *Time.* February 12.

Legman, G. 1941. The language of homosexuality: An American glossary. In G. W. Henry (Ed.), *Sex variants: A study of homosexual patterns.* New York/London: Hoeber.

Leibovich, M. 2014. Did anyone wash dishes in this family? *The New York Times Sunday Magazine.* April 13.

Lemire, E. 2002. *Miscegenation: Making race in America.* Philadelphia: University of Pennsylvania Press.

Leonhardt, D. 2009. Fat tax. *The New York Times Magazine,* August 16.

Leonhardt, D., & Quealy, K. 2014. U.S. middle class no longer world's richest. *The New York Times.* April 23, 2014.

Lepkowska, D. 2004. Model minority tag hides Asian drop-out problem. *Times Educational Supplement,* May 7.

Lesane-Brown, C. L. 2006. A review of race socialization within black families. *Developmental Review, 26,* 400–426.

Lesko, N. 2008. Our guys/good guys: Playing with high school privilege and power. In S. J. Ferguson (Ed.), *Mapping the social landscape.* New York: McGraw-Hill.

Letellier, P. 1996. Gay and bisexual male domestic violence victimization. In L. K. Hamberger & C. Renzetti (Eds.), *Domestic partner abuse.* New York: Springer.

LeVay, S. 1991. A difference in hypothalmic structure between heterosexual and homosexual men. *Science,* August 30, 1034–1037.

Levine, H., & Evans, N. J. 2003. The development of gay, lesbian, and bisexual identities. In K. E. Rosenblum & T. C. Travis (Eds.), *The meaning of difference.* New York: McGraw-Hill.

Lewin, T. 2006. At colleges, women are leaving men in the dust. *The New York Times,* July 9.

Lewin, T. 2012. Black students punished more, data suggests. *The New York Times.* March 6.

Lichtblau, E. 2004. Cracker Barrel agrees to plan to address reports of bias. *The New York Times,* May 4.

Lichtblau, E. 2008. In justice shift, corporate deals replace trials. *The New York Times,* April 9.

Lieberson, S. 1980. *A piece of the pie: Blacks and white immigrants since 1880.* Berkeley: University of California Press.

Lipka, M. 2014. *Young U.S. Catholics overwhelmingly accepting of homosexuality.* Pew Research Center. www.pewresearch.org/fact-tank/2014/10/16/young-u-s-catholics-overwhelmingly-accepting-of-homosexuality/. Accessed January 16, 2015.

Lippmann, L. W. 1922. *Public opinion.* New York: Harcourt Brace Jovanovich.

Liptak, A. 2004. Bans on interracial unions offer perspective on gay ones. *The New York Times,* March 17.

Liptak, A. 2014. Justices' rulings advance gays; women less so. *The New York Times.* August 5.

Liptak, A. 2008. Outside U.S., hate speech can be costly. *New York Times,* June 12.

Little, A. G. 2007. Not in whose backyard? *The New York Times Magazine.* September 2.

Loe, M. 2001. Fixing broken masculinity: Viagra as a technology for the production of gender and sexuality. *Sexuality & Culture, 5,* 97–125.

Longman, J. 2011. Badminton dress code for women criticized as sexist. *The New York Times.* May 26.

Lorber, J. 1998. *Gender inequality: Feminist theories and politics.* Los Angeles: Roxbury.

Lorber, J. 2000. *Gender and the social construction of illness.* Walnut Creek, CA: AltaMira Press.

Lovett, I. 2013. Changing sex, and changing teams. *The New York Times.* May 7.

Lowes, R. 2002. How unhappy are women doctors? In R. H. Lauer & J. C. Lauer (Eds.), *Sociology: Windows on society.* Los Angeles: Roxbury.

Lowrey, A. 2014. Bluegrass-state blues. *The New York Times Magazine.* June 29.

Lucal, B. 1999. What is means to be gendered me: Life on the boundaries of a dichotomous gender system. *Gender & Society, 13,* 781–797.

Lutz, A. 2013. Abercrombie & Fitch refuses to make clothes for large women. *Business Insider.* May 3. www.businessinsider.com/abercrombie-wants-thin-customers-2013-5. Accessed July 1, 2014.

Ma, B. 2010. A trip into the controversy: A study of slum tourism travel motivations. *2009–2010 Penn Humanities Forum on Connections.* repository. upenn.edu/uhf_2012/12. Accessed May 21, 2014.

Macartney, S., Bishaw, A., & Fontenot, K. 2013. *Poverty rates for selected detailed race and Hispanic groups by state and place: 2007–2011.* U.S. Bureau of the Census. ACSBR/11–17. www.census.gov/prod/2013pubs/acsbr11-17.pdf. Accessed June 13, 2014.

MacDonald, K., & Parke, R. G. 1986. Parent-child physical play: The effects of sex and age on children and parents. *Sex Roles, 15,* 367–378.

MacDorman, M. F., Matthews, T. J., & Declercq, E. 2014. Trends in out-of-hospital births in the United States, 1990–2012. *NCHS Data Brief #144.* www.cdc.gov/nchs/data/databriefs/db144.pdf. Accessed July 6, 2014.

MacFarquhar, N. 2011. Food prices worldwide hit record levels, fueled by uncertainty, U.N. says. *The New York Times,* February 4.

Macgillivray, I. K. 2000. Educational equity for gay, lesbian, bisexual, transgendered, and queer/questioning students: The demands of democracy and social justice for America's schools. *Education and Urban Society, 32,* 303–323.

MacMillan, R., & Gartner, R. 1999. When she brings home the bacon: Labor-force participation and the risk of spousal violence against women. *Journal of Marriage and the Family, 61,* 947–959.

Manderey, E. J. 2014. End college legacy preferences. *The New York Times.* April 25.

Mantsios, G. 1995. Media magic: Making class invisible. In P. S. Rothenberg (Ed.), *Race, class and gender in the United States.* New York: St. Martin's Press.

Markowitz, L. 2000. A different kind of queer marriage. *Utne Reader,* September–October.

Markus, H. 2013. Who am I? Race, ethnicity, and identity. In S. Ferguson (ed.), *Race, gender, sexuality, and social class: Dimensions of inequality.* Los Angeles: Sage.

Marmot, M. 2004. *The status syndrome: How social standing affects our health and longevity.* New York: Times Books.

Marriage Equality USA. 2014. *1,138 federal rights.* www.marriageequality.org/1-138-federal-rights. Accessed January 22, 2014.

Marshall, B. L. 2002. "Hard science": Gendered constructions of sexual dysfunction in the "Viagra Age." *Sexualities, 5,* 131–159.

Martin, C. L., Eisenbud, L., & Rose, H. 1995. Children's gender-based reasoning about toys. *Child Development, 66,* 1453–1471.

Martin, C. L., & Ruble, D. 2004. Children's search for gender cues. *Current Directions in Psychological Science, 13,* 67–70.

Martin, C. L., & Ruble, D. 2009. Patterns of gender development. *Annual Review of Psychology, 61,* 353–381.

Martin, M. 2010. *Ahead of census, Arab-American group tells community "You ain't white."* National Public Radio. www.npr.org/templates/story/story.php?storyId=124531038. Accessed May 27, 2010.

Martin, M. 2015. *Fear of the black man: Racial bias could affect crime, labor rates.* National Public Radio. www.npr.org/2015/03/30/396405061/fear-of-the-black-man-how-racial-bias-could-affect-crime-labor-rates. Accessed July 23, 2015.

Martin, P., & Midgley, E. 2010. Immigration in America 2010. *Population Bulletin Update.* www.prb.org/pdf10/immigration-update2010.pdf. Accessed July 6, 2010.

Martinez, E. 2003. Seeing more than black and white: Latinos, racism and the cultural dividers. In T. E. Ore (Ed.), *The social construction of difference and inequality.* New York: McGraw-Hill.

Marx, D. M., Ko, S. J., & Friedman, R. A. 2009. The "Obama Effect": How a salient role model reduces race-based performance differences. *Journal of Experimental Social Psychology, 45,* 953–956.

Marx, K., & Engels, F. 1982. *The communist manifesto.* New York: International Publishers. (Original work published 1848)

Mastrilli, T., & Sardo-Brown, D. 2002. Pre-service teachers' knowledge about Islam: A snapshot post September 11, 2001. *Journal of Institutional Psychology, 4,* 159–173.

Mather, M. & Jarosz, B. 2014. *The demography of inequality in the United States.* Population Reference Bureau. www.prb.org/pdf14/united-states-inequality.pdf. Accessed November 30, 2014.

Mathews, L. 1996. More than identity rides on a new racial category. *The New York Times,* July 6.

Matsuda, M. J. 1993. Public response to racist speech: Considering the victim's story. In M. J. Matsuda, C. R. Lawrence III, R. Delgado, & K. Williams Crenshaw (Eds.), *Words that wound.* Boulder, CO: Westview.

Mauer, M. 2009. *The changing racial dynamics of the war on drugs.* The Sentencing Project. www.sentencingproject.org/doc/dp_raceanddrugs.pdf. Accessed July 2, 2010.

Maume, D. J. 1999. Glass ceilings and glass escalators: Occupational segregation and race and sex differences in managerial promotions. *Work and Occupations, 26,* 483–509.

Mayberry, R., Mili, F., & Ofili, E. 2000. Racial and ethnic differences in access to medical care. *Medical Care Research & Review, 57,* 108–146.

McAuliff, M. 2012. Paul Ryan wants "welfare reform round 2." *Huffington Post.* March 20. www.huffingtonpost.com/2012/03/20/paul-ryan-welfare-reform_n_1368277.html. Accessed June 17, 2014.

McCain, F. 1991. Interview with Franklin McCain. In C. Carson, D. J. Garrow, G. Gill, V. Harding, & D. Clark Hine (Eds.), *The Eyes on the Prize civil rights reader.* New York: Penguin.

McCloskey, D. 1999. *Crossing: A memoir.* Chicago: University of Chicago Press.

McElroy, S. 2014. Homework to find a sense of comfort. *The New York Times.* June 1.

McGee, C. 2010. The open road wasn't quite open to all. *The New York Times,* August 23.

McIntosh, P. 2001. White privilege: Unpacking the invisible knapsack. In P. Rothenberg (Ed.), *Race, class, and gender in the United States.* New York: Worth.

McLeod, J. D., & Owens, T. J. 2004. Psychological well-being in the early life course: Variations by socioeconomic status, gender, and race/ethnicity. *Social Psychology Quarterly, 67,* 257–278.

McLoyd, V. C., Cauce, A. M., Takeuchi, D., & Wilson, L. 2000. Marital processes and parental socialization in families of color: A decade review of research. *Journal of Marriage and the Family, 62,* 1070–1094.

McNeil, D. G. 2004. When real food isn't an option. *New York Times,* May 23.

McNeil, D. G. 2007. Drugs banned, world's poor suffer in pain. *The New York Times,* September 10.

McWhorter, J. 2004. Getting over identity. In T. Jacoby (Ed.), *Reinventing the melting pot.* New York: Basic Books.

Mead, M. 1963. *Sex and temperament.* New York: William Morrow.

Meertens, R. W., & Pettigrew, T. F. 1997. Is subtle prejudice really prejudice? *Public Opinion Quarterly, 61,* 54–71.

Merton, R. 1949. Discrimination and the American creed. In R. M. MacIver (Ed.), *Discrimination and national welfare.* New York: Harper & Row.

Merton, R. 1957. *Social theory and social structure.* New York: Free Press.

Messner, M. 2002. Boyhood, organized sports, and the construction of masculinities. In D. M. Newman & J. O'Brien (Eds.), *Sociology: Exploring the architecture of everyday life (Readings).* Thousand Oaks, CA: Pine Forge Press.

Messner, M., & Bozada-Deas. 2010. Separating the men from the moms: The making of adult gender segregation in youth sports. In D. Newman & J. O'Brien (Eds.), *Sociology: Exploring the architecture of everyday life (Readings).* Thousand Oaks, CA: Pine Forge Press.

Meyer, I. H. 1995. Minority stress and mental health in gay men. *Journal of Health and Social Behavior, 36,* 38–56.

Mezey, N. 2013. The privilege of coming out: Race, class, and lesbians' mothering decisions. In S. Ferguson (Ed.), *Race, gender, sexuality and social class: Dimensions of inequality.* Los Angeles: Sage.

Michael, R. T., Gagnon, J. H., Laumann, E. O., & Kolata, G. 1994. *Sex in America: A definitive survey.* Boston: Little, Brown.

Miller, C. C. 2014. Where are the gay chief executives? *The New York Times.* May 16.

Miller, C. C. 2015. How teacher biases can sway girls from math and science. *The New York Times.* February 7.

Millman, M. 1980. *Such a pretty face.* New York: Norton.

Mintz, S., & Kellogg, S. 1988. *Domestic revolutions.* New York: Free Press.

Mishel, L., Bivens, J., Gould, E., & Shierholz, H. 2013. *The state of working America.* Economic Policy Institute. stateofworkingAmerica.org/subjects/overview/?reader. Accessed May 31, 2013.

Mitford, J. 1993. *The American way of birth.* New York: Plume.

Mokhiber, R., & Weissman, R. 2004. The ten worst corporations of 2004. *Multinational Monitor,* December. pp. 8–21.

Molloy, B. L., & Herzberger, S. D. 1998. Body image and self-esteem: A comparison of African-American and Caucasian women. *Sex Roles, 38,* 631–643.

Monazea, E. M., & Abdel Khalek, E. M. 2010. *Domestic violence high in Egypt, affecting women's reproductive health.* Population Reference Bureau. www.prb.org/Articles/2010/domesticviolence-egypt.aspx. Accessed June 20, 2010.

Mooallem, J. 2010. The love that dare not squawk its name. *The New York Times Magazine,* April 4.

Moore, M. 2011. *Invisible families: Gay identities, relationships, and motherhood among black women.* Berkeley: University of California Press.

Moore, R. B. 1992. Racist stereotyping in the English language. In M. L. Anderson & P. H. Collins (Eds.), *Race, class and gender: An anthology.* Belmont, CA: Wadsworth.

Morello, C. 2011. 9 million Americans estimated to be gay or bisexual, but solid figures elusive. *Washington Post,* April 7.

Morgan, M. 1982. Television and adolescents' sex role stereotypes: A longitudinal study. *Journal of Personality and Social Psychology, 48,* 1173–1190.

Morgan, M. 1987. Television sex role attitudes and sex role behavior. *Journal of Early Adolescence, 7,* 269–282.

Morgan, R. 1996. *Sisterhood is global.* New York: The Feminist Press at the City University of New York.

Morris, E. 2006. *An unexpected minority: White kids in an urban school.* New Brunswick, NJ: Rutgers University Press.

Morrongiello, B. A., & Hogg, K. 2004. Mothers' reactions to children misbehaving in ways that can lead to injury: Implications for gender differences in children's risk taking and injuries. *Sex Roles, 50,* 103–118.

Mui, Y. Q., & Jenkins, C. L. 2014. For some black women, economy and willingness to aid family strains finances. *Washington Post.* February 5.

Murguia, E., & Telles, E. E. 1996. Phenotype and schooling among Mexican Americans. *Sociology of Education, 69,* 276–289.

Murphy, D. E. 2004. Imagining life without illegal immigrants. *The New York Times,* January 11.

Murphy, M. L. 1997. The elusive bisexual: Social categorization and lexico-semantic change. In A. Livia & K. Hall (Eds.), *Queerly phrased: Language, gender, and sexuality.* New York: Oxford University Press.

Nagel, J. 2003. *Race, ethnicity, and sexuality: Intimate intersections, forbidden frontiers.* New York: Oxford University Press.

Nagourney, A. 2014. Honolulu shores up tourism with crackdown on homeless. *The New York Times.* June 23.

Nanda, S. 2003. Hijra and Sādhin: Neither man nor woman in India. In S. LaFont (Ed.), *Constructing sexualities: Readings in sexuality, gender, and culture.* Upper Saddle River, NJ: Prentice Hall.

National Academies. 2013. *Americans have worse health than people in other high-income countries; Health disadvantage is pervasive across age and socio-economic groups.* www8.nationalacademies.org/onpinews/newsitem. aspx?RecordID=13497. Accessed January 10, 2013.

National Alliance to End Homelessness. 2015. *State of homelessness in America 2015.* www.endhomelessness.org/library/entry/the-state-of-homelessness-in-america-2015. Accessed June 2, 2015.

National Association for Single Sex Public Education. 2013. *Single-sex schools/ schools with single-sex classrooms/What's the difference?* www.singlesex-schools.org/schools-schools.htm. Accessed June 23, 2013.

National Association of Black Social Workers. 2003. *Preserving families.* www. nabsw.org/mserver/PreservingFamilies.aspx. Accessed April 13, 2011.

NCAA. 2013. *Estimated probability of competing in athletics beyond the high school interscholastic level.* www.ncaa.org/sites/default/files/Probability-of-going-pro-methodology_Update2013.pdf. Accessed June 2, 2015.

National Center for Education Statistics. 2010. *Status and trends in the education of racial and ethnic minorities.* NCES2010-015. nces.ed.gov/pubs2010/2010015/ tables/table_24_1.asp. Accessed June 17, 2014.

National Center for Education Statistics. 2013. *Characteristics of public and private elementary and secondary school teachers in the United States: Results from the 2011–12 schools and staffing survey.* www.nces.ed.gov/ pubs2013/2013314.pdf. Accessed June 6, 2015.

National Center for Education Statistics. 2014a. *Digest of education statistics.* www.nces.ed.gov/programs/digest/d13/. Accessed June 12, 2015.

National Center for Education Statistics. 2014b. *Fast facts: Graduation rates, Table 326.10.* www.nces.ed.gov/programs/digest/d13/tables/dt13_326.10. asp. Accessed June 6, 2015.

National Center for Fair and Open Testing. 2014. *SAT score trend remains flat; test-fixated school policies have not improved college readiness even as measured by other standardized exams.* www.fairtest.org/sites/default/files/SATScores2014Release.pdf. Accessed May 27, 2015.

National Center for Health Statistics. 2014. *Health: United States: 2013.* www.cdc.gov/nchs/data/hus/hus13.pdf. Accessed July 23, 2015.

National Center for Missing and Exploited Children. 2014. *Child sex trafficking.* www.missisngkids.com/1in6. Accessed May 26, 2015.

National Coalition for the Homeless. 2014. *Vulnerable to hate: A survey of hate crimes and violence committed against homeless people in 2013.* national-homeless.org/wp-content/uploads/2014/06/Hate-Crimes-2013-FINAL.pdf. Accessed August 1, 2014.

National Crime Records Bureau. 2014. *Crime in India: 2013.* ncrb.nic.in/CD-CII-2013/Home.asp. Accessed June 14, 2015.

National Digestive Diseases Information Clearinghouse. 2011. *Hemochromatosis.* http://digestive.niddk.nih.gov/ddiseases/pubs/hemochromatosis. Accessed April 1, 2011.

National Eating Disorders Association. 2011. *Statistics: Eating disorders and their precursors.* www.nationaleatingdisorders.org/informationresources/general-information.php#factsstatistics. Accessed June 20, 2011.

National Eating Disorders Association. 2014. *Diversity.* Ww.nationaleatingdisorders.org/diversity. Accessed July 5, 2014.

National Employment Law Project. 2014. *2013 annual report.* www.nelp.org/page/-/Reports/NELP-2013-Annual-Report.pdf?nocdn=1. Accessed July 8, 2014.

National Employment Law Project. 2015. *It's time to raise the minimum wage.* www.nclp.org/publication/time-raise-minimum-wage/. Accessed June 25, 2015.

National Fair Housing Alliance. 2015. *Where you live matters: 2015 Fair Housing Trends Report.* www.nationalfairhousing.org/LinkClick.aspx?filcticke=SYWmBgwpazA%3d&tabid=3917&mid=5321. Accessed June 3, 2015.

National Law Center on Homelessness and Poverty. 2014. *No safe place: The criminalization of homelessness in U.S. cities.* www.nlchp.org/documents/No_Safe_Place. Accessed July 17, 2014.

National Low Income Housing Coalition. 2015. *Out of reach 2015.* www.nlihc.org/sites/default/files/oor/OOR_2015_FULL.pdf. Accessed May 28, 2015.

National Public Radio. 2009. *In India, skin-whitening creams reflect old biases.* www.npr.org/templates/story/story.php?storyId=120340646. Accessed June 18, 2010.

National Women's Law Center. 2006. *The Paycheck Fairness Act: Helping to close the wage gap for women.* www.pay-equity.org/PDFs/PaycheckFairnessActApr06.pdf. Accessed September 5, 2009.

Neary, I. 1986. Socialist and Communist party attitudes towards discrimination against Japan's Burakumin. *Political Studies, 34,* 556–574.

Neary, I. 2003. Burakumin at the end of history. *Social Research, 70,* 269–294.

Netzhammer, E. C., & Shamp, S. A. 1994. Guilt by association. Homosexuality and AIDS on prime-time television. In R. J. Ringer (Ed.), *Queer words, queer images.* New York: NYU Press.

Neumeister, L. 2015. Suit targets bias of post-9/11 US. *Lewiston Sun Journal.* June 22.h

Newman, D. M. 2017. *Sociology: Exploring the architecture of everyday life.* Thousand Oaks, CA: Pine Forge Press.

NOMAS. 2014. *Statement of principles.* site.nomas.org/principles/. Accessed July 16, 2014.

Nordberg, J. 2010. Where boys are prized, girls live the part. *The New York Times,* September 21.

Nordland, R. 2014. In spite of the law, Afghan "honor killings" of women continue. *The New York Times.* May 3.

Northridge, M. E., Stover, G. N., Rosenthal, J. E., & Sherard, D. 2003. Environmental equity and health: Understanding complexity and moving forward. *American Journal of Public Health, 93,* 209–214.

Norton, M. I., & Sommers, S. R. 2011. Whites see racism as a zero-sum game that they are now losing. *Perspectives in Psychological Science, 6,* 215–218.

Nossiter, A. 2014. Nigeria uses law and whip to "sanitize" gays. *The New York Times.* February 9.

Nossiter, A. 2015. Former captives in Nigeria tell of mass rapes. *The New York Times.* May 19.

O'Brien, J. 1999. *Social prisms: Reflections on everyday myths and paradoxes.* Thousand Oaks, CA: Pine Forge Press.

O'Brien, M., & Huston, A. C. 1985. Development of sex-typed play behavior in toddlers. *Developmental Psychology, 21,* 866–871.

Ocampo, A. C. 2012. Making masculinity: Negotiations of gender presentation among Latino gay men. *Latino Studies, 10,* 448–472.

Omi, M., & Winant, H. 1992. Racial formations. In P. S. Rothenberg (Ed.), *Race, class and gender in the United States.* New York: St. Martin's Press.

Onishi, N. 2001. On the scale of beauty, weight weighs heavily. *The New York Times,* February 12.

Onishi, N. 2009. Japan's outcasts still wait for acceptance. *The New York Times,* January 16.

Ordover, N. 1996. Eugenics, the gay gene, and the science of backlash. *Socialist Review, 26,* 125–144.

Orenstein, P. 2008. Mixed messenger. *The New York Times Magazine,* March 23.

Orenstein, P. 2010. The fat trap. *The New York Times Magazine,* April 18.

Orfield, G., Frankenberg, E., Ee, J., & Kuscera J. 2014. *Brown at 60: Great progress, a long retreat and an uncertain future.* The Civil Rights Project.

civilrightsproject.ucla.edu/research/k-12-education/integration-and-diversity/brown-at-60-great-progress-a-long-retreat-and-an-uncertain-future. Accessed June 10, 2014.

Organ Procurement and Transplantion Network. 2015. *National data*. optn.transplant.hrsa.gov/converge/latestData/step2.asp. Accessed June 3, 2015.

Ortner, S. B. 1996. *Making gender: The politics and erotics of culture*. Boston: Beacon Press.

Ortner, S. B. 1998. Identities: The hidden life of class. *Journal of Anthropological Research, 54*, 1–17.

Oxfam. 2014. *Working for the few: Political capture and economic inequality*. www.oxfam.org/en/policy/working-for-the-few-economic-inequality. Accessed January 21, 2014.

Padavic, I., & Reskin, B. 2004. Moving up and taking charge. In L. Richardson, V. Taylor, & N. Whittier (Eds.), *Feminist frontiers*. New York: McGraw-Hill.

Padawer, R. 2012. What's so bad about a boy who wants to wear a dress? *The New York Times Magazine*. August 8.

Padawer, R. 2014. Sisterhood is complicated. *The New York Times Magazine*. October 19.

Parker, A. 2014a. Gay G.O.P. candidates feature partners in ads. *The New York Times*. June 20.

Parker, A. 2014b. Reclaiming words that smear. *The New York Times*. April 12.

Parker, S., Nichter, M., Nichter, M., Vuckovic, N., Sims, C., & Ritenbaugh, C. 1995. Body image and weight concerns among African American and white adolescent females: Differences that make a difference. *Human Organization, 54*, 103–114.

Parker-Pope, T. 2011. Fat stigma is fast spreading around the globe. *The New York Times*. March 31.

Parker-Pope, T. 2012. Overtreatment is taking a harmful toll. *The New York Times*. August 28.

Parker-Pope, T. 2013. Overweight patients face bias. *The New York Times*. April 30.

Parsons, T. 1951. *The social system*. New York: Free Press.

Parsons, T., & Bales, R. F. 1955. *Family, socialization and interaction process*. Glencoe, IL: Free Press.

Pascoe, C. J. 2010, Dude, you're a fag? Adolescent male homophobia. In S. Ferguson (Ed.), *Mapping the social landscape*. New York: McGraw-Hill.

Passel, J. S., & Cohn, D. 2011. *Unauthorized immigrant population: National and state trends 2010*. Pew Hispanic Center. www.pewhispanic.org/2011/02/01/v-workers/. Accessed June 1, 2014.

Passel, J., Cohn, D., & Gonzalez-Barrera, A. 2012. *Net migration from Mexico falls to zero—and perhaps less*. Pew Hispanic Center. www.pewhispanic.org/2012/04/23/net-migration-from-mexico-falls-to-zero-and-perhaps-less/. Accessed June 28, 2013.

Passel, J. S., Cohn, D., Krogstad, J. M., & Gonzalez-Barrera, A. 2014. *As growth stalls, unauthorized immigrant population becomes more settled.* Pew Research Center. www.pewhispanic.org/files/2014/09/2014-09-03_Unauthorized-Final. pdf. Accessed June 21, 2015.

Patten, E. 2013. *The black-white and urban-rural divides in perceptions of racial fairness.* Pew Research Center. www.pewresearch.org/fact-tank/2013/08/28/ the-black-white-and-urban-rural-divides-in-perceptions-of-racial-fairness/. Accessed July 7, 2014.

Pattillo-McCoy, M. 1999. *Black picket fences: Privilege and peril among the black middle class.* Chicago: University of Chicago Press.

Paul, A. M. 2004. Taming your mood swings. *Shape Magazine,* July.

Payer, L. 1988. *Medicine and culture.* New York: Penguin.

Pear, R. 2000. Studies find research on women lacking. *The New York Times,* April 30.

Pearce, D. 1979. Gatekeepers and homeseekers: Institutional patterns of racial steering. *Social Problems, 26,* 325–342.

Pearce, D. 2014. Competing poverty measures: An analysis. *Footnotes.* January.

Penner, A. M., & Saperstein, A. 2013. Engendering racial perceptions: An inter-sectional analysis of how social status shapes race. *Gender & Society, 27,* 319–344.

Perez-Peña, R. 2003. Study finds asthma in 25% of children in central Harlem. *The New York Times,* April 19.

Pérez-Peña, R. 2015. The odd case of the woman playing black. *The New York Times.* June 13.

Peri, G. 2009. The effect of immigration on productivity: Evidence from U.S. states. *National Bureau of Economic Research Working Paper 15507.* www. nber.org/papers/w15507.pdf?new_window=1. Accessed July 5, 2010.

Perlez, J. 1998. A wall not yet built casts the shadow of racism. *The New York Times,* July 2.

Peters, M. F. 1988. *Parenting in black families with young children: A historical perspective.* In H. P. McAdoo (Ed.), Black families. Newbury Park, CA: Sage.

Peterson, R. R. 1996. A re-evaluation of the economic consequences of divorce. *American Sociological Review, 61,* 528–536.

Peterson, S. B., & Lach, M. A. 1990. Gender stereotypes in children's books: Their prevalence and influence in cognitive and affective development. *Gender and Education, 2,* 185–197.

Pettit, B. 2012. *Invisible men: Mass incarceration and the myth of black progress.* New York: Russell Sage.

Pettit, B., & Western, B. 2004. Mass imprisonment and the life course: Race and class inequality in U.S. incarceration. *American Sociological Review, 69,* 151–169.

Pew Forum on Religion and Public Life. 2008. *U.S. religious landscape survey: Religious affiliation, diverse and dynamic.* http://religions.pewforum.org/pdf/report-religious-landscape-study-full.pdf. Accessed May 30, 2011.

Pew Forum on Religion and Public Life. 2011. *The future of the global Muslim population.* http://pewforum.org/The-Future-of-the-Global-Muslim-Population.aspx. Accessed June 10, 2011.

Pew Research Center. 2009. *Public backs affirmative action, but not minority preferences.* www.pewresearch.org/2009/06/02/public-backs-affirmative-action-but-not-minority-preferences/. Accessed June 18, 2014.

Pew Research Center. 2012a. *Pew Center for the People and the Press Values Survey.* www.people-press.org/question-search?qid=1811628&pic=51&ccid=51#top. Accessed June 1, 2014.

Pew Research Center. 2014a. *For 2016 hopefuls, Washington experience could do more harm than good.* www.people-press.org/files/legacy-pdf/5-19-14%20Presidential%20Traits%20Release.pdf. Accessed May 19, 2014.

Pew Research Center. 2014b. *Sharp racial divisions in reactions to Brown, Garner decisions.* www.people-press.org/2014/12/08/sharp-racial-divisions-in-reactions-to-brown-garner-decisions. Accessed June 2, 2015.

Pew Research Center. 2015a. *America's changing religious landscape.* www.pewforum.org/2015/05/12/americas-changing-religious-landscape/. Accessed May 18, 2015.

Pew Research Center. 2015b. *Broad public support for legal status for undocumented immigrants.* www.people-press.org/files/2015/06/6-4-15-immigration-release.pdf. Accessed June 19, 2015.

Pew Research Center. 2015c. *Multiracial in America: Proud, diverse, and growing in numbers.* www.pewsocialtrends.org/files/2015/06/2015-06-11_multiracial_in_america_final updated.pdf. Accessed June 11, 2015.

Pew Research Center. 2015d. *Support for same-sex marriage at record high, but key segments remain opposed.* www.people press.org/files/2015/06/6-8-15-Same-sex-marriage-release1.pdf. Accessed June 26, 2015.

Phillips, K. 2002. *Wealth and democracy.* New York: Broadway Books.

Phipps, A. 2009. Rape and respectability: Ideas about sexual violence and social class. *Sociology, 43,* 667–683.

Pieterse, J. N. 1995. "White" negroes. In G. Dines & J. M. Humez (Eds.), *Gender, race and class in media.* Thousand Oaks, CA: Sage.

Piketty, T. 2014. *Capital in the twenty-first century.* Cambridge, MA: Belknap Press.

Piper, A. 1992. Passing for white, passing for black. *Transition, 58,* 4–32.

Planty, M., Langton, L., Krebs, C., Berzofsky, M., & Smiley-McDonald, H. 2013. *Female victims of sexual violence 1994–2010.* U.S. Bureau of Justice Statistics. NCJ240655. www.bjs.gov/content/pub/pdf/fvsv9410.pdf. Accessed June 18, 2013.

Polgreen, L. 2005. Ghana's uneasy embrace of slavery's diaspora. *The New York Times,* December 27.

Political correctness. 2004. Wikipedia on-line encyclopedia. http://en.wikipedia. org/wiki/Political_Correctness. Accessed June 18, 2004.

Pollard, K. 2011. *The gender gap in college enrollment and graduation.* Population Reference Bureau. April. www.prb.org/Articles/2011/gender-gap-in-education.aspx?p=1. Accessed April 19, 2011.

Population Reference Bureau. 2004. *The wealth gap in health,* May. www.prg. org. Accessed July 15, 2004.

Population Reference Bureau. 2014a. *Extreme poverty rate falls in many countries.* www.prb.org/Publications/Articles/2014/wpds-2014-extreme-poverty. aspx. Accessed October 21, 2014.

Population Reference Bureau. 2014b. *World population data sheet.* www.prb. org/pdf14/2014-world-population-data-sheet_eng.pdf. Accessed September 7, 2014.

Porter, E. 2005. Illegal immigrants are bolstering Social Security with billions. *The New York Times,* April 5.

Potts, A., Grace, V., Gavey, N., & Vares, T. 2004. "Viagra stories": Challenging erectile dysfunction. *Social Science and Medicine, 59,* 489–499.

Povich, D., Roberts, B., & Mather, M. 2014. *Low-income working mothers and state policy: Investing for a better economic future.* The Working Poor Families Project. www.workingpoorfamilies.org/wp-content/uploads/2014/02/WPFP_Low-Income-Working-Mothers-Report_021214.pdf. Accessed June 18, 2014.

Powell, M. 2009. Suit accuses Wells Fargo of steering blacks to subprime mortgages in Baltimore. *The New York Times,* June 7.

Powell, M. 2012. In police training, a dark film on U.S. Muslims. *The New York Times.* January 24.

Prasad, V., Vandross, A., Toomey, C., Cheung, M., Rho, J., Quinn, S., Chacko, S. J., Borkar, D., Gall, V., Selvarai, S., Ho, N., & Cifu, A. 2013. A decade of reversal: An analysis of 146 contradicted medical practices. *Mayo Clinic Proceedings, 88,* 790–798.

Probe into race link with homelessness. 2002. *Community Care,* September 19.

ProQuest Statistical Abstract. 2013. *Statistical abstract of the United States: 2013 Online edition.* si.conquestsystems.com/sa/index.html?id=5d40ca75-82e1=4194-b9dc-44cd63428eaa#. Accessed January 16, 2013.

ProQuest Statistical Abstract. 2014. *Statistical abstract of the United States: 2013 Online edition.* http://statistical.proquest.com.ezproxy.depauw.edu/statisticalinsight/search/basic/sibasicsearch. Accessed June 1, 2014.

ProQuest Statistical Abstract. 2015. *Statistical abstract of the United States: 2015 Online edition.* http://statabs.proquest.com.ezproxy.depauw.edu/sa/index.html. Accessed July 2, 2015.

Public Policy Polling. 2011. *MS GOP: Bryant for Gov., Barbour or Huckabee for Pres.* April 7. www.publicpolicypolling.com/pdf/PPP_Release_MS_0407915. pdf. Accessed August 1, 2014.

Queen, R. 1997. I don't speak spritch: Locating lesbian language. In A. Livia & K. Hall (Eds.), *Queerly phrased: Language, gender, and sexuality.* New York: Oxford University Press.

Quinney, R. 1970. *The social reality of crime.* Boston: Little, Brown.

Rabin, R. C. 2014a. Ban on medicare coverage of sex-change surgery is lifted. *The New York Times.* May 31.

Rabin, R. C. 2014b. Guideline calls routine pelvic exams unnecessary. *The New York Times.* June 30.

Rabin, R. C. 2014c. Health researchers will get $10.1 million to counter gender bias in studies. *The New York Times,* September 23.

Rabin, R. C. 2014d. Labs are told to start including a neglected variable: females. *The New York Times.* May 15.

Raffaelli, M., & Ontai, L. L. 2004. Gender socialization in Latino/a families: Results from two retrospective studies. *Sex Roles, 50,* 287–299.

Rampell, C. 2010. Women now a majority in American workplaces. *The New York Times,* February 6.

Rankin, S. R. 2003. *Campus climate for gay, lesbian, bisexual, and transgender people: A national perspective.* National Gay and Lesbian Task Force. www.thetaskforce.org/downloads/CampusClimate.pdf. Accessed September 22, 2004.

Ransom, E. I., & Elder, L. K. 2003. *Nutrition of women and adolescent girls: Why it matters.* Population Reference Bureau, July. www.prb.org. Accessed July 15, 2004.

Rattner, S. 2014. Fear not the coming of the robots. *The New York Times.* June 22.

Raven, D. 2015. ISIS: Pregnant girls aged 9 having secret abortions after being raped by twisted Islamic State militants. *The Mirror.* www.mirror.co.uk/news/world-news/isis-pregnant-girls-aged-9-5587288. Accessed June 10, 2015.

Reardon, S. F., Fox, L., & Townsend, J. 2015. Neighborhood income composition by household race and income, 1990–2009. *The Annals of the American Academy of Political and Social Science, 660,* 78–97.

Reddy, G. 2005. *With respect to sex: Negotiating Hijra identity in South Asia.* Chicago: University of Chicago Press.

Reeves, H. 2013. In the old days, you'd smell the milk. *The New York Times Magazine.* November 10.

Reeves, R. 2004. Men remain stuck in cages of their own creation. *The New Statesman,* August 16.

Reiman, J., & Leighton, P. 2013. *The rich get richer and the poor get prison.* Boston: Pearson.

Reinisch, J. M., Rosenblum, L. A., Rubin, D. B., & Schulsinger, M. F. 1997. Sex differences emerge during the first year of life. In M. R. Walsh (Ed.), *Women, men and gender: Ongoing debates.* New Haven, CT: Yale University Press.

Reitzel, L. R., Regan, S. D., Nguyen, N., Cromley, E. K., Strong, L. L., Wetter, D. W., & McNeill, L. H. 2014. Density and proximity of fast food restaurants and body mass index among African Americans. *American Journal of Public Health, 104,* 110–116.

Relethford, J. H., Stern, M. P., Caskill, S. P., & Hazuda, H. P. 1983. Social class, admixture, and skin color variation in Mexican Americans and Anglo Americans living in San Antonio, Texas. *American Journal of Physical Anthropology, 61,* 97–102.

Rennison, C. M., & Welchans, S. 2000. Intimate partner violence. *United States Bureau of Justice Statistics Special Report.* Washington, DC: U.S. Government Printing Office.

Renzetti, C. M., & Curran, D. J. 2003. *Women, men, and society.* Boston: Allyn & Bacon.

Research findings affirm health of women hinges on reform on clinical research. 2003. *Women's Health Weekly,* August 14.

Reuters. 2014. Attorney General Eric Holder: Persistent, subtle racism poses bigger threat than "outbursts of bigotry." *Newsweek.* May 17. www.newsweek.com/attorney-general-eric-holder-persistent-subtle-racism-poses-bigger-threat-outbursts-2513450. Accessed June 12, 2014.

Reyes, L., & Rubie, P. 1994. *Hispanics in Hollywood: An encyclopedia of film and television.* New York: Garland Press.

Rhoden, W. C. 2006. *Forty million dollar slaves: The rise, fall, and redemption of the black athlete.* New York: Crown.

Ribando, C. M. 2007. *Trafficking in persons: U.S. policy and issues for Congress.* www.humantrafficking.org/uploads/publications/20070806_120229_RL30545.pdf. Accessed September 5, 2009.

Rich, M. 2011. Nature? Nurture? Not so fast. . . . *The New York Times,* April 17.

Rich, M. 2014. Old tactic gets new use: Schools segregate boys and girls. *The New York Times.* December 1.

Richardson, L. 1997. An old experiment's legacy: Distrust of AIDS treatment. *The New York Times,* April 21.

Richardson, L. 2004. Gender stereotyping in the English language. In L. Richardson, V. Taylor, & N. Whittier (Eds.), *Feminist frontiers.* New York: McGraw-Hill.

Rimer, S., & Arenson, K. W. 2004. Top colleges take more blacks, but which ones? *The New York Times,* June 24.

Risen, J. 2012. Military has not solved problem of sexual assault, women say. *The New York Times.* November 2.

Risman, B., & Myers, K. 1997. As the twig is bent: Children reared in feminist households. *Qualitative Sociology, 20,* 229–252.

Risman, B., & Seale, E. 2010. Betwixt and be tween: Gender contradictions among middle schoolers. In B. Risman (Ed.), *Families as they really are.* New York: Norton.

Roberts, E. F. S. 2012. *God's laboratory: Assisted reproduction in the Andes.* Berkeley: University of California Press.

Roberts, S. 2008. A nation of none and all of the above. *The New York Times,* August 17.

Roberts, S. 2010a. Births to minorities approach a majority. *The New York Times,* March 12.

Roberts, S. 2010b. Census figures challenge views of race and ethnicity. *The New York Times,* January 21.

Robinson, R. V., & Bell, W. 1978. Equality, success and social justice in England and the United States. *American Sociological Review, 43,* 125–143.

Rodriguez, C. E., & Cordero-Guzman, H. 2004. Placing race in context. In C. A. Gallagher (Ed.), *Rethinking the color line: Readings in race and ethnicity.* New York: McGraw-Hill.

Roediger, D. R. 1998. *Black on white: Black writers on what it means to be white.* New York: Schocken.

Roehling, M. V. 1999. Weight-based discrimination in employment: Psychological and legal aspects. *Personnel Psychology, 52,* 969–1017.

Rogmans, W. 2001. The rich and the poor. *Injury Control and Safety Promotion, 8,* 129–130.

Romano, A., & Samuels, A. 2012. Is Obama making it worse? *Newsweek.* April 16.

Romero, M. 2010. Life as the maid's daughter: An exploration of the everyday boundaries of race, class, and gender. In D. M. Newman & J. O'Brien (Eds.), *Sociology: Exploring the architecture of everyday life (Readings).* Thousand Oaks, CA: Pine Forge Press.

Romesburg, D. 1997. *Thirteen theories to "cure" homosexuality.* www.law.harvard.edu/students/orgs/lambda/1_13theo.html. Accessed January 11, 2005.

Rose, M. 2004. The mind at work: Valuing the intelligence of the American worker. New York: Viking.

Rosenbloom, S. 2014. In pursuit of the "pink dollar." *The New York Times.* June 1.

Ross, P. 2014. "Cinderella surgery" on the rise in US, Women reshape feet to better fit into expensive shoes. *International Business Times.* April 29. www.ibtimes.com/cinderella-surgery-rise-us-women-reshape-feet-better-fit-expensive-heels-157796. Accessed July 2, 2014.

Rothenberg, P. 1992. *Race, class, and gender in the United States.* New York: St. Martin's Press.

Rothenberg, P. 2000. *Invisible privilege: A memoir about race, class, and gender.* Lawrence: University of Kansas Press.

Rothman, B. K. 1984. Women, health and medicine. In J. Freeman (Ed.), *Women: A feminist perspective.* Palo Alto, CA: Mayfield.

Rothman, B. K., & Caschetta, M. B. 1999. Treating health: Women and medicine. In S. J. Ferguson (Ed.), *Mapping the social landscape: Readings in sociology.* Mountain View, CA: Mayfield.

Rothschild, N. 1990. *New York City neighborhoods.* New York: Academic Press.

Rothstein, R. 2014. *The racial achievement gap, segregated schools, and segregated neighborhoods—A constitutional insult.* Economic Policy Institute.

www.epi.org/publication/the-racial-achievement-gap-segregated-schools-and-segregated-neighborhoods-a-constitutional-insult/. Accessed June 4, 2015.

Rubin, J. Z., Provenzano, F. J., & Luria, Z. 1974. The eye of the beholder: Parents' views on sex of newborns. *American Journal of Orthopsychiatry, 44,* 512–519.

Rubin, L. 1990. *Erotic wars: What happened to the sexual revolution?* New York: Harper Perennial.

Rubin, L. 1994. *Families on the fault line.* New York: Harper Perennial.

Rubinstein, S., & Caballero, B. 2000. Is Miss America an undernourished role model? *Journal of the American Medical Association, 283,* 1569.

Rudman, L. A., & Glick, P. 1999. Feminized management and backlash toward agentic women: The hidden costs to women of a kinder, gentler image of middle managers. *Journal of Personality and Social Psychology, 77,* 1004–1010.

Sadker, M., & Sadker, D. 2002. Failing at fairness: Hidden lessons. In S. Ferguson (Ed.), *Mapping the social landscape.* New York: McGraw-Hill.

Sadker, M., Sadker, D., Fox, L., & Salata, M. 2004. Gender equity in the classroom: The unfinished agenda. In M. S. Kimmel (Ed.), *The gendered society reader.* New York: Oxford University Press.

Saez, E. 2012. *Striking it richer: The evolution of top incomes in the United States (updated with 2009 and 2010 estimates).* Working paper. University of California. elsa.berkeley.edu/~saez/saez-UStopincomes-2010.pdf. Accessed June 2, 2013.

Sagal, P. 2015. The fear factor. *Runner's World.* June.

Sage, G. H. 2001. Racial equality and sport. In D. S. Eitzen (Ed.), *Sport in contemporary society.* New York: Worth.

Samuels, A. 2004. Smooth operations. *Newsweek,* July 5.

Sanchez, D. T., & Garcia, J. A. 2012. Putting race in context: Socioeconomic status predicts racial fluidity. In S. T. Fiske & H. R. Markus (Eds.), *Facing social class: How societal rank influences interaction.* New York: Russell Sage.

Sander, T. H. 2005. A friend in need. *Boston Globe,* November 14.

Sanger-Katz, M. 2014. Number of Americans without health insurance is down by about 25 percent. *The New York Times.* October 27.

Saperstein, A., & Penner, A. M. 2010. The race of a criminal record: How incarceration colors racial perceptions. *Social Problems, 57,* 92–113.

Saperstein, A., Penner, A. M., & Light, R. 2013. Racial formation in perspective: Connecting individuals, institutions and power relations. *Annual Review of Sociology, 39,* 359–378.

Saul, J. 2015. Racist CVS managers profiled minorities for shoplifting: suit. *New York Post.* June 3.

Saulnier, C. F. 2002. Deciding who to see: Lesbians discuss their preferences in health and mental health care providers. Social Work, 47, 355–365.

Saulny, S. 2011. Black and white and married in the deep south: A shifting image. *The New York Times.* March 20.

Save the Children. 2014. *State of the world's mothers 2014.* www.savethechildren. org. Accessed July 2, 2014.

Savin-Williams, R. C. 2007. Dating and romantic relationships among gay, lesbian, and bisexual youths. In S. Ferguson (Ed.), *Shifting the center.* New York: McGraw-Hill.

Schafft, K. A., Jensen, E. B., & Hinrichs, C. C. 2009. Food deserts and over-weight schoolchildren: Evidence from Pennsylvania. *Rural Sociology, 74,* 153–177.

Schilt, K. 2009. Tomboy/sissy. In J. O'Brien (Ed.), *Encyclopedia of gender and society.* Thousand Oaks, CA: Sage.

Schnittker, J. 2004. Social distance in the clinical encounter: Interactional and sociodemographic foundations for mistrust in physicians. *Social Psychology Quarterly, 67,* 217–235.

Schooler, C. 1996. Cultural and social structural explanations of cross-national psychological differences. *Annual Review of Sociology, 22,* 323–349.

Schulman, M. 2013. Generation LGBTQIA. *The New York Times.* January 10.

Schwartz, J., Revkin, A. C., & Wald, M. L. 2005. In reviving New Orleans, a challenge of many tiers. The New York Times, September 12.

Schwartzman, L. F. 2007. Does money whiten? Intergenerational changes in racial classification. *American Sociological Review, 72,* 940–963.

Sciolino, E. 2004. Spain mobilizes against scourge of machismo. *The New York Times,* July 14.

Scott, L. D. 2003. The relation of racial identity and racial socialization to coping with discrimination among African American adolescents. *Journal of Black Studies, 33,* 520–538.

Screen Actors Guild. 2007. *A different America on screen.* www.sagaftra.org/ files/sag/documents/CastingDataReport.pdf. Accessed June 2, 2014.

Scully, A., & Favreau, D. 1986. A chance to cut is a chance to cure: Sexual surgery for psychosis in three nineteenth century societies. In S. Spitzer & A. T. Scull (Eds.), *Research in law, deviance and social control (Vol. 8).* Greenwich, CT: JAI Press.

Searcey, D. 2014. For women in midlife, decades of work force gains slip away. *The New York Times.* June 24.

Seelye, K. Q., & Bidgood, J. 2014. Police official in New Hampshire resigns amid uproar over slur against Obama. *The New York Times.* May 20.

Sehgal, P. 2015. Power play. *The New York Times Magazine.* July 19.

Seidman, S. 2004. *Beyond the closet: The transformation of gay and lesbian life.* New York: Routledge.

Seldes, G. 1985. *The great thoughts.* New York: Ballantine.

Sengupta, S. 2004. Relentless attacks on women in West Sudan draw an outcry. *The New York Times,* October 26.

The Sentencing Project. 2014. *Facts about prison and people in prison.* sentencingproject.org/doc/publications/inc_Facts About Prisons.pdf. Accessed June 25, 2014.

Serrano, R. A. 2011. Federal panel OKs shorter sentences for crack offenders. *The Seattle Times.* June 30.

Setoodeh, R. 2010. Straight jacket. *Newsweek,* May 10.

Seuss, Dr. 1961. *The Sneetches and other stories.* New York: Random House.

Severson, K., & Hu, W. 2013. Cut in food stamps forces hard choices on poor. *The New York Times.* November 8.

Sexual harassment support. 2009. *Sexual harassment in the workplace.* www.sexualharassmentsupport.org/SHworkplace.html. Accessed July 2, 2010.

Shakin, M., Shakin, D., & Sternglanz, S. H. 1985. Infant clothing: Sex labeling for strangers. *Sex Roles, 12,* 955–964.

Shanker, T. 2004. Inquiry faults commanders in assaults on cadets. *The New York Times,* December 8.

Shanklin, E. 1994. *Anthropology and race.* Belmont, CA: Wadsworth.

Shapiro, T. M. 2010. The hidden cost of being African American. In S. J. Ferguson (Ed.), *Mapping the social landscape.* New York: McGraw-Hill.

Shipler, D. K. 2004. *The working poor: Invisible in America.* New York: Knopf.

Shoemaker, N. 1997. How Indians got to be red. *American Historical Review, 102,* 625–644.

Shoener, S. 2014. Two-parent households can be lethal. *The New York Times.* June 22.

Short, K. 2012. The research: Supplemental poverty measure, 2011. *Current Population Reports, P60-244.* www.census.gov/prod/2012pubs/p60-244.pdf. Accessed June 1, 2013.

Shugart, H. A. 2003. She shoots, she scores: Mediated construction of contemporary female athletes in coverage of the 1999 US Women's soccer team. *Western Journal of Communication, 67,* 1–31.

Shweder, R. A. 1997. It's called poor health for a reason. *The New York Times,* March 9.

Siddiqui, S. 2014. American's attitudes toward Muslims and Arabs are getting worse, poll finds. *Huffington Post Religion.* www.huffingtonpost.com/2014/07/29/arab-muslim-poll_n_5628919.html. Accessed June 7, 2015.

Sidel, R. 1990. *On her own: Growing up in the shadow of the American Dream.* New York: Penguin.

Siebens, J., & Ryan, C. L. 2012. *Field of Bachelor's degrees in the United States: 2009.* U.S. Bureau of the Census. ACS-18. www.census.gov/prod/2012pubs/acs-18.pdf. Accessed June 10, 2014.

Siegel, R. B. 2004. A short history of sexual harassment. In C. A. MacKinnon & R. B. Siegel (Eds.), *Directions in sexual harassment law.* New Haven, CT: Yale University Press.

Signorielli, N. 1990. Children, television, and gender roles. *Journal of Adolescent Health Care, 11,* 50–58.

Silber, J. H., Rosenbaum, P. R., Clark, A. S., Giantonio, B. J., Ross, R. N., Teng, Y., Wang, M., Niknam, B. A., Ludwig, J. M., Wang, W., Even-Shoshan, O., Fox, K. R., 2013. Characteristics associated with differences in survival among black and white women with breast cancer. *JAMA, 310,* 389–397.

Silberstein, F. B., & Seeman, M. 1959. Social mobility and prejudice. *American Journal of Sociology, 60,* 258–264.

Silverglate, H. A., & Lukianoff, G. 2003. Speech codes: Alive and well at colleges. *Chronicle of Higher Education, 49,* B7–B8.

Simmons, R. 2002. *Odd girl out: The hidden culture of aggression in girls.* Orlando: Harcourt.

Sinclair, S., Huntsinger, J., Skorinko, J., & Hardin, C. D. 2005. Social tuning of the self: Consequences for the self-evaluation of stereotype targets. *Journal of Personality and Social Psychology, 89,* 160–175.

Sinozich, S., & Langton, L. 2014. *Rape and sexual assault victimization among college-age females, 1995–2013.* U.S. Bureau of Justice Statistics, NCJ248421. www.bjs.gov/content/pub/pdf/rsavcaf9513.pdf. Accessed January 6, 2015.

Skolnick, A. 1996. *The intimate environment: Exploring marriage and the family.* New York: HarperCollins.

Slaves of New York. 2007. *The New York Times,* May 20.

Smith, C. S. 2002. Risking limbs for height and success in China. *The New York Times,* May 5.

Smith, M. 2013. "Racial Justice Act" repealed in North Carolina. *CNN Justice.* June 21. www.cnn.com/2013/06/20/justice/north-carolina-death-penalty/. Accessed June 25, 2014.

Smith, T. 2011. *Public attitudes toward homosexuality.* National Opinion Research Center. Univesity of Chicago. www.norc.org/PDFs/2011 GSS Reports/GSS_Public Attitudes Toward Homosexuality_Sept2011.pdf. Accessed June 14, 2014.

Smith, S. L., Choueiti, M., Prescott, A., & Pieper, K. 2012. *Gender roles and occupations: A look at character attributes and job-related aspirations in film and television.* Geena Davis Institute on Gender in Media. www.seejane. org/downloads/KeyFindings_GenderROles.pdf. Accessed January 9, 2013.

Sommers, B. D., Long, S. K., & Baicker, K. 2014. Changes in mortality after Massachusetts health care reform: A quasi-experimental study. *Annals of Internal Medicine, 160,* 585–593.

Sorkin, A. R., & Thee-Brenan, M. 2014. Many feel American dream is out of reach. *The New York Times.* December 11.

Southern Poverty Law Center. 2013. *Hate map.* www.splcenter.org/get-informed/hate-map. Accessed June 12, 2013.

Spencer, M. E. 1994. Multiculturalism, "political correctness," and the politics of identity. *Sociological Forum, 9,* 547–567.

Sperling, S. 1991. Baboons with briefcases: Feminism, functionalism, and sociobiology in the evolution of primate behavior. *Signs, 17,* 1–27.

Squires, N. 2015. "Dung of the devil": Pope Francis denounces capitalism, greed and the pursuit of money. *National Post.* July 12. http://news.nationalpost.com/news/world/dung-of-the-devil-pope-francis-denounces-capitalism-greed-and-the-pursuit-of-money. Accessed July 22, 2015.

St. Jean, Y., & Feagin, J. R. 1998. *Double burden: Black women and everyday racism.* Armonk, NY: M. E. Sharp.

Staggenborg, S. 1998. *Gender, family and social movements.* Thousand Oaks, CA: Pine Forge Press.

Stanley, L. 2002. Should "sex" really be "gender"—or "gender" really be "sex"? In S. Jackson & S. Scott (Eds.), *Gender: A sociological reader.* London: Routledge.

Staples, R. 1992. African American families. In J. M. Henslin (Ed.), *Marriage and family in a changing society.* New York: Free Press.

The State of Obesity. 2014. *Special report: Racial and ethnic disparities in obesity.* www.stateofobesity.org/disparities/. Accessed January 13, 2015.

Steinhauer, J. 2013. Navy hearing in rape case raises alarm. *The New York Times.* September 20.

Steinhauer, J., & Joachim, D. S. 2014. 55 colleges named in federal inquiry into the handling of sexual assault cases. *The New York Times.* May 2.

Stephan, C. W., & Stephan, W. G. 1989. After intermarriage: Ethnic identity among mixed-heritage Japanese-Americans and Hispanics. *Journal of Marriage and the Family, 51,* 507–519.

Stephens-Davidowitz, S. 2013. How many American men are gay? *The New York Times.* December 7.

Stephens-Davidowitz, S. 2014. Google, tell me. Is my son a genius? *The New York Times.* January 18.

Stolberg, S. G. 1998. Live and let die over transplants. *The New York Times,* April 5.

Stolberg, S. G. 2014. Rights bill sought for lesbian, gay, bisexual, and transgender Americans. *The New York Times,* December 5.

Strong, P. T. 2004. The mascot slot: Cultural citizenship, political correctness, and pseudo-Indian sports symbols. *Journal of Sport and Social Issues, 28,* 79–87.

Sullivan, C. M., Tan, C., Basta, J., Rumptz, M., & Davidson, W. S. 1992. An advocacy intervention program for women with abusive partners: Initial evaluation. *American Journal of Community Psychology, 20,* 309–332.

Sunwolf, & Leets, L. 2004. Being left out: Rejecting outsiders and communicating group boundaries in childhood and adolescent peer groups. *Journal of Applied Communication Research, 32,* 195–223.

Super, C. M. 1976. Environmental effects on motor development. *Developmental Medicine and Child Neurology, 18,* 561–567.

Survivor stories. 2001. Protection Project. www.protectionproject.org/main1.htm. Accessed July 28, 2004.

Swarns, R. L. 2004. "African American" becomes a term for debate. *The New York Times,* August 29.

Swarns, R. L. 2008. Bipartisan calls for new federal poverty measure. *The New York Times,* September 2.

Swartz, M. 2007. Shop stewards on Fantasy Island? *The New York Times Magazine,* June 10.

Swartz, M. 2011. Living the good lie. *The New York Times Magazine.* June 16.

Sweeney, G. 2001. The trashing of white trash: Natural Born Killers and the appropriation of the white trash aesthetic. *Quarterly Review of Film and Video, 18,* 143–155.

Swinburn, B. A., Sacks, G., Hall, K. D., McPherson, K., Finegood, D. T., Moodie, M. L., & Gortmaker, S. L. 2011. The global obesity pandemic: Shaped by global drivers and local environments. *The Lancet, 378,* 804–814.

Symmes, P. 2012. Hunted in Alabama. *Newsweek.* February 23.

Talbot, M. 2002. Men behaving badly. *The New York Times Magazine,* October 13.

Talbot, M. 2013. About a boy. *The New Yorker.* March 18.

Tannen, D. 1990. *You just don't understand: Women and men in conversation.* New York: William Morrow.

Tatlow, D. K. 2013. In China, a respected Ms. May be labeled Mr. *The New York Times.* August 29.

Tauber, M. A. 1979. Parental socialization techniques and sex differences in children's play. *Child Development, 50,* 225–234.

Taubes, G. 2012. The new obesity campaigns have it all wrong. *Newsweek.* May 14.

Tavernise, S. 2016. Life spans of the rich leave the poor behind. *The New York Times* February 13.

Tavris, C. 1992. *The mismeasure of woman.* New York: Touchstone.

Tavris, C., & Offir, C. 1984. *The longest war: Sex differences in perspective.* New York: Harcourt Brace Jovanovich.

Telles, E. E., & Murguia, E. 1990. Phenotypic discrimination and income differences among Mexican Americans. *Social Science Quarterly, 71,* 682–696.

Thomas, W. I., & Thomas, D. 1928. *The child in America.* New York: Knopf.

Thompson, H. S., Valdimarsdottir, H. B., Winkel, G., Jandorf, L., & Redd, W. 2004. The group-based medical mistrust scale: Psychometric properties and association with breast cancer screening. *Preventive Medicine, 38,* 209–219.

Thompson, K. 2012. Survey paints portrait of black women in America. *Washington Post.* January 22.

Thompson, M. S., & Keith, V. M. 2004. The blacker the berry: Gender, skin tone, self-esteem, and self-efficacy. In D. M. Newman & J. O'Brien (Eds.),

Sociology: Exploring the architecture of everyday life (Readings). Thousand Oaks, CA: Pine Forge Press.

Thorne, B. 1995. Girls and boys together . . . but mostly apart: Gender arrangements in elementary schools. In D. M. Newman (Ed.), *Sociology: Exploring the architecture of everyday life (Readings)*. Thousand Oaks, CA: Pine Forge Press.

Thornton, M. C. 1997. Strategies of racial socialization among black parents: Mainstreaming, minority, and cultural messages. In R. Taylor, J. Jackson, & L. Chatters (Eds.), *Family life in Black America*. Thousand Oaks, CA: Sage.

Thornton, M. C., Chatters, L. M., Taylor, R. J., & Allen, W. R. 1990. Sociodemographic and environmental correlates of racial socialization by black parents. *Child Development, 61,* 401–409.

Thurlow, C. 2001. Naming the "outsider within": Homophobic pejoratives and the verbal abuse of lesbian, gay, and bisexual high-school pupils. *Journal of Adolescence, 24,* 25–38.

Tittle, C. R. 1994. Theoretical bases for inequality in formal social control. In G. S. Bridges & M. Myers (Eds.), *Inequality, crime, and social control*. Boulder, CO: Westview.

Tjaden, P., & Thoennes, N. 2000. Extent, nature, and consequences of intimate partner violence. *National Institute of Justice Report #NCJ 181867*. www.ncjrs.org/pdffiles1/nij/181867.pdf. Accessed October 12, 2004.

TMZ.com. 2014. L. A. Clippers owner to GF: Don't bring black people to my games . . . including Magic Johnson. April 26. www.tmz.com/2014/04/26/donald-sterling-clippers-owner-black-people-racist-audio-magic-johnson/. Accessed June 12, 2014.

Tonry, M. 1995. *Malign neglect*. New York: Oxford University Press.

Traister, R. 2011. Ladies, we have a problem. *The New York Times Magazine*. July 24.

Transparency Market Research. 2015. *Erectile Dysfunction drugs market (Viagra, Cialis, Levitra/Staxyn, Stendra/Spedra, Zydena, MUSE, Mvix and Helleva)—Global industry analysis, size, share, growth, trends and forecast, 2013–2019*. www.transparencymarketresearch.com/erectile-dysfunction-drugs.htm. Accessed July 22, 2015.

Trepagnier, B. 2013. Silent racism: Passivity in well-meaning white people. In D. Newman & J. O'Brien (Eds.). *Sociology: Exploring the architecture of everyday life (Readings)*. Thousand Oaks, CA: Sage.

Truman, J. L., & Morgan, R. E. 2014. *Nonfatal domestic violence, 2003–2012*. U.S. Bureau of Justice Statistics. NCJ244697. www.bjs.gov/content/pub/pdf/ndv0312.pdf. Accessed June 26, 2014.

Truman, M., & Rand, J. 2010. *Criminal victimization, 2009* (NCJ 231327). U.S. Bureau of Justice Statistics. http://bjs.ojp.usdoj.gov/content/pub/pdf/cv09.pdf. Accessed June 20, 2011.

Tuller, D. 2004. Gentlemen, start your engines? *The New York Times,* June 21.

Tuller, D. 2011. No surprise for bisexual men: Report indicates they exist. *The New York Times.* August 23.

Tumin, M. 1953. Some principles of stratification: A critical analysis. *American Sociological Review, 18,* 387–393.

Uchitelle, L. 2008. The wage that meant middle class. *The New York Times,* April 20.

Udry, J. R. 2000. Biological limits of gender construction. *American Sociological Review, 65,* 443–457.

Uggen, C., & Blackstone, A. 2004. Sexual harassment as a gendered expression of power. *American Sociological Review, 69,* 64–92.

Ukraine bill proposes prison for positive gay depictions. 2012. *The New York Times.* July 24.

Ulrich, L. T. 1990. *A midwife's tale: The life of Martha Ballard, based on her diary, 1785–1812.* New York: Knopf.

UNAIDS 2014. *The gap report.* www.unaids.org/sites/default/files/media_asset/UNAIDS_Gap_report-en.pdf. Accessed May 29, 2015.

Undersecretary of Defense. 2013. *Memorandum for secretaries of the military departments.* www.defense.gov/home/features/2013/docs/Further-Guidance-on-Extending-Benefits-to-Same-Sex-Spouses-of-Military-M.pdf. Accessed June 24, 2014.

UNICEF. 2009. *The state of the world's children 2009.* www.unicef.org/sowc09/docs/SOWC09-FullReport-EN.pdf. Accessed September 5, 2009.

UNICEF/WHO. 2012. *Progress on drinking water and sanitation.* www.unicef.org/media/files/JMPreport2012.pdf. Accessed July 2, 2014.

United States Bureau of the Census. 2011. *Statistical abstract of the United States.* www.census.gov/compendia/statab/2011edition.html. Accessed April 1, 2011.

United States Bureau of the Census, 2014. *2014 national population projections: Summary tables.* www.census.gov/population/projections/data/national/2014/summarytables.html. Accessed December 15, 2014.

United States Bureau of the Census. 2016. *American fact finder.* factfinder.census.gov/faces/nav/jsf/pages/community_facts.xhtml. Accessed February 12, 2016.

United States Bureau of Justice Statistics. 2012. *Sourcebook of criminal justice statistics online.* www.albany.edu/sourcebook/. Accessed January 21, 2013.

United States Bureau of Labor Statistics. 2004. *Women in the labor force.* Report #973. www.bls.gov/cps/wlf-databook.htm. Accessed September 23, 2004.

United States Bureau of Labor Statistics. 2013a. *American Time Use Survey— 2012 results.* USDL-13-1178. www.bls.gov/news.release/atus/nr0.htm. Accessed June 21, 2013.

United States Bureau of Labor Statistics. 2013b. *Median weekly earnings of full-time wage and salary workers by detailed occupation and sex.* www.bls.gov/cps/cpsaat39.pdf. Accessed June 19, 2014.

United States Bureau of Labor Statistics. 2014a. *Consumer expenditures in 2012.* Report #1046. www.bls.gov/cexl. Accessed May 30, 2014.

United States Bureau of Labor Statistics. 2014b. *The employment situation – May 2014.* USDL-14-0987. www.bls.gov/news.release/empsit.nr0.htm. Accessed June 16, 2014.

United States Bureau of Labor Statistics. 2015a. *Census of fatal occupational injuries charts, 1992–2013 (Preliminary data).* www.bls.gov/iif/oshcfoi1. htm#2013. Accessed January 21, 2015.

United States Bureau of Labor Statistics. 2015b. *Median weekly earnings of full-time wage and salary workers by detailed occupation and sex. Table 39.* www.bls.gov/cps/cpsaat39.pdf. Accessed June 14, 2015.

United States Bureau of Labor Statistics. 2015c. *Numbers of non-fatal occupational injuries by identity and case types, 2013.* www.bls.gov/iif/oshwc/osh/os/ost63960.pdf. Accessed January 21, 2015.

United States Bureau of Labor Statistics. 2015d. *Table A6—Employed and unemployed full- and part-time workers by sex and age, seasonally adjusted.* www.bls.gov/web/empsit/cpseea06.htm. Accessed June 14, 2015.

United States Conference of Mayors. 2014. *Hunger and homelessness survey: A status report on hunger and homelessness in America's cities.* www. usmayors.org/pressreleases/uploads/2014/1211-report-hh.pdf. Accessed June 2, 2015.

United States Department of Defense. 2013. *Sexual assault prevention and responses—annual reports.* www.sapr.mil/public/docs/reports/FY12_DoD_SAPRO_Annual_Report_on_Sexual_Assault-VOLUME_ONE.pdf. Accessed June 19, 2013.

United States Department of Education. 2014. *Expansive survey of America's public schools reveals troubling racial disparities.* www.ed.gov/news/press-releases/expansive-survey-americas-public-schools-reveals-troubling-racial-disparities. Accessed June 8, 2014.

United States Department of Health and Human Services. 2009. *Adoption USA: A chartbook based on the 1007 National Survey of Adoptive Parents.* aspe. hhs.gov/hsp/09/nsap/chartbook/chartbook.cfm?id=2. Accessed June 4, 2014.

United States Department of the Interior Bureau of Indian Affairs. 2014. Indian entities recognized and eligible to receive services from the United States Bureau of Indian Affairs. *Federal Register, 79,* 4748. www.bia.gov/WhoWeAre/BIA/OIS/TribalGovernmentServices/TribalDirectory/. Accessed May 31, 2014.

United States Department of Justice. 2009. *UBS enters into deferred prosecution agreement.* www.usdoj.gov/opa/pr/2009/February/09-tax-136.html. Accessed May 21, 2009.

United States Department of Justice. 2012. *Attorney General Eric Holder announces revisions to the Uniform Crime Reports definition of rape.* www. justice.gov/opa/pr/2012/January/12-ag-018.html. Accessed June 30, 2014.

United States Department of State. 2012. *Trafficking in persons report.* www. state.gov/documents/organization/192587.pdf. Accessed May 30, 2013.

United States Equal Employment Opportunity Commission. 2015. *Charges alleging sexual harassment FY2010-FY2014.* www.eeoc.gov/eeoc/statistics/ enforcement/sexual_harassment_new.cfm. Accessed June 9, 2015.

United States Sentencing Commission. 2009. *Sourcebook of federal sentencing statistics.* www.ussc.gov/ANNRPT/2009/SBTOC09.htm. Accessed July 2, 2010.

United States Sentencing Commission. 2011. *2011 Annual Report.* www.ussc. gov/Data_and_Statistics/Annual_Reports_and_Sourcebooks/2011/ar11toc. htm. Accessed January 21, 2013.

United States Sentencing Commission. 2013. *2013 Annual Report.* www.ussc. gov/research-and-publications/annual-reports-sourcebooks/2013/annual-report-2013. Accessed June 25, 2014.

United States Sentencing Commission. 2014a. *Quick facts: Crack cocaine trafficking offenses.* www.ussc.gov/sites/default/files/pdf/research-and-publications/quick-facts/Quick_Facts_Crack_Cocaine.pdf. Accessed January 22, 2015.

United States Sentencing Commission. 2014b. *Quick facts: Powder cocaine trafficking offenses.* www.ussc.gov/sites/default/files/pdf/research-and-publications/quick-facts/Quick_Facts_Powder_Cocaine.pdf. Accessed January 22, 2015.

United States Surgeon General. 2014. *The health consequences of smoking-50 years of progress: A report of the Surgeon General, 2014.* www.surgeongeneral. gov/library/reports/50-years-of-progress/. Accessed June 23, 2014.

UN Women. 2015. *The Beijing Declaration and Platform for Action turns 20.* www.unwomen.org/~/media/headquarters/attachments/sections/library/ publications/2015/sg report_synthesis-en_web.pdf. Accessed March 10, 2015.

Upper bound. 2010. *The Economist,* April 17.

Upton, R. L. 2010. "Fat eggs": Gender and fertility as important factors in HIV/ AIDS prevention in Botswana. *Gender & Development, 18,* 515–524.

U.S. English Foundation. 2014. *US states with official English laws.* www.us-english.org/view/13. Accessed June 1, 2014.

Van Ausdale, D., & Feagin, J. R. 2001. *The first R: How children learn race and racism.* Lanham, MD: Rowman & Littlefield.

Vanek, J. 1980. Work, leisure and family roles: Farm households in the United States: 1920–1955. *Journal of Family History, 5,* 422–431.

Van Ryn, M., & Burke, J. 2000. The effect of patient race and socio-economic status on physicians' perceptions of patients. *Social Science and Medicine, 50,* 813–820.

Vega, T. 2014. Discipline to girls differs between and within races. *The New York Times.* December 11.

Velázquez, N. 2002. In search of justice. In J. B. Schor & B. Taylor (Eds.), *Sustainable planet: Solutions for the twenty-first century.* Boston: Beacon Press.

Vespa, J., Lewis, J. M., & Kreider, R. M. 2013. *America's families and living arrangements: 2012.* U.S. Bureau of the Census. P20-570. www.census.gov/prod/2013pubs/p20-570.pdf. Accessed June 18, 2014.

Vidal de Haymes, M., & Simon, S. 2003. Transracial adoption: Families identify issues and needed support services. *Child Welfare, 82,* 251–272.

Waldman, A. 2003. Broken taboos doom lovers in an Indian village. *The New York Times,* March 28.

Walmsley, R. 2013. *World prison population list.* International Centre for Prison Studies. www.prisonstudies.org/sites/prisonstudies.org/files/resources/downloads/wppl_10.pdf. Accessed June 25, 2014.

Wang, W. 2012. *The rise of intermarriage: Rates, characteristics vary by race and gender.* Pew Research Social and Demographic Trends. www.pewsocialtrends.org/2012/02/16/the-rise-of-intermarriage/. Accessed January 26, 2014.

Ward, L. M. 2003. Understanding the role of entertainment media in the sexual socialization of American youth: A review of empirical research. *Developmental Review, 23,* 347–389.

Ward, L. M., & Friedman, K. 2006. Using TV as a guide: Associations between television viewing and adolescents' sexual attitudes and behavior. *Journal of Research on Adolescence, 16,* 133–156.

Washington, H. A. 2006. *Medical apartheid: The dark history of medical experimentation on black Americans from Colonial times to the present.* New York: Doubleday.

Washington, J. 2010. Black or biracial? Census forces a choice for some. *The Grio.* www.thegrio.com/news/black-or-biracial-census-forces-a-choice-for-some.php. Accessed May 27, 2010.

Washington, J. 2013. Barneys and Macy's racial discrimination cases stir talk of "shopping while black." *Huffington Post.* October 29. www.huffingtonpost.com/2013/10/29/barneys-macys-shopping-while-black-_n_4173929.html. Accessed June 19, 2014.

Waters, M. C. 2010. Optional ethnicities: For whites only? In D. M. Newman & J. O'Brien (Eds.), *Sociology: Exploring the Architecture of Everyday Life (Readings).* Thousand Oaks, CA: Pine Forge Press.

Waxman, S. 2004. Using a racial epithet to combat racism. *The New York Times,* July 3.

Weber, L. 1998. A conceptual framework for understanding race, class, gender, and sexuality. *Psychology of Women Quarterly, 22,* 13–32.

Weber, M. 1970. *From Max Weber: Essays in sociology* (H. H. Gerth & C. W. Mills, Eds.). New York: Oxford University Press.

Weil, E. 2005. Heavy questions. *The New York Times Magazine,* January 2.

Weil, E. 2006. What if it's (sort of) a boy and (sort of) a girl? *The New York Times Magazine,* September 24.

Weinberg, D. H. 2007. Earnings by gender: Evidence from Census 2000. *Monthly Labor Review,* July/August, 26–34.

Weinberg, M. S., Williams, C. J., & Pryor, D. W. 2003. Becoming bisexual. In P. A. Adler & P. Adler (Eds.), *Constructions of deviance: Social power, context, and interaction.* Belmont, CA: Wadsworth.

Weismantel, M. 2005. White. In D. Kulick &. A. Meneley (Eds.), *Fat: The anthropology of an obsession.* New York: Tarcher/Penguin.

Weiss, J. 2000. *To have and to hold: Marriage, the Baby Boom and social change.* Chicago: University of Chicago Press.

Weitzman, L., Eifler, D., Hodada, E., & Ross, C. 1972. Sex-role socialization in picture books for preschool children. *American Journal of Sociology, 77,* 1125–1150.

Weitzman, N., Birns, B., & Friend, R. 1985. Traditional and nontraditional mothers' communication with their daughters and sons. *Child Development, 56,* 894–898.

Welch, B. 2007. Putting a stop to slave labor. *Utne Reader,* March/April.

West, C., & Zimmerman, D. 1987. Doing gender. *Gender & Society, 1,* 135–151.

Western, B., & Pettit, B. 2010. Incarceration and social inequality. *Daedalus, 139,* 8–19.

White, J. E. 1997. Multiracialism: The melding of America. *Time,* May 5.

The White House Council on Women and Girls. 2014. *Rape and sexual assault: A renewed call to action.* www.whitehouse.gov/sites/default/files/docs/sexual_assault_report_1-24-14.pdf. Accessed January 23, 2014.

Wildman, S. M., & Davis, A. D. 2002. Making systems of privilege visible. In P. S. Rothenberg (Ed.), *White privilege: Essential readings on the other side of racism.* New York: Worth.

Wilkins, D. E. 2004. A tour of Indian peoples and Indian lands. In C. A. Gallagher (Ed.), *Rethinking the color line: Readings in race and ethnicity.* New York: McGraw-Hill.

Will, J., Self, P., & Datan, N. 1976. Maternal behavior and perceived sex of infant. *American Journal of Orthopsychiatry, 46,* 135–139.

Williams, C. 2004. Still a man's world: Men who do "women's work." In D. M. Newman & J. O'Brien (Eds.), *Sociology: Exploring the architecture of everyday life (Readings).* Thousand Oaks, CA: Pine Forge Press.

Williams, G. H. 1995. *Life on the color line: The true story of a white boy who discovered he was black.* New York: Dutton.

Williams, J. A., Vernon, J. A., Williams, M. C., & Malecha, K. 1987. Sex role socialization in picture books: An update. *Social Science Quarterly, 68,* 148–156.

Williams, T. C. 2011. Racial bias seen in study of lead dust and children. *The New York Times.* September 16.

Williams, T. C. 2012. As black as we wish to be. *The New York Times.* March 18.

Williams, W. L. 1992. *The spirit and the flesh: Sexual diversity in American Indian culture.* Boston: Beacon Press.

Williamson, R. C. 1984. A partial replication of the Kohn-Gecas-Nye thesis in a German sample. *Journal of Marriage and the Family, 46,* 971–979.

Wilson, D. 2009. Race, ethnicity and care. *The New York Times,* August 30.

Wilson, J. L., Peebles, R., Hardy, K. K., & Litt, I. F. 2006. Surfing for thinness: A pilot study of pro-eating disorder website usage in adolescents with eating disorders. *Pediatrics, 118,* 1635–1643.

Wilson, W. J. 1980. *The declining significance of race.* Chicago: University of Chicago Press.

Wilson, W, J. 2003. Jobless ghettos: The social implications of the disappearance of work in segregated neighborhoods. In T. E. Ore (Ed.), *The social construction of difference and inequality: Race, class, gender, and sexuality.* New York: McGraw-Hill.

Wines, M., & Robles, F. 2014. Key factor in police shootings: "Reasonable fear." *The New York Times.* August 23.

Wingfield, A. H. 2013. Racializing the glass escalator: Reconsidering men's experiences with women's work. In S. Ferguson (Ed.), *Mapping the social landscape.* New York: McGraw-Hill.

Wise, T. 2002. Membership has its privileges: Thoughts on acknowledging and challenging whiteness. In P. S. Rothenberg (Ed.), *White privilege: Essential readings on the other side of racism.* New York: Worth.

Wolfe, A. 2000. Benign multiculturalism. In P. Kivisto & G. Rundblad (Eds.), *Multiculturalism in the United States.* Thousand Oaks, CA: Pine Forge Press.

Wollan, M. 2012. Free speech is one thing, vagrants another. *The New York Times.* October 19.

The Women's Media Center. 2015. *The status of women in the U.S. media 2015.* www.wmc.3cdn.net/83bf6082a319460eb1_hsrm680x2.pdf. Accessed June 11, 2015.

Wong, C. M. 2014. New York's transgender residents will now be able to change birth certificate sex designation without surgery. *Huffington Post.* December 8. www.huffingtonpost.com/2014/12/08/new-york-transgender-birt_n_6290590.html. Accessed July 23, 2015.

Wood, N. 2005. Eight nations agree on plan to lift status of Gypsies. *The New York Times,* February 6.

Woolf, S. H., & Aron, L. 2013. *U.S. health in international perspective: Shorter lives, poorer health.* Washington, DC: National Academy Press.

World Food Programme. 2014. *Hunger.* www.wfp.org/hunger. Accessed June 20, 2014.

World Health Organization. 1995. *World health report 1995—Executive summary.* www.who.int. Accessed June 23, 2001.

World Health Organization. 2013. *Fact sheet on the world malaria report 2013.* www.who.int/malaria/media/world_malaria_report_2013/en/. Accessed July 2, 2014.

World Health Organization. 2014. *Global update on the health sector response to HIV, 2014.* www.who.int/hiv/pub/global-update.pdf. Accessed June 23, 2015.

World Health Organization. 2015. *Tobacco control.* www.who.int/gho/tobacco/en/. Accessed January 22, 2015.

World Hunger Education Service. 2012. *2012 world hunger and poverty facts and statistics.* www.worldhunger.org/articles/Learn/world hunger facts 2002. htm#Footnotes. Accessed June 3, 2013.

Worsnop, R. 1996. Getting into college. *CQ Researcher,* February 23.

Worth, R. F. 2010. Crime (sex) and punishment (stoning). *The New York Times,* August 22.

Wright, E. O. 1976. Class boundaries in advanced capitalist societies. *New Left Review, 98,* 3–41.

Wright, E. O., Costello, C., Hachen, D., & Sprague, J. 1982. The American class structure. *American Sociological Review, 47,* 709–726.

Wright, E. O., & Perrone, L. 1977. Marxist class categories and income inequality. *American Sociological Review, 42,* 32–55.

Wu, F. H. 2002. *Yellow: Race in America beyond black and white.* New York: Basic Books.

Xiao, H. 2000. Class, gender, and parental values in the 1990s. *Gender & Society, 14,* 785–803.

Yamaguchi, M. 2004. In Japan, feudal stigma persists; Burakumin class still encounters bias. *Washington Post,* July 18.

Yardley, J. 2010. In India, castes, honor and killings intertwine. *The New York Times,* July 9.

Yllo, K., & Straus, M. A. 1990. Patriarchy and violence against wives: The impact of structural and normative factors. In M. A. Straus & R. J. Gelles (Eds.), *Physical violence in American families.* New Brunswick, NJ: Transaction.

Yook, H. 2014. Positive stereotypes are hurtful too. *The Daily Californian.* March 10. www.dailycal.org/2014/03/10/positive-stereotypes-hurtful/. Accessed June 11, 2014.

Your most private sex questions. 2004. *CosmoGirl Magazine.* May.

Zhang, S. D., & Odenwald, W. F. 1995. Misexpression of the white gene triggers male-male courtship in Drosophila. *Proceedings of the National Academy of Sciences, 92,* 5525–5529.

Zoepf, K. 2007. A dishonorable affair. *The New York Times Magazine,* September 23.

Zuberi, T. 2001. *Thicker than blood: How racial statistics lie.* Minneapolis: University of Minnesota Press.

Zwicky, A. M. 1997. Two lavender issues for linguists. In A. Livia & K. Hall (Eds.), *Queerly phrased: Language, gender, and sexuality.* New York: Oxford University Press.

**Mc
Graw
Hill
Education**

ISBN 978-1-259-91040-1
MHID 1-259-91040-7

EAN

9 781259 910401

90000

mheducation.com/highered